Federal Habeas Corpus

Cases and Materials

Federal Habeas Corpus

Cases and Materials

Andrea D. Lyon

ASSOCIATE CLINICAL PROFESSOR OF LAW,
DIRECTOR, THE CENTER FOR JUSTICE IN CAPITAL CASES
DEPAUL UNIVERSITY COLLEGE OF LAW

Emily Hughes

ASSOCIATE DIRECTOR,
THE CENTER FOR JUSTICE IN CAPITAL CASES
DEPAUL UNIVERSITY COLLEGE OF LAW

Mary Prosser

ASSISTANT CLINICAL PROFESSOR OF LAW,
FRANK J. REMINGTON CENTER
UNIVERSITY OF WISCONSIN LAW SCHOOL

CAROLINA ACADEMIC PRESS
Durham, North Carolina

Library of Congress Cataloging-in-Publication Data

Lyon, Andrea D.
    Federal habeas corpus : cases and materials / by Andrea Lyon, Emily Hughes,
Mary Prosser.
       p. cm.
    Includes bibliographical references and index.
    ISBN 0-89089-586-4
    1. Habeas corpus--United States. I. Hughes, Emily. II. Prosser, Mary. III. Title.

    KF9011.L96 2004
    347.73'5--dc22

                                        2004007867

CAROLINA ACADEMIC PRESS
700 Kent Street
Durham, North Carolina 27701
Telephone (919) 489-7486
Fax (919) 493-5668
www.cap-press.com

We dedicate this book to
Arnold and John,
to our children,
Will, Samantha, Molly, Hannah, and Ella,
and to the many colleagues and clients who have
generously shared their knowledge and their stories with us.

Summary of Contents

Contents

Foreword

Why Is Habeas Corpus Important?

By John C. Tucker

"Would you write a short introduction for our casebook about why habeas corpus is important?" Professor Lyon asked. "I'd be glad to," I said.

The problem, I soon realized, is how to write anything short about something as fundamental to our legal system as habeas corpus—the law which Blackstone described as "the stable bulwark of our liberties," and which American courts commonly refer to as simply "The Great Writ."

In talking about habeas corpus we can't avoid starting nearly 800 years ago at Runnymede, with the most famous provision of Magna Carta: "No freeman shall be taken or imprisoned except by the lawful judgement of his peers or by the law of the land." Magna Carta Art. 39 (1215). For the next 467 years, English kings periodically ignored that stricture and imprisoned their subjects without due process of law, while English parliaments passed laws designed to prevent it—laws referred to by the Latin phrase "habeas corpus"—loosely, "you have the person, now show a legal justification for keeping him or let him go." Finally, the Habeas Corpus Act of 1679 (the statute Blackstone was talking about) pretty much settled the matter. Unless parliament passed a law temporarily suspending habeas, no citizen of England could be imprisoned without a formal charge and an opportunity to contest it.

Given the importance of habeas corpus as a check on the power of the English monarch, it is not surprising that the American colonists also saw it as their most important guarantee of due process, and were enraged when royal authorities sometimes refused to afford its protections to colonists who challenged their arbitrary conduct. Thus, in Federalist 84, Alexander Hamilton declared that habeas corpus was "the bulwark of the British Constitution" and essential to the protection of liberty in the new nation. Habeas corpus became the only English common-law process explicitly written into our own Constitution, and jurisdiction to enforce the Great Writ was granted to American courts in the first Judiciary Act in 1789, even before the adoption of the Bill of Rights.

From that time forward, the Great Writ has been seen as a cornerstone of American justice. As the Supreme Court declared in *Fay v. Noia*, "there is no higher duty than to maintain it unimpaired."

It was *Gideon v. Wainwright,* another habeas case, which, with the book and movie *Gideon's Trumpet,* became the most famous of the decisions which marked the Warren Court's post World War II effort to extend the protections of the United States Constitution to criminal defendants whose due process rights had previously been left to the less-than-rigorous care of state courts. And while many important cases of that era were decided on direct appeal from state supreme courts, the protections established by cases like *Griffin v. Illinois* (free transcript), *Mapp v. Ohio* (exclusionary rule), *Brady v. Maryland* (exculpatory evidence), *Miranda v. Arizona* (warning of rights) and *Malloy v. Hogan* (Fifth Amendment) were initially most often vindicated by a federal petition for writ of habeas corpus.

If you really want to understand why habeas corpus is so important, the people to talk to are the thousands of criminal defendants who have found themselves convicted and imprisoned in state penitentiaries—sometimes on death row—because of ineffective assistance of counsel, or the concealment of exculpatory evidence, or a confession obtained by artifice or coercion. In the roughly two decades following reinstatement of the death penalty in America, nearly 50% of the cases in which a verdict and sentence of death was imposed and approved by the state courts were set aside in federal court by petition for writ of habeas corpus. And while it is probably impossible to give definitive numbers, there is no question that a majority of the 114 men and women who have been released from death row as a result, in part, of the development of DNA testing which proved them innocent, would have died had their executions not been delayed by operation of the Great Writ. Sometimes a life was saved by a finding that the original verdict or sentence was constitutionally defective, sometimes it was delay alone that saved an innocent life until DNA testing was perfected. Such a result would only be decried by the posturing politicians who in recent years have sought to weaken the protections of habeas corpus as a way of demonstrating their supposed "toughness on crime." The founding fathers—who such politicians shamelessly invoke at every opportunity—would weep.

As lawyers who will handle criminal cases, whether as a significant element of your practice or simply to fulfill your obligation to the profession by accepting appointed cases at the trial or post-trial levels, an understanding of the law of habeas corpus is as essential as anything the users of this book will learn in law school. Indeed, with the increasingly restrictive and complex procedural requirements which have been imposed on the exercise of the writ in recent years by legislators and the Rehnquist Court, an understanding of the intricacies of habeas corpus law is more important than ever, lest the protections of the Great Writ be lost to a client by ignorance or inadvertence.

Finally, we cannot ignore the frontal assault on the writ which our current royalty has mounted in the name of national security and the "war on terror." As I write, the detainee cases are awaiting decision in the Supreme Court. By the time you read this introduction they will have been decided. If the Court rules for the Government, non-citizens may no longer have access to the protections of the writ at all, even when held on American-controlled soil. Even citizens, if arbitrarily designated "enemy combatants," may see the protections of the Great Writ fade like the grin of the Cheshire Cat, until nothing of practical importance remains.

In these times, the ghosts of Runnymede are not grinning, and protection of the Great Writ has never been more important. Whatever is decided in the detainee cases, for ordinary citizens, the Great Writ must remain as a bulwark of our liberties, the ultimate vehicle for protecting our Constitutional rights against the power of government.

A lawyer who does not know how to preserve the rights guaranteed by the Writ and to invoke them for her clients is not fully educated in the law.

John Tucker is a lawyer and the author of May God Have Mercy: A True Story of Crime and Punishment *and* Trial and Error: The Education of a Courtroom Lawyer.

Preface

The three of us are deeply concerned about issues reflected in recent statutory and doctrinal changes in the "Great Writ." We undertook this book in hopes of helping students understand and critically examine the political, legal, and pragmatic effects of the role of habeas corpus in our criminal justice system. At the same time, we hope this book may also be useful to attorneys who wish to familiarize themselves with habeas corpus jurisprudence. While we have tried to fairly present the competing concerns that inform this complex and evocative area of the law, because we are defense attorneys, our experiences representing individual—rather than governmental—interests have undoubtedly shaped our personal perspectives. As we finished reading each case, we would often wonder what happened to the person behind the case, the person whose life and liberty the Court's decision most immediately affected. Many of the cases are thus followed by a brief synopsis of what happened to the defendant after the case was over.

We want to acknowledge the support and assistance our schools provided us while writing this book: the DePaul University College of Law and Dean Glen Weissenberger, as well as the University of Wisconsin Law School and Dean Kenneth B. Davis, Jr. We also acknowledge the important work of Professors James Liebman, Randy Hertz, and Larry Yackle, whose treatises, articles, books, and research continue to be both groundbreaking and foundational. In addition, we sincerely thank Professors Susan Bandes, Walter J. Dickey, Samuel R. Gross, James Liebman, and Marc Weber, as well as Grant Sovern, for their insightful comments and suggestions. A number of current and former law students also assisted us with various phases of the book, including Julie Darr, Erin Hairoupoulos, Byron Lichstein, and Maryam Toghraee. And finally, we extend a special thanks to our proofreader, Susan Burgess, for her patience and diligence.

Permissions

Thanks to the following authors and copyright holders for permission to use their materials:

Various case opinions, contained within the text, are reprinted and/or adapted with the permission of LexisNexis.

Bator, Paul M., Finality in Criminal Law and Federal Habeas Corpus for State Prisoners, 76 Harv. L. Rev. 441 (1963). Reprinted with permission.

Concord Monitor, "Stolen Votes: Wrongly Listing Citizens as Felons Likely Cost Gore Election," Mar. 18, 2002. Reprinted with permission.

Friendly, Henry J., Is Innocence Irrelevant? Collateral Attack on Criminal Judgments, 38 U. Chi. L. Rev. 142 (1970). Reprinted with permission.

Green, Frank, "State Objects to More Testing," Richmond Times-Dispatch, Oct. 7, 2000. Reprinted with permission.

Hertz, Randy, and James S. Liebman, Appendix A, Reprinted with permission from Federal Habeas Corpus Practice and Procedure, 4th Ed. Copyright 2001, Matthew Bender & Company, Inc., a member of the LexisNexis Group. All rights reserved.

Liebman, James S., Jeffrey Fagan and Valerie West, A Broken System: Error Rates in Capital Cases, 1973–1995 (Executive Summary) (June 12, 2000). Reprinted with permission of the author.

Liebman, James S., Jeffrey Fagan, Andrew Gelman, Valerie West, Garth Davies, and Alexander Kiss, A Broken System, Part II: Why There Is So Much Error in Capital Cases, and What Can Be Done About It (Executive Summary) (February 11, 2002). Reprinted with permission of the author.

Palacios, Victoria J., Faith in Fantasy: The Supreme Court's Reliance on Commutation to Ensure Justice in Death Penalty Cases, 49 Vand. L. Rev. 311 (1996). Reprinted with permission.

Rosen, Jeffrey, "Judge Not" in The New Republic, Jan. 26, 2004. Reprinted with permission.

Ryan, George, Text of Governor Ryan's DePaul University College of Law Speech Pardoning Four on Death Row, Delivered on January 10, 2003, at DePaul University College of Law. Reprinted with permission of former Governor Ryan.

Ryan, George, Text of Governor George Ryan's Commutation Announcement Delivered on January 11, 2003, at Northwestern University School of Law. Reprinted with the permission of Northwestern Law News, Northwestern University School of Law, Copyright 2002 Northwestern University.

The Virginian-Pilot, "No Hollywood Ending in Defending the Indigent," Mar. 28, 2003. Reprinted with permission.

The Virginian-Pilot, "Take Off the Blindfold in the Roger Coleman Case," Mar. 6, 2003. Reprinted with permission.

Weiss, Eric M., "DNA Testing By Media Barred: Va. Justices Deny Access in Case of Executed Man," The Washington Post, Nov. 2, 2002. Reprinted with permission.

Part I

Introduction

Chapter 1

The Great Writ

A. Historical Background

The writ of habeas corpus has a long and detailed history, possibly dating as far back as the Roman Empire.[1] The phrase "habeas corpus" is Latin for "you have the body," although in practice, it means a lot more than that. According to Black Law's Dictionary, "habeas corpus" is:

> A writ employed to bring a person before a court, most frequently to ensure that the party's imprisonment or detention is not illegal.... In addition to being used to test the legality of an arrest or commitment, the writ may be used to obtain review of (1) the regularity of extradition process, (2) the right to or amount of bail, or (3) the jurisdiction of a court that has imposed a criminal sentence.

Black's Law Dictionary 715 (7th ed. 1999).

[margin handwritten note: Black's Law Dict]

Essentially, the "Great Writ" is an avenue that the court may use to undo a prisoner's wrongful incarceration. Historically, habeas corpus was viewed as a remedy to be used in the case of extrajudicial detention, such as when the Crown incarcerated someone because of the person's political views rather than for criminal activity. In the United States, the reach of habeas corpus has expanded to include the ability of a person who is convicted in violation of constitutional principles to petition for a writ. Indeed, it is this "look behind the veil" of a state conviction that sometimes causes habeas corpus to be so controversial.

The "Great Writ" came to our country by way of English Common Law[2] and is given explicit recognition in the United States Constitution. U.S. Const. Art. 1, § 9, cl. 2. This casebook explores the nature of the writ, its reach, and its requirements.

[margin handwritten note: Art 1, § 9 cl 2]

The Reach of the Writ

The reach and power of the writ in American courts coincided with two significant events in U.S. history.[3] The first was in 1867, immediately following the Civil War, when

---

1. Albert S. Glass, *Historical Aspects of Habeas Corpus*, 9 St. John's L. Rev. 55–70 (1934).
2. Blackstone called it "the most celebrated writ in the English Law." 3 William Blackstone, Commentaries *129.
3. *See generally* Marshall J. Hartman & Shelvin Singer, *Requiem For Habeas Corpus*, The Champion, Mar. 1994, at 12–20.

the writ was extended to state court defendants. This allowed federal courts to monitor state court proceedings for the first time, thus insuring that the constitutional rights of defendants were not violated.[4] The second event was a series of decisions handed down by the Warren Court during the 1960s that extended the protections of the Bill of Rights to defendants with state convictions through 28 U.S.C. § 2254.[5] In addition to applying to state convictions, the writ of habeas corpus also applies to federal convictions under 28 U.S.C. § 2255. This casebook primarily examines the application of the writ to state convictions.

There are other applications of the writ of habeas corpus. For example, because habeas corpus applies to anyone in government custody, it can be used to challenge a civil commitment order. *See Hopkins v. Lynn*, 888 F.2d 35 (5th Cir. 1989) (an acquittal by reason of insanity could not, without more, be enough to confine a defendant to a mental institution, and so a writ of habeas corpus should issue). Habeas is also applicable to the denial of parole, although the likelihood of a petitioner's success is poor. *See Ohio Adult Parole Authority v. Woodard*, 523 U.S. 272 (1998), *infra*, Chapter 14. A petition for a writ also may issue regarding deportation (*see INS. v. St. Cyr*, 533 U.S. 289 (2001) (holding that the changes made to habeas by the Antiterrorism and Effective Death Penalty Act of 1996 did not preclude habeas review for those facing deportation)),[6] extradition (*see In re Burt*, 737 F.2d 1477 (7th Cir. 1984) (holding that petitioner's due process claim properly could be considered in a habeas review of an extradition proceeding to Germany)), a conviction by a military court (*see, e.g., Murphy v. Garrett*, 729 F. Supp. 461 (W.D. Pa. 1990) (holding that a federal court had habeas jurisdiction over an Article 32 court martial, although declining to grant relief)), and of particular interest in recent times, an executive detention (*see Ogbudimkpa v. Ashcroft*, 342 F.3d 207 (3rd Cir. 2003) (holding that habeas review of executive detention is "at the historical core" of the writ)).

The reach of the writ to state convictions was greatly expanded in 1963. That year, the Supreme Court decided three landmark cases concerning federal habeas corpus: *Fay v. Noia*, 372 U.S. 391 (1963) (*see infra*, Chapter 7); *Townsend v. Sain*, 372 U.S. 293 (1963) (*see infra*, Chapter 6); and *Sanders v. United States*, 373 U.S. 1 (1963) (*see infra*, Chapter 11). These cases caused an unprecedented expansion in the reach of the federal writ, engendered much resentment from the states, and were a large part of the application of the Bill of Rights and civil rights decisions of the 1960s.

Brown v. Allen often is credited as the start of modern habeas corpus jurisprudence.

Brown v. Allen
344 U.S. 443 (1953)

JUSTICE REED delivered the opinion of the Court.

---

4. See generally SHELVIN SINGER & MARSHALL J. HARTMAN, CONSTITUTIONAL CRIMINAL PROCEDURE HANDBOOK, Chapter 1 (1986), for a discussion of the legislative intent of Congress in making the Bill of Rights obligatory on the States through the Fourteenth Amendment.

5. Prior to these cases, the Supreme Court held that the protections guaranteed by the Bill of Rights applied only in federal court. They refused to hold these protections applicable to the states. *See, e.g., Gideon v. Wainright*, 372 U.S. 335 (1963) (requiring the appointment of counsel to the criminally accused in state court); *Miranda v. Arizona*, 384 U.S. 436 (1966) (requiring the recitation of one's right to remain silent and to consult with an attorney while being questioned in state custody).

6. *See* ERWIN CHEMERINSKY, FEDERAL JURISDICTION 172 (4th ed. 2003).

Certiorari was granted to review judgments of the United States Court of Appeals for the Fourth Circuit. ***[7]

[Those] judgments of affirmance were entered October 12, 1951, on appeal from three judgments of the United States District Court for the Eastern District of North Carolina, refusing writs of habeas corpus sought by prisoners convicted in that state. We conclude that all required procedure for state review of the convictions had been exhausted by petitioners in each case before they sought the writs of habeas corpus in the federal courts. In each case petitions for certiorari to this Court for direct review of the state judgments rendered by the highest court of the state in the face of the same federal issues now presented by habeas corpus had been denied. *** It is not necessary in such circumstances for the prisoner to ask the state for collateral relief, based on the same evidence and issues already decided by direct review with another petition for certiorari directed to this Court. *** [After discussing the procedural history of the consolidated cases, the court continues.]

When, in April 1948, Judge Maris presented the Judicial Conference draft of § 2254 to the Senate Judiciary Subcommittee, the language of the revision of 28 U.S.C., on which the hearings [in question] were being held, set out three bases for exercise of federal jurisdiction over applications for habeas corpus from state prisoners. Under the language of the bill as it then read, an application might have been entertained where it appeared (1) that the applicant had exhausted the remedies available in the courts of the state, or (2) where there was no adequate remedy available in such courts, or (3) where such courts had denied the applicant a fair adjudication of the legality of his detention under the Constitution and laws of the United States. In accepting the recommendation of the Judicial Conference, the Congress eliminated the third basis of jurisdiction. ***

If the substitution for "adequate remedy available" of the present definition was intended by the Congress to eliminate the right of a state prisoner to apply for relief by habeas corpus to the lower federal courts, we do not think that the report would have suggested that a remedy for denial of a "fair adjudication" was in the federal court. The suggested elimination of district and circuit courts does not square with the other statutory habeas corpus provisions. *See* 28 U.S.C. §§ 2241, 2242, 2251, 2252, 2253, 3d paragraph. We are unwilling to conclude without a definite congressional direction that so radical a change was intended. In each of these cases the District Court, in determining the propriety of its granting the writ, considered the effect of our refusal of certiorari on the same questions upon direct review of the judgments of the highest court of the state. ***

***

II. Effect of Former Proceedings.

The effect to be given this Court's former refusal of certiorari in these cases was presented to the District Court which heard the applications for federal habeas corpus upon full records of the state proceedings in the trial and appellate courts. ***

***

A. *Effect of Denial of Certiorari.*—In cases such as these, a minority of this Court is of the opinion that there is no reason why a district court should not give consideration

---

7. Throughout this book we use ** to indicate that we omitted a citation or group of citations, and we use *** to indicate we omitted text and/or a footnote.

to the record of the prior certiorari in this Court and such weight to our denial as the District Court feels the record justifies. This is the view of the Court of Appeals.** This is, we think, the teaching of *Ex parte Hawk*, 321 U.S. 114, 118 [(1944),] and *White v. Ragen*, 324 U.S. 760, 764, 765 [(1945)]. We have frequently said that the denial of certiorari "imports no expression of opinion upon the merits of a case." ***

B. *Effect of State Court Adjudications.*—With the above statement of the position of the minority on the weight to be given our denial of certiorari, we turn to another question. The fact that no weight is to be given by the Federal District Court to our denial of certiorari should not be taken as an indication that similar treatment is to be accorded to the orders of the state courts. So far as weight to be given the proceedings in the courts of the state is concerned, a United States district court, with its familiarity with state practice is in a favorable position to recognize adequate state grounds in denials of relief by state courts without opinion. *A fortiori*, where the state action was based on an adequate state ground, no further examination is required, unless no state remedy for the deprivation of federal constitutional rights ever existed. *Mooney v. Holohan*, 294 U.S. 103 [(1935)]; *Ex parte Hawk*, 321 U.S. 114 [(1944)]. Furthermore, where there is material conflict of fact in the transcripts of evidence as to deprivation of constitutional rights, the District Court may properly depend upon the state's resolution of the issue. *Malinski v. New York*, 324 U.S. 401, 404 [(1945)]. In other circumstances the state adjudication carries the weight that federal practice gives to the conclusion of a court of last resort of another jurisdiction on federal constitutional issues. It is not res judicata. ***

Furthermore, in view of the consideration that was given by the District Court to our denial of certiorari in these cases, should we return them to that court for reexamination in the light of this Court's ruling upon the effect to be given to the denial? We think not. From the findings of fact and the judgments of the District Court we cannot see that such consideration as was given by that court to our denials of certiorari could have had any effect on its conclusions as to whether the respective defendants had been denied federal constitutional protection. *** It is true, under the Court's ruling today, that the District Court in each of the three cases erroneously gave consideration to our denial of certiorari. It is also true that its rulings, set out above, show that without that consideration, it found from its examination of the state records and new evidence presented that the conduct of the respective state proceedings was in full accord with due process. Such conclusions make immaterial the fact that the trial court gave consideration to our denial of certiorari.

The District Court and the Court of Appeals recognized the power of the District Court to reexamine federal constitutional issues even after trial and review by a state and refusal of certiorari in this Court. *Darr v. Burford*, 339 U.S. [200,] 214 [(1950)]. The intimation to the contrary in *Speller* [v. Crawford, 99 F. Supp. 92, 95 (E.D.N.C. 1951)], must be read as the Court's opinion after the hearing. "In the review of judicial proceedings the rule is settled that, if the decision below is correct, it must be affirmed, although the lower court relied upon a wrong ground or gave a wrong reason." *** Certainly the consideration given by the District Court to our former refusals of certiorari on the issues presented cannot affect its determinations that there was no merit in any of the applications for habeas corpus. ** Where it is made to appear affirmatively, as here, that the alleged error could not affect the result, such errors may be disregarded even in the review of criminal trials. *** Whether we affirm or reverse in these cases, therefore, does not depend upon the trial court's consideration of our denial of certiorari but upon the soundness of its decisions upon the issues of alleged violation of federal procedural requirements or of petitioner's constitutional rights by the North Carolina proceedings. We now take up those problems.

III. Right to Plenary Hearing.

Petitioner alleges a procedural error in No. 32, *Brown v. Allen*. As we stated in the preceding subdivision, the writ of habeas corpus was refused on the entire record of the respective state and federal courts. ** It is petitioner's contention, however, that the District Court committed error when it took no evidence and heard no argument on the federal constitutional issues. He contends he is entitled to a plenary trial of his federal constitutional issues in the District Court. He argues that the Federal District Court, with jurisdiction of the particular habeas corpus, must exercise its judicial power to hear again the controversy notwithstanding prior determinations of substantially identical federal issues by the highest state court, either on direct review of the conviction or by post-conviction remedy, habeas corpus, coram nobis, delayed appeal or otherwise. ***

Jurisdiction over applications for federal habeas corpus is controlled by statute. *** The Code directs a court entertaining an application to award the writ. *** But an application is not "entertained" by a mere filing. Liberal as the courts are and should be as to practice in setting out claimed violations of constitutional rights, the applicant must meet the statutory test of alleging facts that entitle him to relief. ***

The word "entertain" presents difficulties. Its meaning may vary according to its surroundings. *** In §2243 and §2244 we think it means a federal district court's conclusion, after examination of the application with such accompanying papers as the court deems necessary, that a hearing on the merits, legal or factual, is proper. ***

It is clear by statutory enactment that a federal district court is not required to entertain an application for habeas corpus if it appears that "the legality of such detention has been determined by a judge or court of the United States on a prior application for a writ of habeas corpus." ***

Furthermore, in enacting 28 U.S.C. §2254, dealing with persons in custody under state judgments, Congress made no reference to the power of a federal district court over federal habeas corpus for claimed wrongs previously passed upon by state courts. *** A federal judge on a habeas corpus application is required to "summarily hear and determine the facts, and dispose of the matter as law and justice require." 28 U.S.C. §2243. This has long been the law. ***

Applications to district courts on grounds determined adversely to the applicant by state courts should follow the same principle—a refusal of the writ without more, if the court is satisfied, by the record, that the state process has given fair consideration to the issues and the offered evidence, and has resulted in a satisfactory conclusion. Where the record of the application affords an adequate opportunity to weigh the sufficiency of the allegations and the evidence, and no unusual circumstances calling for a hearing are presented, a repetition of the trial is not required. ** However, a trial may be had in the discretion of the federal court or judge hearing the new application. A way is left open to redress violations of the Constitution. ** Although they have the power, it is not necessary for federal courts to hold hearings on the merits, facts or law a second time when satisfied that federal constitutional rights have been protected. *** It is necessary to exercise jurisdiction to the extent of determining by examination of the record whether or not a hearing would serve the ends of justice. ** As the state and federal courts have the same responsibilities to protect persons from violation of their constitutional rights, we conclude that a federal district court may decline, without a rehearing of the facts, to award a writ of habeas corpus to a state prisoner where the legality of such detention has been determined, on the facts presented, by the highest state court with jurisdiction, whether through affirmance of the judgment on appeal or denial of post-conviction remedies. **

As will presently appear, this case involves no extraordinary situation. Since the complete record was before the District Court, there was no need for rehearing or taking of further evidence. Treating the State's response to the application as a motion to dismiss, the court properly granted that motion. Discharge from conviction through habeas corpus is not an act of judicial clemency but a protection against illegal custody.

The need for argument is a matter of judicial discretion. All issues were adequately presented. There was no abuse.

IV. Disposition of Constitutional Issues.

[The Court proceeds to discuss and ultimately agree with the district court's denial of the writ based on "unconstitutional exclusions of Negroes" from juries in *Brown v. Allen*. The Court then examines and agrees with the district court's rejection of Brown's claim of unconstitutional use of a coerced confession. Next, the Court turns to *Speller v. Allen* and affirms the district court's rejection of Speller's claim of unconstitutional exclusion of black jurors. The analysis of *Speller* continues.]

It is suggested that the record shows that the names of colored persons in the jury box were marked with a dot or period on the scroll. This could be used for unlawful disposition of such scrolls when drawn. Such a scheme would be useless in the circumstances of this case. The record shows that the defendant and his counsel were present when the venire was drawn by a child, aged 5. All of the names drawn were given to the sheriff and summonses were issued. As a matter of fact the special venire contained the names of seven Negroes. Four appeared. None sat as jurors. Therefore the assertion as to the dots, even if true, means no more than that some unknown person desired to interfere with the fair drawing of juries in Vance County. The trial court found against petitioner on this question. The District Court pointed out its immateriality. **

This box was filled by names selected by the clerk of the jury commissioners and corrected by the commissioners. The names put in were substantially those selected by the clerk, who chose them from those on the tax lists who had "the most property." The clerk testified no racial discrimination entered into his selection. Since the effect of this possible objection to the selection of jurors on an economic basis was not raised or developed at the trial, on appeal to the State Supreme Court, on the former certiorari to this Court, or in the petition or brief on the present certiorari to this Court, it is not open to consideration here. *** Such an important national asset as state autonomy in local law enforcement must not be eroded through indefinite charges of unconstitutional actions. ***

　　　***

The trial and district courts, after hearing witnesses, found no racial discrimination in the selection of the prospective jurors. The conviction was upheld as nondiscriminatory by the State Supreme Court, which had once acted to reverse a conviction of this defendant by a jury deemed tainted with racial discrimination, ** and again to reverse a conviction when adequate time for investigation of discrimination had not been given. ** It would require a conviction, by this Court, of violation of equal protection through racial discrimination to set aside this trial. Our delicate and serious responsibility of compelling state conformity to the Constitution by overturning state criminal convictions, should not be exercised without clear evidence of violation.

Disregarding, as we think we should, the clerk's unchallenged selections based on taxable property, there is no evidence of racial discrimination. Negroes' names now appear in the jury box. If the requirement of comparative wealth is eliminated, and the statutory standards employed, the number would increase to the equality justified by their moral and educational qualification for jury service as compared with the white race. We do not think the small number, by comparison, of Negro names in this one jury box, is, in itself, enough to establish racial discrimination.

*** We have the problems presented by No. 20, *Daniels v. Allen*. The two petitioners, Negroes, were indicted and convicted in the North Carolina courts on a charge of murder. Their trial in the Superior Court of Pitt County resulted in a verdict of guilty, and each petitioner was thereafter sentenced to death. There is no issue over guilt under the evidence introduced. In addition to the objections stated above, ** — discrimination in jury lists, coerced confessions and refusal to hear on the merits — there is also objection here to the procedure for determination of the voluntariness of the confessions. As the failure to serve the statement of the case on appeal seems to us decisive, we do not discuss in detail the other constitutional issues tendered and only point out that they were resolved against the petitioners by the sentencing state court and the Federal District Court after full hearing of the evidence offered. ***

***

This situation confronts us. North Carolina furnished a criminal court for the trial of those charged with crime. Petitioners at all times had counsel, chosen by themselves and recognized by North Carolina as competent to conduct the defense. In that court all petitioners' objections and proposals, whether of jury discrimination, admission of confessions, instructions or otherwise, were heard and decided against petitioners. The state furnished an adequate and easily-complied-with method of appeal. This included a means to serve the statement of the case on appeal in the absence of the prosecutor from his office. ** Yet petitioners' appeal was not taken and the State of North Carolina, although the full trial record and statement on appeal were before it, refused to consider the appeal on its merits. ***

The writ of habeas corpus in federal courts is not authorized for state prisoners at the discretion of the federal court. It is only authorized when a state prisoner is in custody in violation of the Constitution of the United States. 28 U.S.C. § 2241, [28 U.S.C.A. § 2241]. That fact is not to be tested by the use of habeas corpus in lieu of an appeal. *** To allow habeas corpus in such circumstances would subvert the entire system of state criminal justice and destroy state energy in the detection and punishment of crime.

Of course, federal habeas corpus is allowed where time has expired without appeal when the prisoner is detained without opportunity to appeal because of lack of counsel, incapacity, or some interference by officials. *** Also, this Court will review state habeas corpus proceedings even though no appeal was taken, if the state treated habeas corpus as permissible. *** Federal habeas corpus is available following our refusal to review such state habeas corpus proceedings. *** Failure to appeal is much like a failure to raise a known and existing question of unconstitutional proceeding or action prior to conviction or commitment. Such failure, of course, bars subsequent objection to conviction on those grounds. ***

North Carolina has applied its law in refusing this out-of-time review. *** This Court applies its jurisdictional statute in the same manner. ** We cannot say that North Carolina's action in refusing review after failure to perfect the case on appeal violates the Federal Constitution. A period of limitation accords with our conception of proper procedure.

Finally, federal courts may not grant habeas corpus for those convicted by the state except pursuant to § 2254. ** We have interpreted § 2254 as not requiring repetitious

applications to state courts for collateral relief, ** but clearly the state's procedure for relief must be employed in order to avoid the use of federal habeas corpus as a matter of
procedural routine to review state criminal rulings. A failure to use a state's available
remedy, in the absence of some interference or incapacity, *** bars federal habeas corpus. The statute requires that the applicant exhaust available state remedies. To show
that the time has passed for appeal is not enough to empower the Federal District Court
to issue the writ. The judgments must be affirmed.

***

The judgments are affirmed.

JUSTICE JACKSON, concurring in the result.

Controversy as to the undiscriminating use of the writ of habeas corpus by federal
judges to set aside state court convictions is traceable to three principal causes: (1) this
Court's use of the generality of the Fourteenth Amendment to subject state courts to
increasing federal control, especially in the criminal law field; (2) *ad hoc* determination
of due process of law issues by personal notions of justice instead of by known rules of
law; and (3) the breakdown of procedural safeguards against abuse of the writ.

***

But, once established, this jurisdiction obviously would grow with each expansion of
the substantive grounds for habeas corpus. The generalities of the Fourteenth Amendment are so indeterminate as to what state actions are forbidden that this Court has
found it a ready instrument, in one field or another, to magnify federal, and inciden-
tally its own, authority over the states. The expansion now has reached a point where
any state court conviction, disapproved by a majority of this Court, thereby becomes
unconstitutional and subject to nullification by habeas corpus. ***

***

JUSTICE BLACK, with whom JUSTICE DOUGLAS concurs, dissenting.

The four petitioners in these cases are under sentences of death imposed by North
Carolina state courts. All are Negroes. Brown and Speller were convicted of raping
white women; the two Daniels, aged 17 when arrested, were convicted of murdering a
white man. The State Supreme Court affirmed and we denied certiorari in all the cases.
These are habeas corpus proceedings which challenge the validity of the convictions.

I agree with the Court that the District Court had habeas corpus jurisdiction in all the
cases including power to release either or all of the prisoners if held as a result of violation of constitutional rights. This I understand to be a reaffirmance of the principle embodied in *Moore v. Dempsey*, 261 U.S. 86 [(1923)]. I also agree that in the exercise of this
jurisdiction the District Court had power to hear and consider all relevant facts bearing
on the constitutional contentions asserted in these cases. I disagree with the Court's conclusion that petitioners failed to establish those contentions. The chief constitutional
claims throughout have been and are: (a) extorted confessions were used to convict; (b)
Negroes were deliberately excluded from service as jurors on account of their race. For
the following reasons I would reverse each of the judgments denying habeas corpus.

First. In denying habeas corpus in all the cases, the District Court felt constrained to
give and did give weight to our prior denials of certiorari. So did the Court of Appeals. I
agree with the Court that this was error but disagree with its holding that the error was
harmless. It is true that after considering our denials of certiorari as a reason for refusing habeas corpus, the district judge attempted to pass upon the constitutional questions just as if we had not declined to review the convictions. But the record shows the

difficulty of his attempt to erase this fact from his mind and I am not willing to act on the assumption that he succeeded in doing so. Both the jury and confession questions raised in these death cases have entirely too much record support to refuse relief on such a questionable assumption. I would therefore reverse and remand all the cases for the district judge to consider and appraise the issues free from his erroneous belief that this Court decided them against petitioners by denying certiorari.

Second. Brown v. Allen, No. 32. Brown's death sentence for rape rests on an indictment returned by a Forsyth County grand jury. We recently reversed five North Carolina convictions on the ground that there had been a systematic racial exclusion of Negroes from Forsyth County's juries for many years prior to 1947. ***

*** [P]roof of a lesser degree of discrimination now than before 1949 is insufficient to show that impartial selection of jurors which the Constitution requires. Negroes are about one-third of Forsyth County's population. Consequently, the number of Negroes now called for jury duty is still glaringly disproportionate to their percentage of citizenship. It is not possible to attribute either the pre-1949 or the post-1949 disproportions entirely to accident. And the state has not produced evidence to show that the partial continuation of the long-standing failure to use Negro jurors is due to some cause other than racial discrimination. ***

Third. Speller v. Allen, No. 22. The jury that tried Speller was drawn from Vance County, North Carolina. Before this trial no Negro had served on a Vance County jury in recent years. No Negro had even been summoned. That this was the result of unconstitutional discrimination is made clear by the fact that Negroes constitute 45% of the county's population and 38% of its taxpayers. The Court holds, however, that this discrimination was completely cured by refilling the jury box with the names of 145 Negroes and 1,981 whites. Such a small number of Negro jurors is difficult to explain except on the basis of racial discrimination. ***

Fourth. Daniels v. Allen, No. 20. Here also evidence establishes an unlawful exclusion of Negroes from juries because of race. The State Supreme Court refused to review this evidence on state procedural grounds. Absence of state court review on this ground is now held to cut off review in federal habeas corpus proceedings. But in the two preceding cases where the State Supreme Court did review the evidence, this Court has also reviewed it. I find it difficult to agree with the soundness of a philosophy which prompts this Court to grant a second review where the state has granted one but to deny any review at all where the state has granted none. The following facts indicate the obviousness of discriminatory Negro exclusion from jury service in Pitt County where this case was tried. Negroes constituted about 47% of the population of the county and about one-third of the taxpayers. But the jury box of 10,000 names included at most 185 Negroes. And up to and including the Daniels' trial no Negro had ever served on a grand jury in modern times. Petitioners made objection in ample time to juries so discriminatorily chosen.

***

*** I read *Moore v. Dempsey, supra*, as standing for the principle that it is never too late for courts in habeas corpus proceedings to look straight through procedural screens in order to prevent forfeiture of life or liberty in flagrant defiance of the Constitution. *Cf. United States v. Kennedy*, 157 F.2d 811, 813 [(2d Cir. 1946)]. Perhaps there is no more exalted judicial function. I am willing to agree that it should not be exercised in cases like these except under special circumstances or in extraordinary situations. But I cannot join in any opinion that attempts to confine the Great Writ within rigid formalistic boundaries.

***

[Concurring and dissenting opinions, in which the justices join with each other on a variety of different points, are omitted.]

Notes

1. *Subsequent case history*

Clyde Brown and Raleigh Speller were both executed in North Carolina on May 29, 1953. Bennie Daniels and Lloyd Ray Daniels were both executed in North Carolina on November 6, 1953. *See* http://www.doc.state.nc.us/DOP/deathpenalty.

2. *The import of* Brown v. Allen

Brown v. Allen is considered by some to have greatly changed the reach of the writ of habeas corpus. Reading this case and the brief history that precedes it, does such an assessment seem to be correct?

3. *Article III*

Article III of the United States Constitution reads, in part: "The Privilege of the Writ of Habeas Corpus shall not be suspended unless when in Cases of Rebellion or Invasion the public Safety may require it." Why does the writ of habeas corpus figure so prominently in the Constitution?

Article III also states: "The judicial Power shall extend to all Cases, in Law and Equity, arising under this Constitution, the Laws of the United States, and Treaties made, or which shall be made, under their Authority." How did this grant of independence of the judiciary affect the decision in *Brown*?

Stages of a Criminal Case

The following is an overview of the stages of a criminal case. It may be useful to place habeas cases in context and to understand the sometimes complex procedural history of a case.

I. Arrest
    A. Charging decision
    B. If charged with a misdemeanor, then the case goes to whichever court hears those cases.
    C. If charged with a felony, then there must be a probable cause determination. This can be made by a grand jury or by a judge after a preliminary hearing.
II. Preliminary hearing
    A. Held to determine
        1. Was a crime committed?
        2. Is it likely or probable that the defendant committed that crime?
    B. If the answer to both questions is "yes," the defendant is "bound over" on the charge(s).
III. Grand jury
    A. A determination of probable cause can be made by a jury that meets in secret and deliberates the same issues as in section II above.
    B. At this hearing, however, the defendant has no right to be present or to have an attorney present to question witnesses.

IV. Pre-trial matters
    A. Both misdemeanors and felonies are placed on a judge's "call" (or docket) and may have one or more than one pre-trial hearing.
    B. At these hearings, there may be plea negotiations.
        1. A plea may be entered.
        2. Many times the plea is to a lesser charge, or for a guaranteed sentence.
    C. There may be pre-trial motions. Examples include:
        1. Motion to quash arrest for lack of probable cause
        2. Motion to suppress a statement due to its involuntary nature
        3. Motion to suppress the identification testimony of a witness due to a tainted identification procedure.
    D. If none of these motions is granted, or if some of them are granted but do not dispose of the case, the case is set for trial.
V. Trial
    A. Bench or jury (Both the prosecution and defense must agree to a jury waiver in most jurisdictions.)
    B. Jury selection
    C. Opening statements
    D. Prosecution's case-in-chief
        1. Witnesses presented
        2. Witnesses cross-examined
    E. There can be (but need not be) a defense case-in-chief.
        1. Witnesses presented
        2. Witnesses cross-examined
    F. The prosecution may present a rebuttal case.
    G. Sometimes the defense presents a surrebuttal case.
    H. Closing arguments
    I. Jury instructions
    J. Deliberation
    K. Verdict
        1. If the verdict is not guilty, that's the end.
        2. If the verdict is guilty, there is a sentencing hearing.
VI. Sentencing
    A. This happens after a plea or a guilty verdict.
    B. Presentence report (In most jurisdictions the probation department or some other arm of the court prepares such a report; however, most jurisdictions with the death penalty do not prepare this report if death is an option.)
    C. Guidelines
    D. Hearing
        1. Victim impact statement
        2. Evidence from defense
    E. Sentence is passed
VII. Right to appeal

B. Reasons for the Writ

Finality in Criminal Law and
Federal Habeas Corpus for State Prisoners
Harvard Law Review
January, 1963
Paul M. Bator
Copyright ©1963 by the Harvard Law Review Association; Paul M. Bator

***

The problem of finality in criminal law raises acute tensions in our society. This should not, of course, occasion surprise. For the processes of the criminal law are, after all, purposefully and designedly awful. Through them society purports to bring citizens to the bar of judgment for condemnation, and those condemned become for that reason subject to governmental power exercised in its acutest forms: loss of property, of liberty, even life. No wonder that our instinct is that we must be sure before we proceed to the end, that we will not write an irrevocable finis on the page until we are somehow truly satisfied that justice has been done.

But the general tendency to hesitate before pronouncing a final judgment *** in a criminal case is, I think, reinforced today by some rather special currents in our thought. Partly, our century has peculiarly sensitized us to and made us fearful of abuses of power exercised through the legal process; we find the claims of liberty, of our residue of autonomy, particularly sweet in an age of dictators, political prosecutions and concentration camps. More crucial, even, is our general and deep-seated uneasiness about the ethical and psychological premises of the criminal process itself. The notion that a criminal litigation has irrevocably ended may have been an acceptable one in an age with a robust confidence in (or, if you prefer, complacency about) the rationality and justice of the basic process itself. But no such confidence or complacency can be said to exist today. For some decades the purposes and methods of our penal law have been the subject of sustained and intensive criticism and debate. The general line of the challenge need not be detailed here; in summary we are told that the criminal law's notion of just condemnation and punishment is a cruel hypocrisy visited by a smug society on the psychologically and economically crippled; that its premise of a morally autonomous will with at least some measure of choice whether to comply with the values expressed in a penal code is unscientific and outmoded; that its reliance on punishment as an educational and deterrent agent is misplaced, particularly in the case of the very members of society most likely to engage in criminal conduct; and that its failure to provide for individualized and humane rehabilitation of offenders is inhuman and wasteful. ***

Although many lawyers—I dare say most lawyers—would disagree with many of these contentions, it cannot be doubted that the challenge has caused profound concern. And the response among many sensitive lawyers, judges and scholars has been, it seems to me, a peculiar receptivity toward claims of injustice which arise within the traditional structure of the system itself; fundamental disagreement and unease about the very bases of the criminal law has, inevitably, created acute pressure at least to expand and liberalize those of its processes and doctrines which serve to make more tentative its judgments or limit its power. In short, our fear (and, in some, conviction) that the entire apparatus of the criminal process may itself be fundamentally unjust makes us peculiarly unwilling to accept the notion that the end has finally come in a particular case;

the impulse is to make doubly, triply, even ultimately sure that the particular judgment is just, that the facts as found are "true" and the law applied "correct."

It is thus not surprising to find that turbulence surrounds the doctrines of the criminal law which determine when, if ever, a judgment of conviction assumes finality. One of the areas of acutest controversy, namely, the proper reach of the federal habeas corpus jurisdiction for state prisoners, is the subject of this essay. The problems created by this jurisdiction are peculiarly difficult because underlying dilemmas with respect to finality in criminal cases are here compounded by the complex demands of a federal system with its two sets of courts applying law derived from two sovereignties. Imbedded in this often murky and technical field of law are fundamental problems about justice: what processes and institutions in a federal system can best assure that the exercise of the powers invoked by a judgment of conviction will be based on premises acceptable politically and morally? When has justice been done?

The ultimate issue I propose to treat is this: under what circumstances should a federal district court on habeas corpus have the power to redetermine the merits of federal questions decided by the state courts in the course of state criminal cases?

Let us briefly review the structure within which this problem arises. A defendant is tried in a state court for an offense against state law. A variety of federal questions may arise in the course of the litigation; thus the accused may claim that the federal constitution precludes the state from introducing a confession which, he alleges, was forcibly extracted from him. It is, of course, the duty of the state court conscientiously to decide this federal question in accordance with the governing federal law, which the command of the supremacy clause *** makes applicable to the case. Let us assume that the state court does so: its decision will turn on findings of fact as to what phenomena existed or occurred bearing on the making of the confession, and on the application of federal legal standards to these facts. Alleged error in the disposition of the federal question may be and is, I further assume, properly raised for appellate review in the state system. On affirmance, the federal issue is subject to direct review by the United States Supreme Court, usually on certiorari, sometimes on appeal. In case of affirmance by that Court or a denial of the writ, the judgment, in the normal operations of the legal system, becomes final and binding. Should then a federal district court, in the face of such a judgment, have jurisdiction in a collateral habeas corpus proceeding to redetermine the federal question which the state court has already decided and which the Supreme Court has had an opportunity to review? The law today seems squarely to answer "yes"; the reigning principle is the striking one that a state prisoner may seek and automatically obtain federal district court collateral review of the merits of all federal (at least constitutional) questions, no matter how fully and fairly these have been litigated in the state-court system. ***

One word of reservation: I assume, in this article, that the defendant in the state case has not forfeited his right to litigate his federal claim by procedural default; in other words, I do not propose to deal with the vexing question whether a state prisoner who fails to raise his federal contentions in accordance with state procedural law loses his right to raise them on federal habeas corpus. ***

I. SOME GENERAL CONSIDERATIONS

A. Finality in Criminal Litigation

The federal writ of habeas corpus has its roots in the common law. *** Its function, in the great phrase, is to test "the legality of the detention of one in the custody of another." *** In our constitutional context this refers, of course, to detentions made illegal by federal law. Power to issue the writ is conferred, and this limitation made explicit, in section 2241 of the Judicial Code. ***

When is a state prisoner held in "violation" of federal law? I suppose that the answer that may first suggest itself is that one is held in violation of federal law whenever the state courts have erroneously decided a federal question bearing dispositively on the judgment authorizing the detention. And if this is the case, the proper reach of the jurisdiction can be tersely summarized: the writ should test the merits of every dispositive federal question in the case. ***

I do not claim that such a *result* is necessarily unsound. The conclusion that a federal court should, at some point, have the power to decide the merits of all federal constitutional questions arising in state criminal proceedings (with a habeas court doing so if the Supreme Court has failed to review the issue) may be a sound one, resting on the specific institutional and political premises of our constitutional federalism. The fourteenth amendment does, after all, direct supervening commands to the states in the management of their criminal law; the Constitution does not accept the state process as "complete." The creation of a remedial framework to ensure effective implementation of these commands is, therefore, one of the important tasks of our system. It is the purpose of the main body of this essay to analyze habeas corpus in terms of this task, to weigh the strength of the claim that federal rights should be tested by federal courts.

In these introductory pages, however, I want to ignore the special demands for a specifically federal forum to which habeas corpus may be responsive, and direct my attention more generally to the problem of finality as it bears on the great task of creating rational institutional schemes for the administration of the criminal law. More particularly, consider some of the general premises which may underlie the demand for relitigation of constitutional questions on habeas corpus. The fundamental assumption often seems to be a generalized version of the notion adverted to above: a prisoner is obviously held in violation of law if the decision to detain was "wrong." It would follow that a detention may not be considered lawful unless the proceedings leading to it were, in some ultimate sense, free of error, unless the facts as found were "really" true and the law "really" correctly applied. If a tribunal finds that the prisoner was not whipped in order to procure a confession, but, in fact, he actually was whipped, he is detained illegally. If the court determines that on the facts as found the confession was admissible, but the "correct" view of the law is that such a confession is not admissible, he is detained illegally. Underlying all the processes is the ultimate reality that he was wrongly condemned. *** And thus to determine the legality of the detention one must, evidently, determine whether the committing tribunal fell into error.

What must be noted, however, is that on this underlying premise the conclusion is inescapable that no detention can ever be finally determined to be lawful; for if legality turns on "actual" freedom from errors of either fact or law, whenever error is alleged the court passing on legality will necessarily have to satisfy itself by determining the merits whether in fact error occurred. After all, there is no ultimate guarantee that *any* tribunal arrived at the correct result; the conclusions of a habeas corpus court, or of any number of habeas corpus courts, that the facts were X and that on X facts Y law applies are not infallible; if the existence *vel non* of mistake determines the lawfulness of the judgment, there can be no escape from a literally endless relitigation of the merits because the possibility of mistake always exists.

In fact, doesn't the dilemma go deeper? As Professor Jaffe has taught us, if the lawfulness of the exercise of the power to detain turns on whether the facts which validate its exercise "actually" happened in some ultimate sense, power can never be exercised law-fully at all, because we can never absolutely recreate past phenomena and thus can never have final certainty as to their existence:

> A court cannot any more than any other human agency break down the barrier between appearance and reality. In short, the court can be wrong. ***

***

*** [I]f a criminal judgment is ever to be final, the notion of legality must at some point include the assignment of final competences to determine legality. But, it may be asked, why should we seek a point at which such a judgment becomes final? Conceding that no process can assure ultimate truth, will not repetition of inquiry stand a better chance of approximating it? In view of the awesomeness of the consequences of convic-tion, shouldn't we allow redetermination of the merits in an attempt to make sure that no error has occurred?

Surely the answer runs, in the first place, in terms of conservation of resources—and I mean not only simple economic resources, but all of the intellectual, moral, and political resources involved in the legal system. The presumption must be, it seems to me, that if a job can be well done once, it should not be done twice. ***

Mere iteration of process can do other kinds of damage. I could imagine nothing more subversive of a judge's sense of responsibility, of the inner subjective conscien-tiousness which is so essential a part of the difficult and subtle art of judging well, than an indiscriminate acceptance of the notion that all the shots will always be called by someone else. Of course this does not mean that we should not have appeals. As we shall see, important functional and ethical purposes are served by allowing recourse to an appellate court in a unitary system, and to a federal supreme court in a federal sys-tem. The acute question is the effect it will have on a trial judge if we then allow still further recourse where these purposes may no longer be relevant. What seems so objec-tionable is second-guessing merely for the sake of second-guessing, in the service of the illusory notion that if we only try hard enough we will find the "truth."

Another point, too, should be remembered. The procedural arrangements we create for the adjudication of criminal guilt have an important bearing on the effectiveness of the substantive commands of the criminal law. I suggest that finality may be a crucial el-ement of this effectiveness. Surely it is essential to the educational and deterrent func-tions of the criminal law that we be able to say that one violating that law will swiftly and certainly become subject to punishment, just punishment. Yet this threat may be under-mined if at the same time we so define the processes leading to just punishment that it can really never be finally imposed at all. A procedural system which permits an endless repetition of inquiry into facts and law in a vain search for ultimate certitude implies a lack of confidence about the possibilities of justice that cannot but war with the effec-tiveness of the underlying substantive commands. *** Furthermore, we should at least tentatively inquire whether an endless reopening of convictions, with its continuing un-derlying implication that perhaps the defendant can escape from corrective sanctions after all, can be consistent with the aim of rehabilitating offenders. *** The first step in achieving that aim may be a realization by the convict that he is justly subject to sanc-tion, that he stands in need of rehabilitation; and a process of reeducation cannot, per-haps, even begin if we make sure that the cardinal moral predicate is missing, if society itself continuously tells the convict that he may not be justly subject to reeducation and treatment in the first place. The idea of just condemnation lies at the heart of the crimi-nal law, and we should not lightly create processes which implicitly belie its possibility.

One further point should be made in this canvass of the general policies which support doctrines of finality in the criminal law. It is a point difficult to formulate because so easily twisted into an expression of mere complacency. Repose is a psychological necessity in a secure and active society, and it should be one of the aims—though, let me make explicit, not the sole aim—of a procedural system to devise doctrines which, in the end, do give us repose, do embody the judgment that we have tried hard enough and thus may take it that justice has been done. There comes a point where a procedural system which leaves matters perpetually open no longer reflects humane concern but merely anxiety and a desire for immobility. *** Somehow, somewhere, we must accept the fact that human institutions are short of infallible; there is reason for a policy which leaves well enough alone and which channels our limited resources of concern toward more productive ends. I want to be careful to stress that I do not counsel a smug acceptance of injustice merely because it is disturbing to worry whether injustice has been done. What I do seek is a general procedural system which does not cater to a perpetual and unreasoned anxiety that there is a possibility that error has been made in every criminal case in the legal system.

B. Limitations on the Policies of Finality

I am aware that my argument may seem to go too far. Nobody contends, and I would not do so either, that the legal system would be better served if all courts of original jurisdiction had final competence to decide all cases. The possibilities of error, oversight, arbitrariness and even venality in any human institution are such that subjecting decisions to review of some kind answers a felt need: it would simply go against the grain, today, to make a matter as sensitive as a criminal conviction subject to unchecked determination by a single institution. ***

                    ***

Let me repeat, then, that the point is not that no court should review any other court. Nor do I suggest at this stage that a federal habeas corpus court should not review the merits of all federal questions litigated in the state court, that valid justifications, rooted in our federalism, of such a jurisdiction may not be forthcoming. All I say is that it is not enough to validate the jurisdiction to assert that some error of fact or law as to the federal question may in fact occur in a state litigation. The point can be put in terms of a limiting (rather than defining) principle: if one set of institutions has been granted the task of finding the facts and applying the law and does so in a manner rationally adapted to the task, in the absence of institutional or functional reasons to the contrary we should accept a presumption against mere repetition of the process on the alleged ground that, after all, error could have occurred.

I should like now to set forth certain limiting principles at the other extreme: general categories where it seems to me plain that the first go-around, whether in a unitary or a federal system, should not count, and where relitigation serves obvious and appropriate ends.

1. *Failure of Process.*—The first category has been implicit throughout the discussion. I have said that, presumptively, a process fairly and rationally adapted to the task of finding the facts and applying the law should not be repeated. This suggests that it is always an appropriate inquiry whether previous process was meaningful process, that is, whether the conditions and tools of inquiry were such as to assure a reasoned probability that the facts were correctly found and the law correctly applied. At the very least if no opportunity at all was provided to litigate a question which the applicable law makes

relevant to the disposition of the case, it is just and useful to have a subsequent "supervisory" jurisdiction, as it were, to furnish such an opportunity. Similarly, if the conditions under which a question was litigated were not fairly and rationally adapted for the reaching of a correct solution of any issue of fact or law, there would seem to be no reason of principle to immunize the solution reached; that issue should be redetermined. Suppose that well-supported allegations are made on collateral attack that the trial judge in a criminal trial was bribed to convict (and that the prisoner did not discover this until the time for appeal had expired). The appropriateness of exercising a collateral jurisdiction would seem beyond question: a "trial" under such circumstances is not a rational method of inquiry into questions of fact or law, and no reason exists to respect its conclusions. The same would be true of a case where a mob is alleged to have dominated the trial court and jury, and no remedy was provided on appeal to test this allegation itself. Again, suppose a prisoner alleges that he was, through torture, forced to plead guilty. Such a finding of "guilt" manifestly should not "count" as a full and fair litigation which forecloses further inquiry; and, if no remedy exists by appeal (as it would not if the coercion was "successful" enough), it is plainly appropriate to test it on collateral attack.

What binds these cases together is that in all of them the inquiry is, initially directed, not at the question whether substantive error of fact or law occurred, but at whether the processes previously employed for determination of questions of fact and law were fairly and rationally adapted to that task. ***

***

We must therefore be wary before assuming too easily that the absence of state process should be cured by using the federal habeas jurisdiction as a backstop, as it were, rather than exercising a more direct control by an affirmative command that the state may not imprison the defendant without itself providing such process. What we have is a question, to be answered in light of the political, institutional and functional considerations, as to which route we should take. ***

One more caution should be added. Even if we conclude that we should have a federal collateral jurisdiction to test the integrity of previous state proceedings, this does not mean that such a jurisdiction should assume the precise form which has been associated traditionally with the writ of habeas corpus. Most significantly, we should be aware that the policies we have been discussing do not support the notion that federal collateral attack should be available without limit of time. The fact that a forum is called for to test an allegation of coercion of a guilty plea or prosecution perjury does not tell us that a prisoner should be free to wait to raise these at his pleasure. The policies of finality and repose must surely play a role even when there has been failure of process, though the role may be the more limited one of placing on the prisoner the obligation to make his allegations within a reasonable time after they have become available to him.

2. *Failure of Jurisdiction.* — The second category which furnishes appropriate limitation on notions of finality in the criminal law is the most traditional one of all, involving the concept, so vexing and difficult on its edges, yet so useful at the core, of "jurisdiction." It is black-letter in civil as well as criminal law that the judgment of a court without at least colorable jurisdiction or competence to deal with the issue it is purporting to decide enjoys no immunity from collateral attack. *** The reason must be plain: it is not that the decision may be erroneous, but that allowing it to "count" would violate the political rules allocating institutional competences to deal with various matters. ***

***

Let me now summarize my conclusions. It has not been my purpose to set up hard and fast touchstones for the habeas corpus jurisdiction. More particularly let me again warn the reader explicitly that what has gone before does not purport to be an analysis of the possible roles which such a jurisdiction can play in a constitutional federalism. It may be entirely justified and appropriate that the question whether a defendant has been deprived of federal constitutional rights should always be decided by a federal constitutional court. That is the question which I will treat in detail in the latter parts of this essay. What I have tried to do so far is simply to canvass some of the underlying general problems of finality, without reference to the special institutional and functional claims of federalism, and to establish a set of limiting notions. In these terms, then, I see the need for a tentative presumption that questions fairly and fully canvassed by institutions with general competence to deal with such questions and making use of processes fairly and rationally adapted to the function of deciding them should not be relitigated *unless* felt functional or institutional requirements call for the repetition. On the other hand, as the proposition implies, subsequent jurisdictions should be free to ignore decisions previously made by institutions without colorable competence in the premises; and should in any event be free to direct inquiry into the question whether the totality of previous proceedings furnished the defendant with a full and fair opportunity to litigate his case.

With this general introduction I turn now to a study of the law of federal habeas corpus itself. The next section of this article describes and analyzes the development of the jurisdiction up to the decision in *Brown v. Allen*, *** which explicitly enthroned the principle that all federal constitutional questions decided in state criminal cases may be redetermined on the merits on federal habeas corpus. The remainder of the article is then devoted to an analysis of the doctrine of that case.

[Section II, wherein Professor Bator discusses the history and body of law pertaining to habeas, is omitted.]

III. *Brown v. Allen* AND ITS JUSTIFICATIONS

A. The Decision and Its Problems

Brown v. Allen *** reached the Supreme Court in the 1951 Term and was decided in 1953. It involved three proceedings: Brown's, Speller's, and Daniels'; only the first two need concern us here. Brown was convicted of rape by a North Carolina court and sentenced to death. In his appeal to the state supreme court he claimed his conviction violated the federal constitution because of the admission of a coerced confession and racial discrimination in the selection of grand and petit juries. These issues had been fully litigated, with the aid of counsel, in the trial court through procedures not themselves alleged to have been in any way unfair. The state supreme court affirmed the conviction, rejecting the defendant's federal contentions on the merits in a reasoned opinion. *** Certiorari was denied. *** The prisoner then sought federal habeas corpus. The district court denied the writ without holding a hearing, and the court of appeals affirmed. ***

Speller, also a capital case, likewise involved a claim of racial discrimination in jury selections which had been fully litigated in the state system. (Indeed, the state courts had twice previously reversed Speller's convictions, first on the ground that such discrimination was shown, and then after retrial because his counsel had not been furnished adequate opportunity to test the question; *** this was, therefore, Speller's third trial.) The state supreme court rejected the allegation on the merits, and certiorari was denied. *** Now Speller, too, sought habeas. The district court took testimony on the discrimination issue in addition to considering the state record, and denied the writ. Again, the court of appeals affirmed. ***

The Supreme Court granted certiorari in both cases and affirmed the convictions. It did so, however, not on the basis of *Frank v. Mangum*, that the state had provided adequate corrective process, but by reaching and rejecting on the merits the federal claims presented which had been previously adjudicated by the state courts. The Court did so without any explicit discussion of the question of jurisdiction or any apparent understanding of how radical this step was: with only Mr. Justice Jackson disagreeing, eight of nine Justices assumed that on habeas corpus federal district courts must provide review of the merits of constitutional claims fully litigated in the state-court system. As Professor Hart says, the decision thus "manifestly broke new ground." It seems to say

> that due process of law in the case of state prisoners is not primarily concerned with the adequacy of the state's corrective process or of the prisoner's personal opportunity to avail himself of this process…but relates essentially to the avoidance in the end of any underlying constitutional error.… ***

And ever since *Brown v. Allen* the Supreme Court has continued to assume, without discussion, that it is the purpose of the federal habeas corpus jurisdiction to redetermine the merits of federal constitutional questions decided in state criminal proceedings. ***

What is the basis of *Brown v. Allen*? The opinions do not cast much light on that question. Mr. Justice Frankfurter, in one of the two opinions of the Court in the case, repeatedly asserts, without discussion, that the act of 1867 compels the conclusion that state consideration "cannot foreclose" federal determination of the merits of constitutional claims; *** he says that as to all legal issues (such as the admissibility of a confession) the district judge "must" exercise his own judgment, *** that Congress has "seen fit" to "give to the lower federal courts power to inquire into federal claims, by way of habeas corpus," and that it would be "inadmissible to deny the use of the writ merely because a State court has passed on a federal constitutional issue." *** But these are mere statements of conclusion; they ignore completely that such a purpose cannot be derived automatically from either the language or history of the 1867 act, and that the act was not so understood in the first eighty years of its history; they ignore, too, the explicit ruling in *In re Wood* *** that at least the question of jury discrimination in violation of the Constitution is not a question open on collateral attack if opportunity to litigate it was afforded in the state system and on direct review.

Oddly enough, much of the discussion in the two majority opinions in *Brown* deals not with the question why a state's adjudication of the law should be disregarded, but why the state's adjudication of the facts should not necessarily be disregarded. Mr. Justice Reed states that no new hearing as to the facts is necessary if the district court is satisfied that the state process has given them "fair consideration" and resulted in a "satisfactory conclusion," if no "unusual circumstances" are present and the record "affords an adequate opportunity" to test the merits of the claim. *** The taking of new evidence by the district court is "in its discretion." *** Mr. Justice Frankfurter says that as to the facts, the state's conclusions "may" be accepted by the district judge "unless a vital flaw be found in the process of ascertaining such facts." *** These ambiguous formulations have created vexing problems as to the scope of review on habeas corpus which I need not canvass here. *** I do suggest, however, that the basic reason why the courts have had such difficulties in defining the scope of review on habeas is that the Court in *Brown* did not provide a principled rationalization of the purpose being served by affording the federal court the right to review the determination of the state court in the first instance. If it is the purpose of the habeas jurisdiction to assure that no error has been made, then there is no reason why the state courts' determinations of fact should be any more sacred than their conclusions of law. In view of the function of appellate courts to make pronouncements of law, it is manifestly sensible to restrict their review to issues of law. But district court jurisdiction on habeas certainly does not serve that purpose; and if the purpose is to assure "correct" determinations, that purpose should not be disregarded when the allegation is that the state court has erred in finding the facts bearing on a constitutional claim. On the other hand, if meaningful process serves as an adequate guarantee of the probability of the correctness of factfindings, we are entitled to some explanation why it does not satisfy us with respect to legal conclusions. ***

There is another aspect of this question which should be noticed. The Court in *Brown* made much of the notion that the integrity of a state's process with respect to factfinding should be respected. But it made clear that this is solely a matter of discretion, that the district judge may redetermine the facts even where there is no "unusual circumstance" or "vital flaw" which casts doubt on the adequacy of those findings; and the Court went out of its way to reaffirm this grant of discretion a few years later. *** But if the federal judge has an impeccable record before him, that is, he has no reason to believe that the factfinding processes of the state courts were in any way inadequate to the task at hand, on what principle should he decide whether to exercise such a discretion? Note that if he does exercise it, he would seem to be completely free to disregard the state-court findings even though the issue may turn on an assessment of the veracity of witnesses; in such a case we have the startling result that a state prisoner is deemed to be held in violation of the Constitution of the United States because a state judge believed the prosecution's witnesses and the federal judge believes those of the defendant.

Nor do the opinions in *Brown v. Allen* deal adequately with the grave problems of federalism created by the doctrine of that case. It is fashionable today to dismiss the resentments created in the states by the existence of an indiscriminate federal habeas jurisdiction; we are told that complaints about intrusion by federal habeas courts into state criminal processes are disingenuous, directed not at the remedy but at the substantive due process doctrines enforced thereby; *** we are further assured that such complaints are in any event beside the mark since very few prisoners are actually released by the federal courts. *** But the very unanimity of the resentment among state law-enforcement officials and judges, *** many of them, surely, as conscientious in their adherence to the Constitution and as intellectually honest as their critics, counsels, not against the jurisdiction, but against its indiscriminate expansion without principled justification. Note further that it was not state officials but the Judicial Conference of the United States, headed by Chief Justice Warren, which in 1955 adopted a report of a committee consisting of Circuit Judges Parker, Phillips and Stephens and District Judges Hooper, Vaught and Wyzanski, which stated that the expansion of the habeas jurisdiction has

> greatly interfered with the procedure of the State courts, delaying in many cases the proper enforcement of their judgments. Where adequate procedure is provided by State law for the handling of such matters, it is clear that the remedy should be sought in the State courts with any review…only by the Supreme Court…

and recommended, *inter alia*, statutory preclusion of the writ where a federal question was "raised and determined" in the state-court system. ***

The point is not that it is unseemly for a federal district judge to reverse the action of the highest court of the state, but that it is unseemly for him to do so without principled institutional justification for his power. This justification was simply not provided by the opinions in *Brown v. Allen*. ***

***

B. The Right to a Federal Forum

***

In fact the result of the rather wooden differentiation we now make between constitutional and nonconstitutional questions is not without its ironies. Why is it, for instance, that we go so far to allow relitigation of constitutional questions (even where the particular issue is closely balanced and technical) and yet do not allow any relitigation of the fundamental question of the factual guilt or innocence of the accused? If a state prisoner claims that he confessed after he was interrogated for six hours, not (as the state court found) for four, the law says he may relitigate the issue and, perhaps, gain release as a consequence, even though the evidence of guilt may be overwhelming. But if a defendant is convicted of murder and ten years later another person confesses to the crime, so that we can be absolutely certain that the defendant was innocent all the time, the law says that he must rely on executive clemency. Why? Why should we pay so little attention to finality with respect to constitutional questions when, in general, the law is so unbending with respect to other questions which, nevertheless, may bear as crucially on justice as any constitutional issue in the case?

In any event, even if we assume that issues bearing on constitutional rights are necessarily "important," this does not automatically validate the claim to a federal forum. Why should a federal court hear cases even if they do involve these important rights? The answer is, of course, clear where state courts will not—and are not compelled to—hear them at all or under fair circumstances. But what if a state court has done so? Is there any sense in which the federal courts will, in the abstract, be more "correct" with respect to issues of federal law than state courts? Surely not. There is no intrinsic reason why the fact that a man is a federal judge should make him more competent, or conscientious, or learned with respect to the applicable federal law than his neighbor in the state courthouse. The federal judge is more "correct" under the present system only because our institutional arrangements make him authoritative. As Justice Jackson pointed out about the Supreme Court itself:

> [R]eversal by a higher court is not proof that justice is thereby better done. There is no doubt that if there were a super-Supreme Court, a substantial proportion of our reversals of state courts would also be reversed. We are not final because we are infallible, but we are infallible only because we are final. ***

***

I do not wish to overstate the argument. Important values may be served by having federal judges pass on federal issues. Even in a very general sense a federal judge, operating within a different system and with a differently defined set of institutional responsibilities, may bring to bear on such issues an objectivity, a freshness and insight which may have been denied to the state judge, no matter how conscientious, whose perspective will be subtly shaped by implicit presumptions derived from his responsi-

bilities within the state institutional framework, who stands within that system. ***
More particular considerations may be mentioned too. The federal judge is independent by constitutional guarantee; the state judge may not be. The difference surely does
bear on conditions necessary for principled judging; it is, at least, a common assumption—perhaps implicit in the Constitution itself—that state courts may be more responsive to local pressures, local prejudices, local politics, than federal judges. *** And
there is, too, the fear that state officials, including judges, will somehow be less sympathetic or generous with respect to federal claims raised by state prisoners than federal
judges.

   ***

   *** If the purpose of the certiorari jurisdiction is to settle conflicts and decide im-
portant cases, the mere fact that in the process the Supreme Court (infallible only because it is final) has authority to make decisions which will be deemed right does not
prove that its jurisdiction is also necessary for the doing of justice, and therefore does
not tell us that without federal review the probabilities that the states will do justice are
unacceptably low.

   What it comes down to, really, is that the state prisoner in an important case does
have one more chance to persuade a set of judges—and judges, perhaps, of superior
objectivity and fresher perspective with respect to matters of federal law—to see the
case his way than the prisoner in an unimportant case. And this is a real difference. The
sense of inequality created by the discretionary certiorari jurisdiction does seem to me a
weighty and important consideration. Whether it serves in itself to justify *Brown v.
Allen*, in view of all the problems created, I am not at all sure. But at least it helps ratio-
nalize and explain it.

   ***

C. The Problem of Inadequate Supreme Court Supervision

   Another line of argument to support the present structure of the habeas corpus jurisdiction rests on the proposition that direct review by the Supreme Court provides inadequate supervision of the state courts' adjudications with respect to state defendants' federal constitutional rights. Of course, whether supervision is "adequate" turns on how one
defines the purposes being served by such supervision. Insofar as we are told that habeas
corpus is necessary because the overcrowding of the Supreme Court's docket makes it impossible for the Court to consider the merits of every case where a prisoner alleges that he
has been deprived of a constitutional right, *** this is but another version of the assertion
that a federal court should decide the merits of every such case. But there does exist another, rather different, problem. It stems from the well-known fact that the typical certiorari petition from a state prisoner, and the record, if any, that accompanies it, are often
wholly inadequate to inform the Supreme Court whether the case should be reviewed.
The petitions, we are told, drafted usually without a lawyer, are frequently unintelligible
and rarely clear; certified records are "almost unknown" and

   > the number of cases in which most of the papers necessary to prove what hap-
   > pened in the State proceedings are not filed is striking. Whether there has been
   > an adjudication or simply a perfunctory denial of a claim below is rarely ascer-
   > tainable. Seldom do we have enough on which to base a solid conclusion as to
   > the adequacy of the State adjudication. Even if we are told something about a
   > trial of the claims the applicant asserts, we almost never have a transcript of
   > these proceedings to assist us in determining whether the trial was adequate. ***

And these messy and often inscrutable petitions come before the Court in very large numbers indeed. ***

***

D. Some Cautions: The Inadequate State Process

The existence, notorious and oft-exhibited, of grave inadequacies in the states' criminal procedures, both original and post-conviction, makes the federal habeas corpus jurisdiction a present necessity. On this bedrock proposition I agree with the writ's defenders. These inadequacies have been explicitly acknowledged by distinguished state judges, including a committee of the Conferences of Chief Justices, whose report, recommending many improvements in state procedures, states that

> responsibility for the unfortunate conditions prevailing in habeas corpus litigation rests upon the State as well as upon the Federal judicial systems, and…the evils presently prevailing can be reduced substantially by action taken at the State level. ***

If any doubt remains as to this point, it should be allayed by Professor Curtis Reitz's admirable article in the University of Pennsylvania Law Review, [*Federal Habeas Corpus*, 108 U. Pa. L. Rev. 461 (1960)], in which he reports on a painstaking canvass of some thirty-five cases from a ten-year period involving state prisoners in which habeas corpus was ultimately granted by a federal court. These cases show beyond a doubt that the states frequently fail to provide a fair and rational setting for the litigation of claims of federal constitutional right, so that habeas turns out to be the only available remedy for the vindication of such claims.

What is, however, so hard for me to grasp is why the existence of habeas to cure failures of state process justifies its present reach to cases where there has not been such a failure of process. Inadequacies of state procedure do not validate the status quo. The issue is not whether the jurisdiction should be abolished but whether its expansion to cases where there is no reasoned basis to suspect failure to provide a rational trial of the federal question, before an unbiased tribunal and through fair procedures, is justified. ***

***

IV. CONCLUSION: THE ROLE OF DISCRETION

What should we conclude about *Brown v. Allen*? I do not pretend to find the answer easy, nor the claims for federal supervision unweighty. Their strength derives from our own historical experience. The last twenty-five years have seen rapid and tremendous expansion and movement in the substantive doctrines derived from the due process clause which limit the power of the states in their administration of criminal justice. It is natural that, in an era of such rapid growth in the substantive federal law, there should be a demand that the remedial system keep pace, that federal supervision be expanded to make sure that the states receive the new doctrines hospitably. And there is, of course, the underlying suspicion that in fact the states have not done so, that if we do not keep a sharp eye out, federal rights will be subtly eroded, verbal respect paid to the principles but the substance robbed of meaning through astringent and unsympathetic application. (The suspicion is surely fed by the knowledge that a substantial proportion of those accused of crime, particularly in the Southern States, will be Negroes.)

Yet we must remember that the remedial system we construct must be tailored for tomorrow as well as today. It is not fanciful to suppose that the law of due process for criminal defendants will, in the foreseeable future, reach a resting point, will become stabilized. ***

Similarly, I resist the notion that sound remedial institutions can be built on the premise that state judges are not in sympathy with federal law. Again we must think in terms of tomorrow as well as today. Hopefully we will reach the day when the suspicion will no longer be justified that state judges—especially Southern state judges—evade their responsibilities by giving only the appearance of fairness in their rulings as to state defendants' federal rights. The unification of the country is, after all, in progress; the day when Southern justice is like Northern justice, justice for the Negro like justice for the white, is no longer out of sight. And our remedial system ought to take account of this motion.

The crucial point, it is worth reiterating, is that the question before us is *not* whether federal supervision of the states' administration of criminal justice is necessary. The question is whether such supervision is inadequate if limited to the very sweeping powers of the Supreme Court on direct review, and of the district courts on habeas to inquire into the fairness of the state's process. Is more than this needed? Must there be further supervision if the Supreme Court has had a chance to review the case and has chosen not to, and if the federal district court finds that the state has afforded fair process for the litigation of federal rights?

True, it will be argued that such supervision cannot ensure that in each case the federal right has in fact been conscientiously protected; it does not guard against cases where there has been the appearance of fairness but not its inner essence. But is it so clear that it is the function of judicial review to give us this ultimate guarantee? *Can* the legal system assure us in any event of this ultimate inner conscientiousness? And may one not speculate that perhaps conscientiousness is a by-product not only of supervision from above but also of responsibility, that it is not the best way to assure honest respect for federal law to relieve the state judge of responsibility?

In sum, it seems to me that the proper verdict on the case made for *Brown v. Allen* is "not proven"—and I do think the burden of proof is on the proponents. I rest partly on the federalist premise, that the abrasions and conflicts created by federal interference with the states' administration of criminal justice should be avoided in the absence of felt need, where the institutional necessities are as dubious as they seem to me to be in this case. I also reason from the very real claims which the need for finality and repose seem to me to make on the criminal process, claims particularly strong in view of what I consider to be philosophically faulty premises about justice which are often at the heart of the demand that we repeat inquiry endlessly to make sure that no mistake has been made. And, finally, *Brown v. Allen* seems to me to be unresponsive to (and even subversive of) what should be our central aim: encouraging reform and improvement in state criminal procedures.

Nevertheless, I cannot pretend that the case the other way is weightless. Our traditional doctrines of judicial review do rest on the premise of good-faith judging. Whenever good faith is questioned, strain is put on the ordinary rules of review; and maybe untraditional and extraordinary accommodations should therefore be made. There is surely appeal in the notion, and perhaps it makes sense at a time when there still is a justified suspicion and distrust of state-court rulings as to federal constitutional rights, to have a jurisdiction with a large and roving commission "to prevent a complete miscarriage of justice"; *** maybe it is well that a writ the historic purpose of which is to furnish "a swift and imperative remedy in all cases of illegal restraint"…should be left fluid and free from the definiteness appropriate to ordinary jurisdictional doctrines. ***

Of course we should not forget that there is already in existence an instrument in the administration of criminal justice whose very purpose is to assure relief where there has been a miscarriage of justice: the power of executive clemency supposedly already gives us a roving commission, usually free of technicalities and jurisdictional limitations, to seek out and right injustice. In fact it is striking how often we lose sight of the pardon as an integral part of the administration of criminal justice; in many cases where judicial relief is sought by way of collateral attack, the question that leaps to mind is: why is not pardon the obvious and sound solution here? Why wasn't executive clemency exercised? Surely it is a sorry thing that in so many states the pardoning power has been allowed to atrophy, and is reserved for highly extraordinary (usually death) cases. And again we have the striking phenomenon that the states' own failure to provide, through the pardon, an effective instrument of justice has prompted a search for a federal substitute, in this case in the form of habeas corpus.

In any event, *Brown v. Allen* may be justified in terms of a need for an extraordinary roving jurisdiction to make sure once more that there has not been, with respect to constitutional rights, a miscarriage of justice; perhaps we do need to grant federal courts the power to redetermine the merits to assure that covert unfairness does not lurk behind the appearance of fairness. But if this is the theory of the jurisdiction, then what is called for, I submit, is a decision, based on all the facts, whether justice really does call for release in the particular case. Suppose, for instance, that a federal district judge finds (1) that the admissibility of a confession has been fully and fairly litigated in the state courts, on an impeccable record giving the Supreme Court a full opportunity to review if it so chooses; (2) that on the merits he disagrees with the state judges as to admissibility; and (3) that the evidence in the record apart from the confession, or, indeed, the trustworthiness of the confession itself, makes it absolutely clear that the defendant was guilty as charged. It is (today's) hornbook law that on direct review there would be automatic reversal, that neither the trustworthiness of the confession nor the other evidence of guilt can cure the error; let us, further, assume the soundness of this doctrine. But is it absolutely clear that the reasons which have moved us to so astringent a rule of law on the merits, as it were, should necessarily apply in a jurisdiction which is concededly extraordinary, the existence of which is justified by the need to make sure once more that justice in the particular case has indeed been done? Remember that I assume that full corrective process has been afforded in the original litigation: the defendant has had a fair opportunity to establish his federal claim. We now give him one more chance, in the fear that justice has miscarried. But has it miscarried if he has had one meaningful go-around and the district judge can be morally assured that he was guilty? I acknowledge that the purpose of the rule of automatic reversal is to deter uncivilized police behavior and to keep the courts' own processes unsullied; but the claims for deterrence do not strike me as so inexorable that we must honor them in cases where our fundamental purpose, in fact our justification for inquiry, is, after all, to do our best by the defendant; nor can I take too seriously the idea that the integrity of the legal process will be sullied if a court in effect finds that for purposes of the extraordinary habeas jurisdiction the admission of the confession—previously tested by fair process—was harmless error. ***

I continue to resist, in sum, the notion that the inquiry on habeas should be mere repetition, an exact replica, of what has gone before. I do not see that as institutionally justified. If we wish to have an ultimate recourse, if we want to grant the federal courts a roving extraordinary commission to undo injustice, then, it seems to me, all the factors which bear on justice should be put on the scales. If *Brown v. Allen* is to remain the law, it should be modified to make clear that where a federal constitutional question has been fully canvassed by fair state process, and meaningfully submitted for possible Supreme Court review, then the federal district judge on habeas, though entitled to redetermine the merits, has a large discretion to decide whether the federal error, if any, was prejudicial, whether justice will be served by releasing the prisoner, taking into account in the largest sense all the relevant factors, including his conscientious appraisal of the guilt or innocence of the accused on the basis of the full record before him.

Notes

1. *Critiquing Brown v. Allen*

Professor Bator writes critically about the decision in *Brown v. Allen*. What informs his criticism? Is his critique legal or political? Why?

2. *"Extraordinary roving jurisdiction"*

Toward the end of the article, Professor Bator states:

> In any event, *Brown v. Allen* may be justified in terms of a need for an extraordinary roving jurisdiction to make sure once more that there has not been, with respect to constitutional rights, a miscarriage of justice; perhaps we do need to grant federal courts the power to redetermine the merits to assure that covert unfairness does not lurk behind the appearance of fairness. But if this is the theory of the jurisdiction, then what is called for, I submit, is a decision, based on all the facts, whether justice really does call for release in the particular case.

Is Professor Bator correct about the "justification" for *Brown v. Allen*? Why or why not?

C. Introduction to the Antiterrorism and Effective Death Penalty Act of 1996 (AEDPA)

In 1996, Congress passed, and President Clinton signed into law, the Antiterrorism and Effective Death Penalty Act of 1996 (AEDPA), which substantially changed habeas corpus. As you work through this casebook you will see the evolution of the writ and the changes wrought by AEDPA. Before the act was passed, procedural rules were being tightened, making it more difficult for a petitioner to be heard in federal court, but after the AEDPA, those rules became even stronger.

The habeas corpus statute before the AEDPA read as follows:

28 U.S.C.A. § 2254:
State Custody; Remedies in Federal Court

(a) The Supreme Court, a Justice thereof, a circuit judge, or a district court shall entertain an application for a writ of habeas corpus in behalf of a person in custody pursuant to the judgment of a State court only on the ground that he is in custody in violation of the Constitution or laws or treaties of the United States.

(b) An application for a writ of habeas corpus in behalf of a person in custody pursuant to the judgment of a State court shall not be granted unless it appears that the applicant has exhausted the remedies available in the courts of the State, or that there is either an absence of available State corrective process or the existence of circumstances rendering such process ineffective to protect the rights of the prisoner.

(c) An applicant shall not be deemed to have exhausted the remedies available in the courts of the State, within the meaning of this section, if he has the right under the law of the State to raise, by any available procedure, the questions presented.

(d) In any proceeding instituted in a Federal court by an application for a writ of habeas corpus by a person in custody pursuant to the judgment of a State court, a determination after a hearing on the merits of a factual issue, made by a State court of competent jurisdiction in a proceeding to which the applicant for the writ and the State or an officer or agent thereof were parties, evidenced by a written finding, written opinion, or other reliable and adequate written indicia, shall be presumed to be correct, unless the applicant shall establish or it shall otherwise appear, or the respondent shall admit

   (1) that the merits of the factual dispute were not resolved in the State court hearing;

   (2) that the factfinding procedure employed by the State court was not adequate to afford a full and fair hearing;

   (3) that the material facts were not adequately developed at the State court hearing;

   (4) that the State court lacked jurisdiction of the subject matter or over the person of the applicant in the State court proceeding;

   (5) that the applicant was an indigent and the State court, in deprivation of his constitutional right, failed to appoint counsel to represent him in the State court proceeding;

   (6) that the applicant did not receive a full, fair, and adequate hearing in the state court proceeding[;] or

   (7) that the applicant was otherwise denied due process of law in the State court proceeding;

   (8) or unless that part of the record of the State court proceeding in which the determination of such factual issue was made, pertinent to a determination of the sufficiency of the evidence to support such factual determination, is produced as provided for hereinafter, and the Federal court on a consideration of such part of the record as a whole concludes that such factual determination is not fairly supported by the record. And in an evidentiary hearing in the proceeding in the Federal court, when due proof of such factual determination has been made, unless the existence of one or more of the circumstances respectively set forth in paragraphs numbered (1) to (7), inclusive, is shown by the applicant, otherwise unless the court concludes pursuant to the provisions of paragraph numbered (8) that the record in the State court proceeding, considered as a whole, does not fairly support such factual determination, the burden shall rest upon the applicant to establish by convincing evidence that the factual determination by the State court was erroneous.

(e) If the applicant challenges the sufficiency of the evidence adduced in such State court proceeding to support the State court's determination of a factual issue made therein, the applicant, if able, shall produce that part of the record pertinent to a determination of the sufficiency of the evidence to support such determination. If the applicant, because of indigency or other reason is unable to produce such part of the record, then the State shall produce such part of the record and the Federal court shall direct the State to do so by order directed to an appropriate State official. If the State cannot provide such pertinent part of the record, then the court shall determine under the existing facts and circumstances what weight shall be given to the State court's factual determination.

(f) A copy of the official records of the State court, duly certified by the clerk of such court to be a true and correct copy of a finding, judicial opinion, or other reliable written indicia showing such a factual determination by the State court shall be admissible in the Federal court proceeding.

Since the AEDPA was enacted, the statute now reads:

28 U.S.C.A. § 2254:
State Custody; Remedies in Federal Court

(a) The Supreme Court, a Justice thereof, a circuit judge, or a district court shall entertain an application for a writ of habeas corpus in behalf of a person in custody pursuant to the judgment of a State court only on the ground that he is in custody in violation of the Constitution or laws or treaties of the United States.

(b)(1) An application for a writ of habeas corpus on behalf of a person in custody pursuant to the judgment of a State court shall not be granted unless it appears that—

(A) the applicant has exhausted the remedies available in the courts of the State; or

(B)(i) there is an absence of available State corrective process; or

(ii) circumstances exist that render such process ineffective to protect the rights of the applicant.

(2) An application for a writ of habeas corpus may be denied on the merits, notwithstanding the failure of the applicant to exhaust the remedies available in the courts of the State.

(3) A State shall not be deemed to have waived the exhaustion requirement or be estopped from reliance upon the requirement unless the State, through counsel, expressly waives the requirement.

(c) An applicant shall not be deemed to have exhausted the remedies available in the courts of the State, within the meaning of this section, if he has the right under the law of the State to raise, by any available procedure, the question presented.

(d) An application for a writ of habeas corpus on behalf of a person in custody pursuant to the judgment of a State court shall not be granted with respect to any claim that was adjudicated on the merits in State court proceedings unless the adjudication of the claim—

(1) resulted in a decision that was contrary to, or involved an unreasonable application of, clearly established Federal law, as determined by the Supreme Court of the United States; or

(2) resulted in a decision that was based on an unreasonable determination of the facts in light of the evidence presented in the State court proceeding.

(e)(1) In a proceeding instituted by an application for a writ of habeas corpus by a person in custody pursuant to the judgment of a State court, a determination of a factual issue made by a State court shall be presumed to be correct. The applicant shall have the burden of rebutting the presumption of correctness by clear and convincing evidence.

(2) If the applicant has failed to develop the factual basis of a claim in State court proceedings, the court shall not hold an evidentiary hearing on the claim unless the applicant shows that—

(A) the claim relies on—

(i) a new rule of constitutional law, made retroactive to cases on collateral review by the Supreme Court, that was previously unavailable; or

(ii) a factual predicate that could not have been previously discovered through the exercise of due diligence; and

(B) the facts underlying the claim would be sufficient to establish by clear and convincing evidence that but for constitutional error, no reasonable factfinder would have found the applicant guilty of the underlying offense.

(f) If the applicant challenges the sufficiency of the evidence adduced in such State court proceeding to support the State court's determination of a factual issue made therein, the applicant, if able, shall produce that part of the record pertinent to a determination of the sufficiency of the evidence to support such determination. If the applicant, because of indigency or other reason is unable to produce such part of the record, then the State shall produce such part of the record and the Federal court shall direct the State to do so by order directed to an appropriate State official. If the State cannot provide such pertinent part of the record, then the court shall determine under the existing facts and circumstances what weight shall be given to the State court's factual determination.

(g) A copy of the official records of the State court, duly certified by the clerk of such court to be a true and correct copy of a finding, judicial opinion, or other reliable written indicia showing such a factual determination by the State court shall be admissible in the Federal court proceeding.

(h) Except as provided in section 408 of the Controlled Substances Act, in all proceedings brought under this section, and any subsequent proceedings on review, the court may appoint counsel for an applicant who is or becomes financially unable to afford counsel, except as provided by a rule promulgated by the Supreme Court pursuant to statutory authority. Appointment of counsel under this section shall be governed by section 3006A of title 18.

(i) The ineffectiveness or incompetence of counsel during Federal or State collateral post-conviction proceedings shall not be a ground for relief in a proceeding arising under section 2254.

Notes

1. Comparing pre- and post-AEDPA

What are some of the differences in the two statutes? What do you think were the reasons for the changes? For further discussion of some of the major changes in the statute, see Larry Yackle, *Federal Evidentiary Hearings Under the New Habeas Corpus Statute*, 6 B.U. Pub. Int. L.J. 135 (1996) (summarizing three paramount issues: "(1) when a federal court must or can hold its own evidentiary hearing; (2) the significance to be attached to previous state court findings of fact; and (3) the consequences of the petitioner's procedural default with respect to fact-finding in state court"; then finding that while the AEDPA has no bearing on the first issue, it has significant implications for the other two).

2. *Does the AEDPA apply to pending habeas petitions?*

If a state prisoner filed a habeas petition in federal district court *before* the AEDPA, but his petition was still pending when the AEDPA was enacted, should the AEDPA apply? See *Leavitt v. Arave*, 927 F. Supp. 394 (D. Idaho 1996), as well as other cases of interest, in *Current Developments in the Law: A Survey of Cases Affecting the Anti-Terrorism and Effective Death Penalty Act of 1996*, 6 B.U. Pub. Int. L.J. 333 (1996).

Chapter 2

Overview of Common Habeas Corpus Claims

The cases in this chapter outline the most common claims litigants raise in habeas corpus petitions. Section A introduces the concept of withholding exculpatory evidence, while Section B discusses ineffective assistance of counsel claims. In addition to discussing the seminal cases in these two arenas, this chapter continues to explore the basic procedural framework for habeas petitions discussed in Chapter 1.

A. Withholding Exculpatory Evidence

One of the cases on which the petitioners in *Strickler v. Greene* and *Kyles v. Whitley* relied to support their claims is *Brady v. Maryland*, 373 U.S. 83 (1963). After separate trials, petitioner Brady and a co-defendant, Boblit, each were found guilty of murder in the first degree and sentenced to death. At Brady's trial, which took place first, Brady took the stand and admitted his participation in the crime but claimed that Boblit did the actual killing. Defense counsel even conceded in closing argument that Brady was guilty of first-degree murder, asking only that the jury return the verdict "without capital punishment." Defense counsel made this admission because, prior to trial, defense counsel had asked the prosecution to allow him to examine Boblit's extra-judicial statements, and several of those statements were shown to him. Although defense counsel thus read several of Boblit's statements, the prosecution withheld a key statement in which Boblit admitted the actual homicide. That statement did not come to Brady's notice until after his conviction had been affirmed. When he later appealed to the United States Supreme Court, the Court held that prosecutorial suppression of evidence favorable to an accused—where the accused had requested such discovery—violates due process if the evidence is material either to guilt or punishment, irrespective of the good faith or bad faith of the prosecution.

In *Strickler v. Greene,* the Court considers a *Brady* violation in the context of a habeas petition. In *Kyles v. Whitley*, the Court discusses the circumstances under which a *Brady* violation that might or might not have been known to the prosecution becomes the prosecution's responsibility.

Strickler v. Greene
527 U.S. 263 (1999)

JUSTICE STEVENS delivered the opinion of the Court.

The District Court for the Eastern District of Virginia granted petitioner's application for a writ of habeas corpus and vacated his capital murder conviction and death sentence on the grounds that the Commonwealth had failed to disclose important exculpatory evidence and that petitioner had not, in consequence, received a fair trial. The Court of Appeals for the Fourth Circuit reversed because petitioner had not raised his constitutional claim at his trial or in state collateral proceedings. In addition, the Fourth Circuit concluded that petitioner's claim was, "in any event, without merit." ** Finding the legal question presented by this case considerably more difficult than the Fourth Circuit, we granted certiorari ** to consider (1) whether the State violated *Brady v. Maryland*, 373 U.S. 83 (1963), and its progeny; (2) whether there was an acceptable "cause" for petitioner's failure to raise this claim in state court; and (3), if so, whether he suffered prejudice sufficient to excuse his procedural default.

I

In the early evening of January 5, 1990, Leanne Whitlock, an African-American sophomore at James Madison University, was abducted from a local shopping center and robbed and murdered. In separate trials, both petitioner and Ronald Henderson were convicted of all three offenses. Henderson was convicted of first-degree murder, a noncapital offense, whereas petitioner was convicted of capital murder and sentenced to death. ***

At both trials, a woman named Anne Stoltzfus testified in vivid detail about Whitlock's abduction. The exculpatory material that petitioner claims should have been disclosed before trial includes documents prepared by Stoltzfus, and notes of interviews with her, that impeach significant portions of her testimony. We begin, however, by noting that, even without the Stoltzfus testimony, the evidence in the record was sufficient to establish petitioner's guilt on the murder charge. Whether petitioner would have been convicted of capital murder and received the death sentence if she had not testified, or if she had been sufficiently impeached, is less clear. To put the question in context, we review the trial testimony at some length.

The Testimony at Trial

At about 4:30 p.m. on January 5, 1990, Whitlock borrowed a 1986 blue Mercury Lynx from her boyfriend, John Dean, who worked in the Valley Shopping Mall in Harrisonburg, Virginia. At about 6:30 or 6:45 p.m., she left her apartment, intending to return the car to Dean at the mall. She did not return the car and was not again seen alive by any of her friends or family.

Petitioner's mother testified that she had driven petitioner and Henderson to Harrisonburg on January 5. She also testified that petitioner always carried a hunting knife that had belonged to his father. Two witnesses, a friend of Henderson's and a security guard, saw petitioner and Henderson at the mall that afternoon. The security guard was informed around 3:30 p.m. that two men, one of whom she identified at trial as petitioner, were attempting to steal a car in the parking lot. She had them under observation during the remainder of the afternoon but lost sight of them at about 6:45.

At approximately 7:30 p.m., a witness named Kurt Massie saw the blue Lynx at a location in Augusta County about 25 miles from Harrisonburg and a short distance from the cornfield where Whitlock's body was later found. Massie identified petitioner as the driver of the vehicle; he also saw a white woman in the front seat and another man in the back. Massie noticed that the car was muddy, and that it turned off Route 340 onto a dirt road.

At about 8 p.m., another witness saw the Lynx at Buddy's Market, with two men sitting in the front seat. The witness did not see anyone else in the car. At approximately 9 p.m., petitioner and Henderson arrived at Dice's Inn, a bar in Staunton, Virginia, where they stayed for about four or five hours. They danced with several women, including four prosecution witnesses: Donna Kay Tudor, Nancy Simmons, Debra Sievers, and Carolyn Brown. While there, Henderson gave Nancy Simmons a watch that had belonged to Whitlock. Petitioner spent most of his time with Tudor, who was later arrested for grand larceny based on her possession of the blue Lynx.

These four women all testified that Tudor had arrived at Dice's at about 8 p.m. Three of them noticed nothing unusual about petitioner's appearance, but Tudor saw some blood on his jeans and a cut on his knuckle. Tudor also testified that she, Henderson, and petitioner left Dice's together after it closed to search for marijuana. Henderson was driving the blue Lynx, and petitioner and Tudor rode in back. Tudor related that petitioner was leaning toward Henderson and talking with him; she overheard a crude conversation that could reasonably be interpreted as describing the assault and murder of a black person with a "rock crusher." Tudor stated that petitioner made a statement that implied that he had killed someone, so they "wouldn't give him no more trouble." ** Tudor testified that while she, petitioner, and Henderson were driving around, petitioner took out his knife and threatened to stab Henderson because he was driving recklessly. Petitioner then began driving.

At about 4:30 or 5 a.m. on January 6, petitioner drove Henderson to Kenneth Workman's apartment in Timberville. *** Henderson went inside to get something, and petitioner and Tudor drove off without waiting for him. Workman testified that Henderson had blood on his pants and stated he had killed a black person.

Petitioner and Tudor then drove to a motel in Blue Ridge. A day or two later they went to Virginia Beach, where they spent the rest of the week. Petitioner gave Tudor pearl earrings that Whitlock had been wearing when she was last seen. Tudor saw Whitlock's driver's license and bank card in the glove compartment of the car. Tudor testified that petitioner unsuccessfully attempted to use Whitlock's bank card when they were in Virginia Beach.

When petitioner and Tudor returned to Augusta County, they abandoned the blue Lynx. On January 11, the police identified the car as Dean's, and found petitioner's and Tudor's fingerprints on both the inside and the outside of the car. They also found shoe impressions that matched the soles of shoes belonging to petitioner. Inside the car, they retrieved a jacket that contained identification papers belonging to Henderson.

The police also recovered a bag at petitioner's mother's house that Tudor testified she and petitioner had left when they returned from Virginia Beach. The bag contained, among other items, three identification cards belonging to Whitlock and a black "tank top" shirt that was later found to have human blood and semen stains on it. **

On January 13, a farmer called the police to advise them that he had found Henderson's wallet; a search of the area led to the discovery of Whitlock's frozen, nude, and battered body. A 69-pound rock, spotted with blood, lay nearby. Forensic evidence indicated that Whitlock's death was caused by "multiple blunt force injuries to the head." ** The location of the rock and the human blood on the rock suggested that it had been used to inflict these injuries. Based on the contents of Whitlock's stomach, the medical examiner determined that she died fewer than six hours after she had last eaten. ***

A number of Caucasian hair samples were found at the scene, three of which were probably petitioner's. Given the weight of the rock, the prosecution argued that one of the killers must have held the victim down while the other struck her with the murder weapon.

Donna Tudor's estranged husband, Jay Tudor, was called by the defense and testified that in March she had told him that she was present at the murder scene and that petitioner did not participate in the murder. Jay Tudor's testimony was inconsistent in several respects with that of other witnesses. For example, he testified that several days elapsed between the time that petitioner, Henderson, and Donna Tudor picked up Whitlock and the time of Whitlock's murder.

Anne Stoltzfus' Testimony

Anne Stoltzfus testified that on two occasions on January 5 she saw petitioner, Henderson, and a blonde girl inside the Harrisonburg mall, and that she later witnessed their abduction of Whitlock in the parking lot. She did not call the police, but a week and a half after the incident she discussed it with classmates at James Madison University, where both she and Whitlock were students. One of them called the police. The next night a detective visited her, and the following morning she went to the police station and told her story to Detective Claytor, a member of the Harrisonburg City Police Department. Detective Claytor showed her photographs of possible suspects, and she identified petitioner and Henderson "with absolute certainty" but stated that she had a slight reservation about her identification of the blonde woman. **

At trial, Stoltzfus testified that, at about 6 p.m. on January 5, she and her 14-year-old daughter were in the Music Land store in the mall looking for a compact disc. While she was waiting for assistance from a clerk, petitioner, whom she described as "Mountain Man," and the blonde girl entered. ** Because petitioner was "revved up" and "very impatient," she was frightened and backed up, bumping into Henderson (whom she called "Shy Guy"), and thought she felt something hard in the pocket of his coat. **

Stoltzfus left the store, intending to return later. At about 6:45, while heading back toward Music Land, she again encountered the threesome: "Shy Guy" walking by himself, followed by the girl, and then "Mountain Man" yelling "Donna, Donna, Donna." The girl bumped into Stoltzfus and then asked for directions to the bus stop. *** The three then left.

At first Stoltzfus tried to follow them because of her concern about petitioner's behavior, but she "lost him" and then headed back to Music Land. The clerk had not returned, so she and her daughter went to their car. While driving to another store, they saw a shiny dark blue car. The driver was "beautiful," "well dressed and she was happy, she was singing...." ** When the blue car was stopped behind a minivan at a stop sign, Stoltzfus saw petitioner for the third time. She testified:

> "'Mountain Man' came tearing out of the Mall entrance door and went up to the driver of the van and... was just really mad and ran back and banged on back of the backside of the van and then went back to the Mall entrance wall where 'Shy Guy' and 'Blonde Girl' was standing... then we left [and before the van and a white-pickup truck could turn] 'Mountain Man' came out again...." **

After first going to the passenger side of the pickup truck, petitioner came back to the black girl's car, "pounded on" the passenger window, shook the car, yanked the door open and jumped in. When he motioned for "Blonde Girl" and "Shy Guy" to get in, the driver stepped on the gas and "just laid on the horn" but she could not go because there were people walking in front of the car. The horn "blew a long time" and petitioner "started hitting her...on the left shoulder, her right shoulder and then it looked like to me that he started hitting her on the head and I was, I just became concerned and upset. So I beeped, honked my horn and then she stopped honking the horn and he stopped hitting her and opened the door again and the 'Blonde Girl' got in the back and 'Shy Guy' followed and got behind him." **

[handwritten margin note: she saw them, her beat her in car in mall (2)]

Stoltzfus pulled her car up parallel to the blue car, got out for a moment, got back in, and leaned over to ask repeatedly if the other driver was "O.K." The driver looked "frozen" and mouthed an inaudible response. Stoltzfus started to drive away and then realized "the only word that it could possibly be, was help." ** The blue car then drove slowly around her, went over the curb with its horn honking, and headed out of the mall. Stoltzfus briefly followed, told her daughter to write the license number on a "3x4 [inch] index card," *** and then left for home because she had an empty gas tank and "three kids at home waiting for supper." **

At trial Stoltzfus identified Whitlock from a picture as the driver of the car and pointed to petitioner as "Mountain Man." When asked if pretrial publicity about the murder had influenced her identification, Stoltzfus replied "absolutely not." She explained: "First of all, I have an exceptionally good memory. I had very close contact with [petitioner] and he made an emotional impression with me because of his behavior and I, he caught my attention and I paid attention. So I have absolutely no doubt of my identification." **

The Commonwealth did not produce any other witnesses to the abduction. Stoltzfus' daughter did not testify.

The Stoltzfus Documents

The materials that provide the basis of petitioner's *Brady* claim consist of notes taken by Detective Claytor during his interviews with Stoltzfus, and letters written by Stoltzfus to Claytor. They cast serious doubt on Stoltzfus' confident assertion of her "exceptionally good memory." Because the content of the documents is critical to petitioner's procedural and substantive claims, we summarize their content.

Exhibit 1 *** is a handwritten note prepared by Detective Claytor after his first interview with Stoltzfus on January 19, 1990, just two weeks after the crime. The note indicates that she could not identify the black female victim. The only person Stoltzfus apparently could identify at this time was the white female. **

Exhibit 2 is a document prepared by Detective Claytor some time after February 1. It contains a summary of his interviews with Stoltzfus conducted on January 19 and January 20, 1990. *** At that time "she was not sure whether she could identify the white males but felt sure she could identify the white female."

Exhibit 3 is entitled "Observations" and includes a summary of the abduction.

Exhibit 4 is a letter written by Stoltzfus to Claytor three days after their first interview "to clarify some of my confusion for you." The letter states that she had not remembered being at the mall, but that her daughter had helped jog her memory. Her description of the abduction includes the comment: "I have a very vague memory that I'm not sure of. It seems as if the wild guy that I saw had come running through the door and up to a bus as the bus was pulling off.... Then the guy I saw came running up to the black girl's window? Were those 2 memories the same person?" ** In a postscript she noted that her daughter "doesn't remember seeing the 3 people get into the black girl's car...." **

Exhibit 5 is a note to Claytor captioned "My Impressions of 'The Car,'" which contains three paragraphs describing the size of the car and comparing it with Stoltzfus' Volkswagen Rabbit, but not mentioning the license plate number that she vividly recalled at the trial. **

Exhibit 6 is a brief note from Stoltzfus to Claytor dated January 25, 1990, stating that after spending several hours with John Dean, Whitlock's boyfriend, "looking at current photos," she had identified Whitlock "beyond a shadow of a doubt." *** The District Court noted that by the time of trial her identification had been expanded to include a description of her clothing and her appearance as a college kid who was "singing" and "happy." **

Exhibit 7 is a letter from Stoltzfus to Detective Claytor, dated January 16, 1990, in which she thanks him for his "patience with my sometimes muddled memories." She states that if the student at school had not called the police, "I never would have made any of the associations that you helped me make." **

In Exhibit 8, which is undated and summarizes the events described in her trial testimony, Stoltzfus commented: "So where is the 3x4 card?... It would have been very nice if I could have remembered all this at the time and had simply gone to the police with the information. But I totally wrote this off as a trivial episode of college kids carrying on and proceeded with my own full-time college load at JMU.... Monday, January 15th. I was cleaning out my car and found the 3x4 card. I tore it into little pieces and put it in the bottom of a trash bag." **

There is a dispute between the parties over whether petitioner's counsel saw Exhibits 2, 7, and 8 before trial. The prosecuting attorney conceded that he himself never saw Exhibits 1, 3, 4, 5, and 6 until long after petitioner's trial, and they were not in the file he made available to petitioner. *** For purposes of this case, therefore, we assume that petitioner proceeded to trial without having seen Exhibits 1, 3, 4, 5, and 6. ***

State Proceedings

Petitioner was tried in Augusta County, where Whitlock's body was found, on charges of capital murder, robbery, and abduction. Because the prosecutor maintained an open file policy, which gave petitioner's counsel access to all of the evidence in the Augusta County prosecutor's files, *** petitioner's counsel did not file a pretrial motion for discovery of possible exculpatory evidence. *** In closing argument, petitioner's lawyer effectively conceded that the evidence was sufficient to support the robbery and abduction charges, as well as the lesser offense of first-degree murder, but argued that the evidence was insufficient to prove that petitioner was guilty of capital murder. **

The judge instructed the jury that petitioner could be found guilty of the capital charge if the evidence established beyond a reasonable doubt that he "jointly participated in the fatal beating" and "was an active and immediate participant in the act or acts that caused the victim's death." ** The jury found petitioner guilty of abduction, robbery, and capital murder. ** After listening to testimony and arguments presented during the sentencing phase, the jury made findings of "vileness" and "future dangerousness," and unanimously recommended the death sentence that the judge later imposed.

The Virginia Supreme Court affirmed the conviction and sentence. ** It held that the trial court had properly instructed the jury on the "joint perpetrator" theory of capital murder and that the evidence, viewed most favorably in support of the verdict, amply supported the prosecution's theory that both petitioner and Henderson were active participants in the actual killing. ***

[margin note: VSC Affirmed]

In December 1991, the Augusta County Circuit Court appointed new counsel to represent petitioner in state habeas corpus proceedings. State habeas counsel advanced an ineffective-assistance-of-counsel claim based, in part, on trial counsel's failure to file a motion under *Brady v. Maryland*, 373 U.S. 83 (1963), "to have the Commonwealth disclose to the defense all exculpatory evidence known to it—or in its possession." ** In answer to that claim, the Commonwealth asserted that such a motion was unnecessary because the prosecutor had maintained an open file policy. ** The Circuit Court dismissed the petition, and the State Supreme Court affirmed. **

[margin note: State Habeas denied IAC claim. VSC affirmed]

Federal Habeas Corpus Proceedings

In March 1996, petitioner filed a federal habeas corpus petition in the Eastern District of Virginia. The District Court entered a sealed, *ex parte* order granting petitioner's counsel the right to examine and to copy all of the police and prosecution files in the case. ** That order led to petitioner's counsel's first examination of the Stoltzfus materials, described above. **

[margin note: FHC. District Ct ordered defense + petitioner to see + copy Stoltzfus material.]

[margin note: didn't find info until FHC.]

Based on the discovery of those exhibits, petitioner for the first time raised a direct claim that his conviction was invalid because the prosecution had failed to comply with the rule of *Brady v. Maryland*. The District Court granted the Commonwealth's motion to dismiss all claims except for petitioner's contention that the Commonwealth violated *Brady*, that he received ineffective assistance of counsel, *** and that he was denied due process of law under the Fifth and Fourteenth Amendments. In its order denying the Commonwealth's motion to dismiss, the District Court found that petitioner had "demonstrated cause for his failure to raise this claim earlier [because] defense counsel had no independent access to this material and the Commonwealth repeatedly withheld it throughout Petitioner's state habeas proceeding." **

After reviewing the Stoltzfus materials, and making the assumption that the three disputed exhibits had been available to the defense, the District Court concluded that the failure to disclose the other five was sufficiently prejudicial to undermine confidence in the jury's verdict. ** It granted summary judgment to petitioner and granted the writ.

[margin note: Dist Ct granted FHC]

The Court of Appeals vacated in part and remanded. It held that petitioner's *Brady* claim was procedurally defaulted because the factual basis for the claim was available to him at the time he filed his state habeas petition. Given that he knew that Stoltzfus had been interviewed by Harrisonburg police officers, the court opined that "reasonably competent counsel would have sought discovery in state court" of the police files, and that in response to this "simple request, it is likely the state court would have ordered the production of the files." ** Therefore, the Court of Appeals reasoned, it could not address the *Brady* claim unless petitioner could demonstrate both cause and actual prejudice.

[margin note: 4th Cir Ct of Appls Reversed + remanded]

[margin note: cause + prejudice]

Under Fourth Circuit precedent a party "cannot establish cause to excuse his default if he should have known of such claims through the exercise of reasonable diligence." ** Having already decided that the claim was available to reasonably competent counsel, the Fourth Circuit stated that the basis for finding procedural default also foreclosed a finding of cause. Moreover, the Court of Appeals reasoned, petitioner could not fault

[margin note: not cause b/c counsel's fault.]

his trial lawyers' failure to make a *Brady* claim because they reasonably relied on the prosecutor's open file policy. **

As an alternative basis for decision, the Court of Appeals also held that petitioner could not establish prejudice because "the Stoltzfus materials would have provided little or no help…in either the guilt or sentencing phases of the trial." ** With respect to guilt, the court noted that Stoltzfus' testimony was not relevant to petitioner's argument that he was only guilty of first-degree murder rather than capital murder because Henderson, rather than he, actually killed Whitlock. With respect to sentencing, the court concluded that her testimony "was of no import" because the findings of future dangerousness and vileness rested on other evidence. Finally, the court noted that even if it could get beyond the procedural default, the *Brady* claim would fail on the merits because of the absence of prejudice. ** The Court of Appeals, therefore, reversed the District Court's judgment and remanded the case with instructions to dismiss the petition.

II

The first question that our order granting certiorari directed the parties to address is whether the State violated the *Brady* rule. We begin our analysis by identifying the essential components of a *Brady* violation.

In *Brady* this Court held "that the suppression by the prosecution of evidence favorable to an accused upon request violates due process where the evidence is material either to guilt or to punishment, irrespective of the good faith or bad faith of the prosecution." *Brady v. Maryland*, 373 U.S. at 87. We have since held that the duty to disclose such evidence is applicable even though there has been no request by the accused, *United States v. Agurs*, 427 U.S. 97, 107 (1976), and that the duty encompasses impeachment evidence as well as exculpatory evidence, *United States v. Bagley*, 473 U.S. 667, 676 (1985). Such evidence is material "if there is a reasonable probability that, had the evidence been disclosed to the defense, the result of the proceeding would have been different." ** Moreover, the rule encompasses evidence "known only to police investigators and not to the prosecutor." ** In order to comply with *Brady*, therefore, "the individual prosecutor has a duty to learn of any favorable evidence known to the others acting on the government's behalf in this case, including the police." **

***

*** Thus the term "*Brady* violation" is sometimes used to refer to any breach of the broad obligation to disclose exculpatory evidence ***—that is, to any suppression of so-called "*Brady* material"—although, strictly speaking, there is never a real "*Brady* violation" unless the nondisclosure was so serious that there is a reasonable probability that the suppressed evidence would have produced a different verdict. There are three components of a true *Brady* violation: The evidence at issue must be favorable to the accused, either because it is exculpatory, or because it is impeaching; that evidence must have been suppressed by the State, either willfully or inadvertently; and prejudice must have ensued.

Two of those components are unquestionably established by the record in this case. The contrast between (a) the terrifying incident that Stoltzfus confidently described in her testimony and (b) her initial perception of that event "as a trivial episode of college kids carrying on" that her daughter did not even notice, suffices to establish the impeaching character of the undisclosed documents. *** Moreover, with respect to at least five of those documents, there is no dispute about the fact that they were known to the State but not disclosed to trial counsel. It is the third

focused on issue of Prejudice

component—whether petitioner has established the prejudice necessary to satisfy the "materiality" inquiry—that is the most difficult element of the claimed *Brady* violation in this case.

Because petitioner acknowledges that his *Brady* claim is procedurally defaulted, we must first decide whether that default is excused by an adequate showing of cause and prejudice. In this case, cause and prejudice parallel two of the three components of the alleged *Brady* violation itself. The suppression of the Stoltzfus documents constitutes one of the causes for the failure to assert a *Brady* claim in the state courts, and unless those documents were "material" for *Brady* purposes, their suppression did not give rise to sufficient prejudice to overcome the procedural default.

III   *CAUSE*

*** [I]t is appropriate to begin the analysis of the "cause" issue by explaining why petitioner's reasons for failing to raise his *Brady* claim at trial are acceptable under this Court's cases.

Three factors explain why trial counsel did not advance this claim: The documents were suppressed by the Commonwealth; the prosecutor maintained an open file policy; *** and trial counsel were not aware of the factual basis for the claim. The first and second factors—*i.e.*, the non-disclosure and the open file policy—are both fairly characterized as conduct attributable to the State that impeded trial counsel's access to the factual basis for making a *Brady* claim. *** [I]t is just such factors that ordinarily establish the existence of cause for a procedural default. ***

If it was reasonable for trial counsel to rely on, not just the presumption that the prosecutor would fully perform his duty to disclose all exculpatory materials, but also the implicit representation that such materials would be included in the open files tendered to defense counsel for their examination, we think such reliance by counsel appointed to represent petitioner in state habeas proceedings was equally reasonable. Indeed, in *Murray [v. Carrier,* 477 U.S. 478 (1986)] we expressly noted that "the standard for cause should not vary depending on the timing of a procedural default." **

***

Although it is true that petitioner's lawyers—both at trial and in post-trial proceedings—must have known that Stoltzfus had had multiple interviews with the police, it by no means follows that they would have known that records pertaining to those interviews, or that the notes that Stoltzfus sent to the detective, existed and had been suppressed. *** Indeed, if the Commonwealth is correct that Exhibits 2, 7, and 8 were in the prosecutor's "open file," it is especially unlikely that counsel would have suspected that additional impeaching evidence was being withheld. The prosecutor must have known about the newspaper articles and Stoltzfus' meetings with Claytor, yet he did not believe that his prosecution file was incomplete.

Furthermore, the fact that the District Court entered a broad discovery order even before federal habeas counsel had advanced a *Brady* claim does not demonstrate that a state court also would have done so. *** Indeed, as we understand Virginia law and the Commonwealth's position, petitioner would not have been entitled to such discovery in state habeas proceedings without a showing of good cause. *** Even pursuant to the broader discovery provisions afforded at trial, petitioner would not have had access to these materials under Virginia law, except as modified by *Brady*. ** Mere speculation that some exculpatory material may have been withheld is unlikely to establish good cause for a discovery request on collateral review. Nor, in our opinion, should such suspicion suffice to impose a duty on counsel to advance a claim for which they have no evidentiary support. ***

The Commonwealth's position on the "cause" issue is particularly weak in this case because the state habeas proceedings confirmed petitioner's justification for his failure to raise a *Brady* claim. As already noted, when he alleged that trial counsel had been incompetent because they had not advanced such a claim, the warden responded by pointing out that there was no need for counsel to do so because they "were voluntarily given full disclosure of everything known to the government." *** Given that representation, petitioner had no basis for believing the Commonwealth had failed to comply with *Brady* at trial. ***

***

In summary, petitioner has established cause for failing to raise a *Brady* claim prior to federal habeas because (a) the prosecution withheld exculpatory evidence; (b) petitioner reasonably relied on the prosecution's open file policy as fulfilling the prosecution's duty to disclose such evidence; and (c) the Commonwealth confirmed petitioner's reliance on the open file policy by asserting during state habeas proceedings that petitioner had already received "everything known to the government." *** We need not decide in this case whether any one or two of these factors would be sufficient to constitute cause, since the combination of all three surely suffices.

IV Prejudice

The differing judgments of the District Court and the Court of Appeals attest to the difficulty of resolving the issue of prejudice. Unlike the Fourth Circuit, we do not believe that "the Stolzfus [sic] materials would have provided little or no help to Strickler in either the guilt or sentencing phases of the trial." ** Without a doubt, Stoltzfus' testimony was prejudicial in the sense that it made petitioner's conviction more likely than if she had not testified, and discrediting her testimony might have changed the outcome of the trial.

That, however, is not the standard that petitioner must satisfy in order to obtain relief. He must convince us that "there is a reasonable probability" that the result of the trial would have been different if the suppressed documents had been disclosed to the defense. ***

The Court of Appeals' negative answer to that question rested on its conclusion that, without considering Stoltzfus' testimony, the record contained ample, independent evidence of guilt, as well as evidence sufficient to support the findings of vileness and future dangerousness that warranted the imposition of the death penalty. The standard used by that court was incorrect. As we made clear in *Kyles*, the materiality inquiry is not just a matter of determining whether, after discounting the inculpatory evidence in light of the undisclosed evidence, the remaining evidence is sufficient to support the jury's conclusions. ** Rather, the question is whether "the favorable evidence could reasonably be taken to put the whole case in such a different light as to undermine confidence in the verdict." **

***

Conviction

Given the record evidence involving Henderson, *** the District Court concluded that, without Stoltzfus' testimony, the jury might have been persuaded that Henderson, rather than petitioner, was the ringleader. He reasoned that a "reasonable probability of conviction" of first-degree, rather than capital, murder sufficed to establish the materiality of the undisclosed Stoltzfus materials and, thus, a *Brady* violation. **

***

Even if Stoltzfus and her testimony had been entirely discredited, the jury might still have concluded that petitioner was the leader of the criminal enterprise because he was the one seen driving the car by Kurt Massie near the location of the murder and the one who kept the car for the following week. *** In addition, Tudor testified that petitioner threatened Henderson with a knife later in the evening.

[margin note: other evidence showed he was leader of crim enterprise]

More importantly, however, petitioner's guilt of capital murder did not depend on proof that he was the dominant partner: Proof that he was an equal participant with Henderson was sufficient under the judge's instructions. *** Accordingly, the strong evidence that Henderson was a killer is entirely consistent with the conclusion that petitioner was also an actual participant in the killing. ***

Furthermore, there was considerable forensic and other physical evidence linking petitioner to the crime. *** The weight and size of the rock, *** and the character of the fatal injuries to the victim, *** are powerful evidence supporting the conclusion that two people acted jointly to commit a brutal murder.

We recognize the importance of eyewitness testimony; Stoltzfus provided the only disinterested, narrative account of what transpired on January 5, 1990. However, Stoltzfus' vivid description of the events at the mall was not the only evidence that the jury had before it. Two other eyewitnesses, the security guard and Henderson's friend, placed petitioner and Henderson at the Harrisonburg Valley Shopping Mall on the afternoon of Whitlock's murder. One eyewitness later saw petitioner driving Dean's car near the scene of the murder.

The record provides strong support for the conclusion that petitioner would have been convicted of capital murder and sentenced to death, even if Stoltzfus had been severely impeached. The jury was instructed on two predicates for capital murder: robbery with a deadly weapon and abduction with intent to defile. ***

*** *[handwritten: Death Pen.]*

Petitioner also maintains that he suffered prejudice from the failure to disclose the Stoltzfus documents because her testimony impacted on the jury's decision to impose the death penalty. Her testimony, however, did not relate to his eligibility for the death sentence and was not relied upon by the prosecution at all during its closing argument at the penalty phase. *** With respect to the jury's discretionary decision to impose the death penalty, it is true that Stoltzfus described petitioner as a violent, aggressive person, but that portrayal surely was not as damaging as either the evidence that he spent the evening of the murder dancing and drinking at Dice's or the powerful message conveyed by the 69-pound rock that was part of the record before the jury. Notwithstanding the obvious significance of Stoltzfus' testimony, petitioner has not convinced us that there is a reasonable probability that the jury would have returned a different verdict if her testimony had been either severely impeached or excluded entirely.

[margin note: 69 lb rock dancing + drinking]

Petitioner has satisfied two of the three components of a constitutional violation under *Brady*: exculpatory evidence and nondisclosure of this evidence by the prosecution. Petitioner has also demonstrated cause for failing to raise this claim during trial or on state postconviction review. However, petitioner has not shown that there is a reasonable probability that his conviction or sentence would have been different had these materials been disclosed. He therefore cannot show materiality under *Brady* or prejudice from his failure to raise the claim earlier. Accordingly, the judgment of the Court of Appeals is

Affirmed.

[A concurrence, in part, by Justice Souter is omitted, as is a dissent, in part, by Justice Souter, joined in part by Justice Kennedy.]

Notes

1. *Subsequent case history*

Tony Strickler was executed by lethal injection on July 21, 1999.

2. *Other opinions*

Justice Souter, with whom Justice Kennedy joined in part, concurred with the Court's opinion in Part III and otherwise dissented. He agreed with the Court that Strickler failed to establish a reasonable probability that, had the materials withheld been disclosed, he would not have been found guilty of capital murder. Justice Souter then emphasized that the prejudice inquiry does not stop at the conviction but also goes to each step of the sentencing process—and there, Justice Souter believed that Strickler had carried his burden. Specifically, Justice Souter believed there was a reasonable probability (which he took to mean a "significant possibility") that disclosure of the Stoltzfus materials would have led the jury to recommend life, not death.

In explaining his position, Justice Souter stated:

> Ultimately, I cannot accept the Court's discount of Stoltzfus in the *Brady* sentencing calculus for the reason I have repeatedly emphasized, the undeniable narrative force of what she said. Against this, it does not matter so much that other witnesses could have placed Strickler at the shopping mall on the afternoon of the murder, ** or that the Stoltzfus testimony did not directly address the aggravating factors found. ** What is important is that her evidence presented a gripping story. ** Its message was that Strickler was the madly energetic leader of two morally apathetic accomplices, who were passive but for his direction. One cannot be reasonably confident that not a single juror would have had a different perspective after an impeachment that would have destroyed the credibility of that story. I would accordingly vacate the sentence and remand for reconsideration, and to that extent I respectfully dissent.

3. *Practical and political implications*

What practical limitations might come into play in identifying any exculpatory evidence that might exist in a case? What political considerations might affect a prosecutor's determination of what evidence should be turned over to the defense? What are the political and practical considerations of *Strickler* on habeas practice for the prosecution? For the defense?

4. *The influence of Giglio*

In addition to *Brady v. Maryland*, another seminal case informing the Court's opinion in *Strickler* is *Giglio v. United States*, 405 U.S. 150 (1972). In *Giglio*, petitioner was convicted of passing forged money orders and sentenced to five years in prison. While an appeal was pending, defense counsel discovered new evidence indicating that the government had failed to disclose an alleged promise made to its key witness, Taliento—a promise that Taliento would not be prosecuted if he testified for the government. Later, the lead prosecutor filed an affidavit stating that he personally had consulted with Taliento and his attorney shortly before trial to emphasize that Taliento definitely would be prosecuted if he did not testify and that if he did testify he would be obliged to rely on the "good judgment and conscience of the Government" as to whether he would be prosecuted. The issue before the Supreme Court was whether the evidence not disclosed was such as to require a new trial under the due process criteria of precedent such as *Brady v. Maryland*, 373 U.S. 83 (1963).

The Supreme Court held that a new trial is not automatically required when evidence useful to the defense is discovered after trial if it would not have likely changed the verdict. Under *Brady*, in order to require a new trial, a finding of materiality of the evidence is required. The Court further stated that whether the nondisclosure of the evidence was purposeful or not does not matter—the prosecutor ultimately is held responsible. Because the government's case against Giglio depended almost entirely on the witness's testimony, and no indictment would have resulted without it, the Court found that the jury was entitled to know about the witness's deal with the prosecution, so the Court ordered a new trial.

Kyles v. Whitley
514 U.S. 419 (1995)

JUSTICE SOUTER delivered the opinion of the Court.

After his first trial in 1984 ended in a hung jury, petitioner Curtis Lee Kyles was tried again, convicted of first-degree murder, and sentenced to death. On habeas review, we follow the established rule that the state's obligation under *Brady v. Maryland*, 373 U.S. 83 (1963), to disclose evidence favorable to the defense, turns on the cumulative effect of all such evidence suppressed by the government, and we hold that the prosecutor remains responsible for gauging that effect regardless of any failure by the police to bring favorable evidence to the prosecutor's attention. Because the net effect of the evidence withheld by the State in this case raises a reasonable probability that its disclosure would have produced a different result, Kyles is entitled to a new trial.

I

Following the mistrial when the jury was unable to reach a verdict, Kyles's subsequent conviction and sentence of death were affirmed on direct appeal. ** On state collateral review, the trial court denied relief, but the Supreme Court of Louisiana remanded for an evidentiary hearing on Kyles's claims of newly discovered evidence. During this state-court proceeding, the defense was first able to present certain evidence, favorable to Kyles, that the State had failed to disclose before or during trial. The state trial court nevertheless denied relief, and the State Supreme Court denied Kyles's application for discretionary review. **

Kyles then filed a petition for habeas corpus in the United States District Court for the Eastern District of Louisiana, which denied the petition. The Court of Appeals for the Fifth Circuit affirmed by a divided vote. ** As we explain, *infra*, there is reason to question whether the Court of Appeals evaluated the significance of undisclosed evidence under the correct standard. Because "our duty to search for constitutional error with painstaking care is never more exacting than it is in a capital case," ** we granted certiorari ** and now reverse.

II

A

The record indicates that, at about 2:20 p.m. on Thursday, September 20, 1984, 60-year-old Dolores Dye left the Schwegmann Brothers' store (Schwegmann's) on Old Gentilly Road in New Orleans after doing some food shopping. As she put her grocery bags into the trunk of her red Ford LTD, a man accosted her and after a short struggle drew a revolver, fired into her left temple, and killed her. The gunman took Dye's keys and drove away in the LTD.

New Orleans police took statements from six eyewitnesses, *** who offered various descriptions of the gunman. They agreed that he was a black man, and four of them said that he had braided hair. The witnesses differed significantly, however, in their descriptions of height, age, weight, build, and hair length. Two reported seeing a man of 17 or 18, while another described the gunman as looking as old as 28. One witness described him as 5'4" or 5'5", medium build, 140–150 pounds; another described the man as slim and close to six feet. One witness said he had a mustache; none of the others spoke of any facial hair at all. One witness said the murderer had shoulder-length hair; another described the hair as "short."

Since the police believed the killer might have driven his own car to Schwegmann's and left it there when he drove off in Dye's LTD, they recorded the license numbers of the cars remaining in the parking lots around the store at 9:15 p.m. on the evening of the murder. Matching these numbers with registration records produced the names and addresses of the owners of the cars, with a notation of any owner's police record. Despite this list and the eyewitness descriptions, the police had no lead to the gunman until the Saturday evening after the shooting.

At 5:30 p.m., on September 22, a man identifying himself as James Joseph called the police and reported that on the day of the murder he had bought a red Thunderbird from a friend named Curtis, whom he later identified as petitioner, Curtis Kyles. He said that he had subsequently read about Dye's murder in the newspapers and feared that the car he purchased was the victim's. He agreed to meet with the police.

A few hours later, the informant met New Orleans Detective John Miller, who was wired with a hidden body microphone, through which the ensuing conversation was recorded. ** The informant now said his name was Joseph Banks and that he was called Beanie. His actual name was Joseph Wallace. ***

His story, as well as his name, had changed since his earlier call. In place of his original account of buying a Thunderbird from Kyles on Thursday, Beanie told Miller that he had not seen Kyles at all on Thursday ** and had bought a red LTD the previous day, Friday. ** Beanie led Miller to the parking lot of a nearby bar, where he had left the red LTD, later identified as Dye's.

Beanie told Miller that he lived with Kyles's brother-in-law (later identified as Johnny Burns), *** whom Beanie repeatedly called his "partner." ** Beanie described Kyles as slim, about 6-feet tall, 24 or 25 years old, with a "bush" hairstyle. ** When asked if Kyles ever wore his hair in plaits, Beanie said that he did but that he "had a bush" when Beanie bought the car. **

During the conversation, Beanie repeatedly expressed concern that he might himself be a suspect in the murder. He explained that he had been seen driving Dye's car on Friday evening in the French Quarter, admitted that he had changed its license plates, and worried that he "could have been charged" with the murder on the basis of his possession of the LTD. ** He asked if he would be put in jail. ** Miller acknowledged that Beanie's possession of the car would have looked suspicious ** but reassured him that he "didn't do anything wrong." **

Beanie seemed eager to cast suspicion on Kyles, who allegedly made his living by "robbing people," and had tried to kill Beanie at some prior time. ** Beanie said that Kyles regularly carried two pistols, a .38 and a .32, and that if the police could "set him up good," they could "get that same gun" used to kill Dye. ** Beanie rode with Miller and Miller's supervisor, Sgt. James Eaton, in an unmarked squad car to Desire Street, where he pointed out the building containing Kyles's apartment. **

Beanie told the officers that after he bought the car, he and his "partner" (Burns) drove Kyles to Schwegmann's about 9 p.m. on Friday evening to pick up Kyles's car, described as an orange four-door Ford. *** When asked where Kyles's car had been parked, Beanie replied that it had been "on the same side [of the lot] where the woman was killed at." ** The officers later drove Beanie to Schwegmann's, where he indicated the space where he claimed Kyles's car had been parked. Beanie went on to say that when he and Burns had brought Kyles to pick up the car, Kyles had gone to some nearby bushes to retrieve a brown purse, ** which Kyles subsequently hid in a wardrobe at his apartment. Beanie said that Kyles had "a lot of groceries" in Schwegmann's bags and a new baby's potty "in the car." ** Beanie told Eaton that Kyles's garbage would go out the next day and that if Kyles was "smart" he would "put [the purse] in [the] garbage." ** Beanie made it clear that he expected some reward for his help, saying at one point that he was not "doing all of this for nothing." ** The police repeatedly assured Beanie that he would not lose the $400 he paid for the car. **

After the visit to Schwegmann's, Eaton and Miller took Beanie to a police station where Miller interviewed him again on the record, which was transcribed and signed by Beanie, using his alias "Joseph Banks." ** This statement, Beanie's third (the telephone call being the first, then the recorded conversation), repeats some of the essentials of the second one: that Beanie had purchased a red Ford LTD from Kyles for $400 on Friday evening; that Kyles had his hair "combed out" at the time of the sale; and that Kyles carried a .32 and a .38 with him "all the time."

Portions of the third statement, however, embellished or contradicted Beanie's preceding story and were even internally inconsistent. Beanie reported that after the sale, he and Kyles unloaded Schwegmann's grocery bags from the trunk and back seat of the LTD and placed them in Kyles's own car. Beanie said that Kyles took a brown purse from the front seat of the LTD and that they then drove in separate cars to Kyles's apartment, where they unloaded the groceries. ** Beanie also claimed that, a few hours later, he and his "partner" Burns went with Kyles to Schwegmann's, where they recovered Kyles's car and a "big brown pocket book" from "next to a building." ** Beanie did not explain how Kyles could have picked up his car and recovered the purse at Schwegmann's, after Beanie had seen Kyles with both just a few hours earlier. The police neither noted the inconsistencies nor questioned Beanie about them.

Although the police did not thereafter put Kyles under surveillance, ** they learned about events at his apartment from Beanie, who went there twice on Sunday. According to a fourth statement by Beanie, this one given to the chief prosecutor in November (between the first and second trials), he first went to the apartment about 2 p.m., after a telephone conversation with a police officer who asked whether Kyles had the gun that was used to kill Dye. Beanie stayed in Kyles's apartment until about 5 p.m., when he left to call Detective John Miller. Then he returned about 7 p.m. and stayed until about 9:30

p.m., when he left to meet Miller, who also asked about the gun. According to this fourth statement, Beanie "rode around" with Miller until 3 a.m. on Monday, September 24. Sometime during those same early morning hours, detectives were sent at Sgt. Eaton's behest to pick up the rubbish outside Kyles's building. As Sgt. Eaton wrote in an interoffice memorandum, he had "reason to believe the victims [sic] personal papers and the Schwegmann's bags will be in the trash." **

At 10:40 a.m., Kyles was arrested as he left the apartment, which was then searched under a warrant. Behind the kitchen stove, the police found a .32-caliber revolver containing five live rounds and one spent cartridge. Ballistics tests later showed that this pistol was used to murder Dye. In a wardrobe in a hallway leading to the kitchen, the officers found a homemade shoulder holster that fit the murder weapon. In a bedroom dresser drawer, they discovered two boxes of ammunition, one containing several .32-caliber rounds of the same brand as those found in the pistol. Back in the kitchen, various cans of cat and dog food, some of them of the brands Dye typically purchased, were found in Schwegmann's sacks. No other groceries were identified as possibly being Dye's, and no potty was found. Later that afternoon at the police station, police opened the rubbish bags and found the victim's purse, identification, and other personal belongings wrapped in a Schwegmann's sack.

The gun, the LTD, the purse, and the cans of pet food were dusted for fingerprints. The gun had been wiped clean. Several prints were found on the purse and on the LTD, but none was identified as Kyles's. Dye's prints were not found on any of the cans of pet food. Kyles's prints were found, however, on a small piece of paper taken from the front passenger-side floorboard of the LTD. The crime laboratory recorded the paper as a Schwegmann's sales slip, but without noting what had been printed on it, which was obliterated in the chemical process of lifting the fingerprints. A second Schwegmann's receipt was found in the trunk of the LTD, but Kyles's prints were not found on it. Beanie's fingerprints were not compared to any of the fingerprints found. **

The lead detective on the case, John Dillman, put together a photo lineup that included a photograph of Kyles (but not of Beanie) and showed the array to five of the six eyewitnesses who had given statements. Three of them picked the photograph of Kyles; the other two could not confidently identify Kyles as Dye's assailant.

B

Kyles was indicted for first-degree murder. Before trial, his counsel filed a lengthy motion for disclosure by the State of any exculpatory or impeachment evidence. The prosecution responded that there was "no exculpatory evidence of any nature," despite the government's knowledge of the following evidentiary items: (1) the six contemporaneous eyewitness statements taken by police following the murder; (2) records of Beanie's initial call to the police; (3) the tape recording of the Saturday conversation between Beanie and officers Eaton and Miller; (4) the typed and signed statement given by Beanie on Sunday morning; (5) the computer printout of license numbers of cars parked at Schwegmann's on the night of the murder, which did not list the number of Kyles's car; (6) the internal police memorandum calling for the seizure of the rubbish after Beanie had suggested that the purse might be found there; and (7) evidence linking Beanie to other crimes at Schwegmann's and to the unrelated murder of one Patricia Leidenheimer, committed in January before the Dye murder.

At the first trial, in November, the heart of the State's case was eyewitness testimony from four people who were at the scene of the crime (three of whom had previously

picked Kyles from the photo lineup). Kyles maintained his innocence, offered supporting witnesses, and supplied an alibi that he had been picking up his children from
school at the time of the murder. The theory of the defense was that Kyles had been
framed by Beanie, who had planted evidence in Kyles's apartment and his rubbish for
the purposes of shifting suspicion away from himself, removing an impediment to ro-
mance with Pinky Burns, and obtaining reward money. Beanie did not testify as a witness for either the defense or the prosecution.

Because the State withheld evidence, its case was much stronger, and the defense case
much weaker, than the full facts would have suggested. Even so, after four hours of delib-
eration, the jury became deadlocked on the issue of guilt, and a mistrial was declared.

After the mistrial, the chief trial prosecutor, Cliff Strider, interviewed Beanie. **
Strider's notes show that Beanie again changed important elements of his story. He said
that he went with Kyles to retrieve Kyles's car from the Schwegmann's lot on Thursday,
the day of the murder, at some time between 5 and 7:30 p.m., not on Friday, at 9 p.m.,
as he had said in his second and third statements. (Indeed, in his second statement,
Beanie said that he had not seen Kyles at all on Thursday. **) He also said, for the first
time, that when they had picked up the car they were accompanied not only by Johnny
Burns but also by Kevin Black, who had testified for the defense at the first trial. Beanie
now claimed that after getting Kyles's car they went to Black's house, retrieved a number
of bags of groceries, a child's potty, and a brown purse, all of which they took to Kyles's
apartment. Beanie also stated that on the Sunday after the murder he had been at Kyles's
apartment two separate times. Notwithstanding the many inconsistencies and varia-
tions among Beanie's statements, neither Strider's notes nor any of the other notes and
transcripts were given to the defense.

In December 1984, Kyles was tried a second time. Again, the heart of the State's case
was the testimony of four eyewitnesses who positively identified Kyles in front of the
jury. The prosecution also offered a blown-up photograph taken at the crime scene soon
after the murder, on the basis of which the prosecutors argued that a seemingly two-
toned car in the background of the photograph was Kyles's. They repeatedly suggested
during cross-examination of defense witnesses that Kyles had left his own car at Schwegmann's on the day of the murder and had retrieved it later, a theory for which they offered no evidence beyond the blown-up photograph. Once again, Beanie did not testify.

As in the first trial, the defense contended that the eyewitnesses were mistaken. Kyles's
counsel called several individuals, including Kevin Black, who testified to seeing Beanie,
with his hair in plaits, driving a red car similar to the victim's about an hour after the
killing. ** Another witness testified that Beanie, with his hair in braids, had tried to sell
him the car on Thursday evening, shortly after the murder. ** Another witness testified
that Beanie, with his hair in a "Jheri curl," had attempted to sell him the car on Friday. **
One witness, Beanie's "partner," Burns, testified that he had seen Beanie on Sunday at
Kyles's apartment, stooping down near the stove where the gun was eventually found,
and the defense presented testimony that Beanie was romantically interested in Pinky
Burns. To explain the pet food found in Kyles's apartment, there was testimony that
Kyles's family kept a dog and cat and often fed stray animals in the neighborhood.

Finally, Kyles again took the stand. Denying any involvement in the shooting, he explained his fingerprints on the cash register receipt found in Dye's car by saying that
Beanie had picked him up in a red car on Friday, September 21, and had taken him to
Schwegmann's, where he purchased transmission fluid and a pack of cigarettes. He suggested that the receipt may have fallen from the bag when he removed the cigarettes.

On rebuttal, the prosecutor had Beanie brought into the courtroom. All of the testi-fying eyewitnesses, after viewing Beanie standing next to Kyles, reaffirmed their previ-ous identifications of Kyles as the murderer. Kyles was convicted of first-degree murder and sentenced to death. Beanie received a total of $1,600 in reward money. **

Following direct appeal, it was revealed in the course of state collateral review that the State had failed to disclose evidence favorable to the defense. After exhausting state remedies, Kyles sought relief on federal habeas, claiming, among other things, that the evidence withheld was material to his defense and that his conviction was thus obtained in violation of *Brady*. Although the United States District Court denied relief and the Fifth Circuit affirmed, *** Judge King dissented, writing that "for the first time in my fourteen years on this court...I have serious reservations about whether the State has sentenced to death the right man." **

III

The prosecution's affirmative duty to disclose evidence favorable to a defendant can trace its origins to early 20th-century strictures against misrepresentation and is of course most prominently associated with this Court's decision in *Brady v. Maryland*, 373 U.S. 83 (1963). ** *Brady* held "that the suppression by the prosecution of evidence favorable to an accused upon request violates due process where the evidence is material either to guilt or to punishment, irrespective of the good faith or bad faith of the prose-cution." 373 U.S. at 87. ** In *United States v. Agurs*, 427 U.S. 97 (1976), however, it be-came clear that a defendant's failure to request favorable evidence did not leave the Gov-ernment free of all obligation. There, the Court distinguished three situations in which a *Brady* claim might arise: first, where previously undisclosed evidence revealed that the prosecution introduced trial testimony that it knew or should have known was per-jured, *** second, where the Government failed to accede to a defense request for dis-closure of some specific kind of exculpatory evidence, ** and third, where the Govern-ment failed to volunteer exculpatory evidence never requested, or requested only in a general way. The Court found a duty on the part of the Government even in this last sit-uation, though only when suppression of the evidence would be "of sufficient signifi-cance to result in the denial of the defendant's right to a fair trial." **

In the third prominent case on the way to current *Brady* law, *United States v. Bagley*, 473 U.S. 667 (1985), the Court disavowed any difference between exculpatory and im-peachment evidence for *Brady* purposes, and it abandoned the distinction between the second and third *Agurs* circumstances, *i.e.*, the "specific-request" and "general- or no-request" situations. *Bagley* held that regardless of request, favorable evidence is mater-ial, and constitutional error results from its suppression by the government, "if there is a reasonable probability that, had the evidence been disclosed to the defense, the result of the proceeding would have been different." **

Four aspects of materiality under *Bagley* bear emphasis. Although the constitutional duty is triggered by the potential impact of favorable but undisclosed evidence, a show-ing of materiality does not require demonstration by a preponderance that disclosure of the suppressed evidence would have resulted ultimately in the defendant's acquittal (whether based on the presence of reasonable doubt or acceptance of an explanation for the crime that does not inculpate the defendant). *** *Bagley*'s touchstone of materiality is a "reasonable probability" of a different result, and the adjective is important. The question is not whether the defendant would more likely than not have received a dif-ferent verdict with the evidence, but whether in its absence he received a fair trial, un-derstood as a trial resulting in a verdict worthy of confidence. A "reasonable probability" of a different result is accordingly shown when the government's evidentiary suppression "undermines confidence in the outcome of the trial." **

The second aspect of *Bagley* materiality bearing emphasis here is that it is not a sufficiency of evidence test. A defendant need not demonstrate that after discounting the inculpatory evidence in light of the undisclosed evidence, there would not have been enough left to convict. The possibility of an acquittal on a criminal charge does not imply an insufficient evidentiary basis to convict. One does not show a *Brady* violation by demonstrating that some of the inculpatory evidence should have been excluded, but by showing that the favorable evidence could reasonably be taken to put the whole case in such a different light as to undermine confidence in the verdict. ***

Third, we note that, contrary to the assumption made by the Court of Appeals, ** once a reviewing court applying *Bagley* has found constitutional error there is no need for further harmless-error review. Assuming, *arguendo*, that a harmless-error enquiry were to apply, a *Bagley* error could not be treated as harmless, since "a reasonable probability that, had the evidence been disclosed to the defense, the result of the proceeding would have been different," ** necessarily entails the conclusion that the suppression must have had "'substantial and injurious effect or influence in determining the jury's verdict.'" ***

The fourth and final aspect of *Bagley* materiality to be stressed here is its definition in terms of suppressed evidence considered collectively, not item by item. *** As Justice Blackmun emphasized in the portion of his opinion written for the Court, the Constitution is not violated every time the government fails or chooses not to disclose evidence that might prove helpful to the defense. ** We have never held that the Constitution demands an open file policy (however such a policy might work out in practice), and the rule in *Bagley* (and, hence, in *Brady*) requires less of the prosecution than the ABA Standards for Criminal Justice, which call generally for prosecutorial disclosures of any evidence tending to exculpate or mitigate. ***

.While the definition of *Bagley* materiality in terms of the cumulative effect of suppression must accordingly be seen as leaving the government with a degree of discretion, it must also be understood as imposing a corresponding burden. On the one side, showing that the prosecution knew of an item of favorable evidence unknown to the defense does not amount to a *Brady* violation, without more. But the prosecution, which alone can know what is undisclosed, must be assigned the consequent responsibility to gauge the likely net effect of all such evidence and make disclosure when the point of "reasonable probability" is reached. This in turn means that the individual prosecutor has a duty to learn of any favorable evidence known to the others acting on the government's behalf in the case, including the police. But whether the prosecutor succeeds or fails in meeting this obligation (whether, that is, a failure to disclose is in good faith or bad faith **) the prosecution's responsibility for failing to disclose known, favorable evidence rising to a material level of importance is inescapable.

The State of Louisiana would prefer an even more lenient rule. It pleads that some of the favorable evidence in issue here was not disclosed even to the prosecutor until after trial, ** and it suggested below that it should not be held accountable under *Bagley* and *Brady* for evidence known only to police investigators and not to the prosecutor. *** To accommodate the State in this manner would, however, amount to a serious change of course from the *Brady* line of cases. In the State's favor it may be said that no one doubts that police investigators sometimes fail to inform a prosecutor of all they know. But neither is there any serious doubt that "procedures and regulations can be established to carry [the prosecutor's] burden and to insure communication of all relevant information on each case to every lawyer who deals with it." ** Since, then, the prosecutor has the means to discharge the government's *Brady* responsibility if he will, any argument for excusing a prosecutor from disclosing what he does not happen to know about boils down to a plea to substitute the police for the prosecutor, and even for the courts themselves, as the final arbiters of the government's obligation to ensure fair trials.

Short of doing that, we were asked at oral argument to raise the threshold of materiality because the *Bagley* standard "makes it difficult...to know" from the "perspective [of the prosecutor at] trial...exactly what might become important later on." ** The State asks for "a certain amount of leeway in making a judgment call" as to the disclosure of any given piece of evidence. **

Uncertainty about the degree of further "leeway" that might satisfy the State's request for a "certain amount" of it is the least of the reasons to deny the request. At bottom, what the State fails to recognize is that, with or without more leeway, the prosecution cannot be subject to any disclosure obligation without at some point having the responsibility to determine when it must act. Indeed, even if due process were thought to be violated by every failure to disclose an item of exculpatory or impeachment evidence (leaving harmless error as the government's only fallback), the prosecutor would still be forced to make judgment calls about what would count as favorable evidence, owing to the very fact that the character of a piece of evidence as favorable will often turn on the context of the existing or potential evidentiary record. Since the prosecutor would have to exercise some judgment even if the State were subject to this most stringent disclosure obligation, it is hard to find merit in the State's complaint over the responsibility for judgment under the existing system, which does not tax the prosecutor with error for any failure to disclose, absent a further showing of materiality. Unless, indeed, the adversary system of prosecution is to descend to a gladiatorial level unmitigated by any prosecutorial obligation for the sake of truth, the government simply cannot avoid responsibility for knowing when the suppression of evidence has come to portend such an effect on a trial's outcome as to destroy confidence in its result.

This means, naturally, that a prosecutor anxious about tacking too close to the wind will disclose a favorable piece of evidence. ** This is as it should be. Such disclosure will serve to justify trust in the prosecutor as "the representative...of a sovereignty...whose interest... in a criminal prosecution is not that it shall win a case, but that justice shall be done." ** And it will tend to preserve the criminal trial, as distinct from the prosecutor's private deliberations, as the chosen forum for ascertaining the truth about criminal accusations. ***

There is room to debate whether the two judges in the majority in the Court of Appeals made an assessment of the cumulative effect of the evidence. Although the majority's *Brady* discussion concludes with the statement that the court was not persuaded of the reasonable probability that Kyles would have obtained a favorable verdict if the jury had been "exposed to any or all of the undisclosed materials," ** the opinion also contains repeated references dismissing particular items of evidence as immaterial and so suggesting that cumulative materiality was not the touchstone. *** The result reached by the Fifth Circuit majority is compatible with a series of independent materiality evaluations, rather than the cumulative evaluation required by *Bagley*, as the ensuing discussion will show.

IV

In this case, disclosure of the suppressed evidence to competent counsel would have made a different result reasonably probable.

A

As the District Court put it, "the essence of the State's case" was the testimony of eye-witnesses, who identified Kyles as Dye's killer. ** Disclosure of their statements would have resulted in a markedly weaker case for the prosecution and a markedly stronger one for the defense. To begin with, the value of two of those witnesses would have been substantially reduced or destroyed.

The State rated Henry Williams as its best witness, who testified that he had seen the struggle and the actual shooting by Kyles. The jury would have found it helpful to probe this conclusion in the light of Williams's contemporaneous statement, in which he told the police that the assailant was "a black male, about 19 or 20 years old, about 5'4" or 5'5", 140 to 150 pounds, medium build" and that "his hair looked like it was platted." ** If cross-examined on this description, Williams would have had trouble explaining how he could have described Kyles, 6-feet tall and thin, as a man more than half a foot shorter with a medium build. *** Indeed, since Beanie was 22 years old, 5'5" tall, and 159 pounds, the defense would have had a compelling argument that Williams's description pointed to Beanie but not to Kyles. ***

The trial testimony of a second eyewitness, Isaac Smallwood, was equally damning to Kyles. He testified that Kyles was the assailant, and that he saw him struggle with Dye. He said he saw Kyles take a ".32, a small black gun" out of his right pocket, shoot Dye in the head, and drive off in her LTD. When the prosecutor asked him whether he actually saw Kyles shoot Dye, Smallwood answered "Yeah." **

Smallwood's statement taken at the parking lot, however, was vastly different. Immediately after the crime, Smallwood claimed that he had not seen the actual murder and had not seen the assailant outside the vehicle. "I heard a lound [sic] pop," he said. "When I looked around I saw a lady laying on the ground, and there was a red car coming toward me." ** Smallwood said that he got a look at the culprit, a black teenage male with a mustache and shoulder-length braided hair, as the victim's red Thunderbird passed where he was standing. When a police investigator specifically asked him whether he had seen the assailant outside the car, Smallwood answered that he had not; the gunman "was already in the car and coming toward me." **

A jury would reasonably have been troubled by the adjustments to Smallwood's original story by the time of the second trial. The struggle and shooting, which earlier he had not seen, he was able to describe with such detailed clarity as to identify the murder weapon as a small black .32-caliber pistol, which, of course, was the type of weapon used. His description of the victim's car had gone from a "Thunderbird" to an "LTD"; and he saw fit to say nothing about the assailant's shoulder-length hair and moustache, details noted by no other eyewitness. These developments would have fueled a withering cross-examination, destroying confidence in Smallwood's story and raising a substantial implication that the prosecutor had coached him to give it. ***

Since the evolution over time of a given eyewitness's description can be fatal to its reliability, ** the Smallwood and Williams identifications would have been severely undermined by use of their suppressed statements. The likely damage is best understood by taking the word of the prosecutor, who contended during closing arguments that Smallwood and Williams were the State's two best witnesses. ** Nor, of course, would the harm to the State's case on identity have been confined to their testimony alone. The fact that neither Williams nor Smallwood could have provided a consistent eyewitness description pointing to Kyles would have undercut the prosecution all the more because the remaining eyewitnesses called to testify (Territo and Kersh) had their best views of the gunman only as he fled the scene with his body partly concealed in Dye's car. And even aside from such important details, the effective impeachment of one eyewitness can call for a new trial even though the attack does not extend directly to others, as we have said before. **

B

Damage to the prosecution's case would not have been confined to evidence of the eyewitnesses, for Beanie's various statements would have raised opportunities to attack not only the probative value of crucial physical evidence and the circumstances in which it was found, but the thoroughness and even the good faith of the investigation, as well. By the State's own admission, Beanie was essential to its investigation and, indeed, "made the case" against Kyles. ** Contrary to what one might hope for from such a source, however, Beanie's statements to the police were replete with inconsistencies and would have allowed the jury to infer that Beanie was anxious to see Kyles arrested for Dye's murder. Their disclosure would have revealed a remarkably uncritical attitude on the part of the police.

If the defense had called Beanie as an adverse witness, he could not have said anything of any significance without being trapped by his inconsistencies. ***

Even if Kyles's lawyer had followed the more conservative course of leaving Beanie off the stand, though, the defense could have examined the police to good effect on their knowledge of Beanie's statements and so have attacked the reliability of the investigation in failing even to consider Beanie's possible guilt and in tolerating (if not countenancing) serious possibilities that incriminating evidence had been planted. ***

By demonstrating the detectives' knowledge of Beanie's affirmatively self-incriminating statements, the defense could have laid the foundation for a vigorous argument that the police had been guilty of negligence. ***

The admitted failure of the police to pursue these pointers toward Beanie's possible guilt could only have magnified the effect on the jury of explaining how the purse and the gun happened to be recovered. In Beanie's original recorded statement, he told the police that "[Kyles's] garbage goes out tomorrow," and that "if he's smart he'll put [the purse] in [the] garbage." ** These statements, along with the internal memorandum stating that the police had "reason to believe" Dye's personal effects and Schwegmann's bags would be in the garbage, would have supported the defense's theory that Beanie was no mere observer, but was determining the investigation's direction and success. The potential for damage from using Beanie's statement to undermine the ostensible integrity of the investigation is only confirmed by the prosecutor's admission at one of Kyles's postconviction hearings, that he did not recall a single instance before this case when police had searched and seized garbage on the street in front of a residence, ** and by Detective John Miller's admission at the same hearing that he thought at the time that it "was a possibility" that Beanie had planted the incriminating evidence in the garbage. ** If a police officer thought so, a juror would have, too. ***

To the same effect would have been an enquiry based on Beanie's apparently revealing remark to police that "if you can set [Kyles] up good, you can get that same gun." ** While the jury might have understood that Beanie meant simply that if the police investigated Kyles, they would probably find the murder weapon, the jury could also have taken Beanie to have been making the more sinister suggestion that the police "set up" Kyles, and the defense could have argued that the police accepted the invitation. ***

C

Next to be considered is the prosecution's list of the cars in the Schwegmann's parking lot at mid-evening after the murder. While its suppression does not rank with the failure to disclose the other evidence discussed here, it would have had some value as exculpation and impeachment, and it counts accordingly in determining whether *Bagley*'s standard of materiality is satisfied. On the police's assumption, argued to the jury, that the killer drove to the lot and left his car there during the heat of the investigation, the list without Kyles's registration would obviously have helped Kyles and would have had some value in countering an argument by the prosecution that a grainy enlargement of a photograph of the crime scene showed Kyles's car in the background. The list would also have shown that the police either knew that it was inconsistent with their informant's second and third statements (in which Beanie described retrieving Kyles's car after the time the list was compiled) or never even bothered to check the informant's story against known fact. Either way, the defense would have had further support for arguing that the police were irresponsible in relying on Beanie to tip them off to the location of evidence damaging to Kyles. ***

D

In assessing the significance of the evidence withheld, one must of course bear in mind that not every item of the State's case would have been directly undercut if the *Brady* evidence had been disclosed. It is significant, however, that the physical evidence remaining unscathed would, by the State's own admission, hardly have amounted to overwhelming proof that Kyles was the murderer. ***

Similarly undispositive is the small Schwegmann's receipt on the front passenger floorboard of the LTD, the only physical evidence that bore a fingerprint identified as Kyles's. Kyles explained that Beanie had driven him to Schwegmann's on Friday to buy cigarettes and transmission fluid, and he theorized that the slip must have fallen out of the bag when he removed the cigarettes. This explanation is consistent with the location of the slip when found and with its small size. The State cannot very well argue that the fingerprint ties Kyles to the killing without also explaining how the 2-inch-long register slip could have been the receipt for a week's worth of groceries, which Dye had gone to Schwegmann's to purchase. ***

The inconclusiveness of the physical evidence does not, to be sure, prove Kyles's innocence, and the jury might have found the eyewitness testimony of Territo and Kersh sufficient to convict, even though less damning to Kyles than that of Smallwood and Williams. *** But the question is not whether the State would have had a case to go to the jury if it had disclosed the favorable evidence, but whether we can be confident that the jury's verdict would have been the same. Confidence that it would have been cannot survive a recap of the suppressed evidence and its significance for the prosecution. The jury would have been entitled to find:

(a) that the investigation was limited by the police's uncritical readiness to accept the story and suggestions of an informant whose accounts were inconsistent to the point, for example, of including four different versions of the discovery of the victim's purse, and whose own behavior was enough to raise suspicions of guilt;

(b) that the lead police detective who testified was either less than wholly candid or less than fully informed;

(c) that the informant's behavior raised suspicions that he had planted both the murder weapon and the victim's purse in the places they were found;

(d) that one of the four eyewitnesses crucial to the State's case had given a description that did not match the defendant and better described the informant;

(e) that another eyewitness had been coached, since he had first stated that he had not seen the killer outside the getaway car, or the killing itself, whereas at trial he claimed to have seen the shooting, described the murder weapon exactly, and omitted portions of his initial description that would have been troublesome for the case;

(f) that there was no consistency to eyewitness descriptions of the killer's height, build, age, facial hair, or hair length.

Since all of these possible findings were precluded by the prosecution's failure to disclose the evidence that would have supported them, "fairness" cannot be stretched to the point of calling this a fair trial. *** This is not the "massive" case envisioned by the dissent; ** it is a significantly weaker case than the one heard by the first jury, which could not even reach a verdict.

The judgment of the Court of Appeals is reversed, and the case is remanded for further proceedings consistent with this opinion.

It is so ordered.

[Concurring opinions by Justice Stevens, joined by Justices Ginsburg and Breyer, and a dissenting opinion by Justice Scalia, joined by Chief Justice Rehnquist and Justices Kennedy and Thomas, are omitted.]

Notes

1. *Subsequent case history*

After this decision, Kyles was tried three more times. Each time the jury hung and the court declared a mistrial. In 1998, the prosecution decided not to try Kyles a sixth time. Nina Rivkind & Steven F. Shatz, CASES AND MATERIALS ON THE DEATH PENALTY 396 (2001), *citing* J. Gill, *Murder Trial's Inglorious End*, THE NEW ORLEANS TIMES-PICAYUNE, Feb. 20, 1998, at B7.

2. *Concurring opinion*

Justice Stevens was joined by Justices Ginsburg and Breyer in his concurrence. He agreed with the Court that the case presents "an important legal issue." "Because Justice Scalia so emphatically disagrees," Justice Stevens added the following response to Justice Scalia's criticism of the Court's decision to grant certiorari:

> Proper management of our certiorari docket, as Justice Scalia notes, ** precludes us from hearing argument on the merits of even a "substantial percentage" of the capital cases that confront us. ** Even aside from its legal importance, however, this case merits "favored treatment" ** for at least three reasons. First, the fact that the jury was unable to reach a verdict at the conclusion of the first trial provides strong reason to believe the significant errors that occurred at the second trial were prejudicial. Second, cases in which the record reveals so many instances of the state's failure to disclose exculpatory evidence are extremely rare. Even if I shared Justice Scalia's appraisal of the evidence in this case—which I do not—I would still believe we should independently review the record to ensure that the prosecution's blatant and repeated violations of a well-settled constitutional obligation did not deprive petitioner of a fair trial. Third, despite my high regard for the diligence and craftsmanship of the

author of the majority opinion in the Court of Appeals, my independent re-view of the case left me with the same degree of doubt about petitioner's guilt expressed by the dissenting judge in that court.

Our duty to administer justice occasionally requires busy judges to engage in a detailed review of the particular facts of a case, even though our labors may not provide posterity with a newly minted rule of law. The current popularity of capital punishment makes this "generalizable principle" ** especially impor-tant. I wish such review were unnecessary, but I cannot agree that our position in the judicial hierarchy makes it inappropriate. Sometimes the performance of an unpleasant duty conveys a message more significant than even the most penetrating legal analysis.

3. *Dissenting opinion*

Justice Scalia's dissent was joined by the Chief Justice, Justice Kennedy, and Justice Thomas. It included the following observations:

In a sensible system of criminal justice, wrongful conviction is avoided by estab-lishing, at the trial level, lines of procedural legality that leave ample margins of safety (for example, the requirement that guilt be proved beyond a reasonable doubt)—not by providing recurrent and repetitive appellate review of whether the facts in the record show those lines to have been narrowly crossed. ***

Since this Court has long shared Justice Jackson's view, today's opinion—which considers a fact-bound claim of error rejected by every court, state and federal, that previously heard it—is, so far as I can tell, wholly unprecedented. The Court has adhered to the policy that, when the petitioner claims only that a concededly correct view of the law was incorrectly applied to the facts, certio-rari should generally (*i.e.*, except in cases of the plainest error) be denied. ** That policy has been observed even when the fact-bound assessment of the federal court of appeals has differed from that of the district court; ** and under what we have called the "two-court rule," the policy has been applied with particular rigor when district court and court of appeals are in agreement as to what conclusion the record requires. ** How much the more should the policy be honored in this case, a federal habeas proceeding where not only both lower federal courts but also the state courts on postconviction review have all reviewed and rejected precisely the fact-specific claim before us. ** In-stead, however, the Court not only grants certiorari to consider whether the Court of Appeals (and all the previous courts that agreed with it) was correct as to what the facts showed in a case where the answer is far from clear, but in the process of such consideration renders new findings of fact and judgments of credibility appropriate to a trial court of original jurisdiction. **
***

The greatest puzzle of today's decision is what could have caused *this* capital case to be singled out for favored treatment. Perhaps it has been randomly se-lected as a symbol, to reassure America that the United States Supreme Court is reviewing capital convictions to make sure no factual error has been made. If so, it is a false symbol, for we assuredly do not do that. At, and during the week preceding, our February 24 Conference, for example, we considered and dis-posed of 10 petitions in capital cases, from seven States. We carefully consid-ered whether the convictions and sentences in those cases had been obtained in reliance upon correct principles of federal law; but if we had tried to consider, in addition, whether those correct principles had been applied, not merely plausibly, but *accurately*, to the particular facts of each case, we would have done nothing else for the week. The reality is that responsibility for factual accuracy, in capital cases as in other cases, rests elsewhere—with trial judges and juries, state appellate courts, and the lower federal courts; we do nothing but encourage foolish reliance to pretend otherwise. ***

Before concluding, Justice Scalia went on to analyze the evidence and to find that the withheld evidence would not have made a difference to the outcome of the case.

As evidenced by Justice Scalia's dissent, the role of evaluation of facts by a reviewing court has been a source of controversy. What are the reasons for this controversy?

4. Recent Supreme Court decision

In February 2004, the Supreme Court applied its holdings in *Strickler* and *Kyles* to *Banks v. Dretke*, 540 U.S. 668 (2004), a case where the prosecution withheld evidence that would have allowed the defendant to discredit two essential prosecution witnesses. Although the defendant did not discover the long-suppressed evidence until he was in federal habeas proceedings—well after he had finished state collateral review—the Court found that it was "incumbent on the State to set the record straight."

B. Ineffective Assistance of Counsel

The cases in this section outline the Supreme Court's standards for deciding when the Constitution requires a conviction or death sentence to be set aside because counsel's assistance at either the trial or the sentencing was ineffective. In *Strickland v. Washington*, 466 U.S. 668 (1984), the Court set forth the seminal standard for deciding what constitutes ineffective assistance of counsel and found that trial counsel was not ineffective.

> First, the defendant must show that counsel's performance was deficient. This requires showing that counsel made errors so serious that counsel was not functioning as the 'counsel' guaranteed the defendant by the Sixth Amendment. Second, the defendant must show that the deficient performance prejudiced the defense. This requires showing that counsel's errors were so serious as to deprive the defendant of a fair trial, a trial whose result is reliable. Unless a defendant makes both showings, it cannot be said that the conviction or death sentence resulted from a breakdown in the adversary process that renders the result unreliable.

Id. at 687.

In *Williams v. Taylor*, the Court applies the *Strickland* standard and determines that trial counsel were ineffective because they failed to investigate and failed to present substantial mitigating evidence during the sentencing portion of the defendant's capital murder trial. In *Wiggins v. Smith*, the court defines what is meant by an adequate investigation, and it finds ineffective assistance of counsel.

Williams v. Taylor
529 U.S. 362 (2000)

JUSTICE STEVENS announced the judgment of the Court and delivered the opinion of the Court with respect to Parts I, III, and IV, and an opinion with respect to Parts

II and V. JUSTICE SOUTER, JUSTICE GINSBURG, and JUSTICE BREYER join this opinion in its entirety. JUSTICE O'CONNOR and JUSTICE KENNEDY join Parts I, III, and IV of this opinion.

The questions presented are whether Terry Williams' constitutional right to the effective assistance of counsel as defined in *Strickland v. Washington*, 466 U.S. 668 (1984), was violated, and whether the judgment of the Virginia Supreme Court refusing to set aside his death sentence "was contrary to, or involved an unreasonable application of, clearly established Federal law, as determined by the Supreme Court of the United States," within the meaning of 28 U.S.C. § 2254(d)(1) (1994 ed., Supp. III). We answer both questions affirmatively.

I

On November 3, 1985, Harris Stone was found dead in his residence on Henry Street in Danville, Virginia. Finding no indication of a struggle, local officials determined that the cause of death was blood alcohol poisoning, and the case was considered closed. Six months after Stone's death, Terry Williams, who was then incarcerated in the "I" unit of the city jail for an unrelated offense, wrote a letter to the police stating that he had killed "'that man down on Henry Street'" and also stating that he "'did it'" to that "'lady down on West Green Street'" and was "'very sorry.'" The letter was unsigned, but it closed with a reference to "I cell." ** The police readily identified Williams as its author, and, on April 25, 1986, they obtained several statements from him. In one Williams admitted that, after Stone refused to lend him "'a couple of dollars,'" he had killed Stone with a mattock and taken the money from his wallet. *** In September 1986, Williams was convicted of robbery and capital murder.

At Williams' sentencing hearing, the prosecution proved that Williams had been convicted of armed robbery in 1976 and burglary and grand larceny in 1982. The prosecution also introduced the written confessions that Williams had made in April. The prosecution described two auto thefts and two separate violent assaults on elderly victims perpetrated after the Stone murder. On December 4, 1985, Williams had started a fire outside one victim's residence before attacking and robbing him. On March 5, 1986, Williams had brutally assaulted an elderly woman on West Green Street — an incident he had mentioned in his letter to the police. That confession was particularly damaging because other evidence established that the woman was in a "vegetative state" and not expected to recover. ** Williams had also been convicted of arson for setting a fire in the jail while awaiting trial in this case. Two expert witnesses employed by the State testified that there was a "high probability" that Williams would pose a serious continuing threat to society. **

The evidence offered by Williams' trial counsel at the sentencing hearing consisted of the testimony of Williams' mother, two neighbors, and a taped excerpt from a statement by a psychiatrist. One of the neighbors had not been previously interviewed by defense counsel, but was noticed by counsel in the audience during the proceedings and asked to testify on the spot. The three witnesses briefly described Williams as a "nice boy" and not a violent person. ** The recorded psychiatrist's testimony did little more than relate Williams' statement during an examination that in the course of one of his earlier robberies, he had removed the bullets from a gun so as not to injure anyone.

In his cross-examination of the prosecution witnesses, Williams' counsel repeatedly emphasized the fact that Williams had initiated the contact with the police that enabled them to solve the murder and to identify him as the perpetrator of the recent assaults, as well as the car thefts. In closing argument, Williams' counsel characterized Williams' confessional statements as "dumb," but asked the jury to give weight to the fact that he had "turned himself in, not on one crime but on four...that the [police otherwise] would not have solved." ** The weight of defense counsel's closing, however, was devoted to explaining that it was difficult to find a reason why the jury should spare Williams' life. ***

The jury found a probability of future dangerousness and unanimously fixed Williams' punishment at death. The trial judge concluded that such punishment was "proper" and "just" and imposed the death sentence. ** The Virginia Supreme Court affirmed the conviction and sentence. ** It rejected Williams' argument that when the trial judge imposed sentence, he failed to give mitigating weight to the fact that Williams had turned himself in. **

State Habeas Corpus Proceedings

In 1988 Williams filed for state collateral relief in the Danville Circuit Court. The petition was subsequently amended, and the Circuit Court (the same judge who had presided over Williams' trial and sentencing) held an evidentiary hearing on Williams' claim that trial counsel had been ineffective. *** Based on the evidence adduced after two days of hearings, Judge Ingram found that Williams' conviction was valid, but that his trial attorneys had been ineffective during sentencing. Among the evidence reviewed that had not been presented at trial were documents prepared in connection with Williams' commitment when he was 11 years old that dramatically described mistreatment, abuse, and neglect during his early childhood, as well as testimony that he was "borderline mentally retarded," had suffered repeated head injuries, and might have mental impairments organic in origin. ** The habeas hearing also revealed that the same experts who had testified on the State's behalf at trial believed that Williams, if kept in a "structured environment," would not pose a future danger to society. **

Counsel's failure to discover and present this and other significant mitigating evidence was "below the range expected of reasonable, professional competent assistance of counsel." ** Counsel's performance thus "did not measure up to the standard required under the holding of *Strickland v. Washington*, 466 U.S. 668 (1984), and [if it had,] there is a reasonable probability that the result of the sentencing phase would have been different." ** Judge Ingram therefore recommended that Williams be granted a rehearing on the sentencing phase of his trial.

The Virginia Supreme Court did not accept that recommendation. ***
***

Federal Habeas Corpus Proceedings

Having exhausted his state remedies, Williams sought a federal writ of habeas corpus pursuant to 28 U.S.C. § 2254 (1994 ed. and Supp. III). After reviewing the state habeas hearing transcript and the state courts' findings of fact and conclusions of law, the federal trial judge agreed with the Virginia trial judge: The death sentence was constitutionally infirm.

After noting that the Virginia Supreme Court had not addressed the question whether trial counsel's performance at the sentencing hearing fell below the range of competence demanded of lawyers in criminal cases, the judge began by addressing that issue in detail. He identified five categories of mitigating evidence that counsel had failed to introduce, *** and he rejected the argument that counsel's failure to conduct an adequate investigation had been a strategic decision to rely almost entirely on the fact that Williams had voluntarily confessed.

***

The Federal Court of Appeals reversed. ** It construed §2254(d)(1) as prohibiting the grant of habeas corpus relief unless the state court " 'decided the question by interpreting or applying the relevant precedent in a manner that reasonable jurists would all agree is unreasonable.' " ** Applying that standard, it could not say that the Virginia Supreme Court's decision on the prejudice issue was an unreasonable application of the tests developed in either *Strickland* or *Lockhart*. *** It explained that the evidence that Williams presented a future danger to society was "simply overwhelming," ** it endorsed the Virginia Supreme Court's interpretation of *Lockhart*, ** and it characterized the state court's understanding of the facts in this case as "reasonable." **

We granted certiorari ** and now reverse.

II

In 1867, Congress enacted a statute providing that federal courts "shall have power to grant writs of habeas corpus in all cases where any person may be restrained of his or her liberty in violation of the constitution, or of any treaty or law of the United States…." Act of Feb. 5, 1867, ch. 28, §1, 14 Stat. 385. Over the years, the federal habeas corpus statute has been repeatedly amended, but the scope of that jurisdictional grant remains the same. *** It is, of course, well settled that the fact that constitutional error occurred in the proceedings that led to a state-court conviction may not alone be sufficient reason for concluding that a prisoner is entitled to the remedy of habeas. *See, e.g., Stone v. Powell*, 428 U.S. 465 (1976); *Brecht v. Abrahamson*, 507 U.S. 619 (1993). On the other hand, errors that undermine confidence in the fundamental fairness of the state adjudication certainly justify the issuance of the federal writ. *See, e.g., Teague v. Lane*, 489 U.S. 288 (1989). ** The deprivation of the right to the effective assistance of counsel recognized in *Strickland* is such an error. *Strickland*, 466 U.S. at 686, 697–698.

The warden here contends that federal habeas corpus relief is prohibited by the amendment to 28 U.S.C. §2254 (1994 ed., Supp. III), enacted as a part of the Antiterrorism and Effective Death Penalty Act of 1996 (AEDPA). The relevant portion of that amendment provides:

> (d) An application for a writ of habeas corpus on behalf of a person in custody pursuant to the judgment of a State court shall not be granted with respect to any claim that was adjudicated on the merits in State court proceedings unless the adjudication of the claim —
>
> > (1) resulted in a decision that was contrary to, or involved an unreasonable application of, clearly established Federal law, as determined by the Supreme Court of the United States….

In this case, the Court of Appeals applied the construction of the amendment [incorrectly]. [The Court then sets forth the incorrect application and explains why it was incorrect.]

As the Fourth Circuit would have it, a state-court judgment is "unreasonable" in the face of federal law only if all reasonable jurists would agree that the state court was unreasonable. Thus, in this case, for example, even if the Virginia Supreme Court misread our opinion in *Lockhart*, we could not grant relief unless we believed that none of the judges who agreed with the state court's interpretation of that case was a "reasonable jurist." But the statute says nothing about "reasonable judges," presumably because all, or virtually all, such judges occasionally commit error; they make decisions that in retrospect may be characterized as "unreasonable." Indeed, it is most unlikely that Congress would deliberately impose such a requirement of unanimity on federal judges. As Congress is acutely aware, reasonable lawyers and lawgivers regularly disagree with one another. Congress surely did not intend that the views of one such judge who might think that relief is not warranted in a particular case should always have greater weight than the contrary, considered judgment of several other reasonable judges.

The inquiry mandated by the amendment relates to the way in which a federal habeas court exercises its duty to decide constitutional questions; the amendment does not alter the underlying grant of jurisdiction in § 2254(a). ** When federal judges exercise their federal-question jurisdiction under the "judicial Power" of Article III of the Constitution, it is "emphatically the province and duty" of those judges to "say what the law is." *Marbury v. Madison*, 5 U.S. 137 (1803). At the core of this power is the federal courts' independent responsibility—independent from its coequal branches in the Federal Government, and independent from the separate authority of the several States—to interpret federal law. A construction of AEDPA that would require the federal courts to cede this authority to the courts of the States would be inconsistent with the practice that federal judges have traditionally followed in discharging their duties under Article III of the Constitution. If Congress had intended to require such an important change in the exercise of our jurisdiction, we believe it would have spoken with much greater clarity than is found in the text of AEDPA.

This basic premise informs our interpretation of both parts of § 2254(d)(1): first, the requirement that the determinations of state courts be tested only against "clearly established Federal law, as determined by the Supreme Court of the United States," and second, the prohibition on the issuance of the writ unless the state court's decision is "contrary to, or involved an unreasonable application of," that clearly established law. We address each part in turn.

The "clearly established law" requirement

In *Teague v. Lane*, 489 U.S. 288 (1989), we held that the petitioner was not entitled to federal habeas relief because he was relying on a rule of federal law that had not been announced until after his state conviction became final. The antiretroactivity rule recognized in *Teague*, which prohibits reliance on "new rules," is the functional equivalent of a statutory provision commanding exclusive reliance on "clearly established law." Because there is no reason to believe that Congress intended to require federal courts to ask both whether a rule sought on habeas is "new" under *Teague*—which remains the law—and also whether it is "clearly established" under AEDPA, it seems safe to assume that Congress had congruent concepts in mind. *** It is perfectly clear that AEDPA codifies *Teague* to the extent that *Teague* requires federal habeas courts to deny relief that is contingent upon a rule of law not clearly established at the time the state conviction became final. ***
    ***

To this, AEDPA has added, immediately following the "clearly established law" requirement, a clause limiting the area of relevant law to that "determined by the Supreme Court of the United States." 28 U.S.C. § 2254(d)(1) (1994 ed., Supp. III). If this Court has not broken sufficient legal ground to establish an asked-for constitutional principle, the lower federal courts cannot themselves establish such a principle with clarity sufficient to satisfy the AEDPA bar. ***
    ***

In the context of this case, we also note that, as our precedent interpreting *Teague* has demonstrated, rules of law may be sufficiently clear for habeas purposes even when they are expressed in terms of a generalized standard rather than as a bright-line rule. As JUSTICE KENNEDY has explained:

> If the rule in question is one which of necessity requires a case-by-case examination of the evidence, then we can tolerate a number of specific applications without saying that those applications themselves create a new rule.... Where the beginning point is a rule of this general application, a rule designed for the specific purpose of evaluating a myriad of factual contexts, it will be the infrequent case that yields a result so novel that it forges a new rule, one not dictated by precedent. *Wright v. West*, 505 U.S. 277, 308–309 (1992) (opinion concurring in judgment). Moreover, the determination whether or not a rule is clearly established at the time a state court renders its final judgment of conviction is a question as to which the "federal courts must make an independent evaluation." *Id.* at 305 (O'CONNOR, J., [concurring in judgment]). **

It has been urged, in contrast, that we should read *Teague* and its progeny to encompass a broader principle of deference requiring federal courts to "validate 'reasonable, good-faith interpretations' of the law" by state courts. ***

Teague, however, does not extend this far. The often repeated language that *Teague* endorses "reasonable, good-faith interpretations" by state courts is an explanation of policy, not a statement of law. The *Teague* cases reflect this Court's view that habeas corpus is not to be used as a second criminal trial, and federal courts are not to run roughshod over the considered findings and judgments of the state courts that conducted the original trial and heard the initial appeals. On the contrary, we have long insisted that federal habeas courts attend closely to those considered decisions, and give them full effect when their findings and judgments are consistent with federal law. See *Thompson v. Keohane*, 516 U.S. 99, 107–116 (1995). But as JUSTICE O'CONNOR explained in *Wright*:

> The duty of the federal court in evaluating whether a rule is 'new' is not the same as deference;... *Teague* does not direct federal courts to spend less time or effort scrutinizing the existing federal law, on the ground that they can assume the state courts interpreted it properly.

> The maxim that federal courts should "give great weight to the considered conclusions of a coequal state judiciary"... does not mean that we have held in the past that federal courts must presume the correctness of a state court's legal conclusions on habeas, or that a state court's incorrect legal determination has ever been allowed to stand because it was reasonable. We have always held that federal courts, even on habeas, have an independent obligation to say what the law is. 505 U.S. at 305 (opinion concurring in judgment).

We are convinced that in the phrase, "clearly established law," Congress did not intend to modify that independent obligation.

The "contrary to, or an unreasonable application of," requirement

The message that Congress intended to convey by using the phrases, "contrary to" and "unreasonable application of" is not entirely clear. The prevailing view in the Circuits is that the former phrase requires de novo review of "pure" questions of law and the latter requires some sort of "reasonability" review of so-called mixed questions of law and fact. **

We are not persuaded that the phrases define two mutually exclusive categories of questions. Most constitutional questions that arise in habeas corpus proceedings—and therefore most "decisions" to be made—require the federal judge to apply a rule of law to a set of facts, some of which may be disputed and some undisputed. For example, an erroneous conclusion that particular circumstances established the voluntariness of a confession, or that there exists a conflict of interest when one attorney represents multiple defendants, may well be described either as "contrary to" or as an "unreasonable application of" the governing rule of law. ** In constitutional adjudication, as in the common law, rules of law often develop incrementally as earlier decisions are applied to new factual situations. ** But rules that depend upon such elaboration are hardly less lawlike than those that establish a bright-line test.

Indeed, our pre-AEDPA efforts to distinguish questions of fact, questions of law, and "mixed questions," and to create an appropriate standard of habeas review for each, generated some not insubstantial differences of opinion as to which issues of law fell into which category of question, and as to which standard of review applied to each. *See Thompson*, 516 U.S., at 110–111 (acknowledging "'that the Court has not charted an entirely clear course in this area'" and that "the proper characterization of a question as one of fact or law is sometimes slippery") (quoting *Miller*, 474 U.S. at 113). ***

The statutory text likewise does not obviously prescribe a specific, recognizable standard of review for dealing with either phrase. Significantly, it does not use any term, such as "de novo" or "plain error," that would easily identify a familiar standard of review. Rather, the text is fairly read simply as a command that a federal court not issue the habeas writ unless the state court was wrong as a matter of law or unreasonable in its application of law in a given case. The suggestion that a wrong state-court "decision"—a legal judgment rendered "after consideration of facts, and...law," Black's Law Dictionary 407 (6th ed.1990)—may no longer be redressed through habeas (because it is unreachable under the "unreasonable application" phrase) is based on a mistaken insistence that the § 2254(d)(1) phrases have not only independent, but mutually exclusive, meanings. Whether or not a federal court can issue the writ "under [the] 'unreasonable application' clause," the statute is clear that habeas may issue under § 2254(d)(1) if a state court "decision" is "contrary to...clearly established Federal law." We thus anticipate that there will be a variety of cases, like this one, in which both phrases may be implicated.

Even though we cannot conclude that the phrases establish "a body of rigid rules," they do express a "mood" that the federal judiciary must respect. ** In this respect, it seems clear that Congress intended federal judges to attend with the utmost care to state-court decisions, including all of the reasons supporting their decisions, before concluding that those proceedings were infected by constitutional error sufficiently serious to warrant the issuance of the writ. Likewise, the statute in a separate provision provides for the habeas remedy when a state-court decision "was based on an unreasonable determination of the facts in light of the evidence presented in the State court proceeding." 28 U.S.C. § 2254(d)(2) (1994 ed., Supp. III). While this provision is not before us in this case, it provides relevant context for our interpretation of § 2254(d)(1); in this respect, it bolsters our conviction that federal habeas courts must make as the starting point of their analysis the state courts' determinations of fact, including that aspect of a "mixed question" that rests on a finding of fact. AEDPA plainly sought to ensure a level of "deference to the determinations of state courts," provided those determinations did not conflict with federal law or apply federal law in an unreasonable way. H.R. Conf.

Rep. No. 104-518, p. 111 (1996). Congress wished to curb delays, to prevent "retrials" on federal habeas, and to give effect to state convictions to the extent possible under law. When federal courts are able to fulfill these goals within the bounds of the law, AEDPA instructs them to do so.

On the other hand, it is significant that the word "deference" does not appear in the text of the statute itself. Neither the legislative history, nor the statutory text suggests any difference in the so-called "deference" depending on which of the two phrases is implicated. *** Whatever "deference" Congress had in mind with respect to both phrases, it surely is not a requirement that federal courts actually defer to a state-court application of the federal law that is, in the independent judgment of the federal court, in error. As Judge Easterbrook noted with respect to the phrase "contrary to":

> Section 2254(d) requires us to give state courts' opinions a respectful reading, and to listen carefully to their conclusions, but when the state court addresses a legal question, it is the law "as determined by the Supreme Court of the United States" that prevails. ***

***

In sum, the statute directs federal courts to attend to every state-court judgment with utmost care, but it does not require them to defer to the opinion of every reasonable state-court judge on the content of federal law. If, after carefully weighing all the reasons for accepting a state court's judgment, a federal court is convinced that a prisoner's custody—or, as in this case, his sentence of death—violates the Constitution, that independent judgment should prevail. Otherwise the federal "law as determined by the Supreme Court of the United States" might be applied by the federal courts one way in Virginia and another way in California. In light of the well-recognized interest in ensuring that federal courts interpret federal law in a uniform way, *** we are convinced that Congress did not intend the statute to produce such a result.

III

In this case, Williams contends that he was denied his constitutionally guaranteed right to the effective assistance of counsel when his trial lawyers failed to investigate and to present substantial mitigating evidence to the sentencing jury. The threshold question under AEDPA is whether Williams seeks to apply a rule of law that was clearly established at the time his state-court conviction became final. That question is easily answered because the merits of his claim are squarely governed by our holding in *Strickland v. Washington*, 466 U.S. 668 (1984).

***

It is past question that the rule set forth in *Strickland* qualifies as "clearly established Federal law, as determined by the Supreme Court of the United States." That the *Strickland* test "of necessity requires a case-by-case examination of the evidence," *Wright*, 505 U.S. at 308 (KENNEDY, J., concurring), obviates neither the clarity of the rule nor the extent to which the rule must be seen as "established" by this Court. This Court's precedent "dictated" that the Virginia Supreme Court apply the *Strickland* test at the time that court entertained Williams' ineffective-assistance claim. *Teague*, 489 U.S. at 301. And it can hardly be said that recognizing the right to effective counsel "breaks new ground or imposes a new obligation on the States," *ibid*. Williams is therefore entitled to relief if the Virginia Supreme Court's decision rejecting his ineffective-assistance claim was either "contrary to, or involved an unreasonable application of," that established law. It was both.

IV

The Virginia Supreme Court erred in holding that our decision in *Lockhart v. Fretwell*, 506 U.S. 364 (1993), modified or in some way supplanted the rule set down in *Strickland*. It is true that while the *Strickland* test provides sufficient guidance for resolving virtually all ineffective-assistance-of-counsel claims, there are situations in which the overriding focus on fundamental fairness may affect the analysis. ***

***

Unlike the Virginia Supreme Court, the state trial judge omitted any reference to *Lockhart* and simply relied on our opinion in *Strickland* as stating the correct standard for judging ineffective-assistance claims. *** The trial judge analyzed the ineffective-assistance claim under the correct standard; the Virginia Supreme Court did not.

We are likewise persuaded that the Virginia trial judge correctly applied both components of that standard to Williams' ineffectiveness claim. Although he concluded that counsel competently handled the guilt phase of the trial, he found that their representation during the sentencing phase fell short of professional standards — a judgment barely disputed by the State in its brief to this Court. The record establishes that counsel did not begin to prepare for that phase of the proceeding until a week before the trial. ** They failed to conduct an investigation that would have uncovered extensive records graphically describing Williams' nightmarish childhood, not because of any strategic calculation but because they incorrectly thought that state law barred access to such records. Had they done so, the jury would have learned that Williams' parents had been imprisoned for the criminal neglect of Williams and his siblings, *** that Williams had been severely and repeatedly beaten by his father, that he had been committed to the custody of the social services bureau for two years during his parents' incarceration (including one stint in an abusive foster home), and then, after his parents were released from prison, had been returned to his parents' custody.

Counsel failed to introduce available evidence that Williams was "borderline mentally retarded" and did not advance beyond sixth grade in school. ** They failed to seek prison records recording Williams' commendations for helping to crack a prison drug ring and for returning a guard's missing wallet, or the testimony of prison officials who described Williams as among the inmates "least likely to act in a violent, dangerous or provocative way." ** Counsel failed even to return the phone call of a certified public accountant who had offered to testify that he had visited Williams frequently when Williams was incarcerated as part of a prison ministry program, that Williams "seemed to thrive in a more regimented and structured environment," and that Williams was proud of the carpentry degree he earned while in prison. **

Of course, not all of the additional evidence was favorable to Williams. The juvenile records revealed that he had been thrice committed to the juvenile system — for aiding and abetting larceny when he was 11 years old, for pulling a false fire alarm when he was 12, and for breaking and entering when he was 15. ** But as the Federal District Court correctly observed, the failure to introduce the comparatively voluminous amount of evidence that did speak in Williams' favor was not justified by a tactical decision to focus on Williams' voluntary confession. Whether or not those omissions were sufficiently prejudicial to have affected the outcome of sentencing, they clearly demonstrate that trial counsel did not fulfill their obligation to conduct a thorough investigation of the defendant's background. See 1 ABA Standards for Criminal Justice 4-4.1, commentary, p. 4–55 (2d ed. 1980).

We are also persuaded, unlike the Virginia Supreme Court, that counsel's unprofessional service prejudiced Williams within the meaning of *Strickland*. After hearing the additional evidence developed in the postconviction proceedings, the very judge who presided at Williams' trial and who once determined that the death penalty was "just" and "appropriate," concluded that there existed "a reasonable probability that the result of the sentencing phase would have been different" if the jury had heard that evidence. ** We do not agree with the Virginia Supreme Court that Judge Ingram's conclusion should be discounted because he apparently adopted "a per se approach to the prejudice element" that placed undue "emphasis on mere outcome determination." ** Judge Ingram did stress the importance of mitigation evidence in making his "outcome determination," but it is clear that his predictive judgment rested on his assessment of the totality of the omitted evidence rather than on the notion that a single item of omitted evidence, no matter how trivial, would require a new hearing.

The Virginia Supreme Court's own analysis of prejudice reaching the contrary conclusion was thus unreasonable in at least two respects. First, as we have already explained, the State Supreme Court mischaracterized at best the appropriate rule, made clear by this Court in *Strickland*, for determining whether counsel's assistance was effective within the meaning of the Constitution. While it may also have conducted an "outcome determinative" analysis of its own, ** it is evident to us that the court's decision turned on its erroneous view that a "mere" difference in outcome is not sufficient to establish constitutionally ineffective assistance of counsel. ** Its analysis in this respect was thus not only "contrary to," but also, inasmuch as the Virginia Supreme Court relied on the inapplicable exception recognized in *Lockhart*, an "unreasonable application of" the clear law as established by this Court.

Second, the State Supreme Court's prejudice determination was unreasonable insofar as it failed to evaluate the totality of the available mitigation evidence—both that adduced at trial, and the evidence adduced in the habeas proceeding—in reweighing it against the evidence in aggravation. See *Clemons v. Mississippi*, 494 U.S. 738, 751–752 (1990). This error is apparent in its consideration of the additional mitigation evidence developed in the postconviction proceedings. The court correctly found that as to "the factual part of the mixed question," there was "really…no…dispute" that available mitigation evidence was not presented at trial. ** As to the prejudice determination comprising the "legal part" of its analysis, ** it correctly emphasized the strength of the prosecution evidence supporting the future dangerousness aggravating circumstance.

But the state court failed even to mention the sole argument in mitigation that trial counsel did advance—Williams turned himself in, alerting police to a crime they otherwise would never have discovered, expressing remorse for his actions, and cooperating with the police after that. While this, coupled with the prison records and guard testimony, may not have overcome a finding of future dangerousness, the graphic description of Williams' childhood, filled with abuse and privation, or the reality that he was "borderline mentally retarded," might well have influenced the jury's appraisal of his moral culpability. See *Boyde v. California*, 494 U.S. 370, 387 (1990). The circumstances recited in his several confessions are consistent with the view that in each case his violent behavior was a compulsive reaction rather than the product of cold-blooded premeditation. Mitigating evidence unrelated to dangerousness may alter the jury's selection of penalty, even if it does not undermine or rebut the prosecution's death-eligibility case. The Virginia Supreme Court did not entertain that possibility. It thus failed to accord appropriate weight to the body of mitigation evidence available to trial counsel.

V

In our judgment, the state trial judge was correct both in his recognition of the established legal standard for determining counsel's effectiveness, and in his conclusion that the entire postconviction record, viewed as a whole and cumulative of mitigation evidence presented originally, raised "a reasonable probability that the result of the sentencing proceeding would have been different" if competent counsel had presented and explained the significance of all the available evidence. It follows that the Virginia Supreme Court rendered a "decision that was contrary to, or involved an unreasonable application of, clearly established Federal law." Williams' constitutional right to the effective assistance of counsel as defined in *Strickland v. Washington*, 466 U.S. 668 (1984), was violated.

Accordingly, the judgment of the Court of Appeals is reversed, and the case is remanded for further proceedings consistent with this opinion.

It is so ordered.

[JUSTICE O'CONNOR concurred in part and concurred in the judgment. She delivered the opinion on behalf of the Court with respect to Part II (except as to the footnote). JUSTICE KENNEDY joined the opinion in its entirety. THE CHIEF JUSTICE and JUSTICE THOMAS joined Part II. JUSTICE SCALIA joined Part II, except as to the footnote. Additionally, THE CHIEF JUSTICE, joined by JUSTICES SCALIA and THOMAS, concurred in part and dissented in part.]

Notes

1. *Subsequent case history*

On November 14, 2000, Terry Williams accepted a life sentence without the possibility of parole. In exchange, the prosecution agreed not to pursue the death penalty. Brooke A. Master, *Deal Gets Inmate Off Death Row*, THE WASHINGTON POST, Nov. 15, 2000, at B1.

2. *From Strickland to Terry Williams*

Why did the Court find Terry Williams' attorneys to be ineffective, while the attorney in *Strickland* was not?

3. *A note about deference*

Footnote 13 in Section II reads:

As Judge Easterbrook has noted, the statute surely does not require the kind of "deference" appropriate in other contexts: "It does not tell us to 'defer' to state decisions, as if the Constitution means one thing in Wisconsin and another in Indiana. Nor does it tell us to treat state courts the way we treat federal administrative agencies. *** Congress did not delegate interpretive or executive power to the state courts. They exercise powers under their domestic law, constrained by the Constitution of the United States. 'Deference' to the jurisdictions bound by those constraints is not sensible." **....

In addition to this footnote, Justice Stevens also observes in Section II:

We all agree that state-court judgments must be upheld unless, after the closest examination of the state-court judgment, a federal court is firmly convinced that a federal constitutional right has been violated. Our difference is as to the cases in which, at first-blush, a state-court judgment seems entirely reasonable, but thorough analysis by a federal court produces a firm conviction that that judgment is infected by constitutional error. In our view, such an erroneous judgment is "unreasonable" within the meaning of the act even though that conclusion was not immediately apparent.

What is the import of these commentaries?

Wiggins v. Smith

reviewing 4th Cir opinion.

539 U.S. 510 (2003)

JUSTICE O'CONNOR delivered the opinion of the Court.

Petitioner, Kevin Wiggins, argues that his attorneys' failure to investigate his background and present mitigating evidence of his unfortunate life history at his capital sentencing proceedings violated his Sixth Amendment right to counsel. In this case, we consider whether the United States Court of Appeals for the Fourth Circuit erred in upholding the Maryland Court of Appeals' rejection of this claim.

IAC

I

A

On September 17, 1988, police discovered 77-year-old Florence Lacs drowned in the bathtub of her ransacked apartment in Woodlawn, Maryland. ** The State indicted petitioner for the crime on October 20, 1988, and later filed a notice of intention to seek the death penalty. Two Baltimore County public defenders, Carl Schlaich and Michelle Nethercott, assumed responsibility for Wiggins' case. In July 1989, petitioner elected to be tried before a judge in Baltimore County Circuit Court. ** On August 4, after a 4-day trial, the court found petitioner guilty of first-degree murder, robbery, and two counts of theft. **

After his conviction, Wiggins elected to be sentenced by a jury, and the trial court scheduled the proceedings to begin on October 11, 1989. On September 11, counsel filed a motion for bifurcation of sentencing in hopes of presenting Wiggins' case in two phases. ** Counsel intended first to prove that Wiggins did not act as a "principal in the first degree," **—*i.e.*, that he did not kill the victim by his own hand. ** Counsel then intended, if necessary, to present a mitigation case. In the memorandum in support of their motion, counsel argued that bifurcation would enable them to present each case in its best light; separating the two cases would prevent the introduction of mitigating evidence from diluting their claim that Wiggins was not directly responsible for the murder. **

On October 12, the court denied the bifurcation motion, and sentencing proceedings commenced immediately thereafter. In her opening statement, Nethercott told the jurors they would hear evidence suggesting that someone other than Wiggins actually killed Lacs. ** Counsel then explained that the judge would instruct them to weigh Wiggins' clean record as a factor against a death sentence. She concluded: "You're going to hear that Kevin Wiggins has had a difficult life. It has not been easy for him. But he's worked. He's tried to be a productive citizen, and he's reached the age of 27 with no convictions for prior crimes of violence and no convictions, period.... I think that's an important thing for you to consider." ** During the proceedings themselves, however, counsel introduced no evidence of Wiggins' life history.

Before closing arguments, Schlaich made a proffer to the court, outside the presence of the jury, to preserve bifurcation as an issue for appeal. He detailed the mitigation case counsel would have presented had the court granted their bifurcation motion. He explained that they would have introduced psychological reports and expert testimony demonstrating Wiggins' limited intellectual capacities and childlike emotional state on the one hand, and the absence of aggressive patterns in his behavior, his capacity for empathy, and his desire to function in the world on the other. ** At no point did Schlaich proffer any evidence of petitioner's life history or family background. On October 18, the court instructed the jury on the sentencing task before it, and later that afternoon, the jury returned with a sentence of death. ** A divided Maryland Court of Appeals affirmed. **

B

In 1993, Wiggins sought postconviction relief in Baltimore County Circuit Court. With new counsel, he challenged the adequacy of his representation at sentencing, arguing that his attorneys had rendered constitutionally defective assistance by failing to investigate and present mitigating evidence of his dysfunctional background. ** To support his claim, petitioner presented testimony by Hans Selvog, a licensed social worker certified as an expert by the court. ** Selvog testified concerning an elaborate social history report he had prepared containing evidence of the severe physical and sexual abuse petitioner suffered at the hands of his mother and while in the care of a series of foster parents. Relying on state social services, medical, and school records, as well as interviews with petitioner and numerous family members, Selvog chronicled petitioner's bleak life history. **

According to Selvog's report, petitioner's mother, a chronic alcoholic, frequently left Wiggins and his siblings home alone for days, forcing them to beg for food and to eat paint chips and garbage. ** Mrs. Wiggins' abusive behavior included beating the children for breaking into the kitchen, which she often kept locked. She had sex with men while her children slept in the same bed and, on one occasion, forced petitioner's hand against a hot stove burner — an incident that led to petitioner's hospitalization. ** At the age of six, the State placed Wiggins in foster care. Petitioner's first and second foster mothers abused him physically, ** and, as petitioner explained to Selvog, the father in his second foster home repeatedly molested and raped him. **

During the postconviction proceedings, Schlaich testified that he did not remember retaining a forensic social worker to prepare a social history, even though the State made funds available for that purpose. ** He explained that he and Nethercott, well in advance of trial, decided to focus their efforts on "retrying the factual case" and disputing Wiggins' direct responsibility for the murder. ** In April 1994, at the close of the proceedings, the judge observed from the bench that he could not remember a capital case in which counsel had not compiled a social history of the defendant, explaining, "not to do a social history, at least to see what you have got, to me is absolute error. I just—I would be flabbergasted if the Court of Appeals said anything else." ** In October 1997, however, the trial court denied Wiggins' petition for postconviction relief. The court concluded that "when the decision not to investigate…is a matter of trial tactics, there is no ineffective assistance of counsel." **

The Maryland Court of Appeals affirmed the denial of relief, concluding that trial counsel had made "a deliberate, tactical decision to concentrate their effort at convincing the jury" that appellant was not directly responsible for the murder. ** The court observed that counsel knew of Wiggins' unfortunate childhood. They had available to them both the presentence investigation (PSI) report prepared by the Division of Parole and Probation, as required by Maryland law, ** as well as "more detailed social service records that recorded incidences of physical and sexual abuse, an alcoholic mother, placements in foster care, and borderline retardation." ** The court acknowledged that this evidence was neither as detailed nor as graphic as the history elaborated in the Selvog report but emphasized that "counsel *did* investigate and *were* aware of appellant's background." ** Counsel knew that at least one uncontested mitigating factor—Wiggins' lack of prior convictions—would be before the jury should their attempt to disprove Wiggins' direct responsibility for the murder fail. As a result, the court concluded, Schlaich and Nethercott "made a reasoned choice to proceed with what they thought was their best defense." **

C

In September 2001, Wiggins filed a petition for writ of habeas corpus in Federal District Court. The trial court granted him relief, holding that the Maryland courts' rejection of his ineffective assistance claim "involved an unreasonable application of clearly established federal law." ** The court rejected the State's defense of counsel's "tactical" decision to "'retry guilt,'" concluding that for a strategic decision to be reasonable, it must be "based upon information the attorney has made after conducting a reasonable investigation." ** The court found that though counsel were aware of some aspects of Wiggins' background, that knowledge did not excuse them from their duty to make a "fully informed and deliberate decision" about whether to present a mitigation case. In fact, the court concluded, their knowledge triggered an obligation to look further. **

Reviewing the District Court's decision *de novo*, the Fourth Circuit reversed, holding that counsel had made a reasonable strategic decision to focus on petitioner's direct responsibility. ** The court contrasted counsel's complete failure to investigate potential mitigating evidence in *Williams* ** with the fact that Schlaich and Nethercott knew at least some details of Wiggins' childhood from the PSI and social services records. ** The court acknowledged that counsel likely knew further investigation "would have resulted in more sordid details surfacing," but agreed with the Maryland Court of Appeals that counsel's knowledge of the avenues of mitigation available to them "was sufficient to make an informed strategic choice" to challenge petitioner's direct responsibility for the murder. ** The court emphasized that conflicting medical testimony with respect to the time of death, the absence of direct evidence against Wiggins, and unexplained forensic evidence at the crime scene supported counsel's strategy. **

We granted certiorari ** and now reverse.

II
A

Petitioner renews his contention that his attorneys' performance at sentencing violated his Sixth Amendment right to effective assistance of counsel. The amendments to 28 U.S.C. §2254, enacted as part of the Antiterrorism and Effective Death Penalty Act of 1996 (AEDPA), circumscribe our consideration of Wiggins' claim and require us to limit our analysis to the law as it was "clearly established" by our precedents at the time of the state court's decision. Section 2254 provides:

> (d) An application for a writ of habeas corpus on behalf of a person in custody pursuant to the judgment of a State court shall not be granted with respect to

any claim that was adjudicated on the merits in State court proceedings unless the adjudication of the claim —

> (1) resulted in a decision that was contrary to, or involved an unreasonable application of, clearly established Federal law, as determined by the Supreme Court of the United States; or

> (2) resulted in a decision that was based on an unreasonable determination of the facts in light of the evidence presented at the State court proceeding."

We have made clear that the "unreasonable application" prong of § 2254(d)(1) permits a federal habeas court to "grant the writ if the state court identifies the correct governing legal principle from this Court's decisions but unreasonably applies that principle to the facts" of petitioner's case. ***

We established the legal principles that govern claims of ineffective assistance of counsel in *Strickland v. Washington*. ** An ineffective assistance claim has two components: A petitioner must show that counsel's performance was deficient, and that the deficiency prejudiced the defense. ** To establish deficient performance, a petitioner must demonstrate that counsel's representation "fell below an objective standard of reasonableness." ** We have declined to articulate specific guidelines for appropriate attorney conduct and instead have emphasized that "the proper measure of attorney performance remains simply reasonableness under prevailing professional norms." **

In this case, as in *Strickland*, petitioner's claim stems from counsel's decision to limit the scope of their investigation into potential mitigating evidence. ** Here, as in *Strickland*, counsel attempt to justify their limited investigation as reflecting a tactical judgment not to present mitigating evidence at sentencing and to pursue an alternate strategy instead. In rejecting Strickland's claim, we defined the deference owed such strategic judgments in terms of the adequacy of the investigations supporting those judgments:

> Strategic choices made after thorough investigation of law and facts relevant to plausible options are virtually unchallengeable; and strategic choices made after less than complete investigation are reasonable precisely to the extent that reasonable professional judgments support the limitations on investigation. In other words, counsel has a duty to make reasonable investigations or to make a reasonable decision that makes particular investigations unnecessary. In any ineffectiveness case, a particular decision not to investigate must be directly assessed for reasonableness in all the circumstances, applying a heavy measure of deference to counsel's judgments. **

***

In light of these standards, our principal concern in deciding whether Schlaich and Nethercott exercised "reasonable professional judgment" ** is not whether counsel should have presented a mitigation case. Rather, we focus on whether the investigation supporting counsel's decision not to introduce mitigating evidence of Wiggins' background *was itself reasonable*. ***

B

1

The record demonstrates that counsel's investigation drew from three sources. **. Counsel arranged for William Stejskal, a psychologist, to conduct a number of tests on petitioner. Stejskal concluded that petitioner had an IQ of 79, had difficulty coping with demanding situations, and exhibited features of a personality disorder. ** These reports revealed nothing, however, of petitioner's life history. **

With respect to that history, counsel had available to them the written PSI, which included a one-page account of Wiggins' "personal history" noting his "misery as a youth," quoting his description of his own background as "'disgusting,'" and observing that he spent most of his life in foster care. ** Counsel also "tracked down" records kept by the Baltimore City Department of Social Services (DSS) documenting petitioner's various placements in the State's foster care system. ** In describing the scope of counsel's investigation into petitioner's life history, both the Fourth Circuit and the Maryland Court of Appeals referred only to these two sources of information. **

Counsel's decision not to expand their investigation beyond the PSI and the DSS records fell short of the professional standards that prevailed in Maryland in 1989. As Schlaich acknowledged, standard practice in Maryland in capital cases at the time of Wiggins' trial included the preparation of a social history report. ** Despite the fact that the Public Defender's office made funds available for the retention of a forensic social worker, counsel chose not to commission such a report. ** Counsel's conduct similarly fell short of the standards for capital defense work articulated by the American Bar Association (ABA)—standards to which we long have referred as "guides to determining what is reasonable." ** The ABA Guidelines provide that investigations into mitigating evidence "should comprise efforts to discover *all reasonably available* mitigating evidence and evidence to rebut any aggravating evidence that may be introduced by the prosecutor." ** Despite these well-defined norms, however, counsel abandoned their investigation of petitioner's background after having acquired only rudimentary knowledge of his history from a narrow set of sources. **

The scope of their investigation was also unreasonable in light of what counsel actually discovered in the DSS records. The records revealed several facts: Petitioner's mother was a chronic alcoholic; Wiggins was shuttled from foster home to foster home and displayed some emotional difficulties while there; he had frequent, lengthy absences from school; and, on at least one occasion, his mother left him and his siblings alone for days without food. ** As the Federal District Court emphasized, any reasonably competent attorney would have realized that pursuing these leads was necessary to making an informed choice among possible defenses, particularly given the apparent absence of any aggravating factors in petitioner's background. ** Indeed, counsel uncovered no evidence in their investigation to suggest that a mitigation case, in its own right, would have been counterproductive, or that further investigation would have been fruitless; this case is therefore distinguishable from our precedents in which we have found limited investigations into mitigating evidence to be reasonable. ***

The record of the actual sentencing proceedings underscores the unreasonableness of counsel's conduct by suggesting that their failure to investigate thoroughly resulted from inattention, not reasoned strategic judgment. Counsel sought, until the day before sentencing, to have the proceedings bifurcated into a retrial of guilt and a mitigation stage. ** On the eve of sentencing, counsel represented to the court that they were prepared to come forward with mitigating evidence ** and that they intended to present such evidence in the event the court granted their motion to bifurcate. In other words, prior to sentencing, counsel never actually abandoned the possibility that they would present a mitigation defense. Until the court denied their motion, then, they had every reason to develop the most powerful mitigation case possible.

Investig + present = unreasonable

What is more, during the sentencing proceeding itself, counsel did not focus exclusively on Wiggins' direct responsibility for the murder. After introducing that issue in her opening statement, ** Nethercott entreated the jury to consider not just what Wiggins "is found to have done," but also "who [he] is." ** Though she told the jury it would "hear that Kevin Wiggins has had a difficult life," **counsel never followed up on that suggestion with details of Wiggins' history. At the same time, counsel called a criminologist to testify that inmates serving life sentences tend to adjust well and refrain from further violence in prison—testimony with no bearing on whether petitioner committed the murder by his own hand. ** Far from focusing exclusively on petitioner's direct responsibility, then, counsel put on a halfhearted mitigation case, taking precisely the type of "shotgun" approach the Maryland Court of Appeals concluded counsel sought to avoid. ** When viewed in this light, the "strategic decision" the state courts and respondents all invoke to justify counsel's limited pursuit of mitigating evidence resembles more a *post-hoc* rationalization of counsel's conduct than an accurate description of their deliberations prior to sentencing.

In rejecting petitioner's ineffective assistance claim, the Maryland Court of Appeals appears to have assumed that because counsel had *some* information with respect to petitioner's background—the information in the PSI and the DSS records—they were in a position to make a tactical choice not to present a mitigation defense. ** In assessing the reasonableness of an attorney's investigation, however, a court must consider not only the quantum of evidence already known to counsel, but also whether the known evidence would lead a reasonable attorney to investigate further. Even assuming Schlaich and Nethercott limited the scope of their investigation for strategic reasons, *Strickland* does not establish that a cursory investigation automatically justifies a tactical decision with respect to sentencing strategy. Rather, a reviewing court must consider the reasonableness of the investigation said to support that strategy. **

The Maryland Court of Appeals' application of *Strickland*'s governing legal principles was objectively unreasonable. Though the state court acknowledged petitioner's claim that counsel's failure to prepare a social history "did not meet the minimum standards of the profession," the court did not conduct an assessment of whether the decision to cease all investigation upon obtaining the PSI and the DSS records actually demonstrated reasonable professional judgment. ***

Additionally, the court based its conclusion, in part, on a clear factual error—that the "social service records...recorded incidences of...sexual abuse." ** As the State and the United States now concede, the records contain no mention of sexual abuse, much less of the repeated molestations and rapes of petitioner detailed in the Selvog report. ** The state court's assumption that the records documented instances of this abuse has been shown to be incorrect by "clear and convincing evidence," 28 U.S.C. § 2254(e)(1), and reflects "an unreasonable determination of the facts in light of the evidence presented in the State court proceeding," § 2254(d)(2). This partial reliance on an erroneous factual finding further highlights the unreasonableness of the state court's decision.

The dissent insists that this Court's hands are tied, under § 2254(d), "by the state court's factual determinations that Wiggins' trial counsel '*did* investigate and *were* aware of [Wiggins'] background.'" ** But as we have made clear, the Maryland Court of Appeals' conclusion that the *scope* of counsel's investigation into petitioner's background met the legal standards set in *Strickland* represented an objectively unreasonable application of our precedent. § 2254(d)(1). Moreover, the court's assumption that counsel learned of a major aspect of Wiggins' background, *i.e.*, the sexual abuse, from the DSS records was clearly erroneous. The requirements of § 2254(d) thus pose no bar to granting petitioner habeas relief.

2

***

We therefore must determine, *de novo*, whether counsel reached beyond the PSI and the DSS records in their investigation of petitioner's background. The record as a whole does not support the conclusion that counsel conducted a more thorough investigation than the one we have described. ***

The State maintained at oral argument that Schlaich's reference to "other people's reports" indicated that counsel learned of the sexual abuse from sources other than the PSI and the DSS records. ** But when pressed repeatedly to identify the sources counsel might have consulted, the State acknowledged that no written reports documented the sexual abuse and speculated that counsel must have learned of it through "oral reports" from Wiggins himself. ** Not only would the phrase "other people's reports" have been an unusual way for counsel to refer to conversations with his client, but the record contains no evidence that counsel ever pursued this line of questioning with Wiggins. ** For its part, the United States emphasized counsel's retention of the psychologist. ** But again, counsel's decision to hire a psychologist sheds no light on the extent of their investigation into petitioner's social background. Though Stejskal based his conclusions on clinical interviews with Wiggins, as well as meetings with Wiggins' family members, ** his final report discussed only petitioner's mental capacities and attributed nothing of what he learned to Wiggins' social history.

To further underscore that counsel did not know, prior to sentencing, of the sexual abuse, as well as of the other incidents not recorded in the DSS records, petitioner directs us to the content of counsel's October 17, 1989, proffer. Before closing statements and outside the presence of the jury, Schlaich proffered to the court the mitigation case counsel would have introduced had the court granted their motion to bifurcate. ** In his statement, Schlaich referred only to the results of the psychologist's test and mentioned nothing of Wiggins' troubled background. Given that the purpose of the proffer was to preserve their pursuit of bifurcation as an issue for appeal, they had every incentive to make their mitigation case seem as strong as possible. Counsel's failure to include in the proffer the powerful evidence of repeated sexual abuse is therefore explicable only if we assume that counsel had no knowledge of the abuse.

Contrary to the dissent's claim, ** we are not accusing Schlaich of lying. His statements at the postconviction proceedings that he knew of this abuse, as well as of the hand-burning incident, may simply reflect a mistaken memory shaped by the passage of time. After all, the state postconviction proceedings took place over four years after Wiggins' sentencing. Ultimately, given counsel's likely ignorance of the history of sexual abuse at the time of sentencing, we cannot infer from Schlaich's postconviction testimony that counsel looked further than the PSI and the DSS records in investigating petitioner's background. Indeed, the record contains no mention of sources other than those it is undisputed counsel possessed. ** We therefore conclude that counsel's investigation of petitioner's background was limited to the PSI and the DSS records.

3

In finding that Schlaich and Nethercott's investigation did not meet *Strickland*'s performance standards, we emphasize that *Strickland* does not require counsel to investigate every conceivable line of mitigating evidence no matter how unlikely the effort would be to assist the defendant at sentencing. Nor does *Strickland* require defense counsel to present mitigating evidence at sentencing in every case. Both conclusions would interfere with the "constitutionally protected independence of counsel" at the heart of *Strickland*. 466 U.S. at 689. We base our conclusion on the much more limited principle that "strategic choices made after less than complete investigation are reasonable" only to the extent that "reasonable professional judgments support the limitations on investigation." ** A decision not to investigate thus "must be directly assessed for reasonableness in all the circumstances." **

***

III

In order for counsel's inadequate performance to constitute a Sixth Amendment violation, petitioner must show that counsel's failures prejudiced his defense. ** In *Strickland*, we made clear that, to establish prejudice, a "defendant must show that there is a reasonable probability that, but for counsel's unprofessional errors, the result of the proceeding would have been different. A reasonable probability is a probability sufficient to undermine confidence in the outcome." ** In assessing prejudice, we reweigh the evidence in aggravation against the totality of available mitigating evidence. In this case, our review is not circumscribed by a state court conclusion with respect to prejudice, as neither of the state courts below reached this prong of the *Strickland* analysis.

The mitigating evidence counsel failed to discover and present in this case is powerful. As Selvog reported based on his conversations with Wiggins and members of his family, ** Wiggins experienced severe privation and abuse in the first six years of his life while in the custody of his alcoholic, absentee mother. He suffered physical torment, sexual molestation, and repeated rape during his subsequent years in foster care. The time Wiggins spent homeless, along with his diminished mental capacities, further augment his mitigation case. Petitioner thus has the kind of troubled history we have declared relevant to assessing a defendant's moral culpability. **

Given both the nature and the extent of the abuse petitioner suffered, we find there to be a reasonable probability that a competent attorney, aware of this history, would have introduced it at sentencing in an admissible form. While it may well have been strategically defensible upon a reasonably thorough investigation to focus on Wiggins' direct responsibility for the murder, the two sentencing strategies are not necessarily mutually exclusive. Moreover, given the strength of the available evidence, a reasonable attorney may well have chosen to prioritize the mitigation case over the direct responsibility challenge, particularly given that Wiggins' history contained little of the double edge we have found to justify limited investigations in other cases. **

***

We further find that had the jury been confronted with this considerable mitigating evidence, there is a reasonable probability that it would have returned with a different sentence. In reaching this conclusion, we need not, as the dissent suggests, ** make the state-law evidentiary findings that would have been at issue at sentencing. Rather, we evaluate the totality of the evidence—"both that adduced at trial, *and the evidence adduced in the habeas proceeding[s]*." **

***

*** Accordingly, the judgment of the United States Court of Appeals for the Fourth Circuit is reversed, and the case is remanded for further proceedings consistent with this opinion.

It is so ordered.

JUSTICE SCALIA, with whom JUSTICE THOMAS joins, dissenting:

The Court today vacates Kevin Wiggins' death sentence on the ground that his trial counsel's investigation of potential mitigating evidence was "incomplete." ** Wiggins' trial counsel testified under oath, however, that he was aware of the basic features of Wiggins' troubled childhood that the Court claims he overlooked. ** The Court chooses to disbelieve this testimony for reasons that do not withstand analysis. Moreover, even if this disbelief could plausibly be entertained, that would certainly not establish (as 28 U.S.C. § 2254(d) requires) that the Maryland Court of Appeals was *unreasonable* in believing it, and in therefore concluding that counsel adequately investigated Wiggins' background. The Court also fails to observe § 2254(e)(1)'s requirement that federal habeas courts respect state-court factual determinations not rebutted by "clear and convincing evidence." The decision sets at naught the statutory scheme we once described as a "highly deferential standard for evaluating state-court rulings." ** I respectfully dissent.

***

II

***

There is no "reasonable probability" that a social-history investigation would have altered the chosen strategy of Wiggins' trial counsel. As noted earlier, Schlaich was well aware—without the benefit of a "social history" report—that Wiggins had a troubled childhood and background. And the Court remains bound, *even after* concluding that Wiggins has satisfied the standards of §§ 2254(d)(1) and (d)(2), by the state court's factual determination that Wiggins' trial attorneys "*were* aware of [Wiggins'] background" ** and "were aware that Wiggins had a most unfortunate childhood." ** See 28 U.S.C. § 2254(e)(1). Wiggins' trial attorneys chose, however, not to present evidence of Wiggins' background to the jury because of their "deliberate, tactical decision to concentrate their effort at convincing the jury that appellant was not a principal in the killing of Ms. Lacs." **

Wiggins has not shown that the incremental information in Hans Selvog's social-history report would have induced counsel to change this course. ***

***

Today's decision is extraordinary—even for our "death is different" jurisprudence. ** It fails to give effect to § 2254(e)(1)'s requirement that state court factual determinations be presumed correct, and disbelieves the sworn testimony of a member of the bar while treating hearsay accounts of statements of a convicted murderer as established fact. I dissent.

Notes

1. *Subsequent case history*

Kevin Wiggins' sentencing in Baltimore County is still pending.

2. *Considering the term "unreasonableness"*

What is your response to Justice Scalia's remark that the Maryland Court of Appeals was not unreasonable in believing the testimony of Wiggins' attorney? Would you agree with Justice Scalia that the Court's decision in *Wiggins* was "extraordinary"?

3. *How far is the Court willing to take the analysis in* Wiggins?

In October 2003, the Supreme Court issued a *per curiam* opinion in *Yarborough v. Gentry*, 540 U.S. 1 (2003), a case in which the Ninth Circuit granted habeas corpus relief on the basis of ineffective assistance of counsel during the closing argument at trial. Lionel Gentry was convicted in a California state court of assault with a deadly weapon for stabbing his girlfriend, who testified against him at trial. The Ninth Circuit reviewed Gentry's attorney's closing argument and criticized him for such errors as not highlighting certain potentially exculpatory pieces of evidence, criticizing his own client, failing to demand that the jury acquit Gentry, and confessing that he could not tell who was telling the truth, either. In reversing the Ninth Circuit's decision, the Supreme Court stated that the "Ninth Circuit's conclusion—not only that [counsel's] performance was deficient, but that any disagreement with that conclusion would be objectively unreasonable—gives too little deference to the state courts that have primary responsibility for supervising defense counsel in state criminal trials."

Based on the bare facts outlined in this note about Gentry's closing argument, what are the main differences between Gentry's case and Wiggins' case that enabled the Court to reach such different results?

Part II

Subject Matter Jurisdiction

Chapter 3

Custody

The very essence of the words *habeas corpus*—"that you have the body"—signifies that when filing a petition for writ of habeas corpus, a person asserts he is in custody. Given the essence of the Great Writ, it comes as no surprise that one of the jurisdictional requirements for habeas review is that the petitioner be "in custody."

Section 2254(a) specifically states:

> The Supreme Court, a Justice thereof, a circuit judge, or a district court shall entertain an application for a writ of habeas corpus in behalf of a person in custody pursuant to the judgment of a State court only on the ground that he is in custody in violation of the Constitution or laws or treaties of the United States.

Although the issue of "custody" may seem simple to resolve, it is more complex than it first appears.

In *Carafas v. LaVallee*, the Court examines whether a person who is in custody when he first applies for a writ of habeas corpus, but who is discharged before the Court issues its writ of certiorari, has federal jurisdiction. In deciding that such a person can pursue his claim, the Court points to amendments to the habeas corpus statute that specifically contemplate the possibility of relief other than immediate release from physical custody. A few days after *Carafas*, the Court states in *Sibron v. New York* that a person who has completed his six-month sentence can continue to pursue a habeas petition he filed before completing his sentence. In so deciding, the Court relies on its holding in *Carafas*. The Court also explains that important constitutional problems sometimes occur in the context of minor offenses that carry short sentences and collateral consequences and that people should be able to avail themselves of constitutional protections and remedies, even if they have completed their sentences before their petitions wind their way through the court process. The final case in this chapter, *Lane v. Williams*, also discusses collateral consequences of a conviction, but it does so in the context of a petitioner challenging his sentence—rather than the conviction itself. The Court finds that when a person only challenges his sentence, expiration of that sentence renders the habeas petition moot.

Carafas v. LaVallee
391 U.S. 234 (1968)

JUSTICE FORTAS delivered the opinion of the Court.

This case has a lengthy procedural history. In 1960, petitioner was convicted of burglary and grand larceny in New York state court proceedings and was sentenced to concurrent terms of three to five years. On direct appeal (following *Mapp v. Ohio*, 367 U.S.

643 (1961)), petitioner claimed that illegally obtained evidence had been introduced against him at trial. The Appellate Division affirmed the conviction without opinion, ** as did the New York Court of Appeals. *** This Court denied a petition for a writ of certiorari. **

Thereafter, complex proceedings took place in which petitioner sought in both federal and state courts to obtain relief by writ of habeas corpus, based on his claim that illegally seized evidence was used against him. ** On November 5, 1965, the United States District Court, as directed by the United States Court of Appeals for the Second Circuit, ** heard petitioner's claim on the merits. It dismissed his petition on the ground that he had failed to show a violation of his Fourth Amendment rights. Petitioner appealed in circumstances hereinafter related. The Court of Appeals for the Second Circuit dismissed the appeal. [We granted the] petition for a writ of certiorari. *** [F]irst we must consider the State's contention that this case is now moot because petitioner has been unconditionally released from custody.

Petitioner applied to the United States District Court for a writ of habeas corpus in June 1963. He was in custody at that time. On March 6, 1967, petitioner's sentence expired, *** and he was discharged from the parole status in which he had been since October 4, 1964. We issued our writ of certiorari on October 16, 1967. **

The issue presented, then, is whether the expiration of petitioner's sentence, before his application was finally adjudicated and while it was awaiting appellate review, terminates federal jurisdiction with respect to the application. Respondent relies upon *Parker v. Ellis*, 362 U.S. 574 (1960), and unless this case is overruled, it stands as an insuperable barrier to our further consideration of petitioner's cause or to the grant of relief upon his petition for a writ of habeas corpus.

Parker v. Ellis held that when a prisoner was released from state prison after having served his full sentence, this Court could not proceed to adjudicate the merits of the claim for relief on his petition for habeas corpus which he had filed with the Federal District Court. This Court held that upon petitioner's unconditional release the case became "moot." Parker was announced in a *per curiam* decision. ***

It is clear that petitioner's cause is not moot. In consequence of his conviction, he cannot engage in certain businesses; *** he cannot serve as an official of a labor union for a specified period of time; *** he cannot vote in any election held in New York State; *** he cannot serve as a juror. *** Because of these "disabilities or burdens (which) may flow from" petitioner's conviction, he has "a substantial stake in the judgment of conviction which survives the satisfaction of the sentence imposed on him." *Fiswick v. United States*, 329 U.S. 211, 222 (1946). On account of these "collateral consequences," *** the case is not moot. *Ginsberg v. New York*, 390 U.S. 629, 633–634 n.2 (1968); *Fiswick v. United States*, *supra*, 329 U.S. at 222, n. 10; *United States v. Morgan*, 346 U.S. 502, 512–513 (1954).

The substantial issue, however, which is posed by *Parker v. Ellis*, is not mootness in the technical or constitutional sense, but whether the statute defining the habeas corpus jurisdiction of the federal judiciary in respect of persons in state custody is available here. In *Parker v. Ellis*, as in the present case, petitioner's application was filed in the Federal District Court when he was in state custody, and in both the petitioner was unconditionally released from state custody before his case could be heard in this Court. For the reasons which we here summarize and which are stated at length in the dissenting opinions in *Parker v. Ellis*, we conclude that under the statutory scheme, once the federal jurisdiction has attached in the District Court, it is not defeated by the release of the petitioner prior to completion of proceedings on such application.

The federal habeas corpus statute requires that the applicant must be "in custody" when the application for habeas corpus is filed. This is required not only by the repeated references in the statute, *** but also by the history of the great writ. *** Its province, shaped to guarantee the most fundamental of all rights, *** is to provide an effective and speedy instrument by which judicial inquiry may be had into the legality of the detention of a person. *See Peyton v. Rowe*, [391 U.S. 54 (1968)]. ***

But the statute does not limit the relief that may be granted to discharge of the applicant from physical custody. Its mandate is broad with respect to the relief that may be granted. It provides that "[t]he court shall... dispose of the matter as law and justice require." 28 U.S.C. § 2243. The 1966 amendments to the habeas corpus statute seem specifically to contemplate the possibility of relief other than immediate release from physical custody. At one point, the new § 2244(b) (1964 ed., Supp. II), speaks in terms of "release from custody or other remedy." *See Peyton v. Rowe, supra; Walker v. Wainwright*, 390 U.S. 335 (1968). **

In the present case, petitioner filed his application shortly after June 20, 1963, while he was in custody. He was not released from custody until March 6, 1967, two weeks before he filed his petition for certiorari here. During the intervening period his application was under consideration in various courts. Petitioner is entitled to consideration of his application for relief on its merits. He is suffering, and will continue to suffer, serious disabilities because of the law's complexities and not because of his fault, if his claim that he has been illegally convicted is meritorious. There is no need in the statute, the Constitution, or sound jurisprudence for denying to petitioner his ultimate day in court. [The Court goes on to hold that because the district court had issued a certificate of probable cause to appeal and waived the filing fee, it was error for the appeals court to deny him the right to appeal in forma pauperis. In so doing, the Court also overrules *Parker v. Ellis*.] ***

Accordingly, the judgment below is vacated and the case is remanded to the United States Court of Appeals for the Second Circuit for further proceedings consistent with this opinion.

It is so ordered.

Judgment vacated and case remanded.

[JUSTICE MARSHALL took no part in the consideration or decision of this case. JUSTICE HARLAN and JUSTICE STEWART concurred.]

Sibron v. New York
Peters v. New York
Nos. 63 & 74
392 U.S. 40 (1968)

CHIEF JUSTICE WARREN delivered the opinion of the Court.

These are companion cases to No. 67, *Terry v. Ohio*, [392 U.S. 1 (1968),] decided today. They present related questions under the Fourth and Fourteenth Amendments, but the cases arise in the context of New York's "stop-and-frisk" law, N.Y. Code Crim. Proc. § 180-a. This statute provides:

> 1. A police officer may stop any person abroad in a public place whom he reasonably suspects is committing, has committed or is about to commit a felony or any of the offenses specified in section five hundred fifty-two of this chapter, and may demand of him his name, address and an explanation of his actions.

2. When a police officer has stopped a person for questioning pursuant to this section and reasonably suspects that he is in danger of life or limb, he may search such person for a dangerous weapon. If the police officer finds such a weapon or any other thing the possession of which may constitute a crime, he may take and keep it until the completion of the questioning, at which time he shall either return it, if lawfully possessed, or arrest such person.

The appellants, Sibron and Peters, were both convicted of crimes in New York state courts on the basis of evidence seized from their persons by police officers. The Court of Appeals of New York held that the evidence was properly admitted, on the ground that the searches which uncovered it were authorized by the statute. ***

Sibron, the appellant in No. 63, was convicted of the unlawful possession of heroin. *** He moved before trial to suppress the heroin seized from his person by the arresting officer, Brooklyn Patrolman Anthony Martin. After the trial court denied his motion, Sibron pleaded guilty to the charge, preserving his right to appeal the evidentiary ruling. *** At the hearing on the motion to suppress, Officer Martin testified that while he was patrolling his beat in uniform on March 9, 1965, he observed Sibron "continually from the hours of 4:00 P.M. to 12:00, midnight…in the vicinity of 742 Broadway." He stated that during this period of time he saw Sibron in conversation with six or eight persons whom he (Patrolman Martin) knew from past experience to be narcotics addicts. The officer testified that he did not overhear any of these conversations, and that he did not see anything pass between Sibron and any of the others. Late in the evening Sibron entered a restaurant. Patrolman Martin saw Sibron speak with three more known addicts inside the restaurant. Once again, nothing was overheard and nothing was seen to pass between Sibron and the addicts. Sibron sat down and ordered pie and coffee, and, as he was eating, Patrolman Martin approached him and told him to come outside. Once outside, the officer said to Sibron, "You know what I am after." According to the officer, Sibron "mumbled something and reached into his pocket." Simultaneously, Patrolman Martin thrust his hand into the same pocket, discovering several glassine envelopes, which, it turned out, contained heroin.

The State has had some difficulty in settling upon a theory for the admissibility of these envelopes of heroin. In his sworn complaint Patrolman Martin stated:

As the officer approached the defendant, the latter being in the direction of the officer and seeing him, he did put his hand in his left jacket pocket and pulled out a tinfoil envelope and did attempt to throw same to the ground. The officer never losing sight of the said envelope seized it from the defendant's left hand, examined it and found it to contain ten glascine [sic] envelopes with a white substance alleged to be Heroin.

This version of the encounter, however, bears very little resemblance to Patrolman Martin's testimony at the hearing on the motion to suppress. In fact, he discarded the abandonment theory at the hearing. *** Nor did the officer ever seriously suggest that he was in fear of bodily harm and that he searched Sibron in self-protection to find weapons. ***

The prosecutor's theory at the hearing was that Patrolman Martin had probable cause to believe that Sibron was in possession of narcotics because he had seen him conversing with a number of known addicts over an eight-hour period. In the absence of any knowledge on Patrolman Martin's part concerning the nature of the intercourse between Sibron and the addicts, however, the trial court was inclined to grant the motion to suppress. ***

***

I

At the outset we must deal with the question whether we have jurisdiction in No. 63. It is asserted that because Sibron has completed service of the six-month sentence imposed upon him as a result of his conviction, the case has become moot under *St. Pierre v. United States*, 319 U.S. 41 (1943). *** We have concluded that the case is not moot.

In the first place, it is clear that the broad dictum with which the Court commenced its discussion in *St. Pierre*—that "the case is moot because, after petitioner's service of his sentence and its expiration, there was no longer a subject matter on which the judgment of this Court could operate" (319 U.S. at 42)—fails to take account of significant qualifications recognized in *St. Pierre* and developed in later cases. Only a few days ago we held unanimously that the writ of habeas corpus was available to test the constitutionality of a state conviction where the petitioner had been in custody when he applied for the writ, but had been released before this Court could adjudicate his claims. *Carafas v. LaVallee*, 391 U.S. 234 (1968). On numerous occasions in the past this Court has proceeded to adjudicate the merits of criminal cases in which the sentence had been fully served or the probationary period during which a suspended sentence could be reimposed had terminated. ** Thus mere release of the prisoner does not mechanically foreclose consideration of the merits by this Court.

St. Pierre itself recognized two possible exceptions to its "doctrine" of mootness, and both of them appear to us to be applicable here. The Court stated that "it does not appear that petitioner could not have brought his case to this Court for review before the expiration of his sentence," noting also that because the petitioner's conviction was for contempt and because his controversy with the Government was a continuing one, there was a good chance that there would be "ample opportunity to review" the important question presented on the merits in a future proceeding. 319 U.S. at 43. This was a plain recognition of the vital importance of keeping open avenues of judicial review of deprivations of constitutional right. *** There was no way for Sibron to bring his case here before his six-month sentence expired. By statute he was precluded from obtaining bail pending appeal, *** and by virtue of the inevitable delays of the New York court system, he was released less than a month after his newly appointed appellate counsel had been supplied with a copy of the transcript and roughly two months before it was physically possible to present his case to the first tier in the state appellate court system. *** This was true despite the fact that he took all steps to perfect his appeal in a prompt, diligent, and timely manner.

Many deep and abiding constitutional problems are encountered primarily at a level of "low visibility" in the criminal process—in the context of prosecutions for "minor" offenses which carry only short sentences. *** We do not believe that the Constitution contemplates that people deprived of constitutional rights at this level should be left utterly remediless and defenseless against repetitions of unconstitutional conduct. A State may not cut off federal review of whole classes of such cases by the simple expedient of a blanket denial of a pending appeal. As *St. Pierre* clearly recognized, a State may not effectively deny a convict access to its appellate courts until he has been released and then argue that his case has been mooted by his failure to do what it alone prevented him from doing. ***

The second exception recognized in *St. Pierre* permits adjudication of the merits of a criminal case where "under neither state or federal law further penalties or disabilities can be imposed...as a result of the judgment which has...been satisfied." 319 U.S. at 43. Subsequent cases have expanded this exception to the point where it may realistically be said that inroads have been made upon the principle itself. *St. Pierre* implied that the burden was upon the convict to show the existence of collateral legal consequences. Three years later in *Fiswick v. United States*, 329 U.S. 211 (1946), however, the Court held that a criminal case had not become moot upon release of the prisoner, noting that the convict, an alien, might be subject to deportation for having committed a crime of "moral turpitude"—even though it had never been held (and the Court refused to hold) that the crime of which he was convicted fell into this category. The Court also pointed to the fact that if the petitioner should in the future decide he wanted to become an American citizen, he might have difficulty proving that he was of "good moral character." ***

    ***

Three years later, in *Pollard v. United States*, 352 U.S. 354 (1957), the Court abandoned all inquiry into the actual existence of specific collateral consequences and in effect presumed that they existed. ***

This case certainly meets that test for survival. Without pausing to canvass the possibilities in detail, we note that New York expressly provides by statute that Sibron's conviction may be used to impeach his character should he choose to put it in issue at any future criminal trial, N.Y. Code Crim. Proc. § 393-c, and that it must be submitted to a trial judge for his consideration in sentencing should Sibron again be convicted of a crime, N.Y. Code Crim. Proc. § 482. There are doubtless other collateral consequences. Moreover, we see no relevance in the fact that Sibron is a multiple offender. *** A judge or jury faced with a question of character, like a sentencing judge, may be inclined to forgive or at least discount a limited number of minor transgressions, particularly if they occurred at some time in the relatively distant past. *** It is impossible for this Court to say at what point the number of convictions on a man's record renders his reputation irredeemable. *** And even if we believed that an individual had reached that point, it would be impossible for us to say that he had no interest in beginning the process of redemption with the particular case sought to be adjudicated. We cannot foretell what opportunities might present themselves in the future for the removal of other convictions from an individual's record. The question of the validity of a criminal conviction can arise in many contexts, compare *Burgett v. Texas*, 389 U.S. 109 (1967), and the sooner the issue is fully litigated the better for all concerned. It is always preferable to litigate a matter when it is directly and principally in dispute, rather than in a proceeding where it is collateral to the central controversy. Moreover, litigation is better conducted when the dispute is fresh and additional facts may, if necessary, be taken without a substantial risk that witnesses will die or memories fade. And it is far better to eliminate the source of a potential legal disability than to require the citizen to suffer the possibly unjustified consequences of the disability itself for an indefinite period of time before he can secure adjudication of the State's right to impose it on the basis of some past action. **

None of the concededly imperative policies behind the constitutional rule against entertaining moot controversies would be served by a dismissal in this case. There is nothing abstract, feigned, or hypothetical about Sibron's appeal. Nor is there any suggestion that either Sibron or the State has been wanting in diligence or fervor in the litigation. We have before us a fully developed record of testimony about contested historical facts, which reflects the "impact of actuality" *** to a far greater degree than many controversies accepted for adjudication as a matter of course under the Federal Declaratory Judgment Act, 28 U.S.C. § 2201.

*** Sibron "has a substantial stake in the judgment of conviction which survives the satisfaction of the sentence imposed on him." *Fiswick v. United States, supra,* [329 U.S.] at 222. The case is not moot.

***

[The Court upheld Peters' conviction but reversed Sibron's conviction on the ground that the heroin was unconstitutionally admitted as evidence against him.]

[JUSTICE DOUGLAS concurred in both Peters' and Sibron's cases; JUSTICES FORTAS and WHITE concurred; JUSTICE HARLAN concurred in the result; and JUSTICE BLACK concurred in Peters' case but dissented in Sibron's case.]

Lane v. Williams
455 U.S. 624 (1982)

JUSTICE STEVENS delivered the opinion of the Court.

In 1975, respondents pleaded guilty in Illinois state court to a charge of burglary, an offense punishable at that time by imprisonment for an indeterminate term of years and a mandatory 3-year parole term. We granted certiorari to consider whether the failure of the trial court to advise respondents of that mandatory parole requirement before accepting their guilty pleas deprived them of due process of law. We are unable to reach that question, however, because we find that respondents' claims for relief are moot.

I

On March 11, 1975, respondent Lawrence Williams appeared in Illinois state court and pleaded guilty to a single count of burglary. Before accepting the guilty plea, the trial judge elicited Williams' understanding of the terms of a plea agreement, in which his attorney and the prosecutor had agreed that Williams would receive an indeterminate sentence of from one to two years in prison in exchange for pleading guilty. The judge informed Williams that he would impose the bargained sentence, and advised him of both the nature of the charge against him and the constitutional rights that he would waive by pleading guilty. After the prosecutor established a factual basis for the plea, Williams indicated that he understood his rights and wished to plead guilty.

At the time that Williams pleaded guilty, Illinois law required every indeterminate sentence for certain felonies, including burglary, to include a special parole term in addition to the term of imprisonment. *** During the plea acceptance hearing, neither the trial judge, the prosecutor, nor defense counsel informed Williams that his negotiated sentence included a mandatory parole term of three years.

Williams was discharged from prison on May 20, 1976, and released on parole. On March 3, 1977, he was arrested for reasons that do not appear in the record and, on March 16, 1977, he was returned to prison as a parole violator. While in custody, Williams filed a petition for a writ of habeas corpus in the United States District Court for the Northern District of Illinois. He alleged that he "was not informed" that a mandatory parole term had attached to his sentence until two months before his discharge from prison and that "his present incarceration is therefore in violation of the Due Process Clause of the 14th Amendment to the U. S. Constitution." ** Williams' petition did not ask the federal court to set aside his conviction and allow him to plead anew. It requested an order "freeing him from the present control" of the Warden and from "all future liability" under his original sentence. ***

On January 4, 1978, the District Court found that Williams' guilty plea had been induced unfairly in violation of the Due Process Clause of the Fourteenth Amendment and ordered Williams released from custody. *United States ex rel. Williams v. Morris*, 447

F. Supp. 95 ([N.D. Ill.] 1978). The court expressly "opted for specific performance" of the plea bargain "rather than nullification of the guilty plea." *Id.* at 101. The relief granted was precisely what Williams had requested.

Williams was not, however, immediately released from custody. The District Court entered a stay to give the State an opportunity to file a motion for reconsideration. Before that stay was lifted, Williams was released from prison on a special 6-month "supervisory release term." The District Court subsequently denied the State's motion to reconsider and the State appealed. *** While that appeal was pending, Williams' 6-month release term expired and he was released from the custody of the Illinois Department of Corrections.

[The Court then explained the facts concerning the other respondent, Southall, which were similar to Williams' case.]

***

II

Respondents claim that their constitutional rights were violated when the trial court accepted their guilty pleas without informing them of the mandatory parole requirement. Assuming, for the sake of argument, that the court's failure to advise respondents of this consequence rendered their guilty pleas void, *** respondents could seek to remedy this error in two quite different ways. They might ask the District Court to set aside their convictions and give them an opportunity to plead anew; in that event, they might either plead not guilty and stand trial or they might try to negotiate a different plea bargain properly armed with the information that any sentence they received would include a special parole term. Alternatively, they could seek relief in the nature of "special enforcement" of the plea agreement as they understood it; in that event, the elimination of the mandatory parole term from their sentences would remove any possible harmful consequence from the trial court's incomplete advice.

If respondents had sought the opportunity to plead anew, this case would not be moot. Such relief would free respondents from all consequences flowing from their convictions, as well as subject them to reconviction with a possibly greater sentence. *Cf. North Carolina v. Pearce*, 395 U.S. 711 [(1969)]. Thus, a live controversy would remain to determine whether a constitutional violation in fact had occurred and whether respondents were entitled to the relief that they sought. ***

Since respondents had completed their previously imposed sentences, however, they did not seek the opportunity to plead anew. *** Rather, they sought to remedy the alleged constitutional violation by removing the consequence that gave rise to the constitutional harm. In the course of their attack, that consequence expired of its own accord. Respondents are no longer subject to any direct restraint as a result of the parole term. They may not be imprisoned on the lesser showing needed to establish a parole violation than to prove a criminal offense. Their liberty or freedom of movement is not in any way curtailed by a parole term that has expired.

Since respondents elected only to attack their sentences, and since those sentences expired during the course of these proceedings, this case is moot. "Nullification of a conviction may have important benefits for a defendant...but urging in a habeas corpus proceeding the correction of a sentence already served is another matter." *North Carolina v. Rice*, 404 U.S. 244, 248 [(1971)].

***

Respondents have never attacked, on either substantive or procedural grounds, the finding that they violated the terms of their parole. Respondent Williams simply sought an order "freeing him from the present control" of the Warden and from "all future liability" under his original sentence; Southall sought his "immediate release" from custody. Through the mere passage of time, respondents have obtained all the relief that they sought. In these circumstances, no live controversy remains.

The Court of Appeals also held that this case was not moot because it was "capable of repetition, yet evading review." *Southern Pacific Terminal Co. v. ICC*, 219 U.S. 498, 515 [(1911)]. That doctrine, however, is applicable only when there is "a reasonable expectation that the same complaining party would be subjected to the same action again." *Weinstein v. Bradford*, 423 U.S. 147, 149 [(1975)]; *Murphy v. Hunt*, [455 U.S. 478,] 482 [(1982)]. Respondents are now acutely aware of the fact that a criminal sentence in Illinois will include a special parole term; any future guilty plea will not be open to the same constitutional attack. The possibility that other persons may litigate a similar claim does not save this case from mootness.

The judgment of the Court of Appeals is vacated. The case should be dismissed as moot.

It is so ordered.

***

[JUSTICE MARSHALL, with whom JUSTICES BRENNAN and BLACKMUN joined, dissented.]

Notes

1. *Dissenting opinion by Justice Marshall (joined by Justice Brennan and Justice Blackmun)*

The dissenting opinion by Justice Marshall includes the following observation:

> The majority announces today that this case is moot because, in its view, no collateral consequences flow from respondents' parole revocations, which were based on findings that respondents had violated the conditions of parole terms declared void by the courts below. I dissent from this holding because I believe it is contrary to this Court's precedents and because it ignores the fact that the State of Illinois does attach collateral consequences to parole revocations, a fact recognized both in the State's brief to the Court of Appeals on the issue of mootness and in state-court decisions in analogous cases.

In light of the Court's discussion of collateral consequences in *Sibron*, do you agree with Justice Marshall that the holding in *Lane v. Williams* is contrary to the Court's precedent? Why or why not?

2. *Collateral consequences under the Federal Sentencing Guidelines*

Lane v. Williams predates the enactment of the Federal Sentencing Guidelines, wherein an individual who is sentenced to even a short period of time (*i.e.*, more than 60 days) is subject to an automatic increase of his criminal history score by two points instead of the one point increase he would receive had he been sentenced to a term of probation. *See United States v. Chavez-Palacios*, 30 F.3d 1290, 1293 (10th Cir. 1994) (discussing sections 4A1.1(b) and (c) of the Federal Sentencing Guidelines). Should such collateral consequences of a sentence already served still render the appeal moot? *See Chavez-Palacios*, 30 F.3d at 1293 (finding the appeal not moot); *United States v. Dickey*, 924 F.2d 836 (9th Cir.), *cert. denied*, 502 U.S. 943 (1991) (same).

3. *Further reading*

There is reason to debate the wisdom of federal courts staying out of cases when the petitioner no longer is in the custody or control of the state. For a thorough examination of the subject, see Marc Mauer's "The Intended and Unintended Consequences of Incarceration-based Sentencing Policies," 16 T.M. Cooley L. Rev. 47 (1999).

4. *Collateral consequences in presidential elections*

Consider the following editorial from the *Concord Monitor*, which documents how Black voters were wrongly turned away from the Florida polls during the Bush v. Gore presidential election in 2000.

Concord Monitor Editorial: "Stolen Votes"
Monday, March 18, 2002
Wrongly listing citizens as felons likely cost Gore election.
Copyright ©2002 by the Concord Monitor

No matter how successful George W. Bush proves to be as president, a pall will forever hang over the 2000 election. In national scrutiny of the way Americans cast and count their ballots, many states were found wanting. The chief among them was Florida, where the outcome, with the help of the U.S. Supreme Court, gave Bush his victory over Al Gore.

Reform efforts are under way, but at least one major flaw in the system should be repaired by Congress before another national election is held. A chilling two-page account in the current issue of *Harper's* magazine by Greg Palast, who investigated the 2000 election for the BBC, illustrates why.

Had thousands of voters not wrongly been turned away from the polls, the outcome in Florida probably would have been different and Gore, not Bush, would be in the White House. Most of the disenfranchised voters were black.

Most states deny prisoners the vote. Only Maine, Massachusetts, Vermont and Utah do not. But only 15 states, including Florida, bar felons who have served their time from voting, according to a 1998 study by the Sentencing Project of the international organization Human Rights Watch.

In Florida, between May 1999 and election day, two secretaries of state loyal to the governor of Florida, President Bush's brother Jeb Bush, ordered 57,700 ex-felons purged from the voter rolls, according to Palast's research.

To create the "scrub" list, a private company, DBT Online, matched voters by name, birth date, gender and race with the names of tens of millions of ex-felons in the United States. The system to filter out mismatches was set to exclude as many voters as possible. The company had proposed using a more complicated and accurate system that took into account people's address histories and financial records but was told this was unnecessary.

Here are a few examples of mistakes Palast documented:

• One voter was barred for a crime committed in 2007.

• One county that checked the 694 names on the disqualified voter list could verify the accuracy of only 34.

• Voters were disqualified for having names identical to a felon in another state, in some cases even when birth dates were different. Many people were disqualified simply for having names so common that a match was likely.

• One county election supervisor threw out the scrub list when she found her own name on it.

• The contract with DBT required the company to contact each voter disqualified as a felon by telephone. The state, however, told the company that was unnecessary.

• One 64-year-old man lost his right to vote for having been convicted in 1959 of sleeping on a bus-stop bench.

In all, the U.S. Commission on Civil Rights estimates that at least 8,000 voters were falsely disqualified from voting because they were listed as felons. Blacks were four times as likely to be disqualified as whites. On Nov. 26, Bush was certified the winner by 537 votes.

That the Florida election verification system was horribly and perhaps purposely inaccurate is clear. The remedy, however, only partially lies in improving its accuracy.

According to the Sentencing Project, the United States is the only democratic nation that bars felons from voting for life. Doing so is not only unfair to people who have paid the debt for their misdeeds, but it also runs counter to efforts to turn criminals into productive, fully functioning members of society. It is also undemocratic.

At least when it comes to federal elections, the right to deny felons the vote should not lie with the states but with the federal government. Congress should create a uniform system that gives the franchise to felons in all states.

Chapter 4

Cognizable Claims

The transplantation of habeas corpus from England into the United States Constitution was largely uneventful. The colonists continued to view habeas corpus as a protection against imprisonment by police or other government officials. Rather than modifying the writ, the colonists were simply concerned that it would endure. Thus, they proclaimed that the "Privilege of the Writ of Habeas Corpus shall not be suspended, unless when in Cases of Rebellion or Invasion the public Safety may require it." U.S. CONST. art. I, § 9, cl. 2.

The view that habeas corpus was simply a protection against police and government officials changed in large degree because of the Civil War. During Reconstruction, the federal government needed to exert control over an angry South. In 1867, Congress broadened the jurisdiction of habeas corpus by extending federal habeas corpus to prisoners held in state custody and declaring "the power to grant writs of habeas corpus in all cases where any person may be restrained of his or her liberty in violation of the constitution, or of any treaty or law of the United States." Act of Feb. 5, 1867, ch. 28, 14 Stat. 385 (1867). This modification of habeas corpus began the process of molding the writ into the post-conviction remedy it is today.

After 1867, the only cognizable claims under a federal writ of habeas corpus were those that challenged the jurisdiction of the trial court. It wasn't until 1874, in *Ex parte Lange*, 85 U.S. 163 (1873), that the Court began to broaden the concept of "jurisdictional defect" to include sentences imposed without statutory authority. *See* discussion in *McCleskey v. Zant*, 499 U.S. 467, 478 (1991). Five years after *Lange*, in *Ex parte Siebold*, the Court continued to expand the kinds of loosely based "jurisdictional defect" claims that were cognizable through a writ of habeas corpus. In *Siebold*, the Court reviewed a federal habeas petition based on a conviction obtained under an unconstitutional statute.

Today, in order to invoke a federal writ of habeas corpus, the petitioner must have federal grounds on which to challenge either the jurisdiction of, or the criminal procedure employed by, the state court. A petitioner's ability to attack a criminal conviction on federal constitutional procedural grounds is as recent as the Court's 1979 decision in *Jackson v. Virginia*, in which the Court applied the due process clause of the Fourteenth Amendment to the states through habeas corpus.

Ex Parte Siebold
100 U.S. 371 (1879)

JUSTICE BRADLEY delivered the opinion of the court.

The petitioners in this case, Albert Siebold, Walter Tucker, Martin C. Burns, Lewis Coleman, and Henry Bowers, were judges of election at different voting precincts in the city of Baltimore, at the election held in that city, and in the State of Maryland, on the fifth day of November, 1878, at which representatives to the Forty-sixth Congress were voted for.

At the November Term of the Circuit Court of the United States for the District of Maryland, an indictment against each of the petitioners was found in said court, for offences alleged to have been committed by them respectively at their respective precincts whilst being such judges of election; upon which indictments they were severally tried, convicted, and sentenced by said court to fine and imprisonment. They now apply to this court for a writ of habeas corpus to be relieved from imprisonment.

[The Court first examined the procedural history of the case, then turned to the question of jurisdiction.]

That this court is authorized to exercise appellate jurisdiction by habeas corpus directly is a position sustained by abundant authority. It has general power to issue the writ, subject to the constitutional limitations of its jurisdiction, which are, that it can only exercise original jurisdiction in cases affecting ambassadors, public ministers and consuls, and cases in which a State is a party; but has appellate jurisdiction in all other cases of Federal cognizance, "with such exceptions and under such regulations as Congress shall make." Having this general power to issue the writ, the court may issue it in the exercise of original jurisdiction where it has original jurisdiction; and may issue it in the exercise of appellate jurisdiction where it has such jurisdiction, which is in all cases not prohibited by law except those in which it has original jurisdiction only. **

There are other limitations of the jurisdiction, however, arising from the nature and objects of the writ itself, as defined by the common law, from which its name and incidents are derived. It cannot be used as a mere writ of error. Mere error in the judgment or proceedings, under and by virtue of which a party is imprisoned, constitutes no ground for the issue of the writ. Hence, upon a return to a habeas corpus, that the prisoner is detained under a conviction and sentence by a court having jurisdiction of the cause, the general rule is, that he will be instantly remanded. No inquiry will be instituted into the regularity of the proceedings, unless, perhaps, where the court has cognizance by writ of error or appeal to review the judgment. In such a case, if the error be apparent and the imprisonment unjust, the appellate court may, perhaps, in its discretion, give immediate relief on habeas corpus, and thus save the party the delay and expense of a writ of error. ** But the general rule is, that a conviction and sentence by a court of competent jurisdiction is lawful cause of imprisonment, and no relief can be given by habeas corpus.

The only ground on which this court, or any court, without some special statute authorizing it, will give relief on habeas corpus to a prisoner under conviction and sentence of another court is the want of jurisdiction in such court over the person or the cause, or some other matter rendering its proceedings void.

[After explaining the historical difference between an "erroneous" judgment and one that is "illegal or void," the Court found that the question raised in the case was proper for consideration on habeas corpus. In doing so, the Court noted that a conviction under an unconstitutional law is not merely erroneous, but is illegal and void. Therefore, such a conviction cannot be a legal cause of imprisonment. The Court also explained that if such a conviction was based on an unconstitutional law, the trial court did not have jurisdiction to impose the conviction. The Court examined the specific statutes in detail before exploring how to balance the authority of both the state and national governments over elections.]

The peculiarity of the case consists in the concurrent authority of the two sovereignties, State and National, over the same subject-matter. This, however, is not entirely without a parallel. The regulation of foreign and inter-state commerce is conferred by the Constitution upon Congress. It is not expressly taken away from the States. But where the subject-matter is one of a national character, or one that requires a uniform rule, it has been held that the power of Congress is exclusive. On the contrary, where neither of these circumstances exist, it has been held that State regulations are not unconstitutional. In the absence of congressional regulation, which would be of paramount authority when adopted, they are valid and binding. ***[The Court then explored whether a conflict would exist when both the State and the federal government appoint officers to oversee elections, but state and federal regulations governing their actions conflicted. The Court found that if a conflict were to exist, the federal officers would have authority to act without obstruction or interference from the officers of the State.]

*** Where there is a disposition to act harmoniously, there is no danger of disturbance between those who have different duties to perform. When the rightful authority of the general government is once conceded and acquiesced in, the apprehended difficulties will disappear. Let a spirit of national as well as local patriotism once prevail, let unfounded jealousies cease, and we shall hear no more about the impossibility of harmonious action between the national and State governments in a matter in which they have a mutual interest.

***

It is objected that Congress has no power to enforce State laws or to punish State officers, and especially has no power to punish them for violating the laws of their own State. As a general proposition, this is undoubtedly true; but when, in the performance of their functions, State officers are called upon to fulfill duties which they owe to the United States as well as to the State, has the former no means of compelling such fulfillment? Yet that is the case here. It is the duty of the States to elect representatives to Congress. The due and fair election of these representatives is of vital importance to the United States. The government of the United States is no less concerned in the transaction than the State government is. It certainly is not bound to stand by as a passive spectator, when duties are violated and outrageous frauds are committed. It is directly interested in the faithful performance, by the officers of election, of their respective duties. Those duties are owed as well to the United States as to the State. This necessarily follows from the mixed character of the transaction—State and national. A violation of duty is an offence against the United States, for which the offender is justly amenable to that government. No official position can shelter him from this responsibility. In view of the fact that Congress has plenary and paramount jurisdiction over the whole subject, it seems almost absurd to say that an officer who receives or has custody of the ballots given for a representative owes no duty to the national government which Congress can enforce; or that an officer who stuffs the ballot-box cannot be made amenable to the United States. If Congress has not, prior to the passage of the present laws, imposed any penalties to prevent and punish frauds and violations of duty committed by officers of election, it has been because the exigency has not been deemed sufficient to require it, and not because Congress had not the requisite power.

The objection that the laws and regulations, the violation of which is made punishable by the acts of Congress, are State laws and have not been adopted by Congress, is no sufficient answer to the power of Congress to impose punishment. It is true that Congress has not deemed it necessary to interfere with the duties of the ordinary officers of election, but has been content to leave them as prescribed by State laws. It has only created additional sanctions for their performance, and provided means of supervision in order more effectually to secure such performance. The imposition of punishment implies a prohibition of the act punished. The State laws which Congress sees no occasion to alter, but which it allows to stand, are in effect adopted by Congress. It simply demands their fulfillment. Content to leave the laws as they are, it is not content with the means provided for their enforcement. It provides additional means for that purpose; and we think it is entirely within its constitutional power to do so. It is simply the exercise of the power to make additional regulations.

    ***

    *** [W]e think it clear that the clause of the Constitution relating to the regulation of such elections contemplates such co-operation [between the state and federal governments] whenever Congress deems it expedient to interfere merely to alter or add to existing regulations of the State. If the two governments had an entire equality of jurisdiction, there might be an intrinsic difficulty in such co-operation. *** But no such equality exists in the present case. The power of Congress, as we have seen, is paramount, and may be exercised at any time, and to any extent which it deems expedient; and so far as it is exercised, and no farther, the regulations effected supersede those of the State which are inconsistent therewith.

    ***

    The next point raised is, that the act of Congress proposes to operate on officers or persons authorized by State laws to perform certain duties under them, and to require them to disobey and disregard State laws when they come in conflict with the act of Congress; that it thereby of necessity produces collision, and is therefore void. This point has been already fully considered. We have shown, as we think, that, where the regulations of Congress conflict with those of the State, it is the latter which are void, and not the regulations of Congress; and that the laws of the State, in so far as they are inconsistent with the laws of Congress on the same subject, cease to have effect as laws.

    ***

    In our judgment, Congress had the power to vest the appointment of the supervisors in question in the circuit courts.

    The doctrine laid down at the close of counsel's brief, that the State and national governments are co-ordinate and altogether equal, on which their whole argument, indeed, is based, is only partially true.

    The true doctrine, as we conceive, is this, that whilst the States are really sovereign as to all matters which have not been granted to the jurisdiction and control of the United States, the Constitution and constitutional laws of the latter are, as we have already said, the supreme law of the land; and, when they conflict with the laws of the States, they are of paramount authority and obligation. This is the fundamental principle on which the authority of the Constitution is based; and unless it be conceded in practice, as well as theory, the fabric of our institutions, as it was contemplated by its founders, cannot stand. The questions involved have respect not more to the autonomy and existence of the States, than to the continued existence of the United States as a government to which every American citizen may look for security and protection in every part of the land.

    We think that the cause of commitment in these cases was lawful, and that the application for the writ of habeas corpus must be denied.

Application denied.

[JUSTICE FIELD's dissenting opinion, joined by JUSTICE CLIFFORD, is omitted.]

Notes

1. *Voidable judgment*

Prior to and for some time after *Siebold*, federal habeas claims were analyzed from the perspective, or at least the rhetoric, of a "void" or "voidable" judgment. What political issues does such an analysis address?

2. *Expansion of federal habeas corpus after* Ex parte Siebold

After *Siebold*, the Court did not address the reach of federal habeas corpus review again until *Frank v. Mangum*, 237 U.S. 309 (1915), when the Court allowed habeas relief to a confined defendant who was convicted in state court without adequate procedural protections.

It was not until *Waley v. Johnston*, 316 U.S. 101 (1942) (per curiam), that the Court specifically held that the use of the writ of habeas corpus in federal courts is not restricted to the lack of jurisdiction of the trial court. The Court specified that it "extends also to those exceptional cases where the conviction has been in disregard of the constitutional rights of the accused, and where the writ is the only effective means of preserving his rights." *Waley*, 316 U.S. at 105.

In reviewing the line of cases from *Ex parte Lange* and *Ex parte Siebold* through *Waley*, the Supreme Court has declared that it was not until *Waley* that the Court "openly discarded the concept of jurisdiction—by then more a fiction than anything else—as a touchstone of the availability of federal habeas review." *Wainwright v. Sykes*, 433 U.S. 72, 79 (1977). Does *Ex parte Siebold* make the necessity of setting forth a claim in federal habeas corpus based on lack of jurisdiction a "fiction"?

3. *Original versus appellate jurisdiction*

The Court began its analysis in *Siebold* by comparing original jurisdiction with appellate jurisdiction and finding that it had "authority to exercise appellate jurisdiction by *habeas corpus* directly."

After Congress passed the Antiterrorism and Effective Death Penalty Act of 1996 (AEDPA), the Court revisited the issue of original versus appellate jurisdiction in habeas corpus in *Felker v. Turpin*, 518 U.S. 651 (1996). Provisions in the AEDPA expressly prevent the Supreme Court's review of a Court of Appeals' order disallowing the filing of a second habeas petition. Nonetheless, the Supreme Court found that the AEDPA did not prevent it from considering an original habeas petition since the gatekeeping functions that the AEDPA assigned to the Court of Appeals did not apply to the Supreme Court's original jurisdiction of habeas petitions.

What are the implications of the *Felker* decision on the kinds of cases the Supreme Court may or may not consider?

Two cases paving the way to the Court's decision in *Jackson v. Virginia* came from an unlikely source for habeas corpus precedence: the juvenile court system.

In *In re Gault*, 387 U.S. 1 (1967), the Court decided that the Fourteenth Amendment does not require that a juvenile adjudicatory hearing must conform with all of the requirements of either a criminal trial or an administrative proceeding. 387 U.S. at 30. While an adjudicatory hearing need not contain "all of the requirements" of an adult criminal trial, the Court held that the due process clause nonetheless required state courts to employ "the essentials of due process and fair treatment." *Id.* at 30–31.

Although *Gault* left open the question of what constituted "essentials of due process and fair treatment," the Court answered that question three years later in *In re Winship*, 397 U.S. 358 (1970). In *Winship*, a 12-year-old boy stole $112 from a woman's purse. At his adjudicatory hearing, the juvenile court found him delinquent by a "preponderance of the evidence." *Id.* at 360. The Supreme Court reversed, finding that the juvenile court should have judged the evidence by "proof beyond a reasonable doubt." *Id.* The basis of the Court's reasoning was that the due process clause of the Fourteenth Amendment protects a juvenile in an adjudicatory hearing—just as it protects an adult defendant in a criminal case—against conviction except upon proof beyond a reasonable doubt.

After deciding that the due process clause applied to adjudicatory hearings in juvenile court, the Court examined the question of whether the due process clause applied to the states through federal habeas corpus in *Jackson v. Virginia*.

Jackson v. Virginia
443 U.S. 307 (1979)

JUSTICE STEWART delivered the opinion of the Court.

The Constitution prohibits the criminal conviction of any person except upon proof of guilt beyond a reasonable doubt. *In re Winship*, 397 U.S. 358 [(1970)]. The question in this case is what standard is to be applied in a federal habeas corpus proceeding when the claim is made that a person has been convicted in a state court upon insufficient evidence.

I

The petitioner was convicted after a bench trial in the Circuit Court of Chesterfield County, Va., of the first-degree murder of a woman named Mary Houston Cole. *** Under Virginia law, murder is defined as "the unlawful killing of another with malice aforethought." ** Premeditation, or specific intent to kill, distinguishes murder in the first from murder in the second degree; proof of this element is essential to conviction of the former offense, and the burden of proving it clearly rests with the prosecution. **

That the petitioner had shot and killed Mrs. Cole was not in dispute at the trial. The State's evidence established that she had been a member of the staff at the local county jail, that she had befriended him while he was imprisoned there on a disorderly conduct charge, and that when he was released she had arranged for him to live in the home of her son and daughter-in-law. Testimony by her relatives indicated that on the day of the killing the petitioner had been drinking and had spent a great deal of time shooting at targets with his revolver. Late in the afternoon, according to their testimony, he had unsuccessfully attempted to talk the victim into driving him to North Carolina. She did drive the petitioner to a local diner. There the two were observed by several police officers, who testified that both the petitioner and the victim had been drinking. The two were observed by a deputy sheriff as they were preparing to leave the diner in her car. The petitioner was then in possession of his revolver, and the sheriff also observed a kitchen knife in the automobile. The sheriff testified that he had offered to keep the revolver until the petitioner sobered up, but that the latter had indicated that this would be unnecessary since he and the victim were about to engage in sexual activity.

Her body was found in a secluded church parking lot a day and a half later, naked from the waist down, her slacks beneath her body. Uncontradicted medical and expert evidence established that she had been shot twice at close range with the petitioner's gun. She appeared not to have been sexually molested. Six cartridge cases identified as having been fired from the petitioner's gun were found near the body.

After shooting Mrs. Cole, the petitioner drove her car to North Carolina, where, after a short trip to Florida, he was arrested several days later. In a postarrest statement, introduced in evidence by the prosecution, the petitioner admitted that he had shot the victim. He contended, however, that the shooting had been accidental. When asked to describe his condition at the time of the shooting, he indicated that he had not been drunk, but had been "pretty high." His story was that the victim had attacked him with a knife when he resisted her sexual advances. He said that he had defended himself by firing a number of warning shots into the ground, and had then reloaded his revolver. The victim, he said, then attempted to take the gun from him, and the gun "went off" in the ensuing struggle. He said that he fled without seeking help for the victim because he was afraid. At the trial, his position was that he had acted in self-defense. Alternatively, he claimed that in any event the State's own evidence showed that he had been too intoxicated to form the specific intent necessary under Virginia law to sustain a conviction of murder in the first degree. ***

The trial judge, declaring himself convinced beyond a reasonable doubt that the petitioner had committed first-degree murder, found him guilty of that offense. The petitioner's motion to set aside the judgment as contrary to the evidence was denied, and he was sentenced to serve a term of 30 years in the Virginia state penitentiary. A petition for writ of error to the Virginia Supreme Court on the ground that the evidence was insufficient to support the conviction was denied. ***

The petitioner then commenced this habeas corpus proceeding in the United States District Court for the Eastern District of Virginia, raising the same basic claim. *** Applying the "no evidence" criterion of *Thompson v. Louisville*, 362 U.S. 199 [(1960)], the District Court found the record devoid of evidence of premeditation and granted the writ. The Court of Appeals for the Fourth Circuit reversed the judgment. *** The court was of the view that some evidence that the petitioner had intended to kill the victim could be found in the facts that the petitioner had reloaded his gun after firing warning shots, that he had had time to do so, and that the victim was then shot not once but twice. The court also concluded that the state trial judge could have found that the petitioner was not so intoxicated as to be incapable of premeditation.

We granted certiorari to consider the petitioner's claim that under *In re Winship*, [397 U.S. 358 (1970),] a federal habeas corpus court must consider not whether there was *any* evidence to support a state-court conviction, but whether there was sufficient evidence to justify a rational trier of the facts to find guilt beyond a reasonable doubt. **

II

Our inquiry in this case is narrow. *** His sole constitutional claim, based squarely upon *Winship*, is that the District Court and the Court of Appeals were in error in not recognizing that the question to be decided in this case is whether any rational factfinder could have concluded beyond a reasonable doubt that the killing for which the petitioner was convicted was premeditated. The question thus raised goes to the basic nature of the constitutional right recognized in the *Winship* opinion.

III
A

This is the first of our cases to expressly consider the question whether the due process standard recognized in *Winship* constitutionally protects an accused against conviction except upon evidence that is sufficient fairly to support a conclusion that every element of the crime has been established beyond a reasonable doubt. Upon examination of the fundamental differences between the constitutional underpinnings of *Thompson v. Louisville, supra,* and of *In re Winship, supra,* the answer to that question, we think, is clear.

It is axiomatic that a conviction upon a charge not made or upon a charge not tried constitutes a denial of due process. *Cole v. Arkansas,* 333 U.S. 196, 201 [(1948)]. ** These standards no more than reflect a broader premise that has never been doubted in our constitutional system: that a person cannot incur the loss of liberty for an offense without notice and a meaningful opportunity to defend. *E.g., Hovey v. Elliott,* 167 U.S. 409, 416–420 [(1897)]. ** A meaningful opportunity to defend, if not the right to a trial itself, presumes as well that a total want of evidence to support a charge will conclude the case in favor of the accused. Accordingly, we held in the *Thompson* case that a conviction based upon a record wholly devoid of any relevant evidence of a crucial element of the offense charged is constitutionally infirm. ** The "no evidence" doctrine of *Thompson v. Louisville* thus secures to an accused the most elemental of due process rights: freedom from a wholly arbitrary deprivation of liberty.

The Court in *Thompson* explicitly stated that the due process right at issue did not concern a question of evidentiary "sufficiency." 362 U.S. at 199. The right established in *In re Winship,* however, clearly stands on a different footing. *Winship* involved an adjudication of juvenile delinquency made by a judge under a state statute providing that the prosecution must prove the conduct charged as delinquent—which in *Winship* would have been a criminal offense if engaged in by an adult—by a preponderance of the evidence. Applying that standard, the judge was satisfied that the juvenile was "guilty," but he noted that the result might well have been different under a standard of proof beyond a reasonable doubt. In short, the record in *Winship* was not totally devoid of evidence of guilt.

The constitutional problem addressed in *Winship* was thus distinct from the stark problem of arbitrariness presented in *Thompson v. Louisville.* In *Winship,* the Court held for the first time that the Due Process Clause of the Fourteenth Amendment protects a defendant in a criminal case against conviction "except upon proof beyond a reasonable doubt of every fact necessary to constitute the crime with which he is charged." 397 U.S. at 364. *** The standard of proof beyond a reasonable doubt, said the Court, "plays a vital role in the American scheme of criminal procedure," because it operates to give "concrete substance" to the presumption of innocence, to ensure against unjust convictions, and to reduce the risk of factual error in a criminal proceeding. 397 U.S. at 363. At the same time, by impressing upon the factfinder the need to reach a subjective state of near certitude of the guilt of the accused, the standard symbolizes the significance that our society attaches to the criminal sanction and thus to liberty itself. *Id.* at 372 (Harlan, J., concurring).

***

B

***

The *Winship* doctrine requires more than simply a trial ritual. A doctrine establishing so fundamental a substantive constitutional standard must also require that the factfinder will rationally apply that standard to the facts in evidence. *** A "reasonable doubt," at a minimum, is one based upon "reason." *** Yet a properly instructed jury may occasionally convict even when it can be said that no rational trier of fact could find guilt beyond a reasonable doubt, and the same may be said of a trial judge sitting as a jury. In a federal trial, such an occurrence has traditionally been deemed to require reversal of the conviction. ** Under *Winship*, which established proof beyond a reasonable doubt as an essential of Fourteenth Amendment due process, it follows that when such a conviction occurs in a state trial, it cannot constitutionally stand.

A federal court has a duty to assess the historic facts when it is called upon to apply a constitutional standard to a conviction obtained in a state court. For example, on direct review of a state-court conviction, where the claim is made that an involuntary confession was used against the defendant, this Court reviews the facts to determine whether the confession was wrongly admitted in evidence. ** The same duty obtains in federal habeas corpus proceedings. See *Townsend v. Sain*, 372 U.S. 293, 318 [(1963)]; *Brown v. Allen*, 344 U.S. 443, 506–507 [(1953)] (opinion of Frankfurter, J.).

After *Winship*, the critical inquiry on review of the sufficiency of the evidence to support a criminal conviction must be not simply to determine whether the jury was properly instructed, but to determine whether the record evidence could reasonably support a finding of guilt beyond a reasonable doubt. *** But this inquiry does not require a court to "ask itself whether *it* believes that the evidence at the trial established guilt beyond a reasonable doubt." *Woodby v. INS*, 385 U.S. [276], 282 [(1966)] (emphasis added). Instead, the relevant question is whether, after viewing the evidence in the light most favorable to the prosecution, *any* rational trier of fact could have found the essential elements of the crime beyond a reasonable doubt. See *Johnson v. Louisiana*, 406 U.S. [356], 362 [(1972)]. This familiar standard gives full play to the responsibility of the trier of fact fairly to resolve conflicts in the testimony, to weigh the evidence, and to draw reasonable inferences from basic facts to ultimate facts. Once a defendant has been found guilty of the crime charged, the factfinder's role as weigher of the evidence is preserved through a legal conclusion that upon judicial review *all of the evidence* is to be considered in the light most favorable to the prosecution. *** The criterion thus impinges upon "jury" discretion only to the extent necessary to guarantee the fundamental protection of due process of law. ***

That the *Thompson* "no evidence" rule is simply inadequate to protect against misapplications of the constitutional standard of reasonable doubt is readily apparent. "[A] mere modicum of evidence may satisfy a 'no evidence' standard...." *Jacobellis v. Ohio*, 378 U.S. 184, 202 [(1964)] (Warren, C.J., dissenting). Any evidence that is relevant — that has any tendency to make the existence of an element of a crime slightly more probable than it would be without the evidence, cf. Fed. Rule Evid. 401 — could be deemed a "mere modicum." But it could not seriously be argued that such a "modicum" of evidence could by itself rationally support a conviction beyond a reasonable doubt. The *Thompson* doctrine simply fails to supply a workable or even a predictable standard for determining whether the due process command of *Winship* has been honored. ***

C

Under 28 U.S.C. §2254, a federal court must entertain a claim by a state prisoner that he or she is being held in "custody in violation of the Constitution or laws or treaties of the United States." Under the *Winship* decision, it is clear that a state prisoner who alleges that the evidence in support of his state conviction cannot be fairly characterized as sufficient to have led a rational trier of fact to find guilt beyond a reasonable doubt has stated a federal constitutional claim. Thus, assuming that state remedies have been exhausted, see 28 U.S.C. §2254(b), and that no independent and adequate state ground stands as a bar, *see, e.g., Estelle v. Williams*, 425 U.S. 501 [(1976)]; ** *Fay v. Noia*, 372 U.S. 391, 438 [(1963)], it follows that such a claim is cognizable in a federal habeas corpus proceeding. ***

***

First, the burden that is likely to follow from acceptance of the *Winship* standard has, we think, been exaggerated. Federal-court challenges to the evidentiary support for state convictions have since *Thompson* been dealt with under §2254. ** A more stringent standard will expand the contours of this type of claim, but will not create an entirely new class of cases cognizable on federal habeas corpus. Furthermore, most meritorious challenges to constitutional sufficiency of the evidence undoubtedly will be recognized in the state courts, and, if the state courts have fully considered the issue of sufficiency, the task of a federal habeas court should not be difficult. *Cf. Brown v. Allen*, 344 U.S. at 463. *** And this type of claim can almost always be judged on the written record without need for an evidentiary hearing in the federal court.

Second, the problems of finality and federal-state comity arise whenever a state prisoner invokes the jurisdiction of a federal court to redress an alleged constitutional violation. A challenge to a state conviction brought on the ground that the evidence cannot fairly be deemed sufficient to have established guilt beyond a reasonable doubt states a federal constitutional claim. Although state appellate review undoubtedly will serve in the vast majority of cases to vindicate the due process protection that follows from *Winship*, the same could also be said of the vast majority of other federal constitutional rights that may be implicated in a state criminal trial. It is the occasional abuse that the federal writ of habeas corpus stands ready to correct. *Brown v. Allen, supra*, at 498–501 (opinion of Frankfurter, J.).

The respondents have argued nonetheless that whenever a person convicted in a state court has been given a "full and fair hearing" in the state system—meaning in this instance state appellate review of the sufficiency of the evidence—further federal inquiry—apart from the possibility of discretionary review by this Court—should be foreclosed. This argument would prove far too much. A judgment by a state appellate court rejecting a challenge to evidentiary sufficiency is of course entitled to deference by the federal courts, as is any judgment affirming a criminal conviction. But Congress in §2254 has selected the federal district courts as precisely the forums that are responsible for determining whether state convictions have been secured in accord with federal constitutional law. The federal habeas corpus statute presumes the norm of a fair trial in the state court and adequate state postconviction remedies to redress possible error. *See* 28 U.S.C. §§2254(b), (d). What it does not presume is that these state proceedings will always be without error in the constitutional sense. The duty of a federal habeas corpus court to appraise a claim that constitutional error did occur—reflecting as it does the belief that the "finality" of a deprivation of liberty through the invocation of the criminal sanction is simply not to be achieved at the expense of a constitutional right—is not one that can be so lightly abjured.

***

We hold that in a challenge to a state criminal conviction brought under 28 U.S.C. § 2254—if the settled procedural prerequisites for such a claim have otherwise been satisfied—the applicant is entitled to habeas corpus relief if it is found that upon the record evidence adduced at the trial no rational trier of fact could have found proof of guilt beyond a reasonable doubt. ***

IV

Turning finally to the specific facts of this case, we reject the petitioner's claim that under the constitutional standard dictated by *Winship* his conviction of first-degree murder cannot stand. A review of the record in the light most favorable to the prosecution convinces us that a rational factfinder could readily have found the petitioner guilty beyond a reasonable doubt of first-degree murder under Virginia law.

***

Only under a theory that the prosecution was under an affirmative duty to rule out every hypothesis except that of guilt beyond a reasonable doubt could this petitioner's challenge be sustained. That theory the Court has rejected in the past. *Holland v. United States*, 348 U.S. 121, 140 [(1954)]. We decline to adopt it today. Under the standard established in this opinion as necessary to preserve the due process protection recognized in *Winship*, a federal habeas corpus court faced with a record of historical facts that supports conflicting inferences must presume—even if it does not affirmatively appear in the record—that the trier of fact resolved any such conflicts in favor of the prosecution, and must defer to that resolution. Applying these criteria, we hold that a rational trier of fact could reasonably have found that the petitioner committed murder in the first degree under Virginia law.

For these reasons, the judgment of the Court of Appeals is affirmed.

It is so ordered.

MR. JUSTICE POWELL took no part in the consideration or decision of this case.

MR. JUSTICE STEVENS, with whom THE CHIEF JUSTICE and MR. JUSTICE REHNQUIST join, concurring in the judgment.

The Constitution prohibits the criminal conviction of any person except upon proof *sufficient to convince the trier of fact* of guilt beyond a reasonable doubt. ** This rule has prevailed in our courts "at least from our early years as a Nation." *In re Winship*, 397 U.S. 358, 361 [(1970)].

Today the Court creates a new rule of law—one that has never prevailed in our jurisprudence. According to the Court, the Constitution now prohibits the criminal conviction of any person—including, apparently, a person against whom the facts have already been found beyond a reasonable doubt by a jury, a trial judge, and one or more levels of state appellate judges—except upon proof sufficient to convince a *federal judge* that a "rational trier of fact could have found the essential elements of the crime beyond a reasonable doubt." **

The adoption of this novel constitutional rule is not necessary to the decision of this case. Moreover, I believe it is an unwise act of lawmaking. Despite its chimerical appeal as a new counterpart to the venerable principle recognized in *Winship*, I am persuaded that its precipitous adoption will adversely affect the quality of justice administered by federal judges. ***

***

Notes

1. The "no evidence" standard

Before *Jackson v. Virginia*, appellate courts employed *Thompson*'s "no evidence" standard to review federal habeas petitions, rather than "proof sufficient to convince the trier of fact of guilt beyond a reasonable doubt." Although concurring with the Court, Justice Stevens stated the following:

> In this case…it would be impossible (and the Court does not even try) to demonstrate that there is an appreciable risk that a factfinding made by a jury beyond a reasonable doubt, and twice reviewed by a trial judge in ruling on directed verdict and post-trial acquittal motions and by one or more levels of appellate courts on direct appeal, as well as by two federal habeas courts under the *Thompson* "no evidence" rule, is likely to be erroneous.

Why did the Court modify the *Thompson* "no evidence" standard?

2. A wise compromise?

Justice Stevens also observed that "[t]ime may prove that the rule the Court has adopted today is the wisest compromise between one extreme that maximizes the protection against the risk that innocent persons will be erroneously convicted and the other extreme that places the greatest faith in the ability of fair procedures to produce just verdicts."

One of the historical bases for habeas relief is that the court's jurisdiction over the petitioner's case is not related to innocence or guilt. Given the Court's analysis in *Jackson v. Virginia*, and in light of its holding in *Winship*, what role should an assessment of the strength of the case play in the Court's assessment of the petitioner's claims? Has time proven Justice Stevens' prophecy to be true?

3. Comity and finality

How does the Court's concern with comity and finality factor into its decision? For example, are state judges better able to evaluate sufficiency claims because they are more familiar with the elements of state offenses than are federal judges? Is the Court's holding an invitation to state prisoners to file federal habeas corpus claims based on sufficiency challenges?

Part III

Habeas Corpus Litigation

Chapter 5

Appointment of Counsel

The concept of the right to counsel is relatively new. It was nearly two hundred years after the establishment of this country before a right to the appointment of counsel for the indigent existed.

In *Gideon v. Wainwright*, 372 U.S. 335 (1963), the Court reversed *Betts v. Brady*, 316 U.S. 455 (1942), by finding that the Sixth Amendment's guarantee of counsel is a fundamental right made applicable to the states by the Fourteenth Amendment to the United States Constitution. In so holding, the Court clarified that, rather than establishing a new precedent, it was returning to "old precedents, sounder we believe than the new,... [by restoring] constitutional principles established to achieve a fair system of justice." 372 U.S. at 344.

Some of the Court's fundamental reasoning in *Gideon* included the following:

> Not only these precedents but also reason and reflection require us to recognize that in our adversary system of criminal justice, any person haled into court, who is too poor to hire a lawyer, cannot be assured a fair trial unless counsel is provided for him. This seems to us to be an obvious truth. Governments, both state and federal, quite properly spend vast sums of money to establish machinery to try defendants accused of crime. Lawyers to prosecute are everywhere deemed essential to protect the public's interest in an orderly society. Similarly, there are few defendants charged with crime, few indeed, who fail to hire the best lawyers they can get to prepare and present their defenses. That government hires lawyers to prosecute and defendants who have the money hire lawyers to defend are the strongest indications of the widespread belief that lawyers in criminal courts are necessities, not luxuries. The right of one charged with crime to counsel may not be deemed fundamental and essential to fair trials in some countries, but it is in ours. From the very beginning, our state and national constitutions and laws have laid great emphasis on procedural and substantive safeguards designed to assure fair trials before impartial tribunals in which every defendant stands equal before the law. This noble ideal cannot be realized if the poor man charged with crime has to face his accusers without a lawyer to assist him.

372 U.S. at 344. Based on the foundation articulated in *Gideon*, the Court also held in *Douglas v. California*, 372 U.S. 353 (1963), that the Fourteenth Amendment guarantees a criminal defendant the right to counsel on his first appeal as of right.

More than twenty years later, in *Evitts v. Lucey*, the Court finds that the due process clause of the Fourteenth Amendment guarantees a criminal defendant the effective assistance of counsel on appeal. In *McFarland v. Scott*, the Court relies on the Anti-Drug Abuse Act of 1988 to hold that there is a right to pre-filing appointment of counsel for a capital habeas petitioner.

Evitts v. Lucey

469 U.S. 387 (1985)

JUSTICE BRENNAN delivered the opinion of the Court.

***

I

On March 21, 1976, a Kentucky jury found respondent guilty of trafficking in controlled substances. His retained counsel filed a timely notice of appeal to the Court of Appeals of Kentucky, the state intermediate appellate court. Kentucky Rule of Appellate Procedure 1.095(a)(1) required appellants to serve on the appellate court the record on appeal and a "statement of appeal" that was to contain the names of appellants and appellees, counsel, and the trial judge, the date of judgment, the date of notice of appeal, and additional information. *** Respondent's counsel failed to file a statement of appeal when he filed his brief and the record on appeal on September 12, 1977. ***

When the Commonwealth filed its brief, it included a motion to dismiss the appeal for failure to file a statement of appeal. The Court of Appeals granted this motion because "appellant has failed to supply the information required by RAP 1.095(a)(1)." ** Respondent moved for reconsideration, arguing that all of the information necessary for a statement of appeal was in fact included in his brief, albeit in a somewhat different format. At the same time, respondent tendered a statement of appeal that formally complied with the Commonwealth Rules. The Court of Appeals summarily denied the motion for reconsideration. Respondent sought discretionary review in the Supreme Court of Kentucky, but the judgment of the Court of Appeals was affirmed in a one-sentence order. In a final effort to gain state appellate review of his conviction, respondent moved the trial court to vacate the judgment or to grant a belated appeal. The trial court denied the motion.

Respondent then sought federal habeas corpus relief in the United States District Court for the Eastern District of Kentucky. He challenged the constitutionality of the Commonwealth's dismissal of his appeal because of his lawyer's failure to file the statement of appeal, on the ground that the dismissal deprived him of his right to effective assistance of counsel on appeal guaranteed by the Fourteenth Amendment. The District Court granted respondent a conditional writ of habeas corpus ordering his release unless the Commonwealth either reinstated his appeal or retried him. *** The Commonwealth appealed to the Court of Appeals for the Sixth Circuit, which reached no decision on the merits but instead remanded the case to the District Court for determination whether respondent had a claim under the Equal Protection Clause. **

On remand, counsel for both parties stipulated that there was no equal protection issue in the case, the only issue being whether the state court's action in dismissing respondent's appeal violated the Due Process Clause. The District Court thereupon reissued the conditional writ of habeas corpus. On January 12, 1984, the Court of Appeals for the Sixth Circuit affirmed the judgment of the District Court. ** We granted the petition for certiorari. ** We affirm.

***

II

Respondent has for the past seven years unsuccessfully pursued every avenue open to him in an effort to obtain a decision on the merits of his appeal and to prove that his conviction was unlawful. The Kentucky appellate courts' refusal to hear him on the merits of his claim does not stem from any view of those merits, and respondent does not argue in this Court that those courts were constitutionally required to render judgment on the appeal in his favor. Rather the issue we must decide is whether the state court's dismissal of the appeal, despite the ineffective assistance of respondent's counsel on appeal, violates the Due Process Clause of the Fourteenth Amendment.

Before analyzing the merits of respondent's contention, it is appropriate to emphasize two limits on the scope of the question presented. First, there is no challenge to the District Court's finding that respondent indeed received ineffective assistance of counsel on appeal. Respondent alleges—and petitioners do not deny in this Court—that his counsel's failure to obey a simple court rule that could have such drastic consequences required this finding. We therefore need not decide the content of appropriate standards for judging claims of ineffective assistance of appellate counsel. ** Second, the stipulation in the District Court on remand limits our inquiry solely to the validity of the state court's action under the Due Process Clause of the Fourteenth Amendment. ***

Respondent's claim arises at the intersection of two lines of cases. In one line, we have held that the Fourteenth Amendment guarantees a criminal appellant pursuing a first appeal as of right certain minimum safeguards necessary to make that appeal "adequate and effective," *see Griffin v. Illinois*, 351 U.S. 12, 20 (1956); among those safeguards is the right to counsel, *see Douglas v. California*, 372 U.S. 353 (1963). In the second line, we have held that the trial-level right to counsel, created by the Sixth Amendment and applied to the States through the Fourteenth Amendment, *see Gideon v. Wainwright*, 372 U.S. 335, 344 (1963), comprehends the right to effective assistance of counsel. ** The question presented in this case is whether the appellate-level right to counsel also comprehends the right to effective assistance of counsel.

A

Almost a century ago, the Court held that the Constitution does not require States to grant appeals as of right to criminal defendants seeking to review alleged trial court errors. *McKane v. Durston*, 153 U.S. 684 (1894). Nonetheless, if a State has created appellate courts as "an integral part of the . . . system for finally adjudicating the guilt or innocence of a defendant," *Griffin v. Illinois*, 351 U.S. at 18, the procedures used in deciding appeals must comport with the demands of the Due Process and Equal Protection Clauses of the Constitution. In *Griffin* itself, a transcript of the trial court proceedings was a prerequisite to a decision on the merits of an appeal. ** We held that the State must provide such a transcript to indigent criminal appellants who could not afford to buy one if that was the only way to assure an "adequate and effective" appeal. **

Just as a transcript may by rule or custom be a prerequisite to appellate review, the services of a lawyer will for virtually every layman be necessary to present an appeal in a form suitable for appellate consideration on the merits. ** Therefore, *Douglas v. California, supra*, recognized that the principles of *Griffin* required a State that afforded a right of appeal to make that appeal more than a "meaningless ritual" by supplying an indigent appellant in a criminal case with an attorney. ** This right to counsel is limited to the first appeal as of right, *see Ross v. Moffitt*, 417 U.S. 600 (1974), and the attorney need not advance *every* argument, regardless of merit, urged by the appellant, *see Jones v. Barnes*, 463 U.S. 745 (1983). But the attorney must be available to assist in preparing and submitting a brief to the appellate court,** and must play the role of an active advocate, rather than a mere friend of the court assisting in a detached evaluation of the appellant's claim. ***

B

Gideon v. Wainwright, supra, held that the Sixth Amendment right to counsel was "'so fundamental and essential to a fair trial, and so, to due process of law, that it is made obligatory upon the States by the Fourteenth Amendment.'" *Id.* at 340, *quoting Betts v. Brady,* 316 U.S. 455, 465 (1942). ** *Gideon* rested on the "obvious truth" that lawyers are "necessities, not luxuries" in our adversarial system of criminal justice. 372 U.S. at 344. ***

***

[T]he constitutional guarantee of effective assistance of counsel at trial applies to every criminal prosecution, without regard to whether counsel is retained or appointed. ** The constitutional mandate is addressed to the action of the State in obtaining a criminal conviction through a procedure that fails to meet the standards of due process of law. "Unless a defendant charged with a serious offense has counsel able to invoke the procedural and substantive safeguards that distinguish our system of justice, a serious risk of injustice infects the trial itself. When a State obtains a criminal conviction through such a trial, it is the State that unconstitutionally deprives the defendant of his liberty."**

C

The two lines of cases mentioned—the cases recognizing the right to counsel on a first appeal as of right and the cases recognizing that the right to counsel at trial includes a right to effective assistance of counsel—are dispositive of respondent's claim. In bringing an appeal as of right from his conviction, a criminal defendant is attempting to demonstrate that the conviction, with its consequent drastic loss of liberty, is unlawful. To prosecute the appeal, a criminal appellant must face an adversary proceeding that—like a trial—is governed by intricate rules that to a layperson would be hopelessly forbidding. An unrepresented appellant—like an unrepresented defendant at trial—is unable to protect the vital interests at stake. To be sure, respondent did have nominal representation when he brought this appeal. But nominal representation on an appeal as of right—like nominal representation at trial—does not suffice to render the proceedings constitutionally adequate; a party whose counsel is unable to provide effective representation is in no better position than one who has no counsel at all.

A first appeal as of right therefore is not adjudicated in accord with due process of law if the appellant does not have the effective assistance of an attorney. ***

Recognition of the right to effective assistance of counsel on appeal requires that we affirm the Sixth Circuit's decision in this case. Petitioners object that this holding will disable state courts from enforcing a wide range of vital procedural rules governing appeals. Counsel may, according to petitioners, disobey such rules with impunity if the state courts are precluded from enforcing them by dismissing the appeal.

Petitioners' concerns are exaggerated. The lower federal courts—and many state courts—overwhelmingly have recognized a right to effective assistance of counsel on appeal. *** These decisions do not seem to have had dire consequences for the States' ability to conduct appeals in accordance with reasonable procedural rules. ***

***

*** A system of appeal as of right is established precisely to assure that only those who are validly convicted have their freedom drastically curtailed. A State may not extinguish this right because another right of the appellant—the right to effective assistance of counsel—has been violated.

III

[In the beginning of this section, the Court outlines the petitioners' three arguments: (1) Because the Commonwealth need not establish a system of appeals as of right, it is immune from constitutional scrutiny when it chooses to do so; (2) respondent had no right to counsel because his appeal was a "conditional" appeal, not an appeal as of right; and (3) even if the Commonwealth's actions were subject to constitutional scrutiny and the appeal was an appeal as of right, the due process clause has no bearing on the Commonwealth's actions in this particular case. In response to the first argument, the Court found that "when a state opts to act in a field where its action has significant discretionary elements, it must nonetheless act in accord with the dictates of the Constitution—and, in particular, in accord with the Due Process Clause." The Court then considered petitioners' second argument.]

B

Petitioners' second argument relies on the holding of *Ross v. Moffitt, supra*, that a criminal defendant has a right to counsel only on appeals as of right, not on discretionary state appeals. According to petitioners, the Kentucky courts permit criminal appeals only on condition that the appellant follow the local rules and statutes governing such appeals. ** Therefore, the system does not establish an appeal as of right, but only a "conditional appeal" subject to dismissal if the state rules are violated. Petitioners conclude that if respondent has no appeal as of right, he has no right to counsel—or to effective assistance of counsel—on his "conditional appeal."

Under any reasonable interpretation of the line drawn in *Ross* between discretionary appeals and appeals as of right, a criminal defendant's appeal of a conviction to the Kentucky Court of Appeals is an appeal as of right. Section 115 of the Kentucky Constitution provides that "[i]n all cases, civil and criminal, there shall be allowed as a matter of right at least one appeal to another court." Unlike the appellant in the discretionary appeal in *Ross*, a criminal appellant in the Kentucky Court of Appeals typically has not had the benefit of a previously prepared trial transcript, a brief on the merits of the appeal, or a previous written opinion. ** In addition, petitioners fail to point to any source of Kentucky law indicating that a decision on the merits in an appeal like that of respondent—unlike the discretionary appeal in *Ross*—is contingent on a discretionary finding by the Court of Appeals that the case involves significant public or jurisprudential issues; the purpose of a first appeal in the Kentucky court system appears to be precisely to determine whether the individual defendant has been lawfully convicted. In short, a criminal defendant bringing an appeal to the Kentucky Court of Appeals has not previously had "an adequate opportunity to present his claims fairly in the context of the State's appellate process." ** It follows that for purposes of analysis under the Due Process Clause, respondent's appeal was an appeal as of right, thus triggering the right to counsel recognized in *Douglas v. California*, 372 U.S. 353 (1963).

C

[In the final section, the Court determines that the due process clause applies.]

Affirmed.

[CHIEF JUSTICE REHNQUIST's dissenting opinion, joined by JUSTICE BURGER, is omitted.]

Notes

1. *Subsequent case history*

The district court's original writ had ordered the Commonwealth of Kentucky to release Lucey, retry him, or restore his appellate rights. Lucey was discharged from custody and his civil rights were restored five days before oral argument in the United States Supreme Court. 469 U.S. at 391. Thus, because Lucey was released, the Commonwealth had already complied with the district court's order and had no obligation to retry Lucey or restore his appellate rights.

2. *Forty years after Gideon*

While the right to an attorney is no longer in question, the consensus of opinion is that the promise of *Gideon* has not been fulfilled. Reproduced below is an op-ed piece from The Virginian-Pilot, published on the fortieth anniversary of *Gideon v. Wainwright*.

No Hollywood Ending in Defending the Indigent

The Virginian-Pilot
Copyright © March 28, 2003 by The Virginian-Pilot

More than four decades ago, Clarence Earl Gideon, a penniless Florida man accused of breaking into a pool hall, requested and was denied a court-appointed lawyer. Behind bars after his self-defense and conviction, Gideon penned a hand-written note to the U.S. Supreme Court, protesting the lack of legal representation and setting in motion one of the great stories of American jurisprudence.

The high court named Abe Fortas, among the nation's most prestigious attorneys, to argue Gideon's claim, and in March 1963 the justices held that even the poorest among us has the right to an attorney in a criminal case.

In the movie, based on the Anthony Lewis book, "Gideon's Trumpet," Henry Fonda played Gideon.

Gideon vs. Wainwright turns 40 this month, which makes it a good time to assess how well the nation is doing in guaranteeing legal representation for the poor. The answer is sobering: better than in 1963, perhaps, but far less well than many hoped and than *Gideon* seemed to promise.

The rash of DNA releases in the past few years has spotlighted cases in which the legal defense fell far short of a reasonable standard. Many more such cases are unheralded. Numerous scholars concur in the assessment of lawyer-professor David Cole: "Much like Dr. Martin Luther King Jr.'s dream of the same year (1963), the dream of *Gideon* has not been realized."

Cole's further assertion, that neither the Supreme Court nor the public appears to have any interest in making the constitutional right announced in *Gideon* a reality, is open to debate. But it is not debatable that the public generally has been unwilling to fund for indigents anywhere near the same quality legal representation that even the middle-class expects.

In Virginia, for instance, the move to public defender offices in some four dozen jurisdictions has provided a more consistent and arguably superior level of defense. But a clue to the public mind-set is the fact that creation of such offices is typically sold politically by stressing the cost savings.

The public defender offices are staffed at levels that create substantial savings over private, court-appointed attorneys. That's true even though Virginia's private-attorney reimbursement rates appear to be the lowest in the nation.

Representing an indigent client in an adult misdemeanor case, or on any juvenile charge in district court, will net a court-appointed attorney the whopping sum of $120, tops. The top payment for misdemeanors in circuit court is $158, which jumps to $445 for felonies punishable by 20 years or less in prison.

And the most a court-appointed attorney could make representing an indigent client on a non-capital charge punishable by more than 20 years in prison is $1,235. Assuming the lawyer spent two 40-hour weeks on the case, a ridiculously low expectation for a good defense, the lawyer would make less than $15 an hour.

The State Crime Commission made a number of recommendations last year to improve this system. Even the most obviously necessary got nowhere: paying attorneys representing juveniles accused of serious crimes at the same level as attorneys representing adults on the same charges; and allowing trial courts to waive the current caps in appropriate cases.

The competition for scarce tax dollars is extreme these days. The defense of indigents has fewer advocates than teacher pay, the environment or care of the mentally ill, none of which is being adequately funded either.

Still, at the 40th anniversary of *Gideon vs. Wainwright*, it is worth remembering how far reality remains from the Hollywood ideal.

Anti-Drug Abuse Act of 1988
21 U.S.C. §§ 848(e) and 848(q)(4)(B)

(e) Death penalty.

(1) In addition to the other penalties set forth in this section—

(A) any person engaging in or working in furtherance of a continuing criminal enterprise, or any person engaging in an offense punishable under section 841(b)(1)(A) or section 960(b)(1) ** who intentionally kills or counsels, commands, induces, procures, or causes the intentional killing of an individual and such killing results, shall be sentenced to any term of imprisonment, which shall not be less than 20 years, and which may be up to life imprisonment, or may be sentenced to death; and

(B) any person, during the commission of, in furtherance of, or while attempting to avoid apprehension, prosecution or service of a prison sentence for, a felony violation of this title or title III who intentionally kills or counsels, commands, induces, procures, or causes the intentional killing of any Federal, State, or local law enforcement officer engaged in, or on account of, the performance of such officer's official duties and such killing results, shall be sentenced to any term of imprisonment, which shall not be less than 20 years, and which may be up to life imprisonment, or may be sentenced to death.

(2) As used in paragraph [(1)(B)], the term "law enforcement officer" means a public servant authorized by law or by a Government agency or Congress to conduct or en-

gage in the prevention, investigation, prosecution or adjudication of an offense, and includes those engaged in corrections, probation, or parole functions.

***

(q) Appeal in capital cases; counsel for financially unable defendants.

***

(4) (B) In any post conviction proceeding under section 2254 or 2255 of Title 28, United States Code, seeking to vacate or set aside a death sentence, any defendant who is or becomes financially unable to obtain adequate representation or investigative, expert, or other reasonably necessary services shall be entitled to the appointment of one or more attorneys and the furnishing of such other services in accordance with paragraphs (5), (6), (7), (8), and (9).

McFarland v. Scott
512 U.S. 849 (1994)

JUSTICE BLACKMUN delivered the opinion of the Court.

In establishing a federal death penalty for certain drug offenses under the Anti-Drug Abuse Act of 1988, 21 U.S.C. §848(e), Congress created a statutory right to qualified legal representation for capital defendants in federal habeas corpus proceedings. §848(q)(4)(B). This case presents the question whether a capital defendant must file a formal habeas corpus petition in order to invoke this statutory right and to establish a federal court's jurisdiction to enter a stay of execution.

I

Petitioner Frank Basil McFarland was convicted of capital murder on November 13, 1989, in the State of Texas and sentenced to death. The Texas Court of Criminal Appeals affirmed the conviction and sentence, ** and this *** Court denied certiorari. ** Two months later, on August 16, 1993, the Texas trial court scheduled McFarland's execution for September 23, 1993. On September 19, McFarland filed a *pro se* motion requesting that the trial court stay or withdraw his execution date to allow the Texas Resource Center an opportunity to recruit volunteer counsel for his state habeas corpus proceeding. Texas opposed a stay of execution, arguing that McFarland had not filed an application for writ of habeas corpus and that the court thus lacked jurisdiction to enter a stay. The trial court declined to appoint counsel, but modified McFarland's execution date to October 27, 1993.

On October 16, 1993, the Resource Center informed the trial court that it had been unable to recruit volunteer counsel and asked the court to appoint counsel for McFarland. Concluding that Texas law did not authorize the appointment of counsel for state habeas corpus proceedings, the trial court refused either to appoint counsel or to modify petitioner's execution date. McFarland then filed a *pro se* motion in the Texas Court of Criminal Appeals requesting a stay and a remand for appointment of counsel. The court denied the motion without comment.

Having failed to obtain either the appointment of counsel or a modification of his execution date in state court, McFarland, on October 22, 1993, commenced the present action in the United States District Court for the Northern District of Texas by filing a *pro se* motion stating that he "wished to challenge [his] conviction and sentence under [the federal habeas corpus statute,] 28 U.S.C. §2254." ** McFarland requested the appointment of counsel under 21 U.S.C. §848(q)(4)(B) and a stay of execution to give that counsel time to prepare and file a habeas corpus petition. ***

The District Court denied McFarland's motion on October 25, 1993, concluding that because no "post conviction proceeding" had been initiated pursuant to 28 U.S.C. §2254 or §2255, petitioner was not entitled to appointment of counsel and the court lacked jurisdiction to enter a stay of execution. ** The court later denied a certificate of probable cause to appeal.

On October 26, the eve of McFarland's scheduled execution, the Court of Appeals for the Fifth Circuit denied his application for stay. ** The court noted that federal law expressly authorizes federal courts to stay state proceedings while a federal habeas corpus proceeding is pending, 28 U.S.C. §2251, but held that no such proceeding was pending, because a "motion for stay and for appointment of counsel [is not] the equivalent of an application for habeas relief." ** The court concluded that any other federal judicial interference in state-court proceedings was barred by the Anti-Injunction Act, 28 U.S.C. §2283.

Shortly before the Court of Appeals ruled, a Federal Magistrate Judge located an attorney willing to accept appointment in McFarland's case and suggested that if the attorney would file a skeletal document entitled "petition for writ of habeas corpus," the District Court might be willing to appoint him and grant McFarland a stay of execution. The attorney accordingly drafted and filed a *pro forma* habeas petition, together with a motion for stay of execution and appointment of counsel. *** [D]espite the fact that Texas did not oppose a stay, the District Court found the petition to be insufficient and denied the motion for stay on the merits. **

On October 27, 1993, this Court granted a stay of execution in McFarland's original suit pending consideration of his petition for certiorari. ** The Court later granted certiorari ** to resolve an apparent conflict with *Brown v. Vasquez.*

II

A

Section 848(q)(4)(B) of Title 21 provides:

> In any *post conviction proceeding* under section 2254 or 2255 of title 28 seeking to vacate or set aside a death sentence, any defendant who is or becomes financially unable to obtain adequate representation or investigative, expert, or other reasonably necessary services *shall be entitled* to the appointment of one or more attorneys and the furnishing of such other services in accordance with paragraphs (5), (6), (7), (8), and (9) (emphasis added).

On its face, this statute grants indigent capital defendants a mandatory right to qualified legal counsel *** and related services "in any [federal] post conviction proceeding." The express language does not specify, however, how a capital defendant's right to counsel in such a proceeding shall be invoked.

Neither the federal habeas corpus statute, 28 U.S.C. §2241 *et seq.*, nor the rules governing habeas corpus proceedings define a "post conviction proceeding" under §2254 or §2255 or expressly state how such a proceeding shall be commenced. Construing §848(q)(4)(B) in light of its related provisions, however, indicates that the right to appointed counsel adheres prior to the filing of a formal, legally sufficient habeas corpus petition. Section 848(q)(4)(B) expressly incorporates 21 U.S.C. §848(q)(9), which entitles capital defendants to a variety of expert and investigative services upon a showing of necessity:

> Upon a finding in ex parte proceedings that investigative, expert or other services are reasonably necessary for the representation of the defendant,...the court *shall authorize* the defendant's attorneys to obtain such services on behalf of the defendant and shall order the payment of fees and expenses therefore (emphasis added).

The services of investigators and other experts may be critical in the preapplication phase of a habeas corpus proceeding, when possible claims and their factual bases are researched and identified. Section 848(q)(9) clearly anticipates that capital defense counsel will have been appointed under §848(q)(4)(B) before the need for such technical assistance arises, since the statute requires "the defendant's attorneys to obtain such services" from the court. §848(q)(9). In adopting §848(q)(4)(B), Congress thus established a right to preapplication legal assistance for capital defendants in federal habeas corpus proceedings.

This interpretation is the only one that gives meaning to the statute as a practical matter. Congress' provision of a right to counsel under §848(q)(4)(B) reflects a determination that quality legal representation is necessary in capital habeas corpus proceedings in light of "the seriousness of the possible penalty and...the unique and complex nature of the litigation." §848(q)(7). An attorney's assistance prior to the filing of a capital defendant's habeas corpus petition is crucial, because "[t]he complexity of our jurisprudence in this area...makes it unlikely that capital defendants will be able to file successful petitions for collateral relief without the assistance of persons learned in the law." **

Habeas corpus petitions must meet heightened pleading requirements, see 28 U.S.C. §2254 Rule 2(c), and comply with this Court's doctrines of procedural default and waiver, *see Coleman v. Thompson*, 501 U.S. 722 (1991). Federal courts are authorized to dismiss summarily any habeas petition that appears legally insufficient on its face, *see* 28 U.S.C. §2254 Rule 4, and to deny a stay of execution where a habeas petition fails to raise a substantial federal claim, *see Barefoot v. Estelle*, 463 U.S. 880, 894 (1983). Moreover, should a defendant's *pro se* petition be summarily dismissed, any petition subsequently filed by counsel could be subject to dismissal as an abuse of the writ. *See McCleskey v. Zant*, 499 U.S. 467, 494 (1991). Requiring an indigent capital petitioner to proceed without counsel in order to obtain counsel thus would expose him to the substantial risk that his habeas claims never would be heard on the merits. Congress legislated against this legal backdrop in adopting §848(q)(4)(B), and we safely assume that it did not intend for the express requirement of counsel to be defeated in this manner.

The language and purposes of §848(q)(4)(B) and its related provisions establish that the right to appointed counsel includes a right to legal assistance in the preparation of a habeas corpus application. We therefore conclude that a "post conviction proceeding" within the meaning of §848(q)(4)(B) is commenced by the filing of a death row defendant's motion requesting the appointment of counsel for his federal habeas corpus proceeding. *** McFarland filed such a motion and was entitled to the appointment of a lawyer.

B

[In Section B, the Court explains that McFarland's motion for appointment of counsel would have been meaningless unless his execution was also stayed, then it finds that the district court had jurisdiction to grant his motion for a stay of execution. The Court noted that Section 2251 does not mandate the entry of a stay but that it does dedicate the exercise of stay jurisdiction to the sound discretion of a federal court. Because "the right to counsel necessarily includes a right for that counsel meaningfully to research and present a defendant's habeas claims[,]...[w]here this opportunity is not afforded, 'approving the execution of a defendant before his [petition] is decided on the merits would clearly be improper.'" ** The Court then goes on to say that "[o]n the other hand, if a dilatory capital defendant inexcusably ignores this opportunity and flouts the available processes, a federal court presumably would not abuse its discretion in denying a stay of execution."]

III

A criminal trial is the "main event" at which a defendant's rights are to be determined, and the Great Writ is an extraordinary remedy that should not be employed to "relitigate state trials." [*Barefoot*,] 463 U.S. at 887. At the same time, criminal defendants are entitled by federal law to challenge their conviction and sentence in habeas corpus proceedings. By providing indigent capital defendants with a mandatory right to qualified legal counsel in these proceedings, Congress has recognized that federal habeas corpus has a particularly important role to play in promoting fundamental fairness in the imposition of the death penalty.

We conclude that a capital defendant may invoke this right to a counseled federal habeas corpus proceeding by filing a motion requesting the appointment of habeas counsel, and that a district court has jurisdiction to enter a stay of execution where necessary to give effect to that statutory right. McFarland filed a motion for appointment of counsel and for stay of execution in this case, and the District Court had authority to grant the relief he sought.

The judgment of the Court of Appeals is reversed.

It is so ordered.

JUSTICE O'CONNOR, concurring in the judgment in part and dissenting in part.

I agree with the Court's conclusion that 21 U.S.C. § 848 entitles capital defendants pursuing federal habeas corpus relief to a properly trained attorney. I also agree that this right includes legal assistance in preparing a habeas petition. Thus, the Court correctly holds that a defendant need not file a habeas petition to invoke the right to counsel. ** I write separately, however, because I disagree with the Court's conclusion that 28 U.S.C. § 2251 allows a district court to stay an execution pending counsel's preparation of an application for a writ of habeas corpus. **

   ***

In my view,...petitioner is not entitled under present law to a stay of execution while counsel prepares a habeas petition. The habeas statute provides in relevant part that "[a] justice or judge of the United States before whom a habeas corpus proceeding is pending, may...stay any proceeding against the person detained in any State court." 28 U.S.C. § 2251. While this provision authorizes a stay in the habeas context, it does not explicitly allow a stay prior to the filing of a petition, and our cases have made it clear that capital defendants must raise at least some colorable federal claim before a stay of execution may be entered. ***

JUSTICE THOMAS, with whom THE CHIEF JUSTICE and JUSTICE SCALIA join, dissenting.

Today the Court holds that a state prisoner under sentence of death may invoke a federal district court's jurisdiction to obtain appointed counsel under 21 U.S.C. § 848(q)(4)(B) and to obtain a stay of execution under 28 U.S.C. §2251 simply by filing a motion for appointment of counsel. In my view, the Court's conclusion is at odds with the terms of both statutory provisions. Each statute allows a federal district court to take action (appointing counsel under §848(q)(4)(B) or granting a stay under §2251) only after a habeas proceeding has been commenced. *** [B]ecause §848(q)(4)(B), like §2251, conditions a court's power to act upon the existence of a habeas proceeding, I would also hold that a district court cannot appoint counsel until an application for habeas relief has been filed. I therefore respectfully dissent.

I

***

The Court appears to acknowledge that a §2254 proceeding must be initiated before counsel can be appointed under §848(q)(4)(B), but asserts that "neither the federal habeas corpus statute...nor the rules governing habeas corpus proceedings define a 'post conviction proceeding' under §2254...or expressly state how such a proceeding shall be commenced." ** It is difficult to imagine, however, how the federal habeas statute could be more "express" on the matter. ***

***

*** Rather than turning to the habeas statute for guidance in determining when a "proceeding under section 2254" commences, the Court bases its examination of the question primarily on what it perceives to be the time at which legal assistance would be most useful to a death-sentenced prisoner. ***

***

In my view, such an oblique reference to "the defendant's attorneys" is a remarkably thin reed upon which to rest Congress' supposed intention to "establish a right to preapplication legal assistance for capital defendants in federal habeas corpus proceedings." *Ibid.* Indeed, had Congress intended to establish such a "right," it surely would have done so in §848(q)(4)(B), which provides for appointment of counsel, rather than in §848(q)(9), which sets forth the mechanics of how "investigative, expert or other services" are to be obtained.

***

II

Had the Court ended its analysis with the ruling that an indigent death-sentenced prisoner is entitled to counsel under §848(q)(4)(B) prior to filing an application for habeas relief, today's decision would have an impact on federal coffers, but would not expand the power of the federal courts to interfere with States' legitimate interests in enforcing the judgments of their criminal justice systems. The Court, however, does not stop with its decision on availability of counsel; rather, it goes on to hold that upon a motion for appointment of counsel, a death-sentenced prisoner is also able to obtain a stay of his execution in order to permit counsel "to research and present [his] habeas claims." *Ante.*

The Court reaches its decision through the sheerest form of bootstrapping. ***

***

In reaching its expansive interpretation of §2251, the Court ignores the fact that the habeas statute provides federal courts with exceptional powers. Federal habeas review "disturbs the State's significant interest in repose for concluded litigation, denies society the right to punish some admitted offenders, and intrudes on state sovereignty to a degree matched by few exercises of federal judicial authority." *Duckworth v. Eagan*, 492 U.S. 195, 210 (1989). ** We should not lightly assume that Congress intended to expand federal courts' habeas power; this is particularly true regarding their power directly to interfere with state proceedings through granting stays.

Moreover, as JUSTICE O'CONNOR observes, in expanding the federal courts' power to grant stays, the Court's decision "conflicts with the sound principle underlying our precedents that federal habeas review exists only to review errors of constitutional dimension." *Ante.* Under the Court's interpretation of § 2251, a prisoner may obtain a stay of execution without presenting a single claim to a federal court. Indeed, under the Court's reading of the statute, a federal district court determining whether to enter a stay will no longer have to evaluate whether a prisoner has presented a potentially meritorious constitutional claim. Rather, the court's task will be to determine whether a "capital defendant" who comes to federal court shortly before his scheduled execution has been "dilatory" in pursuing his "right to counsel." ** If he has not been "dilatory," the district court presumably must enter a stay to preserve his "right to counsel" and his "right for that counsel meaningfully to research and present [his] habeas claims." ** In my view, simply by providing for the appointment of counsel in habeas cases, Congress did not intend to achieve such an extraordinary result. ***

   ***

Notes

1. *Subsequent case history*

Frank McFarland was executed on April 29, 1998. *See* Website of the Death Penalty Information Center, http://www.deathpenaltyinfo.org.

2. *Competing concerns*

What are the competing concerns regarding the appointment of counsel before the filing of a habeas petition? Is there a constitutional basis for the Court's decision in *McFarland*? Is *McFarland* a case that can withstand a change in the statute?

Chapter 6

Right to a Hearing

The cases in this chapter discuss a habeas petitioner's right to a hearing. This chapter begins with *Townsend v. Sain,* in which the Court finds that when the facts in a habeas petition are in dispute, the federal court must hold an evidentiary hearing if the habeas applicant did not receive a full and fair evidentiary hearing in state court and if the petitioner did not deliberately bypass state court proceedings. Nearly thirty years later, in *Keeney v. Tamayo-Reyes,* the Court decided that *Townsend*'s "deliberate bypass standard" no longer was the correct standard for reviewing a habeas petitioner's failure to develop a material fact in state proceedings.

Four years after *Keeney*, the Antiterrorism and Effective Death Penalty Act (AEDPA) introduced new language regarding a habeas petitioner's right to a hearing through section 2254(d) and Discovery Rule 6 of the rules governing section 2254, both of which are included in this chapter. After the AEDPA's enactment, the Court analyzed the impact of the AEDPA on the right to a hearing in *Michael Williams v. Taylor,* in which the Court decided whether a petitioner has a right to an evidentiary hearing in federal court after he has failed to develop his claims in state court. Although analyzing and applying new language from the AEDPA, the Court finds that this new language does not ultimately change the standard by which the Court determines a petitioner's right to a hearing.

Townsend v. Sain

372 U.S. 293 (1963)

CHIEF JUSTICE WARREN delivered the opinion of the Court.

This case, in its present posture raising questions as to the right to a plenary hearing in federal habeas corpus, comes to us once again after a tangle of prior proceedings. In 1955 the petitioner, Charles Townsend, was tried before a jury for murder in the Criminal Court of Cook County, Illinois. At his trial petitioner, through his court-appointed counsel, the public defender, objected to the introduction of his confession on the ground that it was the product of coercion. A hearing was held outside the presence of the jury, and the trial judge denied the motion to suppress. He later admitted the confession into evidence. Further evidence relating to the issue of voluntariness was introduced before the jury. The charge permitted them to disregard the confession if they found that it was involuntary. Under Illinois law the admissibility of the confession is determined solely by the trial judge, but the question of voluntariness, because it bears on the issue of credibility, may also be presented to the jury. ** The jury found petitioner guilty and affixed the death penalty to its verdict. The Supreme Court of Illinois affirmed the conviction, two justices dissenting. **

Petitioner next sought post-conviction collateral relief in the Illinois State courts. The Cook County Criminal Court dismissed his petition without holding an eviden-

jury — guilty death penalty

tiary hearing. The Supreme Court of Illinois by order affirmed, holding that the issue of coercion was res judicata, and this Court again denied certiorari. ** The issue of coercion was pressed at all stages of these proceedings.

Having thoroughly exhausted his state remedies, Townsend petitioned for habeas corpus in the United States District Court for the Northern District of Illinois. That court, considering only the pleadings filed in the course of that proceeding and the opinion of the Illinois Supreme Court rendered on direct appeal, denied the writ. The Court of Appeals for the Seventh Circuit dismissed an appeal. ** However, this Court granted a petition for certiorari, vacated the judgment and remanded for a decision as to whether, in the light of the state-court record, a plenary hearing was required. **

On the remand, the District Court held no hearing and dismissed the petition, finding only that "Justice would not be served by ordering a full hearing or by awarding any or all of [the] relief sought by Petitioner." The judge stated that he was satisfied from the state-court records before him that the decision of the state courts holding the challenged confession to have been freely and voluntarily given by petitioner was correct, and that there had been no denial of federal due process of law. On appeal the Court of Appeals concluded that "[o]n habeas corpus, the district court's inquiry is limited to a study of the undisputed portions of the record" and that the undisputed portions of this record showed no deprivation of constitutional rights. ** We granted certiorari to determine whether the courts below had correctly determined and applied the standards governing hearings in federal habeas corpus. ** The case was first argued during the October Term 1961. Two of the Justices were unable to participate in a decision, and we subsequently ordered it reargued. ** We now have it before us for decision.

The undisputed evidence adduced at the trial-court hearing on the motion to suppress showed the following. Petitioner was arrested by Chicago police shortly before or after 2 a.m. on New Year's Day 1954. They had received information from one Campbell, then in their custody for robbery, that petitioner was connected with the robbery and murder of Jack Boone, a Chicago steelworker and the victim in this case. Townsend was 19 years old at the time, a confirmed heroin addict and a user of narcotics since age 15. He was under the influence of a dose of heroin administered approximately one and one-half hours before his arrest. It was his practice to take injections three to five hours apart. At about 2:30 a.m. petitioner was taken to the second district police station and, shortly after his arrival, was questioned for a period variously fixed from one-half to two hours. During this period, he denied committing any crimes. Thereafter at about 5 a.m. he was taken to the 19th district station where he remained, without being questioned, until about 8:15 p.m. that evening. At that time he was returned to the second district station and placed in a line-up with several other men so that he could be viewed by one Anagnost, the victim of another robbery. When Anagnost identified another man, rather than petitioner, as his assailant, a scuffle ensued, the details of which were disputed by petitioner and the police. Following this incident petitioner was again subjected to questioning. He was interrogated more or less regularly from about 8:45 until 9:30 by police officers. At that time an Assistant State's Attorney arrived. Some time shortly before or after nine o'clock, but before the arrival of the State's attorney, petitioner complained to Officer Cagney that he had pains in his stomach, that he was suffering from other withdrawal symptoms, that he wanted a doctor, and that he was in need of a dose of narcotics. Petitioner clutched convulsively at his stomach a number of times. Cagney, aware that petitioner was a narcotic addict, telephoned for a police physician. There was some dispute between him and the State's Attorney, both prosecution witnesses, as to whether the questioning continued until the doctor arrived.

Cagney testified that it did and the State's Attorney to the contrary. In any event, after the withdrawal symptoms commenced it appears that petitioner was unresponsive to questioning. The doctor appeared at 9:45. In the presence of Officer Cagney he gave Townsend a combined dosage by injection of 1/8-grain of phenobarbital and 1/230-grain of hyoscine. Hyoscine is the same as scopolamine and is claimed by petitioner in this proceeding to have the properties of a "truth serum." The doctor also left petitioner four or five 1/4-grain tablets of phenobarbital. Townsend was told to take two of these that evening and the remainder the following day. The doctor testified that these medications were given to petitioner for the purpose of alleviating the withdrawal symptoms; the police officers and the State's Attorney testified that they did not know what the doctor had given petitioner. The doctor departed between 10 and 10:30. The medication alleviated the discomfort of the withdrawal symptoms, and petitioner promptly responded to questioning.

As to events succeeding this point in time on January 1, the testimony of the prosecution witnesses and of the petitioner irreconcilably conflicts. However, for the purposes of this proceeding both sides agree that the following occurred. After the doctor left, Officer Fitzgerald and the Assistant State's Attorney joined Officer Cagney in the room with the petitioner, where he was questioned for about 25 minutes. They all then went to another room; a court reporter there took down petitioner's statements. The State's Attorney turned the questioning to the Boone case about 11:15. In less than nine minutes a full confession was transcribed. At about 11:45 the questioning was terminated, and petitioner was returned to his cell.

The following day, Saturday, January 2, at about 1 p.m. petitioner was taken to the office of the prosecutor where the Assistant State's Attorney read, and petitioner signed, transcriptions of the statements which he had made the night before. When Townsend again experienced discomfort on Sunday evening, the doctor was summoned. He gave petitioner more 1/4-grain tablets of phenobarbital. On Monday, January 4, Townsend was taken to a coroner's inquest where he was called to the witness stand by the State and, after being advised of his right not to testify, again confessed. At the time of the inquest petitioner was without counsel. The public defender was not appointed to represent him until his arraignment on January 12.

Petitioner testified at the motion to suppress to the following version of his detention. He was initially questioned at the second district police station for a period in excess of two hours. Upon his return from the 19th district and after Anagnost, the robbery victim who had viewed the line-up, had identified another person as the assailant, Officer Cagney accompanied Anagnost into the hall and told him that he had identified the wrong person. Another officer then entered the room, hit the petitioner in the stomach and stated that petitioner knew that he had robbed Anagnost. Petitioner fell to the floor and vomited water and a little blood. Officer Cagney spoke to Townsend 5 or 10 minutes later, Townsend told him that he was sick from the use of drugs, and Cagney offered to call a doctor if petitioner would "cooperate" and tell the truth about the Boone murder. Five minutes later the officer had changed his tack; he told petitioner that he thought him innocent and that he would call the doctor, implying that the doctor would give him a narcotic. The doctor gave petitioner an injection in the arm and five pills. Townsend took three of these immediately. Although he felt better, he felt dizzy and sleepy and his distance vision was impaired. Anagnost was then brought into the room, and petitioner was asked by someone to tell Anagnost that he had robbed him. Petitioner then admitted the robbery, and the next thing he knew was that he was sitting at a desk. He fell asleep but was awakened and handed a pen; he signed his name believing that he was going to be released on bond. Townsend was taken to his cell but was later taken back to the room in which he had been before. He could see "a lot of lights flickering," and someone told him to hold his head up. This went on for a minute or so, and petitioner was then again taken back to his cell. The next morning petitioner's head was much clearer, although he could not really remember what had occurred following the injection on the previous evening. An officer then told petitioner that he had confessed. Townsend was taken into a room and asked about a number of robberies and murders. "I believe I said yes to all of them." He could not hear very well and felt sleepy. That afternoon, after he had taken the remainder of the phenobarbital pills, he was taken to the office of the State's Attorney. Half asleep he signed another paper although not aware of its contents. The doctor gave him six or seven pills of a different color on Sunday evening. He took some of these immediately. They kept him awake all night. The following Monday morning he took more of these pills. Later that day he was taken to a coroner's inquest. He testified at the inquest because the officers had told him to do so.

Essentially the prosecution witnesses contradicted all of the above. They testified that petitioner had been questioned initially for only one-half hour, that he had scuffled with the man identified by Anagnost, and not an officer, and that he had not vomited. The officers and the Assistant State's Attorney also testified that petitioner had appeared to be awake and coherent throughout the evening of the 1st of January and at all relevant times thereafter, and that he had not taken the pills given to him by the doctor on the evening of the 1st. They stated that the petitioner had appeared to follow the statement which he signed and which was read to him at the State's Attorney's office. Finally they denied that any threats or promises of any sort had been made or that Townsend had been told to testify at the coroner's inquest. As stated above counsel was not provided for him at this inquest.

There was considerable testimony at the motion to suppress concerning the probable effects of hyoscine and phenobarbital. Dr. Mansfield, who had prescribed for petitioner on the evening when he had first confessed, testified for the prosecution. He stated that a full therapeutic dose of hyoscine was 1/100 of a grain; that he gave Townsend 1/230 of a grain; that "phenobarbital…reacts very well combined with [hyoscine when]…you want to quiet" a person; that the combination will "pacify" because "it has an effect on the mind"; but that the dosage administered would not put a person to sleep and would not cause amnesia or impairment of eyesight or of mental condition. The doctor denied that he had administered any "truth serum." However, he did not disclose that hyoscine is the same as scopolamine or that the latter is familiarly known as "truth serum." Petitioner's expert was a doctor of physiology, pharmacology and toxicology. He was formerly the senior toxicological chemist of Cook County and at the time of trial was a professor of pharmacology, chemotherapy and toxicology at the Loyola University School of Medicine. He testified to the effect of the injection upon a hypothetical subject, obviously the petitioner. The expert stated that the effect of the prescribed dosage of hyoscine upon the subject, assumed to be a narcotic addict, "would be of such a nature that it could range between absolute sleep… and drowsiness, as one extreme, and the other extreme…would incorporate complete disorientation and excitation…." And, assuming that the subject took 1/8-grain phenobarbital by injection and 1/2-grain orally at the same time, the expert stated that the depressive effect would be accentuated. The expert testified that the subject would suffer partial or total amnesia for five to eight hours and loss of near vision for four to six hours.

The trial judge summarily denied the motion to suppress and later admitted the court reporter's transcription of the confession into evidence. He made no findings of fact and wrote no opinion stating the grounds of his decision. *** Thereafter, for the purpose of testing the credibility of the confession, the evidence relating to coercion was placed before the jury. At that time additional noteworthy testimony was elicited. The identity of hyoscine and scopolamine was established (but no mention of the drug's properties as a "truth serum" was made). An expert witness called by the prosecution testified that Townsend had such a low intelligence that he was a near mental defective and "just a little above moron." Townsend testified that the officers had slapped him on several occasions and had threatened to shoot him. Finally, Officer Corcoran testified that about 9 p.m., Friday evening, before the doctor's arrival, Townsend had confessed to the Boone assault and robbery in response to a question propounded by Officer Cagney in the presence of Officers Fitzgerald, Martin and himself. But although Corcoran, Cagney and Martin had testified extensively at the motion to suppress, none had mentioned any such confession. Furthermore, both Townsend and Officer Fitzgerald at the motion to suppress had flatly said that no statement had been made before the doctor arrived. Although the other three officers testified at the trial, not one of them was asked to corroborate this phase of Corcoran's testimony.

It was established that the homicide occurred at about 6 p.m. on December 18, 1953. Essentially the only evidence which connected petitioner with the crime, other than his confession, was the testimony of Campbell, then on probation for robbery, and of the pathologist who performed the autopsy on Boone. Campbell testified that about the "middle" of December at about 8:30 p.m. he had seen Townsend walking down a street in the vicinity of the murder with a brick in his hand. He was unable to fix the exact date, did not know of the Boone murder at the time and, so far as his testimony revealed, had no reason to suspect that Townsend had done anything unlawful previous to their meeting.

The pathologist testified that death was caused by a "severe blow to the top of his [Boone's] head...." Contrary to the statement in the opinion of the Illinois Supreme Court on direct appeal there was no testimony that the wounds were "located in such a manner as to have been inflicted by a blow with a house brick...." ** In any event, that court characterized the evidence as meagre and noted that "it was brought out by cross-examination that Campbell had informed on the defendant to obtain his own release from custody." ** Prior to petitioner's trial Campbell was placed on probation for robbery. Justice Schaefer, joined by Chief Justice Klingbiel in dissent, found Campbell's testimony "inherently incredible." **

The theory of petitioner's application for habeas corpus did not rest upon allegations of physical coercion. Rather, it relied upon the hitherto undisputed testimony and alleged: (1) that petitioner vomited water and blood at the police station when he became ill from the withdrawal of narcotics; (2) that scopolamine is a "truth serum" and that this fact was not brought out at the motion to suppress or at the trial; (3) that scopolamine "either alone or combined with Phenobarbital, is not the proper medication for a narcotic addict [and that]...[t]he effect of the intravenous injection of hyoscine and phenobarbital...is to produce a physiological and psychological condition adversely affecting the mind and will...[and] a psychic effect which removes the subject thus injected from the scope of reality; so that the person so treated is removed from contact with his environment, he is not able to see and feel properly, he loses proper use of his eye-sight, his hearing and his sense of perception and his ability to withstand interrogation"; (4) that the police doctor willfully suppressed this information and information of the identity of hyoscine and scopolamine, of his knowledge of these things, and of his intention to inject the hyoscine for the purpose of producing in Townsend "a physiological and psychological state...susceptible to interrogation resulting in...confes-

sions…"; (5) that the injection caused Townsend to confess; (6) that on the evening of
January 1, immediately after the injection of scopolamine, petitioner confessed to three
murders and one robbery other than the murder of Boone and the robbery of Anagnost. Although there was some mention of other confessions at the trial, only the confession to the Anagnost robbery was specifically testified to.

***

I

Numerous decisions of this Court have established the standards governing the admissibility of confessions into evidence. If an individual's "will was overborne" *** or if
his confession was not "the product of a rational intellect and a free will," *** his confession is inadmissible because coerced. These standards are applicable whether a confession is the product of physical intimidation or psychological pressure and, of course,
are equally applicable to a drug-induced statement. It is difficult to imagine a situation
in which a confession would be less the product of a free intellect, less voluntary, than
when brought about by a drug having the effect of a "truth serum." *** It is not significant that the drug may have been administered and the questions asked by persons un-
familiar with hyoscine's properties as a "truth serum," if these properties exist. Any
questioning by police officers which in fact produces a confession which is not the
product of a free intellect renders that confession inadmissible. ***

Thus we conclude that the petition for habeas corpus alleged a deprivation of constitutional rights. The remaining question before us then is whether the District Court
was required to hold a hearing to ascertain the facts which are a necessary predicate to a
decision of the ultimate constitutional question.

The problem of the power and duty of federal judges, on habeas corpus, to hold evidentiary hearings—that is, to try issues of fact *** anew—is a recurring one. The Court
last dealt at length with it in *Brown v. Allen*, 344 U.S. 443 [(1953)], in opinions by Justices
Reed and Frankfurter, both speaking for a majority of the Court. Since then, we have but
touched upon it. *** We granted certiorari in the 1959 Term to consider the question, but
ultimately disposed of the case on a more immediate ground. *Rogers v. Richmond*, 365
U.S. 534, 540 [(1961)]. It has become apparent that the opinions in *Brown v. Allen, supra*,
do not provide answers for all aspects of the hearing problem for the lower federal courts,
which have reached widely divergent, in fact often irreconcilable, results. *** We mean to
express no opinion on the correctness of particular decisions. But we think that it is appropriate at this time to elaborate the considerations which ought properly to govern the
grant or denial of evidentiary hearings in federal habeas corpus proceedings.

II

The broad considerations bearing upon the proper interpretation of the power of the
federal courts on habeas corpus are reviewed at length in the Court's opinion in *Fay v.
Noia*, [372 U.S.] 391[(1963)] and need not be repeated here. We pointed out there that
the historic conception of the writ, anchored in the ancient common law and in our
Constitution as an efficacious and imperative remedy for detentions of fundamental illegality, has remained constant to the present day. We pointed out, too, that the Act of
February 5, 1867, c. 28, §1, 14 Stat. 385–386, which in extending the federal writ to
state prisoners described the power of the federal courts to take testimony and determine the facts de novo in the largest terms, restated what apparently was the common-
law understanding. *Fay v. Noia*, [372 U.S.] at 416, n.27. The hearing provisions of the

1867 Act remain substantially unchanged in the present codification. 28 U.S.C. §2243. In construing the mandate of Congress, so plainly designed to afford a trial-type proceeding in federal court for state prisoners aggrieved by unconstitutional detentions, this Court has consistently upheld the power of the federal courts on habeas corpus to take evidence relevant to claims of such detention. "Since *Frank v. Mangum*, 237 U.S. 309, 331[(1915)], this Court has recognized that habeas corpus in the federal courts by one convicted of a criminal offense is a proper procedure 'to safeguard the liberty of all persons within the jurisdiction of the United States against infringement through any violation of the Constitution,' even though the events which were alleged to infringe did not appear upon the face of the record of his conviction." *Hawk v. Olson*, 326 U.S. 271, 274 [(1945)]. *Brown v. Allen* and numerous other cases have recognized this.

The rule could not be otherwise. The whole history of the writ—its unique development—refutes a construction of the federal courts' habeas corpus powers that would assimilate their task to that of courts of appellate review. The function on habeas is different. It is to test by way of an original civil proceeding, independent of the normal channels of review of criminal judgments, the very gravest allegations. State prisoners are entitled to relief on federal habeas corpus only upon proving that their detention violates the fundamental liberties of the person, safeguarded against state action by the Federal Constitution. Simply because detention so obtained is intolerable, the opportunity for redress, which presupposes the opportunity to be heard, to argue and present evidence, must never be totally foreclosed. ** It is the typical, not the rare, case in which constitutional claims turn upon the resolution of contested factual issues. Thus a narrow view of the hearing power would totally subvert Congress' specific aim in passing the Act of February 5, 1867, of affording state prisoners a forum in the federal trial courts for the determination of claims of detention in violation of the Constitution. The language of Congress, the history of the writ, the decisions of this Court, all make clear that the power of inquiry on federal habeas corpus is plenary. Therefore, where an applicant for a writ of habeas corpus alleges facts which, if proved, would entitle him to relief, the federal court to which the application is made has the power to receive evidence and try the facts anew.

III

We turn now to the considerations which in certain cases may make exercise of that power mandatory. The appropriate standard—which must be considered to supersede, to the extent of any inconsistencies, the opinions in *Brown v. Allen*—is this: Where the facts are in dispute, the federal court in habeas corpus must hold an evidentiary hearing if the habeas applicant did not receive a full and fair evidentiary hearing in a state court, either at the time of the trial or in a collateral proceeding. In other words a federal evidentiary hearing is required unless the state-court trier of fact has after a full hearing reliably found the relevant facts. ***

It would be unwise to overly particularize this test. The federal district judges are more intimately familiar with state criminal justice, and with the trial of fact, than are we, and to their sound discretion must be left in very large part the administration of federal habeas corpus. But experience proves that a too general standard—the "exceptional circumstances" and "vital flaw" tests of the opinions in *Brown v. Allen*—does not serve adequately to explain the controlling criteria for the guidance of the federal habeas corpus courts. Some particularization may therefore be useful. We hold that a federal court must grant an evidentiary hearing to a habeas applicant under the following circumstances: If (1) the merits of the factual dispute were not resolved in the state hearing; (2) the state factual determination is not fairly supported by the record as a whole;

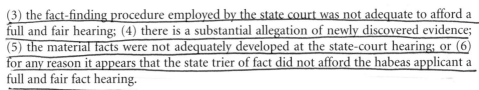

(3) the fact-finding procedure employed by the state court was not adequate to afford a full and fair hearing; (4) there is a substantial allegation of newly discovered evidence; (5) the material facts were not adequately developed at the state-court hearing; or (6) for any reason it appears that the state trier of fact did not afford the habeas applicant a full and fair fact hearing.

(1) There cannot even be the semblance of a full and fair hearing unless the state court actually reached and decided the issues of fact tendered by the defendant. Thus, if no express findings of fact have been made by the state court, the District Court must initially determine whether the state court has impliedly found material facts. No relevant findings have been made unless the state court decided the constitutional claim tendered by the defendant on the merits. If relief has been denied in prior state collateral proceedings after a hearing but without opinion, it is often likely that the decision is based upon a procedural issue—that the claim is not collaterally cognizable—and not on the merits. On the other hand, if the prior state hearing occurred in the course of the original trial—for example, on a motion to suppress allegedly unlawful evidence, as in the instant case—it will usually be proper to assume that the claim was rejected on the merits.

If the state court has decided the merits of the claim but has made no express findings, it may still be possible for the District Court to reconstruct the findings of the state trier of fact, either because his view of the facts is plain from his opinion or because of other indicia. In some cases this will be impossible, and the Federal District Court will be compelled to hold a hearing.

Reconstruction is not possible if it is unclear whether the state finder applied correct constitutional standards in disposing of the claim. Under such circumstances the District Court cannot ascertain whether the state court found the law or the facts adversely to the petitioner's contentions. Since the decision of the state trier of fact may rest upon an error of law rather than an adverse determination of the facts, a hearing is compelled to ascertain the facts. Of course, the possibility of legal error may be eliminated in many situations if the fact finder has articulated the constitutional standards which he has applied. Furthermore, the coequal responsibilities of state and federal judges in the administration of federal constitutional law are such that we think the district judge may, in the ordinary case in which there has been no articulation, properly assume that the state trier of fact applied correct standards of federal law to the facts, in the absence of evidence, such as was present in *Rogers v. Richmond*, that there is reason to suspect that an incorrect standard was in fact applied. *** Thus, if third-degree methods of obtaining a confession are alleged and the state court refused to exclude the confession from evidence, the district judge may assume that the state trier found the facts against the petitioner, the law being, of course, that third-degree methods necessarily produce a coerced confession.

In any event, even if it is clear that the state trier of fact utilized the proper standard, a hearing is sometimes required if his decision presents a situation in which the "so-called facts and their constitutional significance [are]...so blended that they cannot be severed in consideration." *Rogers v. Richmond*, [365 U.S.] at 546. *See Frank v. Mangum*, [237 U.S.] at 347 (Holmes, J., dissenting). Unless the district judge can be reasonably certain that the state trier would have granted relief if he had believed petitioner's allegations, he cannot be sure that the state trier in denying relief disbelieved these allegations. If any combination of the facts alleged would prove a violation of constitutional rights and the issue of law on those facts presents a difficult or novel problem for decision, any hypothesis as to the relevant factual determinations of the state trier involves the purest speculation. The federal court cannot exclude the possibility that the trial judge believed facts which showed a deprivation of constitutional rights and yet (erroneously) concluded that relief should be denied. Under these circumstances it is impossible for the federal court to reconstruct the facts, and a hearing must be held.

(2) This Court has consistently held that state factual determinations not fairly supported by the record cannot be conclusive of federal rights. *Fiske v. Kansas*, 274 U.S. 380, 385 [(1927)]; *Blackburn v. Alabama*, 361 U.S. 199, 208–209 [(1960)]. Where the fundamental liberties of the person are claimed to have been infringed, we carefully scrutinize the state-court record. *See, e.g., Blackburn v. Alabama, supra; Moore v. Michigan*, 355 U.S. 155 [(1957)]. The duty of the Federal District Court on habeas is no less exacting.

(3) However, the obligation of the Federal District Court to scrutinize the state-court findings of fact goes farther than this. Even if all the relevant facts were presented in the state-court hearing, it may be that the factfinding procedure there employed was not adequate for reaching reasonably correct results. If the state trial judge has made serious procedural errors (respecting the claim pressed in federal habeas) in such things as the burden of proof, a federal hearing is required. Even where the procedure employed does not violate the Constitution, if it appears to be seriously inadequate for the ascertainment of the truth, it is the federal judge's duty to disregard the state findings and take evidence anew. Of course, there are procedural errors so grave as to require an appropriate order directing the habeas applicant's release unless the State grants a new trial forthwith. Our present concern is with errors which, although less serious, are nevertheless grave enough to deprive the state evidentiary hearing of its adequacy as a means of finally determining facts upon which constitutional rights depend.

(4) Where newly discovered evidence is alleged in a habeas application, evidence which could not reasonably have been presented to the state trier of facts, the federal court must grant an evidentiary hearing. Of course, such evidence must bear upon the constitutionality of the applicant's detention; the existence merely of newly discovered evidence relevant to the guilt of a state prisoner is not a ground for relief on federal habeas corpus. Also, the district judge is under no obligation to grant a hearing upon a frivolous or incredible allegation of newly discovered evidence.

(5) The conventional notion of the kind of newly discovered evidence which will permit the reopening of a judgment is, however, in some respects too limited to provide complete guidance to the federal district judge on habeas. If, for any reason not attributable to the inexcusable neglect of petitioner, *see Fay v. Noia*, [372 U.S.] at 438 (Part V), evidence crucial to the adequate consideration of the constitutional claim was not developed at the state hearing, a federal hearing is compelled. The standard of inexcusable default set down in *Fay v. Noia* adequately protects the legitimate state interest in orderly criminal procedure, for it does not sanction needless piecemeal presentation of constitutional claims in the form of deliberate by-passing of state procedures. Compare *Price v. Johnston*, 334 U.S. 266, 291 [(1948)]: "The primary purpose of a habeas corpus proceeding is to make certain that a man is not unjustly imprisoned. And if for some justifiable reason he was previously unable to assert his rights or was unaware of the significance of relevant facts, it is neither necessary nor reasonable to deny him all opportunity of obtaining judicial relief."

(6) Our final category is intentionally open-ended because we cannot here anticipate all the situations wherein a hearing is demanded. It is the province of the district judges first to determine such necessities in accordance with the general rules. The duty to try the facts anew exists in every case in which the state court has not after a full hearing reliably found the relevant facts.

IV

It is appropriate to add a few observations concerning the proper application of the test we have outlined.

First. The purpose of the test is to indicate the situations in which the holding of an evidentiary hearing is mandatory. In all other cases where the material facts are in dispute, the holding of such a hearing is in the discretion of the district judge. If he concludes that the habeas applicant was afforded a full and fair hearing by the state court resulting in reliable findings, he may, and ordinarily should, accept the facts as found in the hearing. But he need not. In every case he has the power, constrained only by his sound discretion, to receive evidence bearing upon the applicant's constitutional claim. There is every reason to be confident that federal district judges, mindful of their delicate role in the maintenance of proper federal-state relations, will not abuse that discretion. We have no fear that the hearing power will be used to subvert the integrity of state criminal justice or to waste the time of the federal courts in the trial of frivolous claims.

Second. Although the district judge may, where the state court has reliably found the relevant facts, defer to the state court's findings of fact, he may not defer to its findings of law. It is the district judge's duty to apply the applicable federal law to the state court fact findings independently. The state conclusions of law may not be given binding weight on habeas. That was settled in *Brown v. Allen*, [344 U.S.] at 506 (opinion of Mr. Justice Frankfurter).

Third. A District Court sitting in habeas corpus clearly has the power to compel production of the complete state-court record. Ordinarily such a record—including the transcript of testimony (or if unavailable some adequate substitute, such as a narrative record), the pleadings, court opinions, and other pertinent documents—is indispensable to determining whether the habeas applicant received a full and fair state-court evidentiary hearing resulting in reliable findings. ** Of course, if because no record can be obtained the district judge has no way of determining whether a full and fair hearing which resulted in findings of relevant fact was vouchsafed, he must hold one. So also, there may be cases in which it is more convenient for the district judge to hold an evidentiary hearing forthwith rather than compel production of the record. It is clear that he has the power to do so.

Fourth. It rests largely with the federal district judges to give practical form to the principles announced today. We are aware that the too promiscuous grant of evidentiary hearings on habeas could both swamp the dockets of the District Courts and cause acute and unnecessary friction with state organs of criminal justice, while the too limited use of such hearings would allow many grave constitutional errors to go forever uncorrected. The accommodation of these competing factors must be made on the front line, by the district judges who are conscious of their paramount responsibility in this area.

V

Application of the foregoing principles to the particular litigation before us is not difficult. Townsend received an evidentiary hearing at his original trial, where his confession was held to be voluntary. Having exhausted his state remedies without receiving any further such hearing, he turned to the Federal District Court. Twice now, habeas corpus relief has been denied without an evidentiary hearing. On appeal from the second denial, the Court of Appeals held that "[o]n habeas corpus, the district court's inquiry is limited to a study of the undisputed portions of the record." That formulation was error. And we believe that on this record it was also error to refuse Townsend an evidentiary hearing in the District Court. The state trial judge rendered neither an opinion, conclusions of law, nor findings of fact. He made no charge to the jury setting forth the constitutional standards governing the admissibility of confessions. In short, there are no indicia which would indicate whether the trial judge applied the proper standard of federal law in ruling upon the admissibility of the confession. The Illinois Supreme Court opinion rendered at the time of direct appeal contains statements which might indicate that the court thought the confession was admissible if it satisfied the "coherency" standard. Under that test the confession would be admissible "[s]o long as the accused [was] capable of making a narrative of past events or of stating his own participation in the crime...." ** As we have indicated in Part I of this opinion, this test is not the proper one. Possibly the state trial judge believed that the admissibility of allegedly drug-induced confessions was to be judged by the "coherency" standard. *** However, even if this possibility could be eliminated, and it could be ascertained that correct standards of law were applied, it is still unclear whether the state trial judge would have excluded Townsend's confession as involuntary if he had believed the evidence which Townsend presented at the motion to suppress. The problem which the trial judge faced was novel and by no means without difficulty. We believe that the Federal District Court could not conclude that the state trial judge admitted the confession because he disbelieved the evidence which would show that it was involuntary. We believe that the findings of fact of the state trier could not be successfully reconstructed. We hold that, for this reason, an evidentiary hearing was compelled. ***

Furthermore, a crucial fact was not disclosed at the state-court hearing: that the substance injected into Townsend before he confessed has properties which may trigger statements in a legal sense involuntary. *** This fact was vital to whether his confession was the product of a free will and therefore admissible. To be sure, there was medical testimony as to the general properties of hyoscine, from which might have been inferred the conclusion that Townsend's power of resistance had been debilitated. But the crucially informative characterization of the drug, the characterization which would have enabled the judge and jury, mere laymen, intelligently to grasp the nature of the substance under inquiry, was inexplicably omitted from the medical experts' testimony. Under the circumstances, disclosure of the identity of hyoscine as a "truth serum" was indispensable to a fair, rounded, development of the material facts. And the medical experts' failure to testify fully cannot realistically be regarded as Townsend's inexcusable default. *See Fay v. Noia*, [372 U.S.] at 438 (Part V).

On the remand it would not, of course, be sufficient for the District Court merely to hear new evidence and to read the state-court record. Where an unresolved factual dispute exists, demeanor evidence is a significant factor in adjudging credibility. And questions of credibility, of course, are basic to resolution of conflicts in testimony. To be sure, the state-court record is competent evidence, *** and either party may choose to rely solely upon the evidence contained in that record, but the petitioner, and the State, must be given the opportunity to present other testimonial and documentary evidence relevant to the disputed issues. This was not done here.

In deciding this case as we do, we do not mean to prejudge the truth of the allegations of the petition for habeas corpus. We decide only that on this record the federal district judge was obliged to hold a hearing.

Reversed and remanded.

[JUSTICE GOLDBERG wrote a concurring opinion, which is omitted. A dissenting opinion by JUSTICE STEWART, who was joined by JUSTICE CLARK, JUSTICE HARLAN, and JUSTICE WHITE, also is omitted.]

Notes

1. Subsequent case history

Charles Townsend was convicted and sentenced to death in Cook County, Illinois, in 1955. His conviction and sentence were affirmed by the state courts. The federal district court and the Seventh Circuit Court of Appeals denied his first habeas petition. *United States ex rel. Townsend v. Sain*, 265 F.2d 660 (7th Cir. 1958). The Supreme Court vacated the denial and remanded. 359 U.S. 64 (1958). On remand, the district court once again denied the writ and the Seventh Circuit affirmed. 276 F.2d 324 (7th Cir. 1960). As the above opinion demonstrates, in 1963 the Supreme Court again reversed and required the district court to grant Townsend a hearing on his habeas petition. On remand, the district court held that the confession was voluntary but nonetheless granted the writ based on the existence of new evidence. The Seventh Circuit reversed and ordered the petition dismissed. *United States ex rel. Townsend v. Ogilvie*, 334 F.2d 837 (7th Cir. 1964). In 1971, after Townsend's second habeas petition, the district court ordered Townsend's confession suppressed, reversed his conviction and sentence, and ordered the State of Illinois to retry him. *United States ex. rel. Townsend v. Twomey*, 322 F. Supp. 158 (N.D. Ill. 1971). The Seventh Circuit reversed the order granting a new trial but held that Illinois could not impose the death penalty on Townsend. 452 F.2d 350 (7th Cir. 1971). The Seventh Circuit gave Illinois the option of re-sentencing Townsend, re-trying him, or immediately releasing him. *Id*. at 363.

Charles Townsend was never executed and is not presently incarcerated in Illinois. The Illinois Department of Corrections has no records that appear to match those of Charles Townsend, and the Cook County State's Attorney's Office has no further information on his case.

2. Deliberate bypass

Under *Townsend*, what constitutes a "deliberate bypass"? How does the Court evaluate whether a petitioner has deliberately bypassed state court proceedings?

Keeney v. Tamayo-Reyes

504 U.S. 1 (1992)

JUSTICE WHITE delivered the opinion of the Court.

Respondent is a Cuban immigrant with little education and almost no knowledge of English. In 1984, he was charged with murder arising from the stabbing death of a man who had allegedly attempted to intervene in a confrontation between respondent and his girlfriend in a bar.

Respondent was provided with a defense attorney and interpreter. The attorney recommended to respondent that he plead *nolo contendere* to first-degree manslaughter. **
Respondent signed a plea form that explained in English the rights he was waiving by entering the plea. The state court held a plea hearing, at which petitioner was represented by counsel and his interpreter. The judge asked the attorney and interpreter if they had explained to respondent the rights in the plea form and the consequences of his plea; they responded in the affirmative. The judge then explained to respondent, in English, the rights he would waive by his plea, and asked the interpreter to translate. Respondent indicated that he understood his rights and still wished to plead *nolo contendere*. The judge accepted his plea.

[handwritten margin note: He vanished?]

[handwritten margin note: Didn't speak English]

Later, respondent brought a collateral attack on the plea in a state-court proceeding. He alleged his plea had not been knowing and intelligent and therefore was invalid because his translator had not translated accurately and completely for him the *mens rea* element of manslaughter. He also contended that he did not understand the purposes of the plea form or the plea hearing. He contended that he did not know he was pleading no contest to manslaughter, but rather that he thought he was agreeing to be tried for manslaughter.

After a hearing, the state court dismissed respondent's petition, finding that respondent was properly served by his trial interpreter and that the interpreter correctly, fully, and accurately translated the communications between respondent and his attorney. ** The State Court of Appeals affirmed, and the State Supreme Court denied review.

hearing

Respondent then entered Federal District Court seeking a writ of habeas corpus. Respondent contended that the material facts concerning the translation were not adequately developed at the state-court hearing, implicating the fifth circumstance of *Townsend v. Sain*, 372 U.S. 293, 313 (1963), and sought a federal evidentiary hearing on whether his *nolo contendere* plea was unconstitutional. The District Court found that the failure to develop the critical facts relevant to his federal claim was attributable to inexcusable neglect and that no evidentiary hearing was required. ** Respondent appealed.

The Court of Appeals for the Ninth Circuit recognized that the alleged failure to translate the *mens rea* element of first-degree manslaughter, if proved, would be a basis for overturning respondent's plea** and determined that material facts had not been adequately developed in the state postconviction court, ** apparently due to the negligence of postconviction counsel. The court held that *Townsend v. Sain*, [372 U.S.] at 317, and *Fay v. Noia*, 372 U.S. 391, 438 (1963), required an evidentiary hearing in the District Court unless respondent had deliberately bypassed the orderly procedure of the state courts. Because counsel's negligent failure to develop the facts did not constitute a deliberate bypass, the Court of Appeals ruled that respondent was entitled to an evidentiary hearing on the question whether the *mens rea* element of first-degree manslaughter was properly explained to him. ***

We granted certiorari to decide whether the deliberate bypass standard is the correct standard for excusing a habeas petitioner's failure to develop a material fact in state-court proceedings. ** We reverse.

Because the holding of *Townsend v. Sain* that *Fay v. Noia*'s deliberate bypass standard is applicable in a case like this had not been reversed, it is quite understandable that the Court of Appeals applied that standard in this case. However, in light of more recent decisions of this Court, *Townsend*'s holding in this respect must be overruled. *** *Fay v. Noia* was itself a case where the habeas petitioner had not taken advantage of state remedies by failing to appeal—a procedural default case. Since that time, however, this Court has rejected the deliberate bypass standard in state procedural default cases and has applied instead a standard of cause and prejudice.

[The Court then discussed *Francis v. Henderson*, 425 U.S. 536 (1976) (recognizing that considerations of comity and concerns for the orderly administration of criminal justice may in some circumstances require a federal court to forgo the exercise of its habeas corpus power, and holding that a federal habeas petitioner is required to show cause for his procedural default, as well as actual prejudice); *Wainwright v. Sykes*, 433 U.S. 72 (1977) (rejecting *Fay*'s standard of "knowing waiver" or "deliberate bypass" to excuse a petitioner's failure to comply with a state contemporaneous-objection rule, observing that procedural rules that contribute to error-free state trial proceedings are thoroughly desirable, and applying a cause-and-prejudice standard to a petitioner's failure to object at trial); *McCleskey v. Zant*, 499 U.S. 467 (1991) (recognizing, *inter alia*, that the writ strikes at finality of a state criminal conviction, a matter of particular importance in a federal system, and that federal habeas litigation places a heavy burden on scarce judicial resources, which may give litigants incentives to withhold claims for manipulative purposes and may create disincentives to present claims when evidence is fresh); and *Coleman v. Thompson*, 501 U.S. 722 (1991) (applying the cause-and-prejudice standard uniformly to state procedural defaults, eliminating the "irrational" distinction between *Fay* and subsequent cases).]

The concerns that motivated the rejection of the deliberate bypass standard in *Wainwright*, *Coleman*, and other cases are equally applicable to this case. *** As in cases of state procedural default, application of the cause-and-prejudice standard to excuse a state prisoner's failure to develop material facts in state court will appropriately accommodate concerns of finality, comity, judicial economy, and channeling the resolution of claims into the most appropriate forum.

Applying the cause-and-prejudice standard in cases like this will obviously contribute to the finality of convictions, for requiring a federal evidentiary hearing solely on the basis of a habeas petitioner's negligent failure to develop facts in state-court proceedings dramatically increases the opportunities to relitigate a conviction.

Similarly, encouraging the full factual development in state court of a claim that state courts committed constitutional error advances comity by allowing a coordinate jurisdiction to correct its own errors in the first instance. It reduces the "inevitable friction" that results when a federal habeas court "overturn[s] either the factual or legal conclusions reached by the state-court system." *Sumner v. Mata*, 449 U.S. 539, 550 (1981).

Also, by ensuring that full factual development takes place in the earlier, state-court proceedings, the cause-and-prejudice standard plainly serves the interest of judicial economy. It is hardly a good use of scarce judicial resources to duplicate factfinding in federal court merely because a petitioner has negligently failed to take advantage of opportunities in state-court proceedings.

Furthermore, ensuring that full factual development of a claim takes place in state court channels the resolution of the claim to the most appropriate forum. The state court is the appropriate forum for resolution of factual issues in the first instance, and creating incentives for the deferral of factfinding to later federal-court proceedings can only degrade the accuracy and efficiency of judicial proceedings. This is fully consistent with, and gives meaning to, the requirement of exhaustion. The Court has long held that state prisoners must exhaust state remedies before obtaining federal habeas relief. *Ex parte Royall*, 117 U.S. 241 (1886). The requirement that state prisoners exhaust state remedies before a writ of habeas corpus is granted by a federal court is now incorporated in the federal habeas statute. *** 28 U.S.C. 10 § 2254. Exhaustion means more than notice. In requiring exhaustion of a federal claim in state court, Congress surely meant that exhaustion be serious and meaningful. The purpose of exhaustion is not to create a procedural hurdle on the path to federal habeas court, but to channel claims into an appropriate forum, where meritorious claims may be vindicated and unfounded litigation obviated before resort to federal court. Comity concerns dictate that the requirement of exhaustion is not satisfied by the mere statement of a federal claim in state court. Just as the State must afford the petitioner a full and fair hearing on his federal claim, so must the petitioner afford the State a full and fair opportunity to address and resolve the claim on the merits. **

Finally, it is worth noting that applying the cause-and-prejudice standard in this case also advances uniformity in the law of habeas corpus. There is no good reason to maintain in one area of habeas law a standard that has been rejected in the area in which it was principally enunciated. And little can be said for holding a habeas petitioner to one standard for failing to bring a claim in state court and excusing the petitioner under another, lower standard for failing to develop the factual basis of that claim in the same forum. A different rule could mean that a habeas petitioner would not be excused for negligent failure to object to the introduction of the prosecution's evidence, but nonetheless would be excused for negligent failure to introduce any evidence of his own to support a constitutional claim. ***

Respondent Tamayo-Reyes is entitled to an evidentiary hearing if he can show cause for his failure to develop the facts in state-court proceedings and actual prejudice resulting from that failure. We also adopt the narrow exception to the cause-and-prejudice requirement: A habeas petitioner's failure to develop a claim in state-court proceedings will be excused and a hearing mandated if he can show that a fundamental miscarriage of justice would result from failure to hold a federal evidentiary hearing. *Cf. McCleskey v. Zant*, 499 U.S. at 494. **

The State concedes that a remand to the District Court is appropriate in order to afford respondent the opportunity to bring forward evidence establishing cause and prejudice, ** and we agree that respondent should have that opportunity. Accordingly, the decision of the Court of Appeals is reversed, and the cause is remanded to the District Court for further proceedings consistent with this opinion.

So ordered.

JUSTICE O'CONNOR, with whom JUSTICE BLACKMUN, JUSTICE STEVENS, and JUSTICE KENNEDY join, dissenting.

Under the guise of overruling "a remnant of a decision," ** and achieving "uniformity in the law," ** the Court has changed the law of habeas corpus in a fundamental way by effectively overruling cases decided long before *Townsend v. Sain*, 372 U.S. 293 (1963). I do not think this change is supported by the line of our recent procedural default cases upon which the Court relies: In my view, the balance of state and federal interests regarding whether a federal court will consider a claim raised on habeas cannot be simply lifted and transposed to the different question whether, once the court will consider the claim, it should hold an evidentiary hearing. Moreover, I do not think the Court's decision can be reconciled with 28 U.S.C. §2254(d), a statute Congress enacted three years after *Townsend*.

I

Jose Tamayo-Reyes' habeas petition stated that because he does not speak English he pleaded *nolo contendere* to manslaughter without any understanding of what "manslaughter" means. ** If this assertion is true, his conviction was unconstitutionally obtained, ** and Tamayo-Reyes would be entitled to a writ of habeas corpus. Despite the Court's attempt to characterize his allegation as a technical quibble—"his translator had not translated accurately and completely for him the mens rea element of manslaughter" **—this much is not in dispute. Tamayo-Reyes has alleged a fact that, if true, would entitle him to the relief he seeks.

Tamayo-Reyes initially, and properly, challenged the voluntariness of his plea in a petition for postconviction relief in state court. The court held a hearing, after which it found that "[p]etitioner's plea of guilty was knowingly and voluntarily entered." ** Yet the record of the postconviction hearing hardly inspires confidence in the accuracy of this determination. Tamayo-Reyes was the only witness to testify, but his attorney did not ask him whether his interpreter had translated "manslaughter" for him. Counsel instead introduced the deposition testimony of the interpreter, who admitted that he had translated "manslaughter" only as "less than murder." ** No witnesses capable of assessing the interpreter's performance were called; the attorney instead tried to direct the court's attention to various sections of the interpreter's deposition and attempted to point out where the interpreter had erred. When the prosecutor objected to this discussion on the ground that counsel was not qualified as an expert witness, his "presentation of the issue quickly disintegrated." ** The state court had no other relevant evidence before it when it determined that Tamayo-Reyes actually understood the charge to which he was pleading.

Contrary to the impression conveyed by this Court's opinion, the question whether a federal court should defer to this sort of dubious "factfinding" in addressing a habeas corpus petition is one with a long history behind it, a history that did not begin with *Townsend v. Sain.*

II

A

The availability and scope of habeas corpus have changed over the writ's long history, but one thing has remained constant: Habeas corpus is not an appellate proceeding, but rather an original civil action in a federal court. *See, e.g., Browder v. Director, Dept. of Corrections of Ill.,* 434 U.S. 257, 269 (1978). It was settled over a hundred years ago that "[t]he prosecution against [a criminal defendant] is a criminal prosecution, but the writ of habeas corpus…is not a proceeding in that prosecution. On the contrary, it is a new suit brought by him to enforce a civil right." *Ex parte Tom Tong,* 108 U.S. 556, 559–560 (1883). Any possible doubt about this point has been removed by the statutory procedure Congress has provided for the disposition of habeas corpus petitions, a procedure including such nonappellate functions as the allegation of facts, 28 U.S.C. §2242, the taking of depositions and the propounding of interrogatories, §2246, the introduction of documentary evidence, §2247, and, of course, the determination of facts at evidentiary hearings, §2254(d).

To be sure, habeas corpus has its own peculiar set of hurdles a petitioner must clear before his claim is properly presented to the district court. The petitioner must, in general, exhaust available state remedies, §2254(b), avoid procedural default, *Coleman v. Thompson,* 501 U.S. 722 (1991), not abuse the writ, *McCleskey v. Zant,* 499 U.S. 467 (1991), and not seek retroactive application of a new rule of law, *Teague v. Lane,* 489 U.S. 288 (1989). For much of our history, the hurdles were even higher. *See, e.g., Ex parte Watkins,* [28 U.S.] 3 Pet. 193, 203 (1830) (habeas corpus available only to challenge jurisdiction of trial court). But once they have been surmounted—once the claim is properly before the district court—a habeas petitioner, like any civil litigant, has had a right to a hearing where one is necessary to prove the facts supporting his claim. ** Thus when we observed in *Townsend v. Sain,* 372 U.S. at 312 [(1963)], that "the opportunity for redress…presupposes the opportunity to be heard, to argue and present evidence," we were saying nothing new. We were merely restating what had long been our understanding of the method by which contested factual issues raised on habeas should be resolved.

Habeas corpus has always differed from ordinary civil litigation, however, in one important respect: The doctrine of res judicata has never been thought to apply. *See, e.g.,*

Brown v. Allen, 344 U.S. 443, 458 (1953). ** A state prisoner is not precluded from raising a federal claim on habeas that has already been rejected by the state courts. This is not to say that state court factfinding is entitled to no weight, or that every state prisoner has the opportunity to relitigate facts found against him by the state courts. Concerns of federalism and comity have pushed us from this extreme just as the importance of the writ has repelled us from the opposite extreme, represented by the strict application of res judicata. Instead, we have consistently occupied the middle ground. Even before *Townsend*, federal courts deferred to state court findings of fact where the federal district judge was satisfied that the state court had fairly considered the issues and the evidence and had reached a satisfactory result. *See, e.g., Brown*, [344 U.S.] at 458, 465. ** But where such was not the case, the federal court entertaining the habeas petition would examine the facts anew. *See, e.g., Ex parte Hawk*, 321 U.S. 114, 116, 118 (1944). *** In *Brown*, we explained that a hearing may be dispensed with only "[w]here the record of the application affords an adequate opportunity to weigh the sufficiency of the allegations and the evidence, and no unusual circumstances calling for a hearing are presented." 344 U.S. at 463.

Townsend "did not launch the Court in any new directions," Weisselberg, EVIDENTIARY HEARINGS IN FEDERAL HABEAS CORPUS CASES, 1990 BYU L. Rev. 131, 150, but it clarified how the district court should measure the adequacy of the state court proceeding. *Townsend* specified six circumstances in which one could not be confident that "the state-court trier of fact has after a full hearing reliably found the relevant facts." 372 U.S. at 313. *** That these principles marked no significant departure from our prior understanding of the writ is evident from the view expressed by the four dissenters, who had "no quarrel with the Court's statement of the basic governing principle which should determine whether a hearing is to be had in a federal habeas corpus proceeding," but disagreed only with the Court's attempt "to erect detailed hearing standards for the myriad situations presented by federal habeas corpus applications." 372 U.S. at 326–327 (Stewart, J., dissenting). *Townsend* thus did not alter the federal courts' practice of holding an evidentiary hearing unless the state court had fairly considered the relevant evidence.

The Court expressed concern in *Townsend* that a petitioner might abuse the fifth circumstance described in the opinion, by deliberately withholding evidence from the state factfinder in the hope of finding a more receptive forum in a federal court. *Id.* at 317. To discourage this sort of disrespect for state proceedings, the Court held that such a petitioner would not be entitled to a hearing. *Ibid.* The *Townsend* opinion did not need to address this concern in much detail, because a similar issue was discussed at greater length in another case decided the same day, *Fay v. Noia*, 372 U.S. 391 (1963). The *Townsend* opinion thus merely referred the reader to the discussion in *Fay*, where a similar exception was held to bar a state prisoner from habeas relief where the prisoner had intentionally committed a procedural default in state court. *See Townsend*, [372 U.S.] at 317.

Nearly 30 years later, the Court implies that *Fay* and *Townsend* must stand or fall together. ** But this is not so: The *Townsend* Court did not suggest that the issues in *Townsend* and *Fay* were identical, or that they were so similar that logic required an identical answer to each. *Townsend* did not purport to rely on *Fay* as authority; it merely referred to *Fay*'s discussion as a shorthand device to avoid repeating similar analysis. Indeed, reliance on *Fay* as authority would have been unnecessary. *Townsend* was essentially an elaboration of our prior cases regarding the holding of hearings in federal habeas cases; *Fay* represented an overruling of our prior cases regarding procedural defaults. *See Coleman v. Thompson*, 501 U.S. at 744–747; *Wainwright v. Sykes*, 433 U.S. 72, 82 (1977).

As the Court recognizes, *ante,* ** we have applied *Townsend*'s analysis ever since. ** But we have not, in my view, been unjustifiably clinging to a poorly reasoned precedent. While we properly abandoned *Fay* because it was inconsistent with prior cases that represented a better-reasoned balance of state and federal interests, the same cannot be said of *Townsend*. The Court today holds that even when the reliability of state factfinding is doubtful because crucial evidence was not presented to the state trier of fact, a habeas petitioner is ordinarily not entitled to an opportunity to prove the facts necessary to his claim. This holding, of course, directly overrules a portion of *Townsend*, but more than that, I think it departs significantly from the pre-*Townsend* law of habeas corpus. Even before *Townsend*, when a habeas petitioner's claim was properly before a federal court, and when the accurate resolution of that claim depended on proof of facts that had been resolved against the petitioner in an unreliable state proceeding, the petitioner was entitled to his day in federal court. As Justice Holmes wrote for the Court, in a case where the state courts had rejected—under somewhat suspicious circumstances—the petitioner's allegation that his trial had been dominated by an angry mob: "[I]t does not seem to us sufficient to allow a Judge of the United States to escape the duty of examining the facts for himself when if true as alleged they make the trial absolutely void." *Moore*, 261 U.S. at 92. The class of petitioners eligible to present claims on habeas may have been narrower in days gone by, and the class of claims one might present may have been smaller, but once the claim was properly before the court, the right to a hearing was not construed as narrowly as the Court construes it today.

B

Instead of looking to the history of the right to an evidentiary hearing, the Court simply borrows the cause and prejudice standard from a series of our recent habeas corpus cases. *Ante.* All but one of these cases address the question of when a habeas claim is properly before a federal court despite the petitioner's procedural default. *See Coleman v. Thompson, supra; Murray v. Carrier*, 477 U.S. 478 (1986); *Reed v. Ross*, 468 U.S. 1 (1984); *Engle v. Isaac*, 456 U.S. 107 (1982); *Wainwright v. Sykes, supra; Francis v. Henderson*, 425 U.S. 536 (1976). The remaining case addresses the issue of a petitioner's abuse of the writ. *See McCleskey v. Zant*, 499 U.S. 467 (1991).

These cases all concern the question whether the federal court will consider the merits of the claim, that is, whether the court has the authority to upset a judgment affirmed on direct appeal. So far as this threshold inquiry is concerned, our respect for state procedural rules and the need to discourage abuse of the writ provide the justification for the cause and prejudice standard. As we have said in the former context: "[T]he Great Writ imposes special costs on our federal system. The States possess primary authority for defining and enforcing the criminal law. In criminal trials they also hold the initial responsibility for vindicating constitutional rights. Federal intrusions into state criminal trials frustrate both the States' sovereign power to punish offenders and their good-faith attempts to honor constitutional rights." *Engle*, [456 U.S.] at 128.

The question we are considering here is quite different. Here, the Federal District Court has already determined that it will consider the claimed constitutional violation; the only question is how the court will go about it. When it comes to determining whether a hearing is to be held to resolve a claim that is already properly before a federal court, the federalism concerns underlying our procedural default cases are diminished somewhat. By this point, our concern is less with encroaching on the territory of the state courts than it is with managing the territory of the federal courts in a manner that will best implement their responsibility to consider habeas petitions. Our adoption of a cause and prejudice standard to resolve the first concern should not cause us reflexively to adopt the same standard to resolve the second. Federalism, comity, and finality are all advanced by declining to permit relitigation of claims in federal court in certain circumstances; these interests are less significantly advanced, once relitigation properly occurs, by permitting district courts to resolve claims based on an incomplete record.

III

The Court's decision today cannot be reconciled with subsection (d) of 28 U.S.C. §2254, which Congress enacted only three years after we decided *Townsend*. Subsection (d) provides that state court factfinding "shall be presumed to be correct, unless the applicant shall establish" one of eight listed circumstances. Most of these circumstances are taken word for word from *Townsend*, including the one at issue here; §2254(d)(3) renders the presumption of correctness inapplicable where "the material facts were not adequately developed at the State court hearing." The effect of the presumption is to augment the habeas petitioner's burden of proof. Where state factfinding is presumed correct, the petitioner must establish the state court's error "by convincing evidence"; where state factfinding is not presumed correct, the petitioner must prove the facts necessary to support his claim by only a preponderance of the evidence. *Sumner v. Mata*, 449 U.S. 539, 551 (1981).

Section 2254(d) is not, in the strict sense, a codification of our holding in *Townsend*. The listed circumstances in *Townsend* are those in which a hearing must be held; the nearly identical listed circumstances in §2254(d) are those in which facts found by a state court are not presumed correct. But the two are obviously intertwined. If a habeas petitioner fulfills one of the *Townsend* requirements he will be entitled to a hearing, and by virtue of fulfilling a *Townsend* requirement he will necessarily have also fulfilled one of the §2254(d) requirements, so that at his hearing the presumption of correctness will not apply. On the other hand, if the petitioner has not fulfilled one of the *Townsend* requirements he will generally not have fulfilled the corresponding §2254(d) requirement either, so he will be entitled neither to a hearing nor to an exception from the presumption of correctness. *Townsend* and §2254(d) work hand in hand: Where a petitioner has a right to a hearing he must prove facts by a preponderance of the evidence, but where he has no right to a hearing he must prove facts by the higher standard of convincing evidence. Without the opportunity for a hearing, it is safe to assume that this higher standard will be unattainable for most petitioners. *See* L. Yackle, Postconviction Remedies 508–509 (1981).

In enacting a statute that so closely parallels *Townsend*, Congress established a procedural framework that relies upon *Townsend*'s continuing validity. In general, therefore, overruling *Townsend* would frustrate the evident intent of Congress that the question of when a hearing is to be held should be governed by the same standards as the question of when a federal court should defer to state court factfinding. In particular, the Court's adoption of a "cause and prejudice" standard for determining whether the material facts were adequately developed in state proceedings will frustrate Congress' intent with respect to that *Townsend* circumstance's statutory analog, §2254(d)(3).

For a case to fit within this *Townsend* circumstance but none of *Townsend*'s other circumstances, the case will very likely be like this one, where the material facts were not developed because of attorney error. Any other reason the material facts might not have been developed, such as that they were unknown at the time or that the State denied a full and fair opportunity to develop them, will almost certainly be covered by one of *Townsend*'s other circumstances. *See Townsend*, 372 U.S. at 313. We have already held that attorney error short of constitutionally ineffective assistance of counsel does not amount to "cause." *See Murray v. Carrier*, 477 U.S. at 488. As a result, the practical effect of the Court's ruling today will be that for a case to fall within *Townsend*'s fifth circumstance but no other — for a petitioner to be entitled to a hearing on the ground that the material facts were not adequately developed in state court but on no other ground — the petitioner's attorney must have rendered constitutionally ineffective assistance in presenting facts to the state factfinder.

This effect is more than a little ironic. Where the state factfinding occurs at the trial itself, counsel's ineffectiveness will not just entitle the petitioner to a hearing — it will entitle the petitioner to a new trial. Where, as in this case, the state factfinding occurs at a postconviction proceeding, the petitioner has no constitutional right to the effective assistance of counsel, so counsel's poor performance can never constitute "cause" under the cause and prejudice standard. *Coleman v. Thompson*, 501 U.S. at 752. After today's decision, the only petitioners entitled to a hearing under *Townsend*'s fifth circumstance are the very people who do not need one, because they will have already obtained a new trial or because they will already be entitled to a hearing under one of the other circumstances. The Court has thus rendered unusable the portion of *Townsend* requiring hearings where the material facts were not adequately developed in state court.

As noted above, the fact that § 2254(d)(3) uses language identical to the language we used in *Townsend* strongly suggests that Congress presumed the continued existence of this portion of *Townsend*. Moreover, the Court's application of a cause and prejudice standard creates a conundrum regarding how to interpret § 2254(d)(3). If a cause and prejudice standard applies to §2254(d)(3) as well as *Townsend*'s fifth circumstance, then the Court has rendered § 2254(d)(3) superfluous for the same reason this part of *Townsend* has become superfluous. While we may deprive portions of our own prior decisions of any effect, we generally may not, of course, do the same with portions of statutes. On the other hand, if a cause and prejudice standard does not apply to § 2254(d)(3), we will have uncoupled the statute from the case it was intended to follow, and there will likely be instances where a petitioner will be entitled to an exception from the presumption of correctness but will not be entitled to a hearing. This result does not accord with the evident intent of Congress that the first inquiry track the second. Reconciliation of these two questions is now left to the district courts, who still possess the discretion, which has not been removed by today's opinion, to hold hearings even where they are not mandatory. *See Townsend*, [372 U.S.] at 318.

For these reasons, I think § 2254(d) presumes the continuing validity of our decision in *Townsend*, including the portion of the decision that recognized a "deliberate bypass" exception to a petitioner's right to a hearing where the material facts were not adequately developed in the state court.

Jose Tamayo-Reyes alleges that he pleaded *nolo contendere* to a crime he did not understand. He has exhausted state remedies, has committed no procedural default, has properly presented his claim to a Federal District Court in his first petition for a writ of habeas corpus, and would be entitled to a hearing under the standard set forth in *Townsend*. Given that his claim is properly before the District Court, I would not cut off his right to prove his claim at a hearing. I respectfully dissent.

JUSTICE KENNEDY, dissenting.

By definition, the cases within the ambit of the Court's holding are confined to those in which the factual record developed in the state-court proceedings is inadequate to resolve the legal question. I should think those cases will be few in number. *Townsend v.*

Sain, 372 U.S. 293, 318 (1963), has been the law for almost 30 years and there is no clear evidence that this particular classification of habeas proceedings has burdened the dockets of the federal courts. And in my view, the concept of factual inadequacy comprehends only those petitions with respect to which there is a realistic possibility that an evidentiary hearing will make a difference in the outcome. This serves to narrow the number of cases in a further respect and to ensure that they are the ones, as JUSTICE O'CONNOR points out, in which we have valid concerns with constitutional error.

Our recent decisions in *Coleman v. Thompson*, 501 U.S. 722 (1991), *McCleskey v. Zant*, 499 U.S. 467 (1991), and *Teague v. Lane*, 489 U.S. 288 (1989), serve to protect the integrity of the writ, curbing its abuse and ensuring that the legal questions presented are ones which, if resolved against the State, can invalidate a final judgment. So we consider today only those habeas actions which present questions federal courts are bound to decide in order to protect constitutional rights. We ought not to take steps which diminish the likelihood that those courts will base their legal decision on an accurate assessment of the facts. For these reasons and all those set forth by JUSTICE O'CONNOR, I dissent from the opinion and judgment of the Court.

Notes

1. *Subsequent case history*

Jose Tamayo-Reyes was discharged from custody in November 1993.

2. *Replacing "deliberate bypass" with "cause-and-prejudice"*

In her dissent, Justice O'Connor states that "[u]nder the guise of overruling 'a remnant of a decision' and achieving 'uniformity in the law,' the Court has changed the law of habeas corpus in a fundamental way by effectively overruling cases decided long before *Townsend v. Sain*." In your analysis, what concerns appear to have influenced the Court's decision to replace *Fay* and *Townsend*'s deliberate bypass standard with a cause-and-prejudice analysis?

Antiterrorism and Effective Death Penalty Act § 2254(d)

(d) An application for a writ of habeas corpus on behalf of a person in custody pursuant to the judgment of a State court shall not be granted with respect to any claim that was adjudicated on the merits in State court proceedings unless the adjudication of the claim —

   (1) resulted in a decision that was contrary to, or involved an unreasonable application of, clearly established Federal law, as determined by the Supreme Court of the United States; or

   (2) resulted in a decision that was based on an unreasonable determination of the facts in light of the evidence presented in the State court proceeding.

Discovery: Rule 6 of the Rules Governing § 2254

Rule 6. Discovery

   (a) Leave of court required

   A party shall be entitled to invoke the processes of discovery available under the Federal Rules of Civil Procedure if, and to the extent that, the judge in the exercise of his discretion and for good cause shown grants leave to do so, but not otherwise. If necessary for the effective utilization of discovery procedures, counsel shall be appointed by the judge for a petitioner who qualifies for the appointment of counsel under 18 U.S.C. §3006A(g).

(b) Requests for discovery

Requests for discovery shall be accompanied by a statement of the interrogatories or requests for admission and a list of the documents, if any, sought to be produced.

(c) Expenses

If the respondent is granted leave to take the deposition of the petitioner or any other person the judge may as a condition of taking it direct that the respondent pay the expenses of travel and subsistence and fees of counsel for the petitioner to attend the taking of the deposition.

* * *

Although the analysis of a "right to hearing" and "exhaustion of state remedies" are intertwined, the remainder of this chapter focuses on the question of how the AEDPA impacts a petitioner's right to a hearing. Because the right-to-hearing analysis in *Michael Williams v. Taylor* interweaves with its exhaustion-of-state-remedies analysis, the following excerpt also begins to introduce the concept of exhaustion.

Michael Williams v. Taylor
529 U.S. 420 (2000)

JUSTICE KENNEDY delivered the opinion of the Court.

Petitioner Michael Wayne Williams received a capital sentence for the murders of Morris Keller, Jr., and Keller's wife, Mary Elizabeth. Petitioner later sought a writ of habeas corpus in federal court. Accompanying his petition was a request for an evidentiary hearing on constitutional claims which, he alleged, he had been unable to develop in state-court proceedings. The question in this case is whether 28 U.S.C. §2254(e)(2) (1994 ed., Supp. III), as amended by the Antiterrorism and Effective Death Penalty Act of 1996 (AEDPA), 110 Stat. 1214, bars the evidentiary hearing petitioner seeks. If petitioner "has failed to develop the factual basis of [his] claim[s] in State court proceedings," his case is subject to §2254(e)(2), and he may not receive a hearing because he concedes his inability to satisfy the statute's further stringent conditions for excusing the deficiency.

I

On the evening of February 27, 1993, Verena Lozano James dropped off petitioner and his friend Jeffrey Alan Cruse near a local store in a rural area of Cumberland County, Virginia. The pair planned to rob the store's employees and customers using a .357 revolver petitioner had stolen in the course of a quadruple murder and robbery he had committed two months earlier. Finding the store closed, petitioner and Cruse walked to the Kellers' home. Petitioner was familiar with the couple, having grown up down the road from where they lived. He told Cruse they would have "a couple thousand dollars." ** Cruse, who had been holding the .357, handed the gun to petitioner and knocked on the door. When Mr. Keller opened the door, petitioner pointed the gun at him as the two intruders forced their way inside. Petitioner and Cruse forced Mr.

Keller to the kitchen, where they discovered Mrs. Keller. Petitioner ordered the captives to remove their clothing. While petitioner kept guard on the Kellers, Cruse searched the house for money and other valuables. He found a .38-caliber handgun and bullets. Upon Cruse's return to the kitchen, petitioner had Cruse tie their captives with telephone cords. The Kellers were confined to separate closets while the intruders continued ransacking the house.

When they gathered all they wanted, petitioner and Cruse decided to rape Mrs. Keller. With Mrs. Keller pleading with them not to hurt her or her husband, petitioner raped her. Cruse did the same. Petitioner then ordered the Kellers to shower and dress and "take a walk" with him and Cruse. ** As they were leaving, petitioner told Mrs. Keller he and Cruse were going to burn down the house. Mrs. Keller begged to be allowed to retrieve her marriage license, which she did, guarded by petitioner.

As the prosecution later presented the case, details of the murders were as follows. Petitioner, now carrying the .38, and Cruse, carrying the .357, took the Kellers to a thicket down a dirt road from the house. With petitioner standing behind Mr. Keller and Cruse behind Mrs. Keller, petitioner told Cruse, "We'll shoot at the count of three." ** At the third count, petitioner shot Mr. Keller in the head, and Mr. Keller collapsed to the ground. Cruse did not shoot Mrs. Keller at the same moment. Saying "he didn't want to leave no witnesses," petitioner urged Cruse to shoot Mrs. Keller. ** Cruse fired one shot into her head. Despite his wound, Mr. Keller stood up, but petitioner shot him a second time. To ensure the Kellers were dead, petitioner shot each of them two or three more times.

After returning to the house and loading the stolen property into the Kellers' jeep, petitioner and Cruse set fire to the house and drove the jeep to Fredericksburg, Virginia, where they sold some of the property. They threw the remaining property and the .357 revolver into the Rappahannock River and set fire to the jeep.

***

Petitioner was arrested and charged with robbery, abduction, rape, and the capital murders of the Kellers. At trial in January 1994, Cruse was the Commonwealth's main witness. He recounted the murders as we have just described. Cruse testified petitioner raped Mrs. Keller, shot Mr. Keller at least twice, and shot Mrs. Keller several times after she had been felled by Cruse's bullet. He also described petitioner as the mastermind of the murders. The circumstances of the first plea agreement between the Commonwealth and Cruse and its revocation were disclosed to the jury. ** Testifying on his own behalf, petitioner admitted he was the first to shoot Mr. Keller and it was his idea to rob the store and set fire to the house. He denied, however, raping or shooting Mrs. Keller, and claimed to have shot Mr. Keller only once. Petitioner blamed Cruse for the remaining shots and disputed some other parts of Cruse's testimony.

The jury convicted petitioner on all counts. After considering the aggravating and mitigating evidence presented during the sentencing phase, the jury found the aggravating circumstances of future dangerousness and vileness of the crimes and recommended a death sentence. The trial court imposed the recommended sentence. The Supreme Court of Virginia affirmed petitioner's convictions and sentence, ** and we denied certiorari. ** In a separate proceeding, Cruse pleaded guilty to the capital murder of Mrs. Keller and the first-degree murder of Mr. Keller. After the prosecution asked the sentencing court to spare his life because of his testimony against petitioner, Cruse was sentenced to life imprisonment.

death sentence for double murder

Petitioner filed a habeas petition in state court alleging, in relevant part, that the Commonwealth failed to disclose a second agreement it had reached with Cruse after the first one was revoked. The new agreement, petitioner alleged, was an informal undertaking by the prosecution to recommend a life sentence in exchange for Cruse's testimony. Finding no merit to petitioner's claims, the Virginia Supreme Court dismissed the habeas petition, and we again denied certiorari. **

Petitioner filed a habeas petition in the United States District Court for the Eastern District of Virginia on November 20, 1996. In addition to his claim regarding the alleged undisclosed agreement between the Commonwealth and Cruse, the petition raised three claims relevant to questions now before us. First, petitioner claimed the prosecution had violated *Brady v. Maryland*, 373 U.S. 83 (1963), in failing to disclose a report of a confidential pre-trial psychiatric examination of Cruse. Second, petitioner alleged his trial was rendered unfair by the seating of a juror who at *voir dire* had not revealed possible sources of bias. Finally, petitioner alleged one of the prosecutors committed misconduct in failing to reveal his knowledge of the juror's possible bias.

The District Court granted an evidentiary hearing on the undisclosed agreement and the allegations of juror bias and prosecutorial misconduct but denied a hearing on the psychiatric report. Before the evidentiary hearing could be held, the Commonwealth filed an application for an emergency stay and a petition for a writ of mandamus and prohibition in the Court of Appeals. The Commonwealth argued that petitioner's evidentiary hearing was prohibited by 28 U.S.C. § 2254(e)(2) (1994 ed., Supp. III). A divided panel of the Court of Appeals granted the emergency stay and remanded for the District Court to apply the statute to petitioner's request for an evidentiary hearing. On remand, the District Court vacated its order granting an evidentiary hearing and dismissed the petition, having determined petitioner could not satisfy § 2254(e)(2)'s requirements.

The Court of Appeals affirmed. It first considered petitioner's argument that § 2254(e)(2) did not apply to his case because he had been diligent in attempting to develop his claims in state court. *** The court held, however, that petitioner had not been diligent and so had "failed to develop" in state court the factual bases of his *Brady*, juror bias, and prosecutorial misconduct claims. ** The Court of Appeals concluded petitioner could not satisfy the statute's conditions for excusing his failure to develop the facts and held him barred from receiving an evidentiary hearing. The Court of Appeals ruled in the alternative that, even if § 2254(e)(2) did not apply, petitioner would be ineligible for an evidentiary hearing under the cause and prejudice standard of pre-AEDPA law. **

Addressing petitioner's claim of an undisclosed informal agreement between the Commonwealth and Cruse, the Court of Appeals rejected it on the merits under 28 U.S.C. § 2254(d)(1) and, as a result, did not consider whether § 2254(e)(2) applied. **

On October 18, 1999, petitioner filed an application for stay of execution and a petition for a writ of certiorari. On October 28, we stayed petitioner's execution and granted certiorari to decide whether § 2254(e)(2) precludes him from receiving an evidentiary hearing on his claims. ** We now affirm in part and reverse in part.

II

A

Petitioner filed his federal habeas petition after AEDPA's effective date, so the statute applies to his case. ** The Commonwealth argues AEDPA bars petitioner from receiving an evidentiary hearing on any claim whose factual basis was not developed in state court, absent narrow circumstances not applicable here. Petitioner did not develop, or raise, his claims of juror bias, prosecutorial misconduct, or the prosecution's alleged Brady violation regarding Cruse's psychiatric report until he filed his federal habeas petition. Petitioner explains he could not have developed the claims earlier because he was unaware, through no fault of his own, of the underlying facts. As a consequence, petitioner contends, AEDPA erects no barrier to an evidentiary hearing in federal court.

— didn't raise these 3 claims until federal habeas

Section 2254(e)(2), the provision which controls whether petitioner may receive an evidentiary hearing in federal district court on the claims that were not developed in the Virginia courts, becomes the central point of our analysis. It provides as follows:

> If the applicant has failed to develop the factual basis of a claim in State court proceedings, the court shall not hold an evidentiary hearing on the claim unless the applicant shows that—
>
> (A) the claim relies on —
>
>> (i) a new rule of constitutional law, made retroactive to cases on collateral review by the Supreme Court, that was previously unavailable; or
>>
>> (ii) a factual predicate that could not have been previously discovered through the exercise of due diligence; and
>
> (B) the facts underlying the claim would be sufficient to establish by clear and convincing evidence that but for constitutional error, no reasonable factfinder would have found the applicant guilty of the underlying offense.

By the terms of its opening clause the statute applies only to prisoners who have "failed to develop the factual basis of a claim in State court proceedings." If the prisoner has failed to develop the facts, an evidentiary hearing cannot be granted unless the prisoner's case meets the other conditions of § 2254(e)(2). Here, petitioner concedes his case does not comply with § 2254(e)(2)(B), ** so he may receive an evidentiary hearing only if his claims fall outside the opening clause.

There was no hearing in state court on any of the claims for which petitioner now seeks an evidentiary hearing. That, says the Commonwealth, is the end of the matter. In its view petitioner, whether or not through his own fault or neglect, still "failed to develop the factual basis of a claim in State court proceedings." Petitioner, on the other hand, says the phrase "failed to develop" means lack of diligence in developing the claims, a defalcation he contends did not occur since he made adequate efforts during state-court proceedings to discover and present the underlying facts. The Court of Appeals agreed with petitioner's interpretation of § 2254(e)(2) but believed petitioner had not exercised enough diligence to avoid the statutory bar. ** We agree with petitioner and the Court of Appeals that "failed to develop" implies some lack of diligence; but, unlike the Court of Appeals, we find no lack of diligence on petitioner's part with regard to two of his three claims.

B

We start, as always, with the language of the statute. ** Section 2254(e)(2) begins with a conditional clause, "[i]f the applicant has failed to develop the factual basis of a claim in State court proceedings," which directs attention to the prisoner's efforts in state court. We ask first whether the factual basis was indeed developed in state court, a question susceptible, in the normal course, of a simple yes or no answer. Here the answer is no.

Q1

The Commonwealth would have the analysis begin and end there. Under its no-fault reading of the statute, if there is no factual development in the state court, the federal habeas court may not inquire into the reasons for the default when determining whether the opening clause of §2254(e)(2) applies. We do not agree with the Commonwealth's interpretation of the word "failed."

We do not deny "fail" is sometimes used in a neutral way, not importing fault or want of diligence. So the phrase "We fail to understand his argument" can mean simply "We cannot understand his argument." This is not the sense in which the word "failed" is used here, however.

We give the words of a statute their "'ordinary, contemporary, common meaning,'" absent an indication Congress intended them to bear some different import. ** In its customary and preferred sense, "fail" connotes some omission, fault, or negligence on the part of the person who has failed to do something. ***

Under the opening clause of §2254(e)(2), a failure to develop the factual basis of a claim is not established unless there is lack of diligence, or some greater fault, attributable to the prisoner or the prisoner's counsel. In this we agree with the Court of Appeals and with all other courts of appeals which have addressed the issue. **

Our interpretation of §2254(e)(2)'s opening clause has support in *Keeney v. Tamayo-Reyes*, a case decided four years before AEDPA's enactment. In *Keeney*, a prisoner with little knowledge of English sought an evidentiary hearing in federal court, alleging his *nolo contendere* plea to a manslaughter charge was not knowing and voluntary because of inaccuracies in the translation of the plea proceedings. The prisoner had not developed the facts of his claim in state collateral proceedings, an omission caused by the negligence of his state postconviction counsel. ** The Court characterized this as the "prisoner's failure to develop material facts in state court." ** We required the prisoner to demonstrate cause and prejudice excusing the default before he could receive a hearing on his claim, ** unless the prisoner could "show that a fundamental miscarriage of justice would result from failure to hold a federal evidentiary hearing," **

Section 2254(e)(2)'s initial inquiry into whether "the applicant has failed to develop the factual basis of a claim in State court proceedings" echoes *Keeney* 's language regarding "the state prisoner's failure to develop material facts in state court." In *Keeney*, the Court borrowed the cause and prejudice standard applied to procedurally defaulted claims, ** deciding there was no reason "to distinguish between failing to properly assert a federal claim in state court and failing in state court to properly develop such a claim." ** As is evident from the similarity between the Court's phrasing in *Keeney* and the opening clause of §2254(e)(2), Congress intended to preserve at least one aspect of *Keeney*'s holding: prisoners who are at fault for the deficiency in the state-court record must satisfy a heightened standard to obtain an evidentiary hearing. To be sure, in requiring that prisoners who have not been diligent satisfy §2254(e)(2)'s provisions rather than show cause and prejudice, and in eliminating a freestanding "miscarriage of justice" exception, Congress raised the bar *Keeney* imposed on prisoners who were not diligent in state-court proceedings. Contrary to the Commonwealth's position, however, there is no basis in the text of §2254(e)(2) to believe Congress used "fail" in a different sense than the Court did in *Keeney* or otherwise intended the statute's further, more stringent requirements to control the availability of an evidentiary hearing in a broader class of cases than were covered by *Keeney*'s cause and prejudice standard.

In sum, the opening clause of §2254(e)(2) codifies *Keeney*'s threshold standard of diligence, so that prisoners who would have had to satisfy *Keeney*'s test for excusing the deficiency in the state-court record prior to AEDPA are now controlled by §2254(e)(2). When the words of the Court are used in a later statute governing the same subject matter, it is respectful of Congress and of the Court's own processes to give the words the same meaning in the absence of specific direction to the contrary. **

Interpreting §2254(e)(2) so that "failed" requires lack of diligence or some other fault avoids putting it in needless tension with §2254(d). A prisoner who developed his claim in state court and can prove the state court's decision was "contrary to, or an unreasonable application of, clearly established federal law, as determined by the Supreme Court of the United States," is not barred from obtaining relief by §2254(d)(1). ***

    ***

We are not persuaded by the Commonwealth's further argument that anything less than a no-fault understanding of the opening clause is contrary to AEDPA's purpose to further the principles of comity, finality, and federalism. There is no doubt Congress intended AEDPA to advance these doctrines. Federal habeas corpus principles must inform and shape the historic and still vital relation of mutual respect and common purpose existing between the States and the federal courts. In keeping this delicate balance we have been careful to limit the scope of federal intrusion into state criminal adjudications and to safeguard the States' interest in the integrity of their criminal and collateral proceedings. **

It is consistent with these principles to give effect to Congress' intent to avoid unneeded evidentiary hearings in federal habeas corpus, while recognizing the statute does not equate prisoners who exercise diligence in pursuing their claims with those who do not. Principles of exhaustion are premised upon recognition by Congress and the Court that state judiciaries have the duty and competence to vindicate rights secured by the Constitution in state criminal proceedings. Diligence will require in the usual case that the prisoner, at a minimum, seek an evidentiary hearing in state court in the manner prescribed by state law. "Comity... dictates that when a prisoner alleges that his continued confinement for a state court conviction violates federal law, the state courts should have the first opportunity to review this claim and provide any necessary relief." **

For state courts to have their rightful opportunity to adjudicate federal rights, the prisoner must be diligent in developing the record and presenting, if possible, all claims of constitutional error. If the prisoner fails to do so, himself or herself contributing to the absence of a full and fair adjudication in state court, §2254(e)(2) prohibits an evidentiary hearing to develop the relevant claims in federal court, unless the statute's other stringent requirements are met. Federal courts sitting in habeas are not an alternative forum for trying facts and issues which a prisoner made insufficient effort to pursue in state proceedings. Yet comity is not served by saying a prisoner "has failed to develop the factual basis of a claim" where he was unable to develop his claim in state court despite diligent effort. In that circumstance, an evidentiary hearing is not barred by §2254(e)(2).

III

Now we apply the statutory test. If there has been no lack of diligence at the relevant stages in the state proceedings, the prisoner has not "failed to develop" the facts under §2254(e)(2)'s opening clause, and he will be excused from showing compliance with the balance of the subsection's requirements. We find lack of diligence as to one of the three claims but not as to the other two.

A

[The Court examined the claim that the State violated *Brady v. Maryland* by not disclosing Cruse's psychiatric report.]

As we hold there was a failure to develop the factual basis of this *Brady* claim in state court, we must determine if the requirements in the balance of § 2254(e)(2) are satisfied so that petitioner's failure is excused. Subparagraph (B) of § 2254(e)(2) conditions a hearing upon a showing, by clear and convincing evidence, that no reasonable factfinder would have found petitioner guilty of capital murder but for the alleged constitutional error. Petitioner concedes he cannot make this showing, ** and the case has been presented to us on that premise. For these reasons, we affirm the Court of Appeals' judgment barring an evidentiary hearing on this claim.

B

We conclude petitioner has met the burden of showing he was diligent in efforts to develop the facts supporting his juror bias and prosecutorial misconduct claims in collateral proceedings before the Virginia Supreme Court.

***

The Court of Appeals held state habeas counsel was not diligent because petitioner's investigator on federal habeas discovered the relationships upon interviewing two jurors who referred in passing to Stinnett [who later became the jury foreperson, and who had been divorced from the prosecution's first witness—Deputy Sheriff Claude Meinhard—in 1979] as "Bonnie Meinhard." ** The investigator later confirmed Stinnett's prior marriage to Meinhard by checking Cumberland County's public records. ** We should be surprised, to say the least, if a district court familiar with the standards of trial practice were to hold that in all cases diligent counsel must check public records containing personal information pertaining to each and every juror. Because of Stinnett and Woodson's silence [Woodson was one of the prosecutors, and he had represented Stinnett in her divorce from Meinhard], there was no basis for an investigation into Stinnett's marriage history. Section 2254(e)(2) does not apply to petitioner's related claims of juror bias and prosecutorial misconduct.

We further note the Commonwealth has not argued that petitioner could have sought relief in state court once he discovered the factual bases of these claims some time between appointment of federal habeas counsel on July 2, 1996, and the filing of his federal habeas petition on November 20, 1996. As an indigent, petitioner had 120 days following appointment of state habeas counsel to file a petition with the Virginia Supreme Court. ** State habeas counsel was appointed on August 10, 1995, about a year before petitioner's investigator on federal habeas uncovered the information regarding Stinnett and Woodson. As state postconviction relief was no longer available at the time the facts came to light, it would have been futile for petitioner to return to the Virginia courts. In these circumstances, though the state courts did not have an opportunity to consider the new claims, petitioner cannot be said to have failed to develop them in state court by reason of having neglected to pursue remedies available under Virginia law.

Our analysis should suffice to establish cause for any procedural default petitioner may have committed in not presenting these claims to the Virginia courts in the first instance. Questions regarding the standard for determining the prejudice that petitioner must establish to obtain relief on these claims can be addressed by the Court of Appeals or the District Court in the course of further proceedings. These courts, in light of cases such as *Smith*, [455 U.S. 209], 215 [(1982)] ("[T]he remedy for allegations of juror partiality is a hearing in which the defendant has the opportunity to prove actual bias"), will take due account of the District Court's earlier decision to grant an evidentiary hearing based in part on its belief that "Juror Stinnett deliberately failed to tell the truth on voir dire." **

IV

Petitioner alleges the Commonwealth failed to disclose an informal plea agreement with Cruse. The Court of Appeals rejected this claim on the merits under § 2254(d)(1), so it is unnecessary to reach the question whether § 2254(e)(2) would permit a hearing on the claim.

The judgment of the Court of Appeals is affirmed in part and reversed in part. The case is remanded for further proceedings consistent with this opinion.

It is so ordered.

Notes

1. *Subsequent case history*

On August 22, 2003, Michael Williams was sentenced to life in prison.

2. *Rule 6 of the Discovery Rules Governing Section 2254*

In what way does Rule 6 attempt to balance a restricted, yet flexible, view of habeas corpus?

3. *Definition of "fail"*

Why do you think the Court went to such lengths to define the word "fail" in *Michael Williams v. Taylor*?

4. *Evolution of the Great Writ*

Consider the evolution of the Writ as explained in both Chapter 4 and *Fay v. Noia*, then consider how that history impacted the Court's decision in Michael Williams' case. Did the AEDPA interfere with the historical evolution of the Writ or simply move it along?

Chapter 7

Exhaustion of State Remedies

Not every issue that is cognizable in state court is cognizable in federal court. If a claim is cognizable, exhaustion of state remedies is a prerequisite to consideration of those issues in a habeas proceeding. The theory is that if there has been a violation of federal constitutional law, the state courts should be given the first opportunity to "right the wrong" in the interests of comity. In *Fay v. Noia*, the Supreme Court reviews the historical context of the writ, then evaluates Noia's right to a hearing in federal court by examining whether he has exhausted his claims in state court and, if not, whether he deliberately bypassed the state court proceedings. In its analysis, the concepts of "right to hearing" (*see* Chapter 6, *supra*) and "exhaustion of state remedies" sometimes overlap. In *Rose v. Lundy*, the Court considers the question of what to do with a petition for a writ of habeas corpus that is "mixed," which means that it contains both exhausted and unexhausted claims. In *Granberry v. Greer*, the Court considers whether to draw a bright line rule when the State failed to raise nonexhaustion at its earliest opportunity.

Fay v. Noia
372 U.S. 391(1963)

JUSTICE BRENNAN delivered the opinion of the Court.

This case presents important questions touching the federal habeas corpus jurisdiction, 28 U.S.C. § 2241 *et seq.*, in its relation to state criminal justice. The narrow question is whether the respondent Noia may be granted federal habeas corpus relief from imprisonment under a New York conviction now admitted by the State to rest upon a confession obtained from him in violation of the Fourteenth Amendment, after he was denied state post-conviction relief because the coerced confession claim had been decided against him at the trial and Noia had allowed the time for a direct appeal to lapse without seeking review by a state appellate court.

Noia was convicted in 1942 with Santo Caminito and Frank Bonino in the County Court of Kings County, New York, of a felony murder in the shooting and killing of one Hammeroff during the commission of a robbery. The sole evidence against each defendant was his signed confession. Caminito and Bonino, but not Noia, appealed their convictions to the Appellate Division of the New York Supreme Court. These appeals were unsuccessful, but subsequent legal proceedings resulted in the releases of Caminito and Bonino on findings that their confessions had been coerced and their convictions therefore procured in violation of the Fourteenth Amendment. *** Although it has been stipulated that the coercive nature of Noia's confession was also established, *** the United States District Court for the Southern District of New York held in Noia's federal habeas corpus proceeding that because of his failure to appeal he must be denied

failed to do a direct appeal

he didn't appeal & now wants HC relief

relief under the provision of 28 U.S.C. §2254 whereby "An application for a writ of habeas corpus [on] behalf of a person in custody pursuant to the judgment of a State court shall not be granted unless it appears that the applicant has exhausted the remedies available in the courts of the State." *** The Court of Appeals for the Second Circuit reversed, one judge dissenting, and ordered that Noia's conviction be set aside and that he be discharged from custody unless given a new trial forthwith. ** The Court of Appeals questioned whether §2254 barred relief on federal habeas corpus where the applicant had failed to exhaust state remedies no longer available to him at the time the habeas proceeding was commenced (here a direct appeal from the conviction), but held that in any event exceptional circumstances were present which excused compliance with the section. The court also rejected other arguments advanced in support of the proposition that the federal remedy was unavailable to Noia. ***

We granted certiorari. ** We affirm the judgment of the Court of Appeals but reach that court's result by a different course of reasoning. We hold: (1) Federal courts have power under the federal habeas statute to grant relief despite the applicant's failure to have pursued a state remedy not available to him at the time he applies; the doctrine under which state procedural defaults are held to constitute an adequate and independent state law ground barring direct Supreme Court review is not to be extended to limit the power granted the federal courts under the federal habeas statute. (2) Noia's failure to appeal was not a failure to exhaust "the remedies available in the courts of the State" as required by §2254; that requirement refers only to a failure to exhaust state remedies still open to the applicant at the time he files his application for habeas corpus in the federal court. (3) Noia's failure to appeal cannot under the circumstances be deemed an intelligent and understanding waiver of his right to appeal such as to justify the withholding of federal habeas corpus relief.

I

The question has been much mooted under what circumstances, if any, the failure of a state prisoner to comply with a state procedural requirement, as a result of which the state courts decline to pass on the merits of his federal defense, bars subsequent resort to the federal courts for relief on habeas corpus. *** Plainly it is a question that has important implications for federal-state relations in the area of the administration of criminal justice. It cannot be answered without a preliminary inquiry into the historical development of the writ of habeas corpus.

[The Court then outlined the historical development of the writ. A similar discussion of the history of the writ is included in the introduction to Chapter 4.]

*** Although in form the Great Writ is simply a mode of procedure, its history is inextricably intertwined with the growth of fundamental rights of personal liberty. For its function has been to provide a prompt and efficacious remedy for whatever society deems to be intolerable restraints. Its root principle is that in a civilized society, government must always be accountable to the judiciary for a man's imprisonment: if the imprisonment cannot be shown to conform with the fundamental requirements of law, the individual is entitled to his immediate release. Thus there is nothing novel in the fact that today habeas corpus in the federal courts provides a mode for the redress of denials of due process of law. ***

***

The course of decisions of this Court from *Lange* and *Siebold* to the present makes plain that restraints contrary to our fundamental law, the Constitution, may be challenged on federal habeas corpus even though imposed pursuant to the conviction of a federal court of competent jurisdiction. ***

[The Court continued by explaining more of the historical context of the development of habeas corpus law. Throughout its opinion, the Court also references a case from the 1670s known as "Bushell's Case." Bushell was one of the jurors in the trial of William Penn and William Mead, who were charged with tumultuous assembly and other crimes. The trial was held before the Court of Oyer and Terminer at the Old Bailey. When the jury found the defendants "not guilty," the court ordered the jurors committed for contempt. Bushell sought habeas corpus relief, and the Court of Common Pleas ordered him discharged from custody.]

And so, although almost 300 years have elapsed since *Bushell's Case*, changed conceptions of the kind of criminal proceedings so fundamentally defective as to make imprisonment pursuant to them constitutionally intolerable should not be allowed to obscure the basic continuity in the conception of the writ as the remedy for such imprisonments.

It now remains to consider this principle in the application to the present case. *** Under the conditions of modern society, Noia's imprisonment, under a conviction procured by a confession held by the Court of Appeals in *Caminito v. Murphy* to have been coerced, and which the State here concedes was obtained in violation of the Fourteenth Amendment, is no less intolerable than was Bushell's under the conditions of a very different society; and habeas corpus is no less the appropriate remedy.

II

But, it is argued, a different result is compelled by the exigencies of federalism, which played no role in *Bushell's Case*. We can appraise this argument only in light of the historical accommodation that has been worked out between the state and federal courts respecting the administration of federal habeas corpus. Our starting point is the Judiciary Act of February 5, 1867, c. 28, § 1, 14 Stat. 385–386, which first extended federal habeas corpus to state prisoners generally, and which survives, except for some changes in wording, in the present statutory codification. *** Although the Act of 1867, like its English and American predecessors, nowhere defines habeas corpus, its expansive language and imperative tone, viewed against the background of post-Civil War efforts in Congress to deal severely with the States of the former Confederacy, would seem to make inescapable the conclusion that Congress was enlarging the habeas remedy as previously understood, not only in extending its coverage to state prisoners, but also in making its procedures more efficacious. In 1867, Congress was anticipating resistance to its Reconstruction measures and planning the implementation of the post-war constitutional Amendments. Debated and enacted at the very peak of the Radical Republicans' power, ** the measure that became the Act of 1867 seems plainly to have been designed to furnish a method additional to and independent of direct Supreme Court review of state court decisions for the vindication of the new constitutional guarantees. Congress seems to have had no thought, thus, that a state prisoner should abide state court determination of his constitutional defense—the necessary predicate of direct review by this Court—before resorting to federal habeas corpus. Rather, a remedy almost in the nature of removal from the state to the federal courts of state prisoners' constitutional contentions seems to have been envisaged. ***

The elaborate provisions in the Act for taking testimony and trying the facts anew in habeas hearings *** lend support to this conclusion, as does the legislative history of

House bill No. 605, which became, with slight changes, the Act of February 5, 1867. The bill was introduced in response to a resolution of the House on December 19, 1865, asking the Judiciary Committee to determine "what legislation is necessary to enable the courts of the United States to enforce the freedom of the wives and children of soldiers of the United States *** and also to enforce the liberty of all persons under the operation of the constitutional amendment abolishing slavery." Cong. Globe, 39th Cong., 1st Sess. 87. The terms in which it was described by its proponent, Representative Lawrence of Ohio, leave little doubt of the breadth of its intended scope: "the effect of *** (bill no. 605) is to enlarge the privilege of the writ of [habeas] corpus, and make the jurisdiction of the courts and judges of the United States coextensive with all the powers that can be conferred upon them. It is a bill of the largest liberty." Cong. Globe, 39th Cong., 1st Sess. 4151 (1866). This Court, shortly after the passage of the Act, described it in equally broad terms: "This legislation is of the most comprehensive character. It brings within the habeas corpus jurisdiction of every court and of every judge every possible case of privation of liberty contrary to the National Constitution, treaties, or laws. It is impossible to widen this jurisdiction." *Ex parte McCardle*, 6 Wall. 318, 325–326 (1867).

In thus extending the habeas corpus power of the federal courts evidently to what was conceived to be its constitutional limit, the Act of February 5, 1867, clearly enough portended difficult problems concerning the relationship of the state and federal courts in the area of criminal administration. ***

 ***

 The [Court's prior] decisions fashioned a doctrine of abstention, whereby full play would be allowed the States in the administration of their criminal justice without prejudice to federal rights enwoven in the state proceedings. Thus the Court has frequently held that application for a writ of habeas corpus should have been denied "without prejudice to a renewal of the same after the accused had availed himself of such remedies as the laws of the state afforded." *** *Minnesota v. Brundage*, 180 U.S. 499, 500–501 (1901). ** With refinements, this doctrine requiring the exhaustion of state remedies is now codified in 28 U.S.C. § 2254. *** But its rationale has not changed: "it would be unseemly in our dual system of government for a federal district court to upset a state court conviction without an opportunity to the state courts to correct a constitutional violation. *** Solution was found in the doctrine of comity between courts, a doctrine which teaches that one court should defer action on causes properly within its jurisdiction until the courts of another sovereignty with concurrent powers, and already cognizant of the litigation, have had an opportunity to pass upon the matter." *Darr v. Burford*, 339 U.S. 200, 204 (1950). The rule of exhaustion "is not one defining power but one which relates to the appropriate exercise of power." *Bowen v. Johnston*, 306 U.S. 19, 27 (1939). **

 ***

[The Court next explained how it had not deviated from the general position that after the state courts had decided a federal question on the merits against a habeas petitioner, he could return to the federal court on habeas and there relitigate the question.]

Thus, we have left the weight to be given a particular state court adjudication of a federal claim later pressed on habeas substantially in the discretion of the Federal District Court: "the state adjudication carries the weight that federal practice gives to the conclusion of a court *** of last resort another jurisdiction on federal constitutional issues. It is not res judicata." *Brown v. Allen, supra*, 344 U.S. at 458 (opinion of Justice

Reed). *** (N)o binding weight is to be attached to the State determination. The congressional requirement is greater. The State court cannot have the last say when it, though on fair consideration and what procedurally may be deemed fairness, may have misconceived a federal constitutional right." 344 U.S. at 508 (opinion of Justice Frankfurter). Even if the state court adjudication turns wholly on primary, historical facts, the Federal District Court has a broad power on habeas to hold an evidentiary hearing and determine the facts. *See Brown v. Allen, supra*, 344 U.S. at 478 (opinion of Reed, J.).

The breadth of the federal courts' power of independent adjudication on habeas corpus stems from the very nature of the writ, and conforms with the classic English practice. *** So also, the traditional characterization of the writ of habeas corpus as an original (save perhaps when issued by this Court ***) civil remedy for the enforcement of the right to personal liberty, *** rather than as a stage of the state criminal proceedings or as an appeal therefrom, emphasizes the independence of the federal habeas proceedings from what has gone before. This is not to say that a state criminal judgment resting on a constitutional error is void for all purposes. But conventional notions of finality in criminal litigation cannot be permitted to defeat the manifest federal policy that federal constitutional rights of personal liberty shall not be denied without the fullest opportunity for plenary federal judicial review.

Despite the Court's refusal to give binding weight to state court determinations of the merits in habeas, it has not infrequently suggested that where the state court declines to reach the merits because of a procedural default, the federal courts may be foreclosed from granting the relief sought on habeas corpus. *** But the Court's practice in this area has been far from uniform, *** and even greater divergency has characterized the practice of the lower federal courts. ***

For the present, however, it suffices to note that rarely, if ever, has the Court predicated its deference to state procedural rules on a want of power to entertain a habeas application where a procedural default was committed by the defendant in the state courts. Typically, the Court, like the District Court in the instant case, has approached the problem as an aspect of the rule requiring exhaustion of state remedies, which is not a rule distributing power as between the state and federal courts. *** The point is that the Court, by relying upon a rule of discretion, avowedly flexible, *** yielding always to "exceptional circumstances," *** has refused to concede jurisdictional significance to the abortive state court proceeding.

III

We have reviewed the development of habeas corpus at some length because the question of the instant case has obvious importance to the proper accommodation of a great constitutional privilege and the requirements of the federal system. Our survey discloses nothing to suggest that the Federal District Court lacked the power to order Noia discharged because of a procedural forfeiture he may have incurred under state law. On the contrary, the nature of the writ at common law, the language and purpose of the Act of February 5, 1867, and the course of decisions in this Court extending over nearly a century are wholly irreconcilable with such a limitation. At the time the privilege of the writ was written into the Federal Constitution it was settled that the writ lay to test any restraint contrary to fundamental law, which in England stemmed ultimately from Magna Charta but in this country was embodied in the written Constitution. Congress in 1867 sought to provide a federal forum for state prisoners having constitutional defenses by extending the habeas corpus powers of the federal courts to their constitutional maximum. Obedient to this purpose, we have consistently held that federal court jurisdiction is conferred by the allegation of an unconstitutional restraint and is not defeated by anything that may occur in the state court proceedings. State procedural rules plainly must yield to this overriding federal policy.

A number of arguments are advanced against this conclusion. One, which concedes the breadth of federal habeas power, is that a state prisoner who forfeits his opportunity to vindicate federal defenses in the state court has been given all the process that is constitutionally due him, and hence is not restrained contrary to the Constitution. But this wholly misconceives the scope of due process of law, which comprehends not only the right to be heard but also a number of explicit procedural rights—for example, the right not to be convicted upon evidence which includes one's coerced confession— drawn from the Bill of Rights. ***

*** A defendant by committing a procedural default may be debarred from challenging his conviction in the state courts even on federal constitutional grounds. But a forfeiture of remedies does not legitimize the unconstitutional conduct by which his conviction was procured. Would Noia's failure to appeal have precluded him from bringing an action under the Civil Rights Acts against his inquisitors? The Act of February 5, 1867, like the Civil Rights Acts, was intended to furnish an independent, collateral remedy for certain privations of liberty. *** The very question we face is how completely federal remedies fall with the state remedies; when we have answered this, we shall know in what sense custody may be rendered lawful by a supervening procedural default.

It is a familiar principle that this Court will decline to review state court judgments which rest on independent and adequate state grounds, notwithstanding the co-presence of federal grounds. *See, e.g., N.A.A.C.P. v. Alabama ex rel. Patterson*, 357 U.S. 449 (1958); *Fox Film Corp. v. Muller*, 296 U.S. 207 (1935). *** Thus, a default such as Noia's, if deemed adequate and independent (a question on which we intimate no view), would cut off review by this Court of the state *coram nobis* proceeding in which the New York Court of Appeals refused him relief. It is contended that it follows from this that the remedy of federal habeas corpus is likewise cut off. ***

The fatal weakness of this contention is its failure to recognize that the adequate state-ground rule is a function of the limitations of appellate review. Most of the opinion in the Murdock case is devoted to demonstrating the Court's lack of jurisdiction on direct review to decide questions of state law in cases also raising federal questions. It followed from this holding that if the state question was dispositive of the case, the Court could not decide the federal question. The federal question was moot; nothing turned on its resolution. And so we have held that the adequate state-ground rule is a consequence of the Court's obligation to refrain from rendering advisory opinions or passing upon moot questions.

But while our appellate function is concerned only with the judgments or decrees of state courts, the habeas corpus jurisdiction of the lower federal courts is not so confined. The jurisdictional prerequisite is not the judgment of a state court but detention simpliciter. The entire course of decisions in this Court elaborating the rule of exhaustion of state remedies is wholly incompatible with the proposition that a state court judgment is required to confer federal habeas jurisdiction. And the broad power of the federal courts under 28 U.S.C. § 2243 summarily to hear the application and to "determine the facts, and dispose of the matter as law and justice require," is hardly characteristic of an appellate jurisdiction. Habeas lies to enforce the right of personal liberty; when that right is denied and a person confined, the federal court has the power to release him. Indeed, it has no other power; it cannot revise the state court judgment; it can act only on the body of the petitioner. *In re Medley, Petitioner,* 134 U.S. 160, 173 (1890).

To be sure, this may not be the entire answer to the contention that the adequate state-ground principle should apply to the federal courts on habeas corpus as well as to the Supreme Court on direct review of state judgments. *** For the federal courts to refuse to give effect in habeas proceedings to state procedural defaults might conceivably have some effect upon the States' regulation of their criminal procedures. *** In Noia's case the only relevant substantive law is federal—the Fourteenth Amendment. State law appears only in the procedural framework for adjudicating the substantive federal question. The paramount interest is federal. ** That is not to say that the States have not a substantial interest in exacting compliance with their procedural rules from criminal defendants asserting federal defenses. Of course orderly criminal procedure is a desideratum, and of course there must be sanctions for the flouting of such procedure. But that state interest "competes *** against an ideal *** (the) ideal of fair procedure." Schaefer, *Federalism and State Criminal Procedure*, 70 Harv. L. Rev. 1, 5 (1956). And the only concrete impact the assumption of federal habeas jurisdiction in the face of a procedural default has on the state interest we have described, is that it prevents the State from closing off the convicted defendant's last opportunity to vindicate his constitutional rights, thereby punishing him for his default and deterring others who might commit similar defaults in the future. ***

*** That the Court nevertheless ordinarily gives effect to state procedural grounds may be attributed to considerations which are peculiar to the Court's role and function and have no relevance to habeas corpus proceedings in the Federal District Courts: the unfamiliarity of members of this Court with the minutiae of 50 States' procedures; the inappropriateness of crowding our docket with questions turning wholly on particular state procedures; the web of rules and statutes that circumscribes our appellate jurisdiction; and the inherent and historical limitations of such a jurisdiction.

A practical appraisal of the state interest here involved plainly does not justify the federal courts' enforcing on habeas corpus a doctrine of forfeitures under the guise of applying the adequate state-ground rule. We fully grant, *infra,* that the exigencies of federalism warrant a limitation whereby the federal judge has the discretion to deny relief to one who has deliberately sought to subvert or evade the orderly adjudication of his federal defenses in the state courts. Surely no stricter rule is a realistic necessity. A man under conviction for crime has an obvious inducement to do his very best to keep his state remedies open, and not stake his all on the outcome of a federal habeas proceeding which, in many respects, may be less advantageous to him than a state court proceeding. ** And if because of inadvertence or neglect he runs afoul of a state procedural requirement, and thereby forfeits his state remedies, appellate and collateral, as well as direct review thereof in this Court, those consequences should be sufficient to vindicate the State's valid interest in orderly procedure. Whatever residuum of state interest there may be under such circumstances is manifestly insufficient in the face of the federal policy, drawn from the ancient principles of the writ of habeas corpus, embodied both in the Federal Constitution and in the habeas corpus provisions of the Judicial Code, and consistently upheld by this Court, of affording an effective remedy for restraints contrary to the Constitution. For these several reasons we reject as unsound in principle, as well as not supported by authority, the suggestion that the federal courts are without power to grant habeas relief to an applicant whose federal claims would not be heard on direct review in this Court because of a procedural default furnishing an adequate and independent ground of state decision.

*** Very little support can be found in the long course of previous decisions by this Court elaborating the rule of exhaustion for the proposition that it was regarded at the time of the revision of the Judicial Code as jurisdictional rather than merely as a rule ordering the state and federal proceedings so as to eliminate unnecessary federal-state friction. There is thus no warrant for attributing to Congress, in the teeth of the language of § 2254, intent to work a radical innovation in the law of habeas corpus. We hold that § 2254 is limited in its application to failure to exhaust state remedies still open to the habeas applicant at the time he files his application in federal court. ***

IV

[Noia timely sought and was denied certiorari from the adverse decision of the New York Court of Appeals on his coram nobis application.]

The writ of certiorari, which today provides the usual mode of invoking this Court's appellate jurisdiction of state criminal judgments, "is not a matter of right, but of sound judicial discretion, and will be granted only where there are special and important reasons therefore." Supreme Court Rule 19(1). Review on certiorari therefore does not provide a normal appellate channel in any sense comparable to the writ of error.

***

*** The goal of prompt and fair criminal justice has been impeded because in the overwhelming number of cases the applications for certiorari have been denied for failure to meet the standard of Rule 19. And the demands upon our time in the examination and decision of the large volume of petitions which fail to meet that test have unwarrantably taxed the resources of this Court. Indeed, it has happened that counsel on oral argument has confessed that the record was insufficient to justify our consideration of the case but that he had felt compelled to make the futile time-consuming application in order to qualify for proceeding in a Federal District Court on habeas corpus to make a proper record. *Bullock v. South Carolina*, 365 U.S. 292 (1961). And so in a number of cases the Court has apparently excused compliance with the requirement. ** The same practice has sometimes been followed in the Federal District Courts. ***

Moreover, comity does not demand that such a price in squandered judicial resources be paid; the needs of comity are adequately served in other ways. The requirement that the habeas petitioner exhaust state court remedies available to him when he applies for federal habeas corpus relief gives state courts the opportunity to pass upon and correct errors of federal law in the state prisoner's conviction. And the availability to the States of eventual review on certiorari of such decisions of lower federal courts as may grant relief is always open. Our function of making the ultimate accommodation between state criminal law enforcement and state prisoners' constitutional rights becomes more meaningful when grounded in the full and complete record which the lower federal courts on habeas corpus are in a position to provide.

V

Although we hold that the jurisdiction of the federal courts on habeas corpus is not affected by procedural defaults incurred by the applicant during the state court proceedings, we recognize a limited discretion in the federal judge to deny relief to an applicant under certain circumstances. Discretion is implicit in the statutory command that the judge, after granting the writ and holding a hearing of appropriate scope, "dispose of the matter as law and justice require," 28 U.S.C. § 2243; and discretion was the flexible concept employed by the federal courts in developing the exhaustion rule. Furthermore, habeas corpus has traditionally been regarded as governed by equitable principles. *United States ex rel. Smith. v. Baldi*, 344 U.S. 561, 573 (dissenting opinion) (1953). Among them is the principle that a suitor's conduct in relation to the matter at hand may disentitle him to the relief he seeks. Narrowly circumscribed, in conformity to the historical role of the writ of habeas corpus as an effective and imperative remedy for detentions contrary to fundamental law, the principle is unexceptionable. We therefore hold that the federal habeas judge may in his discretion deny relief to an applicant who has deliberately bypassed the orderly procedure of the state courts and in so doing has forfeited his state court remedies.

But we wish to make very clear that this grant of discretion is not to be interpreted as a permission to introduce legal fictions into federal habeas corpus. The classic definition of waiver enunciated in *Johnson v. Zerbst*, 304 U.S. 458, 464 (1938) — "an intentional relinquishment or abandonment of a known right or privilege" — furnishes the controlling standard. If a habeas applicant, after consultation with competent counsel or otherwise, understandingly and knowingly forewent the privilege of seeking to vindicate his federal claims in the state courts, whether for strategic, tactical, or any other reasons that can fairly be described as the deliberate by-passing of state procedures, then it is open to the federal court on habeas to deny him all relief if the state courts refused to entertain his federal claims on the merits — though of course only after the federal court has satisfied itself, by holding a hearing or by some other means, of the facts bearing upon the applicant's default. *Cf. Price v. Johnston*, 334 U.S. 266, 291 (1948). At all events we wish it clearly understood that the standard here put forth depends on the considered choice of the petitioner. ** A choice made by counsel not participated in by the petitioner does not automatically bar relief. Nor does a state court's finding of waiver bar independent determination of the question by the federal courts on habeas, for waiver affecting federal rights is a federal question. *E.g.*, *Rice v. Olson*, 324 U.S. 786 (1945).

The application of the standard we have adumbrated to the facts of the instant case is not difficult. Under no reasonable view can the State's version of Noia's reason for not appealing support an inference of deliberate by-passing of the state court system. For Noia to have appealed in 1942 would have been to run a substantial risk of electrocution. His was the grisly choice whether to sit content with life imprisonment or to travel the uncertain avenue of appeal which, if successful, might well have led to a retrial and death sentence. *See, e.g., Palko v. Connecticut*, 302 U.S. 319 (1937). He declined to play Russian roulette in this fashion. This was a choice by Noia not to appeal, but under the circumstances it cannot realistically be deemed a merely tactical or strategic litigation step, or in any way a deliberate circumvention of state procedures. This is not to say that in every case where a heavier penalty, even the death penalty, is a risk incurred by taking an appeal or otherwise foregoing a procedural right, waiver as we have defined it cannot be found. Each case must stand on its facts. In the instant case, the language of the judge in sentencing Noia, *** made the risk that Noia, if reconvicted, would be sentenced to death, palpable and indeed unusually acute.

VI

It should be unnecessary to repeat what so often has been said and what so plainly is the case: that the availability of the Great Writ of habeas corpus in the federal courts for persons in the custody of the States offends no legitimate state interest in the enforcement of criminal justice or procedure. Our decision today swings open no prison gates. Today as always few indeed is the number of state prisoners who eventually win their freedom by means of federal habeas corpus. *** Those few who are ultimately successful are persons whom society has grievously wronged and for whom belated liberation is little enough compensation. Surely no fair-minded person will contend that those who have been deprived of their liberty without due process of law ought nevertheless to languish in prison. Noia, no less than his codefendants Caminito and Bonino, is conceded to have been the victim of unconstitutional state action. Noia's case stands on its own; but surely no just and humane legal system can tolerate a result whereby a Caminito and a Bonino are at liberty because their confessions were found to have been coerced yet a Noia, whose confession was also coerced, remains in jail for life. For such anomalies, such affronts to the conscience of a civilized society, habeas corpus is predestined by its historical role in the struggle for personal liberty to be the ultimate remedy. If the States withhold effective remedy, the federal courts have the power and the duty to provide it. Habeas corpus is one of the precious heritages of Anglo-American civilization. We do no more today than confirm its continuing efficacy.

Affirmed.

***

[Dissenting opinion written by JUSTICE HARLAN, joined by JUSTICE CLARK and JUSTICE STEWART, omitted. Dissenting opinion written by JUSTICE CLARK also omitted.]

Notes

1. *Subsequent case history*

Charles Noia was originally convicted in 1942 in Kings County, New York. The Supreme Court granted his writ in 1963 through this case.

2. *Coram nobis*

Coram nobis is an old writ, authorized by the All-Writs Acts (28 U.S.C. § 1651), whereby federal convicts could advance the same claims that they would have otherwise advanced in § 2255 motions. A federal court's power to entertain an application for a writ of *coram nobis* rested on the federal court's original jurisdiction in the criminal prosecution about which the applicant was complaining. Convicts challenging state convictions thus could not seek *coram nobis* relief, but could only pursue a writ of habeas corpus. LARRY YACKLE, FEDERAL COURTS: HABEAS CORPUS 144–45 (Foundation Press: 2003).

3. *Deliberate bypass*

In articulating the deliberate bypass standard (also discussed in Chapter 6, *supra*), Justice Brennan underscored the importance of the petitioner's participation in deciding whether to bypass filing federal claims in state court: "At all events we wish it clearly understood that the standard here put forth depends on the considered choice of the petitioner. A choice made by counsel not participated in by the petitioner does not automatically bar relief." On a practical level, how would a federal court decide whether a petitioner had knowingly decided to bypass filing his federal claims in state court and/or whether the petitioner was merely "sandbagging" those claims in the event his first petition failed?

4. *The overlap of "exhaustion" and "right to a hearing"*

How is the concept of "exhaustion" intertwined with the concept of "right to a hearing"?

5. McCleskey v. Zant *comments on* Fay

Nearly thirty years after *Fay v. Noia*, the Court observed the following in *Mc-Cleskey v. Zant*, 499 U.S. 467, 499 (1991): "The *Fay* standard was based on a conception of federal/state relations that undervalued the important interest in finality served by state procedural rules and the significant harm to the States that results from the failure of the federal courts to respect them." What is your assessment of this statement?

Rose v. Lundy ✓
455 U.S. 509 (1982)

JUSTICE O'CONNOR delivered the opinion of the Court, except as to Part III-C.

In this case we consider whether the exhaustion rule in 28 U.S.C. §§ 2254(b), (c) requires a federal district court to dismiss a petition for a writ of habeas corpus containing any claims that have not been exhausted in the state courts. Because a rule requiring exhaustion of all claims furthers the purposes underlying the habeas statute, we hold that a district court must dismiss such "mixed petitions," leaving the prisoner with the choice of returning to state court to exhaust his claims or of amending or resubmitting the habeas petition to present only exhausted claims to the district court.

H

I

Following a jury trial, respondent Noah Lundy was convicted on charges of rape and crime against nature, and sentenced to the Tennessee State Penitentiary. *** After the Tennessee Court of Criminal Appeals affirmed the convictions and the Tennessee Supreme Court denied review, the respondent filed an unsuccessful petition for post-conviction relief in the Knox County Criminal Court.

The respondent subsequently filed a petition in Federal District Court for a writ of habeas corpus under 28 U.S.C. § 2254, alleging four grounds for relief: (1) that he had been denied the right to confrontation because the trial court limited the defense counsel's questioning of the victim; (2) that he had been denied the right to a fair trial because the prosecuting attorney stated that the respondent had a violent character; (3) that he had been denied the right to a fair trial because the prosecutor improperly remarked in his closing argument that the State's evidence was uncontradicted; and (4) that the trial judge improperly instructed the jury that every witness is presumed to swear the truth. After reviewing the state-court records, however, the District Court concluded that it could not consider claims three and four "in the constitutional framework" because the respondent had not exhausted his state remedies for those grounds. The court nevertheless stated that "in assessing the atmosphere of the cause taken as a whole these items may be referred to collaterally." ***

Apparently in an effort to assess the "atmosphere" of the trial, the District Court reviewed the state trial transcript and identified 10 instances of prosecutorial misconduct, only five of which the respondent had raised before the state courts. *** In addition, although purportedly not ruling on the respondent's fourth ground for relief—that the state trial judge improperly charged that "every witness is presumed to swear the truth"—the court nonetheless held that the jury instruction, coupled with both the restriction of counsel's cross-examination of the victim and the prosecutor's "personal testimony" on the weight of the State's evidence, ** violated the respondent's right to a fair trial. In conclusion, the District Court stated:

***

> ...Under the charge as given, the limitation of cross examination of the victim, and the flagrant prosecutorial misconduct[,] this court is compelled to find that petitioner did not receive a fair trial, his Sixth Amendment rights were violated and the jury poisoned by the prosecutorial misconduct. ***

In short, the District Court considered several instances of prosecutorial misconduct never challenged in the state trial or appellate courts, or even raised in the respondent's habeas petition.

The Sixth Circuit affirmed the judgment of the District Court, ** concluding in an unreported order that the court properly found that the respondent's constitutional rights had been "seriously impaired by the improper limitation of his counsel's cross-examination of the prosecutrix and by the prosecutorial misconduct." The court specifically rejected the State's argument that the District Court should have dismissed the petition because it included both exhausted and unexhausted claims.

II

The petitioner urges this Court to apply a "total exhaustion" rule requiring district courts to dismiss every habeas corpus petition that contains both exhausted and unexhausted claims. *** The petitioner argues at length that such a rule furthers the policy of comity underlying the exhaustion doctrine because it gives the state courts the first opportunity to correct federal constitutional errors and minimizes federal interference and disruption of state judicial proceedings. The petitioner also believes that uniform adherence to a total exhaustion rule reduces the amount of piecemeal habeas litigation.

Under the petitioner's approach, a district court would dismiss a petition containing both exhausted and unexhausted claims, giving the prisoner the choice of returning to state court to litigate his unexhausted claims, or of proceeding with only his exhausted claims in federal court. The petitioner believes that a prisoner would be reluctant to choose the latter route since a district court could, in appropriate circumstances under Habeas Corpus Rule 9(b), dismiss subsequent federal habeas petitions as an abuse of the writ. *** In other words, if the prisoner amended the petition to delete the unexhausted claims or immediately refiled in federal court a petition alleging only his exhausted claims, he could lose the opportunity to litigate his presently unexhausted claims in federal court. This argument is address in Part III-C of this opinion.

In order to evaluate the merits of the petitioner's arguments, we turn to the habeas statute, its legislative history, and the policies underlying the exhaustion doctrine.

III
A

The exhaustion doctrine existed long before its codification by Congress in 1948. In *Ex parte Royall*, 117 U.S. 241, 251 (1886), this Court wrote that as a matter of comity, federal courts should not consider a claim in a habeas corpus petition until after the state courts have had an opportunity to act. ***

Subsequent cases refined the principle that state remedies must be exhausted except in unusual circumstances. *See, e.g., United States ex rel. Kennedy v. Tyler*, 269 U.S. 13, 17–19 (1925) (holding that the lower court should have dismissed the petition because none of the questions had been raised in the state courts ***). In *Ex parte Hawk*, 321 U.S. 114, 117 (1944), this Court reiterated that comity was the basis for the exhaustion doctrine. *** None of these cases, however, specifically applied the exhaustion doctrine to habeas petitions containing both exhausted and unexhausted claims.

In 1948, Congress codified the exhaustion doctrine in 28 U.S.C. §2254, citing *Ex parte Hawk* as correctly stating the principle of exhaustion. *** Because the legislative history of §2254, as well as the pre-1948 cases, contains no reference to the problem of mixed petitions, *** in all likelihood Congress never thought of this problem. *** Consequently, we must analyze the policies underlying the statutory provision to determine its proper scope. ***

B

The exhaustion doctrine is principally designed to protect the state courts' role in the enforcement of federal law and prevent disruption of state judicial proceedings. *** Under our federal system, the federal and state "courts [are] equally bound to guard and protect rights secured by the Constitution." *Ex parte Royall*, 117 U.S. at 251. Because "it would be unseemly in our dual system of government for a federal district court to upset a state court conviction without an opportunity to the state courts to correct a constitutional violation," federal courts apply the doctrine of comity, which "teaches that one court should defer action on causes properly within its jurisdiction until the courts of another sovereignty with concurrent powers, and already cognizant of the litigation, have had an opportunity to pass upon the matter." *Darr v. Burford*, 339 U.S. 200, 204 (1950). ***

A rigorously enforced total exhaustion rule will encourage state prisoners to seek full relief first from the state courts, thus giving those courts the first opportunity to review all claims of constitutional error. As the number of prisoners who exhaust all of their federal claims increases, state courts may become increasingly familiar with and hospitable toward federal constitutional issues. ** Equally as important, federal claims that have been fully exhausted in state courts will more often be accompanied by a complete factual record to aid the federal courts in their review. *Cf.* 28 U.S.C. §2254(d) (requiring a federal court reviewing a habeas petition to presume as correct factual findings made by a state court).

The facts of the present case underscore the need for a rule encouraging exhaustion of all federal claims. In his opinion, the District Court Judge wrote that "there is such mixture of violations that one cannot be separated from and considered independently of the others." Because the two unexhausted claims for relief were intertwined with the exhausted ones, the judge apparently considered all of the claims in ruling on the petition. Requiring dismissal of petitions containing both exhausted and unexhausted claims will relieve the district courts of the difficult if not impossible task of deciding when claims are related, and will reduce the temptation to consider unexhausted claims. ***

Rather than an "adventure in unnecessary lawmaking" (STEVENS, J., *post*), our holdings today reflect our interpretation of a federal statute on the basis of its language and legislative history, and consistent with its underlying policies. *** [O]ur interpretation of §§2254(b), (c) provides a simple and clear instruction to potential litigants: before you bring any claims to federal court, be sure that you first have taken each one to state court. Just as *pro se* petitioners have managed to use the federal habeas machinery, so too should they be able to master this straightforward exhaustion requirement. Those prisoners who misunderstand this requirement and submit mixed petitions nevertheless are entitled to resubmit a petition with only exhausted claims or to exhaust the remainder of their claims.

Rather than increasing the burden on federal courts, strict enforcement of the exhaustion requirement will encourage habeas petitioners to exhaust all of their claims in state court and to present the federal court with a single habeas petition. To the extent that the exhaustion requirement reduces piecemeal litigation, both the courts and the prisoners should benefit, for as a result the district court will be more likely to review all of the prisoner's claims in a single proceeding, thus providing for a more focused and thorough review.

C

The prisoner's principal interest, of course, is in obtaining speedy federal relief on his claims. ** A total exhaustion rule will not impair that interest since he can always amend the petition to delete the unexhausted claims, rather than returning to state court to exhaust all of his claims. By invoking this procedure, however, the prisoner would risk forfeiting consideration of his unexhausted claims in federal court. *** [A] prisoner who decides to proceed only with his exhausted claims and deliberately sets aside his unexhausted claims risks dismissal of subsequent federal petitions.

IV

In sum, because a total exhaustion rule promotes comity and does not unreasonably impair the prisoner's right to relief, we hold that a district court must dismiss habeas petitions containing both exhausted and unexhausted claims. *** Accordingly, the judgment of the Court of Appeals is reversed, and the case is remanded for proceedings consistent with this opinion.

It is so ordered.

JUSTICE BLACKMUN, concurring in the judgment.

The important issue before the Court in this case is whether the conservative "total exhaustion" rule espoused now by two Courts of Appeals, the Fifth and the Ninth Circuits, *see ante*, is required by 28 U.S.C. §§ 2254(b) and (c), or whether the approach adopted by eight other Courts of Appeals—that a district court may review the *exhausted* claims of a mixed petition—is the proper interpretation of the statute. On this basic issue, I firmly agree with the majority of the Courts of Appeals.

I do not dispute the value of comity when it is applicable and productive of harmony between state and federal courts, nor do I deny the principle of exhaustion that §§ 2254(b) and (c) so clearly embrace. What troubles me is that the "total exhaustion" rule, now adopted by this Court, can be read into the statute, as the Court concedes, *ante*, only by sheer force; that it operates as a trap for the uneducated and indigent pro se prisoner-applicant; that it delays the resolution of claims that are not frivolous; and that it tends to increase, rather than to alleviate, the caseload burdens on both state and federal courts. To use the old expression, the Court's ruling seems to me to "throw the baby out with the bath water."

***

I therefore would remand the case, directing that the courts below dismiss respondent's unexhausted claims and examine those that have been properly presented to the state courts in order to determine whether they are interrelated with the unexhausted grounds and, if not, whether they warrant collateral relief.

JUSTICE BRENNAN, with whom JUSTICE MARSHALL joins, concurring in part and dissenting in part.

I join the opinion of the Court (Parts I, II, III-A, III-B, and IV, *ante*), but I do not join in the opinion of the plurality (Part III-C, *ante*). I agree with the Court's holding that the exhaustion requirement of 28 U.S.C. §§ 2254(b), (c) obliges a federal district court to dismiss, without consideration on the merits, a habeas corpus petition from a state prisoner when that petition contains claims that have not been exhausted in the state courts, "leaving the prisoner with the choice of returning to state court to exhaust his claims or of amending or resubmitting the habeas petition to present only exhausted claims to the district court." *Ante*. But I disagree with the plurality's view, in Part III-C, that a habeas petitioner must "risk forfeiting consideration of his unexhausted claims in federal court" if he "decides to proceed only with his exhausted claims and deliberately sets aside his unexhausted claims" in the face of the district court's refusal to consider his "mixed" petition. *Ante*. The issue of Rule 9(b)'s proper application to successive petitions brought as the result of our decision today is not before us—it was not among the questions presented by petitioner, nor was it briefed and argued by the parties. Therefore, the issue should not be addressed until we have a case presenting it. In any event, I disagree with the plurality's proposed disposition of the issue. In my view, Rule 9(b) cannot be read to permit dismissal of a subsequent petition under the circumstances described in the plurality's opinion.

***

I conclude that when a prisoner's original, "mixed" habeas petition is dismissed without any examination of its claims on the merits, and when the prisoner later brings a second petition based on the previously unexhausted claims that had earlier been refused a hearing, then the remedy of dismissal for "abuse of the writ" cannot be employed against that second petition, absent unusual factual circumstances truly suggesting abuse. This conclusion is to my mind inescapably compelled not only by *Sanders [v. United States*, 373 U.S. 1 (1963)], but also by the Advisory Committee explanation of the Rule, and by Congress' subsequent incorporation of the higher, "abusive" standard into the Rule. The plurality's conclusion, in contrast, has no support whatever from any of these sources. Nor, of course, does it have the support of a majority of the Court.

[JUSTICE WHITE rejected the plurality's conclusion in Part III-C, as did JUSTICE BLACKMUN. JUSTICE STEVENS did not reach this issue.]

JUSTICE WHITE, concurring in part and dissenting in part.

I agree with most of JUSTICE BRENNAN's opinion; but like JUSTICE BLACKMUN, I would not require a "mixed" petition to be dismissed in its entirety, with leave to resubmit the exhausted claims. The trial judge cannot rule on the unexhausted issues and should dismiss them. But he should rule on the exhausted claims unless they are intertwined with those he must dismiss or unless the habeas petitioner prefers to have his entire petition dismissed. In any event, if the judge rules on those issues that are ripe and dismisses those that are not, I would not tax the petitioner with abuse of the writ if he returns with the latter claims after seeking state relief.

JUSTICE STEVENS, dissenting.

This case raises important questions about the authority of federal judges. In my opinion the District Judge properly exercised his statutory duty to consider the merits of the claims advanced by respondent that previously had been rejected by the Tennessee courts. The District Judge exceeded, however, what I regard as proper restraints on the scope of collateral review of state-court judgments. Ironically, instead of correcting his error, the Court today fashions a new rule of law that will merely delay the final disposition of this case and, as JUSTICE BLACKMUN demonstrates, impose unnecessary burdens on both state and federal judges.

***

I

***

In my opinion claims of constitutional error are not fungible. There are at least four types. The one most frequently encountered is a claim that attaches a constitutional label to a set of facts that does not disclose a violation of any constitutional right. In my opinion, each of the four claims asserted in this case falls in that category. The second class includes constitutional violations that are not of sufficient import in a particular case to justify reversal even on direct appeal, when the evidence is still fresh and a fair retrial could be promptly conducted. ** A third category includes errors that are important enough to require reversal on direct appeal but do not reveal the kind of fundamental unfairness to the accused that will support a collateral attack on a final judgment. *See, e.g., Stone v. Powell*, 428 U.S. 465 [(1976)]. *** The fourth category includes those errors that are so fundamental that they infect the validity of the underlying judgment itself, or the integrity of the process by which that judgment was obtained. This category cannot be defined precisely; concepts of "fundamental fairness" are not frozen in time. But the kind of error that falls in this category is best illustrated by recalling the classic grounds for the issuance of a writ of habeas corpus—that the proceeding was dominated by mob violence; *** that the prosecutor knowingly made use of perjured testimony; *** or that the conviction was based on a confession extorted from the defendant by brutal methods. *** Errors of this kind justify collateral relief no matter how long a judgment may have been final *** and even though they may not have been preserved properly in the original trial. ***

***

If my appraisal of respondent's exhausted claims is incorrect—if the trial actually was fundamentally unfair to the respondent—postponing relief until another round of review in the state and federal judicial systems has been completed is truly outrageous. The unnecessary delay will make it more difficult for the prosecutor to obtain a conviction on retrial if respondent is in fact guilty; if he is innocent, requiring him to languish in jail because he made a pleading error is callous indeed.

There are some situations in which a district judge should refuse to entertain a mixed petition until all of the prisoner's claims have been exhausted. If the unexhausted claim appears to involve error of the most serious kind and if it is reasonably clear that the exhausted claims do not, addressing the merits of the exhausted claims will merely delay the ultimate disposition of the case. Or if an evidentiary hearing is necessary to decide the merits of both the exhausted and unexhausted claims, a procedure that enables all fact questions to be resolved in the same hearing should be followed. I therefore would allow district judges to exercise discretion to determine whether the presence of an unexhausted claim in a habeas corpus application makes it inappropriate to consider the merits of a properly pleaded exhaustion claim. The inflexible, mechanical rule the Court adopts today arbitrarily denies district judges the kind of authority they need to administer their calendars effectively. ***

II

In recent years federal judges at times have lost sight of the true office of the great writ of habeas corpus. *** The writ of habeas corpus is a fundamental guarantee of liberty. ***

The fact that federal judges have at times construed their power to issue writs of habeas corpus as though it were tantamount to the authority of an appellate court considering a direct appeal from a trial court judgment has had two unfortunate consequences. First, it has encouraged prisoners to file an ever-increasing volume of federal applications that often amount to little more than a request for further review of asserted grounds for reversal that already have been adequately considered and rejected on direct review. Second, it has led this Court into the business of creating special procedural rules for dealing with this floodgate of litigation. The doctrine of nonretroactivity, the emerging "cause and prejudice" doctrine, and today's "total exhaustion" rule are examples of judicial lawmaking that might well have been avoided by confining the availability of habeas corpus relief to cases that truly involve fundamental unfairness.

When that high standard is met, there should be no question about the retroactivity of the constitutional rule being enforced. Nor do I believe there is any need to fashion definitions of "cause" and "prejudice" to determine whether an error that was not preserved at trial or on direct appeal is subject to review in a collateral federal proceeding. *** The availability of habeas corpus relief should depend primarily on the character of the alleged constitutional violation and not on the procedural history underlying the claim. ***

The "total exhaustion" rule the Court crafts today demeans the high office of the great writ. Perhaps a rule of this kind would be an appropriate response to a flood of litigation requesting review of minor disputes. An assumption that most of these petitions are groundless might be thought to justify technical pleading requirements that would provide a mechanism for reducing the sheer number of cases in which the merits must be considered. But the Court's experience has taught us not only that most of these petitions lack merit, but also that there are cases in which serious injustice must be corrected by the issuance of the writ. *** In such cases, the statutory requirement that adequate state remedies be exhausted must, of course, be honored. When a person's liberty is at stake, however, there surely is no justification for the creation of needless procedural hurdles. ***

Procedural regularity is a matter of fundamental importance in the administration of justice. But procedural niceties that merely complicate and delay the resolution of disputes are another matter. In my opinion the federal habeas corpus statute should be construed to protect the former and, whenever possible, to avoid the latter.

I respectfully dissent.

Notes

1. *Subsequent case history*

As noted in the Court's decision, Noah Lundy was sentenced to consecutive terms of 120 years on the rape charge and from 5 to 15 years on the crime against nature charge. *Rose v. Lundy*, 455 U.S. 509, 510 n.1 (1982).

2. *Delaying final disposition and burdening judges*

In his dissenting opinion, Justice Stevens states, "[T]he Court today fashions a new rule of law that will merely delay the final disposition of this case and…impose unnecessary burdens on both state and federal judges." Has Justice Stevens' prediction come true?

3. *Finality*

One of the complaints about federal habeas review of state convictions is the lack of finality and the length of time the case remains "open." How might the *Rose v. Lundy* decision impact these concerns?

4. *"Fairly presenting" federal claims to state courts*

For the purposes of exhausting all available state court remedies to seek federal habeas relief, does a state prisoner "fairly present" his federal claims to a state appellate court when his petition to that court asserts that he received ineffective assistance of both trial and appellate counsel, that his imprisonment was in violation of state law, and that his *trial* counsel's conduct violated several provisions of the federal Constitution—without asserting that his separate *appellate* "ineffective assistance" claim violated federal law?

Would your opinion change if his petition to the state supreme court did not itself alert that court about the federal nature of the appellate "ineffective assistance" claim, but the state supreme court had the opportunity to read the lower state court decision claimed to be in error before deciding whether to grant discretionary review, and *had they read the opinion of the lower state trial court*, the justices would have, or should have, realized that defendant's claim rested upon federal law?

See Baldwin v. Reese, ___ U.S. ___, 124 S.Ct. 1347 (2004) (ordinarily a state prisoner does not "fairly present" a claim to a state court if that court must read beyond a petition or a brief (or a similar document) that does not alert it to the presence of a federal claim in order to find material, such as a lower court opinion in the case, that does so).

Granberry v. Greer
481 U.S. 129 (1987)

JUSTICE STEVENS delivered the opinion of the Court.

Petitioner, a state prisoner, applied to the District Court for the Southern District of Illinois for a writ of habeas corpus pursuant to 28 U.S.C. § 2254. The Magistrate to whom the District Court referred the case ordered the State of Illinois to file an answer; the State instead filed a motion to dismiss under Rule 12(b)(6) of the Federal Rules of Civil Procedure, arguing that the petition failed to state a claim upon which relief could be granted. The District Court adopted the Magistrate's recommendation and dismissed the petition on the merits. When petitioner appealed to the Court of Appeals for the Seventh Circuit, respondent for the first time interposed the defense that petitioner had not exhausted his state remedies. *** In response, petitioner contended that the State had waived that defense by failing to raise it in the District Court. The Court of Appeals rejected the waiver argument and remanded the cause to the District Court with instructions to dismiss without prejudice. ** Because the Courts of Appeals have given different answers to the question whether the State's failure to raise nonexhaustion in the district court constitutes a waiver of that defense in the court of appeals, *** we granted certiorari. **

How an appellate court ought to handle a nonexhausted habeas petition when the State has not raised this objection in the district court is a question that might be answered in three different ways. We might treat the State's silence on the matter as a procedural default precluding the State from raising the issue on appeal. *** At the other extreme, we might treat nonexhaustion as an inflexible bar to consideration of the merits of the petition by the federal court, and therefore require that a petition be dismissed when it appears that there has been a failure to exhaust. *** Or, third, we might adopt an intermediate approach and direct the courts of appeals to exercise discretion in each case to decide whether the administration of justice would be better served by insisting on exhaustion or by reaching the merits of the petition forthwith.

We have already decided that the failure to exhaust state remedies does not deprive an appellate court of jurisdiction to consider the merits of a habeas corpus application. *See Strickland v. Washington*, 466 U.S. 668, 684 (1984) (citing *Rose v. Lundy*, 455 U.S. 509, 515–520 (1982)). ** As the *Strickland* case demonstrates, there are some cases in which it is appropriate for an appellate court to address the merits of a habeas corpus petition notwithstanding the lack of complete exhaustion. Although there is a strong presumption in favor of requiring the prisoner to pursue his available state remedies, his failure to do so is not an absolute bar to appellate consideration of his claims.

We have also expressed our reluctance to adopt rules that allow a party to withhold raising a defense until after the "main event" — in this case, the proceeding in the District Court — is over. *See Wainwright v. Sykes*, 433 U.S. 72, 89–90 (1977). Although the record indicates that the State's failure to raise the nonexhaustion defense in this case was the result of inadvertence, ** rather than a matter of tactics, it seems unwise to adopt a rule that would permit, and might even encourage, the State to seek a favorable ruling on the merits in the district court while holding the exhaustion defense in reserve for use on appeal if necessary. If the habeas petition is meritorious, such a rule would prolong the prisoner's confinement for no other reason than the State's postponement of the exhaustion defense to the appellate level. *** Moreover, if the court of appeals is convinced that the petition has no merit, a belated application of the exhaustion rule might simply require useless litigation in the state courts.

We are not persuaded by either of the extreme positions. The appellate court is not required to dismiss for nonexhaustion notwithstanding the State's failure to raise it, and the court is not obligated to regard the State's omission as an absolute waiver of the claim. Instead, we think the history of the exhaustion doctrine, as recently reviewed in *Rose v. Lundy*, 455 U.S. 509 (1982), points in the direction of a middle course. ***

When the State answers a habeas corpus petition, it has a duty to advise the district court whether the prisoner has, in fact, exhausted all available state remedies. ** As this case demonstrates, however, there are exceptional cases in which the State fails, whether inadvertently or otherwise, to raise an arguably meritorious nonexhaustion defense. The State's omission in such a case makes it appropriate for the court of appeals to take a fresh look at the issue. The court should determine whether the interests of comity and federalism will be better served by addressing the merits forthwith or by requiring a series of additional state and district court proceedings before reviewing the merits of the petitioner's claim.

If, for example, the case presents an issue on which an unresolved question of fact or of state law might have an important bearing, both comity and judicial efficiency may make it appropriate for the court to insist on complete exhaustion to make sure that it may ultimately review the issue on a fully informed basis. On the other hand, if it is perfectly clear that the applicant does not raise even a colorable federal claim, the interests of the petitioner, the warden, the state attorney general, the state courts, and the federal courts will all be well served even if the State fails to raise the exhaustion defense, the district court denies the habeas petition, and the court of appeals affirms the judgment of the district court forthwith. **

Conversely, if a full trial has been held in the district court and it is evident that a miscarriage of justice has occurred, it may also be appropriate for the court of appeals to hold that the nonexhaustion defense has been waived in order to avoid unnecessary delay in granting relief that is plainly warranted. ***

In this case the Court of Appeals simply held that the nonexhaustion defense could not be waived, and made no attempt to determine whether the interests of justice would be better served by addressing the merits of the habeas petition or by requiring additional state proceedings before doing so. Accordingly, we vacate the judgment of the Court of Appeals and remand the case for further proceedings consistent with this opinion. ***

It is so ordered.

Notes

1. *Subsequent case history*

Waldo Granberry is serving a sentence of life in prison without the possibility of parole. *See* http://www.idoc.state.il.us.

2. *Reasons to require exhaustion*

In *Granberry v. Greer*, the Court discusses the reasons to require exhaustion of claims. What is the importance of those reasons? What if one of the claims is that there was no "court" before which to bring the non-exhausted claims? For example, in Virginia, a defendant has only 21 days after conviction to present newly discovered evidence to the state courts. If *Brady* material is discovered later than 21 days after conviction, how can the defendant exhaust his or her claims?

3. *The effect of bedrock constitutional violations on exhaustion*

Should exhaustion be unnecessary when there is a bedrock constitutional violation, such as denial of counsel? What would be the advantages and disadvantages of such an exception?

Chapter 8

When Is a Case Retroactive?

Retroactivity plays an especially important role in habeas jurisprudence. In *Griffith v. Kentucky*, 479 U.S. 314 (1987), the Court considered where to draw the line between when a new rule affecting criminal prosecutions applies retroactively and when it does not. The issue in *Griffith* revolved around the holding in *Batson v. Kentucky*, 476 U.S. 79 (1986), which held that a defendant in a state criminal trial could establish a prima facie case of racial discrimination based on the prosecution's use of peremptory challenges to strike members of the defendant's race from the jury venire. Once the defendant has made a prima facie showing, the burden shifts to the prosecution to come forward with a neutral explanation for those challenges. The defendants in *Griffith* had cases with *Batson* issues in them pending on direct appeal at the time the Court decided *Batson*. The Court held that the new rule applied to any case that was not final on direct appeal at the time the new rule was announced. This meant that a case that was in state post-conviction or federal habeas review would not be able to take advantage of the new rule.

In *Yates v. Aiken*, 484 U.S. 211 (1988), which was decided before the AEDPA, the Court examined whether a case is a new rule for purposes of retroactivity analysis if the rule the case announces derives from a well-settled constitutional principle. In another pre-AEDPA decision, *Teague v. Lane*, 489 U.S. 288 (1989), the Court held that the petitioner could not have the benefit of the ruling in *Batson v. Kentucky* because the petitioner's case was on collateral review at the time *Batson* was announced. The AEDPA essentially codifies the rule announced in *Teague*.

Yates v. Aiken
484 U.S. 211 (1988)

JUSTICE STEVENS delivered the opinion of the Court.

Petitioner and an accomplice robbed a country store in South Carolina in 1981. After petitioner left the store, a fight occurred in which the accomplice and the storekeeper's mother were both killed. Petitioner was convicted of murder and armed robbery and sentenced to death. His conviction and sentence were affirmed by the South Carolina Supreme Court in 1982. **

At his trial, petitioner testified that the victim had not even entered the store before he left and that he had not intended to kill or to harm anyone. The jury, however, was instructed "that malice is implied or presumed from the use of a deadly weapon." *** A few months after petitioner's conviction was affirmed, the South Carolina Supreme Court held that it was error to give such an instruction. ** Thereafter, petitioner sought a writ of habeas corpus from the South Carolina Supreme Court, arguing that the burden-shifting instruction given at his trial was unconstitutional under the state court's reasoning in *Elmore* and under our decision in *Sandstrom v. Montana*, 442 U.S. 510

(1979). While the application for habeas corpus was pending, we decided another case involving a burden-shifting instruction, *Francis v. Franklin*, 471 U.S. 307 (1985), and petitioner promptly called that decision to the attention of the State Supreme Court. The court denied the writ without opinion.

Petitioner then sought a writ of certiorari in this Court. We summarily vacated the judgment of the South Carolina Supreme Court and remanded the case "for further consideration in light of *Francis v. Franklin*." *Yates v. Aiken*, 474 U.S. 896 (1985). On remand, the state court determined that the jury instruction at petitioner's trial "suffered from the same infirmities present in *Elmore* and addressed in *Francis v. Franklin*." ** Nevertheless, the court held that petitioner was not entitled to relief. As an explanation for its holding, the court stated that its decision in *Elmore* should not be applied retroactively to invalidate a conviction that was final when *Elmore* was decided. The opinion did not consider whether the decision in *Francis v. Franklin* might apply retroactively and also did not discuss our decision in *Sandstrom v. Montana*, on which petitioner had relied.

In dissent, Justice Finney reasoned that *Elmore* and *Francis v. Franklin* should be applied retroactively because an instruction that shifts the burden of proof on an element of the offense—particularly in a capital case—substantially impairs the truth-finding function of the jury. Moreover, he reasoned, given our decision in *Sandstrom v. Montana* in 1979, the case did not represent a significant change in the law. ***

We granted certiorari because we were concerned that the South Carolina Supreme Court had not fully complied with our mandate. ** We now reverse.

I

Our order remanding the case for further consideration in the light of *Francis v. Franklin* was predicated entirely on the fact that petitioner's challenge to the jury instruction asserted a substantial federal question. Our opinion in *Francis* explained why a challenge of this kind is supported by the Federal Constitution:

> The Due Process Clause of the Fourteenth Amendment "protects the accused against conviction except upon proof beyond a reasonable doubt of every fact necessary to constitute the crime with which he is charged." *In re Winship*, [397 U.S. 358, 364 (1970)]. This "bedrock, 'axiomatic and elementary' [constitutional] principle," *id.* at 363, prohibits the State from using evidentiary presumptions in a jury charge that have the effect of relieving the State of its burden of persuasion beyond a reasonable doubt of every essential element of a crime. ***

The portion of the state court's opinion concluding that the instruction in petitioner's case was infirm for the reasons "addressed in *Francis*" was responsive to our mandate, but the discussion of the question whether the decision in *Elmore* should be applied retroactively was not. Our mandate contemplated that the state court would consider whether, as a matter of federal law, petitioner's conviction could stand in the light of *Francis*. Since the state court did not decide that question, we shall do so.

II

The South Carolina Attorney General submits that we should adopt Justice Harlan's theory that a newly announced constitutional rule should not be applied retroactively to cases pending on collateral review unless the rule places "certain kinds of primary, private individual conduct beyond the power of the criminal law-making authority to proscribe," *Mackey v. United States*, 401 U.S. 667, 692 (1971) (Harlan, J., concurring in part and dissenting in part), or enunciates a procedural rule that is "implicit in the concept of ordered liberty," *id.* at 693. Under this theory, the Attorney General argues, petitioner would not be entitled to the benefit of our ruling in *Franklin*.

We have already endorsed Justice Harlan's retroactivity analysis for cases pending on direct appeal, *see Griffith v. Kentucky*, 479 U.S. 314, 322 (1987); ** and we have noted, as Justice Harlan did, *Mackey*, [401 U.S.] at 682–687, ** the important distinction between direct review and collateral review. Compare *Allen v. Hardy*, 478 U.S. 255 (1986) (holding that *Batson v. Kentucky*, 476 U.S. 79 (1986) does not apply retroactively to cases on collateral review), with *Griffith*, [479 U.S.] at 322–323 (holding that *Batson* does apply retroactively to cases pending on direct review); *see, e.g., Pennsylvania v. Finley*, 481 U.S. 551 (1987) (right to appointed counsel on direct appeal not applicable in collateral proceedings). To decide this case, however, it is not necessary to determine whether we should go further and adopt Justice Harlan's reasoning as to the retroactivity of cases announcing new constitutional rules to cases pending on collateral review.

Although Justice Harlan believed that most collateral attacks on final judgments should be resolved by reference to the state of the law at the time of the petitioner's conviction, he emphasized the proposition that many "new" holdings are merely applications of principles that were well settled at the time of conviction. As he explained in *Desist*:

> The theory that the habeas petitioner is entitled to the law prevailing at the time of his conviction is, however, one which is more complex than the Court has seemingly recognized. First, it is necessary to determine whether a particular decision has really announced a "new" rule at all or whether it has simply applied a well-established constitutional principle to govern a case which is closely analogous to those which have been previously considered in the prior case law.... One need not be a rigid partisan of Blackstone to recognize that many, though not all, of this Court's constitutional decisions are grounded upon fundamental principles whose content does not change dramatically from year to year, but whose meanings are altered slowly and subtly as generation succeeds generation. In such a context it appears very difficult to argue against the application of the "new" rule in all habeas cases since one could never say with any assurance that this Court would have ruled differently at the time the petitioner's conviction became final. [*Desist v. United States*,] 394 U.S. 244, 263–264 [(1969) (Harlan, J., dissenting)].

This reasoning, which we previously have endorsed, *** is controlling in this case because our decision in *Francis* was merely an application of the principle that governed our decision in *Sandstrom v. Montana*, which had been decided before petitioner's trial took place. We explicitly so held in *Francis* itself:

> The question before the Court in this case is almost identical to that before the Court in *Sandstrom*: "whether the challenged jury instruction had the effect of relieving the State of the burden of proof enunciated in *Winship* on the critical question of...state of mind," 442 U.S. at 521, by creating a mandatory presumption of intent upon proof by the State of other elements of the offense. 471 U.S. at 313.

Sandstrom v. Montana made clear that the Due Process Clause of the Fourteenth Amendment prohibits the State from making use of jury instructions that have the effect of relieving the State of the burden of proof enunciated in *Winship* on the critical question of intent in a criminal prosecution. 442 U.S. at 521. Today we reaffirm the rule of *Sandstrom* and the wellspring due process principle from which it was drawn. The Court of Appeals faithfully and correctly applied this rule, and the court's judgment is therefore affirmed. *Id.* at 326–327.

III

Respondents also argue that South Carolina has the authority to establish the scope of its own habeas corpus proceedings and to refuse to apply a new rule of federal constitutional law retroactively in such a proceeding. We reject this argument for two reasons. First, as we have just explained, *Francis* did not announce a new rule. Second, we do not read the South Carolina Supreme Court's opinion as having placed any limit on the issues that it will entertain in collateral proceedings. Since it has considered the merits of the federal claim, it has a duty to grant the relief that federal law requires.

The judgment is reversed, and the case is remanded for further proceedings not inconsistent with this opinion.

It is so ordered.

Teague v. Lane
489 U.S. 288 (1989)

JUSTICE O'CONNOR announced the judgment of the Court and delivered the opinion of the Court with respect to Parts I, II, and III, and an opinion with respect to Parts IV and V, in which THE CHIEF JUSTICE, JUSTICE SCALIA, and JUSTICE KENNEDY join.

In *Taylor v. Louisiana*, 419 U.S. 522 (1975), this Court held that the Sixth Amendment required that the jury venire be drawn from a fair cross section of the community. The Court stated, however, that "in holding that petit juries must be drawn from a source fairly representative of the community we impose no requirement that petit juries actually chosen must mirror the community and reflect the various distinctive groups in the population. Defendants are not entitled to a jury of any particular composition." *Id.* at 538. The principal question presented in this case is whether the Sixth Amendment's fair cross section requirement should now be extended to the petit jury. Because we adopt Justice Harlan's approach to retroactivity for cases on collateral review, we leave the resolution of that question for another day.

I

Petitioner, a black man, was convicted by an all-white Illinois jury of three counts of attempted murder, two counts of armed robbery, and one count of aggravated battery. During jury selection for petitioner's trial, the prosecutor used all 10 of his peremptory challenges to exclude blacks. Petitioner's counsel used one of his 10 peremptory challenges to exclude a black woman who was married to a police officer. After the prosecutor had struck six blacks, petitioner's counsel moved for a mistrial. The trial court denied the motion. ** When the prosecutor struck four more blacks, petitioner's counsel again moved for a mistrial, arguing that petitioner was "entitled to a jury of his peers." ** The prosecutor defended the challenges by stating that he was trying to achieve a balance of men and women on the jury. The trial court denied the motion, reasoning that the jury "appear[ed] to be a fair [one]." **

On appeal, petitioner argued that the prosecutor's use of peremptory challenges denied him the right to be tried by a jury that was representative of the community. The Illinois Appellate Court rejected petitioner's fair cross section claim. ** The Illinois Supreme Court denied leave to appeal, and we denied certiorari. **

Petitioner then filed a petition for a writ of habeas corpus in the United States District Court for the Northern District of Illinois. Petitioner repeated his fair cross section claim, and argued that the opinions of several Justices concurring in, or dissenting from, the denial of certiorari in *McCray v. New York*, 461 U.S. 961 (1983), had invited a reexamination of *Swain v. Alabama*, 380 U.S. 202 (1965), which prohibited States from purposefully and systematically denying blacks the opportunity to serve on juries. He also argued, for the first time, that under *Swain* a prosecutor could be questioned about his use of peremptory challenges once he volunteered an explanation. The District Court, though sympathetic to petitioner's arguments, held that it was bound by *Swain* and Circuit precedent. **

On appeal, petitioner repeated his fair cross section claim and his *McCray* argument. A panel of the Court of Appeals agreed with petitioner that the Sixth Amendment's fair cross section requirement applied to the petit jury and held that petitioner had made out a prima facie case of discrimination. A majority of the judges on the Court of Appeals voted to rehear the case en banc, and the panel opinion was vacated. ** Rehearing was postponed until after our decision in *Batson v. Kentucky*, 476 U.S. 79 (1986), which overruled a portion of *Swain*. After *Batson* was decided, the Court of Appeals held that petitioner could not benefit from the rule in that case because *Allen v. Hardy*, 478 U.S. 255 (1986) (*per curiam*), had held that *Batson* would not be applied retroactively to cases on collateral review. ** The Court of Appeals also held that petitioner's *Swain* claim was procedurally barred and in any event meritless. ** The Court of Appeals rejected petitioner's fair cross section claim, holding that the fair cross section requirement was limited to the jury venire. ** Judge Cudahy dissented, arguing that the fair cross section requirement should be extended to the petit jury. **

[handwritten margin note: new Batson case]

II *[handwritten: SC grants cert.]*

Petitioner's first contention is that he should receive the benefit of our decision in *Batson* even though his conviction became final before *Batson* was decided. Before addressing petitioner's argument, we think it helpful to explain how *Batson* modified *Swain*. *Swain* held that a "State's purposeful or deliberate denial" to blacks of an opportunity to serve as jurors solely on account of race violates the Equal Protection Clause of the Fourteenth Amendment. 380 U.S. at 203–204. In order to establish a prima facie case of discrimination under *Swain*, a defendant had to demonstrate that the peremptory challenge system had been "perverted." A defendant could raise an inference of purposeful discrimination if he showed that the prosecutor in the county where the trial was held "in case after case, whatever the circumstances, whatever the crime and whoever the defendant or the victim may be," has been responsible for the removal of qualified blacks who had survived challenges for cause, with the result that no blacks ever served on petit juries. *Id.* at 223.

[handwritten margin note: Swain]

In *Batson*, the Court overruled that portion of *Swain* setting forth the evidentiary showing necessary to make out a prima facie case of racial discrimination under the

[handwritten margin note: Batson]

Equal Protection Clause. The Court held that a defendant can establish a prima facie case by showing that he is a "member of a cognizable racial group," that the prosecutor exercised "peremptory challenges to remove from the venire members of the defendant's race," and that those "facts and any other relevant circumstances raise an inference that the prosecutor used that practice to exclude the veniremen from the petit jury on account of their race." 476 U.S. at 96. Once the defendant makes out a prima facie case of discrimination, the burden shifts to the prosecutor "to come forward with a neutral explanation for challenging black jurors." Id. at 97.

In *Allen v. Hardy*, the Court held that *Batson* constituted an "explicit and substantial break with prior precedent" because it overruled a portion of *Swain*. 478 U.S. at 258. Employing the retroactivity standard of *Linkletter v. Walker*, 381 U.S. 618, 636 (1965), the Court concluded that the rule announced in *Batson* should not be applied retroactively on collateral review of convictions that became final before *Batson* was announced. The Court defined final to mean a case "'where the judgment of conviction was rendered, the availability of appeal exhausted, and the time for petition for certiorari had elapsed before our decision in' *Batson*...." 478 U.S. at 258 n.1.

Petitioner's conviction became final 2 1/2 years prior to *Batson*, thus depriving petitioner of any benefit from the rule announced in that case. Petitioner argues, however, that *Batson* should be applied retroactively to all cases pending on direct review at the time certiorari was denied in *McCray* because the opinions filed in *McCray* destroyed the precedential effect of *Swain*. ** The issue in *McCray* and its companion cases was whether the Constitution prohibited the use of peremptory challenges to exclude members of a particular group from the jury, based on the prosecutor's assumption that they would be biased in favor of other members of that same group. Justices Marshall and Brennan dissented from the denial of certiorari, expressing the views that *Swain* should be reexamined and that the conduct complained of violated a defendant's Sixth Amendment right to be tried by an impartial jury drawn from a fair cross section of the community. ** Justices Stevens, Blackmun, and Powell concurred in the denial of certiorari. They agreed that the issue was an important one, but stated that it was a "sound exercise of discretion for the Court to allow the various States to serve as laboratories in which the issue receives further study before it is addressed." **

We reject the basic premise of petitioner's argument. As we have often stated, the "denial of a writ of certiorari imports no expression of opinion upon the merits of the case." *United States v. Carver*, 260 U.S. 482, 490 (1923) (Holmes, J.). *Accord Hughes Tool Co. v. Trans World Airlines, Inc.*, 409 U.S. 363, 366 n.1 (1973); *Brown v. Allen*, 344 U.S. 443, 489–497 (1953). The "variety of considerations [that] underlie denials of the writ," *Maryland v. Baltimore Radio Show*, 338 U.S. 912, 917 (1950) (opinion of Frankfurter, J.), counsels against according denials of certiorari any precedential value. Concomitantly, opinions accompanying the denial of certiorari cannot have the same effect as decisions on the merits. We find that *Allen v. Hardy* is dispositive, and that petitioner cannot benefit from the rule announced in *Batson*.

***

IV

Petitioner's third and final contention is that the Sixth Amendment's fair cross section requirement applies to the petit jury. As we noted at the outset, *Taylor* expressly stated that the fair cross section requirement does not apply to the petit jury. ** Petitioner nevertheless contends that the *ratio decidendi* of *Taylor* cannot be limited to the jury venire, and he urges adoption of a new rule. <u>Because we hold that the rule urged by petitioner should not be applied retroactively to cases on collateral review, we decline to address petitioner's contention.</u>

A

In the past, the Court has, without discussion, often applied a new constitutional rule of criminal procedure to the defendant in the case announcing the new rule, and has confronted the question of retroactivity later when a different defendant sought the benefit of that rule. ** In several cases, however, the Court has addressed the retroactivity question in the very case announcing the new rule. *See Morrissey v. Brewer*, 408 U.S. 471, 490 (1972); *Witherspoon v. Illinois*, 391 U.S. 510, 523 n.22 (1968). <u>These two lines of cases do not have a unifying theme, and we think it is time to clarify how the question of retroactivity should be resolved for cases on collateral review.</u>

The question of retroactivity with regard to petitioner's fair cross section claim has been raised only in an *amicus* brief. ** Nevertheless, that question is not foreign to the parties, who have addressed retroactivity with respect to petitioner's *Batson* claim. ** Moreover, our *sua sponte* consideration of retroactivity is far from novel. In *Allen v. Hardy*, we addressed the retroactivity of *Batson* even though that question had not been presented by the petition for certiorari or addressed by the lower courts. *See* 478 U.S. at 261–262 (Marshall, J., dissenting). *See also Mapp v. Ohio*, 367 U.S. 643, 646 n.3 (1961) (applying exclusionary rule to the States even although such a course of action was urged only by *amicus curiae*).

In our view, the question "whether a decision [announcing a new rule should] be given prospective or retroactive effect should be faced at the time of [that] decision." Mishkin, FOREWORD: THE HIGH COURT, THE GREAT WRIT, AND THE DUE PROCESS OF TIME AND LAW, 79 Harv. L. Rev. 56, 64 (1965). *Cf. Bowen v. United States*, 422 U.S. 916, 920 (1975) (when "issues of both retroactivity and application of constitutional doctrine are raised," the retroactivity issue should be decided first). Retroactivity is properly treated as a threshold question, for, once a new rule is applied to the defendant in the case announcing the rule, evenhanded justice requires that it be applied retroactively to all who are similarly situated. Thus, before deciding whether the fair cross section requirement should be extended to the petit jury, we should ask whether such a rule would be applied retroactively to the case at issue. This retroactivity determination would normally entail application of the *Linkletter* standard, but we believe that our approach to retroactivity for cases on collateral review requires modification.

It is admittedly often difficult to determine when a case announces a new rule, and we do not attempt to define the spectrum of what may or may not constitute a new rule for retroactivity purposes. <u>In general, however, a case announces a new rule when it breaks new ground or imposes a new obligation on the States or the Federal Government.</u> *See, e.g., Rock v. Arkansas*, 483 U.S. 44, 62 (1987) (*per se* rule excluding all hypnotically refreshed testimony infringes impermissibly on a criminal defendant's right to testify on his behalf); *Ford v. Wainwright*, 477 U.S. 399, 410 (1986) (Eighth Amendment prohibits the execution of prisoners who are insane). <u>To put it differently, a case announces a new rule if the result was not *dictated* by precedent existing at the time the defendant's conviction became final.</u> *See generally Truesdale v. Aiken*, 480 U.S. 527, 528–529 (1987) (Powell, J., dissenting). Given the strong language in *Taylor* and our statement in *Akins v. Texas*, 325 U.S. 398, 403 (1945), that "[f]airness in [jury] selection has never been held to require proportional representation of races upon a jury," application of the fair cross section requirement to the petit jury would be a new rule. ***

Not all new rules have been uniformly treated for retroactivity purposes. Nearly a quarter of a century ago, in *Linkletter*, the Court attempted to set some standards by which to determine the retroactivity of new rules. The question in *Linkletter* was whether *Mapp v. Ohio*, which made the exclusionary rule applicable to the States, should be applied retroactively to cases on collateral review. The Court determined that the retroactivity of *Mapp* should be determined by examining the purpose of the exclusionary rule, the reliance of the States on prior law, and the effect on the administration of justice of a retroactive application of the exclusionary rule. Using that standard, the Court held that *Mapp* would only apply to trials commencing after that case was decided. 381 U.S. at 636–640.

The *Linkletter* retroactivity standard has not led to consistent results. Instead, it has been used to limit application of certain new rules to cases on direct review, other new rules only to the defendants in the cases announcing such rules, and still other new rules to cases in which trials have not yet commenced. *See Desist v. United States*, 394 U.S. 244, 256–257 (1969) (Harlan, J., dissenting) (citing examples). Not surprisingly, commentators have "had a veritable field day" with the *Linkletter* standard, with much of the discussion being "more than mildly negative." Beytagh, *Ten Years of Non-Retroactivity: A Critique and a Proposal*, 61 Va. L. Rev. 1557, 1558, and n.3 (1975) (citing sources).

Application of the *Linkletter* standard led to the disparate treatment of similarly situated defendants on direct review. For example, in *Miranda v. Arizona*, 384 U.S. 436, 467–473 (1966), the Court held that, absent other effective measures to protect the Fifth Amendment privilege against self-incrimination, a person in custody must be warned prior to interrogation that he has certain rights, including the right to remain silent. The Court applied that new rule to the defendants in *Miranda* and its companion cases, and held that their convictions could not stand because they had been interrogated without the proper warnings. *Id.* at 491–499. In *Johnson v. New Jersey*, 384 U.S. 719, 733–735 (1966), the Court held, under the *Linkletter* standard, that *Miranda* would only be applied to trials commencing after that decision had been announced. Because the defendant in *Johnson*, like the defendants in *Miranda*, was on direct review of his conviction, *see* 384 U.S. at 721, the Court's refusal to give *Miranda* retroactive effect resulted in unequal treatment of those who were similarly situated. This inequity also generated vehement criticism. *See, e.g.*, A. Bickel, The Supreme Court and the Idea of Progress 54–57 (1978) (decrying the "plain" injustice in *Johnson* and suggesting that the Court should have distinguished between direct and collateral review for purposes of retroactivity).

Dissatisfied with the *Linkletter* standard, Justice Harlan advocated a different approach to retroactivity. He argued that new rules should always be applied retroactively to cases on direct review, but that generally they should not be applied retroactively to criminal cases on collateral review. *See Mackey v. United States*, 401 U.S. 667, 675 (1971) (opinion concurring in judgments in part and dissenting in part); *Desist*, 394 U.S. at 256 (dissenting opinion).

In *Griffith v. Kentucky*, 479 U.S. 314 (1987), we rejected as unprincipled and inequitable the *Linkletter* standard for cases pending on direct review at the time a new rule is announced, and adopted the first part of the retroactivity approach advocated by Justice Harlan. We agreed with Justice Harlan that "failure to apply a newly declared constitutional rule to criminal cases pending on direct review violates basic norms of constitutional adjudication." 479 U.S. at 322. We gave two reasons for our decision. First, because we can only promulgate new rules in specific cases and cannot possibly decide all cases in which review is sought, "the integrity of judicial review" requires the application of the new rule to "all similar cases pending on direct review." *Id.* at 323. We quoted approvingly from Justice Harlan's separate opinion in *Mackey, supra,* 401 U.S. at 679:

> If we do not resolve all cases before us on direct review in light of our best understanding of governing constitutional principles, it is difficult to see why we should so adjudicate any case at all.... In truth, the Court's assertion of power to disregard current law in adjudicating cases before us that have not already run the full course of appellate review is quite simply an assertion that our constitutional function is not one of adjudication but in effect of legislation. 479 U.S. at 323.

Second, because "selective application of new rules violates the principle of treating similarly situated defendants the same," we refused to continue to tolerate the inequity that resulted from not applying new rules retroactively to defendants whose cases had not yet become final. *Id.* at 323–324 (*citing Desist,* [394 U.S.] at 258–259 (Harlan, J., dissenting)). Although new rules that constituted clear breaks with the past generally were not given retroactive effect under the *Linkletter* standard, we held that "a new rule for the conduct of criminal prosecutions is to be applied retroactively to all cases, state or federal, pending on direct review or not yet final, with no exception for cases in which the new rule constitutes a 'clear break' with the past." 479 U.S. at 328.

The *Linkletter* standard also led to unfortunate disparity in the treatment of similarly situated defendants on collateral review. An example will best illustrate the point. In *Edwards v. Arizona,* 451 U.S. 477, 484–487 (1981), the Court held that once a person invokes his right to have counsel present during custodial interrogation, a valid waiver of that right cannot be inferred from the fact that the person responded to police-initiated questioning. It was not until *Solem v. Stumes,* 465 U.S. 638 (1984), that the Court held, under the *Linkletter* standard, that *Edwards* was not to be applied retroactively to cases on collateral review. In the interim, several lower federal courts had come to the opposite conclusion and had applied *Edwards* to cases that had become final before that decision was announced. ** Thus, some defendants on collateral review whose *Edwards* claims were adjudicated prior to *Stumes* received the benefit of *Edwards,* while those whose *Edwards* claims had not been addressed prior to *Stumes* did not. This disparity in treatment was a product of two factors: our failure to treat retroactivity as a threshold question and the *Linkletter* standard's inability to account for the nature and function of collateral review. Having decided to rectify the first of those inadequacies, ** we now turn to the second.

B

Justice Harlan believed that new rules generally should not be applied retroactively to cases on collateral review. He argued that retroactivity for cases on collateral review could "be responsibly [determined] only by focusing, in the first instance, on the nature, function, and scope of the adjudicatory process in which such cases arise. The relevant frame of reference, in other words, is not the purpose of the new rule whose benefit the [defendant] seeks, but instead the purposes for which the writ of habeas corpus is made available." *Mackey,* 401 U.S. at 682 (opinion concurring in judgments in part and dissenting in part). With regard to the nature of habeas corpus, Justice Harlan wrote:

> Habeas corpus always has been a *collateral* remedy, providing an avenue for upsetting judgments that have become otherwise final. It is not designed as a

substitute for direct review. The interest in leaving concluded litigation in a state of repose, that is, reducing the controversy to a final judgment not subject to further judicial revision, may quite legitimately be found by those responsible for defining the scope of the writ to outweigh in some, many, or most instances the competing interest in readjudicating convictions according to all legal standards in effect when a habeas petition is filed. *Id.* at 682–683.

Given the "broad scope of constitutional issues cognizable on habeas," Justice Harlan argued that it is "sounder, in adjudicating habeas petitions, generally to apply the law prevailing at the time a conviction became final than it is to seek to dispose of [habeas] cases on the basis of intervening changes in constitutional interpretation." *Id.* at 689. As he had explained in *Desist*, "the threat of habeas serves as a necessary additional incentive for trial and appellate courts throughout the land to conduct their proceedings in a manner consistent with established constitutional standards. In order to perform this deterrence function,…the habeas court need only apply the constitutional standards that prevailed at the time the original proceedings took place." 394 U.S. at 262–263. **

Justice Harlan identified only two exceptions to his general rule of nonretroactivity for cases on collateral review. First, a new rule should be applied retroactively if it places "certain kinds of primary, private individual conduct beyond the power of the criminal law-making authority to proscribe." *Mackey*, 401 U.S. at 692. Second, a new rule should be applied retroactively if it requires the observance of "those procedures that…are 'implicit in the concept of ordered liberty.'" *Id.* at 693 (*quoting Palko v. Connecticut*, 302 U.S. 319, 325 (1937) (Cardozo, J.)).

Last Term, in *Yates v. Aiken*, 484 U.S. 211 (1988), we were asked to decide whether the rule announced in *Francis v. Franklin*, 471 U.S. 307 (1985), should be applied to a defendant on collateral review at the time that case was decided. We held that *Francis* did not announce a new rule because it "was merely an application of the principle that governed our decision in *Sandstrom v. Montana*, [442 U.S. 510 (1979),] which had been decided before [the defendant's] trial took place." 484 U.S. at 216–217. We therefore found it unnecessary to adopt Justice Harlan's view of retroactivity for cases on collateral review. We stated, however, that our recent decisions had noted, as had Justice Harlan, "the important distinction between direct review and collateral review." *Id.* at 215. *See also Pennsylvania v. Finley*, 481 U.S. 551, 555 (1987) (distinguishing between direct and collateral review for purposes of Sixth Amendment right to counsel on appeal). Indeed, we have expressly reconciled some of our retroactivity decisions with Justice Harlan's approach. *See Shea v. Louisiana*, 470 U.S. 51, 58 n.4 (1985) (giving *Edwards* retroactive effect on direct, but not collateral, review "is fully congruent with both aspects of the approach to retroactivity propounded by Justice Harlan").

We agree with Justice Harlan's description of the function of habeas corpus. "[T]he Court never has defined the scope of the writ simply by reference to a perceived need to assure that an individual accused of crime is afforded a trial free of constitutional error." *Kuhlmann v. Wilson*, 477 U.S. 436, 447 (1986) (plurality opinion). Rather, we have recognized that interests of comity and finality must also be considered in determining the proper scope of habeas review. Thus, if a defendant fails to comply with state procedural rules and is barred from litigating a particular constitutional claim in state court, the claim can be considered on federal habeas only if the defendant shows cause for the default and actual prejudice resulting therefrom. *See Wainwright v. Sykes*, 433 U.S. at 87–91. We have declined to make the application of the procedural default rule dependent on the magnitude of the constitutional claim at issue, *see Engle v. Isaac*, 456 U.S.

[107,] 129 [1982], or on the State's interest in the enforcement of its procedural rule, *see* *Murray v. Carrier*, 477 U.S. 478, 493–496 (1986).

This Court has not "always followed an unwavering line in its conclusions as to the availability of the Great Writ. Our development of the law of federal habeas corpus has been attended, seemingly, with some backing and filling." *Fay v. Noia*, 372 U.S. 391, 411–412, (1963). *See also Stone v. Powell*, 428 U.S. 465, 475–476 (1976). Nevertheless, it has long been established that a final civil judgment entered under a given rule of law may withstand subsequent judicial change in that rule. In *Chicot County Drainage District v. Baxter State Bank*, 308 U.S. 371 (1940), the Court held that a judgment based on a jurisdictional statute later found to be unconstitutional could have res judicata effect. The Court based its decision in large part on finality concerns. ***

These underlying considerations of finality find significant and compelling parallels in the criminal context. Application of constitutional rules not in existence at the time a conviction became final seriously undermines the principle of finality which is essential to the operation of our criminal justice system. Without finality, the criminal law is deprived of much of its deterrent effect. The fact that life and liberty are at stake in criminal prosecutions "shows only that 'conventional notions of finality' should not have *as much* place in criminal as in civil litigation, not that they should have *none*." Friendly, *Is Innocence Irrelevant? Collateral Attack on Criminal Judgments*, 38 U. Chi. L. Rev. 142, 150 (1970). "[I]f a criminal judgment is ever to be final, the notion of legality must at some point include the assignment of final competence to determine legality." Bator, *Finality in Criminal Law and Federal Habeas Corpus for State Prisoners*, 76 Harv. L. Rev. 441, 450–451 (1963) (emphasis omitted). **

***

The "costs imposed upon the State[s] by retroactive application of new rules of constitutional law on habeas corpus…generally far outweigh the benefits of this application." *Stumes*, 465 U.S. at 654 (Powell, J., concurring in judgment). In many ways the application of new rules to cases on collateral review may be more intrusive than the enjoining of criminal prosecutions, *cf. Younger v. Harris*, 401 U.S. 37, 43–54 (1971), for it *continually* forces the States to marshal resources in order to keep in prison defendants whose trials and appeals conformed to then-existing constitutional standards. Furthermore, as we recognized in *Engle v. Isaac*, "[s]tate courts are understandably frustrated when they faithfully apply existing constitutional law only to have a federal court discover, during a [habeas] proceeding, new constitutional commands." 456 U.S. at 128 n.33. *See also Brown v. Allen*, 344 U.S. at 534 (Jackson, J., concurring in result) (state courts cannot "anticipate, and so comply with, this Court's due process requirements or ascertain any standards to which this Court will adhere in prescribing them").

We find these criticisms to be persuasive, and we now adopt Justice Harlan's view of retroactivity for cases on collateral review. Unless they fall within an exception to the general rule, new constitutional rules of criminal procedure will not be applicable to those cases which have become final before the new rules are announced.

V

Petitioner's conviction became final in 1983. As a result, the rule petitioner urges would not be applicable to this case, which is on collateral review, unless it would fall within an exception.

The first exception suggested by Justice Harlan—that a new rule should be applied retroactively if it places "certain kinds of primary, private individual conduct beyond the power of the criminal law-making authority to proscribe," *Mackey*, 401 U.S. at 692 (opinion concurring in judgments in part and dissenting in part) — is not relevant here. Application of the fair cross section requirement to the petit jury would not accord constitutional protection to any primary activity whatsoever.

The second exception suggested by Justice Harlan — that a new rule should be applied retroactively if it requires the observance of "those procedures that . . . are 'implicit in the concept of ordered liberty,'" *id.* at 693 (*quoting Palko*, 302 U.S. at 325) — we apply with a modification. The language used by Justice Harlan in *Mackey* leaves no doubt that he meant the second exception to be reserved for watershed rules of criminal procedure:

> Typically, it should be the case that any conviction free from federal constitutional error at the time it became final, will be found, upon reflection, to have been fundamentally fair and conducted under those procedures essential to the substance of a full hearing. However, in some situations it might be that time and growth in social capacity, as well as judicial perceptions of what we can rightly demand of the adjudicatory process, will properly alter our understanding of the *bedrock procedural elements* that must be found to vitiate the fairness of a particular conviction. For example, such, in my view, is the case with the right to counsel at trial now held a necessary condition precedent to any conviction for a serious crime. 401 U.S. at 693–694 (emphasis added).

In *Desist*, Justice Harlan had reasoned that one of the two principal functions of habeas corpus was "to assure that no man has been incarcerated under a procedure which creates an impermissibly large risk that the innocent will be convicted," and concluded "from this that all 'new' constitutional rules which significantly improve the pre-existing fact-finding procedures are to be retroactively applied on habeas." 394 U.S. at 262. In *Mackey*, Justice Harlan gave three reasons for shifting to the less defined *Palko* approach. First, he observed that recent precedent, particularly *Kaufman v. United States*, 394 U.S. 217 (1969) (permitting Fourth Amendment claims to be raised on collateral review), led "ineluctably . . . to the conclusion that it is not a principal purpose of the writ to inquire whether a criminal convict did in fact commit the deed alleged." 401 U.S. at 694. Second, he noted that cases such as *Coleman v. Alabama*, 399 U.S. 1 (1970) (invalidating lineup procedures in the absence of counsel), gave him reason to doubt the marginal effectiveness of claimed improvements in factfinding. 401 U.S. at 694–695. Third, he found "inherently intractable the purported distinction between those new rules that are designed to improve the factfinding process and those designed principally to further other values." *Id.* at 695.

We believe it desirable to combine the accuracy element of the *Desist* version of the second exception with the *Mackey* requirement that the procedure at issue must implicate the fundamental fairness of the trial. *** Moreover, since *Mackey* was decided, our cases have moved in the direction of reaffirming the relevance of the likely accuracy of convictions in determining the available scope of habeas review. *See, e.g., Kuhlmann v. Wilson*, 477 U.S. at 454 (plurality opinion) (a successive habeas petition may be entertained only if the defendant makes a "colorable claim of factual innocence"); *Murray v. Carrier*, 477 U.S. at 496 ("[W]here a constitutional violation has probably resulted in the conviction of one who is actually innocent, a federal habeas court may grant the writ even in the absence of a showing of cause for the procedural default"); *Stone v. Powell*, 428 U.S. at 491–492 n.31 (removing Fourth Amendment claims from the scope of federal habeas review if the State has provided a full and fair opportunity for litigation creates no danger of denying a "safeguard against compelling an innocent man to suffer an unconstitutional loss of liberty"). Finally, we believe that Justice Harlan's concerns about the difficulty in identifying both the existence and the value of accuracy-enhancing procedural rules can be addressed by limiting the scope of the second exception to those new procedures without which the likelihood of an accurate conviction is seriously diminished.

Because we operate from the premise that such procedures would be so central to an accurate determination of innocence or guilt, we believe it unlikely that many such components of basic due process have yet to emerge. We are also of the view that such rules are "best illustrated by recalling the classic grounds for the issuance of a writ of habeas corpus—that the proceeding was dominated by mob violence; that the prosecutor knowingly made use of perjured testimony; or that the conviction was based on a confession extorted from the defendant by brutal methods." *Rose v. Lundy*, 455 U.S. 509, 544 (1982) (Stevens, J., dissenting) (footnotes omitted). ***

An examination of our decision in *Taylor* applying the fair cross section requirement to the jury venire leads inexorably to the conclusion that adoption of the rule petitioner urges would be a far cry from the kind of absolute prerequisite to fundamental fairness that is "implicit in the concept of ordered liberty." The requirement that the jury venire be composed of a fair cross section of the community is based on the role of the jury in our system. Because the purpose of the jury is to guard against arbitrary abuses of power by interposing the commonsense judgment of the community between the State and the defendant, the jury venire cannot be composed only of special segments of the population. "Community participation in the administration of the criminal law...is not only consistent with our democratic heritage but is also critical to public confidence in the fairness of the criminal justice system." *Taylor*, 419 U.S. at 530. But as we stated in *Daniel v. Louisiana*, 420 U.S. 31, 32 (1975), which held that *Taylor* was not to be given retroactive effect, the fair cross section requirement "[does] not rest on the premise that every criminal trial, or any particular trial, [is] necessarily unfair because it [is] not conducted in accordance with what we determined to be the requirements of the Sixth Amendment." Because the absence of a fair cross section on the jury venire does not undermine the fundamental fairness that must underlie a conviction or seriously diminish the likelihood of obtaining an accurate conviction, we conclude that a rule requiring that petit juries be composed of a fair cross section of the community would not be a "bedrock procedural element" that would be retroactively applied under the second exception we have articulated.

Were we to recognize the new rule urged by petitioner in this case, we would have to give petitioner the benefit of that new rule even though it would not be applied retroactively to others similarly situated. In the words of Justice Brennan, such an inequitable result would be "an unavoidable consequence of the necessity that constitutional adjudications not stand as mere dictum." *Stovall v. Denno*, 388 U.S. [293,] 301 [(1967)]. But the harm caused by the failure to treat similarly situated defendants alike cannot be exaggerated: such inequitable treatment "hardly comports with the ideal of 'administration of justice with an even hand.'" *Hankerson v. North Carolina*, 432 U.S. 233, 247 (1977) (Powell, J., concurring in judgment) (*quoting Desist*, 394 U.S. at 255 (Douglas, J., dissenting)). *See also Fuller v. Alaska*, 393 U.S. 80, 82 (1968) (Douglas, J., dissenting) (if a rule is applied to the defendant in the case announcing the rule, it should be applied to all others similarly situated). Our refusal to allow such disparate treatment in the direct review context led us to adopt the first part of Justice Harlan's retroactivity approach in *Griffith*. "The fact that the new rule may constitute a clear break with the past has no bearing on the 'actual inequity that results' when only one of many similarly situated defendants receives the benefit of the new rule." 479 U.S. at 327–328.

If there were no other way to avoid rendering advisory opinions, we might well agree that the inequitable treatment described above is "an insignificant cost for adherence to sound principles of decision-making." *Stovall v. Denno*, 388 U.S. at 301. But there is a more principled way of dealing with the problem. We can simply refuse to announce a new rule in a given case unless the rule would be applied retroactively to the defendant in the case and to all others similarly situated. *Cf. Bowen v. United States*, 422 U.S. at 920 ("This Court consistently has declined to address unsettled questions regarding the scope of decisions establishing new constitutional doctrine in cases in which it holds those decisions nonretroactive. This practice is rooted in our reluctance to decide constitutional questions unnecessarily") (citations omitted). We think this approach is a sound one. Not only does it eliminate any problems of rendering advisory opinions, it also avoids the inequity resulting from the uneven application of new rules to similarly situated defendants. We therefore hold that, implicit in the retroactivity approach we adopt today, is the principle that habeas corpus cannot be used as a vehicle to create new constitutional rules of criminal procedure unless those rules would be applied retroactively to *all* defendants on collateral review through one of the two exceptions we have articulated. Because a decision extending the fair cross section requirement to the petit jury would not be applied retroactively to cases on collateral review under the approach we adopt today, we do not address petitioner's claim.

For the reasons set forth above, the judgment of the Court of Appeals is affirmed.

It is so ordered.

JUSTICE WHITE, concurring in part and concurring in the judgment.

I join Parts I, II, and III of Justice O'Connor's opinion. Otherwise, I concur only in the judgment.

***

I regret the course the Court has taken to this point, but cases like *Johnson*, *Shea*, and *Griffith* have been decided, and I have insufficient reason to continue to object to them. In light of those decisions, the result reached in Parts IV and V of Justice O'Connor's opinion is an acceptable application in collateral proceedings of the theories embraced by the Court in cases dealing with direct review, and I concur in that result. If we are wrong in construing the reach of the habeas corpus statutes, Congress can of course correct us; but because the Court's recent decisions dealing with direct review appear to have constitutional underpinnings, *see e.g., Griffith v. Kentucky*, [479 U.S.] at 322–323, correction of our error, if error there is, perhaps lies with us, not Congress.

JUSTICE BLACKMUN, concurring in part and concurring in the judgment.

I join Part I of Justice Stevens' opinion, *post*, concurring in part and concurring in the judgment. So far as the petitioner's claim based upon *Swain v. Alabama*, 380 U.S. 202 (1965), is concerned, I concur in the judgment.

JUSTICE STEVENS, with whom JUSTICE BLACKMUN joins as to Part I, concurring in part and concurring in the judgment.

I

For the reasons stated in Part III of Justice BRENNAN's dissent, *post*, I am persuaded this petitioner has alleged a violation of the Sixth Amendment. *** I also believe the Court should decide that question in his favor. I do not agree with Justice O'Connor's assumption that a ruling in petitioner's favor on the merits of the Sixth Amendment issue would require that his conviction be set aside. *See ante*.

When a criminal defendant claims that a procedural error tainted his conviction, an appellate court often decides whether error occurred before deciding whether that error requires reversal or should be classified as harmless. I would follow a parallel approach in cases raising novel questions of constitutional law on collateral review, first determining whether the trial process violated any of the petitioner's constitutional rights and then deciding whether the petitioner is entitled to relief. If error occurred, factors relating to retroactivity—most importantly, the magnitude of unfairness—should be examined before granting the petitioner relief. Proceeding in reverse, a plurality of the Court today declares that a new rule should not apply retroactively without ever deciding whether there is such a rule. ***

[Justice Stevens then states his "general" agreement with Justice Harlan's retroactivity analysis.]

I do not agree, however, with the plurality's dicta proposing a "modification" of Justice Harlan's fundamental fairness exception. *See ante.* "[I]t has been the law, presumably for at least as long as anyone currently in jail has been incarcerated," Justice Harlan wrote, "that procedures utilized to convict them must have been fundamentally fair, that is, in accordance with the command of the Fourteenth Amendment that '[n]o State shall…deprive any person of life, liberty, or property, without due process of law.'" *Mackey*, 401 U.S. at 689. ***

***

As a matter of first impression, therefore, I would conclude that a guilty verdict delivered by a jury whose impartiality might have been eroded by racial prejudice is fundamentally unfair. Constraining that conclusion is the Court's holding in *Allen v. Hardy*, 478 U.S. 255 (1986) (*per curiam*)—an opinion I did not join—that *Batson v. Kentucky*, 476 U.S. 79 (1986), cannot be applied retroactively to permit collateral review of convictions that became final before it was decided. It is true that the *Batson* decision rested on the Equal Protection Clause of the Fourteenth Amendment and that this case raises a Sixth Amendment issue. In both cases, however, petitioners pressed their objections to the jury selection on both grounds. *See ante; Batson v. Kentucky, supra*, at 83. Both cases concern the constitutionality of allowing the use of peremptories to yield a jury that may be biased against a defendant on account of race. Identical practical ramifications will ensue from our holdings in both cases. Thus if there is no fundamental unfairness in denying retroactive relief to a petitioner denied his Fourteenth Amendment right to a fairly chosen jury, as the Court held in *Allen*, *** there cannot be fundamental unfairness in denying this petitioner relief for the violation of his Sixth Amendment right to an impartial jury. I therefore agree that the judgment of the Court of Appeals must be affirmed. ***

***

JUSTICE BRENNAN, with whom JUSTICE MARSHALL joins, dissenting.

Today a plurality of this Court, without benefit of briefing and oral argument, adopts a novel threshold test for federal review of state criminal convictions on habeas corpus. It does so without regard for—indeed, without even mentioning—our contrary decisions over the past 35 years delineating the broad scope of habeas relief. The plurality further appears oblivious to the importance we have consistently accorded the principle of *stare decisis* in nonconstitutional cases. Out of an exaggerated concern for treating similarly situated habeas petitioners the same, the plurality would for the first time preclude the federal courts from considering on collateral review a vast range of important constitutional challenges; where those challenges have merit, it would bar

the vindication of personal constitutional rights and deny society a check against further violations until the same claim is presented on direct review. In my view, the plurality's "blind adherence to the principle of treating like cases alike" amounts to "letting
the tail wag the dog" when it stymies the resolution of substantial and unheralded constitutional questions. *Griffith v. Kentucky*, 479 U.S. 314, 332 (1987) (White, J., dissenting). Because I cannot acquiesce in this unprecedented curtailment of the reach of the
Great Writ, particularly in the absence of any discussion of these momentous changes
by the parties or the lower courts, I dissent.

***

II

Unfortunately, the plurality turns its back on established case law and would erect a
formidable new barrier to relief. Any time a federal habeas petitioner's claim, if successful, would result in the announcement of a new rule of law, the plurality says, it may
only be adjudicated if that rule would "plac[e] 'certain kinds of primary, private individual conduct beyond the power of the criminal law-making authority to proscribe,'"
ante, quoting *Mackey v. United States*, 401 U.S. 667, 692 (1971). ***

Astonishingly, the plurality adopts this novel precondition to habeas review without
benefit of oral argument on the question and with no more guidance from the litigants
than a three-page discussion in an *amicus* brief. *** Although the plurality's approach
builds upon two opinions written by Justice Harlan some years ago, *see Mackey v.
United States*, [401 U.S.] at 675 (opinion concurring in judgments in part and dissenting in part); *Desist v. United States*, 394 U.S. 244, 256 (1969) (dissenting opinion), it declines fully to embrace his views. No briefing or argument at all was devoted to the
points at which the plurality departs from his proposals. It is indeed ironic that in en-
dorsing the bulk of Justice Harlan's approach to the provision of federal habeas relief,
the Court ignores his reminder that our "obligation of orderly adherence to our own
processes would demand that we seek that aid which adequate briefing and argument
lends to the determination of an important issue." *Mapp v. Ohio*, 367 U.S. 643, 677
(1961) (dissenting opinion). Before breaking so sharply with precedent, the plurality
would have done well, I think, to recall what we said in *Ladner v. United States*, 358 U.S.
169, 173 (1958): "The question of the scope of collateral attack upon criminal sentences
is an important and complex one.... We think that we should have the benefit of a full
argument before dealing with the question."

B

Equally disturbing, in my view, is the plurality's infidelity to the doctrine of *stare decisis*. That doctrine "demands respect in a society governed by the rule of law," *Akron v.
Akron Center for Reproductive Health, Inc.*, 462 U.S. 416, 419–420 (1983), because it enhances the efficiency of judicial decisionmaking, allowing judges to rely on settled law
without having to reconsider the wisdom of prior decisions in every case they confront,
and because it fosters predictability in the law, permitting litigants and potential litigants
to act in the knowledge that precedent will not be overturned lightly and ensuring that
they will not be treated unfairly as a result of frequent or unanticipated changes in the
law. We have therefore routinely imposed on those asking us to overrule established lines
of cases "the heavy burden of persuading the Court that changes in society or in the law
dictate that the values served by *stare decisis* yield in favor of a greater objective." **

***

C

The plurality does not so much as mention *stare decisis*. Indeed, from the plurality's exposition of its new rule, one might infer that its novel fabrication will work no great change in the availability of federal collateral review of state convictions. Nothing could be further from the truth. Although the plurality declines to "define the spectrum of what may or may not constitute a new rule for retroactivity purposes," it does say that generally "a case announces a new rule when it breaks new ground or imposes a new obligation on the States or the Federal Government." ** Otherwise phrased, "a case announces a new rule if the result was not *dictated* by precedent existing at the time the defendant's conviction became final." ** This account is extremely broad. *** Few decisions on appeal or collateral review are "*dictated*" by what came before. Most such cases involve a question of law that is at least debatable, permitting a rational judge to resolve the case in more than one way. Virtually no case that prompts a dissent on the relevant legal point, for example, could be said to be "*dictated*" by prior decisions. By the plurality's test, therefore, a great many cases could only be heard on habeas if the rule urged by the petitioner fell within one of the two exceptions the plurality has sketched. Those exceptions, however, are narrow. Rules that place "'certain kinds of primary, private individual conduct beyond the power of the criminal lawmaking authority to proscribe,'" *ante, quoting Mackey v. United States*, 401 U.S. at 692 (Harlan, J., concurring in judgments in part and dissenting in part), are rare. And rules that would require "new procedures without which the likelihood of an accurate conviction is seriously diminished," *ante*, are not appreciably more common. The plurality admits, in fact, that it "believe[s] it unlikely that many such components of basic due process have yet to emerge." *Ibid*. The plurality's approach today can thus be expected to contract substantially the Great Writ's sweep.

***

D

These are massive changes, unsupported by precedent. *** They also lack a reasonable foundation. By exaggerating the importance of treating like cases alike and granting relief to all identically positioned habeas petitioners or none, "the Court acts as if it has no choice but to follow a mechanical notion of fairness without pausing to consider 'sound principles of decisionmaking.'" *Griffith v. Kentucky*, 479 U.S. at 332–333 (White, J., dissenting), *quoting Stovall v. Denno*, 388 U.S. 293, 301 (1967). Certainly it is desirable, in the interest of fairness, to accord the same treatment to all habeas petitioners with the same claims. Given a choice between deciding an issue on direct or collateral review that might result in a new rule of law that would not warrant retroactive application to persons on collateral review other than the petitioner who brought the claim, we should ordinarily grant certiorari and decide the question on direct review. Following our decision in *Griffith v. Kentucky, supra*, a new rule would apply equally to all persons whose convictions had not become final before the rule was announced, whereas habeas petitioners other than the one whose case we decided might not benefit from such a rule if we adopted it on collateral review. Taking cases on direct review ahead of those on habeas is especially attractive because the retrial of habeas petitioners usually places a heavier burden on the States than the retrial of persons on direct review. Other things being equal, our concern for fairness and finality ought to therefore lead us to render our decision in a case that comes to us on direct review.

Other things are not always equal, however. Sometimes a claim which, if successful, would create a new rule not appropriate for retroactive application on collateral review is better presented by a habeas case than by one on direct review. In fact, sometimes the claim is *only* presented on collateral review. In that case, while we could forgo deciding the issue in the hope that it would eventually be presented squarely on direct review, that hope might be misplaced, and even if it were in time fulfilled, the opportunity to check constitutional violations and to further the evolution of our thinking in some area of the law would in the meanwhile have been lost. In addition, by preserving our right and that of the lower federal courts to hear such claims on collateral review, we would not discourage their litigation on federal habeas corpus and thus not deprive ourselves and society of the benefit of decisions by the lower federal courts when we must resolve these issues ourselves.

The plurality appears oblivious to these advantages of our settled approach to collateral review. Instead, it would deny itself these benefits because adherence to precedent would occasionally result in one habeas petitioner's obtaining redress while another petitioner with an identical claim could not qualify for relief. *** In my view, the uniform treatment of habeas petitioners is not worth the price the plurality is willing to pay. Permitting the federal courts to decide novel habeas claims not substantially related to guilt or innocence has profited our society immensely. Congress has not seen fit to withdraw those benefits by amending the statute that provides for them. And although a favorable decision for a petitioner might not extend to another prisoner whose identical claim has become final, it is at least arguably better that the wrong done to one person be righted than that none of the injuries inflicted on those whose convictions have become final be redressed, despite the resulting inequality in treatment. ***

***

Notes

1. *Subsequent case history*

Dale Robert Yates was originally convicted and sentenced to death in 1981. The South Carolina Supreme Court affirmed the conviction and sentence in 1982. That court then denied Yates' petition for a writ of habeas corpus, but in 1985, the United States Supreme Court vacated that decision and remanded the case to the South Carolina Supreme Court. 474 U.S. 896 (1985). On remand in 1986, the South Carolina Supreme Court nonetheless affirmed the denial of the writ once again. In 1988, in the decision included above, the United States Supreme Court again reversed and remanded to the South Carolina Supreme Court. On remand, the South Carolina Supreme Court again denied the writ. 391 S.E.2d 530 (S.C. 1989). In 1991, the United States Supreme Court reversed the South Carolina Supreme Court for the third time. 500 U.S. 391 (1991). Yates is currently serving life in prison. He became eligible for parole in 2002. *See* Website of the South Carolina Department of Corrections, http://www.state.sc.us/scdc.

Frank Dean Teague, Jr., was sentenced to a total of 30 years in prison on February 5, 1977. He was paroled on May 27, 1992, and discharged on July 22, 1993. *See* Website of Illinois Department of Corrections, http://www.idoc.state.il.us.

2. *A "new rule"*

In *Teague* the plurality opinion states that "a case announces a new rule if the result was not dictated by precedent existing at the time the defendant's conviction became final." What problems might this definition engender?

3. *Capital cases and the rule in Teague*

The plurality in *Teague* also states,

> Because petitioner is not under sentence of death, we need not, and do not, express any views as to how the retroactivity approach we adopt today is to be applied in the capital sentencing context. We do, however, disagree with Justice Stevens' suggestion that the finality concerns underlying Justice Harlan's approach to retroactivity are limited to "making convictions final," and are therefore "wholly inapplicable to the capital sentencing context." *Post.* As we have often stated, a criminal judgment necessarily includes the sentence imposed upon the defendant. ***

Does this statement mean that the Court will not view capital cases differently for purposes of retroactivity analysis?

The Antiterrorism and Effective Death Penalty Act of 1996

When Congress passed the Antiterrorism and Effective Death Penalty Act of 1996, it changed the reach of the writ of habeas corpus. The following comparison of the habeas statute pre- and post-AEDPA is taken from Appendix A of Professors Hertz and Liebman's *Federal Habeas Corpus Practice and Procedure* (Lexis 2001). As you read, pay special attention to §2254(d)(1) and how it compares to the rule in *Teague*.

FEDERAL POSTCONVICTION STATUTES AS AMENDED BY THE ANTITERRORISM AND EFFECTIVE DEATH PENALTY ACT OF 1996

Copyright ©2001 by Matthew Bender & Company, Inc.,
a member of the LexisNexis group

[Deletions made by the 1996 Act are indicated by strikeouts; additions made by the Act are indicated by italics.]

§2241. Power to grant writ

(a) Writs of habeas corpus may be granted by the Supreme Court, any justice thereof, the district courts and any circuit judge within their respective jurisdictions. The order of a circuit judge shall be entered in the records of the district court of the district wherein the restraint complained of is had.

(b) The Supreme Court, any justice thereof, and any circuit judge may decline to entertain an application for a writ of habeas corpus and may transfer the application for hearing and determination to the district court having jurisdiction to entertain it.

(c) The writ of habeas corpus shall not extend to a prisoner unless—

(1) He is in custody under or by color of the authority of the United States or is committed for trial before some court thereof; or

(2) He is in custody for an act done or omitted in pursuance of an Act of Congress, or an order, process, judgment or decree of a court or judge of the United States; or

(3) He is in custody in violation of the Constitution or laws or treaties of the United States; or

(4) He, being a citizen of a foreign state and domiciled therein is in custody for an act done or omitted under any alleged right, title, authority, privilege, protection, or exemption claimed under the commission, order or sanction of any foreign state, or under color thereof, the validity and effect of which depend upon the law of nations; or

(5) It is necessary to bring him into court to testify or for trial.

(d) Where an application for a writ of habeas corpus is made by a person in custody under the judgment and sentence of a State court of a State which contains two or more federal judicial districts, the application may be filed in the district court for the district wherein such person is in custody or in the district court for the district within which the State court was held which convicted and sentenced him and each of such district courts shall have concurrent jurisdiction to entertain the application. The district court for the district wherein such an application is filed in the exercise of its discretion and in furtherance of justice may transfer the application to the other district court for hearing and determination.

§ 2242. Application

Application for a writ of habeas corpus shall be in writing signed and verified by the person for whose relief it is intended or by someone acting in his behalf.

It shall allege the facts concerning the applicant's commitment or detention, the name of the person who has custody over him and by virtue of what claim or authority, if known.

It may be amended or supplemented as provided in the rules of procedure applicable to civil actions.

If addressed to the Supreme Court, a justice thereof or a circuit judge it shall state the reasons for not making application to the district court of the district in which the applicant is held.

§ 2243. Issuance of writ; return; hearing; decision

A court, justice or judge entertaining an application for a writ of habeas corpus shall forthwith award the writ or issue an order directing the respondent to show cause why the writ should not be granted, unless it appears from the application that the applicant or person detained is not entitled thereto.

The writ, or order to show cause shall be directed to the person having custody of the person detained. It shall be returned within three days unless for good cause additional time, not exceeding twenty days, is allowed.

The person to whom the writ or order is directed shall make a return certifying the true cause of the detention.

When the writ or order is returned a day shall be set for hearing, not more than five days after the return unless for good cause additional time is allowed.

Unless the application for the writ and the return present only issues of law the person to whom the writ is directed shall be required to produce at the hearing the body of the person detained.

The applicant or the person detained may, under oath, deny any of the facts set forth in the return or allege any other material facts.

The return and all suggestions made against it may be amended, by leave of court, before or after being filed.

The court shall summarily hear and determine the facts, and dispose of the matter as law and justice require.

§ 2244. Finality of determination

(a) No circuit or district judge shall be required to entertain an application for a writ of habeas corpus to inquire into the detention of a person pursuant to a judgment of a court of the United States if it appears that the legality of such detention has been determined by a judge or court of the United States on a prior application for a writ of habeas corpus, ~~and the petition presents no new ground not theretofore presented and determined, and the judge or court is satisfied that the ends of justice will not be served by such inquiry~~ *except as provided in section 2255.*

(b) (1) A claim presented in a second or successive habeas corpus application under section 2254 that was presented in a prior application shall be dismissed.

(2) A claim presented in a second or successive habeas corpus application under section 2254 that was not presented in a prior application shall be dismissed unless—

(A) the applicant shows that the claim relies on a new rule of constitutional law, made retroactive to cases on collateral review by the Supreme Court, that was previously unavailable; or

(B) (i) the factual predicate for the claim could not have been discovered previously through the exercise of due diligence; and

(ii) the facts underlying the claim, if proven and viewed in light of the evidence as a whole, would be sufficient to establish by clear and convincing evidence that, but for constitutional error, no reasonable fact finder would have found the applicant guilty of the underlying offense.

(3) (A) Before a second or successive application permitted by this section is filed in the district court, the applicant shall move in the appropriate court of appeals for an order authorizing the district court to consider the application.

(B) A motion in the court of appeals for an order authorizing the district court to consider a second or successive application shall be determined by a three-judge panel of the court of appeals.

(C) The court of appeals may authorize the filing of a second or successive application only if it determines that the application makes a prima facie showing that the application satisfies the requirements this subsection.

(D) The court of appeals shall grant or deny the authorization to file a second or successive application not later than 30 days after the filing of the motion.

(E) The grant or denial of an authorization by a court of appeals to file a second or successive application shall not be appealable and

shall not be the subject of a petition for rehearing or for a writ of certiorari.

(4) A district court shall dismiss any claim presented in a second or successive application that the court of appeals has authorized to be filed unless the applicant shows that the claim satisfies the requirements of this section.

~~(b) When after an evidentiary hearing on the merits of a material factual issue, or after a hearing on the merits of an issue of law, a person in custody pursuant to the judgment of a State court has been denied by a court of the United States or a justice or judge of the United States release from custody or other remedy on an application for a writ of habeas corpus, a subsequent application for a writ of habeas corpus in behalf of such person need not be entertained by a court of the United States or a justice or judge of the United States unless the application alleges and is predicated on a factual or other ground not adjudicated on the hearing of the earlier application for the writ, and unless the court, justice, or judge is satisfied that the applicant has not in the earlier application deliberately withheld the newly asserted ground or otherwise abused the writ.~~

(c) In a habeas corpus proceeding brought in behalf of a person in custody pursuant to the judgment of a State court, a prior judgment of the Supreme Court of the United States on an appeal or review by a writ of certiorari at the instance of the prisoner of the decision of such State court, shall be conclusive as to all issues of fact or law with respect to an asserted denial of a Federal right which constitutes ground for discharge in a habeas corpus proceeding, actually adjudicated by the Supreme Court therein, unless the applicant for the writ of habeas corpus shall plead and the court shall find the existence of a material and controlling fact which did not appear in the record of the proceeding in the Supreme Court and the court shall further find that the applicant for the writ of habeas corpus could not have caused such fact to appear in such record by the exercise of reasonable diligence.

(d) (1) A 1-year period of limitation shall apply to an application for a writ of habeas corpus by a person in custody pursuant to the judgment of a State court. The limitation period shall run from the latest of—

(A) the date on which the judgment became final by the conclusion of direct review or the expiration of the time for seeking such review;

(B) the date on which the impediment to filing an application created by State action in violation of the Constitution or laws of the United States is removed, if the applicant was prevented from filing by such State action;

(C) the date on which the constitutional right asserted was initially recognized by the Supreme Court, if the right has been newly recognized by the Supreme Court and made retroactively applicable to cases on collateral review; or

(D) the date on which the factual predicate of the claim or claims presented could have been discovered through the exercise of due diligence.

(2) The time during which a properly filed application for State postconviction or other collateral review with respect to the pertinent judg-

ment or claim is pending shall not be counted toward any period of limitation under this subsection.

§ 2245. Certificate of trial judge admissible in evidence

On the hearing of an application for a writ of habeas corpus to inquire into the legality of the detention of a person pursuant to a judgment the certificate of the judge who presided at the trial resulting in the judgment, setting forth the facts occurring at the trial, shall be admissible in evidence. Copies of the certificate shall be filed with the court in which the application is pending and in the court in which the trial took place.

§ 2246. Evidence; depositions; affidavits

On application for a writ of habeas corpus, evidence may be taken orally or by deposition, or, in the discretion of the judge, by affidavit. If affidavits are admitted any party shall have the right to propound written interrogatories to the affiants, or to file answering affidavits.

§ 2247. Documentary evidence

On application for a writ of habeas corpus documentary evidence, transcripts of proceedings upon arraignment, plea and sentence and a transcript of the oral testimony introduced on any previous similar application by or in behalf of the same petitioner, shall be admissible in evidence.

§ 2248. Return or answer; conclusiveness

The allegations of a return to the writ of habeas corpus or of an answer to an order to show cause in a habeas corpus proceeding, if not traversed, shall be accepted as true except to the extent that the judge finds from the evidence that they are not true.

§ 2249. Certified copies of indictment, plea and judgment; duty of respondent

On application for a writ of habeas corpus to inquire into the detention of any person pursuant to a judgment of a court of the United States, the respondent shall promptly file with the court certified copies of the indictment, plea of petitioner and the judgment or such of them as may be material to the questions raised, if the petitioner fails to attach them to his petition, and same shall be attached to the return to the writ, or to the answer to the order to show cause.

§ 2250. Indigent petitioner entitled to documents without cost

If on any application for a writ of habeas corpus an order has been made permitting the petitioner to prosecute the application in forma pauperis, the clerk of any court of the United States shall furnish to the petitioner without cost certified copies of such documents or parts of the record on file in his office as may be required by order of the judge before whom the application is pending.

§2251. Stay of State court proceedings

A justice or judge of the United States before whom a habeas corpus proceeding is pending, may, before final judgment or after final judgment of discharge, or pending appeal, stay any proceeding against the person detained in any State court or by or under the authority of any State for any matter involved in the habeas corpus proceeding. After the granting of such a stay, any such proceeding in any State court or by or under the authority of any State shall be void. If no stay is granted, any such proceeding shall be as valid as if no habeas corpus proceedings or appeal were pending.

§2252. Notice

Prior to the hearing of a habeas corpus proceeding in behalf of a person in custody of State officers or by virtue of State laws notice shall be served on the attorney general or other appropriate officer of such State as the justice or judge at the time of issuing the writ shall direct.

§2253. Appeal

(a) In a habeas corpus proceeding or a proceeding under section 2255 before a district judge, the final order shall be subject to review, on appeal, by the court of appeals for the circuit in which the proceeding is held.

(b) There shall be no right of appeal from a final order in a proceeding to test the validity of a warrant to remove to another district or place for commitment or trial a person charged with a criminal offense against the United States, or to test the validity of such person's detention pending removal proceedings.

(c) (1) Unless a circuit justice or judge issues a certificate of appealability, an appeal may not to be taken to the court of appeals from

(A) the final order in a habeas corpus proceeding in which the detention complained of arises out of a process issued by a State court; or

(B) the final order in a proceeding under section 2255.

(2) A certificate of appealability may issue under paragraph (1) only if the applicant has made a substantial showing of the denial of a constitutional right.

(3) The certificate of appealability under paragraph (1) shall indicate which specific issue or issues satisfy the showing required by paragraph (2).

~~§2253. Appeal~~

~~In a habeas corpus proceeding before a circuit or district judge, the final order shall be subject to review, on appeal, by the court of appeals for the circuit where the proceeding is had.~~

~~There shall be no right of appeal from such an order in a proceeding to test the validity of a warrant to remove, to another district or place for commitment or trial, a person charged with a criminal offense against the United States, or to test the validity of his detention pending removal proceedings.~~

~~An appeal may not be taken to the court of appeals from the final order in a habeas corpus proceeding where the detention complained of arises out of process issued by a State court, unless the justice or judge who rendered the order or a circuit justice or judge issues a certificate of probable cause.~~

§2254. State custody; remedies in Federal courts

(a) The Supreme Court, a Justice thereof, a circuit judge, or a district court shall entertain an application for a writ of habeas corpus in behalf of a person in custody pursuant to the judgment of a State court only on the ground that he is in custody in violation of the Constitution or laws or treaties of the United States.

(b) (1) An application for a writ of habeas corpus on behalf of a person in custody pursuant to the judgment of a State court shall not be granted unless it appears that—

> *(A) the applicant has exhausted the remedies available in the courts of the State; or*

> *(B) (i) there is an absence of available State corrective process; or*

>> *(ii) circumstances exist that render such process ineffective to protect the rights of the applicant.*

(2) An application for a writ of habeas corpus may be denied on the merits, notwithstanding the failure of the applicant to exhaust the remedies available in the courts of the State.

(3) A State shall not be deemed to have waived the exhaustion requirement or be estopped from reliance upon the requirement unless the State, through counsel, expressly waives the requirement.

~~(b) An application for a writ of habeas corpus in behalf of a person in custody pursuant to the judgment of a State court shall not be granted unless it appears that the applicant has exhausted the remedies available in the courts of the State, or that there is either an absence of available State corrective process or the existence of circumstances rendering such process ineffective to protect the rights of the prisoner.~~

(c) An applicant shall not be deemed to have exhausted the remedies available in the courts of the State, within the meaning of this section, if he has the right under the law of the State to raise, by any available procedure, the question presented.

(d) An application for a writ of habeas corpus on behalf of a person in custody pursuant to the judgment of a State court shall not be granted with respect to any claim that was adjudicated on the merits in State court proceedings unless the adjudication of the claim—

> *(1) resulted in a decision that was contrary to, or involved an unreasonable application of clearly established Federal law, as determined by the Supreme Court of the United States; or*

> *(2) resulted in a decision that was based on an unreasonable determination of the facts in light of the evidence presented in the State court proceeding.*

(e) (1) In a proceeding instituted by an application for a writ of habeas corpus by a person in custody pursuant to the judgment of a State court, a determination of a factual issue made by a State court shall be presumed to be correct. The applicant shall have the burden of rebutting the presumption of correctness by clear and convincing evidence.

> *(2) If the applicant has failed to develop the factual basis of a claim in State court proceedings, the court shall not hold an evidentiary hearing on the claim unless the applicant shows that—*

>> *(A) the claim relies on—*

(i) a new rule of constitutional law, made retroactive to cases on collateral review by the Supreme Court, that was previously unavailable; or

(ii) a factual predicate that could not have been previously discovered through the exercise of due diligence; and

(B) the facts underlying the claim would be sufficient to establish by clear and convincing evidence that but for constitutional error, no reasonable factfinder would have found the applicant guilty of the underlying offense.

~~(d) In any proceeding instituted in a Federal court by an application for a writ of habeas corpus by a person in custody pursuant to the judgment of a State court, a determination after a hearing on the merits of a factual issue, made by a State court of competent jurisdiction in a proceeding to which the applicant for the writ and the State or an officer or agent thereof were parties, evidenced by a written finding, written opinion, or other reliable and adequate written indicia, shall be presumed to be correct, unless the applicant shall establish or it shall otherwise appear, or the respondent shall admit~~

~~(1) that the merits of the factual dispute were not resolved in the State court hearing;~~

~~(2) that the factfinding procedure employed by the State court was not adequate to afford a full and fair hearing;~~

~~(3) that the material facts were not adequately developed at the State court hearing;~~

~~(4) that the state court lacked jurisdiction of the subject matter or over the person of the applicant in the State court proceeding;~~

~~(5) that the applicant was an indigent and the State court, in deprivation of his constitutional right, failed to appoint counsel to represent him in the State court proceeding;~~

~~(6) that the applicant did not receive a full, fair, and adequate hearing in the state court proceeding, or~~

~~(7) that the applicant was as otherwise denied due process of law in the State court proceeding;~~

~~(8) or unless that part of the record of the State court proceeding in which the determination of such factual issue was made, pertinent to a determination of the sufficiency of the evidence to support such factual determination, is produced as provided for hereinafter, and the Federal court on a consideration of such part of the record as a whole concludes that such factual determination is not fairly supported by the record. And in an evidentiary hearing in the proceeding in the Federal court, when due proof of such factual determination has been made, unless the existence of one or more of the circumstances respectively set forth in paragraphs numbered (1) to (7), inclusive, is shown by the applicant, otherwise unless the court concludes pursuant to the provisions of paragraph numbered (8) that the record in the State court proceeding, considered as a whole, does not fairly support such factual determination,~~

~~the burden shall rest upon the applicant to establish by convincing evidence that the factual determination by the State court was erroneous.~~

(f) ~~(e)~~ If the applicant challenges the sufficiency of the evidence adduced in such State court proceeding to support the State court's determination of a factual issue made therein, the applicant, if able, shall produce that part of the record pertinent to a determination of the sufficiency of the evidence to support such determination. If the applicant, because of indigency or other reason is unable to produce such part of the record, then the State shall produce such part of the record and the Federal court shall direct the State to do so by order directed to an appropriate State official. If the State cannot provide such pertinent part of the record, then the court shall determine under the existing facts and circumstances what weight shall be given to the State court's factual determination.

(g) ~~(f)~~ A copy of the official records of the State court, duly certified by the clerk of such court to be a true and correct copy of a finding, judicial opinion, or other reliable written indicia showing such a factual determination by the State court shall be admissible in the Federal court proceeding.

(h) Except as provided in section 408 of the Controlled Substances Act, in all proceedings brought under this section, and any subsequent proceedings on review, the court may appoint counsel for an applicant who is or becomes financially unable to afford counsel, except as provided by a rule promulgated by the Supreme Court pursuant to statutory authority. Appointment of counsel under this section shall be governed by section 3006A of title 18.

(i) The ineffectiveness or incompetence of counsel during Federal or State collateral post-conviction proceedings shall not be a ground for relief in a proceeding arising under section 2254.

§ 2255. Federal custody; remedies on motion attacking sentence

A prisoner in custody under sentence of a court established by Act of Congress claiming the right to be released upon the ground that the sentence was imposed in violation of the Constitution or laws of the United States, or that the court was without jurisdiction to impose such sentence, or that the sentence was in excess of the maximum authorized by law, or is otherwise subject to collateral attack, may move the court which imposed the sentence to vacate, set aside or correct the sentence.

~~A motion for such relief may be made at any time.~~

Unless the motion and the files and records of the case conclusively show that the prisoner is entitled to no relief, the court shall cause notice thereof to be served upon the United States attorney, grant a prompt hearing thereon, determine the issues and make findings of fact and conclusions of law with respect thereto. If the court finds that the judgment was rendered without jurisdiction, or that the sentence imposed was not authorized by law or otherwise open to collateral attack, or that there has been such a denial or infringement of the constitutional rights of the prisoner as to render the judgment vulnerable to collateral attack, the court shall vacate and set the judgment aside and shall discharge the prisoner or resentence him or grant a new trial or correct the sentence as may appear appropriate.

A court may entertain and determine such motion without requiring the production of the prisoner at the hearing.

~~The sentencing court shall not be required to entertain a second or successive motion for similar relief on behalf of the same prisoner.~~

An appeal may be taken to the court of appeals from the order entered on the motion as from a final judgment on application for a writ of habeas corpus.

An application for a writ of habeas corpus in behalf of a prisoner who is authorized to apply for relief by motion pursuant to this section, shall not be entertained if it appears that the applicant has failed to apply for relief, by motion, to the court which sentenced him, or that such court has denied him relief, unless it also appears that the remedy by motion is inadequate or ineffective to test the legality of his detention.

A 1-year period of limitation shall apply to a motion under this section. The limitation period shall run from the latest of—

> *(1) the date on which the judgment of conviction becomes final;*
>
> *(2) the date on which the impediment to making a motion created by governmental action in violation of the Constitution or laws of the United States is removed, if the movant was prevented from making a motion by such governmental action;*
>
> *(3) the date on which the right asserted was initially recognized by the Supreme Court, if that right has been newly recognized by the Supreme Court and made retroactively applicable to cases on collateral review; or*
>
> *(4) the date on which the facts supporting the claim or claims presented could have been discovered through the exercise of due diligence.*

Except as provided in section 408 of the Controlled Substances Act, in all proceedings brought under this section, and any subsequent proceedings on review, the court may appoint counsel, except as provided by a rule promulgated by the Supreme Court pursuant to statutory authority. Appointment of counsel under this section shall be governed by section 3006A of title 18.

A second or successive motion must be certified as provided in section 2244 by a panel of the appropriate court of appeals to contain—

> *(1) newly discovered evidence that, if proven and viewed in light of the evidence as a whole, would be sufficient to establish by clear and convincing evidence that no reasonable factfinder would have found the movant guilty of the offense; or*
>
> *(2) a new rule of constitutional law, made retroactive to cases on collateral review by the Supreme Court that was previously unavailable.*

CHAPTER 154—
SPECIAL HABEAS CORPUS PROCEDURES IN CAPITAL CASES

Sec.

2261. Prisoners in State custody subject to capital sentence; appointment of counsel; requirement of rule of court or statute; procedures for appointment.

2262. Mandatory stay of execution; duration; limits on stays of execution; successive petitions.

2263. Filing of habeas corpus application; time requirements; tolling rules.

2264. Scope of Federal review; district court adjudications.

2265. Application to State unitary review procedure.

2266. Limitation periods for determining applications and motions.

§ 2261. Prisoners in State custody subject to capital sentence; appointment of counsel; requirement of rule of court or statute; procedures for appointment

(a) *This chapter shall apply to cases arising under section 2254 brought by prisoners in State custody who are subject to a capital sentence. It shall apply only if the provisions of subsections (b) and (c) are satisfied.*

(b) *This chapter is applicable if a State establishes by statute, rule of its court of last resort, or by another agency authorized by State law, a mechanism for the appointment, compensation, and payment of reasonable litigation expenses of competent counsel in State post-conviction proceedings brought by indigent prisoners whose capital convictions and sentences have been upheld on direct appeal to the court of last resort in the State or have otherwise become final for State law purposes. The rule of court or statute must provide standards of competency for the appointment of such counsel.*

(c) *Any mechanism for the appointment, compensation, and reimbursement of counsel as provided in subsection (b) must offer counsel to all State prisoners under capital sentence and must provide for the entry of an order by a court of record—*

(1) *appointing one or more counsels to represent the prisoner upon a finding that the prisoner is indigent and accepted the offer or is unable competently to decide whether to accept or reject the offer;*

(2) *finding, after a hearing if necessary, that the prisoner rejected the offer of counsel and made the decision with an understanding of its legal consequences; or*

(3) *denying the appointment of counsel upon a finding that the prisoner is not indigent.*

(d) *No counsel appointed pursuant to subsections (b) and (c) to represent a State prisoner under capital sentence shall have previously represented the prisoner at trial or on direct appeal in the case for which the appointment is made unless the prisoner and counsel expressly request continued representation.*

(e) *The ineffectiveness or incompetence of counsel during State or Federal post-conviction proceedings in a capital case shall not be a ground for relief in a proceeding arising under section 2254. This limitation shall not preclude the appointment of different counsel, on the court's own motion or at the request of the prisoner, at any phase of State or Federal post-conviction proceedings on the basis of the ineffectiveness or incompetence of counsel in such proceedings.*

§2262. Mandatory stay of execution; duration; limits on stays of execution; successive petitions

(a) Upon the entry in the appropriate State court of record of an order under section 2261(c), a warrant or order setting an execution date for a State prisoner shall be stayed upon application to any court that would have jurisdiction over any proceedings filed under section 2254. The application shall recite that the State has invoked the post-conviction review procedures of this chapter and that the scheduled execution is subject to stay.

(b) A stay of execution granted pursuant to subsection (a) shall expire if—

(1) a State prisoner fails to file a habeas corpus application under section 2254 within the time required in section 2263;

(2) before a court of competent jurisdiction, in the presence of counsel unless the prisoner has competently and knowingly waived such counsel, and after having been advised of the consequences, a State prisoner under capital sentence waives the right to pursue habeas corpus review under section 2254; or

(3) a State prisoner files a habeas corpus petition under section 2254 within the time required by section 2263 and fails to make a substantial showing of the denial of a Federal right or is denied relief in the district court or at any subsequent stage of review.

(c) If one of the conditions in subsection (b) has occurred, no Federal court thereafter shall have the authority to enter a stay of execution in the case, unless the court of appeals approves the filing of a second or successive application under section 2244(b).

§2263. Filing of habeas corpus application; time requirements; tolling rules

(a) Any application under this chapter for habeas corpus relief under section 2254 must be filed in the appropriate district court not later than 180 days after final State court affirmance of the conviction and sentence on direct review or the expiration of the time for seeking such review.

(b) The time requirements established by subsection (a) shall be tolled—

(1) from the date that a petition for certiorari is filed in the Supreme Court until the date of final disposition of the petition if a State prisoner files the petition to secure review by the Supreme Court of the affirmance of a capital sentence on direct review by the court of last resort of the State or other final State court decision on direct review;

(2) from the date on which the first petition for postconviction review or other collateral relief is filed until the final State court disposition of such petition; and

(3) during an additional period not to exceed 30 days, if—

(A) a motion for an extension of time is filed in the Federal district court that would have jurisdiction over the case upon the filing of a habeas corpus application under section 2254; and

(B) a showing of good cause is made for the failure to file the habeas corpus application within the time period established by this section.

§ 2264. Scope of Federal review; district court adjudications

(a) Whenever a State prisoner under capital sentence files a petition for habeas corpus relief to which this chapter applies, the district court shall only consider a claim or claims that have been raised and decided on the merits in the State courts, unless the failure to raise the claim properly is—

(1) the result of State action in violation of the Constitution or laws of the United States;

(2) the result of the Supreme Court's recognition of a new Federal right that is made retroactively applicable; or

(3) based on a factual predicate that could not have been discovered through the exercise of due diligence in time to present the claim for State or Federal post-conviction review.

(b) Following review subject to subsections (a), (d), and (e) of section 2254, the court shall rule on the claims properly before it.

§ 2265. Application to State unitary review procedure

(a) For purposes of this section, a "unitary review" procedure means a State procedure that authorizes a person under sentence of death to raise, in the course of direct review of the judgment, such claims as could be raised on collateral attack. This chapter shall apply, as provided in this section, in relation to a State unitary review procedure if the State establishes by rule of its court of last resort or by statute a mechanism for the appointment, compensation, and payment of reasonable litigation expenses of competent counsel in the unitary review proceedings, including expenses relating to the litigation of collateral claims in the proceedings. The rule of court or statute must provide standards of competency for the appointment of such counsel.

(b) To qualify under this section, a unitary review procedure must include an offer of counsel following trial for the purpose of representation on unitary review, and entry of an order, as provided in section 2261(c), concerning appointment of counsel or waiver or denial of appointment of counsel for that purpose. No counsel appointed to represent the prisoner in the unitary review proceedings shall have previously represented the prisoner at trial in the case for which the appointment is made unless the prisoner and counsel expressly request continued representation.

(c) Sections 2262, 2263, 2264, and 2266 shall apply in relation to cases involving a sentence of death from any State having a unitary review procedure that qualifies under this section. References to State "postconviction review" and "direct review" in such sections shall be understood as referring to unitary review under the State procedure. The reference in section 2262(a) to an "order under section 2261(c)" shall be understood as referring to the post-trial order under subsection (b) concerning representation in the unitary review proceedings, but if a transcript of the trial proceedings is unavailable at the time of the filing of such an order in the appropriate State court, then the start of the 180-day limitation period under section 2263 shall be deferred until a transcript is made available to the prisoner or counsel of the prisoner.

§ 2266. Limitation periods for determining applications and motions.

(a) The adjudication of any application under section 2254 that is subject to this chapter, and the adjudication of any motion under section 2255 by a person under sentence of death, shall be given priority by the district court and by the court of appeals over all noncapital matters.

(b) (1) (A) A district court shall render a final determination and enter a final judgment on any application for a writ of habeas corpus brought under this chapter in a capital case not later than 180 days after the date on which the application is filed.

(B) A district court shall afford the parties at least 120 days in which to complete all actions, including the preparation of all pleadings and briefs, and if necessary, a hearing, prior to the submission of the case for decision.

(C) (i) A district court may delay for not more than one additional 30-day period beyond the period specified in subparagraph (A), the rendering of a determination of an application for a writ of habeas corpus if the court issues a written order making a finding, and stating the reasons for the finding, that the ends of justice that would be served by allowing the delay outweigh the best interests of the public and the applicant in a speedy disposition of the application.

(ii) The factors, among others, that a court shall consider in determining whether a delay in the disposition of an application is warranted are as follows:

(I) Whether the failure to allow the delay would be likely to result in a miscarriage of justice.

(II) Whether the case is so unusual or so complex, due to the number of defendants, the nature of the prosecution, or the existence of novel questions of fact or law, that it is unreasonable to expect adequate briefing within the time limitations established by subparagraph (A).

(III) Whether the failure to allow a delay in a case that, taken as a whole, is not so unusual or so complex as described in subclause (II), but would otherwise deny the applicant reasonable time to obtain counsel, would unreasonably deny the applicant or the government continuity of counsel, or would deny counsel for the applicant or the government the reasonable time necessary for elective preparation, taking into account the exercise of due diligence.

(iii) No delay in disposition shall be permissible because of general congestion of the court's calendar.

(iv) The court shall transmit a copy of any order issued under clause (i) to the Director of the Administrative Office of the United States Courts for inclusion in the report under paragraph (5).

(2) The time limitations under paragraph (1) shall apply to—

(A) an initial application for a writ of habeas corpus;

(B) any second or successive application for a writ of habeas corpus; and

(C) any redetermination of an application for a writ of habeas corpus following a remand by the court of appeals or the Supreme Court for further proceedings, in which case the limitation period shall run from the date the remand is ordered.

(3) (A) The time limitation under this section shall not be construed to entitle an applicant to a stay of execution, to which the applicant would otherwise not be entitled, for the purpose of litigating any application or appeal.

(B) No amendment to an application for a writ of habeas corpus under this chapter shall be permitted after the filing of the answer to the application, except on the grounds specified in section 2244(b).

(4) (A) The failure of a court to meet or comply with a time limitation under this section shall not be a ground for granting relief from a judgment of conviction or sentence.

(B) The State may enforce a time limitation under this section by petitioning for a writ of mandamus to the court of appeals. The court of appeals shall act on the petition for a writ of mandamus not later than 30 days after the filing of the petition.

(5) (A) The Administrative Office of United States Courts shall submit to Congress an annual report on the compliance by the district courts with the time limitations under this section.

(B) The report described in subparagraph (A) shall include copies of the orders submitted by the district courts under paragraph (1)(B)(iv).

(c) (1) (A) A court of appeals shall hear and render a final determination of any appeal of an order granting or denying, in whole or in part, an application brought under this chapter in a capital case not later than 120 days after the date on which the reply brief is filed, or if no reply brief is filed, not later than 120 days after the date on which the answering brief is filed.

(B) (i) A court of appeals shall decide whether to grant a petition for rehearing or other request for rehearing en banc not later than 30 days after the date on which the petition for rehearing is filed unless a responsive pleading is required, in which case the court shall decide whether to grant the petition not later than 30 days after the date on which the responsive pleading is filed.

(ii) If a petition for rehearing or rehearing en banc is granted, the court of appeals shall hear and render a final determination of the appeal not later than 120 days after the date on which the order granting rehearing en banc is entered.

(2) The time limitations under paragraph (1) shall apply to—

(A) an initial application for a writ of habeas corpus;

(B) any second or successive application for a writ of habeas corpus; and

(C) any redetermination of an application for a writ of habeas corpus or related appeal following a remand by the court of appeals en banc or the Supreme Court for further proceedings, in which case the limitation period shall run from the date the remand is ordered.

(3) The time limitations under this section shall not be construed to entitle an applicant to a stay of execution, to which the applicant would otherwise not be entitled, for the purpose of litigating any application or appeal.

(4) (A) The failure of a court to meet or comply with a time limitation under this section shall not be a ground for granting relief from a judgment of conviction or sentence.

(B) The State may enforce a time limitation under this section by applying for a writ of mandamus to the Supreme Court.

(5) The Administrative Office of United States Courts shall submit to Congress an annual report on the compliance by the courts of appeals with the time limitations under this section.

Section 107(c) of the Antiterrorism and Effective Death Penalty Act of 1996:

(c) EFFECTIVE DATE—Chapter 154 of title 28, United States Code (as added by subsection (a)) shall apply to cases pending on or after the date of enactment of this Act.

Notes

1. *Codifying* Teague

In their learned treatise, *Federal Habeas Corpus Practice and Procedure*, Professors Hertz and Liebman state that §2254(d)(1) of the Antiterrorism and Effective Death Penalty Act codified *Teague v. Lane*, although the rule does not appear to be jurisdictional. In what ways did the AEDPA codify *Teague*? What does it mean that the rule is not jurisdictional?

2. *Preserving issues for appeal*

In *Hopkins v. Reeves*, 524 U.S. 88 (1998), the Court decided whether a state court must give a lesser-included-offense instruction at a capital trial, even when no such lesser-included offense existed under state law. One of the questions on which the Court originally granted certiorari was whether the Eighth Circuit Court of Appeals' holding—requiring Nebraska trial courts to give a capital defendant charged with felony murder a lesser-included-offense instruction on second-degree murder and manslaughter, even when state law said that second-degree murder and manslaughter were not lesser-included offenses of felony murder—was a "new rule" under *Teague v. Lane*. 524 U.S. at 94 n.3. Since the State raised the "new rule" argument for the first time in its petition for a writ of certiorari, however, the Court chose to decide the case on the merits, rather than on the retroactivity question. *Id.*

Does the AEDPA specify when such an issue must be raised in order to be preserved?

3. *Equal protection concerns*

In *James B. Beam Distilling Company v. Georgia*, 501 U.S. 529 (1991), Beam Distilling Company sought the return of taxes they had paid under a Georgia statute requiring "an excise tax on imported alcohol and distilled spirits at a rate double that imposed on alcohol and distilled spirits manufactured from Georgia-grown products." A nearly identical statute had been invalidated as unconstitutional in *Bacchus Imports, Ltd. v. Dias*, 468 U.S. 263 (1984), which was a Hawaii case. The Georgia courts declined to refund the money for the years the statute had been in effect before the *Bacchus* decision. The Court overruled the Georgia courts, holding that "when the Court has applied a rule of law to litigants in one case it must do so with respect to all others not barred by procedural requirements or res judicata." 501 U.S. at 543. Although the Court as a whole could not agree on a single opinion, six members of the Court agreed that *Bacchus* applied retroactively to James Beam. Justice Souter, joined by Justice Stevens, announced the judgment of the Court in an opinion that included a brief analysis implying the existence of equal protection concerns for habeas litigants:

> [R]etroactive application could hardly have been denied the litigant in the law-changing decision itself. A criminal defendant usually seeks one thing only on appeal, the reversal of his conviction; future application would provide little in the way of solace. In this context, without retroactivity at least to the first successful litigant, the incentive to seek review would be diluted if not lost altogether.

> But selective prospectivity also breaches the principle that litigants in similar situations should be treated the same, a fundamental component of *stare decisis* and the rule of law generally. ** "We depart from this basic judicial tradition when we simply pick and choose from among similarly situated defendants those who alone will receive the benefit of a 'new' rule of constitutional law." *Desist v. United States*, 394 U.S. 244, 258–259 (1969) (Harlan, J., dissenting).

501 U.S. at 537–538.

Is equal protection implicated in the AEDPA's codification of *Teague v. Lane*?

Chapter 9

Adequate and Independent State Grounds

In the cases in this chapter, the Supreme Court explains how a state court's adherence to state procedural rules as a basis for denying relief interacts with the availability of federal habeas corpus review.

In *Brown v. Allen*, 344 U.S. 443 (1953) (*see* Chapter 1), the Court explained that a state prisoner's challenge to the trial court's resolution of dispositive federal issues is always fair game on federal habeas. Then in *Fay v. Noia*, 372 U.S. 391 (1963) (*see* Chapter 7), the Court further clarified that "the doctrine under which state procedural defaults are held to constitute an adequate and independent state law ground barring direct Supreme Court review is not to be extended to limit the power granted the federal courts under the federal habeas statute." In so doing, the Court articulated a "deliberate bypass" standard whereby a federal judge had discretion to deny relief to an applicant who had deliberately bypassed the orderly procedure of the state courts and thus forfeited his state court remedies.

In the first case in this chapter, *Wainwright v. Sykes*, the "deliberate bypass standard" from *Fay* gives way to a "cause and prejudice" requirement. The Court explains that an "adequate and independent" finding of procedural default bars federal habeas review of a federal claim unless the habeas petitioner can show "cause" and "prejudice." Then in *Coleman v. Thompson*, the Supreme Court acknowledges that its decision in *Sykes* had left open the question of whether *Fay's* deliberate bypass standard would continue to apply in a case in which a state prisoner defaulted his entire appeal. *Coleman* answers that question by explaining that in all cases in which a state prisoner has defaulted his federal claims in state court pursuant to an independent and adequate state procedural rule, federal habeas review of the claims is barred unless the prisoner can demonstrate either (1) cause and prejudice, or (2) that failure to consider the claims will result in a fundamental miscarriage of justice.

Wainwright v. Sykes
433 U.S. 72 (1977)

JUSTICE REHNQUIST delivered the opinion of the Court.

We granted certiorari to consider the availability of federal habeas corpus to review a state convict's claim that testimony was admitted at his trial in violation of his rights under *Miranda v. Arizona*, 384 U.S. 436 (1966), a claim which the Florida courts have previously refused to consider on the merits because of noncompliance with a state contemporaneous-objection rule. Petitioner Wainwright, on behalf of the State of Florida, here challenges a decision of the Court of Appeals for the Fifth Circuit ordering a hearing in state court on the merits of respondent's contention.

Respondent Sykes was convicted of third-degree murder after a jury trial in the Circuit Court of DeSoto County. He testified at trial that on the evening of January 8, 1972, he told his wife to summon the police because he had just shot Willie Gilbert. Other evidence indicated that when the police arrived at respondent's trailer home, they found Gilbert dead of a shotgun wound, lying a few feet from the front porch. Shortly after their arrival, respondent came from across the road and volunteered that he had shot Gilbert, and a few minutes later respondent's wife approached the police and told them the same thing. Sykes was immediately arrested and taken to the police station.

Once there, it is conceded that he was read his *Miranda* rights, and that he declined to seek the aid of counsel and indicated a desire to talk. He then made a statement, which was admitted into evidence at trial through the testimony of the two officers who heard it, *** to the effect that he had shot Gilbert from the front porch of his trailer home. There were several references during the trial to respondent's consumption of alcohol during the preceding day and to his apparent state of intoxication, facts which were acknowledged by the officers who arrived at the scene. At no time during the trial, however, was the admissibility of any of respondent's statements challenged by his counsel on the ground that respondent had not understood the *Miranda* warnings. *** Nor did the trial judge question their admissibility on his own motion or hold a factfinding hearing bearing on that issue.

Respondent appealed his conviction, but apparently did not challenge the admissibility of the inculpatory statements. *** He later filed in the trial court a motion to vacate the conviction and, in the State District Court of Appeals and Supreme Court, petitions for habeas corpus. These filings, apparently for the first time, challenged the statements made to police on grounds of involuntariness. In all of these efforts respondent was unsuccessful.

Having failed in the Florida courts, respondent initiated the present action under 28 U.S.C. §2254, asserting the inadmissibility of his statements by reason of his lack of understanding of the *Miranda* warnings. *** The United States District Court for the Middle District of Florida ruled that *Jackson v. Denno*, 378 U.S. 368 (1964), requires a hearing in a state criminal trial prior to the admission of an inculpatory out-of-court statement by the defendant. It held further that respondent had not lost his right to assert such a claim by failing to object at trial or on direct appeal, since only "exceptional circumstances" of "strategic decisions at trial" can create such a bar to raising federal constitutional claims in a federal habeas action. The court stayed issuance of the writ to allow the state court to hold a hearing on the "voluntariness" of the statements.

***

The court then directed its attention to the effect on respondent's right of Florida Rule Crim. Proc. 3.190(i), *** which it described as "a contemporaneous objection rule" applying to motions to suppress a defendant's inculpatory statements *** and concluded that the failure to comply with the rule requiring objection at the trial would only bar review of the suppression claim where the right to object was deliberately bypassed for reasons relating to trial tactics. *** It found that prejudice is "inherent" in any situation, like the present one, where the admissibility of an incriminating statement is concerned. Concluding that "[t]he failure to object in this case cannot be dismissed as a trial tactic, and thus a deliberate by-pass," the court affirmed the District Court order that the State hold a hearing on whether respondent knowingly waived his *Miranda* rights at the time he made the statements.

The simple legal question before the Court calls for a construction of the language of 28 U.S.C. §2254(a), which provides that the federal courts shall entertain an application for a writ of habeas corpus "in behalf of a person in custody pursuant to the judgment of a state court only on the ground that he is in custody in violation of the Constitution or laws or treaties of the United States." But, to put it mildly, we do not write on a clean slate in construing this statutory provision. *** Its earliest counterpart, applicable only to prisoners detained by federal authority, is found in the Judiciary Act of 1789. Construing that statute for the Court in *Ex parte Watkins*, 3 Pet. 193, 202, 7 L. Ed. 650 (1830), Chief Justice Marshall said:

> An imprisonment under a judgment cannot be unlawful, unless that judgment be an absolute nullity; and it is not a nullity if the Court has general jurisdiction of the subject, although it should be erroneous.

See Ex parte Kearney, 7 Wheat. 38, 5 L. Ed. 391 (1822).

In 1867, Congress expanded the statutory language so as to make the writ available to one held in state as well as federal custody. For more than a century since the 1867 amendment, this Court has grappled with the relationship between the classical common-law writ of habeas corpus and the remedy provided in 28 U.S.C. § 2254. Sharp division within the Court has been manifested on more than one aspect of the perplexing problems which have been litigated in this connection. Where the habeas petitioner challenges a final judgment of conviction rendered by a state court, this Court has been called upon to decide no fewer than four different questions, all to a degree interrelated with one another: (1) What types of federal claims may a federal habeas court properly consider? (2) Where a federal claim is cognizable by a federal habeas court, to what extent must that court defer to a resolution of the claim in prior state proceedings? (3) To what extent must the petitioner who seeks federal habeas exhaust state remedies before resorting to the federal court? (4) In what instances will an adequate and independent state ground bar consideration of otherwise cognizable federal issues on federal habeas review?

Each of these four issues has spawned its share of litigation. With respect to the first, the rule laid down in *Ex parte Watkins, supra*, was gradually changed by judicial decisions expanding the availability of habeas relief beyond attacks focused narrowly on the jurisdiction of the sentencing court. ** *Ex parte Siebold*, 100 U.S. 371 (1880), authorized use of the writ to challenge a conviction under a federal statute where the statute was claimed to violate the United States Constitution. *Frank v. Mangum*, 237 U.S. 309 (1915), and *Moore v. Dempsey*, 261 U.S. 86 (1923), though in large part inconsistent with one another, together broadened the concept of jurisdiction to allow review of a claim of "mob domination" of what was in all other respects a trial in a court of competent jurisdiction.

In *Johnson v. Zerbst*, 304 U.S. 458, 463 (1938), an indigent federal prisoner's claim that he was denied the right to counsel at his trial was held to state a contention going to the "power and authority" of the trial court, which might be reviewed on habeas. Finally, in *Waley v. Johnston*, 316 U.S. 101 (1942), the Court openly discarded the concept of jurisdiction—by then more a fiction than anything else—as a touchstone of the availability of federal habeas review, and acknowledged that such review is available for claims of "disregard of the constitutional rights of the accused, and where the writ is the only effective means of preserving his rights." *Id.* at 104–105. In *Brown v. Allen*, 344 U.S. 443 (1953), it was made explicit that a state prisoner's challenge to the trial court's resolution of dispositive federal issues is always fair game on federal habeas. ***

The degree of deference to be given to a state court's resolution of a federal-law issue was elaborately canvassed in the Court's opinion in *Brown v. Allen, supra*. Speaking for the Court, Justice Reed stated: "[Such] state adjudication carries the weight that federal practice gives to the conclusion of a court of last resort of another jurisdiction on federal constitutional issues. It is not *res judicata*." ***

The exhaustion-of-state-remedies requirement was first articulated by this Court in the case of *Ex parte Royall*, 117 U.S. 241 (1886). There, a state defendant sought habeas in advance of trial on a claim that he had been indicted under an unconstitutional statute. The writ was dismissed by the District Court, and this Court affirmed, stating that while there was power in the federal courts to entertain such petitions, as a matter of comity they should usually stay their hand pending consideration of the issue in the normal course of the state trial. ***

***

*** The application of this principle in the context of a federal habeas proceeding has therefore excluded from consideration any questions of state *substantive* law, and thus effectively barred federal habeas review where questions of that sort are either the only ones raised by a petitioner or are in themselves dispositive of his case. The area of controversy which has developed has concerned the reviewability of federal claims which the state court has declined to pass on because not presented in the manner prescribed by its procedural rules. The adequacy of such an independent state procedural ground to prevent federal habeas review of the underlying federal issue has been treated very differently than where the state-law ground is substantive. The pertinent decisions marking the Court's somewhat tortuous efforts to deal with this problem are: *Ex parte Spencer*, 228 U.S. 652 (1913); *Brown v. Allen*, 344 U.S. 443 (1953); *Fay v. Noia*[, 372 U.S. 391 (1963)]; *Davis v. United States*, 411 U.S. 233 (1973); and *Francis v. Henderson*, 425 U.S. 536 (1976).

In *Brown, supra*, petitioner Daniels' lawyer had failed to mail the appeal papers to the State Supreme Court on the last day provided by law for filing, and hand delivered them one day after that date. Citing the state rule requiring timely filing, the Supreme Court of North Carolina refused to hear the appeal. This Court, relying in part on its earlier decision in *Ex parte Spencer, supra*, held that federal habeas was not available to review a constitutional claim which could not have been reviewed on direct appeal here because it rested on an independent and adequate state procedural ground. 344 U.S. at 486–487.

In *Fay v. Noia, supra*, respondent Noia sought federal habeas to review a claim that his state-court conviction had resulted from the introduction of a coerced confession in violation of the Fifth Amendment to the United States Constitution. While the convictions of his two co-defendants were reversed on that ground in collateral proceedings following their appeals, Noia did not appeal and the New York courts ruled that his subsequent *coram nobis* action was barred on account of that failure. This Court held that petitioner was nonetheless entitled to raise the claim in federal habeas, and thereby overruled its decision 10 years earlier in *Brown v. Allen, supra* :

> [T]he doctrine under which state procedural defaults are held to constitute an adequate and independent state law ground barring direct Supreme Court review is not to be extended to limit the power granted the federal courts under the federal habeas statute. 372 U.S. at 399.

As a matter of comity but not of federal power, the Court acknowledged "a limited discretion in the federal judge to deny relief…to an applicant who had deliberately bypassed the orderly procedure of the state courts and in so doing has forfeited his state court remedies." *Id.* at 438. In so stating, the Court made clear that the waiver must be knowing and actual—"'an intentional relinquishment or abandonment of a known right or privilege.'" *Id.* at 439, *quoting Johnson v. Zerbst*, 304 U.S. at 464. Noting petitioner's "grisly choice" between acceptance of his life sentence and pursuit of an appeal which might culminate in a sentence of death, the Court concluded that there had been no deliberate bypass of the right to have the federal issues reviewed through a state appeal. ***

A decade later we decided *Davis v. United States, supra,* in which a federal prisoner's application under 28 U.S.C. §2255 sought for the first time to challenge the makeup of the grand jury which indicted him. The Government contended that he was barred by the requirement of Fed. Rule Crim. Proc. 12(b)(2) providing that such challenges must be raised "by motion before trial." The Rule further provides that failure to so object constitutes a waiver of the objection, but that "the court for cause shown may grant relief from the waiver." We noted that the Rule "promulgated by this Court and, pursuant to 18 U.S.C. §3771, 'adopted' by Congress, governs by its terms the manner in which the claims of defects in the institution of criminal proceedings may be waived," 411 U.S. at 241, and held that this standard contained in the Rule, rather than the *Fay v. Noia* concept of waiver, should pertain in federal habeas as on direct review. Referring to previous constructions of Rule 12(b)(2), we concluded that review of the claim should be barred on habeas, as on direct appeal, absent a showing of cause for the noncompliance and some showing of actual prejudice resulting from the alleged constitutional violation.

***

To the extent that the dicta of *Fay v. Noia* may be thought to have laid down an all-inclusive rule rendering state contemporaneous-objection rules ineffective to bar review of underlying federal claims in federal habeas proceedings—absent a "knowing waiver" or a "deliberate bypass" of the right to so object—its effect was limited by *Francis,* which applied a different rule and barred a habeas challenge to the makeup of a grand jury. Petitioner Wainwright in this case urges that we further confine its effect by applying the principle enunciated in *Francis* to a claimed error in the admission of a defendant's confession.

Respondent first contends that any discussion as to the effect that noncompliance with a state procedural rule should have on the availability of federal habeas is quite unnecessary because in his view Florida did not actually have a contemporaneous-objection rule. He would have us interpret Florida Rule Crim. Proc. 3.190(i), *** which petitioner asserts is a traditional "contemporaneous objection rule," to place the burden on the trial judge to raise on his own motion the question of the admissibility of any inculpatory statement. Respondent's approach is, to say the least, difficult to square with the language of the Rule, which in unmistakable terms and with specified exceptions requires that the motion to suppress be raised before trial. Since all of the Florida appellate courts refused to review petitioner's federal claim on the merits after his trial, and since their action in so doing is quite consistent with a line of Florida authorities interpreting the rule in question as requiring a contemporaneous objection, we accept the State's position on this point. **

Respondent also urges that a defendant has a right under *Jackson v. Denno,* 378 U.S. 368 (1964), to a hearing as to the voluntariness of a confession, even though the defendant does not object to its admission. But we do not read Jackson as creating any such requirement. In that case the defendant's objection to the use of his confession was brought to the attention of the trial court, ** and nothing in the Court's opinion suggests that a hearing would have been required even if it had not been. To the contrary, the Court prefaced its entire discussion of the merits of the case with a statement of the constitutional rule that was to prove dispositive—that a defendant has a "right at some stage in the proceedings to object to the use of the confession and to have a fair hearing and a reliable determination on the issue of voluntariness...." ** Language in subsequent decisions of this Court has reaffirmed the view that the Constitution does not require a voluntariness hearing absent some contemporaneous challenge to the use of the confession. ***

We therefore conclude that Florida procedure did, consistently with the United States Constitution, require that respondents' confession be challenged at trial or not at all, and thus his failure to timely object to its admission amounted to an independent and adequate state procedural ground which would have prevented direct review here. *See Henry v. Mississippi*, 379 U.S. 443 (1965). We thus come to the crux of this case. Shall the rule of *Francis v. Henderson, supra*, barring federal habeas review absent a showing of "cause" and "prejudice" attendant to a state procedural waiver, be applied to a waived objection to the admission of a confession at trial? *** We answer that question in the affirmative.

As earlier noted in the opinion, since *Brown v. Allen*, 344 U.S. 443 (1953), it has been the rule that the federal habeas petitioner who claims he is detained pursuant to a final judgment of a state court in violation of the United States Constitution is entitled to have the federal habeas court make its own independent determination of his federal claim, without being bound by the determination on the merits of that claim reached in the state proceedings. This rule of *Brown v. Allen* is in no way changed by our holding today. Rather, we deal only with contentions of federal law which were *not* resolved on the merits in the state proceeding due to respondent's failure to raise them there as required by state procedure. We leave open for resolution in future decisions the precise definition of the "cause"-and-"prejudice" standard, and note here only that it is narrower than the standard set forth in dicta in *Fay v. Noia*, which would make federal habeas review generally available to state convicts absent a knowing and deliberate waiver of the federal constitutional contention. It is the sweeping language of *Fay v. Noia*, going far beyond the facts of the case eliciting it, which we today reject. ***

The reasons for our rejection of it are several. The contemporaneous-objection rule itself is by no means peculiar to Florida, and deserves greater respect than *Fay* gives it, both for the fact that it is employed by a coordinate jurisdiction within the federal system and for the many interests which it serves in its own right. A contemporaneous objection enables the record to be made with respect to the constitutional claim when the recollections of witnesses are freshest, not years later in a federal habeas proceeding. It enables the judge who observed the demeanor of those witnesses to make the factual determinations necessary for properly deciding the federal constitutional question. While the 1966 amendment to § 2254 requires deference to be given to such determinations made by state courts, the determinations themselves are less apt to be made in the first instance if there is no contemporaneous objection to the admission of the evidence on federal constitutional grounds.

    ***

The failure of the federal habeas courts generally to require compliance with a contemporaneous-objection rule tends to detract from the perception of the trial of a criminal case in state court as a decisive and portentous event. A defendant has been accused of a serious crime, and this is the time and place set for him to be tried by a jury of his peers and found either guilty or not guilty by that jury. To the greatest extent possible all issues which bear on this charge should be determined in this proceeding: the accused is in the courtroom, the jury is in the box, the judge is on the bench, and the witnesses, having been subpoenaed and duly sworn, await their turn to testify. Society's resources have been concentrated at that time and place in order to decide, within the limits of human fallibility, the question of guilt or innocence of one of its citizens. Any procedural rule which encourages the result that those proceedings be as free of error as possible is thoroughly desirable, and the contemporaneous-objection rule surely falls within this classification.

We believe the adoption of the *Francis* rule in this situation will have the salutary effect of making the state trial on the merits the "main event," so to speak, rather than a "tryout on the road" for what will later be the determinative federal habeas hearing. There is nothing in the Constitution or in the language of § 2254 which requires that the state trial on the issue of guilt or innocence be devoted largely to the testimony of fact witnesses directed to the elements of the state crime, while only later will there occur in a federal habeas hearing a full airing of the federal constitutional claims which were not raised in the state proceedings. If a criminal defendant thinks that an action of the state trial court is about to deprive him of a federal constitutional right there is every reason for his following state procedure in making known his objection.

The "cause"-and-"prejudice" exception of the *Francis* rule will afford an adequate guarantee, we think, that the rule will not prevent a federal habeas court from adjudicating for the first time the federal constitutional claim of a defendant who in the absence of such an adjudication will be the victim of a miscarriage of justice. Whatever precise content may be given those terms by later cases, we feel confident in holding without further elaboration that they do not exist here. Respondent has advanced no explanation whatever for his failure to object at trial, *** and, as the proceeding unfolded, the trial judge is certainly not to be faulted for failing to question the admission of the confession himself. The other evidence of guilt presented at trial, moreover, was substantial to a degree that would negate any possibility of actual prejudice resulting to the respondent from the admission of his inculpatory statement.

We accordingly conclude that the judgment of the Court of Appeals for the Fifth Circuit must be reversed, and the cause remanded to the United States District Court for the Middle District of Florida with instructions to dismiss respondent's petition for a writ of habeas corpus.

It is so ordered.

[Concurring opinions by CHIEF JUSTICE BURGER, JUSTICE STEVENS, and JUSTICE WHITE, omitted.]

JUSTICE BRENNAN, with whom JUSTICE MARSHALL joins, dissenting.

Over the course of the last decade, the deliberate-bypass standard announced in *Fay v. Noia*, 372 U.S. 391, 438–439 (1963), has played a central role in efforts by the federal judiciary to accommodate the constitutional rights of the individual with the States' interests in the integrity of their judicial procedural regimes. The Court today decides that this standard should no longer apply with respect to procedural defaults occurring during the trial of a criminal defendant. In its place, the Court adopts the two-part "cause"-and-"prejudice" test originally developed in *Davis v. United States*, 411 U.S. 233 (1973), and *Francis v. Henderson*, 425 U.S. 536 (1976). As was true with these earlier cases, *** however, today's decision makes no effort to provide concrete guidance as to the content of those terms. More particularly, left unanswered is the thorny question that must be recognized to be central to a realistic rationalization of this area of law: How should the federal habeas court treat a procedural default in a state court that is attributable purely and simply to the error or negligence of a defendant's trial counsel?

Because this key issue remains unresolved, I shall attempt in this opinion a re-examination of the policies *** that should inform—and in *Fay* did inform—the selection of the standard governing the availability of federal habeas corpus jurisdiction in the face of an intervening procedural default in the state court.

I

I begin with the threshold question: What is the meaning and import of a procedural default? If it could be assumed that a procedural default more often than not is the product of a defendant's conscious refusal to abide by the duly constituted, legitimate processes of the state courts, then I might agree that a regime of collateral review weighted in favor of a State's procedural rules would be warranted. *** *Fay*, however, recognized that such rarely is the case; and therein lies *Fay*'s basic unwillingness to embrace a view of habeas jurisdiction that results in "an airtight system of [procedural] forfeitures." 372 U.S. at 432.

This, of course, is not to deny that there are times when the failure to heed a state procedural requirement stems from an intentional decision to avoid the presentation of constitutional claims to the state forum. *Fay* was not insensitive to this possibility. Indeed, the very purpose of its bypass test is to detect and enforce such intentional procedural forfeitures of outstanding constitutionally based claims. *** For this reason, the Court's assertion that it "think[s]" that the *Fay* rule encourages intentional "sandbagging" on the part of the defense lawyers is without basis, *ante*; certainly the Court points to no cases or commentary arising during the past 15 years of actual use of the *Fay* test to support this criticism. Rather, a consistent reading of case law demonstrates that the bypass formula has provided a workable vehicle for protecting the integrity of state rules in those instances when such protection would be both meaningful and just. ***

But having created the bypass exception to the availability of collateral review, *Fay* recognized that intentional, tactical forfeitures are not the norm upon which to build a rational system of federal habeas jurisdiction. In the ordinary case, litigants simply have no incentive to slight the state tribunal, since constitutional adjudication on the state and federal levels are not mutually exclusive. *Brown v. Allen*, 344 U.S. 443 (1953). ** Under the regime of collateral review recognized since the days of *Brown v. Allen*, and enforced by the *Fay* bypass test, no rational lawyer would risk the "sandbagging" feared by the Court. *** If a constitutional challenge is not properly raised on the state level, the explanation generally will be found elsewhere than in an intentional tactical decision.

   ***

Fay's answer thus is plain: the bypass test simply refuses to credit what is essentially a lawyer's mistake as a forfeiture of constitutional rights. I persist in the belief that the interests of Sykes and the State of Florida are best rationalized by adherence to this test, and by declining to react to inadvertent defaults through the creation of an "airtight system of forfeitures."

II

What are the interests that Sykes can assert in preserving the availability of federal collateral relief in the face of his inadvertent state procedural default? Two are paramount.

As is true with any federal habeas applicant, Sykes seeks access to the federal court for the determination of the validity of his federal constitutional claim. Since at least *Brown v. Allen*, it has been recognized that the "fair effect [of] the habeas corpus jurisdiction as enacted by Congress" entitles a state prisoner to such federal review. 344 U.S.

at 500 (opinion of Frankfurter, J.). While some of my Brethen may feel uncomfortable with this congressional choice of policy, *see, e.g.*, *Stone v. Powell*, 428 U.S. 465 (1976), the Legislative Branch nonetheless remains entirely free to determine that the constitutional rights of an individual subject to state custody, like those of the civil rights plaintiff suing under 42 U.S.C. § 1983, are best preserved by "interpos[ing] the federal courts between the States and the people, as guardians of the people's federal rights...." *Mitchum v. Foster*, 407 U.S. 225, 242 (1972).

***

Thus, I remain concerned that undue deference to local procedure can only serve to undermine the ready access to a federal court to which a state defendant otherwise is entitled. But federal review is not the full measure of Sykes' interest, for there is another of even greater immediacy: assuring that his constitutional claims can be addressed to *some* court. For the obvious consequence of barring Sykes from the federal courthouse is to insulate Florida's alleged constitutional violation from any and all judicial review because of a lawyer's mistake. From the standpoint of the habeas petitioner, it is a harsh rule indeed that denies him "any review at all where the state has granted none," *Brown v. Allen*, 344 U.S. at 552 (Black, J., dissenting), particularly when he would have enjoyed both state and federal consideration had his attorney not erred.

***

In sum, I believe that *Fay*'s commitment to enforcing intentional but not inadvertent procedural defaults offers a realistic measure of protection for the habeas corpus petitioner seeking federal review of federal claims that were not litigated before the State. The threatened creation of a more "airtight system of forfeitures" would effectively deprive habeas petitioners of the opportunity for litigating their constitutional claims before any forum and would disparage the paramount importance of constitutional rights in our system of government. Such a restriction of habeas corpus jurisdiction should be countenanced, I submit, only if it fairly can be concluded that *Fay*'s focus on knowing and voluntary forfeitures unduly interferes with the legitimate interests of state courts or institutions. The majority offers no suggestion that actual experience has shown that *Fay*'s bypass test can be criticized on this score. And, as I now hope to demonstrate, any such criticism would be unfounded.

***

IV

***

One final consideration deserves mention. Although the standards recently have been relaxed in various jurisdictions, *** it is accurate to assert that most courts, this one included, *** traditionally have resisted any realistic inquiry into the competency of trial counsel. There is nothing unreasonable, however, in adhering to the proposition that it is the responsibility of a trial lawyer who takes on the defense of another to be aware of his client's basic legal rights and of the legitimate rules of the forum in which he practices his profession. *** If he should unreasonably permit such rules to bar the assertion of the colorable constitutional claims of his client, then his conduct may well fall below the level of competence that can fairly be expected of him. *** For almost 40 years it has been established that inadequacy of counsel undercuts the very competence and jurisdiction of the trial court and is always open to collateral review. *Johnson v. Zerbst*, 304 U.S. 458 (1938). *** Obviously, as a practical matter, a trial counsel cannot procedurally waive his own inadequacy. If the scope of habeas jurisdiction previously governed by *Fay v. Noia* is to be redefined so as to enforce the errors and neglect of lawyers with unnecessary and unjust rigor, the time may come when conscientious and fairminded federal and state courts, in adhering to the teaching of *Johnson v. Zerbst*, will have to reconsider whether they can continue to indulge the comfortable fiction that all lawyers are skilled or even competent craftsmen in representing the fundamental rights of their clients.

Notes

1. *Concurring opinion by Chief Justice Burger*

In his concurring opinion, Chief Justice Burger wrote separately to emphasize that in his view, "the 'deliberate bypass' standard enunciated in *Fay v. Noia*, 372 U.S. 391 (1963), was never designed for, and is inapplicable to, errors—even of constitutional dimension—alleged to have been committed during trial." He explained:

> In *Fay v. Noia*, the Court applied the "deliberate bypass" standard to a case where the critical procedural decision—whether to take a criminal appeal—was entrusted to a convicted defendant. Although Noia, the habeas petitioner, was represented by counsel, he himself had to make the decision whether to appeal or not; the role of the attorney was limited to giving advice and counsel. In giving content to the new deliberate-bypass standard, *Fay* looked to the Court's decision in *Johnson v. Zerbst*, 304 U.S. 458 (1938), a case where the defendant had been called upon to make the decision whether to request representation by counsel in his federal criminal trial. Because in both *Fay* and *Zerbst*, important rights hung in the balance of the defendant's own decision, the Court required that a waiver impairing such rights be a knowing and intelligent decision by the defendant himself. ***
>
> ***
>
> Since trial decisions are of necessity entrusted to the accused's attorney, the *Fay-Zerbst* standard of "knowing and intelligent waiver" is simply inapplicable. The dissent in this case, written by the author of *Fay v. Noia*, implicitly recognizes as much. According to the dissent, *Fay* imposes the knowing-and-intelligent-waiver standard "where possible" during the course of the trial. In an extraordinary modification of *Fay*, Justice Brennan would now require "that the lawyer actually exercis[e] his expertise and judgment in his client's service, and with his client's knowing and intelligent participation *where possible*"; he does not intimate what guidelines would be used to decide when or under what circumstances this would actually be "possible." ***

Should the standard of a "knowing and intelligent waiver" be inapplicable because trial decisions are necessarily entrusted to the accused's attorney?

Chief Justice Burger criticizes Justice Brennan's dissent for not explaining what guidelines would be used to decide the circumstances under which it would be possible for a lawyer to exercise his expertise and judgment in his client's service and with his client's knowing and intelligent participation. What guidelines might make such an assessment possible?

2. *Concurring opinion by Justice Stevens*

In his concurrence, Justice Stevens explained that "[a]lthough the Court's decision today may be read as a significant departure from the 'deliberate bypass' standard announced in *Fay v. Noia*," he was "persuaded that the holding is consistent with the way other federal courts have actually been applying *Fay*." Because "[m]atters such as the competence of counsel, the procedural context in which the asserted waiver occurred, the character of the constitutional right at stake, and the overall fairness of the entire proceeding, may be more significant than the language of the test the Court purports to apply," Justice Stevens believed the Court had "wisely refrained from attempting to give precise content to its 'cause' and 'prejudice' exception."

In what ways did the Court refrain from giving precise content to its cause-and-prejudice exception? Was Justice Stevens correct that such ambiguity was wise?

After *Wainwright v. Sykes*, a conflict emerged among the Courts of Appeals over the standard for determining whether a state court's ambiguous invocation of a procedural default barred federal habeas review. The Court resolved this conflict in *Harris v. Reed*, 489 U.S. 255, 260 (1989). In *Harris*, the Court articulated a "plain statement" rule for determining whether a state court has relied on adequate and independent state grounds: "a procedural default does not bar consideration of a federal claim on either direct or habeas review unless the last state court rendering a judgment in the case 'clearly and expressly' states that its judgment rests on a state procedural bar." 489 U.S. at 263.

After articulating this bright-line rule, the Court clarified what it meant by "clearly and expressly," stating in *Ylst v. Nunnemaker*, 501 U.S. 797 (1991), and *Coleman v. Thompson* that a judgment rests on a state procedural bar.

Nunnemaker was tried in California state court for murder and raised the defense of diminished capacity. In response, the State introduced—without objection from defense counsel—statements Nunnemaker had made to a psychiatrist who had interviewed him. After the jury found him guilty, Nunnemaker appealed by claiming for the first time that the State's psychiatric testimony was inadmissible because Nunnemaker had not been given a *Miranda* warning before his interview with the State psychiatrist. The California Court of Appeal affirmed the conviction on the basis of a state procedural rule that "an objection based upon a *Miranda* violation cannot be raised for the first time on appeal." *Id.* at 799.

After the California Supreme Court denied discretionary review, Nunnemaker filed various petitions for collateral relief, state habeas corpus, and a petition for writ of federal habeas corpus that either were denied or were dismissed without prejudice. It was not until Nunnemaker filed his second petition for habeas relief in federal court that the Court of Appeals for the Ninth Circuit held that because the California Supreme Court did not "'clearly and expressly state its reliance on Nunnemaker's procedural default,'" the federal court could not say that the Supreme Court's order "was based on a procedural default rather than on the underlying merits of Nunnemaker's claims." *Id.* at 801.

Justice Scalia held that "[w]here there has been one reasoned state judgment rejecting a federal claim, later unexplained orders upholding that judgment or rejecting the same claim rest upon the same ground." ** This means that if the "last reasoned opinion on the claim explicitly imposes a procedural default, [the Court] will presume that a later decision rejecting the claim did not silently disregard that bar and consider the merits." **

Although the Court issued *Ylst* and *Coleman* on the same day, most of the Court's reasoning is found in *Coleman*.

Coleman v. Thompson

501 U.S. 722 (1991)

JUSTICE O'CONNOR delivered the opinion of the Court.

This is a case about federalism. It concerns the respect that federal courts owe the States and the States' procedural rules when reviewing the claims of state prisoners in federal habeas corpus.

A Buchanan County, Virginia, jury convicted Roger Keith Coleman of rape and capital murder and fixed the sentence at death for the murder. The trial court imposed the death sentence, and the Virginia Supreme Court affirmed both the convictions and the sentence. ** This Court denied certiorari. **

Coleman then filed a petition for a writ of habeas corpus in the Circuit Court for Buchanan County, raising numerous federal constitutional claims that he had not raised on direct appeal. After a 2-day evidentiary hearing, the Circuit Court ruled against Coleman on all claims. ** The court entered its final judgment on September 4, 1986.

Coleman filed his notice of appeal with the Circuit Court on October 7, 1986, 33 days after the entry of final judgment. Coleman subsequently filed a petition for appeal in the Virginia Supreme Court. The Commonwealth of Virginia, as appellee, filed a motion to dismiss the appeal. The sole ground for dismissal urged in the motion was that Coleman's notice of appeal had been filed late. Virginia Supreme Court Rule 5:9(a) provides that no appeal shall be allowed unless a notice of appeal is filed with the trial court within 30 days of final judgment.

The Virginia Supreme Court did not act immediately on the Commonwealth's motion, and both parties filed several briefs on the subject of the motion to dismiss and on the merits of the claims in Coleman's petition. On May 19, 1987, the Virginia Supreme Court issued the following order, dismissing Coleman's appeal:

> On December 4, 1986 came the appellant, by counsel, and filed a petition for appeal in the above-styled case.
>
> Thereupon came the appellee, by the Attorney General of Virginia, and filed a motion to dismiss the petition for appeal; on December 19, 1986 the appellant filed a memorandum in opposition to the motion to dismiss; on December 19, 1986 the appellee filed a reply to the appellant's memorandum; on December 23, 1986 the appellee filed a brief in opposition to the petition for appeal; on December 23, 1986 the appellant filed a surreply in opposition to the appellee's motion to dismiss; and on January 6, 1987 the appellant filed a reply brief.
>
> Upon consideration whereof, the motion to dismiss is granted and the petition for appeal is dismissed. **

This Court again denied certiorari. **

Coleman next filed a petition for writ of habeas corpus in the United States District Court for the Western District of Virginia. In his petition, Coleman presented four federal constitutional claims he had raised on direct appeal in the Virginia Supreme Court and seven claims he had raised for the first time in state habeas. The District Court concluded that, by virtue of the dismissal of his appeal by the Virginia Supreme Court in state habeas, Coleman had procedurally defaulted the seven claims. ** The District

Court nonetheless went on to address the merits of all 11 of Coleman's claims. The court ruled against Coleman on all of the claims and denied the petition. **

The United States Court of Appeals for the Fourth Circuit affirmed. ** The court held that Coleman had defaulted all of the claims that he had presented for the first time in state habeas. Coleman argued that the Virginia Supreme Court had not "clearly and expressly" stated that its decision in state habeas was based on a procedural default, and therefore the federal courts could not treat it as such under the rule of *Harris v. Reed*, 489 U.S. 255 (1989). The Fourth Circuit disagreed. It concluded that the Virginia Supreme Court had met the "plain statement" requirement of *Harris* by granting a motion to dismiss that was based solely on procedural grounds. ** The Fourth Circuit held that the Virginia Supreme Court's decision rested on independent and adequate state grounds and that Coleman had not shown cause to excuse the default. ** As a consequence, federal review of the claims Coleman presented only in the state habeas proceeding was barred. ** We granted certiorari ** to resolve several issues concerning the relationship between state procedural defaults and federal habeas review, and now affirm.

II
A

This Court will not review a question of federal law decided by a state court if the decision of that court rests on a state law ground that is independent of the federal question and adequate to support the judgment. *See, e. g., Fox Film Corp. v. Muller*, 296 U.S. 207, 210 (1935). ** This rule applies whether the state law ground is substantive or procedural. ** In the context of direct review of a state court judgment, the independent and adequate state ground doctrine is jurisdictional. Because this Court has no power to review a state law determination that is sufficient to support the judgment, resolution of any independent federal ground for the decision could not affect the judgment and would therefore be advisory. **

We have applied the independent and adequate state ground doctrine not only in our own review of state court judgments, but in deciding whether federal district courts should address the claims of state prisoners in habeas corpus actions. The doctrine applies to bar federal habeas when a state court declined to address a prisoner's federal claims because the prisoner had failed to meet a state procedural requirement. In these cases, the state judgment rests on independent and adequate state procedural grounds. *See Wainwright v. Sykes*, 433 U.S. 72, 81, 87 (1977). **

The basis for application of the independent and adequate state ground doctrine in federal habeas is somewhat different than on direct review by this Court. When this Court reviews a state court decision on direct review pursuant to 28 U.S.C. § 1257, it is reviewing the *judgment*; if resolution of a federal question cannot affect the judgment, there is nothing for the Court to do. This is not the case in habeas. When a federal district court reviews a state prisoner's habeas corpus petition pursuant to 28 U.S.C. § 2254, it must decide whether the petitioner is "in custody in violation of the Constitution or laws or treaties of the United States." *Ibid.* The court does not review a judgment, but the lawfulness of the petitioner's custody *simpliciter*. *See Fay v. Noia*, 372 U.S. 391, 430 (1963).

Nonetheless, a state prisoner is in custody *pursuant* to a judgment. When a federal habeas court releases a prisoner held pursuant to a state court judgment that rests on an independent and adequate state ground, it renders ineffective the state rule just as completely as if this Court had reversed the state judgment on direct review. *See id.* at 469

(Harlan, J., dissenting). In such a case, the habeas court ignores the State's legitimate reasons for holding the prisoner.

In the habeas context, the application of the independent and adequate state ground doctrine is grounded in concerns of comity and federalism. Without the rule, a federal district court would be able to do in habeas what this Court could not do on direct review; habeas would offer state prisoners whose custody was supported by independent and adequate state grounds an end run around the limits of this Court's jurisdiction and a means to undermine the State's interest in enforcing its laws.

When the independent and adequate state ground supporting a habeas petitioner's custody is a state procedural default, an additional concern comes into play. This Court has long held that a state prisoner's federal habeas petition should be dismissed if the prisoner has not exhausted available state remedies as to any of his claims. *See Ex parte Royall,* 117 U.S. 241 (1886). *See also Rose v. Lundy,* 455 U.S. 509 (1982); ** 28 U.S.C. §2254(b) (codifying the rule). This exhaustion requirement is also grounded in principles of comity; in a federal system, the States should have the first opportunity to address and correct alleged violations of state prisoner's federal rights. As we explained in *Rose, supra:*

> The exhaustion doctrine is principally designed to protect the state courts' role in the enforcement of federal law and prevent disruption of state judicial proceedings. ** Under our federal system, the federal and state "courts [are] equally bound to guard and protect rights secured by the Constitution." *Ex parte Royall,* 117 U.S. at 251. Because "it would be unseemly in our dual system of government for a federal district court to upset a state court conviction without an opportunity to the state courts to correct a constitutional violation," federal courts apply the doctrine of comity, which "teaches that one court should defer action on causes properly within its jurisdiction until the courts of another sovereignty with concurrent powers, and already cognizant of the litigation, have had an opportunity to pass upon the matter." **

These same concerns apply to federal claims that have been procedurally defaulted in state court. Just as in those cases in which a state prisoner fails to exhaust state remedies, a habeas petitioner who has failed to meet the State's procedural requirements for presenting his federal claims has deprived the state courts of an opportunity to address those claims in the first instance. A habeas petitioner who has defaulted his federal claims in state court meets the technical requirements for exhaustion; there are no state remedies any longer "available" to him. *See* 28 U. S. C. §2254(b). ** In the absence of the independent and adequate state ground doctrine in federal habeas, habeas petitioners would be able to avoid the exhaustion requirement by defaulting their federal claims in state court. The independent and adequate state ground doctrine ensures that the States' interest in correcting their own mistakes is respected in all federal habeas cases.

B

It is not always easy for a federal court to apply the independent and adequate state ground doctrine. State court opinions will, at times, discuss federal questions at length and mention a state law basis for decision only briefly. In such cases, it is often difficult to determine if the state law discussion is truly an independent basis for decision or merely a passing reference. In other cases, state opinions purporting to apply state constitutional law will derive principles by reference to federal constitutional decisions from this Court. Again, it is unclear from such opinions whether the state law decision is independent of federal law.

In *Michigan v. Long*, 463 U.S. 1032 (1983), we provided a partial solution to this problem in the form of a conclusive presumption. *** [I]n order to minimize the costs associated with resolving ambiguities in state court decisions while still fulfilling our obligation to determine if there was an independent and adequate state ground for the decision, we established a conclusive presumption of jurisdiction in these cases:

> When, as in this case, a state court decision fairly appears to rest primarily on federal law, or to be interwoven with the federal law, and when the adequacy and independence of any possible state law ground is not clear from the face of the opinion, we will accept as the most reasonable explanation that the state court decided the case the way it did because it believed that federal law required it to do so. *Id.* at 1040–1041.

After *Long*, a state court that wishes to look to federal law for guidance or as an alternative holding while still relying on an independent and adequate state ground can avoid the presumption by stating "clearly and expressly that [its decision] is…based on bona fide separate, adequate, and independent grounds." *Id.* at 1041.

In *Caldwell v. Mississippi*, 472 U.S. 320 (1985), we applied the *Long* presumption in the context of an alleged independent and adequate state procedural ground. Caldwell, a criminal defendant, challenged at trial part of the prosecutor's closing argument to the jury, but he did not raise the issue on appeal to the Mississippi Supreme Court. That court raised the issue *sua sponte*, discussing this federal question at length in its opinion and deciding it against Caldwell. The court also made reference to its general rule that issues not raised on appeal are deemed waived. The State argued to this Court that the procedural default constituted an independent and adequate state ground for the Mississippi court's decision. We rejected this argument, noting that the state decision "'fairly appears to rest primarily on federal law,'" and there was no clear and express statement that the Mississippi Supreme Court was relying on procedural default as an independent ground. *Id.* at 327, *quoting Long, supra*, at 1040.

Long and *Caldwell* were direct review cases. We first considered the problem of ambiguous state court decisions in the application of the independent and adequate state ground doctrine in a federal habeas case in *Harris v. Reed*, 489 U.S. 255 (1989). Harris, a state prisoner, filed a petition for state postconviction relief, alleging that his trial counsel had rendered ineffective assistance. The state trial court dismissed the petition, and the Appellate Court of Illinois affirmed. In its order, the Appellate Court referred to the Illinois rule that "'those [issues] which could have been presented [on direct appeal], but were not, are considered waived.'" *Id.* at 258. The court concluded that Harris could have raised his ineffective assistance claims on direct review. Nonetheless, the court considered and rejected Harris' claims on the merits. Harris then petitioned for federal habeas.

The situation presented to this Court was nearly identical to that in *Long* and *Caldwell*: a state court decision that fairly appeared to rest primarily on federal law in a context in which a federal court has an obligation to determine if the state court decision rested on an independent and adequate state ground. "Faced with a common problem, we adopted a common solution." *Harris, supra*, at 263. *Harris* applied in federal habeas the presumption this Court adopted in *Long* for direct review cases. Because the Illinois Appellate Court did not "clearly and expressly" rely on waiver as a ground for rejecting Harris' ineffective assistance of counsel claims, the *Long* presumption applied and Harris was not barred from federal habeas. *Harris, supra*, at 266.

After *Harris*, federal courts on habeas corpus review of state prisoner claims, like this Court on direct review of state court judgments, will presume that there is no independent and adequate state ground for a state court decision when the decision "fairly appears to rest primarily on federal law, or to be interwoven with the federal law, and when the adequacy and independence of any possible state law ground is not clear from the face of the opinion." *Long, supra,* at 1040–1041. In habeas, if the decision of the last state court to which the petitioner presented his federal claims fairly appeared to rest primarily on resolution of those claims, or to be interwoven with those claims, and did not clearly and expressly rely on an independent and adequate state ground, a federal court may address the petition. ***

III

A

Coleman contends that the presumption of *Long* and *Harris* applies in this case and precludes a bar to habeas because the Virginia Supreme Court's order dismissing Coleman's appeal did not "clearly and expressly" state that it was based on state procedural grounds. Coleman reads *Harris* too broadly. A predicate to the application of the *Harris* presumption is that the decision of the last state court to which the petitioner presented his federal claims must fairly appear to rest primarily on federal law or to be interwoven with federal law.

Coleman relies on other language in *Harris*. That opinion announces that "a procedural default does not bar consideration of a federal claim on either direct or habeas review unless the last state court rendering a judgment in the case clearly and expressly states that its judgment rests on a state procedural bar." *Harris, supra,* at 263 (internal quotation marks omitted). Coleman contends that this rule, by its terms, applies to all state court judgments, not just those that fairly appear to rest primarily on federal law.

Coleman has read the rule out of context. It is unmistakably clear that *Harris* applies the same presumption in habeas that *Long* and *Caldwell* adopted in direct review cases in this Court. ** Indeed, the quoted passage purports to state the rule "on either direct or habeas review." *Harris*, being a federal habeas case, could not change the rule for direct review; the reference to both direct and habeas review makes plain that *Harris* applies precisely the same rule as *Long*. *Harris* describes the *Long* presumption, and hence its own, as applying only in those cases in which " 'it fairly appears that the state court rested its decision primarily on federal law.' " *Harris, supra,* at 261, *quoting Long,* 463 U.S. at 1040. That in one particular exposition of its rule *Harris* does not mention the predicate to application of the presumption does not change the holding of the opinion.

Coleman urges a broader rule: that the presumption applies in all cases in which a habeas petitioner presented his federal claims to the state court. This rule makes little sense. In direct review cases, "it is... incumbent upon this Court... to ascertain for itself... whether the asserted non-federal ground independently and adequately supports the [state court] judgment.' " *Long, supra,* at 1038. Similarly, federal habeas courts must ascertain for themselves if the petitioner is in custody pursuant to a state court judgment that rests on independent and adequate state grounds. In cases in which the *Long* and *Harris* presumption applies, federal courts will conclude that the relevant state court judgment does not rest on an independent and adequate state ground. The presumption, like all conclusive presumptions, is designed to avoid the costs of excessive inquiry where a *per se* rule will achieve the correct result in almost all cases. ***

Per se rules should not be applied, however, in situations where the generalization is incorrect as an empirical matter; the justification for a conclusive presumption disappears when application of the presumption will not reach the correct result most of the time. The *Long* and *Harris* presumption works because in the majority of cases in which a state court decision fairly appears to rest primarily on federal law or to be interwoven with such law, and the state court does not plainly state that it is relying on an independent and adequate state ground, the state court decision did not in fact rest on an independent and adequate state ground. We accept errors in those small number of cases where there was nonetheless an independent and adequate state ground in exchange for a significant reduction in the costs of inquiry.

The tradeoff is very different when the factual predicate does not exist. In those cases in which it does not fairly appear that the state court rested its decision primarily on federal grounds, it is simply not true that the "most reasonable explanation" is that the state judgment rested on federal grounds. ** Yet Coleman would have the federal courts apply a conclusive presumption of no independent and adequate state grounds in every case in which a state prisoner presented his federal claims to a state court, regardless of whether it fairly appears that the state court addressed those claims. We cannot accept such a rule, for it would greatly and unacceptably expand the risk that federal courts will review the federal claims of prisoners in custody pursuant to judgments resting on independent and adequate state grounds. Any efficiency gained by applying a conclusive presumption, and thereby avoiding inquiry into state law, is simply not worth the cost in the loss of respect for the State that such a rule would entail.

It may be argued that a broadly applicable presumption is not counterfactual after it is announced: Once state courts know that their decisions resting on independent and adequate state procedural grounds will be honored in federal habeas only if there is a clear and express statement of the default, these courts will provide such a statement in all relevant cases. This argument does not help Coleman. Even assuming that *Harris* can be read as establishing a presumption in all cases, the Virginia Supreme Court issued its order dismissing Coleman's appeal *before* this Court decided *Harris*. As to this state court order, the absence of an express statement of procedural default is not very informative.

In any event, we decline to establish such a rule here, for it would place burdens on the States and state courts in exchange for very little benefit to the federal courts. We are, as an initial matter, far from confident that the empirical assumption of the argument for such a rule is correct. It is not necessarily the case that state courts will take pains to provide a clear and express statement of procedural default in all cases, even after announcement of the rule. State courts presumably have a dignitary interest in seeing that their state law decisions are not ignored by a federal habeas court, but most of the price paid for federal review of state prisoner claims is paid by the State. When a federal habeas court considers the federal claims of a prisoner in state custody for independent and adequate state law reasons, it is the State that must respond. It is the State that pays the price in terms of the uncertainty and delay added to the enforcement of its criminal laws. It is the State that must retry the petitioner if the federal courts reverse his conviction. If a state court, in the course of disposing of cases on its overcrowded docket, neglects to provide a clear and express statement of procedural default, or is insufficiently motivated to do so, there is little the State can do about it. Yet it is primarily respect for the State's interests that underlies the application of the independent and adequate state ground doctrine in federal habeas.

A broad presumption would also put too great a burden on the state courts. It remains the duty of the federal courts, whether this Court on direct review, or lower federal courts in habeas, to determine the scope of the relevant state court judgment. We can establish a *per se* rule that eases the burden of inquiry on the federal courts in those cases where there are few costs to doing so, but we have no power to tell state courts how they must write their opinions. We encourage state courts to express plainly, in every decision potentially subject to federal review, the grounds upon which their judgments rest, but we will not impose on state courts the responsibility for using particular language in every case in which a state prisoner presents a federal claim—every state appeal, every denial of state collateral review—in order that federal courts might not be bothered with reviewing state law and the record in the case.

Nor do we believe that the federal courts will save much work by applying the *Harris* presumption in all cases. The presumption at present applies only when it fairly appears that a state court judgment rested primarily on federal law or was interwoven with federal law, that is, in those cases where a federal court has good reason to question whether there is an independent and adequate state ground for the decision. In the rest of the cases, there is little need for a conclusive presumption. In the absence of a clear indication that a state court rested its decision on federal law, a federal court's task will not be difficult.

There is, in sum, little that the federal courts will gain by applying a presumption of federal review in those cases where the relevant state court decision does not fairly appear to rest primarily on federal law or to be interwoven with such law, and much that the States and state courts will lose. We decline to so expand the *Harris* presumption.

B

The *Harris* presumption does not apply here. Coleman does not argue, nor could he, that it "fairly appears" that the Virginia Supreme Court's decision rested primarily on federal law or was interwoven with such law. The Virginia Supreme Court stated plainly that it was granting the Commonwealth's motion to dismiss the petition for appeal. That motion was based solely on Coleman's failure to meet the Supreme Court's time requirements. There is no mention of federal law in the Virginia Supreme Court's three-sentence dismissal order. It "fairly appears" to rest primarily on state law.

Coleman concedes that the Virginia Supreme Court dismissed his state habeas appeal as untimely, applying a state procedural rule. ** He argues instead that the court's application of this procedural rule was not independent of federal law.

Virginia Supreme Court Rule 5:5(a) declares that the 30-day requirement for filing a notice of appeal is "mandatory." The Virginia Supreme Court has reiterated the unwaivable nature of this requirement. ** Despite these forthright pronouncements, Coleman contends that in this case the Virginia Supreme Court did not automatically apply its time requirement. Rather, Coleman asserts, the court first considered the merits of his federal claims and applied the procedural bar only after determining that doing so would not abridge one of Coleman's constitutional rights. In *Ake v. Oklahoma*, 470 U.S. 68 (1985), this Court held that a similar Oklahoma rule, excusing procedural default in cases of "fundamental trial error," was not independent of federal law so as to bar direct review because "the State had made application of the procedural bar depend on an antecedent ruling on federal law." *Id.* at 75. For the same reason, Coleman argues, the Virginia Supreme Court's time requirement is not independent of federal law.

Ake was a direct review case. We have never applied its rule regarding independent state grounds in federal habeas. But even if *Ake* applies here, it does Coleman no good because the Virginia Supreme Court relied on an independent state procedural rule.

***

*** [T]he notice of appeal is a document filed *with the trial court* that notifies that court and the Virginia Supreme Court, as well as the parties, that there will be an appeal; it is a purely ministerial document. ** The notice of the appeal must be filed within 30 days of the final judgment of the trial court. ** Coleman has cited no authority indicating that the Virginia Supreme Court has recognized an exception to the time requirement for filing a notice of appeal.

***

Coleman contends also that the procedural bar was not adequate to support the judgment. Coleman did not petition for certiorari on this question, and we therefore accept the Court of Appeals' conclusion that the bar was adequate. **

IV

In *Daniels v. Allen*, the companion case to *Brown v. Allen*, 344 U.S. 443 (1953), we confronted a situation nearly identical to that here. Petitioners were convicted in a North Carolina trial court and then were one day late in filing their appeal as of right in the North Carolina Supreme Court. That court rejected the appeals as procedurally barred. We held that federal habeas was also barred unless petitioners could prove that they were "detained without opportunity to appeal because of lack of counsel, incapacity, or some interference by officials." *Id.* at 485–486.

Fay v. Noia, 372 U.S. 391 (1963), overruled this holding. Noia failed to appeal at all in state court his state conviction, and then sought federal habeas review of his claim that his confession had been coerced. This Court held that such a procedural default in state court does not bar federal habeas review unless the petitioner has deliberately bypassed state procedures by intentionally forgoing an opportunity for state review. *Id.* at 438–439. *Fay* thus created a presumption in favor of federal habeas review of claims procedurally defaulted in state court. The Court based this holding on its conclusion that a State's interest in orderly procedure is sufficiently vindicated by the prisoner's forfeiture of his state remedies. "Whatever residuum of state interest there may be under such circumstances is manifestly insufficient in the face of the federal policy…of affording an effective remedy for restraints contrary to the Constitution." *Id.* at 433–434.

Our cases after *Fay* that have considered the effect of state procedural default on federal habeas review have taken a markedly different view of the important interests served by state procedural rules. *Francis v. Henderson*, 425 U.S. 536 (1976), involved a Louisiana prisoner challenging in federal habeas the composition of the grand jury that had indicted him. Louisiana law provided that any such challenge must be made in advance of trial or it would be deemed waived. Because Francis had not raised a timely objection, the Louisiana courts refused to hear his claim. In deciding whether this state procedural default would also bar review in federal habeas, we looked to our decision in *Davis v. United States*, 411 U.S. 233 (1973). Davis, a federal prisoner, had defaulted an identical federal claim pursuant to Federal Rule of Criminal Procedure 12(b)(2). We held that a federal court on collateral review could not hear the claim unless Davis could show "cause" for his failure to challenge the composition of the grand jury before trial and actual prejudice as a result of the alleged constitutional violations. *Id.* at 242–245.

The *Francis* Court noted the important interests served by the pretrial objection requirement of Rule 12(b)(2) and the parallel state rule: the possible avoidance of an unnecessary trial or of a retrial, the difficulty of making factual determinations concerning grand juries long after the indictment has been handed down and the grand jury disbanded, and the potential disruption to numerous convictions of finding a defect in a grand jury only after the jury has handed down indictments in many cases. *Francis*, *supra*, at 540–541. These concerns led us in *Davis* to enforce Rule 12(b)(2) in collateral review. We concluded in *Francis* that a proper respect for the States required that federal courts give to the state procedural rule the same effect they give to the federal rule:

> If, as *Davis* held, the federal courts must give effect to these important and legitimate concerns in §2255 proceedings, then surely considerations of comity and federalism require that they give no less effect to the same clear interests when asked to overturn state criminal convictions. These considerations require that recognition be given "to the legitimate interests of both State and National Governments, and...[that] the National Government, anxious though it may be to vindicate and protect federal rights and federal interests, always [endeavor] to do so in ways that will not unduly interfere with the legitimate activities of the States." *Younger v. Harris*, 401 U.S. 37, 44 (1971). "Plainly the interest in finality is the same with regard to both federal and state prisoners.... There is no reason to...give greater preclusive effect to procedural defaults by federal defendants than to similar defaults by state defendants. To hold otherwise would reflect an anomalous and erroneous view of federal-state relations." *Kaufman v. United States*, 394 U.S. 217, 228 [(1969)]." *Francis*, 425 U.S. at 541–542.

We held that Francis' claim was barred in federal habeas unless he could establish cause and prejudice. *Id.* at 542.

Wainwright v. Sykes, 433 U.S. 72 (1977), applied the cause and prejudice standard more broadly. Sykes did not object at trial to the introduction of certain inculpatory statements he had earlier made to the police. Under Florida law, this failure barred state courts from hearing the claim on either direct appeal or state collateral review. We recognized that this contemporaneous objection rule served strong state interests in the finality of its criminal litigation. *Id.* at 88–90. To protect these interests, we adopted the same presumption against federal habeas review of claims defaulted in state court for failure to object at trial that *Francis* had adopted in the grand jury context: the cause and prejudice standard. "We believe the adoption of the *Francis* rule in this situation will have the salutary effect of making the state trial on the merits the 'main event,' so to speak, rather than a 'tryout on the road' for what will later be the determinative federal habeas hearing." *Id.* at 90.

In so holding, *Sykes* limited *Fay* to its facts. The cause and prejudice standard in federal habeas evinces far greater respect for state procedural rules than does the deliberate bypass standard of *Fay*. These incompatible rules are based on very different conceptions of comity and of the importance of finality in state criminal litigation. In *Sykes*, we left open the question whether the deliberate bypass standard still applied to a situation like that in *Fay*, where a petitioner has surrendered entirely his right to appeal his state conviction. ** We rejected explicitly, however, "the sweeping language of *Fay v. Noia*, going far beyond the facts of the case eliciting it." **

Our cases since *Sykes* have been unanimous in applying the cause and prejudice standard. *Engle v. Isaac*, 456 U.S. 107 (1982), held that the standard applies even in cases in which the alleged constitutional error impaired the truthfinding function of the trial. Respondents had failed to object at trial to jury instructions that placed on them the burden of proving self-defense. Ohio's contemporaneous objection rule barred respondents' claim on appeal that the burden should have been on the State. We held that this independent and adequate state ground barred federal habeas as well, absent a showing of cause and prejudice.

Recognizing that the writ of habeas corpus "is a bulwark against convictions that violate fundamental fairness," we also acknowledged that "the Great Writ entails significant costs." *Id.* at 126 (internal quotation marks omitted). The most significant of these is the cost to finality in criminal litigation that federal collateral review of state convictions entails:

> As Justice Harlan once observed, "both the individual criminal defendant and society have an interest in insuring that there will at some point be the certainty that comes with an end to litigation, and that attention will ultimately be focused not on whether a conviction was free from error but rather on whether the prisoner can be restored to a useful place in the community." *Sanders v. United States*, 373 U.S. 1, 24–25 (1963) (dissenting opinion). *Id.* at 127.

Moreover, "federal intrusions into state criminal trials frustrate both the States' sovereign power to punish offenders and their good-faith attempts to honor constitutional rights." *Id.* at 128. These costs are particularly high, we explained, when a state prisoner, through a procedural default, prevents adjudication of his constitutional claims in state court. Because these costs do not depend on the type of claim the prisoner raised, we reaffirmed that a state procedural default of any federal claim will bar federal habeas unless the petitioner demonstrates cause and actual prejudice. *Id.* at 129. We also explained in *Engle* that the cause and prejudice standard will be met in those cases where review of a state prisoner's claim is necessary to correct "a fundamental miscarriage of justice." *Id.* at 135. *See also Murray v. Carrier*, 477 U.S. 478, 496 (1986) ("Where a constitutional violation has probably resulted in the conviction of one who is actually innocent, a federal habeas court may grant the writ even in the absence of a showing of cause for the procedural default").

***

*** In *Carrier*, as in *Sykes*, we left open the question whether *Fay*'s deliberate bypass standard continued to apply under the facts of that case, where a state prisoner has defaulted his entire appeal. *See Carrier, supra*, at 492; *Sykes*, supra, at 88 n.12. We are now required to answer this question. By filing late, Coleman defaulted his entire state collateral appeal. This was no doubt an inadvertent error, and respondent concedes that Coleman did not "understandingly and knowingly" forgo the privilege of state collateral appeal. *See Fay*, 372 U.S. at 439. Therefore, if the *Fay* deliberate bypass standard still applies, Coleman's state procedural default will not bar federal habeas.

In *Harris*, we described in broad terms the application of the cause and prejudice standard, hinting strongly that *Fay* had been superseded[.]

***

We now make it explicit: In all cases in which a state prisoner has defaulted his federal claims in state court pursuant to an independent and adequate state procedural rule, federal habeas review of the claims is barred unless the prisoner can demonstrate cause for the default and actual prejudice as a result of the alleged violation of federal law, or demonstrate that failure to consider the claims will result in a fundamental miscarriage of justice. *Fay* was based on a conception of federal/state relations that under-valued the importance of state procedural rules. The several cases after *Fay* that applied the cause and prejudice standard to a variety of state procedural defaults represent a different view. We now recognize the important interest in finality served by state procedural rules, and the significant harm to the States that results from the failure of federal courts to respect them. **

Carrier applied the cause and prejudice standard to the failure to raise a particular claim on appeal. There is no reason that the same standard should not apply to a failure to appeal at all. All of the State's interests—in channeling the resolution of claims to the most appropriate forum, in finality, and in having an opportunity to correct its own errors—are implicated whether a prisoner defaults one claim or all of them. A federal court generally should not interfere in either case. By applying the cause and prejudice standard uniformly to all independent and adequate state procedural defaults, we eliminate the irrational distinction between *Fay* and the rule of cases like *Francis, Sykes, Engle,* and *Carrier.*

We also eliminate inconsistency between the respect federal courts show for state procedural rules and the respect they show for their own. This Court has long understood the vital interest served by *federal* procedural rules, even when they serve to bar federal review of constitutional claims. ***

*** No less respect should be given to state rules of procedure. **

V
A

Coleman maintains that there was cause for his default. The late filing was, he contends, the result of attorney error of sufficient magnitude to excuse the default in federal habeas.

Murray v. Carrier considered the circumstances under which attorney error constitutes cause. Carrier argued that his attorney's inadvertence in failing to raise certain claims in his state appeal constituted cause for the default sufficient to allow federal habeas review. We rejected this claim, explaining that the costs associated with an ignorant or inadvertent procedural default are no less than where the failure to raise a claim is a deliberate strategy: It deprives the state courts of the opportunity to review trial errors. When a federal habeas court hears such a claim, it undercuts the State's ability to enforce its procedural rules just as surely as when the default was deliberate. 477 U.S. at 487. We concluded: "So long as a defendant is represented by counsel whose performance is not constitutionally ineffective under the standard established in *Strickland v. Washington,* 466 U.S. 668 (1984), we discern no inequity in requiring him to bear the risk of attorney error that results in a procedural default." *Id.* at 488.

Applying the *Carrier* rule as stated, this case is at an end. There is no constitutional right to an attorney in state post-conviction proceedings. *Pennsylvania v. Finley,* 481 U.S. 551 (1987). ** Consequently, a petitioner cannot claim constitutionally ineffective assistance of counsel in such proceedings. *See Wainwright v. Torna,* 455 U.S. 586 (1982) (where there is no constitutional right to counsel there can be no deprivation of effective assistance). Coleman contends that it was his attorney's error that led to the late filing of his state habeas appeal. This error cannot be constitutionally ineffective; therefore Coleman must "bear the risk of attorney error that results in a procedural default."

Coleman attempts to avoid this reasoning by arguing that *Carrier* does not stand for such a broad proposition. He contends that *Carrier* applies by its terms only in those situations where it is possible to state a claim for ineffective assistance of counsel. Where there is no constitutional right to counsel, Coleman argues, it is enough that a petitioner demonstrate that his attorney's conduct would meet the *Strickland* standard, even though no independent Sixth Amendment claim is possible.

This argument is inconsistent not only with the language of *Carrier*, but with the logic of that opinion as well. We explained clearly that "cause" under the cause and prejudice test must be something *external* to the petitioner, something that cannot fairly be attributed to him: "We think that the existence of cause for a procedural default must ordinarily turn on whether the prisoner can show that some objective factor external to the defense impeded counsel's efforts to comply with the State's procedural rule." 477 U.S. at 488. For example, "a showing that the factual or legal basis for a claim was not reasonably available to counsel, . . . or that 'some interference by officials'. . . made compliance impracticable, would constitute cause under this standard." *Ibid. See also id.* at 492 ("Cause for a procedural default on appeal ordinarily requires a showing of some external impediment preventing counsel from constructing or raising the claim").

Attorney ignorance or inadvertence is not "cause" because the attorney is the petitioner's agent when acting, or failing to act, in furtherance of the litigation, and the petitioner must "bear the risk of attorney error." *Id.* at 488. ** Attorney error that constitutes ineffective assistance of counsel is cause, however. This is not because, as Coleman contends, the error is so bad that "the lawyer ceases to be an agent of the petitioner." ** In a case such as this, where the alleged attorney error is inadvertence in failing to file a timely notice, such a rule would be contrary to well-settled principles of agency law. ** Rather, as *Carrier* explains, "if the procedural default is the result of ineffective assistance of counsel, the Sixth Amendment itself requires that responsibility for the default be imputed to the State." 477 U.S. at 488. In other words, it is not the gravity of the attorney's error that matters, but that it constitutes a violation of petitioner's right to counsel, so that the error must be seen as an external factor, *i.e.,* "imputed to the State." **

Where a petitioner defaults a claim as a result of the denial of the right to effective assistance of counsel, the State, which is responsible for the denial as a constitutional matter, must bear the cost of any resulting default and the harm to state interests that federal habeas review entails. A different allocation of costs is appropriate in those circumstances where the State has no responsibility to ensure that the petitioner was represented by competent counsel. As between the State and the petitioner, it is the petitioner who must bear the burden of a failure to follow state procedural rules. In the absence of a constitutional violation, the petitioner bears the risk in federal habeas for all attorney errors made in the course of the representation, as *Carrier* says explicitly.

B

Among the claims Coleman brought in state habeas, and then again in federal habeas, is ineffective assistance of counsel during trial, sentencing, and appeal. Coleman contends that, at least as to these claims, attorney error in state habeas must constitute cause. This is because, under Virginia law at the time of Coleman's trial and direct appeal, ineffective assistance of counsel claims related to counsel's conduct during trial or appeal could be brought only in state habeas. ** Coleman argues that attorney error in failing to file timely in the first forum in which a federal claim can be raised is cause.

We reiterate that counsel's ineffectiveness will constitute cause only if it is an independent constitutional violation. *Finley* and [*Murray v.*] *Giarratano* [, 492 U.S. 1

(1989),] established that there is no right to counsel in state collateral proceedings. For Coleman to prevail, therefore, there must be an exception to the rule of *Finley* and *Giarratano* in those cases where state collateral review is the first place a prisoner can present a challenge to his conviction. We need not answer this question broadly, however, for one state court has addressed Coleman's claims: the state habeas trial court. The effectiveness of Coleman's counsel before that court is not at issue here. Coleman contends that it was the ineffectiveness of his counsel during the appeal from that determination that constitutes cause to excuse his default. We thus need to decide only whether Coleman had a constitutional right to counsel on appeal from the state habeas trial court judgment. We conclude that he did not.

Douglas v. California, 372 U.S. 353 (1963), established that an indigent criminal defendant has a right to appointed counsel in his first appeal as of right in state court. *Evitts v. Lucey*, [469 U.S. 387 (1985),] held that this right encompasses a right to effective assistance of counsel for all criminal defendants in their first appeal as of right. We based our holding in *Douglas* on that "equality demanded by the Fourteenth Amendment." 372 U.S. at 358. Recognizing that "absolute equality is not required," we nonetheless held that "where the merits of *the one and only appeal* an indigent has as of right are decided without benefit of counsel, we think an unconstitutional line has been drawn between rich and poor." *Id.* at 357 (emphasis in original).

Coleman has had his "one and only appeal," if that is what a state collateral proceeding may be considered; the Buchanan County Circuit Court, after a 2-day evidentiary hearing, addressed Coleman's claims of trial error, including his ineffective assistance of counsel claims. What Coleman requires here is a right to counsel on appeal from *that* determination. Our case law will not support it.

In *Ross v. Moffitt*, 417 U.S. 600 (1974), and *Pennsylvania v. Finley*, 481 U.S. 551 (1987), we declined to extend the right to counsel beyond the first appeal of a criminal conviction. We held in *Ross* that neither the fundamental fairness required by the Due Process Clause nor the Fourteenth Amendment's equal protection guarantee necessitated that States provide counsel in state discretionary appeals where defendants already had one appeal as of right. "The duty of the State under our cases is not to duplicate the legal arsenal that may be privately retained by a criminal defendant in a continuing effort to reverse his conviction, but only to assure the indigent defendant an adequate opportunity to present his claims fairly in the context of the State's appellate process." 417 U.S. at 616. Similarly, in *Finley* we held that there is no right to counsel in state collateral proceedings after exhaustion of direct appellate review. 481 U.S. at 556 (citing *Ross, supra*).

These cases dictate the answer here. Given that a criminal defendant has no right to counsel beyond his first appeal in pursuing state discretionary or collateral review, it would defy logic for us to hold that Coleman had a right to counsel to appeal a state collateral determination of his claims of trial error.

Because Coleman had no right to counsel to pursue his appeal in state habeas, any attorney error that led to the default of Coleman's claims in state court cannot constitute cause to excuse the default in federal habeas. As Coleman does not argue in this Court that federal review of his claims is necessary to prevent a fundamental miscarriage of justice, he is barred from bringing these claims in federal habeas. Accordingly, the judgment of the Court of Appeals is

Affirmed.

[Concurring opinion by JUSTICE WHITE omitted.]

JUSTICE BLACKMUN, with whom JUSTICE MARSHALL and JUSTICE STEVENS join, dissenting.

Federalism; comity; state sovereignty; preservation of state resources; certainty: The majority methodically inventories these multifarious state interests before concluding that the plain-statement rule of *Michigan v. Long*, 463 U.S. 1032 (1983), does not apply to a summary order. One searches the majority's opinion in vain, however, for any mention of petitioner Coleman's right to a criminal proceeding free from constitutional defect or his interest in finding a forum for his constitutional challenge to his conviction and sentence of death. Nor does the majority even allude to the "important need for uniformity in federal law," *id.* at 1040, which justified this Court's adoption of the plain-statement rule in the first place. Rather, displaying obvious exasperation with the breadth of substantive federal habeas doctrine and the expansive protection afforded by the Fourteenth Amendment's guarantee of fundamental fairness in state criminal proceedings, the Court today continues its crusade to erect petty procedural barriers in the path of any state prisoner seeking review of his federal constitutional claims. Because I believe that the Court is creating a Byzantine morass of arbitrary, unnecessary, and unjustifiable impediments to the vindication of federal rights, I dissent.

I

The Court cavalierly claims that "this is a case about federalism" ** and proceeds without explanation to assume that the purposes of federalism are advanced whenever a federal court refrains from reviewing an ambiguous state-court judgment. Federalism, however, has no inherent normative value: It does not, as the majority appears to assume, blindly protect the States from any incursion by the federal courts. Rather, federalism secures to citizens the liberties that derive from the diffusion of sovereign power. *** In this context, it cannot lightly be assumed that the interests of federalism are fostered by a rule that impedes federal review of federal constitutional claims.

Moreover, the form of federalism embraced by today's majority bears little resemblance to that adopted by the Framers of the Constitution and ratified by the original States. The majority proceeds as if the sovereign interests of the States and the Federal Government were coequal. Ours, however, is a federal republic, conceived on the principle of a supreme federal power and constituted first and foremost of citizens, not of sovereign States. ***

Federal habeas review of state-court judgments, respectfully employed to safeguard federal rights, is no invasion of state sovereignty. *** Thus, the considered exercise by federal courts—in vindication of fundamental constitutional rights—of the habeas jurisdiction conferred on them by Congress exemplifies the full expression of this Nation's federalism.
  ***

II

  ***

B

*** In its attempt to justify a blind abdication of responsibility by the federal courts, the majority's opinion marks the nadir of the Court's recent habeas jurisprudence, where the discourse of rights is routinely replaced with the functional dialect of interests. The Court's habeas jurisprudence now routinely, and without evident reflection, subordinates fundamental constitutional rights to mere utilitarian interests. *See, e.g.,* *McCleskey v. Zant*, 499 U.S. 467 (1991). Such unreflective cost-benefit analysis is inconsistent with the very idea of rights. ** The Bill of Rights is not, after all, a collection of technical interests, and "surely it is an abuse to deal too casually and too lightly with rights guaranteed" therein. *Brown v. Allen*, 344 U.S. [433, 498 (1953)] (opinion of Frankfurter, J.).

It is well settled that the existence of a state procedural default does not divest a federal court of jurisdiction on collateral review. *See Wainwright v. Sykes*, 433 U.S. 72, 82–84 (1977). Rather, the important office of the federal courts in vindicating federal rights gives way to the States' enforcement of their procedural rules to protect the States' interest in being an equal partner in safeguarding federal rights. This accommodation furthers the values underlying federalism in two ways. First, encouraging a defendant to assert his federal rights in the appropriate state forum makes it possible for transgressions to be arrested sooner and before they influence an erroneous deprivation of liberty. Second, thorough examination of a prisoner's federal claims in state court permits more effective review of those claims in federal court, honing the accuracy of the writ as an implement to eradicate unlawful detention. *See Rose v. Lundy*, 455 U.S. 509, 519 (1982); *Brown v. Allen*, 344 U.S. at 500–501 (opinion of Frankfurter, J.). The majority ignores these purposes in concluding that a State need not bear the burden of making clear its intent to rely on such a rule. When it is uncertain whether a state-court judgment denying relief from federal claims rests on a procedural bar, it is inconsistent with federalism principles for a federal court to exercise discretion to decline to review those federal claims.

***

Even if the majority correctly attributed the relevant state interests, they are, nonetheless, misconceived. The majority appears most concerned with the financial burden that a retrial places on the States. Of course, if the initial trial conformed to the mandate of the Federal Constitution, not even the most probing federal review would necessitate a retrial. Thus, to the extent the State must "pay the price" of retrying a state prisoner, that price is incurred as a direct result of the State's failure scrupulously to honor his federal rights, not as a consequence of unwelcome federal review. **

***

C

***

The Court's decisions in this case and in *Ylst v. Nunnemaker*, [501 U.S. 797 (1991),] well reveal the illogic of the ad hoc approach. In this case, to determine whether the admittedly ambiguous state-court judgment rests on an adequate and independent state ground, the Court looks to the "nature of the disposition" and the "surrounding circumstances" that "indicate" that the basis [of the decision] was procedural default. *Ylst* [501 U.S.] at 802. This method of searching for "clues" to the meaning of a facially ambiguous order is inherently indeterminate. Tellingly, both the majority and concurring opinions in this case concede that it remains uncertain whether the state court relied on a procedural default. ** The plain-statement rule effectively and equitably eliminates this unacceptable uncertainty. I cannot condone the abandonment of such a rule when the result is to foreclose federal habeas review of federal claims based on conjecture as to the "meaning" of an unexplained order.

The Court's decision in *Ylst* demonstrates that we are destined to relive the period where we struggled to develop principles to guide the interpretation of ambiguous state-court orders. In *Ylst*, the last state court to render a judgment on Nunnemaker's federal claims was the California Supreme Court. Nunnemaker had filed a petition for habeas corpus in that court, invoking its original jurisdiction. Accordingly, the court was not sitting to review the judgment of another state court, but to entertain, as an original matter, Nunnemaker's collateral challenge to his conviction. The court's order denying relief was rendered without explanation or citation. Rejecting the methodology employed just today by the *Coleman* majority, the *Ylst* Court does not look to the pleadings filed in the original action to determine the "meaning" of the unexplained order. Rather, the Court adopts a broad *per se* presumption that "where there has been one reasoned state judgment rejecting a federal claim, later unexplained orders upholding that judgment or rejecting the same claim rest upon the same ground." *Ylst*, [501 U.S.] at 803. This presumption does not purport to distinguish between unexplained judgments that are entered on review of the reasoned opinion and those that are independent thereof.

The *Ylst* Court demonstrates the employment of the presumption by simply ignoring the judgment of the highest court of California, and by looking back to an intermediate court judgment rendered 12 years earlier to conclude that Nunnemaker's federal claims have been procedurally defaulted. In so concluding, the Court determines that an intervening order by the California Supreme Court, which, with citations to two state-court decisions, denied Nunnemaker's earlier petition invoking the court's original jurisdiction, is not "informative with respect to the question," [501 U.S.] at 805, whether a state court has considered the merits of Nunnemaker's claims since the procedural default was recognized. Thus, the Court dismisses two determinations of the California Supreme Court, rendered not in review of an earlier state-court judgment but as an exercise of its original jurisdiction, because it finds those determinations not "informative." While the Court may comfort itself by labeling this exercise "looking through," *see* [501 U.S.] at 804, it cannot be disputed that the practice represents disrespect for the State's determination of how best to structure its mechanisms for seeking postconviction relief.

Moreover, the presumption adopted by the *Ylst* Court further complicates the efforts of state courts to understand and accommodate this Court's federal habeas jurisprudence. Under *Long*, a state court need only recognize that it must clearly express its intent to rely on a state procedural default in order to preclude federal habeas review in most cases. After today, however, a state court that does not intend to rely on a procedural default but wishes to deny a meritless petition in a summary order must now remember that its unexplained order will be ignored by the federal habeas court. Thus, the state court must review the procedural history of the petitioner's claim and determine which state-court judgment a federal habeas court is likely to recognize. It then must determine whether that judgment expresses the substance that the court wishes to convey in its summary order, and react accordingly. If the previous reasoned judgment rests on a procedural default, and the subsequent court wishes to forgive that default, it now must clearly and expressly indicate that its judgment *does not* rest on a state procedural default. I see no benefit in abandoning a clear rule to create chaos.

III

***

The majority's conclusion that Coleman's allegations of ineffective assistance of counsel, if true, would not excuse a procedural default that occurred in the state postconviction proceeding is particularly disturbing because, at the time of Coleman's appeal, state law precluded defendants from raising certain claims on direct appeal. As the majority acknowledges, under state law as it existed at the time of Coleman's trial and appeal, Coleman could raise his ineffective-assistance-of-counsel claim with respect to counsel's conduct during trial and appeal only in state habeas. ** This Court has made clear that the Fourteenth Amendment obligates a State " 'to assure the indigent defendant an adequate opportunity to present his claims fairly in the context of the State's appellate process,' " *Pennsylvania v. Finley*, 481 U.S. at 556, ** and "require[s] that the state appellate system be 'free from unreasoned distinctions,' " *id.* at 612. While the State may have wide latitude to structure its appellate process as it deems most effective, it cannot, consistent with the Fourteenth Amendment, structure it in such a way as to deny indigent defendants meaningful access. Accordingly, if a State desires to remove from the process of direct appellate review a claim or category of claims, the Fourteenth Amendment binds the State to ensure that the defendant has effective assistance of counsel for the entirety of the procedure where the removed claims may be raised. Similarly, fundamental fairness dictates that the State, having removed certain claims from the process of direct review, bear the burden of ineffective assistance of counsel in the proceeding to which the claim has been removed.

Ultimately, the Court's determination that ineffective assistance of counsel cannot constitute cause of a procedural default in a state postconviction proceeding is patently unfair. In concluding that it was not inequitable to apply the cause and prejudice standard to procedural defaults that occur on appeal, the *Murray* Court took comfort in the "additional safeguard against miscarriages of justice in criminal cases": the right to effective assistance of counsel. [*Murray v. Carrier*,] 477 U.S. [478,] 496 [(1986)]. The Court reasoned: "The presence of such a safeguard may properly inform this Court's judgment in determining 'what standards should govern the exercise of the habeas court's equitable discretion' with respect to procedurally defaulted claims." *Ibid.* ** "Fundamental fairness is the central concern of the writ of habeas corpus." *Strickland v. Washington*, 466 U.S. 668, 697 (1984). It is the quintessence of inequity that the Court today abandons that safeguard while continuing to embrace the cause and prejudice standard.

I dissent.

Notes

1. *Subsequent case history*

Roger Coleman was executed on May 20, 1992, by electric chair in Virginia.

2. *Concurring opinion*

Justice White noted in his concurring opinion that if it were true that "on occasion" the Virginia Supreme Court waived the untimeliness rule, then "the rule would not be an adequate and independent state ground barring direct or habeas review." At the same time, Justice White stated that he was not "convinced that there is a practice of waiving the rule when constitutional issues are at stake, even fundamental ones. The evidence is too scanty to permit a conclusion that the rule is no longer an adequate and independent state ground barring federal review."

What kind of evidence would help to prove whether a procedural rule a state court invoked to deny relief was a rule that the court waived "on occasion"? How many times would a court have to waive the rule to constitute waiving it "on occasion"?

3. *Additional reading*

For an extensive and unforgettable analysis of the facts and history behind Roger Coleman's case, see John C. Tucker's *May God Have Mercy: A True Story of Crime and Punishment* (1998).

4. *Subsequent decision*

In <u>Lee v. Kemna</u>, 534 U.S. 362 (2002), the Supreme Court recognized that while a violation of "'firmly established and regularly followed'" state rules ordinarily is adequate to foreclose review of a federal claim, "<u>[t]here are, however, exceptional cases in which exorbitant application of a generally sound rule renders the state ground inadequate to stop consideration of a federal question</u>." ** Lee asserted an alibi defense to the charge of first-degree murder and a related crime, but when it came time to present his alibi defense, his witnesses—who were all family—had inexplicably left the courthouse. Defense counsel moved for an overnight continuance to find his witnesses, but the trial court denied his motion and the jury found Lee guilty. ** The Missouri Court of Appeals relied on two state procedural rules to bar him relief: (1) A state supreme court rule requiring such applications be written and accompanied by an affidavit, and (2) a state supreme court rule stating that a denial of a motion to continue based on a "deficient application" does not constitute an abuse of discretion. ** These procedural oversights were first raised more than two and half years after Lee's trial. **

The Court recognized three considerations that, in combination, led the Court to conclude that the asserted state grounds were inadequate to block adjudication of a federal claim. First, the trial judge who denied Lee's motion to continue did not state he was denying his motion because it was not in writing. Instead, he said that he would not be available the next day because his daughter was in the hospital and that he could not continue Lee's trial until the next business day because he already had scheduled another trial to begin then. Second, "no published Missouri decision direct[ed] flawless compliance with [the state procedural rules relied upon to deny him relief] in the unique circumstances this case present[ed]—the sudden, unanticipated, and at the time unexplained disappearance of critical, subpoenaed witnesses on what became the trial's last day. Lee's predicament *** was one Missouri courts had not confronted before." Third, and most important according to the Court, "given 'the realities of trial,' ** Lee substantially complied with Missouri's key Rule." **

Is the Court's decision in *Lee v. Kemna* consistent with its decision in *Coleman*?

5. *The debate continues over the* Coleman *case*

Even though Roger Coleman was executed in 1992, the debate continues over the possibility of using DNA testing to prove his guilt or innocence. The following articles summarize some of the divergent opinions on the issue. At the time this book went to press, Governor Warner had not yet ordered testing of Coleman's DNA. See http://www.vadp.org for more information.

State Objects to More Testing
DNA Work Sought on Executed Man
Richmond Times-Dispatch — October 7, 2000
Copyright ©2000 by the Richmond Times-Dispatch

Frank Green
Times-Dispatch Staff Writer

The Virginia attorney general's office is objecting to DNA testing that could prove the guilt or innocence of Roger Keith Coleman, executed in 1992, because, among other reasons, it says the public does not have a "right to know."

The Boston Globe and Centurion Ministries are seeking to have another DNA test on spermatozoa on a vaginal swab taken from Wanda McCoy, who was raped and murdered in Grundy in 1981. Coleman always maintained his innocence of the crime.

Many agreed with him, and the case attracted international media attention. Coleman even appeared on the cover of Time Magazine.

The evidence was DNA tested years after Coleman's trial on behalf of Coleman. The test showed Coleman could not be excluded as the rapist. New DNA testing techniques might definitively prove his guilt or innocence, argues the newspaper and Centurion, a New Jersey-based group that works to help free innocent inmates.

But the attorney general's office is opposing any new tests of the evidence being kept in a lab in Richmond, Calif., by DNA expert Edward T. Blake, who performed the original test in 1991.

Citing case law, Assistant Attorney General Pamela A. Rumpz wrote Buchanan County Circuit Judge Keary Williams that "regarding the public's 'right to know,' that right 'focuses on the public's interest in important matters.'"

"Twenty years after the crime and more than eight years after the execution of the culprit, there simply is no 'important' interest in retesting the very DNA evidence which already limited the perpetrator to .2% of the Caucasian population—including Coleman," she argued.

The state also argued that neither the Globe nor Centurion have any legal standing to challenge Williams' Sept. 7 order to Blake to have the material sent back to Virginia and state custody.

The Globe has expressed concerns that the evidence could be damaged in transit. Rumpz said the state had no objection to Williams amending his ruling to make sure the evidence is protected.

John A. Farrell, a Globe reporter, said the newspaper is seeking DNA tests in cases in other states as well in light of accusations made by opponents of capital punishment that innocent people may be executed.

"By using DNA technology to test the results of previous executions, we can test that theory and arrive at some answers," he said. The Globe has already won the first such court order in the country in a Georgia case, Farrell said.

The attorney general's office cited a Buchanan County court order dated Jan. 28, 1991, which notes that Blake had assured the state that "Dr. Blake will maintain and preserve the evidence at his laboratory until further order of the court."

Paul F. Enzinna, a Washington lawyer representing Centurion Ministries, said he sees "common ground here that could form the basis for an agreement by all the parties." He believes the state is leaving the door open to test the material.

Enzinna said he has told the governor's office that Centurion does not want the state to surrender the evidence, "all we want is that the evidence gets tested, and if that means Paul Ferrara testing it, that's fine." Ferrara is the head of the state's Division of Forensic Science.

"We're interested in getting this stuff tested and however we can do that that best satisfies everybody who's interested in this is fine with us. Whether Dr. Blake does the testing and Dr. Ferrara goes out there and watches him do it, or Dr. Ferrara does the testing here and we get to observe that," said Enzinna.

Rumpz said there is no remaining factual issue as to Coleman's guilt. Evidence presented at his trial included that pubic hairs matching Coleman's were found on the victim's body, Coleman had type B blood and so did the attacker, and the same type of blood as the victim's was found on Coleman's jeans.

The 1991 DNA testing bolstered the case against him, said the attorney general's office. In addition, Coleman, shortly before he was executed, took and failed a polygraph examination.

"Under all these circumstances, the Globe's allegation that there is a legitimate public debate regarding Coleman's guilt rings entirely hollow and is entitled to no credit," Rumpz wrote.

DNA Testing by Media Barred
Va. Justices Deny Access in Case of Executed Man
Copyright ©2002 by the Washingtom Post

Eric M. Weiss
The Washington Post
Saturday, November 2, 2002

The Virginia Supreme Court yesterday refused to allow new DNA testing of evidence left over from the case of executed killer Roger Keith Coleman, ruling that doing so would unduly expand the public's right of access.

A group of newspapers, including The Washington Post, and a New Jersey charity had asked the court to allow them to use new technology to answer lingering questions about Coleman's guilt. They asked for the evidence left from the 1981 rape and murder of Coleman's sister-in-law, Wanda McCoy, so they could perform advanced DNA analysis that was not available before Coleman's execution in 1992.

The state opposed the request, saying that the papers didn't have the legal standing to obtain and analyze the evidence and that new tests would not contribute to public confidence in the application of the death penalty.

The newspapers argued that the public interest in knowing whether Virginia put an innocent man to death greatly outweighed the state's interest in preventing the testing.

"I'm disappointed that the Supreme Court didn't use this opportunity to test this evidence," said Margaret Stone, an attorney for the newspapers. She said the evidence has been preserved in a laboratory setting and would provide a good sample for the most up-to-date DNA analysis.

A lower court had previously rejected the request, finding that the newspapers and the charity did not have standing to make the request. Yesterday's state Supreme Court decision went even further, saying that new testing would venture far beyond what is considered rightful public access in criminal proceedings, perhaps opening the door to testing of other evidence, such as assault weapons or illegal drugs.

"Certainly, the right to test evidence in a criminal case has not been historically extended to the press and general public," Justice Donald W. Lemons wrote for the unanimous court. The testing of the remaining DNA would "generate a new scientific report, thereby altering, manipulating, and/or destroying existing evidence in order to create new evidence," Lemons wrote.

Tim Murtaugh, a spokesman for Attorney General Jerry W. Kilgore (R), applauded the ruling. "The bottom line is that in 1981, Roger Keith Coleman raped and murdered Wanda McCoy," he said. "He was tried, convicted, sentenced and punished. And today the Virginia Supreme Court has spoken."

The Post, together with the Richmond Times-Dispatch, the Virginian-Pilot of Norfolk, the Boston Globe and Centurion Ministries, a New Jersey charity that investigates claims of wrongful convictions, offered to pay for new testing that would compare genetic material found on McCoy's body with Coleman's.

The court also found that the physical evidence in criminal cases is not considered open under state freedom of information laws. "Clearly the biological material recovered on swabs from the…victim does not meet the test of a 'public record.' Even if it did, the VFOIA allows for inspection and copying, not testing," the opinion said.

Stone said the court was accurate in saying that allowing the testing would expand First Amendment rights, "but we argued that there would be safeguards and limitations so that the court could deal with problems as they arise."

Coleman, a coal miner from Southwest Virginia, was convicted largely on the basis of hair evidence and a jailhouse informant. Early DNA testing on Coleman in 1990 and 1991 was inconclusive, but strongly suggested he was the killer. And on the morning of his execution, Coleman failed a polygraph test. But he said he had an alibi, and his claims of innocence drew national attention.

In some of his last words, Coleman said, "When my innocence is proven, I hope Americans will realize the injustice of the death penalty as all other civilized countries have."

Virginia judges have rejected similar post-execution requests in the capital cases of Joseph R. O'Dell and Derek R. Barnabei.

More than 100 convicted felons, including six Virginia inmates, were cleared through DNA testing during the past 13 years, according to the New York-based Innocence Project.

DNA Testing of Executed Virginia Inmate Urged

Take off the blindfold in the Roger Coleman case
Copyright ©2003 by The Virginian-Pilot

The Virginian-Pilot
March 6, 2003

A request for the posthumous testing of Roger Keith Coleman's DNA is on its way to Gov. Mark Warner's desk.

Given what the nation now knows about the reality of erroneous convictions, even in crimes serious enough to trigger the death penalty, Warner should bring clarity to this muddled case by ordering the test.

Ever since his face appeared on a Time magazine cover, Coleman has been at the center of a fierce national debate over the validity of his conviction. He was executed in 1992 for the 1981 murder in Grundy of his sister-in-law.

Coleman's supporters argue that, given what is known about his whereabouts on the night of the murder, he simply did not have enough time to rape and kill Wanda McCoy. Detractors observe that Coleman was convicted in a fair trial and that DNA testing shortly before his death put him in a tiny subset of people who could have contributed the genetic material left at the crime scene.

To suggest that there's no useful purpose in revisiting this matter, however, is akin to refusing to study history. How are humans to be guided by their mistakes if they refuse to entertain the possibility of error? In what other field would policy-makers reject the opportunity to subject their actions to pure, unbiased scientific scrutiny?

It is, after all, just as likely—perhaps more so, given the earlier DNA test—that Coleman will be shown to be guilty.

Attorney General Jerry Kilgore argues against retesting, observing that Wanda McCoy's family deserves finality. That logic has two flaws.

First, doubts about Coleman's guilt are so extensive, even spawning a widely distributed book, that finality has never existed in this case. And second, if Coleman was not the murderer, wouldn't her family want to know? In that case, the real killer has gone free.

DNA testing is a powerful tool that has developed substantially since Roger Coleman's execution. It should be possible now to say with certainty whether he was executed justly. Part of the reluctance to test the evidence is the outside chance that the state executed the wrong man.

Gov. Warner holds the key that can unlock this mystery. Nothing other than a misguided loyalty that elevates process over truth could keep him from using it.

Chapter 10

Full and Fair Opportunity to Litigate

The cases in this chapter discuss whether a petitioner's ability to fully and fairly litigate an issue in state court should preclude the petitioner's ability to raise that issue again in federal habeas. Despite the seemingly straightforward terminology, the phrase "full and fair opportunity to litigate" is a term of art, the meaning of which becomes somewhat fluid depending on the context of how it is used within a specific case.

Stone v. Powell presents the Court with a state prisoner's Fourth Amendment claim. After finding that the state court had provided a full and fair opportunity to litigate the Fourth Amendment claim, the Court holds that the state prisoner may not be granted federal habeas corpus relief on the ground that evidence obtained in an unconstitutional search or seizure was introduced at his trial. *Kimmelman v. Morrision* shifts focus from a straight Fourth Amendment claim to a Sixth Amendment claim incorporating a Fourth Amendment claim: whether a Sixth Amendment denial of effective representation claim, based on counsel's failure to file a timely motion to suppress evidence allegedly obtained in violation of the Fourth Amendment, may form the basis of a federal habeas claim. In the final case, *Withrow v. Williams*, the Court examines when federal courts can entertain a habeas petition based on a Fifth Amendment claim when a statement was obtained in violation of *Miranda*.

Stone v. Powell
428 U.S. 465 (1976)

JUSTICE POWELL delivered the opinion of the Court.

Respondents in these cases were convicted of criminal offenses in state courts, and their convictions were affirmed on appeal. The prosecution in each case relied upon evidence obtained by searches and seizures alleged by respondents to have been unlawful. Each respondent subsequently sought relief in a Federal District Court by filing a petition for a writ of federal habeas corpus under 28 U.S.C. § 2254. The question presented is whether a federal court should consider, in ruling on a petition for habeas corpus relief filed by a state prisoner, a claim that evidence obtained by an unconstitutional search or seizure was introduced at his trial, when he has previously been afforded an opportunity for full and fair litigation of his claim in the state courts. The issue is of considerable importance to the administration of criminal justice.

I

We summarize first the relevant facts and procedural history of these cases.

241

A

Respondent Lloyd Powell was convicted of murder in June 1968 after trial in a California state court. At about midnight on February 17, 1968, he and three companions entered the Bonanza Liquor Store in San Bernardino, Cal., where Powell became involved in an altercation with Gerald Parsons, the store manager, over the theft of a bottle of wine. In the scuffling that followed Powell shot and killed Parsons' wife. Ten hours later an officer of the Henderson, Nev., Police Department arrested Powell for violation of the Henderson vagrancy ordinance, *** and in the search incident to the arrest discovered a .38-caliber revolver with six expended cartridges in the cylinder.

Powell was extradited to California and convicted of second-degree murder in the Superior Court of San Bernardino County. Parsons and Powell's accomplices at the liquor store testified against him. A criminologist testified that the revolver found on Powell was the gun that killed Parsons' wife. The trial court rejected Powell's contention that testimony by the Henderson police officer as to the search and the discovery of the revolver should have been excluded because the vagrancy ordinance was unconstitutional. In October 1969, the conviction was affirmed by a California District Court of Appeal. Although the issue was duly presented, that court found it unnecessary to pass upon the legality of the arrest and search because it concluded that the error, if any, in admitting the testimony of the Henderson officer was harmless beyond a reasonable doubt under *Chapman v. California*, 386 U.S. 18 (1967). The Supreme Court of California denied Powell's petition for habeas corpus relief.

In August, 1971 Powell filed an amended petition for a writ of federal habeas corpus under 28 U.S.C. § 2254 in the United States District Court for the Northern District of California, contending that the testimony concerning the .38-caliber revolver should have been excluded as the fruit of an illegal search. He argued that his arrest had been unlawful because the Henderson vagrancy ordinance was unconstitutionally vague, and that the arresting officer lacked probable cause to believe that he was violating it. The District Court concluded that the arresting officer had probable cause and held that even if the vagrancy ordinance was unconstitutional, the deterrent purpose of the exclusionary rule does not require that it be applied to bar admission of the fruits of a search incident to an otherwise valid arrest. In the alternative, that court agreed with the California District Court of Appeal that the admission of the evidence concerning Powell's arrest, if error, was harmless beyond a reasonable doubt.

In December 1974, the Court of Appeals for the Ninth Circuit reversed. ** The court concluded that the vagrancy ordinance was unconstitutionally vague, *** that Powell's arrest was therefore illegal, and that although exclusion of the evidence would serve no deterrent purpose with regard to police officers who were enforcing statutes in good faith, exclusion would serve the public interest by deterring legislators from enacting unconstitutional statutes. ** After an independent review of the evidence the court concluded that the admission of the evidence was not harmless error since it supported the testimony of Parsons and Powell's accomplices. **

B

Respondent David Rice was convicted of murder in April 1971 after trial in a Nebraska state court. At 2:05 a.m. on August 17, 1970, Omaha police received a telephone call that a woman had been heard screaming at 2867 Ohio Street. As one of the officers sent to that address examined a suitcase lying in the doorway, it exploded, killing him instantly. By August 22 the investigation of the murder centered on Duane Peak, a 15-

year-old member of the National Committee to Combat Fascism (NCCF), and that afternoon a warrant was issued for Peak's arrest. The investigation also focused on other known members of the NCCF, including Rice, some of whom were believed to be planning to kill Peak before he could incriminate them. In their search for Peak, the police went to Rice's home at 10:30 that night and found lights and a television on, but there was no response to their repeated knocking. While some officers remained to watch the premises, a warrant was obtained to search for explosives and illegal weapons believed to be in Rice's possession. Peak was not in the house, but upon entering the police discovered, in plain view, dynamite, blasting caps, and other materials useful in the construction of explosive devices. Peak subsequently was arrested, and on August 27, Rice voluntarily surrendered. The clothes Rice was wearing at that time were subjected to chemical analysis, disclosing dynamite particles.

Rice was tried for first-degree murder in the District Court of Douglas County. At trial Peak admitted planting the suitcase and making the telephone call, and implicated Rice in the bombing plot. As corroborative evidence the State introduced items seized during the search, as well as the results of the chemical analysis of Rice's clothing. The court denied Rice's motion to suppress this evidence. On appeal the Supreme Court of Nebraska affirmed the conviction, holding that the search of Rice's home had been pursuant to a valid search warrant. **

In September 1972 Rice filed a petition for a writ of habeas corpus in the United States District Court for Nebraska. Rice's sole contention was that his incarceration was unlawful because the evidence underlying his conviction had been discovered as the result of an illegal search of his home. The District Court concluded that the search warrant was invalid, as the supporting affidavit was defective under *Spinelli v. United States*, 393 U.S. 410 (1969), and *Aguilar v. Texas*, 378 U.S. 108 (1964). *** The court also rejected the State's contention that even if the warrant was invalid the search was justified because of the valid arrest warrant for Peak and because of the exigent circumstances. *** The court reasoned that the arrest warrant did not justify the entry as the police lacked probable cause to believe Peak was in the house, and further concluded that the circumstances were not sufficiently exigent to justify an immediate warrantless search. *** The Court of Appeals for the Eighth Circuit affirmed, substantially for the reasons stated by the District Court. **

Petitioners Stone and Wolff, the wardens of the respective state prisons where Powell and Rice are incarcerated, petitioned for review of these decisions, raising questions concerning the scope of federal habeas corpus and the role of the exclusionary rule upon collateral review of cases involving Fourth Amendment claims. We granted their petitions for certiorari. *** We now reverse.

II

The authority of federal courts to issue the writ of habeas corpus *ad subjiciendum* *** was included in the first grant of federal-court jurisdiction, made by the Judiciary Act of 1789, c. 20, § 14, 1 Stat. 81, with the limitation that the writ extend only to prisoners held in custody by the United States. The original statutory authorization did not define the substantive reach of the writ. It merely stated that the courts of the United States "shall have power to issue writs of...Habeas corpus...." *Ibid.* The courts defined the scope of the writ in accordance with the common law and limited it to an inquiry as to the jurisdiction of the sentencing tribunal. **

In 1867 the writ was extended to state prisoners. ** Under the 1867 Act federal courts were authorized to give relief in "all cases where any person may be restrained of his or her liberty in violation of the constitution, or of any treaty or law of the United States...." But the limitation of federal habeas corpus jurisdiction to consideration of the jurisdiction of the sentencing court persisted. ** And, although the concept of "jurisdiction" was subjected to considerable strain as the substantive scope of the writ was expanded, *** this expansion was limited to only a few classes of cases *** until *Frank v. Mangum*, 237 U.S. 309, in 1915.

    ***

In the landmark decision in *Brown v. Allen*, 344 U.S. 443, 482–487 (1953), the scope of the writ was expanded still further. *** In that case and its companion case, *Daniels v. Allen*, prisoners applied for federal habeas corpus relief claiming that the trial courts had erred in failing to quash their indictments due to alleged discrimination in the selection of grand jurors and in ruling certain confessions admissible. In *Brown*, the highest court of the State had rejected these claims on direct appeal, ** and this Court had denied certiorari. ** Despite the apparent adequacy of the state corrective process, the Court reviewed the denial of the writ of habeas corpus and held that Brown was entitled to a full reconsideration of these constitutional claims, including, if appropriate, a hearing in the Federal District Court. In *Daniels*, however, the State Supreme Court on direct review had refused to consider the appeal because the papers were filed out of time. This Court held that since the state-court judgment rested on a reasonable application of the State's legitimate procedural rules, a ground that would have barred direct review of his federal claims by this Court, the District Court lacked authority to grant habeas corpus relief. *See* 344 U.S. at 458, 486.

[The] final barrier to broad collateral re-examination of state criminal convictions in federal habeas corpus proceedings was removed in *Fay v. Noia*, 372 U.S. 391 (1963). *** This Court affirmed the grant of the writ, narrowly restricting the circumstances in which a federal court may refuse to consider the merits of federal constitutional claims. ***

During the period in which the substantive scope of the writ was expanded, the Court did not consider whether exceptions to full review might exist with respect to particular categories of constitutional claims. Prior to the Court's decision in *Kaufman v. United States*, 394 U.S. 217 (1969), however, a substantial majority of the Federal Courts of Appeals had concluded that collateral review of search-and-seizure claims was inappropriate on motions filed by federal prisoners under 28 U.S.C. §2255, the modern postconviction procedure available to federal prisoners in lieu of habeas corpus. *** The primary rationale advanced in support of those decisions was that Fourth Amendment violations are different in kind from denials of Fifth or Sixth Amendment rights in that claims of illegal search and seizure do not "impugn the integrity of the fact-finding process or challenge evidence as inherently unreliable; rather, the exclusion of illegally seized evidence is simply a prophylactic device intended generally to deter Fourth Amendment violations by law enforcement officers." 394 U.S. at 224. **

Kaufman rejected this rationale and held that search-and-seizure claims are cognizable in §2255 proceedings. The Court noted that "the federal habeas remedy extends to state prisoners alleging that unconstitutionally obtained evidence was admitted against them at trial," 394 U.S. at 225 ** and concluded, as a matter of statutory construction, that there was no basis for restricting "access by federal prisoners with illegal search-and-seizure claims to federal collateral remedies, while placing no similar restriction on access by state prisoners," 394 U.S. at 226. Although in recent years the view has been expressed that the Court should re-examine the substantive scope of federal habeas jurisdiction and limit collateral review of search-and-seizure claims "solely to the question of whether the petitioner was provided a fair opportunity to raise and have adjudicated the question in state courts," *Schneckloth v. Bustamonte*, 412 U.S. 218, 250 (1973) (POWELL, J., concurring), *** the Court, without discussion or consideration of the issue, has continued to accept jurisdiction in cases raising such claims. **

The discussion in *Kaufman* of the scope of federal habeas corpus rests on the view that the effectuation of the Fourth Amendment, as applied to the States through the Fourteenth Amendment, requires the granting of habeas corpus relief when a prisoner has been convicted in state court on the basis of evidence obtained in an illegal search or seizure since those Amendments were held in *Mapp v. Ohio*, 367 U.S. 643 (1961), to require exclusion of such evidence at trial and reversal of conviction upon direct review. *** Until these cases we have not had occasion fully to consider the validity of this view. ** Upon examination, we conclude, in light of the nature and purpose of the Fourth Amendment exclusionary rule, that this view is unjustified. *** We hold, therefore, that where the State has provided an opportunity for full and fair litigation of a Fourth Amendment claim, the Constitution does not require that a state prisoner be granted federal habeas corpus relief on the ground that evidence obtained in an unconstitutional search or seizure was introduced at his trial. ***

III

The Fourth Amendment assures the "right of the people to be secure in their persons, houses, papers, and effects, against unreasonable searches and seizures." The Amendment was primarily a reaction to the evils associated with the use of the general warrant in England and the writs of assistance in the Colonies ** and was intended to protect the "sanctity of a man's home and the privacies of life," *Boyd v. United States*, 116 U.S. 616, 630 (1886), from searches under unchecked general authority. ***

The exclusionary rule was a judicially created means of effectuating the rights secured by the Fourth Amendment. Prior to the Court's decisions in *Weeks v. United States*, 232 U.S. 383 (1914), and *Gouled v. United States*, 255 U.S. 298 (1921), there existed no barrier to the introduction in criminal trials of evidence obtained in violation of the Amendment. *See Adams v. New York*, 192 U.S. 585 (1904). *** In *Weeks* the Court held that the defendant could petition before trial for the return of property secured through an illegal search or seizure conducted by federal authorities. In *Gouled* the Court held broadly that such evidence could not be introduced in a federal prosecution. *See Warden v. Hayden*, 387 U.S. 294, 304–305 (1967). ** Thirty-five years after *Weeks* the Court held in *Wolf v. Colorado*, 338 U.S. 25 (1949), that the right to be free from arbitrary intrusion by the police that is protected by the Fourth Amendment is "implicit in 'the concept of ordered liberty' and as such enforceable against the States through the [Fourteenth Amendment] Due Process Clause." *Id.* at 27–28. The Court concluded, however, that the *Weeks* exclusionary rule would not be imposed upon the States as "an essential ingredient of [that] right." 338 U.S. at 29. The full force of *Wolf* was eroded in subsequent decisions, ** and a little more than a decade later the exclusionary rule was held applicable to the States in *Mapp v. Ohio*, 367 U.S. 643 (1961).

Decisions prior to *Mapp* advanced two principal reasons for application of the rule in federal trials. The Court in *Elkins*, for example, in the context of its special supervisory role over the lower federal courts, referred to the "imperative of judicial integrity," suggesting that exclusion of illegally seized evidence prevents contamination of the judicial process. 364 U.S. at 222. *** But even in that context a more pragmatic ground was emphasized:

> The rule is calculated to prevent, not to repair. Its purpose is to deter—to compel respect for the constitutional guaranty in the only effectively available way—by removing the incentive to disregard it. *Id.* at 217.

The *Mapp* majority justified the application of the rule to the States on several grounds, *** but relied principally upon the belief that exclusion would deter future unlawful police conduct. 367 U.S. at 658.

Although our decisions often have alluded to the "imperative of judicial integrity," *e.g.*, *United States v. Peltier*, 422 U.S. 531, 536–539 (1975), they demonstrate the limited role of this justification in the determination whether to apply the rule in a particular context. *** Logically extended this justification would require that courts exclude unconstitutionally seized evidence despite lack of objection by the defendant, or even over his assent. *Cf. Henry v. Mississippi*, 379 U.S. 443 (1965). It also would require abandonment of the standing limitations on who may object to the introduction of unconstitutionally seized evidence, *Alderman v. United States*, 394 U.S. 165 (1969), and retreat from the proposition that judicial proceedings need not abate when the defendant's person is unconstitutionally seized, *Gerstein v. Pugh*, 420 U.S. 103, 119 (1975); *Frisbie v. Collins*, 342 U.S. 519 (1952). Similarly, the interest in promoting judicial integrity does not prevent the use of illegally seized evidence in grand jury proceedings. *United States v. Calandra*, 414 U.S. 338 (1974). Nor does it require that the trial court exclude such evidence from use for impeachment of a defendant, even though its introduction is certain to result in conviction in some cases. *Walder v. United States*, 347 U.S. 62 (1954). The teaching of these cases is clear. While courts, of course, must ever be concerned with preserving the integrity of the judicial process, this concern has limited force as a justification for the exclusion of highly probative evidence. *** The force of this justification becomes minimal where federal habeas corpus relief is sought by a prisoner who previously has been afforded the opportunity for full and fair consideration of his search-and-seizure claim at trial and on direct review.

The primary justification for the exclusionary rule then is the deterrence of police conduct that violates Fourth Amendment rights. Post-*Mapp* decisions have established that the rule is not a personal constitutional right. It is not calculated to redress the injury to the privacy of the victim of the search or seizure, for any "[r]eparation comes too late." *Linkletter v. Walker*, 381 U.S. 618, 637 (1965). Instead, "the rule is a judicially created remedy designed to safeguard Fourth Amendment rights generally through its deterrent effect...." *United States v. Calandra*, [414 U.S.] at 348. **

***

IV

We turn now to the specific question presented by these cases. Respondents allege violations of Fourth Amendment rights guaranteed them through the Fourteenth Amendment. The question is whether state prisoners—who have been afforded the opportunity for full and fair consideration of their reliance upon the exclusionary rule with respect to seized evidence by the state courts at trial and on direct review—may invoke their claim again on federal habeas corpus review. The answer is to be found by weighing the utility of the exclusionary rule against the costs of extending it to collateral review of Fourth Amendment claims.

The costs of applying the exclusionary rule even at trial and on direct review are well known: *** the focus of the trial, and the attention of the participants therein, are diverted from the ultimate question of guilt or innocence that should be the central concern in a criminal proceeding. *** Moreover, the physical evidence sought to be excluded is typically reliable and often the most probative information bearing on the guilt or innocence of the defendant. As Mr. Justice Black emphasized in his dissent in *Kaufman*:

> A claim of illegal search and seizure under the Fourth Amendment is crucially different from many other constitutional rights; ordinarily the evidence seized can in no way have been rendered untrustworthy by the means of its seizure and indeed often this evidence alone establishes beyond virtually any shadow of a doubt that the defendant is guilty. 394 U.S. at 237.

Application of the rule thus deflects the truth-finding process and often frees the guilty. The disparity in particular cases between the error committed by the police officer and the windfall afforded a guilty defendant by application of the rule is contrary to the idea of proportionality that is essential to the concept of justice. *** Thus, although the rule is thought to deter unlawful police activity in part through the nurturing of respect for Fourth Amendment values, if applied indiscriminately it may well have the opposite effect of generating disrespect for the law and administration of justice. *** These long-recognized costs of the rule persist when a criminal conviction is sought to be overturned on collateral review on the ground that a search-and-seizure claim was erroneously rejected by two or more tiers of state courts. ***

Evidence obtained by police officers in violation of the Fourth Amendment is excluded at trial in the hope that the frequency of future violations will decrease. Despite the absence of supportive empirical evidence, *** we have assumed that the immediate effect of exclusion will be to discourage law enforcement officials from violating the Fourth Amendment by removing the incentive to disregard it. More importantly, over the long term, this demonstration that our society attaches serious consequences to violation of constitutional rights is thought to encourage those who formulate law enforcement policies, and the officers who implement them, to incorporate Fourth Amendment ideals into their value system. ***

We adhere to the view that these considerations support the implementation of the exclusionary rule at trial and its enforcement on direct appeal of state-court convictions. But the additional contribution, if any, of the consideration of search-and-seizure claims of state prisoners on collateral review is small in relation to the costs. ***

In sum, we conclude that where the State has provided an opportunity for full and fair litigation of a Fourth Amendment claim, *** a state prisoner may not be granted federal habeas corpus relief on the ground that evidence obtained in an unconstitutional search or seizure was introduced at his trial. *** In this context the contribution of the exclusionary rule, if any, to the effectuation of the Fourth Amendment is minimal, and the substantial societal costs of application of the rule persist with special force. ***

Accordingly, the judgments of the Courts of Appeals are

Reversed.

[A concurring opinion by CHIEF JUSTICE BURGER, a dissenting opinion by JUSTICE BRENNAN, in which JUSTICE MARSHALL joined, and a dissenting opinion by JUSTICE WHITE are omitted.]

Notes

1. *Subsequent case history*

David Rice began serving a life sentence in Nebraska on April 17, 1971, and is still incarcerated. *See* http://www.corrections.state.ne.us (then search on "inmate locator"). No information is available about Lloyd Powell.

2. *The rationale behind the exclusionary rule*

After stating that "despite the broad deterrent purpose of the exclusionary rule, it has never been interpreted to proscribe the introduction of illegally seized evidence in all proceedings or against all persons," Justice Powell cites the following observation by Professor Tony Amsterdam:

> The rule is unsupportable as reparation or compensatory dispensation to the injured criminal; its sole rational justification is the experience of its indispensability in "exert[ing] general legal pressures to secure obedience to the Fourth Amendment on the part of…law-enforcing officers." As it serves this function, the rule is a needed, but grud[g]ingly taken, medicament; no more should be swallowed than is needed to combat the disease. Granted that so many criminals must go free as will deter the constables from blundering, pursuance of this policy of liberation beyond the confines of necessity inflicts gratuitous harm on the public interest….

428 U.S. at 487 n.24, *quoting Search, Seizure, and Section 2255: A Comment*, 112 U. Pa. L. Rev. 378, 388–389 (1964) (footnotes omitted).

Do you agree with Professor Amsterdam that the exclusionary rule is "unsupportable as reparation or compensatory dispensation to the injured criminal"? If one is to assume that the exclusionary rule should be applied only to the extent necessary to exert legal pressure on law enforcement to obey the Fourth Amendment, where should that line be drawn?

3. *Dissenting opinion by Justice Brennan*

In his dissenting opinion, with whom Justice Marshall concurs, Justice Brennan makes the following observation:

> The Court's opinion does not specify the particular basis on which it denies federal habeas jurisdiction over claims of Fourth Amendment violations brought by state prisoners. The Court insists that its holding is based on the Constitution, ** but in light of the explicit language of 28 U.S.C. §2254 *** (significantly not even mentioned by the Court), I can only presume that the Court intends to be understood to hold either that respondents are not, as a matter of statutory construction, "in custody in violation of the Constitution or laws…of the United States," or that "'considerations of comity and concern for the orderly administration of criminal justice'" *** are sufficient to allow this Court to rewrite jurisdictional statutes enacted by Congress. Neither ground of decision is tenable; the former is simply illogical, and the latter is an arrogation of power committed solely to the Congress.

On what basis does the Court ground its decision? If you agree with Justice Brennan that one of the only rationales for the Court's holding is "considerations of comity and concern for the orderly administration of criminal justice," do you believe such concerns justify the result the Court reached? Why or why not?

4. Dissenting opinion by Justice White

Justice White's dissent begins with the following paragraph:

> For many of the reasons stated by MR. JUSTICE BRENNAN, I cannot agree that the writ of habeas corpus should be any less available to those convicted of state crimes where they allege Fourth Amendment violations than where other constitutional issues are presented to the federal court. Under the amendments to the habeas corpus statute, which were adopted after *Fay v. Noia*, 372 U.S. 391 (1963), and represented an effort by Congress to lend a modicum of finality to state criminal judgments, I cannot distinguish between Fourth Amendment and other constitutional issues.

What distinction does the Court draw between Fourth Amendment violations and other constitutional issues? What is your assessment of that distinction?

Kimmelman v. Morrison
477 U.S. 365 (1986)

JUSTICE BRENNAN delivered the opinion of the Court.

The question we address in this case is whether the restrictions on federal habeas review of Fourth Amendment claims announced in *Stone v. Powell*, 428 U.S. 465 (1976), should be extended to Sixth Amendment claims of ineffective assistance of counsel where the principal allegation and manifestation of inadequate representation is counsel's failure to file a timely motion to suppress evidence allegedly obtained in violation of the Fourth Amendment.

I

Respondent, Neil Morrison, was convicted by the State of New Jersey of raping a 15-year-old girl. The case presented by the State at respondent's bench trial consisted of scientific evidence and of the testimony of the victim, her mother, and the police officers who handled the victim's complaint.

The victim testified that Morrison, who was her employer, had taken her to his apartment, where he forced her onto his bed and raped her. Upon returning home, the girl related the incident to her mother, who, after first summoning Morrison and asking for his account of events, phoned the police. The police came to the victim's home and transported her to the hospital, where she was examined and tested for indicia of a sexual assault.

The State also called as a witness Detective Dolores Most, one of the officers who investigated the rape complaint. Most testified that she accompanied the victim to Morrison's apartment building a few hours after the rape. Morrison was not at home, but another tenant in the building let them into respondent's one-room apartment. While there, Most stated, she seized a sheet from respondent's bed.

At this point in the testimony respondent's counsel objected to the introduction of the sheet and to any testimony concerning it on the ground that Most had seized it without a search warrant. New Jersey Court Rules, however, require that suppression motions be made within 30 days of indictment unless the time is enlarged by the trial court for good cause. ** Because the 30-day deadline had long since expired, the trial judge ruled that counsel's motion was late. Defense counsel explained to the court that he had not heard of the seizure until the day before, when trial began, and that his client could not have known of it because the police had not left a receipt for the sheet. The prosecutor responded that defense counsel, who had been on the case from the beginning, had never asked for *any* discovery. Had trial counsel done so, the prosecutor observed, police reports would have revealed the search and seizure. The prosecutor stated further that one month before trial he had sent defense counsel a copy of the laboratory report concerning the tests conducted on stains and hairs found on the sheets.

Asked repeatedly by the trial court why he had not conducted any discovery, respondent's attorney asserted that it was the State's obligation to inform him of its case against his client, even though he made no request for discovery. The judge rejected this assertion and stated: "I hate to say it, but I have to say it, that you were remiss. I think this evidence was there and available to you for examination and inquiry." ** Defense counsel then attempted to justify his omission on the ground that he had not expected to go to trial because he had been told that the victim did not wish to proceed. The judge rejected this justification also, reminding counsel that once an indictment is handed down, the decision to go through with the complaint no longer belongs to the victim, and that it requires a court order to dismiss an indictment. ** While the judge agreed that defense counsel had "[brought] about a very valid basis...for suppression...if the motion had been brought and timely made," he refused "to entertain a motion to suppress in the middle of the trial." **

The State then called a number of expert witnesses who had conducted laboratory tests on the stains and hairs found on the sheet, on a stain found on the victim's underpants, and on blood and hair samples provided by the victim and respondent. This testimony established that the bedsheet had been stained with semen from a man with type O blood, that the stains on the victim's underwear similarly exhibited semen from a man with type O blood, that the defendant had type O blood, that vaginal tests performed on the girl at the hospital demonstrated the presence of sperm, and that hairs recovered from the sheet were morphologically similar to head hair of both Morrison and the victim. Defense counsel aggressively cross-examined all of the expert witnesses.

The defense called four friends and acquaintances of the defendant and the defendant himself in an attempt to establish a different version of the facts. The defense theory was that the girl and her mother fabricated the rape in order to punish respondent for being delinquent with the girl's wages. According to Morrison, the girl and her mother had not intended to go through with the prosecution, but ultimately they found it impossible to extricate themselves from their lies. Morrison admitted that he had taken the girl to his apartment, but denied having had intercourse with her. He claimed that his sexual activity with other women accounted for the stains on his sheet, and that a hair from the girl's head was on his sheet because she had seated herself on his bed. Defense counsel also implied that the girl's underwear and vaginal secretions tested positive for semen and sperm because she probably had recently engaged in relations with the father of her baby. Counsel did not, however, call the girl's boyfriend to testify or have him tested for blood type, an omission upon which the prosecution commented in closing argument.

The trial judge, in rendering his verdict, noted: "As in most cases nothing is cut and dry. There are discrepancies in the State's case, there are discrepancies in the defense as it's presented." ** After pointing out some of the more troublesome inconsistencies in the testimony of several of the witnesses, the judge declared his conclusion that the State had proved its case beyond a reasonable doubt.

After trial, respondent dismissed his attorney and retained new counsel for his appeal. On appeal, respondent alleged ineffective assistance of counsel and error in the trial court's refusal to entertain the suppression motion during trial. The appeals court announced summarily that it found no merit in either claim and affirmed respondent's conviction. The Supreme Court of New Jersey subsequently denied respondent's petition for discretionary review. Respondent then sought postconviction relief in the New Jersey Superior Court, from the same judge who had tried his case. There Morrison presented the identical issues he had raised on direct appeal. The court denied relief on the ground that it was bound by the appellate court's resolution of those issues against respondent.

Respondent then sought a writ of habeas corpus in Federal District Court, again raising claims of ineffective assistance of counsel and erroneous admission of illegally seized evidence. The District Court ruled that because respondent did not allege that the State had denied him an opportunity to litigate his Fourth Amendment claim fully and fairly, direct consideration of this claim on federal habeas review was barred by *Stone v. Powell*, 428 U.S. 465 (1976). ** The District Court did find respondent's ineffective-assistance claim meritorious.

[The Court then discusses the fact that although this case was decided before *Strickland v. Washington*, 466 U.S. 668 (1984), the precedent relied on matched the reasoning in *Strickland*.]

***

The District Court then determined that, measured by the harmless-beyond-a-reasonable-doubt standard prescribed by [*United States v.*] *Baynes*, [687 F.2d 659 (1982)], respondent had been prejudiced by counsel's ineffectiveness and issued a conditional writ of habeas corpus ordering Morrison's release unless New Jersey should retry him.

Although the District Court did not address the relevance of *Stone, supra,* to respondent's Sixth Amendment ineffective-assistance-of-counsel claim, the Court of Appeals did. Relying on both the language of *Stone* and the different natures of Fourth and Sixth Amendment claims, the Court of Appeals concluded that *Stone* should not be extended to bar federal habeas consideration of Sixth Amendment claims based on counsel's alleged failure competently to litigate Fourth Amendment claims. ** Because *Strickland* had recently been decided by this Court, the Court of Appeals reviewed the District Court's determination of ineffective assistance under *Strickland*'s test. The Court of Appeals determined that respondent's trial counsel had been "grossly ineffective" ** but vacated and remanded for the District Court to consider whether, under the standards set forth in *Strickland, supra,* respondent had been prejudiced by his attorney's incompetence.

Petitioners, the Attorney General of New Jersey and the Superintendent of Rahway State Prison, petitioned for certiorari. We granted their petition ** and now affirm.

II

Petitioners urge that the Sixth Amendment veil be lifted from respondent's habeas petition to reveal what petitioners argue it really is—an attempt to litigate his defaulted Fourth Amendment claim. They argue that because respondent's claim is in fact, if not in form, a Fourth Amendment one, *Stone* directly controls here. Alternatively, petitioners maintain that even if Morrison's Sixth Amendment claim may legitimately be considered distinct from his defaulted Fourth Amendment claim, the rationale and purposes of *Stone* are fully applicable to ineffective-assistance claims where the principal allegation of inadequate representation is counsel's failure to file a timely motion to suppress evidence allegedly obtained in violation of the Fourth Amendment. *Stone,* they argue, will be emasculated unless we extend its bar against federal habeas review to this sort of Sixth Amendment claim. Finally, petitioners maintain that consideration of defaulted Fourth Amendment claims in Sixth Amendment federal collateral proceedings would violate principles of comity and federalism and would seriously interfere with the State's interest in the finality of its criminal convictions. ***

A

We do not share petitioners' perception of the identity between respondent's Fourth and Sixth Amendment claims. While defense counsel's failure to make a timely suppression motion is the primary manifestation of incompetence and source of prejudice advanced by respondent, the two claims are nonetheless distinct, both in nature and in the requisite elements of proof.

Although it is frequently invoked in criminal trials, the Fourth Amendment is not a trial right; the protection it affords against governmental intrusion into one's home and affairs pertains to all citizens. The gravamen of a Fourth Amendment claim is that the complainant's legitimate expectation of privacy has been violated by an illegal search or seizure. *See, e.g., Katz v. United States*, 389 U.S. 347 (1967). In order to prevail, the complainant need prove only that the search or seizure was illegal and that it violated his reasonable expectation of privacy in the item or place at issue. *See, e.g., Rawlings v. Kentucky*, 448 U.S. 98, 104 (1980).

The right to counsel is a fundamental right of criminal defendants; it assures the fairness, and thus the legitimacy, of our adversary process. *E.g., Gideon v. Wainwright*, 372 U.S. 335, 344 (1963). The essence of an ineffective-assistance claim is that counsel's unprofessional errors so upset the adversarial balance between defense and prosecution that the trial was rendered unfair and the verdict rendered suspect. *See, e.g., Strickland v. Washington*, 466 U.S. at 686; *United States v. Cronic*, 466 U.S. 648, 655–657 (1984). In order to prevail, the defendant must show both that counsel's representation fell below an objective standard of reasonableness, *Strickland*, 466 U.S. at 688, and that there exists a reasonable probability that, but for counsel's unprofessional errors, the result of the proceeding would have been different. *Id.* at 694. Where defense counsel's failure to litigate a Fourth Amendment claim competently is the principal allegation of ineffectiveness, the defendant must also prove that his Fourth Amendment claim is meritorious and that there is a reasonable probability that the verdict would have been different absent the excludable evidence in order to demonstrate actual prejudice. Thus, while respondent's defaulted Fourth Amendment claim is one element of proof of his Sixth Amendment claim, the two claims have separate identities and reflect different constitutional values.

B

We also disagree with petitioners' contention that the reasoning and purposes of *Stone* are fully applicable to a Sixth Amendment claim which is based principally on defense counsel's failure to litigate a Fourth Amendment claim competently.

At issue in *Stone* was the proper scope of federal collateral protection of criminal defendants' right to have evidence, seized in violation of the Fourth Amendment, excluded at trial in state court. In determining that federal courts should withhold habeas review where the State has provided an opportunity for full and fair litigation of a Fourth Amendment claim, the Court found it crucial that the remedy for Fourth Amendment violations provided by the exclusionary rule "is not a personal constitutional right." 428 U.S. at 486; *see also id.* at 495 n.37. The Court expressed the understanding that the rule "is not calculated to redress the injury to the privacy of the victim of the search or seizure," *id.* at 486; instead, the Court explained, the exclusionary rule is predominately a "'judicially created'" structural remedy "designed to safeguard Fourth Amendment rights generally through its deterrent effect.'" *Ibid.* (*quoting United States v. Calandra*, 414 U.S. 338, 348 (1974)).

The Court further noted that "[as] in the case of any remedial device, 'the application of the rule has been restricted to those areas where its remedial objectives are thought most efficaciously served,'" 428 U.S. at 486–487 (*quoting Calandra*,[414 U.S.] at 348) and that the rule has not been extended to situations such as grand jury proceedings, 428 U.S. at 486–487 (*citing Calandra, supra*), and impeachment of a defendant who testifies broadly in his own behalf, 428 U.S. at 488 (*citing Walder v. United States*, 347 U.S. 62, 74 (1954)), where the rule's costs would outweigh its utility as a deterrent to police misconduct. Applying this "pragmatic analysis," 428 U.S. at 488, to the question whether prisoners who have been afforded a full and fair opportunity in state court to invoke the exclusionary rule may raise their Fourth Amendment claims on federal habeas review, the Court determined that they may not. While accepting that the exclusionary rule's deterrent effect outweighs its costs when enforced at trial and on direct appeal, the Court found any "additional contribution...of the consideration of search-and-seizure claims...on collateral review, *id.* at 493, to be too small in relation to the costs to justify federal habeas review. *Id.* at 492–495.

In *Stone* the Court also made clear that its "decision...[was] *not* concerned with the scope of the habeas corpus statute as authority for litigating constitutional claims generally." *Id.* at 495 n.37 (emphasis in original). Rather, the Court simply "reaffirm[ed] that the exclusionary rule is a judicially created remedy rather than a personal constitutional right...and...emphasiz[ed] the minimal utility of the rule" in the context of federal collateral proceedings. *Ibid.* **

In contrast to the habeas petitioner in *Stone*, who sought merely to avail himself of the exclusionary rule, Morrison seeks direct federal habeas protection of his personal right to effective assistance of counsel.

The right of an accused to counsel is beyond question a fundamental right. *See, e.g., Gideon*, 372 U.S. at 344 ("The right of one charged with crime to counsel may not be deemed fundamental and essential to fair trials in some countries, but it is in ours"). Without counsel the right to a fair trial itself would be of little consequence, *see, e.g., Cronic*, [466 U.S.] at 653, ** for it is through counsel that the accused secures his other rights. *Maine v. Moulton*, 474 U.S. 159, 168–170 (1985); *Cronic, supra*, at 653. ** The constitutional guarantee of counsel, however, "cannot be satisfied by mere formal appointment," *Avery v. Alabama*, 308 U.S. 444, 446 (1940). "An accused is entitled to be assisted by an attorney, whether retained or appointed, who plays the role necessary to ensure that the trial is fair." *Strickland*, [466 U.S.] at 685. In other words, the right to counsel is the right to effective assistance of counsel. *Evitts v. Lucey*, 469 U.S. 387, 395–396 (1985); *Strickland*, [466 U.S.] at 686; *Cronic*, 466 U.S. at 654. ** [The Court then includes the following footnote: As we held only last Term, the right to effective assistance of counsel is not confined to trial, but extends also to the first appeal as of right. *Evitts v. Lucey*, 469 U.S. 387 (1985).]

Because collateral review will frequently be the only means through which an accused can effectuate the right to counsel, restricting the litigation of some Sixth Amendment claims to trial and direct review would seriously interfere with an accused's right to effective representation. A layman will ordinarily be unable to recognize counsel's errors and to evaluate counsel's professional performance; ** consequently a criminal defendant will rarely know that he has not been represented competently until after trial or appeal, usually when he consults another lawyer about his case. Indeed, an accused will often not realize that he has a meritorious ineffectiveness claim until he begins collateral review proceedings, particularly if he retained trial counsel on direct appeal. Were we to extend *Stone* and hold that criminal defendants may not raise ineffective-assistance claims that are based primarily on incompetent handling of Fourth Amendment issues on federal habeas, we would deny most defendants whose trial attorneys performed incompetently in this regard the opportunity to vindicate their right to effective trial counsel. We would deny all defendants whose appellate counsel performed inadequately with respect to Fourth Amendment issues the opportunity to protect their right to effective appellate counsel. *See Evitts, supra.* Thus, we cannot say, as the Court was able to say in *Stone*, that restriction of federal habeas review would not severely interfere with the protection of the constitutional right asserted by the habeas petitioner. ***

Furthermore, while the Court may be free, under its analysis in *Stone*, to refuse for reasons of prudence and comity *** to burden the State with the costs of the exclusionary rule in contexts where the Court believes the price of the rule to exceed its utility, the Constitution constrains our ability to allocate as we see fit the costs of ineffective assistance. The Sixth Amendment mandates that the State bear the risk of constitutionally deficient assistance of counsel. **

We also reject the suggestion that criminal defendants should not be allowed to vindicate through federal habeas review their right to effective assistance of counsel where counsel's primary error is failure to make a timely request for the exclusion of illegally seized evidence—evidence which is "typically reliable and often the most probative information bearing on the guilt or innocence of the defendant." *Stone*, 428 U.S. at 490. While we have recognized that the "'premise of our adversary system of criminal justice...that partisan advocacy...will best promote the ultimate objective that the guilty be convicted and the innocent go free,'" *Evitts*, 469 U.S. at 394, ** underlies and gives meaning to the right to effective assistance, *Cronic*, [466 U.S.] at 655–656, we have never intimated that the right to counsel is conditioned upon actual innocence. The constitutional rights of criminal defendants are granted to the innocent and the guilty alike. Consequently, we decline to hold either that the guarantee of effective assistance of counsel belongs solely to the innocent or that it attaches only to matters affecting the determination of actual guilt. *** Furthermore, petitioners do not suggest that an ineffective-assistance claim asserted on direct review would fail for want of actual prejudice whenever counsel's primary error is failure to make a meritorious objection to the admission of reliable evidence the exclusion of which might have affected the outcome of the proceeding. We decline to hold that the scope of the right to effective assistance of counsel is altered in this manner simply because the right is asserted on federal habeas review rather than on direct review.

C

Stone's restriction on federal habeas review, petitioners warn, will be stripped of all practical effect unless we extend it to Sixth Amendment claims based principally on defense counsel's incompetent handling of Fourth Amendment issues. Petitioners predict that every Fourth Amendment claim that fails or is defaulted in state court will be fully litigated in federal habeas proceedings in Sixth Amendment guise and that, as a result, many state-court judgments will be disturbed. They seem to believe that a prisoner need only allege ineffective assistance, and if he has an underlying,

meritorious Fourth Amendment claim, the writ will issue and the State will be obligated to retry him without the challenged evidence. Because it ignores the rigorous
standard which *Strickland* erected for ineffective-assistance claims, petitioners' fore-
cast is simply incorrect.

In order to establish ineffective representation, the defendant must prove both incompetence and prejudice. *** 466 U.S. at 688. There is a strong presumption that
counsel's performance falls within the "wide range of professional assistance," *id.* at 689;
the defendant bears the burden of proving that counsel's representation was unreasonable under prevailing professional norms and that the challenged action was not sound
strategy. *Id.* at 688–689. The reasonableness of counsel's performance is to be evaluated
from counsel's perspective at the time of the alleged error and in light of all the circumstances, and the standard of review is highly deferential. *Id.* at 689. The defendant
shows that he was prejudiced by his attorney's ineffectiveness by demonstrating that
"there is a reasonable probability that, but for counsel's unprofessional errors, the result
of the proceeding would have been different." *Id.* at 694. *See also id.* at 695 (Where a defendant challenges his conviction, he must show that there exists "a reasonable probability that, absent the errors, the factfinder would have had a reasonable doubt respecting guilt"). And, in determining the existence *vel non* of prejudice, the court "must
consider the totality of the evidence before the judge or jury." *Ibid.*

As is obvious, *Strickland*'s standard, although by no means insurmountable, is highly
demanding. More importantly, it differs significantly from the elements of proof applicable to a straightforward Fourth Amendment claim. Although a meritorious Fourth
Amendment issue is necessary to the success of a Sixth Amendment claim like respondent's, a good Fourth Amendment claim alone will not earn a prisoner federal habeas
relief. Only those habeas petitioners who can prove under *Strickland* that they have
been denied a fair trial by the gross incompetence of their attorneys will be granted the
writ and will be entitled to retrial without the challenged evidence. ***

D

In summary, we reject petitioners' argument that *Stone*'s restriction on federal
habeas review of Fourth Amendment claims should be extended to Sixth Amendment
ineffective-assistance-of-counsel claims which are founded primarily on incompetent
representation with respect to a Fourth Amendment issue. Where a State obtains a
criminal conviction in a trial in which the accused is deprived of the effective assistance
of counsel, the "State … unconstitutionally deprives the defendant of his liberty." *Cuyler*
[*v. Sullivan*], 446 U.S. 335, 343 [(1980)]. The defendant is thus "in custody in violation
of the Constitution," 28 U.S.C. §2254(a), and federal courts have habeas jurisdiction
over his claim. We hold that federal courts may grant habeas relief in appropriate cases,
regardless of the nature of the underlying attorney error.

III

Petitioners also argue that respondent has not satisfied either the performance or the
prejudice prong of the test for ineffective assistance of counsel set forth in *Strickland*.
We address each component of that test in turn.

A

With respect to the performance component of the *Strickland* test, petitioners contend that Morrison has not overcome the strong presumption of attorney competence

established by *Strickland*. While acknowledging that this Court has said that a single, serious error may support a claim of ineffective assistance of counsel, *** petitioners argue that the mere failure to file a timely suppression motion alone does not constitute a *per se* Sixth Amendment violation. They maintain that the record "amply reflects that trial counsel crafted a sound trial strategy" and that, "[v]iewed in its entirety, counsel's pretrial investigation, preparation and trial performance were professionally reasonable." ** While we agree with petitioners' view that the failure to file a suppression motion does not constitute *per se* ineffective assistance of counsel, we disagree with petitioners' assessment of counsel's performance.

***

The trial record in this case clearly reveals that Morrison's attorney failed to file a timely suppression motion, not due to strategic considerations, but because, until the first day of trial, he was unaware of the search and of the State's intention to introduce the bedsheet into evidence. Counsel was unapprised of the search and seizure because he had conducted no pretrial discovery. Counsel's failure to request discovery, again, was not based on "strategy," but on counsel's mistaken beliefs that the State was obliged to take the initiative and turn over all of its inculpatory evidence to the defense and that the victim's preferences would determine whether the State proceeded to trial after an indictment had been returned.

Viewing counsel's failure to conduct any discovery from his perspective at the time he decided to forgo that stage of pretrial preparation and applying a "heavy measure of deference," [*Strickland*, 466 U.S. at 691,] to his judgment, we find counsel's decision unreasonable, that is, contrary to prevailing professional norms. The justifications Morrison's attorney offered for his omission betray a startling ignorance of the law—or a weak attempt to shift blame for inadequate preparation. "[C]ounsel has a duty to make reasonable investigations or to make a reasonable decision that makes particular investigations unnecessary." *Ibid.* Respondent's lawyer neither investigated, nor made a reasonable decision not to investigate, the State's case through discovery. Such a complete lack of pretrial preparation puts at risk both the defendant's right to an "'ample opportunity to meet the case of the prosecution,'" *id.* at 685 (*quoting Adams*, [317 U.S.] at 275), and the reliability of the adversarial testing process. *See* 466 U.S. at 688.

***

*** We therefore agree with the District Court and the Court of Appeals that the assistance rendered respondent by his trial counsel was constitutionally deficient.

B

1

Petitioners also argue that respondent suffered no prejudice from his attorney's failure to make a timely suppression motion and that the Third Circuit erred in remanding the case to the District Court for a determination of prejudice under *Strickland*'s standard. ***

***

Because it cannot fairly be said that the "merits of the factual dispute," § 2254(d)(1), regarding the existence of prejudice were resolved in the bail hearing, we conclude that the statements of the judge regarding the relative importance of the sheet are not findings of fact subject to § 2254(d) deference. ***

2

Respondent also criticizes the Court of Appeals' decision to remand for redetermination of prejudice. He argues that the record is sufficiently complete to enable this Court to apply *Strickland*'s prejudice prong directly to the facts of his case and urges that we do so.

We decline respondent's invitation. While the existing record proved adequate for our application of *Strickland*'s competency standard, it is incomplete with respect to prejudice. No evidentiary hearing has ever been held on the merits of respondent's Fourth Amendment claim. Because the State has not conceded the illegality of the search and seizure, ** it is entitled to an opportunity to establish that Officer Most's search came within one of the exceptions we have recognized to the Fourth Amendment's prohibition against warrantless searches. Even if not, respondent may be unable to show that absent the evidence concerning the bedsheet there is a reasonable probability that the trial judge would have had a reasonable doubt as to his guilt. If respondent could not make this showing, a matter on which we express no view, there would of course be no need to hold an evidentiary hearing on his Fourth Amendment claim.

The judgment of the Court of Appeals is

Affirmed.

[A concurring opinion by JUSTICE POWELL, in which CHIEF JUSTICE BURGER and JUSTICE REHNQUIST joined, is omitted.]

Notes

1. *Subsequent case history*

On remand, the district court granted Neil Morrison a new trial. *Morrison v. Kimmelman*, 650 F. Supp. 801 (N.J. Dist. Ct. 1986).

2. *Allocating costs of Fourth Amendment and Sixth Amendment violations*

In reaching its decision, the Court states that while it "may be free, under its analysis in *Stone*, to refuse for reasons of prudence and comity to burden the State with the costs of the exclusionary rule" in certain contexts, "[t]he Sixth Amendment mandates that the State bear the risk of constitutionally deficient assistance of counsel." What is your opinion of this distinction?

3. *Personal right versus fundamental rights*

Underlying the Court's rationale is the assessment that the exclusionary rule in *Stone* is a structural remedy created to protect Fourth Amendment rights, while the right to effective assistance of counsel in *Kimmelman* is a fundamental personal right. Do you agree with this assessment?

4. *"Sandbagging" critical claims*

Anticipating possible concerns that an attorney might "sandbag" an issue in hopes of gaining more favorable review of the claim in federal habeas corpus proceedings, Justice Brennan makes the following observation:

> We have no reason to believe that defense attorneys will "sandbag"—that is, consciously default or poorly litigate their clients' Fourth Amendment claims in state court in the hope of gaining more favorable review of these claims in Sixth Amendment federal habeas proceedings. First, it is virtually inconceivable that an attorney would deliberately invite the judgment that his perfor-

mance was constitutionally deficient in order to win federal collateral review
for his client. Second, counsel's client has little, if anything, to gain and everything to lose through such a strategy. It should be remembered that only incompetently litigated and defaulted Fourth Amendment claims that could lead
to a reversal of the defendant's conviction on Sixth Amendment grounds are
potentially outcome-determinative claims. No reasonable lawyer would forgo
competent litigation of meritorious, possibly decisive claims on the remote
chance that his deliberate dereliction might ultimately result in federal habeas
review.

477 U.S. at 387 n.7. Is Justice Brennan's rationale describing why attorneys would not
"sandbag" a Fourth Amendment issue reasonable?

Withrow v. Williams
507 U.S. 680 (1993)

JUSTICE SOUTER delivered the opinion of the Court.

In *Stone v. Powell*, 428 U.S. 465 (1976), we held that when a State has given a full and
fair chance to litigate a Fourth Amendment claim, federal habeas review is not available
to a state prisoner alleging that his conviction rests on evidence obtained through an
unconstitutional search or seizure. Today we hold that *Stone*'s restriction on the exercise
of federal habeas jurisdiction does not extend to a state prisoner's claim that his conviction rests on statements obtained in violation of the safeguards mandated by *Miranda v.
Arizona*, 384 U.S. 436 (1966).

I

Police officers in Romulus, Michigan, learned that respondent, Robert Allen
Williams, Jr., might have information about a double murder committed on April 6,
1985. On April 10, two officers called at Williams's house and asked him to the police
station for questioning. Williams agreed to go. The officers searched Williams, but did
not handcuff him, and they all drove to the station in an unmarked car. One officer,
Sergeant David Early, later testified that Williams was not under arrest at this time, although a contemporaneous police report indicates that the officers arrested Williams at
his residence. **

At the station, the officers questioned Williams about his knowledge of the crime.
Although he first denied any involvement, he soon began to implicate himself, and the
officers continued their questioning, assuring Williams that their only concern was the
identity of the "shooter." After consulting each other, the officers decided not to advise
Williams of his rights under *Miranda v. Arizona, supra*. ** When Williams persisted in
denying involvement, Sergeant Early reproved him:

> You know everything that went down. You just don't want to talk about it.
> What it's gonna amount to is you can talk about it now and give us the truth
> and we're gonna check it out and see if it fits or else we're simply gonna charge
> you and lock you up and you can just tell it to a defense attorney and let him
> try and prove differently. *Ibid.*

The reproof apparently worked, for Williams then admitted he had furnished the
murder weapon to the killer, who had called Williams after the crime and told him
where he had discarded the weapon and other incriminating items. Williams maintained that he had not been present at the crime scene.

Only at this point, some 40 minutes after they began questioning him, did the officers advise Williams of his *Miranda* rights. Williams waived those rights and during subsequent questioning made several more inculpatory statements. Despite his prior denial, Williams admitted that he had driven the murderer to and from the scene of the crime, had witnessed the murders, and had helped the murderer dispose of incriminating evidence. The officers interrogated Williams again on April 11 and April 12, and, on April 12, the State formally charged him with murder.

Before trial, Williams moved to suppress his responses to the interrogations, and the trial court suppressed the statements of April 11 and April 12 as the products of improper delay in arraignment under Michigan law. ** The court declined to suppress the statements of April 10, however, ruling that the police had given Williams a timely warning of his *Miranda* rights. ** A bench trial led to Williams's conviction on two counts each of first-degree murder and possession of a fire-arm during the commission of a felony and resulted in two concurrent life sentences. The Court of Appeals of Michigan affirmed the trial court's ruling on the April 10 statements, ** and the Supreme Court of Michigan denied leave to appeal. ** We denied the ensuing petition for writ of certiorari. **

Williams then began this action *pro se* by petitioning for a writ of habeas corpus in the District Court, alleging a violation of his *Miranda* rights as the principal ground for relief. ** The District Court granted relief, finding that the police had placed Williams in custody for *Miranda* purposes when Sergeant Early had threatened to "lock [him] up," and that the trial court should accordingly have excluded all statements Williams had made between that point and his receipt of the *Miranda* warnings. ** The court also concluded, though neither Williams nor petitioner had addressed the issue, that Williams's statements after receiving the *Miranda* warnings were involuntary under the Due Process Clause of the Fourteenth Amendment and thus likewise subject to suppression. ** The court found that the totality of circumstances, including repeated promises of lenient treatment if he told the truth, had overborne Williams's will. ***

The Court of Appeals affirmed, ** holding the District Court correct in determining the police had subjected Williams to custodial interrogation before giving him the requisite *Miranda* advice, and in finding the statements made after receiving the *Miranda* warnings involuntary. ** The Court of Appeals summarily rejected the argument that the rule in *Stone v. Powell,* 428 U.S. 465 (1976), should apply to bar habeas review of Williams's *Miranda* claim. ** We granted certiorari to resolve the significant issue thus presented. **

II

We have made it clear that *Stone*'s limitation on federal habeas relief was not jurisdictional in nature, *** but rested on prudential concerns counseling against the application of the Fourth Amendment exclusionary rule on collateral review. *See Stone,* [428 U.S.] at 494–495 n.37. ** We simply concluded in *Stone* that the costs of applying the exclusionary rule on collateral review outweighed any potential advantage to be gained by applying it there. *Stone, supra,* at 489–495.

We recognized that the exclusionary rule, held applicable to the States in *Mapp v. Ohio,* 367 U.S. 643 (1961), "is not a personal constitutional right"; it fails to redress "the injury to the privacy of the victim of the search or seizure" at issue, "for any 'reparation comes too late.'" *Stone,* [428 U.S.] at 486 (*quoting Linkletter v. Walker,* 381 U.S. 618, 637 (1965)). The rule serves instead to deter future Fourth Amendment violations, and we reasoned that its application on collateral review would only marginally advance this interest in deterrence. *Stone*, 428 U.S. at 493. On the other side of the ledger, the costs of applying the exclusionary rule on habeas were comparatively great. We reasoned that doing so would not only exclude reliable evidence and divert attention from the central question of guilt, but would also intrude upon the public interest in "'(i) the most effective utilization of limited judicial resources, (ii) the necessity of finality in criminal trials, (iii) the minimization of friction between our federal and state systems of justice, and (iv) the maintenance of the constitutional balance upon which the doctrine of federalism is founded.'" *Id.* at 491 n.31. **

Over the years, we have repeatedly declined to extend the rule in *Stone* beyond its original bounds. In *Jackson v. Virginia*, 443 U.S. 307 (1979), for example, we denied a request to apply *Stone* to bar habeas consideration of a Fourteenth Amendment due process claim of insufficient evidence to support a state conviction. We stressed that the issue was "central to the basic question of guilt or innocence," *Jackson*, 443 U.S. at 323, unlike a claim that a state court had received evidence in violation of the Fourth Amendment exclusionary rule, and we found that to review such a claim on habeas imposed no great burdens on the federal courts. *Id.* at 321–322.

After a like analysis, in *Rose v. Mitchell*, 443 U.S. 545 (1979), we decided against extending *Stone* to foreclose habeas review of an equal protection claim of racial discrimination in selecting a state grand-jury foreman. A charge that state adjudication had violated the direct command of the Fourteenth Amendment implicated the integrity of the judicial process, we reasoned, *Rose*, 443 U.S. at 563, and failed to raise the "federalism concerns" that had driven the Court in *Stone*. 443 U.S. at 562. Since federal courts had granted relief to state prisoners upon proof of forbidden discrimination for nearly a century, we concluded, "confirmation that habeas corpus remains an appropriate vehicle by which federal courts are to exercise their Fourteenth Amendment responsibilities" would not likely raise tensions between the state and federal judicial systems. *Ibid.*

In a third instance, in *Kimmelman v. Morrison*, [477 U.S. 365 (1986)], we again declined to extend *Stone*, in that case to bar habeas review of certain claims of ineffective assistance of counsel under the Sixth Amendment. We explained that unlike the Fourth Amendment, which confers no "trial right," the Sixth confers a "fundamental right" on criminal defendants, one that "assures the fairness, and thus the legitimacy, of our adversary process." 477 U.S. at 374. We observed that because a violation of the right would often go unremedied except on collateral review, "restricting the litigation of some Sixth Amendment claims to trial and direct review would seriously interfere with an accused's right to effective representation." *Id.* at 378.

In this case, the argument for extending *Stone* again falls short. *** To understand why, a brief review of the derivation of the *Miranda* safeguards, and the purposes they were designed to serve, is in order.

The Self-Incrimination Clause of the Fifth Amendment guarantees that no person "shall be compelled in any criminal case to be a witness against himself." U.S. Const., Amdt. 5. In *Bram v. United States*, 168 U.S. 532 (1897), the Court held that the Clause barred the introduction in federal cases of involuntary confessions made in response to custodial interrogation. We did not recognize the Clause's applicability to state cases until 1964, however, *see Malloy v. Hogan*, 378 U.S. 1 [(1964)]; and, over the course of 30 years, beginning with the decision in *Brown v. Mississippi*, 297 U.S. 278 (1936), we analyzed the admissibility of confessions in such cases as a question of due process under the Fourteenth Amendment. ** Under this approach, we examined the totality of circumstances to determine whether a confession had been "'made freely, voluntarily and without compulsion or inducement of any sort.'" *Haynes v. Washington*, 373 U.S. 503, 513 (1963). ** *See generally* 1 W. LaFave & J. Israel, Criminal Procedure § 6.2 (1984). Indeed, we continue to employ the totality-of-circumstances approach when addressing a claim that the introduction of an involuntary confession has violated due process. *E.g., Arizona v. Fulminante*, 499 U.S. 279 (1991); *Miller v. Fenton*, 474 U.S. 104, 109–110 (1985).

In *Malloy*, we recognized that the Fourteenth Amendment incorporates the Fifth Amendment privilege against self-incrimination, and thereby opened *Bram*'s doctrinal avenue for the analysis of state cases. So it was that two years later we held in *Miranda* that the privilege extended to state custodial interrogations. In *Miranda*, we spoke of the privilege as guaranteeing a person under interrogation "the right 'to remain silent unless he chooses to speak in the unfettered exercise of his own will,'" 384 U.S. at 460 (quoting *Malloy*, [378 U.S.] at 8, and held that "without proper safeguards the process of in-custody interrogation...contains inherently compelling pressures which work to undermine the individual's will to resist and to compel him to speak where he would not otherwise do so freely." 384 U.S. at 467. To counter these pressures we prescribed, absent "other fully effective means," the now-familiar measures in aid of a defendant's Fifth Amendment privilege. *** Unless the prosecution can demonstrate the warnings and waiver as threshold matters, we held, it may not overcome an objection to the use at trial of statements obtained from the person in any ensuing custodial interrogation. *See ibid.* **

Petitioner, supported by the United States as *amicus curiae*, argues that *Miranda*'s safeguards are not constitutional in character, but merely "prophylactic," and that in consequence habeas review should not extend to a claim that a state conviction rests on statements obtained in the absence of those safeguards. ** We accept petitioner's premise for purposes of this case, but not her conclusion.

The *Miranda* Court did of course caution that the Constitution requires no "particular solution for the inherent compulsions of the interrogation process," and left it open to a State to meet its burden by adopting "other procedures...at least as effective in apprising accused persons" of their rights. 384 U.S. at 467. The Court indeed acknowledged that, in barring introduction of a statement obtained without the required warnings, *Miranda* might exclude a confession that we would not condemn as "involuntary in traditional terms," *id.* at 457, and for this reason we have sometimes called the *Miranda* safeguards "prophylactic" in nature. ** Calling the *Miranda* safeguards "prophylactic," however, is a far cry from putting *Miranda* on all fours with *Mapp*, or from rendering *Miranda* subject to *Stone*.

As we explained in *Stone*, the *Mapp* rule "is not a personal constitutional right," but serves to deter future constitutional violations; although it mitigates the juridical consequences of invading the defendant's privacy, the exclusion of evidence at trial can do nothing to remedy the completed and wholly extrajudicial Fourth Amendment violation. *Stone*, 428 U.S. at 486. Nor can the *Mapp* rule be thought to enhance the soundness of the criminal process by improving the reliability of evidence introduced at trial. Quite the contrary, as we explained in *Stone*, the evidence excluded under *Mapp* "is typically reliable and often the most probative information bearing on the guilt or innocence of the defendant." 428 U.S. at 490.

Miranda differs from *Mapp* in both respects. "Prophylactic" though it may be, in protecting a defendant's Fifth Amendment privilege against self-incrimination, *Miranda* safeguards "a fundamental *trial right,*" *United States v. Verdugo-Urquidez*, 494 U.S. 259, 264 (1990) (emphasis added). ** The privilege embodies "principles of humanity and civil liberty, which had been secured in the mother country only after years of struggle," *Bram*, 168 U.S. at 544, and reflects

[handwritten margin note: unlike HA Stone]

> many of our fundamental values and most noble aspirations:...our preference for an accusatorial rather than an inquisitorial system of criminal justice; our fear that self-incriminating statements will be elicited by inhumane treatment and abuses; our sense of fair play which dictates "a fair state-individual balance by requiring the government to leave the individual alone until good cause is shown for disturbing him and by requiring the government in its contest with the individual to shoulder the entire load;" our respect for the inviolability of the human personality and of the right of each individual "to a private enclave where he may lead a private life;" our distrust of self-deprecatory statements; and our realization that the privilege, while sometimes "a shelter to the guilty," is often "a protection to the innocent." *Murphy v. Waterfront Comm'n of New York Harbor*, 378 U.S. 52, 55 (1964) (citations omitted).

[handwritten margin note: + 5A]

Nor does the Fifth Amendment "trial right" protected by *Miranda* serve some value necessarily divorced from the correct ascertainment of guilt. "'[A] system of criminal law enforcement which comes to depend on the "confession" will, in the long run, be less reliable and more subject to abuses' than a system relying on independent investigation." *Michigan v. Tucker*, 417 U.S. [443,] 448 [(1974)]. ** By bracing against "the possibility of unreliable statements in every instance of in-custody interrogation," *Miranda* serves to guard against "the use of unreliable statements at trial." *Johnson v. New Jersey*, 384 U.S. 719, 730 (1966). **

Finally, and most importantly, eliminating review of *Miranda* claims would not significantly benefit the federal courts in their exercise of habeas jurisdiction, or advance the cause of federalism in any substantial way. As one *amicus* concedes, eliminating habeas review of *Miranda* issues would not prevent a state prisoner from simply converting his barred *Miranda* claim into a due process claim that his conviction rested on an involuntary confession. ** Indeed, although counsel could provide us with no empirical basis for projecting the consequence of adopting petitioner's position, ** it seems reasonable to suppose that virtually all *Miranda* claims would simply be recast in this way. ***

If that is so, the federal courts would certainly not have heard the last of *Miranda* on collateral review. Under the due process approach, as we have already seen, courts look to the totality of circumstances to determine whether a confession was voluntary. Those potential circumstances include not only the crucial element of police coercion, *Colorado v. Connelly*, 479 U.S. 157, 167 (1986); the length of the interrogation, *Ashcraft v. Tennessee*, 322 U.S. 143, 153–154 (1944); its location, *see Reck v. Pate*, 367 U.S. 433, 441(1961); its continuity, *Leyra v. Denno*, 347 U.S. 556, 561 (1954); the defendant's maturity, *Haley v. Ohio*, 332 U.S. 596, 599–601 (1948) (opinion of Douglas, J.); education, *Clewis v. Texas*, 386 U.S. 707, 712 (1967); physical condition, *Greenwald v. Wisconsin*, 390 U.S. 519, 520–521 (1968) (*per curiam*); and mental health, *Fikes v. Alabama*, 352 U.S. 191, 196 (1957). They also include the failure of police to advise the defendant of his rights to remain silent and to have counsel present during custodial interrogation. *Haynes v. Washington*, 373 U.S. 503, 516–517 (1963). ** We could lock the front door against *Miranda*, but not the back.

We thus fail to see how abdicating *Miranda*'s bright-line (or, at least, brighter-line) rules in favor of an exhaustive totality-of-circumstances approach on habeas would do much of anything to lighten the burdens placed on busy federal courts. ** We likewise fail to see how purporting to eliminate *Miranda* issues from federal habeas would go very far to relieve such tensions as *Miranda* may now raise between the two judicial systems. Relegation of habeas petitioners to straight involuntariness claims would not likely reduce the amount of litigation, and each such claim would in any event present a legal question requiring an "independent federal determination" on habeas. *Miller v. Fenton*, 474 U.S. at 112.

One might argue that tension results between the two judicial systems whenever a federal habeas court overturns a state conviction on finding that the state court let in a voluntary confession obtained by the police without the *Miranda* safeguards. And one would have to concede that this has occurred in the past, and doubtless will occur again. It is not reasonable, however, to expect such occurrences to be frequent enough to amount to a substantial cost of reviewing *Miranda* claims on habeas or to raise federal-state tensions to an appreciable degree. ** We must remember in this regard that *Miranda* came down some 27 years ago. In that time, law enforcement has grown in constitutional as well as technological sophistication, and there is little reason to believe that the police today are unable, or even generally unwilling, to satisfy *Miranda*'s requirements. ** And if, finally, one should question the need for federal collateral review of requirements that merit such respect, the answer simply is that the respect is sustained in no small part by the existence of such review. "It is the occasional abuse that the federal writ of habeas corpus stands ready to correct." *Jackson*, 443 U.S. at 322.

III

One final point should keep us only briefly. As he had done in his state appellate briefs, on habeas Williams raised only one claim going to the admissibility of his statements to the police: that the police had elicited those statements without satisfying the *Miranda* requirements. ** In her answer, petitioner addressed only that claim. ** The District Court, nonetheless, without an evidentiary hearing or even argument, went beyond the habeas petition and found the statements Williams made after receiving the *Miranda* warnings to be involuntary under due process criteria. Before the Court of Appeals, petitioner objected to the District Court's due process enquiry on the ground that the habeas petition's reference to *Miranda* rights had given her insufficient notice to address a due process claim. **

Williams effectively concedes that his habeas petition raised no involuntariness claim, but he argues that the matter was tried by the implied consent of the parties under Federal Rule of Civil Procedure 15(b), *** and that petitioner can demonstrate no prejudice from the District Court's action. ** The record, however, reveals neither thought, word, nor deed of petitioner that could be taken as any sort of consent to the determination of an independent due process claim, and petitioner was manifestly prejudiced by the District Court's failure to afford her an opportunity to present evidence bearing on that claim's resolution. The District Court should not have addressed the involuntariness question in these circumstances. ***

IV

The judgment of the Court of Appeals is affirmed in part and reversed in part, and the case is remanded for further proceedings consistent with this opinion.

It is so ordered.

[An opinion by JUSTICE O'CONNOR, concurring in part and dissenting in part, in which CHIEF JUSTICE REHNQUIST joined, is omitted. An opinion by JUSTICE

SCALIA, concurring in part and dissenting in part, in which JUSTICE THOMAS joined, is also omitted.]

Notes

1. *Subsequent case history*

No information is available about the status of Robert Allen Williams after remand and retrial.

2. *Justice O'Connor's observations*

Justice O'Connor, concurring in part and dissenting in part, joined by Chief Justice Rehnquist, makes the following observation:

> Today the Court permits the federal courts to overturn on habeas the conviction of a double murderer, not on the basis of an inexorable constitutional or statutory command, but because it believes the result desirable from the standpoint of equity and judicial administration. Because the principles that inform our habeas jurisprudence—finality, federalism, and fairness—counsel decisively against the result the Court reaches, I respectfully dissent from this holding.
>
>   ***
>
> In our federal system, state courts have primary responsibility for enforcing constitutional rules in their own criminal trials. When a case comes before the federal courts on habeas rather than on direct review, the judicial role is "significantly different." ** Most important here, federal courts on direct review adjudicate every issue of federal law properly presented; in contrast, "federal courts have never had a similar obligation on habeas corpus." ** As the Court explains today, federal courts exercising their habeas powers may refuse to grant relief on certain claims because of "prudential concerns" such as equity and federalism. ** This follows not only from the express language of the habeas statute, which directs the federal courts to "dispose of [habeas petitions] as law and justice require," 28 U.S.C. § 2243, but from our precedents as well. In *Francis v. Henderson*, 425 U.S. 536 (1976), we stated that "[t]his Court has long recognized that in some circumstances considerations of comity and concerns for the orderly administration of criminal justice require a federal court to forgo the exercise of its habeas corpus power." *Id.* at 539. ** *Fay v. Noia*, [372 U.S.] at 438 ("[H]abeas corpus has traditionally been regarded as governed by equitable principles"). **

Do you agree that habeas review should be more limited than other review? In your opinion, does the gravity of the offense inform the judicial reaction to issues presented in the case? Should it have any affect?

3. *The dependability of state courts*

Justice O'Connor also states,

> As the Court emphasizes today, *Miranda*'s prophylactic rule is now 27 years old; the police and the state courts have indeed grown accustomed to it. ** But it is precisely because the rule is well accepted that there is little further benefit to enforcing it on habeas. We can depend on law enforcement officials to administer warnings in the first instance and the state courts to provide a remedy when law enforcement officers err. None of the Court's asserted justifications

for enforcing *Miranda*'s prophylactic rule through habeas—neither reverence for the Fifth Amendment nor the concerns of reliability, efficiency, and federalism—counsel in favor of the Court's chosen course. Indeed, in my view they cut in precisely the opposite direction. The Court may reconsider its decision when presented with empirical data. ** But I see little reason for such a costly delay. Logic and experience are at our disposal now. And they amply demonstrate that applying *Miranda*'s prophylactic rule on habeas does not increase the amount of justice dispensed; it only increases the frequency with which the admittedly guilty go free. ***

Do you agree with Justice O'Connor that "[w]e can depend on...the state courts to provide a remedy when law enforcement officers err"? Why or why not? What do you think of Justice O'Connor's position that logic and experience "demonstrate that applying *Miranda*'s prophylactic rule on habeas does not increase the amount of justice dispensed"?

4. *Extending* Stone v. Powell

Justice Scalia argues in his dissent that the rule in *Stone v. Powell* should extend to all claims on federal habeas review, that is, that a fully litigated constitutional motion in state court should not be cognizable on habeas. What are the justifications for such a rule? The dangers?

Chapter 11

Successive Petitions

One of the complaints about habeas litigation is that it seems to "never end." The question of when, how, or whether a successive petition may be filed has been answered differently by the courts at different times. In *Sanders v. United States*, the Court interprets the section of 28 U.S.C. §2255 (a writ by a federal prisoner) that reads "[t]he sentencing court shall not be required to entertain a second or successive motion for similar relief on behalf of the same prisoner." In *Kuhlmann v. Wilson*, the Court describes under what circumstances federal courts should even hear a state prisoner's petition for a writ of habeas corpus that raises previously rejected claims. In *McClesky v. Zant*, the Court defines abuse of the writ in successive petitions, including the applicability of the "deliberate abandonment" doctrine.

Sanders v. United States
373 U.S. 1 (1963)

JUSTICE BRENNAN delivered the opinion of the Court.

We consider here the standards which should guide a federal court in deciding whether to grant a hearing on a motion of a federal prisoner under 28 U.S.C. §2255. *** Under that statute, a federal prisoner who claims that his sentence was imposed in violation of the Constitution or laws of the United States may seek relief from the sentence by filing a motion in the sentencing court stating the facts supporting his claim. "[A] prompt hearing" on the motion is required "[u]nless the motion and the files and records of the case conclusively show that the prisoner is entitled to no relief." *** The section further provides that "[t]he sentencing court shall not be required to entertain a second or successive motion for similar relief on behalf of the same prisoner."

The petitioner is serving a 15-year sentence for robbery of a federally insured bank in violation of 18 U.S.C. §2113(a). He filed two motions under §2255. The first alleged no facts but only bare conclusions in support of his claim. The second, filed eight months after the first, alleged facts which, if true, might entitle him to relief. Both motions were denied, without hearing, by the District Court for the Northern District of California. On appeal from the denial of the second motion, the Court of Appeals for the Ninth Circuit affirmed. ** We granted leave to proceed *in forma pauperis* and certiorari. **

On January 19, 1959, petitioner was brought before the United States District Court for the Northern District of California, and was handed a copy of a proposed information charging him with the robbery. He appeared without counsel. In response to inquiries of the trial judge, petitioner stated that he wished to waive assistance of counsel and to proceed by information rather than indictment; *** he signed a waiver of indictment, and then pleaded guilty to the charge in the information. On February 10 he was sentenced. Before sentence was pronounced, petitioner said to the judge: "If possible, your Honor, I would like to go to Springfield or Lexington for addiction cure. I have been using narcotics off and on for quite a while." The judge replied that he was "willing to recommend that."

On January 4, 1960, petitioner, appearing *pro se*, filed his first motion. He alleged no facts but merely the conclusions that (1) the "Indictment" was invalid, (2) "Appellant was denied adequate assistance of Counsel as guaranteed by the Sixth Amendment," and (3) the sentencing court had "allowed the Appellant to be intimidated and coerced into intering [sic] a plea without Counsel, and any knowledge of the charges lodged against the Appellant." He filed with the motion an application for a writ of *habeas corpus ad testificandum* requiring the prison authorities to produce him before the court to testify in support of his motion. On February 3 the District Court denied both the motion and the application. In a memorandum accompanying the denial, the court explained that the motion, "although replete with conclusions, sets forth no facts upon which such conclusions can be founded. For this reason alone, this motion may be denied without a hearing." Nevertheless, the court stated further that the motion "sets forth nothing but unsupported charges, which are completely refuted by the files and records of this case. Since the motion and the files and records of the case conclusively show that the prisoner is entitled to no relief, no hearing on the motion is necessary." No appeal was taken by the petitioner from this denial.

On September 8 petitioner, again appearing *pro se*, filed his second motion. This time he alleged that at the time of his trial and sentence he was mentally incompetent as a result of narcotics administered to him while he was held in the Sacramento County Jail pending trial. He stated in a supporting affidavit that he had been confined in the jail from on or about January 16, 1959, to February 18, 1959; that during this period and during the period of his "trial" he had been intermittently under the influence of narcotics; and that the narcotics had been administered to him by the medical authorities in attendance at the jail because of his being a known addict. The District Court denied the motion without hearing, stating: "As there is no reason given, or apparent to this Court, why petitioner could not, and should not, have raised the issue of mental incompetency at the time of his first motion, the Court will refuse, in the exercise of its statutory discretion, to entertain the present petition." ** The court also stated that "petitioner's complaints are without merit in fact." On appeal from the order denying this motion, the Court of Appeals for the Ninth Circuit affirmed. ** The Court of Appeals said in a *per curiam* opinion: "Where, as here, it is apparent from the record that at the time of filing the first motion the movant knew the facts on which the second motion is based, yet in the second motion set forth no reason why he was previously unable to assert the new ground and did not allege that he had previously been unaware of the significance of the relevant facts, the district court, may, in its discretion, decline to entertain the second motion." **

We reverse. We hold that the sentencing court should have granted a hearing on the second motion.

I

The statute in terms requires that a prisoner shall be granted a hearing on a motion which alleges sufficient facts to support a claim for relief unless the motion and the files and records of the case "conclusively show" that the claim is without merit. This is the first case in which we have been called upon to determine what significance, in deciding whether to grant a hearing, the sentencing court should attach to any record of proceedings on prior motions for relief which may be among the files and records of the case, in light of the provision that: "The sentencing court shall not be required to entertain a second or successive motion for similar relief on behalf of the same prisoner." ***

At common law, the denial by a court or judge of an application for habeas corpus was not *res judicata*. ***

It has been suggested ** that this principle derives from the fact that at common law habeas corpus judgments were not appealable. But its roots would seem to go deeper. Conventional notions of finality of litigation have no place where life or liberty is at stake and infringement of constitutional rights is alleged. If "government [is] always [to] be accountable to the judiciary for a man's imprisonment," *Fay v. Noia*, [372 U.S. 391], 402 [(1963)], access to the courts on habeas must not be thus impeded. The inapplicability of *res judicata* to habeas, then, is inherent in the very role and function of the writ.

***

Very shortly after the *Price* [*v. Johnston*, 334 U.S. 266 (1948)] decision, as part of the 1948 revision of the Judicial Code, the Court's statement in *Salinger* [*v. Loisel*, 265 U.S. 224 (1924)] of the governing principle in the treatment of a successive application was given statutory form. 28 U.S.C. § 2244. *** There are several things to be observed about this codification.

First, it plainly was not intended to change the law as judicially evolved. Not only does the Reviser's Note disclaim any such intention, but language in the original bill which would have injected *res judicata* into federal habeas corpus was deliberately eliminated from the Act as finally passed. ***

Second, even with respect to successive applications on which hearings may be denied because the ground asserted was previously heard and decided, as in *Salinger*, § 2244 is faithful to the Court's phrasing of the principle in *Salinger*, and does not enact a rigid rule. The judge is permitted, not compelled, to decline to entertain such an application, and then only if he "is satisfied that the ends of justice will not be served" by inquiring into the merits.

Third, § 2244 is addressed only to the problem of successive applications based on grounds previously heard and decided. It does not cover a second or successive application containing a ground "not theretofore presented and determined," and so does not touch the problem of abuse of the writ. ***

***

II

We think the judicial and statutory evolution of the principles governing successive applications for federal habeas corpus and motions under § 2255 has reached the point at which the formulation of basic rules to guide the lower federal courts is both feasible and desirable. ** Since the motion procedure is the substantial equivalent of federal habeas corpus, we see no need to differentiate the two for present purposes. It should be noted that these rules are not operative in cases where the second or successive application is shown, on the basis of the application, files, and records of the case alone, conclusively to be without merit. ** In such a case the application should be denied without a hearing.

A. Successive Motions on Grounds Previously Heard and Determined.

Controlling weight may be given to denial of a prior application for federal habeas corpus or § 2255 relief *** only if (1) the same ground presented in the subsequent application was determined adversely to the applicant on the prior application, (2) the prior determination was on the merits, and (3) the ends of justice would not be served by reaching the merits of the subsequent application.

(1) By "ground," we mean simply a sufficient legal basis for granting the relief sought by the applicant. For example, the contention that an involuntary confession was admitted in evidence against him is a distinct ground for federal collateral relief. But a claim of involuntary confession predicated on alleged psychological coercion does not raise a different "ground" than does one predicated on alleged physical coercion. In other words, identical grounds may often be proved by different factual allegations. So also, identical grounds may often be supported by different legal arguments. ** Should doubts arise in particular cases as to whether two grounds are different or the same, they should be resolved in favor of the applicant.

(2) The prior denial must have rested on an adjudication of the merits of the ground presented in the subsequent application. ** This means that if factual issues were raised in the prior application, and it was not denied on the basis that the files and records conclusively resolved these issues, an evidentiary hearing was held. **

(3) Even if the same ground was rejected on the merits on a prior application, it is open to the applicant to show that the ends of justice would be served by permitting the redetermination of the ground. If factual issues are involved, the applicant is entitled to a new hearing upon showing that the evidentiary hearing on the prior application was not full and fair; we canvassed the criteria of a full and fair evidentiary hearing recently in *Townsend v. Sain*, [372 U.S. 289 (1963)], and that discussion need not be repeated here. If purely legal questions are involved, the applicant may be entitled to a new hearing upon showing an intervening change in the law or some other justification for having failed to raise a crucial point or argument in the prior application. Two further points should be noted. *First*, the foregoing enumeration is not intended to be exhaustive; the test is "the ends of justice" and it cannot be too finely particularized. *Second*, the burden is on the applicant to show that, although the ground of the new application was determined against him on the merits on a prior application, the ends of justice would be served by a redetermination of the ground.

B. The Successive Application Claimed to be an Abuse of Remedy.

***

To say that it is open to the respondent to show that a second or successive application is abusive is simply to recognize that "habeas corpus has traditionally been regarded as governed by equitable principles. ** Among them is the principle that a suitor's conduct in relation to the matter at hand may disentitle him to the relief he seeks. Narrowly circumscribed, in conformity to the historical role of the writ of habeas corpus as an effective and imperative remedy for detentions contrary to fundamental law, the principle is unexceptionable." *Fay v. Noia*, [372 U.S.] at 438. Thus, for example, if a prisoner deliberately withholds one of two grounds for federal collateral relief at the time of filing his first application, in the hope of being granted two hearings rather than one or for some other such reason, he may be deemed to have waived his right to a hearing on a second application presenting the withheld ground. The same may be true *** if the prisoner deliberately abandons one of his grounds at the first hearing. Nothing in the traditions of habeas corpus requires the federal courts to tolerate needless piecemeal litigation, or to entertain collateral proceedings whose only purpose is to vex, harass, or delay.

***

*** The principles governing both justifications for denial of a hearing on a successive application are addressed to the sound discretion of the federal trial judges. Theirs is the major responsibility for the just and sound administration of the federal collateral remedies, and theirs must be the judgment as to whether a second or successive application shall be denied without consideration of the merits. Even as to such an application, the federal judge clearly has the power—and, if the ends of justice demand, the duty—to reach the merits. ** We are confident that this power will be soundly applied.

III

***

On remand, a hearing will be required. This is not to say, however, that it will automatically become necessary to produce petitioner at the hearing to enable him to testify. Not every colorable allegation entitles a federal prisoner to a trip to the sentencing court. Congress, recognizing the administrative burden involved in the transportation of prisoners to and from a hearing in the sentencing court, provided in § 2255 that the application may be entertained and determined "without requiring the production of the prisoner at the hearing." This does not mean that a prisoner can be prevented from testifying in support of a substantial claim where his testimony would be material. However, we think it clear that the sentencing court has discretion to ascertain whether the claim is substantial before granting a full evidentiary hearing. In this connection, the sentencing court might find it useful to appoint counsel to represent the applicant. ***

***

The need for great care in criminal collateral procedure is well evidenced by the instant case. Petitioner was adjudged guilty of a crime carrying a heavy penalty in a summary proceeding at which he was not represented by counsel. Very possibly, the proceeding was constitutionally adequate. But by its summary nature, and because defendant was unrepresented by counsel, a presumption of adequacy is obviously less compelling than it would be had there been a full criminal trial. Moreover, the nature of the proceeding was such as to preclude direct appellate review. In such a case it is imperative that a fair opportunity for collateral relief be afforded. An applicant for such relief ought not to be held to the niceties of lawyers' pleadings or be cursorily dismissed because his claim seems unlikely to prove meritorious. That his application is vexatious or repetitious, or that his claim lacks any substance, must be fairly demonstrated.

Finally, we remark that the imaginative handling of a prisoner's first motion would in general do much to anticipate and avoid the problem of a hearing on a second or successive motion. The judge is not required to limit his decision on the first motion to the grounds narrowly alleged, or to deny the motion out of hand because the allegations are vague, conclusional, or inartistically expressed. He is free to adopt any appropriate means for inquiry into the legality of the prisoner's detention in order to ascertain all possible grounds upon which the prisoner might claim to be entitled to relief. Certainly such an inquiry should be made if the judge grants a hearing on the first motion and allows the prisoner to be present. The disposition of all grounds for relief ascertained in this way may then be spread on the files and records of the case. Of course, to the extent the files and records "conclusively show" that the prisoner is entitled to no relief on any such grounds, no hearing on a second or successive motion, to the extent of such grounds, would be necessary.

The judgment of the Court of Appeals is reversed and the case is remanded to the District Court for a hearing consistent with this opinion.

It is so ordered.

***

Notes

1. *Subsequent case history*

Charles Edward Sanders was originally sentenced to fifteen years in prison in February of 1959. After the Supreme Court's reversal, the district court set aside the original proceeding, after which the State once again indicted Sanders. After a jury convicted him, the district court sentenced Sanders to twenty years in prison. 272 F. Supp. 245 (Cal. D.C. 1967). Sanders unsuccessfully challenged the increase in sentence.

2. *Dissenting opinion by Justice Harlan*

JUSTICE HARLAN, whom JUSTICE CLARK joins, dissenting.

This case, together with *Townsend v. Sain* and *Fay v. Noia*, form a trilogy of "guideline" decisions in which the Court has undertaken to restate the responsibilities of the federal courts in federal post-conviction proceedings. *Sain* and *Noia* relate to federal habeas corpus proceedings arising out of state criminal convictions. The present case involves successive § 2255 applications (and similar habeas corpus proceedings under § 2244, which the Court finds sets the pattern for § 2255) arising out of federal convictions.

The over-all effect of this trilogy of pronouncements is to relegate to a back seat, as it affects state and federal criminal cases finding their way into federal post-conviction proceedings, the principle that there must be some end to litigation.

***

III

***

I seriously doubt the wisdom of these "guideline" decisions. They suffer the danger of pitfalls that usually go with judging in a vacuum. However carefully written, they are apt in their application to carry unintended consequences which once accomplished are not always easy to repair. Rules respecting matters daily arising in the federal courts are ultimately likely to find more solid formulation if left to focused adjudication on a case-by-case basis, or to the normal rule-making processes of the Judicial Conference, rather than to *ex cathedra* pronouncements by this Court, which is remote from the arena.

In dealing with cases of this type, I think we do better to confine ourselves to the particular issues presented, and on that basis I would affirm the judgment of the Court of Appeal.

Is the dissent's concern with finality a legitimate concern? Why or why not?

3. *Expanding the reach of habeas corpus?*

Did it seem that the Court expanded the reach of habeas in this case? What are the political ramifications of its decision?

Kuhlmann v. Wilson

477 U.S. 436 (1986)

JUSTICE POWELL announced the judgment of the Court and delivered the opinion of the Court with respect to Parts I, IV, and V, and an opinion with respect to Parts II and III in which THE CHIEF JUSTICE, JUSTICE REHNQUIST, and JUSTICE O'-CONNOR join.

This case requires us to define the circumstances under which federal courts should entertain a state prisoner's petition for writ of habeas corpus that raises claims rejected on a prior petition for the same relief.

I

In the early morning of July 4, 1970, respondent and two confederates robbed the Star Taxicab Garage in the Bronx, New York, and fatally shot the night dispatcher. Shortly before, employees of the garage had observed respondent, a former employee there, on the premises conversing with two other men. They also witnessed respondent fleeing after the robbery, carrying loose money in his arms. After eluding the police for four days, respondent turned himself in. Respondent admitted that he had been present when the crimes took place, claimed that he had witnessed the robbery, gave the police a description of the robbers, but denied knowing them. Respondent also denied any involvement in the robbery or murder, claiming that he had fled because he was afraid of being blamed for the crimes.

After his arraignment, respondent was confined in the Bronx House of Detention, where he was placed in a cell with a prisoner named Benny Lee. Unknown to respondent, Lee had agreed to act as a police informant. Respondent made incriminating statements that Lee reported to the police. Prior to trial, respondent moved to suppress the statements on the ground that they were obtained in violation of his right to counsel. The trial court held an evidentiary hearing on the suppression motion, which revealed that the statements were made under the following circumstances.

Before respondent arrived in the jail, Lee had entered into an arrangement with Detective Cullen, according to which Lee agreed to listen to respondent's conversations and report his remarks to Cullen. Since the police had positive evidence of respondent's participation, the purpose of placing Lee in the cell was to determine the identities of respondent's confederates. Cullen instructed Lee not to ask respondent any questions, but simply to "keep his ears open" for the names of the other perpetrators. Respondent first spoke to Lee about the crimes after he looked out the cellblock window at the Star Taxicab Garage, where the crimes had occurred. Respondent said, "someone's messing with me," and began talking to Lee about the robbery, narrating the same story that he had given the police at the time of his arrest. Lee advised respondent that this explanation "didn't sound too good," *** but respondent did not alter his story. Over the next few days, however, respondent changed details of his original account. Respondent then received a visit from his brother, who mentioned that members of his family were upset because they believed that respondent had murdered the dispatcher. After the visit, respondent again described the crimes to Lee. Respondent now admitted that he and two other men, whom he never identified, had planned and carried out the robbery, and had murdered the dispatcher. Lee informed Cullen of respondent's statements and furnished Cullen with notes that he had written surreptitiously while sharing the cell with respondent.

After hearing the testimony of Cullen and Lee, *** the trial court found that Cullen had instructed Lee "to ask no questions of [respondent] about the crime but merely to listen as to what [respondent] might say in his presence." The court determined that Lee obeyed these instructions, that he "at no time asked any questions with respect to the crime," and that he "only listened to [respondent] and made notes regarding what [respondent] had to say." The trial court also found that respondent's statements to Lee were "spontaneous" and "unsolicited." Under state precedent, a defendant's volunteered statements to a police agent were admissible in evidence because the police were not required to prevent talkative defendants from making incriminating statements. ** The trial court accordingly denied the suppression motion.

The jury convicted respondent of common-law murder and felonious possession of a weapon. On May 18, 1972, the trial court sentenced him to a term of 20 years to life on the murder count and to a concurrent term of up to 7 years on the weapons count. The Appellate Division affirmed without opinion, ** and the New York Court of Appeals denied respondent leave to appeal.

On December 7, 1973, respondent filed a petition for federal habeas corpus relief. Respondent argued, among other things, that his statements to Lee were obtained pursuant to police investigative methods that violated his constitutional rights [under] *Massiah v. United States*, 377 U.S. 201 (1964) [but], the District Court for the Southern District of New York denied the writ on January 7, 1977. [The judge found the] record demonstrated "no interrogation whatsoever" by Lee and "only spontaneous statements" from respondent. In the District Court's view, these "fact[s] preclude[d] any Sixth Amendment violation."

A divided panel of the Court of Appeals for the Second Circuit affirmed. ** The court noted that a defendant is denied his Sixth Amendment rights when the trial court admits in evidence incriminating statements that state agents " 'had deliberately elicited from him after he had been indicted and in the absence of counsel.' " ** *Massiah*, [377 U.S.] at 206. Relying in part on *Brewer v. Williams*, 430 U.S. 387 (1977), the court reasoned that the "deliberately elicited" test of *Massiah* requires something more than incriminating statements uttered in the absence of counsel. On the facts found by the state trial court, which were entitled to a presumption of correctness under 28 U.S.C. §2254(d), the court held that respondent had not established a violation of his Sixth Amendment rights. *** We denied a petition for a writ of certiorari. **

Following this Court's decision in *United States v. Henry*, 447 U.S. 264 (1980), which applied the *Massiah* test to suppress statements made to a paid jailhouse informant, respondent decided to relitigate his Sixth Amendment claim. On September 11, 1981, he filed in state trial court a motion to vacate his conviction. The judge denied the motion, on the grounds that *Henry* was factually distinguishable from this case, *** and that under state precedent *Henry* was not to be given retroactive effect. ** The Appellate Division denied respondent leave to appeal.

On July 6, 1982, respondent returned to the District Court for the Southern District of New York on a habeas petition, again arguing that admission in evidence of his incriminating statements to Lee violated his Sixth Amendment rights. Respondent contended that the decision in *Henry* constituted a new rule of law that should be applied retroactively to this case. The District Court found it unnecessary to consider retroactivity because it decided that *Henry* did not undermine the Court of Appeals' prior disposition of respondent's Sixth Amendment claim. Noting that *Henry* reserved the question whether the Constitution forbade admission in evidence of an accused's statements to an informant who made "no effort to stimulate conversations about the crime charged," ** the District Court believed that this case presented that open question and that the question must be answered negatively. The District Court noted that the trial court's findings were presumptively correct ** and were fully supported by the record. The court concluded that these findings were "fatal" to respondent's claim under *Henry* since they showed that Lee made no "affirmative effort" of any kind "to elicit information" from respondent.

A different, and again divided, panel of the Court of Appeals reversed. ** As an initial matter, the court stated that, under *Sanders v. United States*, 373 U.S. 1 (1963), the "ends of justice" required consideration of this petition, notwithstanding the fact that the prior panel had determined the merits adversely to respondent. ** The court then reasoned that the circumstances under which respondent made his incriminating statements to Lee were indistinguishable from the facts of *Henry*. Finally, the court decided that *Henry* was fully applicable here because it did not announce a new constitutional rule, but merely applied settled principles to new facts. ** Therefore, the court concluded that all of the judges who had considered and rejected respondent's claim had erred, and remanded the case to the District Court with instructions to order respondent's release from prison unless the State elected to retry him. ***

We granted certiorari ** to consider the Court of Appeals' decision that the "ends of justice" required consideration of this successive habeas corpus petition and that court's application of our decision in *Henry* to the facts of this case. We now reverse.

II

A

In concluding that it was appropriate to entertain respondent's successive habeas corpus petition, the Court of Appeals relied upon *Sanders v. United States*, 373 U.S. 1 (1963), which announced guidelines for the federal courts to follow when presented with habeas petitions or their equivalent claimed to be "successive" or an "abuse of the writ." *** The narrow question in *Sanders* was whether a federal prisoner's motion under 28 U.S.C. § 2255 was properly denied without a hearing on the ground that the motion constituted a successive application. ** The Court undertook not only to answer that question, but also to explore the standard that should govern district courts' consideration of successive petitions. *Sanders* framed the inquiry in terms of the requirements of the "ends of justice," advising district courts to dismiss habeas petitions or their equivalent raising claims determined adversely to the prisoner on a prior petition if "the ends of justice would not be served by reaching the merits of the subsequent application." ** While making clear that the burden of proof on this issue rests on the prisoner, ** the Court in *Sanders* provided little specific guidance as to the kind of proof that a prisoner must offer to establish that the "ends of justice" would be served by relitigation of the claims previously decided against him.

The Court of Appeals' decision in this case demonstrates the need for this Court to provide that guidance. The opinion of the Court of Appeals sheds no light on this important threshold question, merely declaring that the "ends of justice" required successive federal habeas corpus review. Failure to provide clear guidance leaves district judges "at large in disposing of applications for a writ of habeas corpus," creating the danger that they will engage in "the exercise not of law but of arbitrariness." ** This Court therefore must now define the considerations that should govern federal courts' disposition of successive petitions for habeas corpus.

B

Since 1867, when Congress first authorized the federal courts to issue the writ on behalf of persons in state custody, *** this Court often has been called upon to interpret the language of the statutes defining the scope of that jurisdiction. It may be helpful to review our cases construing these frequently used statutes before we answer the specific question before us today.

Until the early years of this century, the substantive scope of the federal habeas corpus statutes was defined by reference to the scope of the writ at common law, where the courts' inquiry on habeas was limited exclusively "to the jurisdiction of the sentencing tribunal." *Stone v. Powell*, 428 U.S. 465, 475 (1976). *See Wainwright v. Sykes*, 433 U.S. 72, 78, 79 (1977). ** Thus, the finality of the judgment of a committing court of competent jurisdiction was accorded absolute respect on habeas review. ** During this century, the Court gradually expanded the grounds on which habeas corpus relief was available, authorizing use of the writ to challenge convictions where the prisoner claimed a violation of certain constitutional rights. *See Wainwright v. Sykes*, [433 U.S.] at 79–80; *Stone v. Powell*, [428 U.S.] at 475–478. The Court initially accomplished this expansion while purporting to adhere to the inquiry into the sentencing court's jurisdiction. *Wainwright v. Sykes*, 433 U.S. at 79. Ultimately, the Court abandoned the concept of jurisdiction and acknowledged that habeas "review is available for claims of 'disregard of the constitutional rights of the accused, and where the writ is the only effective means of preserving his rights.'" [*Id.*] **

Our decisions have not been limited to expanding the scope of the writ. Significantly, in *Stone v. Powell*, we removed from the reach of the federal habeas statutes a state prisoner's claim that "evidence obtained in an unconstitutional search or seizure was introduced at his trial" unless the prisoner could show that the State had failed to provide him "an opportunity for full and fair litigation" of his Fourth Amendment claim. ** Although the Court previously had accepted jurisdiction of search and seizure claims, ** we were persuaded that any "advance of the legitimate goal of furthering Fourth Amendment rights" through application of the judicially created exclusionary rule on federal habeas was "outweighed by the acknowledged costs to other values vital to a rational system of criminal justice." [*Stone v. Powell*, 428 U.S.] at 494. Among those costs were diversion of the attention of the participants at a criminal trial "from the ultimate question of guilt or innocence," and exclusion of reliable evidence that was "often the most probative information bearing on the guilt or innocence of the defendant." *Id.* at 490. Our decision to except this category of claims from habeas corpus review created no danger that we were denying a "safeguard against compelling an innocent man to suffer an unconstitutional loss of liberty." *Id.* at 491–492, n.31. Rather, a convicted defendant who pressed a search and seizure claim on collateral attack was "usually asking society to redetermine an issue that ha[d] no bearing on the basic justice of his incarceration." *Id.* at 492, n.31.

In decisions of the past two or three decades construing the reach of the habeas statutes, whether reading those statutes broadly or narrowly, the Court has reaffirmed that "habeas corpus has traditionally been regarded as governed by equitable principles." *Fay v. Noia*, 372 U.S. 391, 438 (1963). ** The Court uniformly has been guided by the proposition that the writ should be available to afford relief to those "persons whom society has grievously wronged" in light of modern concepts of justice. *Fay v. Noia*, [372 U.S.] at 440–441. ** Just as notions of justice prevailing at the inception of habeas corpus were offended when a conviction was issued by a court that lacked jurisdiction, so the modern conscience found intolerable convictions obtained in violation of certain constitutional commands. But the Court never has defined the scope of the writ simply by reference to a perceived need to assure that an individual accused of crime is afforded a trial free of constitutional error. Rather, the Court has performed its statutory task through a sensitive weighing of the interests implicated by federal habeas corpus adjudication of constitutional claims determined adversely to the prisoner by the state courts. **

III

A

The Court in *Sanders* drew the phrase "ends of justice" directly from the version of 28 U.S.C. § 2244 in effect in 1963. The provision, which then governed petitions filed by both federal and state prisoners, stated in relevant part that no federal judge "shall be required to entertain an application for a writ of habeas corpus to inquire into the detention of a person...., if it appears that the legality of such detention has been determined" by a federal court "on a prior application for a writ of habeas corpus and the petition presents no new ground not theretofore presented and determined, and the judge... is satisfied that the *ends of justice will not be served by such inquiry*." 28 U.S.C. § 2244 (1964 ed.) (emphasis added). Accordingly, in describing guidelines for successive petitions, *Sanders* did little more than quote the language of the then-pertinent statute, leaving for another day the task of giving that language substantive content.

In 1966, Congress carefully reviewed the habeas corpus statutes and amended their provisions, including § 2244. Section 2244(b), which we construe today, governs successive petitions filed by state prisoners. The section makes no reference to the "ends of justice," *** and provides that the federal courts "need not" entertain "subsequent applications" from state prisoners "unless the application alleges and is predicated on a factual or other ground not adjudicated on" the prior application "and unless the court... is satisfied that the applicant has not on the earlier application deliberately withheld the newly asserted ground or otherwise abused the writ." *** In construing this language, we are cognizant that Congress adopted the section in light of the need— often recognized by this Court—to weigh the interests of the individual prisoner against the sometimes contrary interests of the State in administering a fair and rational system of criminal laws. ***

The legislative history demonstrates that Congress intended the 1966 amendments, including those to § 2244(b), to introduce "a greater degree of finality of judgments in habeas corpus proceedings." *** The House also expressed concern that the increasing number of habeas applications from state prisoners "greatly interfered with the procedures and processes of the State courts by delaying, in many cases, the proper enforcement of their judgments." **

Based on the 1966 amendments and their legislative history, petitioner argues that federal courts no longer must consider the "ends of justice" before dismissing a successive petition. We reject this argument. It is clear that Congress intended for district courts, as the general rule, to give preclusive effect to a judgment denying on the merits a habeas petition alleging grounds identical in substance to those raised in the subsequent petition. But the permissive language of § 2244(b) gives federal courts discretion to entertain successive petitions under some circumstances. Moreover, Rule 9(b) of the Rules Governing Section 2254 Cases in the United States District Courts, which was amended in 1976, contains similar permissive language, providing that the district court "may" dismiss a "second or successive petition" that does not "allege new or different grounds for relief." Consistent with Congress' intent in enacting § 2244(b), however, the Advisory Committee Note to Rule 9(b), 28 U.S.C., p. 358, states that federal courts should entertain successive petitions only in "rare instances." *** Unless those "rare instances" are to be identified by whim or caprice, district judges must be given guidance for determining when to exercise the limited discretion granted them by § 2244(b). Accordingly, as a means of identifying the rare case in which federal courts should exercise their discretion to hear a successive petition, we continue to rely on the reference in *Sanders* to the "ends of justice." Our task is to provide a definition of the "ends of justice" that will accommodate Congress' intent to give finality to federal habeas judgments with the historic function of habeas corpus to provide relief from unjust incarceration.

B

We now consider the limited circumstances under which the interests of the prisoner in relitigating constitutional claims held meritless on a prior petition may outweigh the countervailing interests served by according finality to the prior judgment. We turn first to the interests of the prisoner.

The prisoner may have a vital interest in having a second chance to test the fundamental justice of his incarceration. Even where, as here, the many judges who have reviewed the prisoner's claims in several proceedings provided by the State and on his first petition for federal habeas corpus have determined that his trial was free from constitutional error, a prisoner retains a powerful and legitimate interest in obtaining his release from custody if he is innocent of the charge for which he was incarcerated. That interest does not extend, however, to prisoners whose guilt is conceded or plain. ***

Balanced against the prisoner's interest in access to a forum to test the basic justice of his confinement are the interests of the State in administration of its criminal statutes. Finality serves many of those important interests. Availability of unlimited federal collateral review to guilty defendants frustrates the State's legitimate interest in deterring crime, since the deterrent force of penal laws is diminished to the extent that persons contemplating criminal activity believe there is a possibility that they will escape punishment through repetitive collateral attacks. *** Similarly, finality serves the State's goal of rehabilitating those who commit crimes because "[r]ehabilitation demands that the convicted defendant realize that 'he is justly subject to sanction, that he stands in need of rehabilitation.'" ** Finality also serves the State's legitimate punitive interests. When a prisoner is freed on a successive petition, often many years after his crime, the State may be unable successfully to retry him. *** This result is unacceptable if the State must forgo conviction of a guilty defendant through the "erosion of memory" and "dispersion of witnesses" that occur with the passage of time that invariably attends collateral attack. ***

In the light of the historic purpose of habeas corpus and the interests implicated by successive petitions for federal habeas relief from a state conviction, we conclude that the "ends of justice" require federal courts to entertain such petitions only where the prisoner supplements his constitutional claim with a colorable showing of factual innocence. *** We adopt this standard now to effectuate the clear intent of Congress that successive federal habeas review should be granted only in rare cases, but that it should be available when the ends of justice so require. The prisoner may make the requisite showing by establishing that under the probative evidence he has a colorable claim of factual innocence. The prisoner must make his evidentiary showing even though—as argued in this case—the evidence of guilt may have been unlawfully admitted. ***

C

Applying the foregoing standard in this case, we hold that the Court of Appeals erred in concluding that the "ends of justice" would be served by consideration of respondent's successive petition. The court conceded that the evidence of respondent's guilt "was nearly overwhelming." ** The constitutional claim argued by respondent does not itself raise any question as to his guilt or innocence. The District Court and the Court of Appeals should have dismissed this successive petition under § 2244(b) on the ground that the prior judgment denying relief on this identical claim was final. ***

IV

Even if the Court of Appeals had correctly decided to entertain this successive habeas petition, we conclude that it erred in holding that respondent was entitled to relief under *United States v. Henry*, 447 U.S. 264 (1980). As the District Court observed, *Henry* left open the question whether the Sixth Amendment forbids admission in evidence of an accused's statements to a jailhouse informant who was "placed in close proximity but [made] no effort to stimulate conversations about the crime charged." *** Our review of the line of cases beginning with *Massiah v. United States*, 377 U.S. 201 (1964), shows that this question must, as the District Court properly decided, be answered negatively.

A

The decision in *Massiah* had its roots in two concurring opinions written in *Spano v. New York*, 360 U.S. 315 (1959). ** Following his indictment for first-degree murder, the defendant in *Spano* retained a lawyer and surrendered to the authorities. Before leaving the defendant in police custody, counsel cautioned him not to respond to interrogation. The prosecutor and police questioned the defendant, persisting in the face of his repeated refusal to answer and his repeated request to speak with his lawyer. The lengthy interrogation involved improper police tactics, and the defendant ultimately confessed. Following a trial at which his confession was admitted in evidence, the defendant was convicted and sentenced to death. ** Agreeing with the Court that the confession was involuntary and thus improperly admitted in evidence under the Fourteenth Amendment, the concurring Justices also took the position that the defendant's right to counsel was violated by the secret interrogation. ** As Justice Stewart observed, an indicted person has the right to assistance of counsel throughout the proceedings against him. ** The defendant was denied that right when he was subjected to an "all-night inquisition," during which police ignored his repeated requests for his lawyer. **

The Court in *Massiah* adopted the reasoning of the concurring opinions in *Spano* and held that, once a defendant's Sixth Amendment right to counsel has attached, he is denied that right when federal agents "deliberately elicit" incriminating statements from him in the absence of his lawyer. ** The Court adopted this test, rather than one that turned simply on whether the statements were obtained in an "interrogation," to protect accused persons from "'indirect and surreptitious interrogations as well as those conducted in the jailhouse. In this case, Massiah was more seriously imposed upon…because he did not even know that he was under interrogation by a government agent.'" ** Thus, the Court made clear that it was concerned with interrogation or investigative techniques that were equivalent to interrogation, and that it so viewed the technique in issue in *Massiah*. ***

In *United States v. Henry*, the Court applied the *Massiah* test to incriminating statements made to a jailhouse informant. The Court of Appeals in that case found a violation of *Massiah* because the informant had engaged the defendant in conversations and "had developed a relationship of trust and confidence with [the defendant] such that [the defendant] revealed incriminating information." 447 U.S. at 269. This Court affirmed, holding that the Court of Appeals reasonably concluded that the Government informant "deliberately used his position to secure incriminating information from [the defendant] when counsel was not present." *Id.* at 270. Although the informant had not questioned the defendant, the informant had "stimulated" conversations with the defendant in order to "elicit" incriminating information. *Id.* at 273. ** The Court emphasized that those facts, like the facts of *Massiah*, amounted to "'indirect and surreptitious interrogation[]'" of the defendant. 447 U.S. at 273.

Earlier this Term, we applied the *Massiah* standard in a case involving incriminating statements made under circumstances substantially similar to the facts of *Massiah* itself. In *Maine v. Moulton*, 474 U.S. 159 (1985), the defendant made incriminating statements in a meeting with his accomplice, who had agreed to cooperate with the police. During that meeting, the accomplice, who wore a wire transmitter to record the conversation, discussed with the defendant the charges pending against him, repeatedly asked the defendant to remind him of the details of the crime, and encouraged the defendant to describe his plan for killing witnesses. ** The Court concluded that these investigatory techniques denied the defendant his right to counsel on the pending charges. *** Significantly, the Court emphasized that, because of the relationship between the defendant and the informant, the informant's engaging the defendant "in active conversation about their upcoming trial was certain to elicit" incriminating statements from the defendant. [474 U.S.] at 177, n.13. Thus, the informant's participation "in this conversation was 'the functional equivalent of interrogation.'" [474 U.S.] at 177, n.13. **

As our recent examination of this Sixth Amendment issue in *Moulton* makes clear, the primary concern of the *Massiah* line of decisions is secret interrogation by investigatory techniques that are the equivalent of direct police interrogation. Since "the Sixth Amendment is not violated whenever—by luck or happenstance—the State obtains incriminating statements from the accused after the right to counsel has attached," ** a defendant does not make out a violation of that right simply by showing that an informant, either through prior arrangement or voluntarily, reported his incriminating statements to the police. Rather, the defendant must demonstrate that the police and their informant took some action, beyond merely listening, that was designed deliberately to elicit incriminating remarks.

B

It is thus apparent that the Court of Appeals erred in concluding that respondent's right to counsel was violated under the circumstances of this case. Its error did not stem from any disagreement with the District Court over appropriate resolution of the question reserved in *Henry*, but rather from its implicit conclusion that this case did not present that open question. That conclusion was based on a fundamental mistake, namely, the Court of Appeals' failure to accord to the state trial court's factual findings the presumption of correctness expressly required by 28 U.S.C. § 2254(d). **

The state court found that Officer Cullen had instructed Lee only to listen to respondent for the purpose of determining the identities of the other participants in the robbery and murder. The police already had solid evidence of respondent's participation. *** The court further found that Lee followed those instructions, that he "at no time asked any questions" of respondent concerning the pending charges, and that he "only listened" to respondent's "spontaneous" and "unsolicited" statements. The only remark made by Lee that has any support in this record was his comment that respondent's initial version of his participation in the crimes "didn't sound too good." Without holding that any of the state court's findings were not entitled to the presumption of correctness under § 2254(d), *** the Court of Appeals focused on that one remark and gave a description of Lee's interaction with respondent that is completely at odds with the facts found by the trial court. In the Court of Appeals' view, "[s]ubtly and slowly, but surely, Lee's ongoing verbal intercourse with [respondent] served to exacerbate [respondent's] already troubled state of mind." *** After thus revising some of the trial court's findings, and ignoring other more relevant findings, the Court of Appeals concluded that the police "deliberately elicited" respondent's incriminating statements. ** This conclusion conflicts with the decision of every other state and federal judge who reviewed this record, and is clear error in light of the provisions and intent of § 2254(d).

V

The judgment of the Court of Appeals is reversed, and the case is remanded for further proceedings consistent with this opinion.

It is so ordered.

[Dissenting opinion by JUSTICE BRENNAN, joined by JUSTICE MARSHALL, is omitted. A concurrence by CHIEF JUSTICE BURGER and a dissent by JUSTICE STEVENS are also omitted.]

Notes

1. *Subsequent case history*

Joseph Allan Wilson was paroled on August 29, 1990, after serving eighteen years in prison. *See* http://nysdocslookup.docs.state.ny.us/kinqw00.

2. *What the "ends of justice" require*

At the end of section III(B), Justice Powell writes:

> In the light of the historic purpose of habeas corpus and the interests implicated by successive petitions for federal habeas relief from a state conviction, we conclude that the "ends of justice" require federal courts to entertain such petitions only where the prisoner supplements his constitutional claim with a colorable showing of factual innocence. *** We adopt this standard now to effectuate the clear intent of Congress that successive federal habeas review should be granted only in rare cases, but that it should be available when the ends of justice so require. The prisoner may make the requisite showing by establishing that under the probative evidence he has a colorable claim of factual innocence. The prisoner must make his evidentiary showing even though — as argued in this case — the evidence of guilt may have been unlawfully admitted. ***

Why did the Supreme Court choose to differentiate between constitutional violations that stand on their own and those that are connected to "colorable claims of innocence"?

3. *Drawing distinctions*

Chief Justice Burger's concurrence makes the following observation: "There is a vast difference between placing an 'ear' in the suspect's cell and placing a voice in the cell to encourage conversation for the 'ear' to record." Do you agree?

4. *Dissenting opinion by Justice Stevens*

In Justice Stevens's dissent, he states,

> When a district court is confronted with the question whether the "ends of justice" would be served by entertaining a state prisoner's petition for habeas corpus raising a claim that has been rejected on a prior federal petition for the same relief, one of the facts that may properly be considered is whether the petitioner has advanced a "colorable claim of innocence." But I agree with JUSTICE BRENNAN that this is not an essential element of every just disposition of a successive petition. More specifically, I believe that the District Court did not abuse its discretion in entertaining the petition in this case, although I would also conclude that this is one of those close cases in which the District Court could have properly decided that a second review of the same contention was not required despite the intervening decision in *United States v Henry*, 447 U.S. 264 (1980).

Why do you think Justice Stevens dissented, given that he finds the "colorable claim of innocence" standard to be appropriate?

McCleskey v. Zant
499 U.S. 467 (1991)

JUSTICE KENNEDY delivered the opinion of the Court.

The doctrine of abuse of the writ defines the circumstances in which federal courts decline to entertain a claim presented for the first time in a second or subsequent petition for a writ of habeas corpus. Petitioner Warren McCleskey in a second federal habeas petition presented a claim under *Massiah v. United States*, 377 U.S. 201 (1964), that he failed to include in his first federal petition. The Court of Appeals for the Eleventh Circuit held that assertion of the *Massiah* claim in this manner abused the writ. Though our analysis differs from that of the Court of Appeals, we agree that the petitioner here abused the writ, and we affirm the judgment.

I

McCleskey and three other men, all armed, robbed a Georgia furniture store in 1978. One of the robbers shot and killed an off duty policeman who entered the store in the midst of the crime. McCleskey confessed to the police that he participated in the robbery. When on trial for both the robbery and the murder, however, McCleskey renounced his confession after taking the stand with an alibi denying all involvement. To rebut McCleskey's testimony, the prosecution called Offie Evans, who had occupied a jail cell next to McCleskey's. Evans testified that McCleskey admitted shooting the officer during the robbery and boasted that he would have shot his way out of the store even in the face of a dozen policemen.

Although no one witnessed the shooting, further direct and circumstantial evidence supported McCleskey's guilt of the murder. An eyewitness testified that someone ran from the store carrying a pearl-handled pistol soon after the robbery. Other witnesses testified that McCleskey earlier had stolen a pearl-handled pistol of the same caliber as the bullet that killed the officer. Ben Wright, one of McCleskey's accomplices, confirmed that during the crime McCleskey carried a white-handled handgun matching the caliber of the fatal bullet. Wright also testified that McCleskey admitted shooting the officer. Finally, the prosecutor introduced McCleskey's confession of participation in the robbery.

In December 1978, the jury convicted McCleskey of murder and sentenced him to death. Since his conviction, McCleskey has pursued direct and collateral remedies for more than a decade. We describe this procedural history in detail, both for a proper understanding of the case and as an illustration of the context in which allegations of abuse of the writ arise.

On direct appeal to the Supreme Court of Georgia, McCleskey raised six grounds of error. ** The portion of the appeal relevant for our purposes involves McCleskey's attack on Evans' rebuttal testimony. McCleskey contended that the trial court "erred in allowing evidence of [McCleskey's] oral statement admitting the murder made to [Evans] in the next cell, because the prosecutor had deliberately withheld such statement" in violation of *Brady v. Maryland*, 373 U.S. 83 (1963). ** A unanimous Georgia Supreme Court acknowledged that the prosecutor did not furnish Evans' statement to the defense, but ruled that because the undisclosed evidence was not exculpatory, McCleskey suffered no material prejudice and was not denied a fair trial under *Brady*. ** The court noted, moreover, that the evidence McCleskey wanted to inspect was "introduced to the jury in its entirety" through Evans' testimony, and that McCleskey's argument that "the evidence was needed in order to prepare a proper defense or impeach other witnesses ha[d] no merit because the evidence requested was statements made by [McCleskey] himself." ** The court rejected McCleskey's other contentions and affirmed his conviction and sentence. ** We denied certiorari. **

McCleskey then initiated postconviction proceedings. In January 1981, he filed a petition for state habeas corpus relief. The amended petition raised 23 challenges to his murder conviction and death sentence. ** Three of the claims concerned Evans' testimony. First, McCleskey contended that the State violated his due process rights under *Giglio v. United States*, 405 U.S. 150 (1972), by its failure to disclose an agreement to drop pending escape charges against Evans in return for his cooperation and testimony. ** Second, McCleskey reasserted his *Brady* claim that the State violated his due process rights by the deliberate withholding of the statement he made to Evans while in jail. ** Third, McCleskey alleged that admission of Evans' testimony violated the Sixth Amendment right to counsel as construed in *Massiah v. United States, supra*. On this theory, "[t]he introduction into evidence of [his] statements to [Evans], elicited in a situation created to induce [McCleskey] to make incriminating statements without the assistance of counsel, violated [McCleskey's] right to counsel under the Sixth Amendment to the Constitution of the United States." **

At the state habeas corpus hearing, Evans testified that one of the detectives investigating the murder agreed to speak a word on his behalf to the federal authorities about certain federal charges pending against him. The state habeas court ruled that the *ex parte* recommendation did not implicate *Giglio*, and it denied relief on all other claims. The Supreme Court of Georgia denied McCleskey's application for a certificate of probable cause, and we denied his second petition for a writ of certiorari. **

In December 1981, McCleskey filed his first federal habeas corpus petition in the United States District Court for the Northern District of Georgia, asserting 18 grounds for relief. ** The petition failed to allege the *Massiah* claim, but it did reassert the *Giglio* and *Brady* claims. Following extensive hearings in August and October 1983, the District Court held that the detective's statement to Evans was a promise of favorable treatment, and that failure to disclose the promise violated *Giglio*. ** The District Court further held that Evans' trial testimony may have affected the jury's verdict on the charge of malice murder. On these premises it granted relief. **

The Court of Appeals reversed the District Court's grant of the writ. ** The court held that the State had not made a promise to Evans of the kind contemplated by *Giglio*, and that in any event the *Giglio* error would be harmless. ** The court affirmed the District Court on all other grounds. We granted certiorari limited to the question whether Georgia's capital sentencing procedures were constitutional, and denied relief. **

McCleskey continued his postconviction attacks by filing a second state habeas corpus action in 1987 which, as amended, contained five claims for relief. ** One of the claims again centered on Evans' testimony, alleging that the State had an agreement with Evans that it had failed to disclose. The state trial court held a hearing and dismissed the petition. The Supreme Court of Georgia denied McCleskey's application for a certificate of probable cause.

In July 1987, McCleskey filed a second federal habeas action, the one we now review. In the District Court, McCleskey asserted seven claims, including a *Massiah* challenge to the introduction of Evans' testimony. ** McCleskey had presented a *Massiah* claim, it will be recalled, in his first state habeas action when he alleged that the conversation recounted by Evans at trial had been "elicited in a situation created to induce" him to make an incriminating statement without the assistance of counsel. The first federal petition did not present a *Massiah* claim. The proffered basis for the *Massiah* claim in the second federal petition was a 21-page signed statement that Evans made to the Atlanta Police Department on August 1, 1978, two weeks before the trial began. The department furnished the document to McCleskey one month before he filed his second federal petition.

The statement related pretrial jailhouse conversations that Evans had with McCleskey and that Evans overheard between McCleskey and Bernard Dupree. By the statement's own terms, McCleskey participated in all the reported jail-cell conversations. Consistent with Evans' testimony at trial, the statement reports McCleskey admitting and boasting about the murder. It also recounts that Evans posed as Ben Wright's uncle and told McCleskey he had talked with Wright about the robbery and the murder.

In his second federal habeas petition, McCleskey asserted that the statement proved Evans "was acting in direct concert with State officials" during the incriminating conversations with McCleskey, and that the authorities "deliberately elicited" inculpatory admissions in violation of McCleskey's Sixth Amendment right to counsel. ** Among other responses, the State of Georgia contended that McCleskey's presentation of a *Massiah* claim for the first time in the second federal petition was an abuse of the writ. **

The District Court held extensive hearings in July and August 1987 focusing on the arrangement the jailers had made for Evans' cell assignment in 1978. Several witnesses denied that Evans had been placed next to McCleskey by design or instructed to overhear conversations or obtain statements from McCleskey. McCleskey's key witness was Ulysses Worthy, a jailer at the Fulton County Jail during the summer of 1978. McCleskey's lawyers contacted Worthy after a detective testified that the 1978 Evans statement was taken in Worthy's office. The District Court characterized Worthy's testimony as "often confused and self-contradictory." ** Worthy testified that someone at some time requested permission to move Evans near McCleskey's cell. He contradicted himself, however, concerning when, why, and by whom Evans was moved, and about whether he overheard investigators urging Evans to engage McCleskey in conversation. **

On December 23, 1987, the District Court granted McCleskey relief based upon a violation of *Massiah*. ** The court stated that the Evans statement "contains strong indication of an *ab initio* relationship between Evans and the authorities." ** In addition, the court credited Worthy's testimony suggesting that the police had used Evans to obtain incriminating information from McCleskey. Based on the Evans statement and portions of Worthy's testimony, the District Court found that the jail authorities had placed Evans in the cell adjoining McCleskey's "for the purpose of gathering incriminating information"; that "Evans was probably coached in how to approach McCleskey and given critical facts unknown to the general public"; that Evans talked with McCleskey and eavesdropped on McCleskey's conversations with others; and that Evans reported what he had heard to the authorities. ** These findings, in the District Court's view, established a *Massiah* violation.

In granting habeas relief, the District Court rejected the State's argument that McCleskey's assertion of the *Massiah* claim for the first time in the second federal petition constituted an abuse of the writ. The court ruled that McCleskey did not deliberately abandon the claim after raising it in his first state habeas petition. "This is not a case," the District Court reasoned, "where petitioner has reserved his proof or deliberately withheld his claim for a second petition." ** The District Court also determined that when McCleskey filed his first federal petition, he did not know about either the 21-page Evans document or the identity of Worthy, and that the failure to discover the evidence for the first federal petition "was not due to [McCleskey's] inexcusable neglect." **

The Eleventh Circuit reversed, holding that the District Court abused its discretion by failing to dismiss McCleskey's *Massiah* claim as an abuse of the writ. ** The Court of Appeals agreed with the District Court that the petitioner must "show that he did not deliberately abandon the claim and that his failure to raise it [in the first federal habeas proceeding] was not due to inexcusable neglect." ** Accepting the District Court's findings that at the first petition stage McCleskey knew neither the existence of the Evans statement nor the identity of Worthy, the court held that the District Court "misconstru[ed] the meaning of deliberate abandonment." ** Because McCleskey included a *Massiah* claim in his first state petition, dropped it in his first federal petition, and then reasserted it in his second federal petition, he "made a knowing choice not to pursue the claim after having raised it previously" that constituted a prima facie showing of "deliberate abandonment." ** The court further found the State's alleged concealment of the Evans statement irrelevant because it "was simply the catalyst that caused counsel to pursue the *Massiah* claim more vigorously" and did not itself "demonstrate the existence of a *Massiah* violation." ** The court concluded that McCleskey had presented no reason why counsel could not have discovered Worthy earlier. ** Finally, the court ruled that McCleskey's claim did not fall within the ends of justice exception to the abuse-of-the-writ doctrine because any *Massiah* violation that may have been committed would have been harmless error. **

McCleskey petitioned this Court for a writ of certiorari, alleging numerous errors in the Eleventh Circuit's abuse-of-the-writ analysis. In our order granting the petition, we requested the parties to address the following additional question: "Must the State demonstrate that a claim was deliberately abandoned in an earlier petition for a writ of habeas corpus in order to establish that inclusion of that claim in a subsequent habeas petition constitutes abuse of the writ?" **

II

The parties agree that the government has the burden of pleading abuse of the writ, and that once the government makes a proper submission, the petitioner must show that he has not abused the writ in seeking habeas relief. ** Much confusion exists though, on the standard for determining when a petitioner abuses the writ. Although the standard is central to the proper determination of many federal habeas corpus actions, we have had little occasion to define it. Indeed, there is truth to the observation that we have defined abuse of the writ in an oblique way, through dicta and denials of certiorari petitions or stay applications. ** Today we give the subject our careful consideration. ***

[The Court then discusses the history of the writ of habeas corpus.]
***

III

Our discussion demonstrates that the doctrine of abuse of the writ refers to a complex and evolving body of equitable principles informed and controlled by historical usage, statutory developments, and judicial decisions. Because of historical changes and the complexity of the subject, the Court has not "always followed an unwavering line in its conclusions as to the availability of the Great Writ." *Fay v. Noia*, 372 U.S. [391], 411–412 [(1963)]. Today we attempt to define the doctrine of abuse of the writ with more precision.

Although our decisions on the subject do not all admit of ready synthesis, one point emerges with clarity: Abuse of the writ is not confined to instances of deliberate abandonment. *Sanders* mentioned deliberate abandonment as but one example of conduct that disentitled a petitioner to relief. *Sanders* cited a passage in *Townsend v. Sain*, 372 U.S. [293], 317 [(1963)], which applied the principle of inexcusable neglect, and noted that this principle also governs in the abuse-of-the-writ context. **

As *Sanders'* reference to *Townsend* demonstrates, as many Courts of Appeals recognize, ** and as McCleskey concedes, ** a petitioner may abuse the writ by failing to raise a claim through inexcusable neglect. Our recent decisions confirm that a petitioner can abuse the writ by raising a claim in a subsequent petition that he could have raised in his first, regardless of whether the failure to raise it earlier stemmed from a deliberate choice. **

The inexcusable neglect standard demands more from a petitioner than the standard of deliberate abandonment. But we have not given the former term the content necessary to guide district courts in the ordered consideration of allegedly abusive habeas corpus petitions. For reasons we explain below, a review of our habeas corpus precedents leads us to decide that the same standard used to determine whether to excuse state procedural defaults should govern the determination of inexcusable neglect in the abuse-of-the-writ context.

The prohibition against adjudication in federal habeas corpus of claims defaulted in state court is similar in purpose and design to the abuse-of-the-writ doctrine, which in general prohibits subsequent habeas consideration of claims not raised, and thus defaulted, in the first federal habeas proceeding. The terms "abuse of the writ" and "inexcusable neglect," on the one hand, and "procedural default," on the other, imply a background norm of procedural regularity binding on the petitioner. This explains the presumption against habeas adjudication both of claims defaulted in state court and of claims defaulted in the first round of federal habeas. A federal habeas court's power to excuse these types of defaulted claims derives from the court's equitable discretion. ** In habeas, equity recognizes that "a suitor's conduct in relation to the matter at hand may disentitle him to the relief he seeks." ** For these reasons, both the abuse-of-the-writ doctrine and our procedural default jurisprudence concentrate on a petitioner's acts to determine whether he has a legitimate excuse for failing to raise a claim at the appropriate time.

The doctrines of procedural default and abuse of the writ implicate nearly identical concerns flowing from the significant costs of federal habeas corpus review. To begin with, the writ strikes at finality. One of the law's very objects is the finality of its judgments. Neither innocence nor just punishment can be vindicated until the final judgment is known. "Without finality, the criminal law is deprived of much of its deterrent effect." *Teague v. Lane*, 489 U.S. 288, 309 (1989). And when a habeas petitioner succeeds in obtaining a new trial, the "'erosion of memory' and 'dispersion of witnesses' that occur with the passage of time" ** prejudice the government and diminish the chances of a reliable criminal adjudication. Though *Fay v. Noia, supra,* may have cast doubt upon these propositions, since *Fay* we have taken care in our habeas corpus decisions to reconfirm the importance of finality. **

Finality has special importance in the context of a federal attack on a state conviction. ** Reexamination of state convictions on federal habeas "frustrates…'both the States' sovereign power to punish offenders and their good-faith attempts to honor constitutional rights.'" ** Our federal system recognizes the independent power of a State to articulate societal norms through criminal law; but the power of a State to pass laws means little if the State cannot enforce them.

Habeas review extracts further costs. Federal collateral litigation places a heavy burden on scarce federal judicial resources, and threatens the capacity of the system to resolve primary disputes. ** Finally, habeas corpus review may give litigants incentives to withhold claims for manipulative purposes and may establish disincentives to present claims when evidence is fresh. **

Far more severe are the disruptions when a claim is presented for the first time in a second or subsequent federal habeas petition. If "[c]ollateral review of a conviction extends the ordeal of trial for both society and the accused," ** the ordeal worsens during subsequent collateral proceedings. Perpetual disrespect for the finality of convictions disparages the entire criminal justice system. ***

If reexamination of a conviction in the first round of federal habeas stretches resources, examination of new claims raised in a second or subsequent petition spreads them thinner still. These later petitions deplete the resources needed for federal litigants in the first instance, including litigants commencing their first federal habeas action. ***

The federal writ of habeas corpus overrides all these considerations, essential as they are to the rule of law, when a petitioner raises a meritorious constitutional claim in a proper manner in a habeas petition. Our procedural default jurisprudence and abuse-of-the-writ jurisprudence help define this dimension of procedural regularity. Both doctrines impose on petitioners a burden of reasonable compliance with procedures designed to discourage baseless claims and to keep the system open for valid ones; both recognize the law's interest in finality; and both invoke equitable principles to define the court's discretion to excuse pleading and procedural requirements for petitioners who could not comply with them in the exercise of reasonable care and diligence. It is true that a habeas court's concern to honor state procedural default rules rests in part on respect for the integrity of procedures "employed by a coordinate jurisdiction within the federal system" ** and that such respect is not implicated when a petitioner defaults a claim by failing to raise it in the first round of federal habeas review. Nonetheless, the doctrines of procedural default and abuse of the writ are both designed to lessen the injury to a State that results through reexamination of a state conviction on a ground that the State did not have the opportunity to address at a prior, appropriate time; and both doctrines seek to vindicate the State's interest in the finality of its criminal judgments.

We conclude from the unity of structure and purpose in the jurisprudence of state procedural defaults and abuse of the writ that the standard for excusing a failure to raise a claim at the appropriate time should be the same in both contexts. We have held that a procedural default will be excused upon a showing of cause and prejudice. ** We now hold that the same standard applies to determine if there has been an abuse of the writ through inexcusable neglect.

In procedural default cases, the cause standard requires the petitioner to show that "some objective factor external to the defense impeded counsel's efforts" to raise the claim in state court. *Murray v. Carrier*, 477 U.S. [478], 488 [(1986)]. Objective factors that constitute cause include "'interference by officials'" that makes compliance with the State's procedural rule impracticable, and "a showing that the factual or legal basis for a claim was not reasonably available to counsel." *Ibid.* In addition, constitutionally "[i]neffective assistance of counsel...is cause." *Ibid.* Attorney error short of ineffective assistance of counsel, however, does not constitute cause and will not excuse a procedural default. *Id.* at 486–488. Once the petitioner has established cause, he must show "'actual prejudice' resulting from the errors of which he complains." **

Federal courts retain the authority to issue the writ of habeas corpus in a further, narrow class of cases despite a petitioner's failure to show cause for a procedural default. These are extraordinary instances when a constitutional violation probably has caused the conviction of one innocent of the crime. We have described this class of cases as implicating a fundamental miscarriage of justice. **

The cause and prejudice analysis we have adopted for cases of procedural default applies to an abuse-of-the-writ inquiry in the following manner. When a prisoner files a second or subsequent application, the government bears the burden of pleading abuse of the writ. The government satisfies this burden if, with clarity and particularity, it notes petitioner's prior writ history, identifies the claims that appear for the first time, and alleges that petitioner has abused the writ. The burden to disprove abuse then becomes petitioner's. To excuse his failure to raise the claim earlier, he must show cause for failing to raise it and prejudice therefrom as those concepts have been defined in our procedural default decisions. The petitioner's opportunity to meet the burden of cause and prejudice will not include an evidentiary hearing if the district court determines as a matter of law that petitioner cannot satisfy the standard. If petitioner cannot show cause, the failure to raise the claim in an earlier petition may nonetheless be excused if he or she can show that a fundamental miscarriage of justice would result from a failure to entertain the claim. Application of the cause and prejudice standard in the abuse-of-the-writ context does not mitigate the force of *Teague v. Lane*, 489 U.S. 288 (1989), which prohibits, with certain exceptions, the retroactive application of new law to claims raised in federal habeas. Nor does it imply that there is a constitutional right to counsel in federal habeas corpus. **

*** We now apply these principles to the case before us.

IV

McCleskey based the *Massiah* claim in his second federal petition on the 21-page Evans document alone. Worthy's identity did not come to light until the hearing. The District Court found, based on the document's revelation of the tactics used by Evans in engaging McCleskey in conversation (such as his pretending to be Ben Wright's uncle and his claim that he was supposed to participate in the robbery), that the document established an *ab initio* relationship between Evans and the authorities. It relied on the finding and on Worthy's later testimony to conclude that the State committed a *Massiah* violation.

This ruling on the merits cannot come before us or any federal court if it is premised on a claim that constitutes an abuse of the writ. We must consider, therefore, the preliminary question whether McCleskey had cause for failing to raise the *Massiah* claim in his first federal petition. The District Court found that neither the 21-page document nor Worthy were known or discoverable before filing the first federal petition. Relying on these findings, McCleskey argues that his failure to raise the *Massiah* claim in the first petition should be excused. For reasons set forth below, we disagree.

That McCleskey did not possess, or could not reasonably have obtained, certain evidence fails to establish cause if other known or discoverable evidence could have supported the claim in any event. "[C]ause...requires a showing of some external impediment *preventing* counsel from constructing or raising the claim." *Murray v. Carrier*, 477 U.S. [478], 492 [(1986)]. For cause to exist, the external impediment, whether it be government interference or the reasonable unavailability of the factual basis for the claim, must have prevented petitioner from raising the claim. ** Abuse of the writ doctrine examines *petitioner's* conduct: The question is whether petitioner possessed, or by reasonable means could have obtained, a sufficient basis to allege a claim in the first petition and pursue the matter through the habeas process. ** The requirement of cause in the abuse-of-the-writ context is based on the principle that petitioner must conduct a reasonable and diligent investigation aimed at including all relevant claims and grounds for relief in the first federal habeas petition. If what petitioner knows or could discover upon reasonable investigation supports a claim for relief in a federal habeas petition, what he does not know is irrelevant. Omission of the claim will not be excused merely because evidence discovered later might also have supported or strengthened the claim.

In applying these principles, we turn first to the 21-page signed statement. It is essential at the outset to distinguish between two issues: (1) Whether petitioner knew about or could have discovered the 21-page document; and (2) whether he knew about or could have discovered the evidence the document recounted, namely, the jail-cell conversations. The District Court's error lies in its conflation of the two inquiries, an error petitioner would have us perpetuate here.

The 21-page document unavailable to McCleskey at the time of the first petition does not establish that McCleskey had cause for failing to raise the *Massiah* claim at the outset. Based on testimony and questioning at trial, McCleskey knew that he had confessed the murder during jail-cell conversations with Evans, knew that Evans claimed to be a relative of Ben Wright during the conversations, and knew that Evans told the police about the conversations. Knowledge of these facts alone would put McCleskey on notice to pursue the *Massiah* claim in his first federal habeas petition as he had done in the first state habeas petition.

But there was more. The District Court's finding that the 21-page document established an *ab initio* relationship between Evans and the authorities rested in its entirety on conversations in which McCleskey himself participated. Though at trial McCleskey denied the inculpatory conversations, his current arguments presuppose them. Quite apart from the inequity in McCleskey's reliance on that which he earlier denied under oath, the more fundamental point remains that because McCleskey participated in the conversations reported by Evans, he knew everything in the document that the District

Court relied upon to establish the *ab initio* connection between Evans and the police. McCleskey has had at least constructive knowledge all along of the facts he now claims to have learned only from the 21-page document. The unavailability of the document did not prevent McCleskey from raising the *Massiah* claim in the first federal petition and is not cause for his failure to do so. And of course, McCleskey cannot contend that his false representations at trial constitute cause for the omission of a claim from the first federal petition.

The District Court's determination that jailer Worthy's identity and testimony could not have been known prior to the first federal petition does not alter our conclusion. It must be remembered that the 21-page statement was the only new evidence McCleskey had when he filed the *Massiah* claim in the second federal petition in 1987. Under McCleskey's own theory, nothing was known about Worthy even then. If McCleskey did not need to know about Worthy and his testimony to press the *Massiah* claim in the second petition, neither did he need to know about him to assert it in the first. Ignorance about Worthy did not prevent McCleskey from raising the *Massiah* claim in the first federal petition and will not excuse his failure to do so.

     ***

We do address whether the Court should nonetheless exercise its equitable discretion to correct a miscarriage of justice. That narrow exception is of no avail to McCleskey. The *Massiah* violation, if it be one, resulted in the admission at trial of truthful inculpatory evidence which did not affect the reliability of the guilt determination. The very statement McCleskey now seeks to embrace confirms his guilt. As the District Court observed:

> After having read [the Evans statement], the court has concluded that nobody short of William Faulkner could have contrived that statement, and as a consequence finds the testimony of Offie Evans absolutely to be true, and the court states on the record that it entertains absolutely no doubt as to the guilt of Mr. McCleskey. **

We agree with this conclusion. McCleskey cannot demonstrate that the alleged *Massiah* violation caused the conviction of an innocent person. **

The history of the proceedings in this case, and the burden upon the State in defending against allegations made for the first time in federal court some nine years after the trial, reveal the necessity for the abuse-of-the-writ doctrine. The cause and prejudice standard we adopt today leaves ample room for consideration of constitutional errors in a first federal habeas petition and in a later petition under appropriate circumstances. Petitioner has not satisfied this standard for excusing the omission of the *Massiah* claim from his first petition. The judgment of the Court of Appeals is

Affirmed.

[Appendix to Opinion of the Court is omitted.]

JUSTICE MARSHALL, with whom JUSTICE BLACKMUN and JUSTICE STEVENS join, dissenting.

Today's decision departs drastically from the norms that inform the proper judicial function. Without even the most casual admission that it is discarding longstanding legal principles, the Court radically redefines the content of the "abuse of the writ" doctrine, substituting the strict-liability "cause and prejudice" standard of *Wainwright v. Sykes*, 433 U.S. 72 (1977), for the good-faith "deliberate abandonment" standard of *Sanders v. United States*, 373 U.S. 1 (1963). This doctrinal innovation, which repudiates a line of judicial decisions codified by Congress in the governing statute and procedural rules, was by no means foreseeable when the petitioner in this case filed his first federal habeas application. Indeed, the new rule announced and applied today was not even *requested* by respondent at any point in this litigation. Finally, rather than remand this case for reconsideration in light of its new standard, the majority performs an independent reconstruction of the record, disregarding the factual findings of the District Court and applying its new rule in a manner that encourages state officials to *conceal* evidence that would likely prompt a petitioner to raise a particular claim on habeas. Because I cannot acquiesce in this unjustifiable assault on the Great Writ, I dissent.

***

II

The real question posed by the majority's analysis is not *whether* the cause-and-prejudice test departs from the principles of *Sanders*—for it clearly does—but whether the majority has succeeded in *justifying* this departure as an exercise of this Court's common-lawmaking discretion. In my view, the majority does not come close to justifying its new standard.

***

B

Even if the fusion of cause-and-prejudice into the abuse-of-the-writ doctrine were not foreclosed by the will of Congress, the majority fails to demonstrate that such a rule would be a wise or just exercise of the Court's common-lawmaking discretion. In fact, the majority's abrupt change in law subverts the policies underlying § 2244(b) and unfairly prejudices the petitioner in this case.

The majority premises adoption of the cause-and-prejudice test almost entirely on the importance of "finality." ** At best, this is an insufficiently developed justification for cause-and-prejudice or any other possible conception of the abuse-of-the-writ doctrine. For the very essence of the Great Writ is our criminal justice system's commitment to suspending "[c]onventional notions of finality of litigation … where life or liberty is at stake and infringement of constitutional rights is alleged." ** To recognize this principle is not to make the straw-man claim that the writ must be accompanied by "'[a] procedural system which permits an endless repetition of inquiry into facts and law in a vain search for ultimate certitude.'" ** Rather, it is only to point out the plain fact that we may not, "[u]nder the guise of fashioning a procedural rule, … wip[e] out the practical efficacy of a jurisdiction conferred by Congress on the District Courts." **

***

This injustice is compounded by the Court's activism in fashioning its new rule. The applicability of *Sykes'* cause-and-prejudice test was not litigated in either the District Court or the Court of Appeals. The additional question that we requested the parties to address reasonably could have been read to relate merely to the burden of proof under the abuse-of-the-writ doctrine; *** it evidently did not put the parties on notice that this Court was contemplating a change in the governing legal standard, since respondent did not even mention *Sykes* or cause-and-prejudice in his brief or at oral argument, much less request the Court to adopt this standard. *** In this respect, too, today's decision departs from norms that inform the proper judicial function. *** It cannot be said that McCleskey had a fair opportunity to challenge the reasoning that the majority today invokes to strip him of his *Massiah* claim.

III

The manner in which the majority applies its new rule is as objectionable as the manner in which the majority creates that rule. As even the majority acknowledges, ** the standard that it announces today is not the one employed by the Court of Appeals, which purported to rely on *Sanders.* ** Where, as here, application of a different standard from the one applied by the lower court requires an in-depth review of the record, the ordinary course is to remand so that the parties have a fair opportunity to address, and the lower court to consider, all of the relevant issues. **

    ***

To appreciate the hollowness—and the dangerousness—of this reasoning, it is necessary to recall the District Court's central finding: that the State *did* covertly plant Evans in an adjoining cell for the purpose of eliciting incriminating statements that could be used against McCleskey at trial. ** Once this finding is credited, it follows that the State affirmatively misled McCleskey and his counsel throughout their unsuccessful pursuit of the *Massiah* claim in state collateral proceedings and their investigation of that claim in preparing for McCleskey's first federal habeas proceeding. McCleskey's counsel deposed or interviewed the assistant district attorney, various jailers, and other government officials responsible for Evans' confinement, all of whom denied any knowledge of an agreement between Evans and the State. **

Against this background of deceit, the State's withholding of Evans' 21-page statement assumes critical importance. The majority overstates McCleskey's and his counsel's awareness of the statement's contents. For example, the statement relates that state officials were present when Evans made a phone call at McCleskey's request to McCleskey's girlfriend, ** a fact that McCleskey and his counsel had no reason to know and that strongly supports the District Court's finding of an *ab initio* relationship between Evans and the State. But in any event, the importance of the statement lay much less in what the statement said than in its simple *existence.* Without the statement, McCleskey's counsel had nothing more than his client's testimony to back up counsel's own suspicion of a possible *Massiah* violation; given the state officials' adamant denials of any arrangement with Evans, and given the state habeas court's rejection of the *Massiah* claim, counsel quite reasonably concluded that raising this claim in McCleskey's first habeas petition would be futile. All this changed once counsel finally obtained the statement, for at that point, there was credible, independent corroboration of counsel's suspicion. This additional evidence not only gave counsel the reasonable expectation of success that had previously been lacking, but also gave him a basis for conducting further investigation into the underlying claim. Indeed, it was by piecing together the circumstances under which the statement had been transcribed that McCleskey's counsel was able to find Worthy, a state official who was finally willing to admit that Evans had been planted in the cell adjoining McCleskey's. ***

    ***

IV

Ironically, the majority seeks to defend its doctrinal innovation on the ground that it will promote respect for the "rule of law." ** Obviously, respect for the rule of law must start with those who are responsible for *pronouncing* the law. The majority's invocation of "'the orderly administration of justice'" ** rings hollow when the majority itself tosses aside established precedents without explanation, disregards the will of Congress, fashions rules that defy the reasonable expectations of the persons who must conform their conduct to the law's dictates, and applies those rules in a way that rewards state misconduct and deceit. Whatever "abuse of the writ" today's decision is designed to avert pales in comparison with the majority's own abuse of the norms that inform the proper judicial function.

I dissent.

Notes

1. *Subsequent case history*

Warren McCleskey was executed on September 5, 1991, by electrocution.

2. *The reach of* McCleskey

When a United States District Court re-characterizes a pro se federal prisoner's first post conviction motion as a habeas petition under 28 U.S.C. § 2255, does such re-characterization place the prisoner's subsequent attempt to file a "second or successive petition" within the purview of the AEDPA? *See Castro v. United States*, 540 U.S. 375 (December 15, 2003).

3. *Public policy concerns*

Justice Marshall's dissent discusses the public policy concerns engendered by the concealment of evidence by police. How does the majority opinion confront this problem?

Chapter 12

Harmless Error

Errors are the insects in the world of law, traveling through it in swarms, often unnoticed in their endless procession. Many are plainly harmless; some appear ominously harmful. Some, for all the benign appearance of their spindly traces, mark the way for a plague of followers that deplete trials of fairness.

The well-being of the law encompasses a tolerance for harmless errors adrift in an imperfect world. Its well-being must also encompass the capacity to ward off the destroyers. So an inquiry into what makes an error harmless, though one of philosophical tenor, is also an intensely practical inquiry into the health and sanitation of the law.

*** From the traffic pattern of errors we have much to learn about judicial discretion in the countless leeways where judges can raise or lower the standards of judicial responsibility.[1]

One of the most controversial of legal concepts is "harmless error." If error occurred at trial but the result of the trial would have been the same even if the error had not occurred, the error is deemed "harmless" and the judgment below should remain undisturbed. As a general matter, the appellant (or petitioner) has the burden to show that the error complained of is indeed harmful and warrants reversal; however, some errors of constitutional magnitude shift the burden of persuasion to the appellee (or respondent) to show the error is harmless beyond a reasonable doubt. Given that a petition for a writ of habeas corpus is premised on constitutional issues, the question of harmless error is central to the resolution of many, if not most, claims.

In *Greer v. Miller*, the Court examines whether a prosecutor whose cross-examination of a defendant at trial includes a question about his post-arrest silence requires reversal of his conviction. In *Arizona v. Fulminante*, the Court decides whether the admission at trial of a coerced confession can be subject to harmless-error analysis. And in *Brecht v. Abrahamson*, the Court returns to the issue of using a defendant's post-*Miranda* silence for impeachment purposes—in violation of the *Doyle* due process requirements—this time expressly deciding whether the harmless-error analysis applies in determining whether petitioner is entitled to habeas corpus relief.

---

1. ROGER J. TRAYNOR, THE RIDDLE OF HARMLESS ERROR (forward) (1970).

Greer v. Miller

483 U.S. 756 (1987)

JUSTICE POWELL delivered the opinion of the Court.

The question before us is whether a prosecutor's question at trial concerning a criminal defendant's post-arrest silence requires reversal of the defendant's conviction.

I

In 1980, Neil Gorsuch was kidnapped, robbed, and murdered after leaving a bar in Jacksonville, Illinois. Three men were charged with the crimes: Randy Williams, Clarence Armstrong, and the respondent, Charles Miller. Williams confessed, and later entered into a plea agreement under which most of the charges against him were dropped in return for his testimony at the separate trials of Armstrong and Miller.

At Miller's trial, Williams testified that he, his brother, and Armstrong had met Gorsuch in a tavern on the evening of February 8. Armstrong offered the victim a ride back to his hotel, and the four men left together at about 1:30 a.m. After Williams' brother was dropped off, Armstrong began beating Gorsuch in the back seat of the car. According to Williams' testimony, the group stopped briefly at Williams' parents' home to pick up a shotgun, and the men then drove to the trailer home where Miller was staying. Williams testified that Miller joined the group, and that they then traveled to a bridge on an isolated road. Williams stated that once there each of the three men shot Gorsuch in the head with the shotgun.

Respondent Miller took the stand on his own behalf and told a different story. On direct examination he testified that he had taken no part in the crime, but that Armstrong and Williams had come to the trailer home after the murder was committed seeking Miller's advice. Miller testified that Armstrong confessed that he and Williams had beaten and robbed Gorsuch, and that they had killed him to avoid being identified as the perpetrators.

The prosecutor began his cross-examination of Miller as follows:

Q: Mr. Miller, how old are you?

A: 23.

Q: Why didn't you tell this story to anybody when you got arrested? **

Defense counsel immediately objected. Out of the hearing of the jury, Miller's lawyer requested a mistrial on the ground that the prosecutor's question violated Miller's right to remain silent after arrest. The trial judge denied the motion, but immediately sustained the objection and instructed the jury to "ignore [the] question, for the time being." ** The prosecutor did not pursue the issue further, nor did he mention it during his closing argument. At the conclusion of the presentation of evidence, defense counsel did not renew his objection or request an instruction concerning the prosecutor's question. Moreover, the judge specifically instructed the jury to "disregard questions...to which objections were sustained." ** Miller was convicted of murder, aggravated kidnapping, and robbery, and sentenced to 80 years in prison.

On appeal the State argued that if the prosecutor's question about Miller's post-arrest silence was prohibited by this Court's decision in *Doyle v. Ohio*, 426 U.S. 610 (1976), the error was harmless under the standards of *Chapman v. California*, 386 U.S. 18 (1967). *** The Illinois Appellate Court rejected the argument and reversed the conviction, concluding that the evidence against Miller "was not so overwhelming as to preclude all reasonable doubts about the effect of the prosecutor's comment." ** The Supreme Court of Illinois disagreed and reinstated the trial court's decision. ** The court noted that the prosecutor's question was an isolated comment made in the course of a lengthy trial, that the jury had been instructed to disregard the question, and that the evidence properly admitted was sufficient to establish Miller's guilt beyond a reasonable doubt. ** It therefore held that the error did not require reversal of the conviction.

Miller then filed a petition for a writ of habeas corpus in the Federal District Court for the Central District of Illinois. The District Court denied the petition, finding "no possibility that the prosecutor's questioning on post-arrest silence could have contributed to the conviction." ** A divided panel of the Court of Appeals for the Seventh Circuit reversed the District Court's decision, ** as did the full court on reargument en banc. ** The en banc court found that because Miller had received *Miranda* *** warnings at the time of his arrest for the offenses in question, "[t]he prosecutor's reference to Miller's silence at the time of his arrest...violated his constitutional right to a fair trial." ** The court further held that the error was not harmless beyond a reasonable doubt under *Chapman v. California, supra,* because "[t]he evidence against Miller was not overwhelming, his story was not implausible, and the trial court's cautionary instruction was insufficient to cure the error." ** Three judges dissented, concluding that under the harmless-error standard, "this fifteen-second colloquy, alleviated by the trial judge's immediately sustaining the defendant's objection and instructing the jury to ignore the prosecutor's improper question and by a threshold jury instruction to disregard questions to which objections were sustained, did not affect the verdict." ** Judge Easterbrook also dissented. In his view, the harmless-error standard of *Chapman* is too stringent to be applied to this case for a number of reasons: the rule of *Doyle* is prophylactic rather than innocence-protecting; the issue is presented on collateral, rather than on direct, review; the error in this case could have been cured more fully had defense counsel so requested at trial; and the violation should be viewed as prosecutorial misconduct that requires reversal only if it rendered the trial fundamentally unfair. **

We granted certiorari to review the Court of Appeals' determination that the prosecutor's question about the criminal defendant's post-arrest silence requires reversal of the conviction in this case. *** We disagree with the Court of Appeals and now reverse.

II

The starting point of our analysis is *Doyle v. Ohio,* 426 U.S. 610 (1976). The petitioners in *Doyle* were arrested for selling marijuana. They were given *Miranda* warnings and made no post-arrest statements about their involvement in the crime. They contended at trial that they had been framed by the government informant. As part of his cross-examination, the prosecutor repeatedly asked petitioners why, if they were innocent, they did not give the explanation that they proffered at their separate trials to the police at the time of their arrest. *** Defense counsel's timely objections to this line of questioning were overruled. Also over timely objections, the trial court allowed the prosecutor to argue petitioners' post-arrest silence to the jury. 426 U.S. at 613–615 & n.5. On review, this Court found that the *Miranda* decision "compel[led] rejection" of the contention that such questioning and argument are proper means of impeachment. 426 U.S. at 617. The Court noted that post-arrest silence may not be particularly probative of guilt. We also found that because *Miranda* warnings contain an implicit assurance "that silence will carry no penalty," 426 U.S. at 618, "'it does not comport with due process to permit the prosecution during the trial to call attention to [the defendant's] silence at the time of arrest and to insist that because he did not speak about the facts of the case at that time, as he was told he need not do, an unfavorable inference might be drawn as to the truth of his trial testimony,'" *id.* at 619. ** Accordingly the Court in *Doyle* held that "the use for impeachment purposes of petitioners' silence, at the time of arrest and after receiving *Miranda* warnings, violated the Due Process Clause of the Fourteenth Amendment." 426 U.S. at 619.

This Court has applied the holding of *Doyle* in a number of subsequent cases. These later holdings confirm that "*Doyle* rests on 'the fundamental unfairness of implicitly assuring a suspect that his silence will not be used against him and then using his silence to impeach an explanation subsequently offered at trial.'" *Wainwright v. Greenfield*, 474 U.S. 284, 291 (1986). ** Thus, "absen[t] the sort of affirmative assurances embodied in the *Miranda* warnings," the Constitution does not prohibit the use of a defendant's post-arrest silence to impeach him at trial. *Fletcher v. Weir*, 455 U.S. 603, 607 (1982). **

There is no question that Miller received the "implicit assurance" of *Miranda* warnings in this case. Thus, this prerequisite of a *Doyle* violation was met. But the holding of *Doyle* is that the Due Process Clause bars "*the use* for impeachment purposes" of a defendant's post-arrest silence. 426 U.S. at 619 (emphasis added). The Court noted that "'it does not comport with due process *to permit* the prosecution during trial to call attention to [the defendant's] silence.'" *Ibid.* ** It is significant that in each of the cases in which this Court has applied *Doyle*, the trial court has permitted specific inquiry or argument respecting the defendant's *post-Miranda* silence. *See Jenkins v. Anderson*, [447 U.S. 231], 233–234 [(1980)]; *Anderson v. Charles*, [447 U.S. 404], 405–406 [(1980)]; *Fletcher v. Weir*, [455 U.S.] at 603–604. **

In contrast to these cases, the trial court in this case did not permit the inquiry that *Doyle* forbids. Instead, the court explicitly sustained an objection to the only question that touched upon Miller's post-arrest silence. No further questioning or argument with respect to Miller's silence occurred, and the court specifically advised the jury that it should disregard any questions to which an objection was sustained. *** Unlike the prosecutor in *Doyle*, the prosecutor in this case was not "allowed to undertake impeachment on," or "permit[ted]...to call attention to," Miller's silence. 426 U.S. at 619 & n.10. The fact of Miller's post-arrest silence was not submitted to the jury as evidence from which it was allowed to draw any permissible inference, and thus no *Doyle* violation occurred in this case. ***

III

Although the prosecutor's question did not constitute a *Doyle* violation, the fact remains that the prosecutor attempted to violate the rule of *Doyle* by asking an improper question in the presence of the jury. This Court has recognized that prosecutorial misconduct may "so infec[t] the trial with unfairness as to make the resulting conviction a denial of due process." *Donnelly v. DeChristoforo*, 416 U.S. 637, 643 (1974). To constitute a due process violation, the prosecutorial misconduct must be "'of sufficient significance to result in the denial of the defendant's right to a fair trial.'" *United States v. Bagley*, 473 U.S. 667, 676 (1985) (quoting *United States v. Agurs*, 427 U.S. 97, 108 (1976)).

The Illinois Supreme Court, applying the analysis of *Chapman v. California*, 386 U.S. 18 (1967), found that the prosecutor's question was harmless beyond a reasonable doubt. ** We thus are convinced that it would find no due process violation under the facts of this case. *** When a defendant contends that a prosecutor's question rendered his trial fundamentally unfair, it is important "as an initial matter to place th[e] remar[k] in context." *Darden v. Wainwright*, 477 U.S. 168, 179 (1986). *See Donnelly v. DeChristoforo*, [416 U.S.] at 639 (determining whether "remarks, in the context of the entire trial, were sufficiently prejudicial to violate respondent's due process rights"). The sequence of events in this case—a single question, an immediate objection, and two curative instructions ***—clearly indicates that the prosecutor's improper question did not violate Miller's due process rights. The Illinois Supreme Court's determination that the properly admitted evidence at trial "was sufficient to prove defendant's guilt beyond a reasonable doubt" ** further supports this result. ***

IV

We reverse the judgment of the Court of Appeals for the Seventh Circuit and remand for proceedings consistent with this opinion.

It is so ordered.

JUSTICE STEVENS, concurring in the judgment.

Having dissented in *Doyle v. Ohio*, 426 U.S. 610, 620–635 (1976), I can readily understand why the Court might want to overrule that case. But if there is to be a rule that prohibits a prosecutor's use of a defendant's post-*Miranda* silence, it should be a clearly defined rule. Whether the trial court sustains an objection to an impermissible question, or whether the prosecutor is allowed to refer to the defendant's silence in his or her closing arguments, are questions that are relevant to the harmless-error inquiry, or to deciding whether the error made the trial fundamentally unfair. But they play no role in deciding whether a prosecutor violated the implicit promise of *Miranda*—as understood in *Doyle*—that the defendant's silence will not be used against him.

I, therefore, agree with the 10 Illinois judges and 12 federal judges who have concluded that the rule of the *Doyle* case was violated when the prosecutor called the jury's attention to respondent's silence. Moreover, for the reasons stated by the Court of Appeals, I think the violation was serious enough to support that court's conclusion that the error was not harmless beyond a reasonable doubt. ** Were this case here on direct appeal, therefore, I would vote to reverse the conviction. Nonetheless, I concur in the Court's judgment because I believe the question presented in the certiorari petition— whether a federal court should apply a different standard in reviewing *Doyle* errors *in a habeas corpus action*—should be answered in the affirmative. In *Rose v. Lundy*, 455 U.S. 509 (1982), I argued that there are at least four types of alleged constitutional errors.

> The one most frequently encountered is a claim that attaches a constitutional label to a set of facts that does not disclose a violation of any constitutional right.... The second class includes constitutional violations that are not of sufficient import in a particular case to justify reversal even on direct appeal, when the evidence is still fresh and a fair retrial could be promptly conducted. ** A third category includes errors that are important enough to require reversal on direct appeal but do not reveal the kind of fundamental unfairness to the accused that will support a collateral attack on a final judgment. *See, e.g., Stone v. Powell*, 428 U.S. 465 [(1976)]. The fourth category includes those errors that are so fundamental that they infect the validity of the underlying judgment itself, or the integrity of the process by which that judgment was obtained. *Id.* at 543–544 (dissenting opinion) (footnote omitted).

In my view, *Doyle* violations which cannot be deemed harmless beyond a reasonable doubt typically fall within the third of these categories. On *direct review*, a conviction should be reversed if a defendant can demonstrate that a *Doyle* error occurred at trial, and the State cannot demonstrate that it is harmless beyond a reasonable doubt. But, in typical *collateral attacks*, such as today's, *Doyle* errors are not so fundamentally unfair that convictions must be reversed whenever the State cannot bear the heavy burden of proving that the error was harmless beyond a reasonable doubt. On the other hand, there may be extraordinary cases in which the *Doyle* error is so egregious, or is combined with other errors or incidents of prosecutorial misconduct, that the integrity of the process is called into question. In such an event, habeas corpus relief should be afforded. ***

In sum, although I agree with the Court's judgment, and the standard that it applies here, I would apply this standard only to *Doyle* violations being considered on collateral review. On direct appeal, a *Doyle* error should give rise to reversal of the conviction unless the State can prove that the error was harmless beyond a reasonable doubt.

JUSTICE BRENNAN, with whom JUSTICE MARSHALL and JUSTICE BLACK-MUN join, dissenting.

Today the Court holds that a prosecutor may comment on a defendant's post-arrest silence in an attempt to impeach his credibility without thereby violating the rule of *Doyle v. Ohio*, 426 U.S. 610 (1976). The Court arrives at this surprising conclusion only by confusing the question whether a *Doyle* violation occurred with the question whether that violation was harmless beyond a reasonable doubt. The holding is remarkable not only because it radically departs from the settled practice of the lower courts, but also because it is founded on a point conceded below and not raised here.

Until today, the common understanding of "our opinion in *Doyle v. Ohio*...[was that it] shields from *comment* by a prosecutor a defendant's silence after receiving *Miranda* warnings." *Wainwright v. Greenfield*, 474 U.S. 284, 296 (1986) (REHNQUIST, J., concurring in result) (emphasis added). Accordingly, a defendant has been able to establish a *Doyle* violation simply by showing that the prosecutor "'call[ed] attention to'" the defendant's post-arrest silence. *Doyle*, [426 U.S.] at 619. "The standard is strict; virtually any description of a defendant's silence following arrest and a *Miranda* warning will constitute a *Doyle* violation." *United States v. Shaw*, 701 F.2d 367, 382 (5th Cir. 1983). ** In light of this authority and the prosecutor's "clear-cut" attempt to use the defendant's post-arrest silence to impeach his credibility, *United States ex rel. Miller v. Greer*, 789 F.2d 438, 447 (7th Cir. 1986), it is not surprising that the five other courts that examined this case found a *Doyle* violation.

To support its decision that no *Doyle* violation occurred in this case, the Court argues in effect that a single comment cannot be sufficient to constitute a *Doyle* violation. A single comment, the Court suggests, does not amount to the "use" of a defendant's silence for impeachment purposes, and is not equivalent to an "inquiry or argument respecting the defendant's post-*Miranda* silence." *Ante*. What the Court overlooks, however, is the fact that a single comment is all the prosecutor needs to notify the jury that the defendant did not "tell his story" promptly after his arrest. Although silence at the time of arrest is "insolubly ambiguous" and may be "consistent with...an exculpatory explanation," *Doyle*, [426 U.S.] at 617, 618 & n.8, nevertheless "the jury is likely to draw" a "strong negative inference" from the fact of a defendant's post-arrest silence. *United States v. Hale*, 422 U.S. 171, 180 (1975). Thus, as the lower courts have consistently found, a prosecutor may in a single comment effectively use a defendant's post-arrest silence to impeach his or her credibility. **

The Court also notes that the trial court sustained defendant's objection to the prosecutor's improper question, and that the court later instructed the jury to disregard all questions to which an objection had been sustained. These actions minimized the harm this particular comment might have caused, the Court implies, and also distinguish this case from previous cases in which this Court has applied *Doyle*. *Ante*. In the case on which *Doyle* was squarely based, however, the Court reversed a conviction because of improper questioning regarding post-*Miranda* silence even though the jury was immediately instructed to disregard that questioning. *See United States v. Hale*, [422 U.S.] at 175 n.3. Moreover, the lower courts have routinely addressed similar situations, and in no case in which the prosecutor has commented on the defendant's silence have these courts found contemporaneous objections or curative instructions sufficient *automatically* to preclude finding a *Doyle* violation. Instead, the Courts of Appeals have examined the comment in context, and considered it along with the weight of the evidence against the defendant and the importance of the defendant's credibility to the defense, in determining whether a *Doyle* violation was harmless beyond a reasonable doubt. ***

The approach taken by the lower courts reflects both the serious impact of *Doyle* violations on the fairness of a trial, and the inherent difficulty in undoing the harm that they cause. With respect to their impact, more than one Circuit has recognized that "*Doyle* violations are rarely harmless." *Williams v. Zahradnick*, 632 F.2d 353, 364 (4th Cir. 1980) (citing practice in the Fifth Circuit with approval). This is because "questions of guilt and credibility [are often] inextricably bound together," *Morgan v. Hall*, [569 F.2d 1161], 1168 [1st Cir. 1978], and because comments upon a defendant's failure to tell his or her story promptly after arrest may significantly undermine the defendant's credibility in the jury's eyes. This case illustrates the potential for harm. The only testimony the State offered that linked the defendant to the crime was that of an alleged accomplice. Jurors often give accomplice testimony reduced weight, particularly when the accomplice has received in return a promise of significant leniency. *** Here the State's case depended entirely on whether the jury believed the defendant or the alleged accomplice. The prosecutor's second question on cross-examination—"Why didn't you tell this story to anybody when you got arrested?"—thus struck directly at the heart of Miller's defense: his credibility. If the rationale of *Doyle* is to have any force, defendants must be protected from such tactics.

Lower courts have also recognized that once the prosecutor calls attention to the defendant's silence, the resultant harm is not easily cured. First, the jury is made aware of the fact of post-arrest silence, and a foundation is laid for subsequent, more subtle attacks. *** Second, "curative" instructions themselves call attention to defendant's silence, and may in some cases serve to exacerbate the harm. In a related context, involving a prosecutor's statement calling attention to the defendant's decision not to testify at trial, JUSTICE STEVENS has argued that "[i]t is unrealistic to assume that instructions on the right to silence always have a benign effect." *Lakeside v. Oregon*, 435 U.S. 333, 347 (1978) (dissenting opinion).

***

Courts below have therefore considered prompt objections and curative instructions relevant to the question whether a comment on a defendant's silence is harmless error, but irrelevant to the question whether the comment violates *Doyle*. The Court today confuses the two inquiries, and thereby eliminates much of the protection afforded by *Doyle*.

Today's radical departure from established practice is particularly inappropriate because this ground for decision was not presented either to the courts below or to this

Court. The State "concede[d]" in the Court of Appeals that "any comment referring to [defendant's] silence after that arrest [for murder] would be improper." *** It sought review in this Court not of the question whether a *Doyle* violation occurred, but whether, assuming the existence of a *Doyle* violation, the standard for appellate review should be more lenient than harmless error. *** The question decided today was therefore *not* "fairly included in the question presented for review." ** Moreover, the Court's contention that this question was argued in the briefs appears to me simply mistaken. *** The Court has overturned the judgment below, and upset the settled practice of the lower courts, on a point which the State conceded below and did not raise here, and on which respondent has had no opportunity to be heard.

Today's decision saps *Doyle* of much of its vitality. I would adhere to *Doyle*'s principles, and to the established practice of the lower courts. I dissent.

Notes

1. *Case history*

Although the accomplice, Randy Williams, admitted shooting the victim, in return for Williams's testimony, the State dropped charges of murder, aggravated kidnapping, and robbery and agreed to a sentence of two years probation. *United States ex rel. Miller v. Greer*, 789 F.2d 438, 440, 446 n.7 (7th Cir. 1986). Charles Miller was sentenced to 80 years for murder, 30 years for aggravated kidnapping, and 7 years for robbery. *Id.* at 441. The jury was aware that a "deal" between the State and Williams had been struck. 483 U.S. at 772 n.2 (Brennan, J., dissenting).

2. *The* Doyle *comments*

As part of his cross-examination of the co-defendants in *Doyle*, the prosecutor asked the following questions:

> Q. If that is all you had to do with this and you are innocent, when [the agent] arrived on the scene why didn't you tell him? **.... You are innocent?
>
> A. I am innocent. Yes Sir.
>
> Q. That's why you told the police department and [the agent] when they arrived — ...about your innocence?
>
> A.... I didn't tell them about my innocence. No. **
>
> Q. You said instead of protesting your innocence, as you do today, you said in response to a question of [the agent], — "I don't know what you are talking about."
>
> A. I believe what I said, — "What's this all about?"
>
> Q. All right, — But you didn't protest your innocence at that time?
>
> A. Not until I knew what was going on. **

Greer v. Miller, 483 U.S. at 763 n.4. How do the *Doyle* questions compare to what the prosecutor asked Miller?

3. *The curative instruction given at Miller's trial*

Many practitioners do not believe that a curative instruction really can fix the problem when an improper matter is placed before the jury, in other words, that one cannot "unring the bell." What are the reasons to think that a curative instruction will fix the problem? What are the reasons to think that it won't?

Arizona v. Fulminante

499 U.S. 279 (1991)

JUSTICE WHITE delivered an opinion, Parts I, II, and IV of which are the opinion of the Court, and Part III of which is a dissenting opinion. [JUSTICE MARSHALL, Justice BLACKMUN and JUSTICE STEVENS join this opinion in its entirety; JUSTICE SCALIA joins Parts I and II; and JUSTICE KENNEDY joins Parts I and IV.]

The Arizona Supreme Court ruled in this case that respondent Oreste Fulminante's confession, received in evidence at his trial for murder, had been coerced and that its use against him was barred by the Fifth and Fourteenth Amendments to the United States Constitution. The court also held that the harmless-error rule could not be used to save the conviction. We affirm the judgment of the Arizona court, although for different reasons than those upon which that court relied.

[handwritten margin note: Murder / Confession was coerced + is inadmissible]

I

Early in the morning of September 14, 1982, Fulminante called the Mesa, Arizona, Police Department to report that his 11-year-old stepdaughter, Jeneane Michelle Hunt, was missing. He had been caring for Jeneane while his wife, Jeneane's mother, was in the hospital. Two days later, Jeneane's body was found in the desert east of Mesa. She had been shot twice in the head at close range with a large caliber weapon, and a ligature was around her neck. Because of the decomposed condition of the body, it was impossible to tell whether she had been sexually assaulted.

Fulminante's statements to police concerning Jeneane's disappearance and his relationship with her contained a number of inconsistencies, and he became a suspect in her killing. When no charges were filed against him, Fulminante left Arizona for New Jersey. Fulminante was later convicted in New Jersey on federal charges of possession of a firearm by a felon.

Fulminante was incarcerated in the Ray Brook Federal Correctional Institution in New York. There he became friends with another inmate, Anthony Sarivola, then serving a 60-day sentence for extortion. The two men came to spend several hours a day together. Sarivola, a former police officer, had been involved in loansharking for organized crime but then became a paid informant for the Federal Bureau of Investigation. While at Ray Brook, he masqueraded as an organized crime figure. After becoming friends with Fulminante, Sarivola heard a rumor that Fulminante was suspected of killing a child in Arizona. Sarivola then raised the subject with Fulminante in several conversations, but Fulminante repeatedly denied any involvement in Jeneane's death. During one conversation, he told Sarivola that Jeneane had been killed by bikers looking for drugs; on another occasion, he said he did not know what had happened. Sarivola passed this information on to an agent of the Federal Bureau of Investigation, who instructed Sarivola to find out more.

Sarivola learned more one evening in October 1983, as he and Fulminante walked together around the prison track. Sarivola said that he knew Fulminante was "starting to get some tough treatment and whatnot" from other inmates because of the rumor. ** Sarivola offered to protect Fulminante from his fellow inmates, but told him, "'You have to tell me about it,' you know. I mean, in other words, 'For me to give you any help.'" ** Fulminante then admitted to Sarivola that he had driven Jeneane to the desert on his motorcycle, where he choked her, sexually assaulted her, and made her beg for her life, before shooting her twice in the head. **

[handwritten margin note: told him he'd protect him if told him what happened]

Sarivola was released from prison in November 1983. Fulminante was released the following May, only to be arrested the next month for another weapons violation. On September 4, 1984, Fulminante was indicted in Arizona for the first-degree murder of Jeneane.

Prior to trial, Fulminante moved to suppress the statement he had given Sarivola in prison, as well as a second confession he had given to Donna Sarivola, then Anthony Sarivola's fiancee and later his wife, following his May 1984 release from prison. He asserted that the confession to Sarivola was coerced, and that the second confession was the "fruit" of the first. ** Following the hearing, the trial court denied the motion to suppress, specifically finding that, based on the stipulated facts, the confessions were voluntary. ** The State introduced both confessions as evidence at trial, and on December 19, 1985, Fulminante was convicted of Jeneane's murder. He was subsequently sentenced to death.

Fulminante appealed, arguing, among other things, that his confession to Sarivola was the product of coercion and that its admission at trial violated his rights to due process under the Fifth and Fourteenth Amendments to the United States Constitution. After considering the evidence at trial as well as the stipulated facts before the trial court on the motion to suppress, the Arizona Supreme Court held that the confession was coerced, but initially determined that the admission of the confession at trial was harmless error, because of the overwhelming nature of the evidence against Fulminante. ** Upon Fulminante's motion for reconsideration, however, the court ruled that this Court's precedent precluded the use of the harmless-error analysis in the case of a coerced confession. ** The court therefore reversed the conviction and ordered that Fulminante be retried without the use of the confession to Sarivola. *** Because of differing views in the state and federal courts over whether the admission at trial of a coerced confession is subject to a harmless-error analysis, we granted the State's petition for certiorari. ** Although a majority of this Court finds that such a confession is subject to a harmless-error analysis, for the reasons set forth below, we affirm the judgment of the Arizona court.

II

We deal first with the State's contention that the court below erred in holding Fulminante's confession to have been coerced. The State argues that it is the totality of the circumstances that determines whether Fulminante's confession was coerced, *cf. Schneckloth v. Bustamonte*, 412 U.S. 218, 226 (1973), but contends that rather than apply this standard, the Arizona court applied a "but for" test, under which the court found that but for the promise given by Sarivola, Fulminante would not have confessed. ** In support of this argument, the State points to the Arizona court's reference to *Bram v. United States*, 168 U.S. 532 (1897). Although the Court noted in *Bram* that a confession cannot be obtained by " 'any direct or implied promises, however slight, nor by the exertion of any improper influence,' " *id.* at 542–543, ** it is clear that this passage from *Bram*, which under current precedent does not state the standard for determining the voluntariness of a confession, was not relied on by the Arizona court in reaching its conclusion. Rather, the court cited this language as part of a longer quotation from an Arizona case which accurately described the State's burden of proof for establishing voluntariness. ** Indeed, the Arizona Supreme Court stated that a "determination regarding the voluntariness of a confession…must be viewed in a totality of the circumstances" ** and under that standard plainly found that Fulminante's statement to Sarivola had been coerced.

In applying the totality of the circumstances test to determine that the confession to Sarivola was coerced, the Arizona Supreme Court focused on a number of relevant facts. First, the court noted that "because [Fulminante] was an alleged child murderer, he was in danger of physical harm at the hands of other inmates." ** In addition, Sarivola was aware that Fulminante had been receiving "'rough treatment from the guys.'" ** Using his knowledge of these threats, Sarivola offered to protect Fulminante in exchange for a confession to Jeneane's murder, ** and "[i]n response to Sarivola's offer of protection, [Fulminante] confessed." ** Agreeing with Fulminante that "Sarivola's promise was 'extremely coercive,'" ** the Arizona court declared: "[T]he confession was obtained as a direct result of extreme coercion and was tendered in the belief that the defendant's life was in jeopardy if he did not confess. This is a true coerced confession in every sense of the word." **

We normally give great deference to the factual findings of the state court. *Davis v. North Carolina*, 384 U.S. 737, 741 (1966). ** Nevertheless, "the ultimate issue of 'voluntariness' is a legal question requiring independent federal determination." *Miller v. Fenton*, 474 U.S. 104, 110 (1985). **

Although the question is a close one, we agree with the Arizona Supreme Court's conclusion that Fulminante's confession was coerced. *** The Arizona Supreme Court found a credible threat of physical violence unless Fulminante confessed. Our cases have made clear that a finding of coercion need not depend upon actual violence by a government agent; *** a credible threat is sufficient. As we have said, "coercion can be mental as well as physical, and...the blood of the accused is not the only hallmark of an unconstitutional inquisition." *Blackburn v. Alabama*, 361 U.S. 199, 206 (1960). ** As in *Payne v. Arkansas*, 356 U.S. 560, 561 (1958)], where the Court found that a confession was coerced because the interrogating police officer had promised that if the accused confessed, the officer would protect the accused from an angry mob outside the jailhouse door, [*id.*] at 564–565, 567, so too here, the Arizona Supreme Court found that it was fear of physical violence, absent protection from his friend (and Government agent) Sarivola, which motivated Fulminante to confess. Accepting the Arizona court's finding, permissible on this record, that there was a credible threat of physical violence, we agree with its conclusion that Fulminante's will was overborne in such a way as to render his confession the product of coercion.

III

Four of us, Justices Marshall, Blackmun, Stevens, and myself, would affirm the judgment of the Arizona Supreme Court on the ground that the harmless-error rule is inapplicable to erroneously admitted coerced confessions. We thus disagree with the Justices who have a contrary view.

The majority today abandons what until now the Court has regarded as the "axiomatic [proposition] that a defendant in a criminal case is deprived of due process of law if his conviction is founded, in whole or in part, upon an involuntary confession, without regard for the truth or falsity of the confession, *Rogers v. Richmond*, 365 U.S. 534 (1961), and even though there is ample evidence aside from the confession to support the conviction." ** *Jackson v. Denno*, 378 U.S. 368, 376 (1964). The Court has repeatedly stressed that the view that the admission of a coerced confession can be harmless error because of the other evidence to support the verdict is "an impermissible doctrine," *Lynumn v. Illinois*, 372 U.S. 528, 537 (1963); for "the admission in evidence, over objection, of the coerced confession vitiates the judgment because it violates the Due Process Clause of the Fourteenth Amendment," *Payne*, [356 U.S.] at 568. *** [T]he rule was the same even when another confession of the defendant had been properly admitted into evidence. Today, a majority of the Court, without any justification, *cf.*

[handwritten margin note: harmless-error rule is inapplicable to erroneously admitted coerced confession (4-5)]

Arizona v. Rumsey, 467 U.S. 203, 212 (1984), overrules this vast body of precedent without a word and in so doing dislodges one of the fundamental tenets of our criminal justice system.

In extending to coerced confessions the harmless-error rule of *Chapman v. California, supra,* the majority declares that because the Court has applied that analysis to numerous other "trial errors," there is no reason that it should not apply to an error of this nature as well. The four of us remain convinced, however, that we should abide by our cases that have refused to apply the harmless-error rule to coerced confessions, for a coerced confession is fundamentally different from other types of erroneously admitted evidence to which the rule has been applied. Indeed, as the majority concedes, *Chapman* itself recognized that prior cases "have indicated that there are some constitutional rights so basic to a fair trial that their infraction can *never* be treated as harmless error," and it placed in that category the constitutional rule against using a defendant's coerced confession against him at his criminal trial. 386 U.S. at 23 & n.8 (emphasis added). ***

Chapman specifically noted three constitutional errors that could not be categorized as harmless error: using a coerced confession against a defendant in a criminal trial, depriving a defendant of counsel, and trying a defendant before a biased judge. The majority attempts to distinguish the use of a coerced confession from the other two errors listed in *Chapman* first by distorting the decision in *Payne,* and then by drawing a meaningless dichotomy between "trial errors" and "structural defects" in the trial process. Viewing *Payne* as merely rejecting a test whereby the admission of a coerced confession could stand if there were "sufficient evidence," other than the confession, to support the conviction, the majority suggests that the Court in *Payne* might have reached a different result had it been considering a harmless-error test. ** It is clear, though, that in *Payne* the Court recognized that *regardless* of the amount of other evidence, "the admission in evidence, over objection, of the coerced confession vitiates the judgment," because "where, as here, a coerced confession constitutes a part of the evidence before the jury and a general verdict is returned, no one can say what credit and weight the jury gave to the confession." 356 U.S. at 568. The inability to assess its effect on a conviction causes the admission at trial of a coerced confession to "defy analysis by 'harmless-error' standards," *cf. post,* ** just as certainly as do deprivation of counsel and trial before a biased judge.

The majority also attempts to distinguish "trial errors" which occur "during the presentation of the case to the jury," ** and which it deems susceptible to harmless-error analysis, from "structural defects in the constitution of the trial mechanism," ** which the majority concedes cannot be so analyzed. This effort fails, for our jurisprudence on harmless error has not classified so neatly the errors at issue. For example, we have held susceptible to harmless-error analysis the failure to instruct the jury on the presumption of innocence, *Kentucky v. Whorton,* 441 U.S. 786 (1979), while finding it impossible to analyze in terms of harmless error the failure to instruct a jury on the reasonable-doubt standard. *Jackson v. Virginia,* 443 U.S. 307, 320 n.14 (1979). These cases cannot be reconciled by labeling the former "trial error" and the latter not, for both concern the exact same stage in the trial proceedings. Rather, these cases can be reconciled only by considering the nature of the right at issue and the effect of an error upon the trial. A jury instruction on the presumption of innocence is not constitutionally required in every case to satisfy due process, because such an instruction merely offers an additional safeguard beyond that provided by the constitutionally required instruction on reasonable doubt. *See Whorton,* [441 U.S.] at 789. ** While it may be possible to analyze as harmless the omission of a presumption of innocence instruction when the required reasonable-doubt instruction has been given, it is impossible to assess the effect on the jury of the omission of the more fundamental instruction on reasonable doubt. In addition, omission of a reasonable-doubt instruction, though a "trial error," distorts the very structure of the trial because it creates the risk that the jury will convict the defendant even if the State has not met its required burden of proof. *Cf. In re Winship*, 397 U.S. 358, 364 (1970). **

These same concerns counsel against applying harmless-error analysis to the admission of a coerced confession. A defendant's confession is "probably the most probative and damaging evidence that can be admitted against him," *Cruz v. New York*, 481 U.S. 186, 195 (1987) (White, J., dissenting), so damaging that a jury should not be expected to ignore it even if told to do so, *Bruton v. United States*, 391 U.S. 123, 140 (1968) (White, J., dissenting), and because in any event it is impossible to know what credit and weight the jury gave to the confession. *Cf. Payne*, [356 U.S.] at 568. Concededly, this reason is insufficient to justify a *per se* bar to the use of *any* confession. Thus, *Milton v. Wainwright*, 407 U.S. 371 (1972), applied harmless-error analysis to a confession obtained and introduced in circumstances that violated the defendant's Sixth Amendment right to counsel. *** Similarly, the Courts of Appeals have held that the introduction of incriminating statements taken from defendants in violation of *Miranda v. Arizona*, 384 U.S. 436 (1966), is subject to treatment as harmless error. ***

Nevertheless, in declaring that it is "impossible to create a meaningful distinction between confessions elicited in violation of the Sixth Amendment and those in violation of the Fourteenth Amendment," ** the majority overlooks the obvious. Neither *Milton v. Wainwright* nor any of the other cases upon which the majority relies involved a defendant's *coerced* confession, nor were there present in these cases the distinctive reasons underlying the exclusion of coerced incriminating statements of the defendant. *** First, some coerced confessions may be untrustworthy. *Jackson v. Denno*, 378 U.S. at 385–386. ** Consequently, admission of coerced confessions may distort the truth-seeking function of the trial upon which the majority focuses. More importantly, however, the use of coerced confessions, "whether true or false," is forbidden "because the methods used to extract them offend an underlying principle in the enforcement of our criminal law: that ours is an accusatorial and not an inquisitorial system—a system in which the State must establish guilt by evidence independently and freely secured and may not by coercion prove its charge against an accused out of his own mouth," *Rogers v. Richmond*, 365 U.S. at 540–541. ** This reflects the "strongly felt attitude of our society that important human values are sacrificed where an agency of the government, in the course of securing a conviction, wrings a confession out of an accused against his will," *Blackburn v. Alabama*, 361 U.S. at 206–207, as well as "the deep-rooted feeling that the police must obey the law while enforcing the law; that in the end life and liberty can be as much endangered from illegal methods used to convict those thought to be criminals as from the actual criminals themselves," *Spano* [*v. New York*, 360 U.S. 315,] 320–321 [(1959)]. Thus, permitting a coerced confession to be part of the evidence on which a jury is free to base its verdict of guilty is inconsistent with the thesis that ours is not an inquisitorial system of criminal justice. *Cf. Chambers v. Florida*, 309 U.S. [227,] 235–238 [1940].

As the majority concedes, there are other constitutional errors that invalidate a conviction even though there may be no reasonable doubt that the defendant is guilty and would be convicted absent the trial error. For example, a judge in a criminal trial "is prohibited from entering a judgment of conviction or directing the jury to come forward with such a verdict, ** regardless of how overwhelmingly the evidence may point in that direction." ** A defendant is entitled to counsel at trial, *Gideon v. Wainwright*, 372 U.S. 335 (1963), and as *Chapman* recognized, violating this right can never be harmless error. 386 U.S. at 23 & n.8. *See also White v. Maryland*, 373 U.S. 59 (1963), where a conviction was set aside because the defendant had not had counsel at a preliminary hearing without regard to the showing of prejudice. In *Vasquez v. Hillery*, 474 U.S. 254 (1986), a defendant was found guilty beyond reasonable doubt, but the conviction had been set aside because of the unlawful exclusion of members of the defendant's race from the grand jury that indicted him, despite overwhelming evidence of his guilt. The error at the grand jury stage struck at fundamental values of our society and "undermine[d] the structural integrity of the criminal tribunal itself, and [was] not amenable to harmless-error review." *Id.* at 263–264. *Vasquez*, like *Chapman*, also noted that rule of automatic reversal when a defendant is tried before a judge with a financial interest in the outcome, ** despite a lack of any indication that bias influenced the decision. *Waller v. Georgia*, 467 U.S. 39, 49 (1984), recognized that violation of the guarantee of a public trial required reversal without any showing of prejudice and even though the values of a public trial may be intangible and unprovable in any particular case.

The search for truth is indeed central to our system of justice, but "certain constitutional rights are not, and should not be, subject to harmless-error analysis because those rights protect important values that are unrelated to the truth-seeking function of the trial." *Rose v. Clark*, 478 U.S. [570,] 587 [(1986)] (Stevens, J., concurring in judgment). The right of a defendant not to have his coerced confession used against him is among those rights, for using a coerced confession "abort[s] the basic trial process" and "render[s] a trial fundamentally unfair." *Id.* at 577, 578 n.6.

For the foregoing reasons the four of us would adhere to the consistent line of authority that has recognized as a basic tenet of our criminal justice system, before and after both *Miranda* and *Chapman*, the prohibition against using a defendant's coerced confession against him at his criminal trial. *Stare decisis* is "of fundamental importance to the rule of law," *Welch v. Texas Dept. of Highways and Public Transportation*, 483 U.S. 468, 494 (1987); the majority offers no convincing reason for overturning our long line of decisions requiring the exclusion of coerced confessions.

IV

Since five Justices have determined that harmless-error analysis applies to coerced confessions, it becomes necessary to evaluate under that ruling the admissibility of Fulminante's confession to Sarivola. ** *Chapman v. California*, 386 U.S. at 24, made clear that "before a federal constitutional error can be held harmless, the court must be able to declare a belief that it was harmless beyond a reasonable doubt." The Court has the power to review the record *de novo* in order to determine an error's harmlessness. *See ibid.* ** In so doing, it must be determined whether the State has met its burden of demonstrating that the admission of the confession to Sarivola did not contribute to Fulminante's conviction. *Chapman*, [386 U.S.] at 26. Five of us are of the view that the State has not carried its burden and accordingly affirm the judgment of the court below reversing respondent's conviction.

A confession is like no other evidence. Indeed, "the defendant's own confession is probably the most probative and damaging evidence that can be admitted against him.... [T]he admissions of a defendant come from the actor himself, the most knowledgeable and unimpeachable source of information about his past conduct. Certainly, confessions have profound impact on the jury, so much so that we may justifiably doubt its ability to put them out of mind even if told to do so." *Bruton v. United States*, 391 U.S. at 139–140 (White, J., dissenting). ** While some statements by a defendant may concern isolated aspects of the crime or may be incriminating only when linked to other evidence, a full confession in which the defendant discloses the motive for and means of the crime may tempt the jury to rely upon that evidence alone in reaching its decision. In the case of a coerced confession such as that given by Fulminante to Sarivola, the risk that the confession is unreliable, coupled with the profound impact that the confession has upon the jury, requires a reviewing court to exercise extreme caution before determining that the admission of the confession at trial was harmless.

In the Arizona Supreme Court's initial opinion, in which it determined that harmless-error analysis could be applied to the confession, the court found that the admissible second confession to Donna Sarivola rendered the first confession to Anthony Sarivola cumulative. ** The court also noted that circumstantial physical evidence concerning the wounds, the ligature around Jeneane's neck, the location of the body, and the presence of motorcycle tracks at the scene corroborated the second confession. *Ibid.* The court concluded that "due to the overwhelming evidence adduced from the second confession, if there had not been a first confession, the jury would still have had the same basic evidence to convict" Fulminante. **

We have a quite different evaluation of the evidence. Our review of the record leads us to conclude that the State has failed to meet its burden of establishing, beyond a reasonable doubt, that the admission of Fulminante's confession to Anthony Sarivola was harmless error. Three considerations compel this result.

First, the transcript discloses that both the trial court and the State recognized that a successful prosecution depended on the jury believing the two confessions. Absent the confessions, it is unlikely that Fulminante would have been prosecuted at all, because the physical evidence from the scene and other circumstantial evidence would have been insufficient to convict. Indeed, no indictment was filed until nearly two years after the murder. *** Although the police had suspected Fulminante from the beginning, as the prosecutor acknowledged in his opening statement to the jury, "[W]hat brings us to Court, what makes this case fileable, and prosecutable and triable is that later, Mr. Fulminante confesses this crime to Anthony Sarivola and later, to Donna Sarivola, his wife." ** After trial began, during a renewed hearing on Fulminante's motion to suppress, the trial court opined, "You know, I think from what little I know about this trial, the character of this man [Sarivola] for truthfulness or untruthfulness and his credibility is the centerpiece of this case, is it not?" The prosecutor responded, "It's very important, there's no doubt." ** Finally, in his closing argument, the prosecutor prefaced his discussion of the two confessions by conceding: "[W]e have a lot of [circumstantial] evidence that indicates that this is our suspect, this is the fellow that did it, but it's a little short as far as saying that it's proof that he actually put the gun to the girl's head and killed her. So it's a little short of that. We recognize that." **

Second, the jury's assessment of the confession to Donna Sarivola could easily have depended in large part on the presence of the confession to Anthony Sarivola. Absent the admission at trial of the first confession, the jurors might have found Donna Sarivola's story unbelievable. Fulminante's confession to Donna Sarivola allegedly occurred in May 1984, on the day he was released from Ray Brook, as she and Anthony Sarivola drove Fulminante from New York to Pennsylvania. Donna Sarivola testified that Fulminante, whom she had never before met, confessed in detail about Jeneane's brutal murder in response to her casual question concerning why he was going to visit friends in

Pennsylvania instead of returning to his family in Arizona. ** Although she testified that she was "disgusted" by Fulminante's disclosures, ** she stated that she took no steps to notify authorities of what she had learned. ** In fact, she claimed that she barely discussed the matter with Anthony Sarivola, who was in the car and overheard Fulminante's entire conversation with Donna. ** Despite her disgust for Fulminante, Donna Sarivola later went on a second trip with him. ** Although Sarivola informed authorities that he had driven Fulminante to Pennsylvania, he did not mention Donna's presence in the car or her conversation with Fulminante. ** Only when questioned by authorities in June 1985 did Anthony Sarivola belatedly recall the confession to Donna more than a year before, and only then did he ask if she would be willing to discuss the matter with authorities. **

Although some of the details in the confession to Donna Sarivola were corroborated by circumstantial evidence, many, including details that Jeneane was choked and sexually assaulted, were not. ** As to other aspects of the second confession, including Fulminante's motive and state of mind, the *only* corroborating evidence was the first confession to Anthony Sarivola. *** Thus, contrary to what the Arizona Supreme Court found, it is clear that the jury might have believed that the two confessions reinforced and corroborated each other. For this reason, one confession was *not* merely cumulative of the other. While in some cases two confessions, delivered on different occasions to different listeners, might be viewed as being independent of each other, *cf. Milton v. Wainwright*, 407 U.S. 371 (1972), it strains credulity to think that the jury so viewed the two confessions in this case, especially given the close relationship between Donna and Anthony Sarivola.

The jurors could also have believed that Donna Sarivola had a motive to lie about the confession in order to assist her husband. Anthony Sarivola received significant benefits from federal authorities, including payment for information, immunity from prosecution, and eventual placement in the federal Witness Protection Program. ** In addition, the jury might have found Donna motivated by her own desire for favorable treatment, for she, too, was ultimately placed in the Witness Protection Program. **

Third, the admission of the first confession led to the admission of other evidence prejudicial to Fulminante. For example, the State introduced evidence that Fulminante knew of Sarivola's connections with organized crime in an attempt to explain why Fulminante would have been motivated to confess to Sarivola in seeking protection. ** Absent the confession, this evidence would have had no relevance and would have been inadmissible at trial. The Arizona Supreme Court found that the evidence of Sarivola's connections with organized crime reflected on Sarivola's character, not Fulminante's, and noted that the evidence could have been used to impeach Sarivola. ** This analysis overlooks the fact that had the confession not been admitted, there would have been no reason for Sarivola to testify and thus no need to impeach his testimony. Moreover, we cannot agree that the evidence did not reflect on Fulminante's character as well, for it depicted him as someone who willingly sought out the company of criminals. It is quite possible that this evidence led the jury to view Fulminante as capable of murder. ***

Finally, although our concern here is with the effect of the erroneous admission of the confession on Fulminante's conviction, it is clear that the presence of the confession also influenced the sentencing phase of the trial. Under Arizona law, the trial judge is the sentencer. ** At the sentencing hearing, the admissibility of information regarding aggravating circumstances is governed by the rules of evidence applicable to criminal trials. ** In this case, "based upon admissible evidence produced at the trial," ** the judge found that only one aggravating circumstance existed beyond a reasonable doubt, *i.e.*, that the murder was committed in "an *especially* heinous, cruel, and depraved manner." ** In reaching this conclusion, the judge relied heavily on evidence concerning the manner of the killing and Fulminante's motives and state of mind which could only be found in the two confessions. For example, in labeling the murder "cruel," the judge focused in part on Fulminante's alleged statements that he choked Jeneane and made her get on her knees and beg before killing her. ** Although the circumstantial evidence was not inconsistent with this determination, neither was it sufficient to make such a finding beyond a reasonable doubt. Indeed, the sentencing judge acknowledged that the confessions were only partly corroborated by other evidence. **

In declaring that Fulminante "acted with an especially heinous and depraved state of mind," the sentencing judge relied solely on the two confessions. ** While the judge found that the statements in the confessions regarding the alleged sexual assault on Jeneane should not be considered on the issue of cruelty because they were not corroborated by other evidence, the judge determined that they were worthy of belief on the issue of Fulminante's state of mind. The judge then focused on Anthony Sarivola's statement that Fulminante had made vulgar references to Jeneane during the first confession, and on Donna Sarivola's statement that Fulminante had made similar comments to her. ** Finally, the judge stressed that Fulminante's alleged comments to the Sarivolas concerning torture, choking, and sexual assault, "whether they all occurred or not," depicted "a man who was bragging and relishing the crime he committed."

Although the sentencing judge might have reached the same conclusions even without the confession to Anthony Sarivola, it is impossible to say so beyond a reasonable doubt. Furthermore, the judge's assessment of Donna Sarivola's credibility, and hence the reliability of the second confession, might well have been influenced by the corroborative effect of the erroneously admitted first confession. Indeed, the fact that the sentencing judge focused on the similarities between the two confessions in determining that they were reliable suggests that either of the confessions alone, even when considered with all the other evidence, would have been insufficient to permit the judge to find an aggravating circumstance beyond a reasonable doubt as a requisite prelude to imposing the death penalty.

Because a majority of the Court has determined that Fulminante's confession to Anthony Sarivola was coerced and because a majority has determined that admitting this confession was not harmless beyond a reasonable doubt, we agree with the Arizona Supreme Court's conclusion that Fulminante is entitled to a new trial at which the confession is not admitted. Accordingly the judgment of the Arizona Supreme Court is

Affirmed.

[CHIEF JUSTICE REHNQUIST's dissent, and JUSTICE KENNEDY's concurrence in the judgment, are omitted.]

Notes

1. *Subsequent case history*

At his new trial, Oreste Fulminante was once again convicted and sentenced to death; however, the Arizona Supreme Court again reversed the conviction and ordered a new trial. *Arizona v. Fulminante*, 975 P.2d 75 (Ariz. 1999). On September 8, 1999, Fulminante pled guilty to murder and kidnapping and was sentenced to thirty-three years in prison.

2. *Additional facts*

In footnote 2, the Court states:

There are additional facts in the record, not relied upon by the Arizona Supreme Court, which also support a finding of coercion. Fulminante possesses low average to average intelligence; he dropped out of school in the fourth grade. ** He is short in stature and slight in build. ** Although he had been in prison before, ** he had not always adapted well to the stress of prison life. While incarcerated at the age of 26, he had "felt threatened by the [prison] population," ** and he therefore requested that he be placed in protective custody. Once there, however, he was unable to cope with the isolation and was admitted to a psychiatric hospital. ***

The Court observed that it has previously recognized that factors such as the ones in this case are relevant in determining whether a defendant's will has been overborne. *See, e.g., Payne v. Arkansas*, 356 U.S. 560, 567 (1958) (lack of education); *Reck v. Pate*, 367 U.S. 433, 441 (1961) (low intelligence). *Cf. Schneckloth v. Bustamonte*, 412 U.S. 218, 226 (1973) (listing potential factors). To what degree did such factors influence the Court's ultimate decision in this case?

3. *Interlocking problems with the evidence*

In footnote 9, the Court observed,

The inadmissible confession to Anthony Sarivola was itself subject to serious challenge. Sarivola's lack of moral integrity was demonstrated by his testimony that he had worked for organized crime during the time he was a uniformed police officer. ** His overzealous approach to gathering information for which he would be paid by authorities ** was revealed by his admission that he had fabricated a tape recording in connection with an earlier, unrelated FBI investigation. ** He received immunity in connection with the information he provided. ** His eagerness to get in and stay in the federal Witness Protection Program provided a motive for giving detailed information to authorities. ** During his first report of the confession, Sarivola failed to hint at numerous details concerning an alleged sexual assault on Jeneane; he mentioned them for the first time more than a year later during further interrogation, at which he also recalled, for the first time, the confession to Donna Sarivola. ***

After explaining the difficulties in the admissibility of the confession, the Court then explained that "[t]he impeaching effect of each of these factors was undoubtedly undercut by the presence of the second confession, which, not surprisingly, recounted a quite similar story and thus corroborated the first confession. Thus, each confession, though easily impeachable if viewed in isolation, became difficult to discount when viewed in conjunction with the other."

What is your assessment of why the Court relegated this observation to a footnote, rather than including it within the text of the opinion?

Brecht v. Abrahamson
507 U.S. 619 (1993)

CHIEF JUSTICE REHNQUIST delivered the opinion of the Court.

In *Chapman v. California*, 386 U.S. 18, 24 (1967), we held that the standard for determining whether a conviction must be set aside because of federal constitutional error is whether the error "was harmless beyond a reasonable doubt." In this case we must decide whether the *Chapman* harmless-error standard applies in determining whether the prosecution's use for impeachment purposes of petitioner's post-*Miranda* *** silence, in violation of due process under *Doyle v. Ohio*, 426 U.S. 610 (1976), entitles petitioner to habeas corpus relief. We hold that it does not. Instead, the standard for determining whether habeas relief must be granted is whether the *Doyle* error "had substantial and injurious effect or influence in determining the jury's verdict." *Kotteakos v. United States*, 328 U.S. 750, 776 (1946). The *Kotteakos* harmless-error standard is better tailored to the nature and purpose of collateral review than the *Chapman* standard, and application of a less onerous harmless-error standard on habeas promotes the considerations underlying our habeas jurisprudence. Applying this standard, we conclude that petitioner is not entitled to habeas relief.

Petitioner Todd A. Brecht was serving time in a Georgia prison for felony theft when his sister and her husband, Molly and Roger Hartman, paid the restitution for petitioner's crime and assumed temporary custody of him. The Hartmans brought petitioner home with them to Alma, Wisconsin, where he was to reside with them before entering a halfway house. This caused some tension in the Hartman household because Roger Hartman, a local district attorney, disapproved of petitioner's heavy drinking habits and homosexual orientation, not to mention his previous criminal exploits. To make the best of the situation, though, the Hartmans told petitioner, on more than one occasion, that he was not to drink alcohol or engage in homosexual activities in their home. Just one week after his arrival, however, petitioner violated this house rule.

While the Hartmans were away, petitioner broke into their liquor cabinet and began drinking. He then found a rifle in an upstairs room and began shooting cans in the backyard. When Roger Hartman returned home from work, petitioner shot him in the back and sped off in Mrs. Hartman's car. Hartman crawled to a neighbor's house to summon help. (The downstairs phone in the Hartmans' house was inoperable because petitioner had taken the receiver on the upstairs phone off the hook.) Help came, but Hartman's wound proved fatal. Meanwhile, petitioner had driven Mrs. Hartman's car into a ditch in a nearby town. When a police officer stopped to offer assistance, petitioner told him that his sister knew about his car mishap and had called a tow truck. Petitioner then hitched a ride to Winona, Minnesota, where he was stopped by police. At first he tried to conceal his identity, but he later identified himself and was arrested. When he was told that he was being held for the shooting, petitioner replied that "it was a big mistake" and asked to talk with "somebody that would understand [him]." ** Petitioner was returned to Wisconsin, and thereafter was given his *Miranda* warnings at an arraignment.

Then petitioner was charged with first-degree murder. At trial in the Circuit Court for Buffalo County, he took the stand and admitted shooting Hartman, but claimed it was an accident. According to petitioner, when he saw Hartman pulling into the driveway on the evening of the shooting, he ran to replace the gun in the upstairs room where he had found it. But as he was running toward the stairs in the downstairs hallway, he tripped, causing the rifle to discharge the fatal shot. After the shooting, Hartman disappeared, so petitioner drove off in Mrs. Hartman's car to find him. Upon spotting Hartman at his neighbor's door, however, petitioner panicked and drove away.

The State argued that petitioner's account was belied by the fact that he had failed to get help for Hartman, fled the Hartmans' home immediately after the shooting, and lied to the police officer who came upon him in the ditch about having called Mrs. Hartman. In addition, the State pointed out that petitioner had failed to mention anything about the shooting being an accident to the officer who found him in the ditch, the man who gave him a ride to Winona, or the officers who eventually arrested him.

Over the objections of defense counsel, the State also asked petitioner during cross-examination whether he had told anyone at any time before trial that the shooting was an accident, to which petitioner replied "no," and made several references to petitioner's pretrial silence during closing argument. *** Finally, the State offered extrinsic evidence tending to contradict petitioner's story, including the path the bullet traveled through Mr. Hartman's body (horizontal to slightly downward) and the location where the rifle was found after the shooting (outside), as well as evidence of motive (petitioner's hostility toward Mr. Hartman because of his disapproval of petitioner's sexual orientation).

The jury returned a guilty verdict, and petitioner was sentenced to life imprisonment. The Wisconsin Court of Appeals set the conviction aside on the ground that the State's references to petitioner's post-*Miranda* silence ** violated due process under *Doyle v. Ohio*, 426 U.S. 610 * (1976), and that this error was sufficiently "prejudicial" to require reversal. ** The Wisconsin Supreme Court reinstated the conviction. Although it agreed that the State's use of petitioner's post-*Miranda* silence was impermissible, the court determined that this error "'was harmless beyond a reasonable doubt.'" *State v. Brecht*, 421 N.W.2d 96, 104 (1988) (*quoting Chapman v. California*, 386 U.S. 18, 24 (1967)). In finding the *Doyle* violation harmless, the court noted that the State's "improper references to Brecht's silence were infrequent," in that they "comprised less than two pages of a 900 page transcript, or a few minutes in a four day trial in which twenty-five witnesses testified," and that the State's evidence of guilt was compelling. **

Petitioner then sought a writ of habeas corpus under 28 U.S.C. § 2254, reasserting his *Doyle* claim. The District Court agreed that the State's use of petitioner's post-*Miranda* silence violated *Doyle*, but disagreed with the Wisconsin Supreme Court that this error was harmless beyond a reasonable doubt, and set aside the conviction. ** The District Court based its harmless-error determination on its view that the State's evidence of guilt was not "overwhelming," and that the State's references to petitioner's post-*Miranda* silence, though "not extensive," were "crucial" because petitioner's defense turned on his credibility. ** The Court of Appeals for the Seventh Circuit reversed. It, too, concluded that the State's references to petitioner's post-*Miranda* silence violated *Doyle*, but it disagreed with both the standard that the District Court had applied in conducting its harmless-error inquiry and the result it reached. **

The Court of Appeals held that the *Chapman* harmless-error standard does not apply in reviewing *Doyle* error on federal habeas. Instead, because of the "prophylactic" nature of the *Doyle* rule, ** as well as the costs attendant to reversing state convictions on collateral review, ** the Court of Appeals held that the standard for determining whether petitioner was entitled to habeas relief was whether the *Doyle* violation "'had substantial and injurious effect or influence in determining the jury's verdict.'" ** Applying this standard, the Court of Appeals concluded that petitioner was not entitled to relief because, "given the many more, and entirely proper, references to [petitioner's] silence preceding arraignment," he could not contend with a "straight face" that the State's use of his post-*Miranda* silence had a "substantial and injurious effect" on the jury's verdict. **

We granted certiorari to resolve a conflict between Courts of Appeals on the question whether the *Chapman* harmless-error standard applies on collateral review of *Doyle* violations *** and now affirm.

We are the sixth court to pass on the question whether the State's use for impeachment purposes of petitioner's post-*Miranda* silence requires reversal of his murder conviction. Petitioner urges us to even the count, and decide matters in his favor once and for all. He argues that the *Chapman* harmless-error standard applies with equal force on collateral review of *Doyle* error. According to petitioner, the need to prevent state courts from relaxing their standards on direct review of *Doyle* claims, and the confusion which would ensue were we to adopt the *Kotteakos* harmless-error standard on collateral review, require application of the *Chapman* standard here. Before considering these arguments, however, we must first characterize the nature of *Doyle* error itself.

In *Doyle v. Ohio*, 426 U.S. at 619, we held that "the use for impeachment purposes of [a defendant's] silence, at the time of arrest and after receiving *Miranda* warnings, violate[s] the Due Process Clause of the Fourteenth Amendment." This rule "rests on 'the fundamental unfairness of implicitly assuring a suspect that his silence will not be used against him and then using his silence to impeach an explanation subsequently offered at trial.'" *Wainwright v. Greenfield*, 474 U.S. 284, 291 (1986). ** The "implicit assurance" upon which we have relied in our *Doyle* line of cases is the right-to-remain-silent component of *Miranda*. Thus, the Constitution does not prohibit the use for impeachment purposes of a defendant's silence prior to arrest, *Jenkins v. Anderson*, 447 U.S. 231, 239 (1980), or after arrest if no *Miranda* warnings are given, *Fletcher v. Weir*, 455 U.S. 603, 606–607 (1982) (*per curiam*). Such silence is probative and does not rest on any implied assurance by law enforcement authorities that it will carry no penalty. *See* 447 U.S. at 239.

This case illustrates the point well. The first time petitioner claimed that the shooting was an accident was when he took the stand at trial. It was entirely proper—and probative—for the State to impeach his testimony by pointing out that petitioner had failed to tell anyone before the time he received his *Miranda* warnings at his arraignment about the shooting being an accident. Indeed, if the shooting was an accident, petitioner had every reason—including to clear his name and preserve evidence supporting his version of the events—to offer his account immediately following the shooting. On the other hand, the State's references to petitioner's silence after that point in time, or more generally to petitioner's failure to come forward with his version of events at any time before trial, ** crossed the *Doyle* line. For it is conceivable that, once petitioner had been given his *Miranda* warnings, he decided to stand on his right to remain silent because he believed his silence would not be used against him at trial.

The Court of Appeals characterized *Doyle* as "a prophylactic rule." ** It reasoned that, since the need for *Doyle* stems from the implicit assurance that flows from *Miranda* warnings, and "the warnings required by *Miranda* are not themselves part of the Constitution," "*Doyle* is...a prophylactic rule designed to protect another prophylactic rule from erosion or misuse." ** But *Doyle* was not simply a further extension of the *Miranda* prophylactic rule. Rather, as we have discussed, it is rooted in fundamental fairness and due process concerns. However real these concerns, *Doyle* does not "'overprotect[]'" them. *Duckworth v. Eagan*, 492 U.S. 195, 209 (1989) (O'CONNOR, J., concurring). Under the rationale of *Doyle*, due process is violated whenever the prosecution uses for impeachment purposes a defendant's post-*Miranda* silence. *Doyle* thus does not bear the hallmarks of a prophylactic rule.

Instead, we think *Doyle* error fits squarely into the category of constitutional violations which we have characterized as "'trial error.'" *See Arizona v. Fulminante*, 499 U.S. 279, 307 (1991). Trial error "occur[s] during the presentation of the case to the jury," and is amenable to harmless-error analysis because it "may...be quantitatively assessed in the context of other evidence presented in order to determine [the effect it had on the trial]." *Id.* at 307–308. At the other end of the spectrum of constitutional errors lie "structural defects in the constitution of the trial mechanism, which defy analysis by 'harmless-error' standards." *Id.* at 309. The existence of such defects—deprivation of the right to counsel, *** for example—requires automatic reversal of the conviction be-cause they infect the entire trial process. *See id.* at 309–310. Since our landmark deci-sion in *Chapman v. California,* 386 U.S. 18 (1967), we have applied the harmless-be-yond-a-reasonable-doubt standard in reviewing claims of constitutional error of the trial type.

In *Chapman,* we considered whether the prosecution's reference to the defendants' failure to testify at trial, in violation of the Fifth Amendment privilege against self-in-crimination, *** required reversal of their convictions. We rejected the argument that the Constitution requires a blanket rule of automatic reversal in the case of constitu-tional error, and concluded instead that "there may be some constitutional errors which in the setting of a particular case are so unimportant and insignificant that they may, consistent with the Federal Constitution, be deemed harmless." *Id.* at 22. After examin-ing existing harmless-error rules, including the federal rule (28 U.S.C. §2111), we held that "before a federal constitutional error can be held harmless, the court must be able to declare a belief that it was harmless beyond a reasonable doubt." 386 U.S. at 24. The State bears the burden of proving that an error passes muster under this standard.

Chapman reached this Court on direct review, as have most of the cases in which we have applied its harmless-error standard. Although we have applied the *Chapman* stan-dard in a handful of federal habeas cases, *see, e.g., Yates v. Evatt,* 500 U.S. 391 (1991); *Rose v. Clark,* 478 U.S. 570 (1986); *Milton v. Wainwright,* 407 U.S. 371 (1972); ** we have yet squarely to address its applicability on collateral review. *** Petitioner contends that we are bound by these habeas cases, by way of *stare decisis,* from holding that the *Kotteakos* harmless-error standard applies on habeas review of *Doyle* error. But since we have never squarely addressed the issue, and have at most assumed the applicability of the *Chapman* standard on habeas, we are free to address the issue on the merits. *See Edelman v. Jordan,* 415 U.S. 651 (1974).

The federal habeas corpus statute is silent on this point. It permits federal courts to en-tertain a habeas petition on behalf of a state prisoner "only on the ground that he is in custody in violation of the Constitution or laws or treaties of the United States," 28 U.S.C. §2254(a), and directs simply that the court "dispose of the matter as law and justice re-quire," §2243. The statute says nothing about the standard for harmless-error review in habeas cases. Respondent urges us to fill this gap with the *Kotteakos* standard, under which an error requires reversal only if it "had substantial and injurious effect or influ-ence in determining the jury's verdict." *Kotteakos v. United States,* 328 U.S. at 776. This standard is grounded in the federal harmless-error statute. 28 U.S.C. §2111 ("On the hearing of any appeal or writ of certiorari in any case, the court shall give judgment after an examination of the record without regard to errors or defects which do not affect the substantial rights of the parties"). *** On its face §2111 might seem to address the situa-tion at hand, but to date we have limited its application to claims of nonconstitutional error in federal criminal cases. *See, e.g., United States v. Lane,* 474 U.S. 438 (1986).

Petitioner asserts that Congress' failure to enact various proposals since *Chapman* was decided that would have limited the availability of habeas relief amounts to legisla-tive disapproval of application of a less stringent harmless-error standard on collateral review of constitutional error. Only one of these proposals merits discussion here. In 1972, a bill was proposed that would have amended 28 U.S.C. §2254 to require habeas petitioners to show that "'a different result would probably have obtained if such con-stitutional violation had not occurred.'" 118 Cong. Rec. 24,936 (1972) (*quoting* S. 3833, 92d Cong., 2d Sess. (1972)). In response, the Attorney General suggested that the above provision be modified to make habeas relief available only where the petitioner "'suffered a substantial deprivation of his constitutional rights at his trial.'" 118 Cong. Rec. 24,939 (1972) (*quoting* letter from Richard G. Kleindienst, Attorney General, to Emanuel Celler, Chairman of the House Committee on the Judiciary (June 21, 1972)). This language of course parallels the federal harmless-error rule. But neither the Attorney General's suggestion nor the proposed bill itself was ever enacted into law.

As a general matter, we are "reluctant to draw inferences from Congress' failure to act." *Schneidewind v. ANR Pipeline Co.*, 485 U.S. 293, 306 (1988). ** We find no reason to depart from this rule here. In the absence of any express statutory guidance from Congress, it remains for this Court to determine what harmless-error standard applies on collateral review of petitioner's *Doyle* claim. We have filled the gaps of the habeas corpus statute with respect to other matters, *see, e.g., McCleskey v. Zant*, 499 U.S. 467, 487 (1991); *Wainwright v. Sykes*, 433 U.S. 72, 81 (1977); *Sanders v. United States*, 373 U.S. 1, 15 (1963); *Townsend v. Sain*, 372 U.S. 293, 312–313 (1963), and find it necessary to do so here. As always, in defining the scope of the writ, we look first to the considerations underlying our habeas jurisprudence, and then determine whether the proposed rule would advance or inhibit these considerations by weighing the marginal costs and benefits of its application on collateral review.

The principle that collateral review is different from direct review resounds throughout our habeas jurisprudence. *See, e.g., Wright v. West*, 505 U.S. 277, 292–293 (1992); *Pennsylvania v. Finley*, 481 U.S. 551, 556–557 (1987). ** Direct review is the principal avenue for challenging a conviction. "When the process of direct review— which, if a federal question is involved, includes the right to petition this Court for a writ of certiorari—comes to an end, a presumption of finality and legality attaches to the conviction and sentence. The role of federal habeas proceedings, while important in assuring that constitutional rights are observed, is secondary and limited. Federal courts are not forums in which to relitigate state trials." *Barefoot v. Estelle*, 463 U.S. 880, 887 (1983).

In keeping with this distinction, the writ of habeas corpus has historically been regarded as an extraordinary remedy, "a bulwark against convictions that violate 'fundamental fairness.'" *Engle v. Isaac*, 456 U.S. 107, 126 (1982) (*quoting Wainwright v. Sykes*, [433 U.S.] at 97, (STEVENS, J., concurring)). "Those few who are ultimately successful [in obtaining habeas relief] are persons whom society has grievously wronged and for whom belated liberation is little enough compensation." *Fay v. Noia*, 372 U.S. 391, 440–441 (1963). *See also Kuhlmann v. Wilson*, 477 U.S. 436, 447 (1986) (plurality opinion) ("The Court uniformly has been guided by the proposition that the writ should be available to afford relief to those 'persons whom society has grievously wronged' in light of modern concepts of justice") (*quoting Fay v. Noia, supra*, at 440–441); *Jackson v. Virginia*, 443 U.S. 307, 332 n.5 (1979) (STEVENS, J., concurring in judgment) (Habeas corpus "is designed to guard against extreme malfunctions in the state criminal justice systems"). Accordingly, it hardly bears repeating that "'an error that may justify reversal on direct appeal will not necessarily support a collateral attack on a final judgment.'" *United States v. Frady*, 456 U.S. 152, 165 (1982). ***

Recognizing the distinction between direct and collateral review, we have applied different standards on habeas than would be applied on direct review with respect to matters other than harmless-error analysis. Our recent retroactivity jurisprudence is a prime example. Although new rules always have retroactive application to criminal cases on direct review, *Griffith v. Kentucky*, 479 U.S. 314, 320–328 (1987), we have held that they seldom have retroactive application to criminal cases on federal habeas, *Teague v. Lane*, 489 U.S. [288,] 305–310 (opinion of O'CONNOR, J.). Other examples abound throughout our habeas cases. *See, e.g., Pennsylvania v. Finley*, 481 U.S. 551, 555–556 (1987) (Although the Constitution guarantees the right to counsel on direct appeal, *Douglas v. California*, 372 U.S. 353, 355 (1963), there is no "right to counsel when mounting collateral attacks"); *United States v. Frady, supra,* at 162–169 (While the federal "plain error" rule applies in determining whether a defendant may raise a claim for the first time on direct appeal, the "cause and prejudice" standard applies in determining whether that same claim may be raised on habeas); *Stone v. Powell*, 428 U.S. 465, 489–496 (1976) (Claims under *Mapp v. Ohio*, 367 U.S. 643 (1961), are not cognizable on habeas as long as the state courts have provided a full and fair opportunity to litigate them at trial or on direct review).

The reason most frequently advanced in our cases for distinguishing between direct and collateral review is the State's interest in the finality of convictions that have survived direct review within the state court system. *See, e.g.,* ** *McCleskey v. Zant*, 499 U.S. at 491; *Wainwright v. Sykes*, 433 U.S. at 90. We have also spoken of comity and federalism. "The States possess primary authority for defining and enforcing the criminal law. In criminal trials they also hold the initial responsibility for vindicating constitutional rights. Federal intrusions into state criminal trials frustrate both the States' sovereign power to punish offenders and their good-faith attempts to honor constitutional rights." *Engle v. Isaac, supra,* at 128. *See also Coleman v. Thompson*, 501 U.S. 722, 748 (1991); *McCleskey, supra,* at 491. Finally, we have recognized that "[l]iberal allowance of the writ...degrades the prominence of the trial itself," *Engle, supra,* at 127, and at the same time encourages habeas petitioners to relitigate their claims on collateral review, *see Rose v. Lundy*, 455 U.S. 509, 547, (1982) (STEVENS, J., dissenting).

In light of these considerations, we must decide whether the same harmless-error standard that the state courts applied on direct review of petitioner's *Doyle* claim also applies in this habeas proceeding. We are the sixth court to pass on the question whether the State's use for impeachment purposes of petitioner's post-*Miranda* silence in this case requires reversal of his conviction. Each court that has reviewed the record has disagreed with the court before it as to whether the State's *Doyle* error was "harmless." State courts are fully qualified to identify constitutional error and evaluate its prejudicial effect on the trial process under *Chapman*, and state courts often occupy a superior vantage point from which to evaluate the effect of trial error. *See Rushen v. Spain*, 464 U.S. 114, 120 (1983) (*per curiam*). For these reasons, it scarcely seems logical to require federal habeas courts to engage in the identical approach to harmless-error review that *Chapman* requires state courts to engage in on direct review.

Petitioner argues that application of the *Chapman* harmless-error standard on collateral review is necessary to deter state courts from relaxing their own guard in reviewing constitutional error and to discourage prosecutors from committing error in the first place. Absent affirmative evidence that state-court judges are ignoring their oath, we discount petitioner's argument that courts will respond to our ruling by violating their Article VI duty to uphold the Constitution. ** Federalism, comity, and the constitutional obligation of state and federal courts all counsel against any presumption that a decision of this Court will "deter" lower federal or state courts from fully performing their sworn duty. ** In any event, we think the costs of applying the *Chapman* standard on federal habeas outweigh the additional deterrent effect, if any, that would be derived from its application on collateral review.

Overturning final and presumptively correct convictions on collateral review because the State cannot prove that an error is harmless under *Chapman* undermines the States' interest in finality and infringes upon their sovereignty over criminal matters. Moreover, granting habeas relief merely because there is a " 'reasonable possibility' " that trial error contributed to the verdict, *see Chapman v. California*, 386 U.S. at 24, ** is at odds with the historic meaning of habeas corpus — to afford relief to those whom society has "grievously wronged." Retrying defendants whose convictions are set aside also imposes significant "social costs," including the expenditure of additional time and resources for all the parties involved, the "erosion of memory" and "dispersion of witnesses" that accompany the passage of time and make obtaining convictions on retrial more difficult, and the frustration of "society's interest in the prompt administration of justice." *United States v. Mechanik*, 475 U.S. 66, 72 (1986) (internal quotation marks omitted). And since there is no statute of limitations governing federal habeas, and the only laches recognized is that which affects the State's ability to defend against the claims raised on habeas, retrials following the grant of habeas relief ordinarily take place much later than do retrials following reversal on direct review.

The imbalance of the costs and benefits of applying the *Chapman* harmless-error standard on collateral review counsels in favor of applying a less onerous standard on habeas review of constitutional error. The *Kotteakos* standard, we believe, fills the bill. The test under *Kotteakos* is whether the error "had substantial and injurious effect or influence in determining the jury's verdict." 328 U.S. at 776. Under this standard, habeas petitioners may obtain plenary review of their constitutional claims, but they are not entitled to habeas relief based on trial error unless they can establish that it resulted in "actual prejudice." *See United States v. Lane*, 474 U.S. 438 (1986). The *Kotteakos* standard is thus better tailored to the nature and purpose of collateral review and more likely to promote the considerations underlying our recent habeas cases. Moreover, because the *Kotteakos* standard is grounded in the federal harmless-error rule, 28 U.S.C. § 2111, federal courts may turn to an existing body of case law in applying it. Therefore, contrary to the assertion of petitioner, application of the *Kotteakos* standard on collateral review is unlikely to confuse matters for habeas courts.

For the foregoing reasons, then, we hold that the *Kotteakos* harmless-error standard applies in determining whether habeas relief must be granted because of constitutional error of the trial type. *** All that remains to be decided is whether petitioner is entitled to relief under this standard based on the State's *Doyle* error. Because the Court of Appeals applied the *Kotteakos* standard below, we proceed to this question ourselves rather than remand the case for a new harmless-error determination. ** At trial, petitioner admitted shooting Hartman, but claimed it was an accident. The principal question before the jury, therefore, was whether the State met its burden in proving beyond a reasonable doubt that the shooting was intentional. Our inquiry here is whether, in light of the record as a whole, the State's improper use for impeachment purposes of petitioner's post-*Miranda* silence ** "had substantial and injurious effect or influence in determining the jury's verdict." We think it clear that it did not.

The State's references to petitioner's post-*Miranda* silence were infrequent, comprising less than two pages of the 900-page trial transcript in this case. And in view of the State's extensive and permissible references to petitioner's pre-*Miranda* silence — i.e., his failure to mention anything about the shooting being an accident to the officer who found him in the ditch, the man who gave him a ride to Winona, or the officers who eventually arrested him — its references to petitioner's post-*Miranda* silence were, in effect, cumulative. Moreover, the State's evidence of guilt was, if not overwhelming, cer-

Other evidence against him was very weighty

tainly weighty. The path of the bullet through Mr. Hartman's body was inconsistent with petitioner's testimony that the rifle had discharged as he was falling. The police officers who searched the Hartmans' home found nothing in the downstairs hallway that could have caused petitioner to trip. The rifle was found outside the house (where Hartman was shot), not inside where petitioner claimed it had accidentally fired, and there was a live round rammed in the gun's chamber, suggesting that petitioner had tried to fire a second shot. Finally, other circumstantial evidence, including the motive proffered by the State, also pointed to petitioner's guilt.

In light of the foregoing, we conclude that the *Doyle* error that occurred at petitioner's trial did not "substantial[ly]...influence" the jury's verdict. Petitioner is therefore not entitled to habeas relief, and the judgment of the Court of Appeals is

Affirmed.

[A concurring opinion by JUSTICE STEVENS, in which JUSTICES WHITE AND BLACKMUN join, and in which JUSTICE SOUTER joins in part and dissents in part, is omitted.]

Notes

1. *Subsequent case history*

Todd Brecht began serving a life sentence in 1986. He was eligible for parole in July 2004.

2. *Excerpt from Stevens's concurrence*

Justice Stevens's concurrence includes the following observation:

> We disagree, however, about whether the same form of harmless-error analysis should apply in a collateral attack as on a direct appeal, and, if not, what the collateral attack standard should be for an error of this kind. The answer to the first question follows from our long history of distinguishing between collateral and direct review ** and confining collateral relief to cases that involve fundamental defects or omissions inconsistent with the rudimentary demands of fair procedure. ** The Court answers the second question by endorsing Justice Rutledge's thoughtful opinion for the Court in *Kotteakos v. United States*, 328 U.S. 750 (1946). ** Because that standard accords with the statutory rule for reviewing other trial errors that affect substantial rights; places the burden on prosecutors to explain why those errors were harmless; requires a habeas court to review the entire record *de novo* in determining whether the error influenced the jury's deliberations; and leaves considerable latitude for the exercise of judgment by federal courts, I am convinced that our answer is correct. I write separately only to emphasize that the standard is appropriately demanding.

Why did Justice Stevens choose to write separately to note that the standard is "appropriately demanding"?

3. *Dissent by Justice White*

Justice White (joined by Justice Blackmun and, in part, Justice Souter) dissented. His dissent includes concerns about the remedy a petitioner would have if the state appellate courts erroneously analyzed an error of this magnitude.

> If, however, the state courts erroneously concluded that no violation had occurred or (as is the case here) that it was harmless beyond a reasonable doubt,

and supposing further that certiorari was either not sought or not granted, the majority would foreclose relief on federal habeas review. As a result of today's decision, in short, the fate of one in state custody turns on whether the state courts properly applied the Federal Constitution as then interpreted by decisions of this Court, and on whether we choose to review his claim on certiorari.

Is Justice White's concern legitimate? Why or why not?

4. *What the jury heard*

In footnote 2, the Court notes that the State's cross-examination of petitioner included the following exchange:

Q. In fact the first time you have ever told this story is when you testified here today was it not?

A. You mean the story of actually what happened?

Q. Yes.

A. I knew what happened, I'm just telling it the way it happened, yes, I didn't have a chance to talk to anyone, I didn't want to call somebody from a phone and give up my rights, so I didn't want to talk about it, no sir. **

Then on re-cross-examination, the State further inquired:

Q. Did you tell anyone about what had happened in Alma?

A. No I did not. **

The Court then documents some of the remarks the prosecutor made during closing arguments:

[T]he State urged the jury to "remember that Mr. Brecht never volunteered until in this courtroom what happened in the Hartman residence...." ** It also made the following statement with regard to petitioner's pretrial silence: "He sits back here and sees all of our evidence go in and then he comes out with this crazy story...." ** Finally, during its closing rebuttal, the State said: "I know what I'd say [had I been in petitioner's shoes], I'd say, 'hold on, this was a mistake, this was an accident, let me tell you what happened,' but he didn't say that did he. No, he waited until he hears our story." **

After reading these summaries of the State's questions and comments, what would the jury's most likely response to them have been? Should that matter?

Chapter 13

Special Issues in Capital Habeas Petitions

Many of the cases in habeas corpus jurisprudence involve capital cases. The fact that a petitioner might actually be put to death both complicates the analysis and adds an element of urgency to the petition. This chapter includes three cases that reveal the framework within which the Court assesses a capital habeas petition: *Parker v. Dugger*, *Calderon v. Coleman*, and *Autry v. Estelle*. In order to place these cases within a larger context, it is helpful to review briefly the seminal cases underlying the Court's modern capital jurisprudence.

In *Furman v. Georgia*, 408 U.S. 238 (1972), the Court invalidated all then-existing death penalty statutes because of concerns over their arbitrary and capricious applications. While none of the Justices agreed about the precise reason for invalidating then-existing statutes, a majority agreed that they were invalid. The response of many states to this decision was to immediately pass new death penalty statutes that were intended to address the concerns of the *Furman* majority: arbitrariness, the need for narrowing the class of persons eligible for the death penalty, and individualized consideration for capital defendants.

Just four years after *Furman*, the Court allowed reinstatement of the death penalty. In *Gregg v. Georgia*, 428 U.S. 153 (1976), the Court found that Georgia's newly modified capital sentencing scheme was constitutional because the Georgia statute had a bifurcated procedure (a separate trial and penalty hearing), because the prosecution had to prove aggravating factors in order to narrow the class of persons convicted of first-degree murder who could face the death penalty, and because the Georgia Supreme Court automatically reviewed all death sentences. That same year, in *Woodson v. North Carolina*, 428 U.S. 280 (1976), the Court held that the North Carolina statute, which made the death penalty mandatory upon a conviction of capital murder, was not constitutional because it failed to provide for individualized consideration of the defendant's history and circumstances. Both *Gregg* and *Woodson* arose from the context of a grant of certiorari on direct review, rather than after a habeas proceeding.

Capital cases in the habeas context present a different set of challenges for the parties and courts. In *Parker v. Dugger*, the Court considers the question of what effect a trier of fact must give mitigating evidence, which is evidence mandated by the requirement of individualized consideration of the defendant. In *Calderon v. Coleman*, the Court examines a jury instruction that admittedly is unconstitutional but that might or might not constitute reversible error. And in *Autry v. Estelle*, the interplay between a stay of execution and a petition for a writ of habeas corpus is at issue.

Parker v. Dugger

498 U.S. 308 (1991)

JUSTICE O'CONNOR delivered the opinion of the Court.

This case requires us to determine precisely what effect the Florida courts gave to the evidence petitioner presented in mitigation of his death sentence, and consequently to determine whether his death sentence meets federal constitutional requirements.

I

On the afternoon of February 6, 1982, petitioner Robert Parker and several others set off to recover money owed them for the delivery of illegal drugs. There followed a nightmarish series of events that ended in the early morning hours of February 7 with the deaths of Richard Padgett, Jody Dalton, and Nancy Sheppard.

A Duval County, Florida, grand jury indicted Parker, his former wife Elaine, Tommy Groover, and William Long for the first-degree murders of Padgett, Dalton, and Sheppard. Elaine Parker and Long entered negotiated pleas to second degree murder. A jury convicted Groover of all three first-degree murders, and the judge sentenced him to death on two counts and life imprisonment on the third.

Parker's jury convicted him of first-degree murder for the killings of Padgett and Sheppard and third-degree murder for the Dalton killing. At the advisory sentencing hearing, Parker presented evidence in mitigation of a death sentence and argued that such evidence also had been presented at trial. The jury found that sufficient aggravating circumstances existed to justify a death sentence as to both the Padgett and Sheppard murders, but that sufficient mitigating circumstances existed that outweighed these aggravating factors. The jury therefore recommended that Parker be sentenced to life imprisonment on both first-degree counts.

The trial judge, who has ultimate sentencing authority under Florida law, accepted the jury's recommendation for the Padgett murder. The judge overrode the jury's recommendation for the Sheppard murder, however, and sentenced Parker to death. The judge's sentencing order explained that "this Court has carefully studied and considered all the evidence and testimony at trial and at advisory sentence proceedings." ** After reviewing the evidence of the various aggravating and mitigating circumstances defined by Florida statute, the judge found six aggravating circumstances present as to the Sheppard murder and no statutory mitigating circumstances. In the sentencing order, the judge did not discuss evidence of, or reach any explicit conclusions concerning, nonstatutory mitigating evidence. He did conclude that "there are no mitigating circumstances that outweigh the aggravating circumstances in the first count (Padgett murder) and the second count (Sheppard murder)." **

On direct appeal, the Florida Supreme Court affirmed Parker's convictions and sentences. ** The court concluded, however, that there was insufficient evidence to support two of the aggravating circumstances that the trial judge had relied upon in sentencing Parker to death: that the Sheppard murder was "especially heinous, atrocious and cruel," and that the murder was committed during a robbery. ** Nonetheless, the court affirmed the death sentence, its entire written analysis consisting of the following:

> The trial court found no mitigating circumstances to balance against the aggravating factors, of which four were properly applied. In light of these findings the facts suggesting the sentence of death are so clear and convincing that vir-

tually no reasonable person could differ. ** The jury override was proper and the facts of this case clearly place it within the class of homicides for which the death penalty has been found appropriate. **

Parker pursued state collateral review without success, and then filed a petition for a writ of habeas corpus in the United States District Court for the Middle District of Florida. That court denied Parker's petition as to his convictions, but granted the petition as to the imposition of the death penalty. ** The court concluded that the trial judge had found no nonstatutory mitigating circumstances. The court also found that there was sufficient evidence in the record to support a finding of nonstatutory mitigating circumstances, and, in particular, to support the jury's recommendation of a life sentence for the Sheppard murder. Because, under Florida law, a sentencing judge is to override a jury's recommendation of life imprisonment only when "virtually no reasonable person could differ," ** the District Court concluded that the failure of the trial judge to find the presence of nonstatutory mitigating circumstances fairly supported by the record rendered the death sentence unconstitutional. ** The District Court also speculated that the trial judge might have failed even to *consider* nonstatutory mitigating circumstances, thereby violating the rule of *Hitchcock v. Dugger*, 481 U.S. 393 (1987). ** The court ordered the State of Florida to hold a resentencing hearing within 120 days, or to vacate the death sentence and impose a lesser sentence. *Id.* at 146.

The Court of Appeals for the Eleventh Circuit reversed. ** That court agreed with the District Court that there was "copious evidence of nonstatutory mitigating circumstances presented by Parker during the sentencing phase." ** As a consequence, however, the Court of Appeals refused to read the trial judge's silence as to nonstatutory mitigating circumstances as an indication that the judge did not consider or find such circumstances: "Under the facts of this case the only reasonable conclusion is that the trial judge found at least some mitigating factors to be present, but also found that they were *outweighed* by the aggravating factors also present. In his sentencing order, the judge wrote that 'there are no mitigating circumstances that *outweigh* the aggravating circumstances in the second count (Sheppard murder)[]' (emphasis added)." ** The Court of Appeals found no constitutional error in Parker's convictions or death sentence. We granted certiorari ** and now reverse the judgment of the Court of Appeals and remand for further proceedings.

II

Parker presents several related challenges to his death sentence. The crux of his contentions is that the Florida courts acted in an arbitrary and capricious manner by failing to treat adequately the evidence he presented in mitigation of the sentence. This case is somewhat unusual in that we are required to reconstruct that which we are to review. The trial judge's order imposing the challenged sentence does not state explicitly what effect the judge gave Parker's nonstatutory mitigating evidence. We must first determine what precisely the trial judge found.

A Florida statute defines certain aggravating and mitigating circumstances relevant to the imposition of the death penalty. ** The death penalty may be imposed only where sufficient aggravating circumstances exist that outweigh mitigating circumstances. ** A jury makes an initial sentencing recommendation to the judge; the judge imposes the sentence. ** Both may consider only those aggravating circumstances described by statute. ** In counterbalance, however, they may consider any mitigating evidence, whether or not it goes to a statutory mitigating circumstance. ** If the jury recommends a life sentence rather than the death penalty, the judge may override that recommendation and impose a sentence of death only where "the facts suggesting a sentence of death [are] so clear and convincing that virtually no reasonable person could differ." **

The jury here recommended a life sentence for the Sheppard murder. The trial judge overrode that recommendation. In his sentencing order, the judge described in detail his factfinding as to each of the eight statutory aggravating and seven statutory mitigating circumstances. The judge found six aggravating circumstances present as to the Sheppard murder, and no statutory mitigating circumstances. ** The sentencing order makes no specific mention of nonstatutory mitigating circumstances. Under "Findings of the Court," the order states: "There are no mitigating circumstances that outweigh the aggravating circumstances." **

What did the trial judge conclude about nonstatutory mitigating evidence? There is no question that Parker presented such evidence. For example, several witnesses at trial, including witnesses for the State, testified that Parker was under the influence of large amounts of alcohol and various drugs, including LSD, during the murders. ** At the sentencing hearing, Parker's attorney emphasized to the jury that none of Parker's accomplices received a death sentence for the Sheppard murder. Billy Long, who admitted shooting Nancy Sheppard, had been allowed to plead guilty to second-degree murder. ** Finally, numerous witnesses testified on Parker's behalf at the sentencing hearing concerning his background and character. Their testimony indicated both a difficult childhood, including an abusive, alcoholic father, and a positive adult relationship with his own children and with his neighbors. **

We must assume that the trial judge considered all this evidence before passing sentence. For one thing, he said he did. The sentencing order states: "Before imposing sentence, this Court has carefully studied and considered *all the evidence and testimony at trial and at advisory sentence proceedings*, the presentence Investigation Report, the applicable Florida Statutes, the case law, and all other factors touching upon this case." ** Under both federal and Florida law, the trial judge could not refuse to consider any mitigating evidence. ** In his instructions to the jury concerning its sentencing recommendation, the judge explained that, in addition to the statutory mitigating factors, the jury could consider "any other aspect of the defendant's character or record, and any other circumstances of the crime." ** Moreover, Parker's nonstatutory mitigating evidence— drug and alcohol intoxication, more lenient sentencing for the perpetrator of the crime, character and background—was of a type that the Florida Supreme Court had in other cases found sufficient to preclude a jury override. ** The trial judge must have at least taken this evidence into account before passing sentence.

We also conclude that the trial judge credited much of this evidence, although he found that it did not outweigh the aggravating circumstances. The judge instructed the jurors at the end of the sentencing hearing that they need be only "reasonably convinced" that a mitigating circumstance exists to consider it established. ** We assume the judge applied the same standard himself. He must, therefore, have found at least some nonstatutory mitigating circumstances. The evidence of Parker's intoxication at the time of the murders was uncontroverted. There is also no question that Long, despite being the triggerman for the Sheppard murder, received a lighter sentence than Parker. Respondent conceded this fact in oral argument before this Court. ** And, as noted, there was extensive evidence going to Parker's personal history and character that might have provided some mitigation.

In addition, every court to have reviewed the record here has determined that the evidence supported a finding of nonstatutory mitigating circumstances. Both the District

Court and the Court of Appeals, in reviewing Parker's habeas petition, concluded that there was more than enough evidence in this record to support such a finding. ** We agree. We note also that the jury found sufficient mitigating circumstances to outweigh the aggravating circumstances in the Sheppard murder. The Florida Supreme Court did not make its own determination whether the evidence supported a finding of nonstatutory mitigating circumstances. ** To the extent there is ambiguity in the sentencing order, we will not read it to be against the weight of the evidence.

Perhaps the strongest indication that the trial judge found nonstatutory mitigating circumstances is that the judge overrode the jury's sentencing recommendation for the Sheppard murder, but not for the Padgett murder. The jury recommended a life sentence for both murders. The judge explicitly found six aggravating circumstances related to the Sheppard murder and five aggravating circumstances related to the Padgett murder. ** The judge found no statutory mitigating circumstances as to either murder. ** Yet he sentenced Parker to death for the Sheppard murder, but accepted the jury's recommendation as to the Padgett murder. If the judge had found no nonstatutory mitigating circumstances, he would have had nothing to balance against the aggravating circumstances for either murder, and the judge presumably would have overridden both recommendations.

It must be that the judge sentenced differentially for the two murders because he believed that the evidence in the Sheppard murder was so "clear and convincing that virtually no reasonable person could differ" about the sentence of death, ** whereas the evidence in the Padgett murder did not meet this test. Perhaps this decision was based solely on the fact that the judge had found six aggravating circumstances in the Sheppard murder but only five in the Padgett murder. Far more likely, however, is that the judge found nonstatutory mitigating circumstances, at least as to the Padgett murder. But, as the nonstatutory mitigating evidence was in general directed to both murders, there is no reason to think the judge did not find mitigation as to both.

***

In light of the substantial evidence, much of it uncontroverted, favoring mitigation, the differential sentences for the Sheppard and Padgett murders, and the fact that the judge indicated that he found no mitigating circumstances "that outweigh" aggravating circumstances, we must conclude, as did the Court of Appeals, that the trial court found and weighed nonstatutory mitigating circumstances before sentencing Parker to death.

III

The Florida Supreme Court did not consider the evidence of nonstatutory mitigating circumstances. On direct review of Parker's sentence, the Florida Supreme Court struck two of the aggravating circumstances on which the trial judge had relied. The Supreme Court nonetheless upheld the death sentence because "the trial court found no mitigating circumstances to balance against the aggravating factors." ** The Florida Supreme Court erred in its characterization of the trial judge's findings, and consequently erred in its review of Parker's sentence.

As noted, Florida is a weighing State; the death penalty may be imposed only where specified aggravating circumstances outweigh all mitigating circumstances. ** In a weighing State, when a reviewing court strikes one or more of the aggravating factors on which the sentencer relies, the reviewing court may, consistent with the Constitution, reweigh the remaining evidence or conduct a harmless error analysis. *Clemons v. Mississippi*, 494 U.S. 738, 741 (1990). It is unclear what the Florida Supreme Court did here. It certainly did not conduct an independent reweighing of the evidence. In affirming Parker's sentence, the court explicitly relied on what it took to be the trial judge's finding of no mitigating circumstances. ** Had it conducted an independent review of the evidence, the court would have had no need for such reliance. More to the point, the Florida Supreme Court has made it clear on several occasions that it does not reweigh the evidence of aggravating and mitigating circumstances. **

The Florida Supreme Court may have conducted a harmless error analysis. At the time it heard Parker's appeal, this was its general practice in cases in which it had struck aggravating circumstances and the trial judge had found no mitigating circumstances. ** Perhaps the Florida Supreme Court conducted a harmless error analysis here: Believing that the trial judge properly had found four aggravating circumstances, and no mitigating circumstances to weigh against them, the Florida Supreme Court may have determined that elimination of two additional aggravating circumstances would have made no difference to the sentence.

But, as we have explained, the trial judge must have found mitigating circumstances. The Florida Supreme Court's practice in such cases—where the court strikes one or more aggravating circumstances relied on by the trial judge and mitigating circumstances are present—is to remand for a new sentencing hearing. ** Following *Clemons*, a reviewing court is not compelled to remand. It may instead reweigh the evidence or conduct a harmless error analysis based on what the sentencer actually found. What the Florida Supreme Court could not do, but what it did, was to ignore the evidence of mitigating circumstances in the record and misread the trial judge's findings regarding mitigating circumstances, and affirm the sentence based on a mischaracterization of the trial judge's findings.

In *Wainwright v. Goode*, 464 U.S. 78 (1983), the Court held that a federal court on habeas review must give deference to a state appellate court's resolution of an ambiguity in a state trial court statement. We did not decide in *Goode* whether the issue resolved by the state appellate court was properly characterized as one of law or of fact. In this case, we conclude that a determination of what the trial judge found is an issue of historical fact. It depends on an examination of the transcript of the trial and sentencing hearing, and the sentencing order. This is not a legal issue; no determination of the legality of Parker's sentence under Florida law necessarily follows from a resolution of the question of what the trial judge found.

Because it is a factual issue, the deference we owe is that designated by 28 U.S.C. § 2254. In ruling on a petition for a writ of habeas corpus, a federal court is not to overturn a factual conclusion of a state court, including a state appellate court, unless the conclusion is not "fairly supported by the record." ** For the reasons stated, we find that the Florida Supreme Court's conclusion that the trial judge found no mitigating circumstances is not fairly supported by the record in this case.

IV

"If a State has determined that death should be an available penalty for certain crimes, then it must administer that penalty in a way that can rationally distinguish between those individuals for whom death is an appropriate sanction and those for whom it is not." *Spaziano v. Florida*, 468 U.S. 447, 460 (1984). The Constitution prohibits the arbitrary or irrational imposition of the death penalty. ** We have emphasized repeatedly the crucial role of meaningful appellate review in ensuring that the death penalty is not imposed arbitrarily or irrationally. *** The Florida Supreme Court did not conduct an independent review here. In fact, there is a sense in which the court did not review Parker's sentence at all.

It cannot be gainsaid that meaningful appellate review requires that the appellate court consider the defendant's actual record. "What is important...is an *individualized* determination on the basis of the character of the individual and the circumstances of the crime." *Zant v. Stephens*, 462 U.S. 862, 879 (1983). ***

The jury found sufficient mitigating circumstances to outweigh the aggravating circumstances and recommended that Parker be sentenced to life imprisonment for the Sheppard murder. The trial judge found nonstatutory mitigating circumstances related to the Sheppard murder. The judge also declined to override the jury's recommendation as to the Padgett murder, even though he found five statutory aggravating circumstances and no statutory mitigating circumstances related to that crime. The Florida Supreme Court then struck two of the aggravating circumstances on which the trial judge had relied. On these facts, the Florida Supreme Court's affirmance of Parker's death sentence based on four aggravating circumstances and the trial judge's "finding" of no mitigating circumstances was arbitrary.

This is not simply an error in assessing the mitigating evidence. Had the Florida Supreme Court conducted its own examination of the trial and sentencing hearing records and concluded that there were no mitigating circumstances, a different question would be presented. Similarly, if the trial judge had found no mitigating circumstances and the Florida Supreme Court had relied on that finding, our review would be very different. ***

V

We reverse the judgment of the Court of Appeals and remand with instructions to return the case to the District Court to enter an order directing the State of Florida to initiate appropriate proceedings in state court so that Parker's death sentence may be reconsidered in light of the entire record of his trial and sentencing hearing and the trial judge's findings. The District Court shall give the State a reasonable period of time to initiate such proceedings. We express no opinion as to whether the Florida courts must order a new sentencing hearing.

***

It is so ordered.

Notes

1. *Subsequent case history*

Robert Parker is currently serving life in prison. *See* www.dc.state.fl.us.

2. *The role of advisory juries*

In this case, the advisory jury voted for life over death on all of the convictions. What effect did the fact that the judge was overriding a jury recommendation of life have on the Supreme Court, if any?

3. *Dissent of Justice White*

In his dissent, Justice White (joined by Chief Justice Rehnquist and Justices Scalia and Kennedy) expresses his concern that the Court has ventured into an area of "reconstructing" the record, an undertaking he opines is best left to the states:

The entire weight of the Court's opinion rests on a reconstruction of the record the likes of which has rarely, if ever, been performed before in this Court. Once armed with its dubious reconstruction of the facts, the Court proceeds to determine that the Florida Supreme Court's conclusion that the trial judge found no nonstatutory mitigating circumstances is not "'fairly supported by the record.'" ** The Court then relies on that determination to assert that the Florida Supreme Court "did not conduct an independent review here," ** even though the Court admits that the Florida Supreme Court's review was at least thorough enough to cause it to strike down two aggravating factors found by the trial judge. ** The Court ultimately concludes that Parker was deprived of "meaningful appellate review" which, for reasons not fully explained, apparently entitles him to relief under the Eighth Amendment of the Constitution. As I see it, these actions conflict with two lines of the Court's precedent.

First, the Court's application of the "fairly supported by the record" standard of § 2254(d)(8) is inconsistent with the way that standard has been applied in other cases and gives far too little deference to state courts that are attempting to apply their own law faithfully and responsibly. ***

    ***

Even more troubling in this case is the Court's creation of a new and unexplained "meaningful appellate review" standard for federal courts to apply in habeas proceedings. The Court suggests that the Florida Supreme Court's "error" in "misreading" the trial judge's findings is conclusive evidence that the court did not independently review Parker's claims and that this failure rendered Parker's sentence "arbitrary" in violation of the Eighth Amendment to the Constitution.

Are Justice White's concerns valid? Why or why not?

Calderon v. Coleman

525 U.S. 141 (1998)

PER CURIAM.

After a jury trial in a state court in California, respondent Russell Coleman was convicted of the September 5, 1979, rape, sodomy, and murder of Shirley Hill. The jury's two special circumstances findings of rape and sodomy made Coleman death-penalty eligible under California law. **

At the penalty phase of Coleman's trial, the trial judge gave the jury a so-called Briggs instruction, then required by California law, which informed the jury of the Governor's power to commute a sentence of life without possibility of parole to some lesser sentence that might include the possibility of parole. After giving the standard Briggs instruction, the state trial court instructed the jury that it was not to consider the Governor's commutation power in reaching its verdict. Thus, the full jury instruction on commutation was as follows:

> You are instructed that under the State Constitution, a Governor is empowered to grant a reprieve, pardon or commutation of a sentence following conviction of the crime.

> Under this power, a Governor may in the future commute or modify a sentence of life imprisonment without the possibility of parole to a lesser sentence that would include the possibility of parole.

So that you will have no misunderstandings relating to a sentence of life without possibility of parole, you have been informed generally as to the Governor's commutation modification power. You are now instructed, however, that the matter of a Governor's commutation power is not to be considered by you in determining the punishment for this defendant.

You may not speculate as to if or when a Governor would commute the sentence to a lesser one which includes the possibility of parole.

I instruct you again that you are to consider only those aggravating and mitigating factors which I have already read to you in determining which punishment shall be imposed on this defendant. **

In an unrelated case, we had upheld the Briggs instruction against a federal constitutional challenge. *California v. Ramos*, 463 U.S. 992 (1983). On direct appeal, however, Coleman argued that giving the Briggs instruction in his case was reversible error under the California Supreme Court's decision in *California v. Ramos*, 689 P.2d 430 (1984). There the California Supreme Court held, on remand from this Court, that the Briggs instruction violates the California Constitution because, in the California Supreme Court's view, it is misleading, invites the jury to consider irrelevant and speculative matters, and diverts the jury from its proper function.

The California Supreme Court rejected Coleman's argument and upheld his death sentence. ** While the court found that the giving of the Briggs instruction was error under California law, it held the error was not prejudicial because the additional instruction told the jury it should not consider the possibility of commutation in determining Coleman's sentence. **

Coleman then sought a federal writ of habeas corpus. Although the District Court acknowledged this Court's holding that giving the Briggs instruction does not violate the Federal Constitution and does not mislead or inappropriately divert the jury, the court nonetheless granted the writ as to Coleman's death sentence. ** Relying on recent Ninth Circuit precedent, the District Court found the Briggs instruction was inaccurate as applied to Coleman because it did not mention a limitation on the Governor's power to commute Coleman's sentence. ** Under the California Constitution, the Governor may not commute the sentence of a prisoner who, like Coleman, is a twice-convicted felon without the approval of four judges of the California Supreme Court. **

The District Court found that, because the Briggs instruction did not mention this limitation on the Governor's commutation power, it violated the Eighth and Fourteenth Amendments by "g[iving] the jury inaccurate information and potentially divert[ing] its attention from the mitigation evidence presented." ** The court also found that, in the context of the case—particularly, the prosecutor's arguments of future dangerousness, "the commutation instruction would likely have prevented the jury from giving due effect to Coleman's mitigating evidence." ** The court did not in express terms consider the effect of the additional instruction, which instructed the jury not to consider commutation, but it noted that the Ninth Circuit had held in a similar case ** "that the trial court did not cure the error by instructing the jury not to consider commutation." **

The Court of Appeals for the Ninth Circuit affirmed the District Court's grant of the writ as to Coleman's sentence. ** The Court of Appeals agreed with the District Court's finding that the instruction, as applied to Coleman, gave the jury inaccurate information about the Governor's commutation power. ** And, in a sweeping pronouncement, the court declared, "[a] commutation instruction is unconstitutional when it is inaccurate." ** The instruction at issue was fatally flawed, the court held, because it "dramatically overstate[d] the possibility of commuting the life sentence of a person such as Coleman" (by creating "the false impression that the Governor, acting alone," could commute the sentence) and thus prevented the jurors from "understand[ing] the choice they [we]re asked to make" and "'invited [them] to speculate' that Coleman could be effectively isolated from the community only through a sentence of death." **

Having concluded that the giving of the instruction was constitutional error, the Court of Appeals then took up the State's argument that, even if the instruction was unconstitutional, it "did not have a 'substantial and injurious effect or influence' on the jury's sentence of death," ** as required by *Brecht v. Abrahamson*, 507 U.S. 619, 637 (1993). The court explained:

> To decide this question, we look to *Boyde v. California*, 494 U.S. 370 (1990). When the inaccuracy undermines the jury's understanding of sentencing options, "there is a reasonable likelihood that the jury has applied the challenged instruction in a way that prevents the consideration of constitutionally relevant evidence." **

> We conclude the district court did not err in holding that Coleman was denied due process by the state trial court's inaccurate commutation instruction. **

Though the Court of Appeals' constitutional analysis of the jury instruction, and the Circuit precedent on which it relied, have not been approved by this Court, we do not consider the validity of that analysis here because the State has not asked us to do so. We will simply assume at this stage that the instruction did not meet constitutional standards. The State does contend, however, that the Court of Appeals erred by failing to apply the harmless-error analysis of *Brecht*. We agree.

We held in *Brecht* a federal court may grant habeas relief based on trial error only when that error "'had substantial and injurious effect or influence in determining the jury's verdict.'" ** This standard reflects the "presumption of finality and legality" that attaches to a conviction at the conclusion of direct review. ** It protects the State's sovereign interest in punishing offenders and its "good-faith attempts to honor constitutional rights," ** while ensuring that the extraordinary remedy of habeas corpus is available to those "'whom society has grievously wronged.'" **

A federal court upsets this careful balance when it sets aside a state-court conviction or sentence without first determining that the error had a substantial and injurious effect on the jury's verdict. The social costs of retrial or resentencing are significant, and the attendant difficulties are acute in cases such as this one, where the original sentencing hearing took place in November 1981, some 17 years ago. ** The State is not to be put to this arduous task based on mere speculation that the defendant was prejudiced by trial error; the court must find that the defendant was actually prejudiced by the error. ** As a consequence, once the Court of Appeals determined that the giving of the Briggs instruction was constitutional error, it was bound to apply the harmless-error analysis mandated by *Brecht*.

The *Boyde* test that the Court of Appeals applied instead is not a harmless-error test at all. It is, rather, the test for determining, in the first instance, whether constitutional error occurred when the jury was given an ambiguous instruction that it might have interpreted to prevent consideration of constitutionally relevant evidence. ** In such cases, constitutional error exists only if "there is a reasonable likelihood" that the jury so interpreted the instruction.

Although the *Boyde* test for constitutional error, like the *Brecht* harmless-error test, furthers the "strong policy against retrials years after the first trial where the claimed error amounts to no more than speculation," ** it is not a substitute for the *Brecht* harmless-error test. The *Boyde* analysis does not inquire into the actual effect of the error on the jury's verdict; it merely asks whether constitutional error has occurred. If the Court of Appeals had viewed the jury instruction as ambiguous on the issue whether the Governor had the power alone to commute defendant's sentence, it might have inquired—as in *Boyde*—whether there was a reasonable likelihood that the jury understood the instruction as stating the Governor had that power. If the court found that possibility to be a reasonable one, it would determine then whether the instruction, so understood, was unconstitutional as applied to the defendant. Even if the court found a constitutional violation, however, it could not grant the writ without further inquiry. As the Court has recognized on numerous occasions, some constitutional errors do not entitle the defendant to relief, particularly habeas relief. ** The court must find that the error, in the whole context of the particular case, had a substantial and injurious effect or influence on the jury's verdict.

The motion of respondent for leave to proceed *in forma pauperis* and the petition for a writ of certiorari are granted, the judgment of the Court of Appeals for the Ninth Circuit is reversed, and the case is remanded for further proceedings consistent with this opinion.

It is so ordered.

JUSTICE STEVENS, with whom JUSTICE SOUTER, JUSTICE GINSBURG, and JUSTICE BREYER join, dissenting.

Busy appellate judges sometimes write imperfect opinions. The failure adequately to explain the resolution of one issue in an opinion that answers several questions is not a matter of serious consequence if the decision is correct. In this case, there might have been a slight flaw in the Court of Appeals' brief explanation of why the invalid instruction given to the jury was not harmless, but, as I shall explain, the court's ruling was unquestionably correct.

The State does not challenge the conclusion that the jury was given an unconstitutional instruction. It merely argues that this trial error should not "command automatic reversal...without application of the harmless error test of *Brecht v. Abrahamson*, 507 U.S. 619 (1993). *** And respondent Coleman does not contend that *Brecht* is inapplicable. He merely argues that the Court of Appeals actually performed the *Brecht* inquiry, albeit in an expedited fashion. Thus, the only controversy before this Court is whether the Court of Appeals was faithful to *Brecht* and sufficiently explicit in its adherence.

Three aspects of the *Brecht* test for harmless error are significant here: (1) The test requires the reviewing judge to evaluate the error in the context of the entire record; (2) it asks whether the constitutional trial error at issue had a "'substantial and injurious effect or influence in determining the jury's verdict;'" ** and (3) if the judge has grave doubt about whether the error was harmless, the uncertain judge should conclude that the error affected the jury's deliberations and grant relief, *see O'Neal v. McAninch*, 513 U.S. 432 (1995).

In this case, it is undisputed that both the District Court and the Court of Appeals made a thorough examination of the entire record. The District Court's 117-page opinion carefully analyzed each of the respondent's nonfrivolous attacks on his conviction and concluded that the judgment of guilt should stand. With respect to the death penalty, however, the District Judge decided that the inaccurate and misleading instruction describing the Governor's commutation power was unconstitutional and "would likely have prevented the jury from giving due effect to Coleman's mitigating evidence."

*** Although the judge did not use the exact words that this Court used in its opinions in *Kotteakos*, *Brecht*, and *O'Neal*, it is perfectly clear that he was convinced that the instruction had a "substantial and injurious effect" on the jury's deliberations. This conclusion is reinforced by the statement of a juror explaining how the invalid instruction had, in fact, affected the jury's deliberations.

Because there is no reason to believe that the District Court's evaluation of the impact of the invalid instruction was incorrect, it is not surprising that the Court of Appeals affirmed without writing extensively about the harmless-error issue. It reasoned, in brief, that if there was a reasonable likelihood that the jury had applied an invalid instruction in a way that prevented the consideration of constitutionally relevant evidence, the error necessarily satisfied the *Brecht* test. Instead of spelling out its reasoning at length, it merely cited an earlier en banc decision of the Ninth Circuit that came to a similar conclusion. ***

Perhaps there may be cases in which a more detailed and written analysis of the harmless-error issue should precede an appellate court's decision to affirm a trial court's conclusion that an unconstitutional jury instruction in a capital sentencing proceeding was not harmless. But even if that be true, there are three good reasons for not requiring the Court of Appeals to take a second look at the issue in this case.

First, in the context of the entire record as analyzed by the District Court, the result here is correct. Second, a fair reading of The Chief Justice's opinion for the Court in *Boyde v. California*, 494 U.S. 370 (1990), indicates that the heightened "reasonable likelihood" standard endorsed in that case was intended to determine whether an instructional error "require[s] reversal." ** There is little reason to question the soundness—at least in most applications—of the reasoning of the en banc opinion in *McDowell* on which the Court of Appeals relied in this case. Third, there is a strong interest in bringing all litigation, and especially capital cases, to a prompt conclusion. This Court's ill-conceived summary disposition will needlessly prolong this proceeding.

Whatever the shortcomings of the Court of Appeals' review, they surely are not so great as to warrant an expenditure of this Court's time and resources. This is especially so because our decision today is unlikely to change the result below. Ordinarily, we demand far more indication that a lower court has departed from settled law, or has reached an issue of some national significance, before we grant review. The purported error in this case does not satisfy that standard.

Accordingly, I would deny the petition for writ of certiorari and, therefore, respectfully dissent.

Notes

1. *Subsequent case history*

After the Court remanded the case to the Ninth Circuit to determine whether the erroneous jury instruction given by the trial court was harmless, the Ninth Circuit held that it was not harmless error and affirmed the district court's decision granting Coleman's habeas petition as to his death sentence. *Coleman v. Calderon*, 210 F.3d 1047, 1048 (9th Cir. 2000). Because the Court did not grant Coleman relief from his conviction, however, Coleman was not released from custody. On February 8, 2002, Russell Coleman was sentenced to life in prison without the possibility of parole.

2. Assessing whether a "substantial and injurious" effect exists

In its *per curiam* opinion, the Court states that a petitioner must "find that the error, in the whole context of the particular case, had a substantial and injurious effect or influence on the jury's verdict." Does the Court explain how to make such an assessment? Recalling the "harmless error" analysis from Chapter 12, does the Court delineate what factors should comprise this analysis? Is the analysis (or should the analysis be) any different within the context of a capital habeas petition? *See Coleman v. Calderon*, 210 F.3d 1047 (9th Cir. 2000) (concluding that the instruction in Coleman's case had a substantial and injurious effect on the jury's verdict).

3. Stevens's dissent

In footnote 3 of Justice Stevens's dissent, he quotes from the Brief in Opposition, noting:

> [A]ccording to juror Verda New, the possibility of parole was a much discussed topic in deciding whether respondent should live or die:

> "[The jurors] openly discussed that Russell Coleman would be released from prison unless we sentenced him to death. Several jurors stated that he could be paroled if we sentenced him to life in prison.... Many of the jurors expressed their fear that if we failed to sentence Mr. Coleman to death, the courts or the Governor could allow him to be released from prison. This was the most significant part of our discussions regarding the appropriate penalty."

Does it seem likely that the issue of commutation would be discussed by jurors in deliberations on whether to sentence someone to death? Why or why not? If it is likely that such an issue would be part of the decision-making process, could such an instruction ever be constitutional?

Autry v. Estelle
464 U.S. 1 (1983)

PER CURIAM.

Applicant was sentenced to death for killing two people while robbing a convenience store. His conviction and sentence were affirmed by the Texas Court of Criminal Appeals. ** We denied certiorari. ** Applicant then sought habeas corpus in the state system; that request was denied. He then filed for habeas corpus in the Federal District Court, presenting some of the same claims that had been unavailing in the state courts. The District Court held a hearing and filed an opinion denying the writ. In a detailed opinion, the Court of Appeals for the Fifth Circuit affirmed the judgment of the District Court. ** It denied rehearing, as well as a stay pending the filing of a petition for certiorari in this Court. Applicant then sought a stay from the Circuit Justice, who referred the application to the Court. Absent a stay, applicant will be executed on October 5.

The application for stay is denied. The grounds on which applicant would request certiorari are amply evident from his application and from the opinions and the proceedings in the District Court and the Court of Appeals. Had applicant convinced four Members of the Court that certiorari would be granted on any of his claims, a stay would issue. But this is not the case; fewer than four Justices would grant certiorari. Applicant thus fails to satisfy one of the basic requirements for the issuance of a stay.

Nor are we inclined to adopt a rule calling for an automatic stay, regardless of the merits of the claims presented, where the applicant is seeking review of the denial of his first federal habeas corpus petition. Applicant has twice sought relief in the state court system. He has also presented his claims to the United States District Court and to the Court of Appeals. None of these judges found sufficient merit in any of applicant's claims to warrant setting aside applicant's conviction or his death sentence. Nor did any of the judges of the Court of Appeals believe that a stay pending certiorari was warranted. Those judges, stating that they were "fully sensitive to the consequence of our judgment and our oaths," ** found each of applicant's claims to be without merit and affirmed the dismissal of his habeas corpus petition. In these circumstances, it is quite appropriate to deny a stay of applicant's sentence, just as we do in other criminal cases that we are convinced do not merit review in this Court. As the Court said just last Term in *Barefoot v. Estelle*, 463 U.S. 880, 887–888 (1983):

> [It] must be remembered that direct appeal is the primary avenue for review of a conviction or sentence, and death penalty cases are no exception. When the process of direct review—which, if a federal question is involved, includes the right to petition this Court for a writ of certiorari—comes to an end, a presumption of finality and legality attaches to the conviction and sentence. The role of federal habeas proceedings, while important in assuring that constitutional rights are observed, is secondary and limited. Federal courts are not forums in which to relitigate state trials. Even less is federal habeas a means by which a defendant is entitled to delay an execution indefinitely. The procedures adopted to facilitate the orderly consideration and disposition of habeas petitions are not legal entitlements that a defendant has a right to pursue irrespective of the contribution these procedures make toward uncovering constitutional error.

JUSTICE BRENNAN, with whom JUSTICE MARSHALL joins, dissenting.

I join JUSTICE STEVENS' dissent, and because I continue to adhere to my view that the death penalty is in all circumstances cruel and unusual punishment prohibited by the Eighth and Fourteenth Amendments, *Gregg v. Georgia*, 428 U.S. 153, 227 (1976) (BRENNAN, J., dissenting), I would, in any case, grant the application for a stay of execution.

JUSTICE STEVENS, with whom JUSTICE BRENNAN, JUSTICE MARSHALL, and JUSTICE BLACKMUN join, dissenting.

Last year the applicant's death sentence was affirmed by the Texas Court of Criminal Appeals. ** On January 14, 1983, the United States District Court for the Eastern District of Texas denied the applicant's first petition for a writ of habeas corpus pursuant to 28 U.S.C. § 2254 after holding an evidentiary hearing. On June 17, 1983, after full briefing and argument, the United States Court of Appeals for the Fifth Circuit issued a carefully prepared 16-page opinion affirming the District Court's denial of the petition. ** Rehearing was denied on August 4, 1983, and on September 1, 1983, Texas authorities scheduled the applicant to be executed on October 5, 1983. He has applied for a stay of execution pending filing and disposition of a petition for a writ of certiorari. The Texas Attorney General does not oppose the stay application.

The time in which the applicant may file a petition for a writ of certiorari in this Court will not expire until November 2, 1983—four weeks after his scheduled execution. Thus, unless a stay is granted, the applicant will be executed before the applicant's time for petitioning this Court for a writ of certiorari expires.

The stay application makes it clear that the applicant's claims are not frivolous. Moreover, since this is the applicant's first federal habeas corpus proceeding, we are not confronted with the prospect of indefinite delay of execution which exists when an applicant has burdened the judicial system with successive federal petitions. On the other hand, on the basis of the papers that have been filed to date, I must acknowledge that I am presently of the opinion that this applicant will be unable to establish that a writ of certiorari should issue. My opinion, however, is necessarily tentative because the stay application contains only a synopsis of the arguments that counsel intends to make in a certiorari petition that has yet to be filed.

The decision to grant or to deny a stay pending the filing of a petition for a writ of certiorari depends on our assessment of the likelihood that such a petition will be granted and a balancing of the relative hardships of the parties. When a denial of a stay merely subjects the applicant to a continuing harm pending our decision on a subsequently filed certiorari petition, it is appropriate to deny the application unless the applicant demonstrates a likelihood that his petition will be granted. If it transpires that our tentative assessment of his case was incorrect, that error can be corrected by granting the subsequently filed certiorari petition, though naturally nothing can eliminate the interim harm the applicant suffered. In the instant case, however, a decision on the application is a final decision on the certiorari question—a decision to deny the stay renders a petition moot. The impact of our decision is therefore in no sense tentative, but our assessment of the case can only be a tentative one because it is based on probability rather than actuality. Accordingly, a preliminary negative evaluation of the certiorari question should not be the end of our analysis; we should also balance the relative hardships on the parties. I would strike that balance in favor of any applicant raising a nonfrivolous challenge to his capital conviction in his first federal habeas proceeding. In such a case, the importance of fully informed consideration of the certiorari question predominates over the interests of the State in expeditious execution of its judgment.

In one sense, the practical question that is raised by this stay application is whether the Court should give habeas petitioners on death row the same time to prepare and file certiorari petitions that other litigants receive. Unless the claims are frivolous, I believe that the overriding interest in the evenhanded administration of justice would be served by according an individual raising his first federal habeas challenge to his capital conviction the same opportunity to seek review in this Court as is accorded to other individuals.

The practice adopted by the majority effectively confers upon state authorities the power to dictate the period in which these federal habeas petitioners may seek review in this Court by scheduling an execution prior to the expiration of the period for filing a certiorari petition. Shortening the period allowed for filing a petition on such an ad hoc basis injects uncertainty and disparity into the review procedure, adds to the burdens of counsel, distorts the deliberative process within this Court, and increases the risk of error. Procedural shortcuts are always dangerous. *** Greater—surely not lesser—care should be taken to avoid the risk of error when its consequences are irreversible.

I respectfully dissent.

Notes

1. *Subsequent case history*

The Court issued its decision in *Autry* on October 3, 1983. Autry's execution was scheduled for October 5, 1983. The same day that the Court denied the stay, Autry immediately filed a second petition for habeas corpus that raised grounds not presented in his first habeas petition and were therefore not before the Court when it denied his stay of execution on October 3. The district court held an evidentiary hearing on October 4, 1983, then denied both the writ and the certificate of probable cause. After oral argument conducted by a conference telephone call, the Fifth Circuit Court of Appeals also denied both the certificate of probable cause and the stay. *Id.* at 1301–1302; *see also Autry v. McKaskle*, 727 F.2d 358, 359 (5th Cir. 1984). "Within minutes, and minutes before the planned execution, Justice White granted a certificate of probable cause and stay of execution." *Autry v. McKaskle*, 727 F.2d at 359.

One of the grounds on which Autry sought relief in his second habeas petition was the "failure of the Texas Court of Criminal Appeals to compare his case with other cases in order to determine whether his death sentence is disproportionate to the punishment imposed on others." *Autry v. Estelle*, 464 U.S. at 1302. Because the Court had recently granted certiorari in a comparative proportionality case out of California, *Pulley v. Harris*, 460 U.S. 1036 (1983), and was rescheduled to hear argument in that case in November 1983, Justice White stated that he "[could not] say that the issue lacks substance" and therefore issued a certificate of probable cause to stay Autry's execution. *Autry v. Estelle*, 464 U.S. 1301, 1302 (1983).

Because the Court's "resolution of the proportionality issue would not be forthcoming for some months," *Autry v. McKaskle*, 727 F.2d at 359, the Fifth Circuit remanded the case to the district court to "allow Autry an opportunity to present all new claims as well as to supplement the record regarding his earlier presented claims." *Id.* at 359–360. The district court conducted a third evidentiary hearing on January 19, 1984, and on "January 23, 1984, the Supreme Court rejected the contention that a proportionality review was constitutionally required." *Id.* at 360, *citing Pulley v. Harris*, 465 U.S. 37 (1984). Autry promptly abandoned his proportionality claim and was thus left with two remaining claims: ineffective of assistance of counsel and cruel and unusual punishment based on his being "placed on the gurney an entire hour prior to the time when respondent had a legal entitlement to end his life…and…misled into believing that a stay had in fact not been obtained and that his death was therefore imminent…amount[ing] to psychological torture." *Id.* at 360. The Fifth Circuit affirmed the district court's denial of both the stay of execution and application for certificate of probable cause. *Id.* at 364.

Twelve days later, on March 13, 1984, the Court denied certiorari. *Autry v. McKaskle*, 465 U.S. 1085 (1984). Justice Marshall, joined by Justice Brennan, dissented from the denial of certiorari with the following observation:

> Despite the fact that the petition [for certiorari] was still pending in this Court, the State set the date for petitioner's execution during our recess. Aware that the State cannot execute petitioner while his various petitions are pending in this Court, *cf. United States v. Shipp*, 203 U.S. 563 (1906), and yet unwilling to postpone petitioner's scheduled execution even a day or so, the Court has cut short its consideration of petitioner's multifarious claims. I, for one, feel unfairly pressed by the Court's insistence upon expedited procedures in death cases.

465 U.S. at 1086 (Marshall, J., dissenting).

James David Autry was executed on March 14, 1984, by lethal injection.

2. *Barefoot v. Estelle*

Three months before *Autry v. Estelle*, the Court decided *Barefoot v. Estelle*, 463 U.S. 880 (1983), which included the issue of "'the appropriate standard for granting or denying a stay of execution pending disposition of an appeal by a federal court of appeals by a death-sentenced federal habeas corpus petitioner.'" *Id.* at 887. In addition to the language quoted at length in the *per curiam* opinion in *Autry*, the Court made the following observation:

> "It is natural that counsel for the condemned in a capital case should lay hold of every ground which, in their judgment, might tend to the advantage of their client, but the administration of justice ought not to be interfered with on mere pretexts." ** Furthermore, unlike a term of years, a death sentence cannot begin to be carried out by the State while substantial legal issues remain outstanding. Accordingly, federal courts must isolate the exceptional cases where constitutional error requires retrial or resentencing as certainly and swiftly as orderly procedures will permit. They need not, and should not, however, fail to give nonfrivolous claims of constitutional error the careful attention that they deserve.

464 U.S. at 888. How can the Court's observation in *Barefoot* be reconciled with the Court's decision in *Autry*, which specified that the role of federal habeas proceedings is "secondary and limited" and that the "procedures adopted to facilitate the orderly consideration and disposition of habeas petitions are not legal entitlements that a defendant has a right to pursue irrespective of the contribution these procedures make toward uncovering constitutional error"? *Autry*, 484 U.S. at 3. How should a federal court isolate "exceptional cases" or "nonfrivolous claims of constitutional error"?

Part IV

Beyond
Habeas Corpus

Chapter 14

Clemency

Because clemency considerations factor into the Court's habeas analysis—especially when it involves capital habeas petitions—this chapter bridges Chapter 13's discussion of special issues that arise in capital cases with Chapters 15 and 16's discussions of politics, race, and innocence. While not a "legal" remedy, clemency has long had a place in the American criminal justice system. For example, the Supreme Court relies on clemency as a fail-safe for otherwise unreachable miscarriages of justice (as highlighted in the innocence cases discussed in Chapter 16), and political pressures influence both clemency and innocence (as discussed in Chapter 15).

In the first case in this chapter, *Ohio Adult Parole Authority v. Woodard*, the Court considers whether certain constitutional rights adhere to the clemency process in capital cases in Ohio. Professor Victoria Palacios then explores whether such reliance is justified in her article "Faith in Fantasy: The Supreme Court's Reliance on Commutation to Ensure Justice in Death Penalty Cases." The final selections contain the texts of two speeches given by outgoing Illinois Governor George Ryan in January of 2003. In his January 10, 2003, address given at DePaul University College of Law, Ryan pardoned—on the basis of innocence—four death row inmates. In his January 11, 2003, speech delivered at Northwestern University School of Law, Ryan commuted the death sentences of all prisoners remaining on Illinois' death row to either life in prison or a term of years.

Ohio Adult Parole Authority v. Woodard
523 U.S. 272 (1998)

CHIEF JUSTICE REHNQUIST announced the judgment of the Court and delivered the opinion of the Court with respect to Parts I and III, and an opinion with respect to Part II in which JUSTICE SCALIA, JUSTICE KENNEDY, and JUSTICE THOMAS join.

This case requires us to resolve two inquiries as to constitutional limitations on state clemency proceedings. The first is whether an inmate has a protected life or liberty interest in clemency proceedings, under either *Connecticut Bd. of Pardons v. Dumschat*, 452 U.S. 458 (1981), or *Evitts v. Lucey*, 469 U.S. 387 (1985). The second is whether giving inmates the option of voluntarily participating in an interview as part of the clemency process violates an inmate's Fifth Amendment rights.

We reaffirm our holding in *Dumschat*, *supra*, that "pardon and commutation decisions have not traditionally been the business of courts; as such, they are rarely, if ever, appropriate subjects for judicial review." ** The Due Process Clause is not violated where, as here, the procedures in question do no more than confirm that the clemency and pardon powers are committed, as is our tradition, to the authority of the executive. *** We further hold that a voluntary inmate interview does not violate the Fifth Amendment.

I

The Ohio Constitution gives the Governor the power to grant clemency upon such conditions as he thinks proper. ** The Ohio General Assembly cannot curtail this discretionary decision-making power, but it may regulate the application and investigation process. ** The General Assembly has delegated in large part the conduct of clemency review to petitioner Ohio Adult Parole Authority (Authority). **

In the case of an inmate under death sentence, the Authority must conduct a clemency hearing within 45 days of the scheduled date of execution. Prior to the hearing, the inmate may request an interview with one or more parole board members. Counsel is not allowed at that interview. The Authority must hold the hearing, complete its clemency review, and make a recommendation to the Governor, even if the inmate subsequently obtains a stay of execution. If additional information later becomes available, the Authority may in its discretion hold another hearing or alter its recommendation.

Respondent Eugene Woodard was sentenced to death for aggravated murder committed in the course of a carjacking. His conviction and sentence were affirmed on appeal, ** and this Court denied certiorari. ** When respondent failed to obtain a stay of execution more than 45 days before his scheduled execution date, the Authority commenced its clemency investigation. It informed respondent that he could have a clemency interview on September 9, 1994, if he wished, and that his clemency hearing would be on September 16, 1994.

Respondent did not request an interview. Instead, he objected to the short notice of the interview and requested assurances that counsel could attend and participate in the interview and hearing. When the Authority failed to respond to these requests, respondent filed suit in United States District Court on September 14, alleging under Rev. Stat. § 1979, 42 U.S.C. § 1983, that Ohio's clemency process violated his Fourteenth Amendment right to due process and his Fifth Amendment right to remain silent.

The District Court granted the State's motion for judgment on the pleadings. The Court of Appeals for the Sixth Circuit affirmed in part and reversed in part. ** That court determined that under a "first strand" of due process analysis, arising out of the clemency proceeding itself, respondent had failed to establish a protected life or liberty interest. It noted that our decision in *Dumschat* ** "decisively rejected the argument that federal law can create a liberty interest in clemency." **

The Court of Appeals further concluded that there was no state-created life or liberty interest in clemency. ** Since the Governor retains complete discretion to make the final decision, and the Authority's recommendation is purely advisory, the State has not created a protected interest. ** The Court of Appeals went on to consider, however, a "second strand" of due process analysis centered on "the role of clemency in the entire punitive scheme." ** The court relied on our statement in *Evitts* that "if a State has created appellate courts as 'an integral part of the...system for finally adjudicating the guilt or innocence of a defendant,' ...the procedures used in deciding appeals must comport with the demands of" due process. ** The court thought this reasoning logically applied to subsequent proceedings, including discretionary appeals, postconviction proceedings, and clemency.

Due process thus protected respondent's "original" life and liberty interests that he possessed before trial at each proceeding. But the amount of process due was in proportion to the degree to which the stage was an "integral part" of the trial process. Clemency, while not required by the Due Process Clause, was a significant, traditionally available remedy for preventing miscarriages of justice when judicial process was exhausted. It therefore came within the *Evitts* framework as an "integral part" of the adjudicatory system. However, since clemency was far removed from trial, the process due could be minimal. The Court did not itself decide what that process should be, but remanded to the District Court for that purpose.

Finally, the Court of Appeals also agreed with respondent that the voluntary interview procedure presented him with a "Hobson's choice" between asserting his Fifth Amendment rights and participating in the clemency review process, raising the specter of an unconstitutional condition. ** There was no compelling state interest that would justify forcing such a choice on the inmate. On the other hand, the inmate had a measurable interest in avoiding incrimination in ongoing postconviction proceedings, as well as with respect to possible charges for other crimes that could be revealed during the interview. While noting some uncertainties surrounding application of the unconstitutional conditions doctrine, the Court of Appeals concluded the doctrine could be applied in this case.

The dissenting judge would have affirmed the District Court's judgment. ** He agreed with the majority's determination that there was no protected interest under *Dumschat*. But he thought that the majority's finding of a due process interest under *Evitts*, *supra*, was necessarily inconsistent with the holding and rationale of *Dumschat*. *Evitts* did not purport to overrule *Dumschat*. He also concluded that respondent's Fifth Amendment claim was too speculative, given the voluntary nature of the clemency interview. We granted certiorari, ** and we now reverse.

II

Respondent argues first, in disagreement with the Court of Appeals, that there is a life interest in clemency broader in scope than the "original" life interest adjudicated at trial and sentencing. ** This continuing life interest, it is argued, requires due process protection until respondent is executed. *** Relying on Eighth Amendment decisions holding that additional procedural protections are required in capital cases, ** respondent asserts that *Dumschat* does not control the outcome in this case because it involved only a liberty interest. Justice Stevens' dissent agrees on both counts. **

In *Dumschat*, an inmate claimed Connecticut's clemency procedure violated due process because the Connecticut Board of Pardons failed to provide an explanation for its denial of his commutation application. The Court held that "an inmate has 'no constitutional or inherent right' to commutation of his sentence." ** It noted that, unlike probation decisions, "pardon and commutation decisions have not traditionally been the business of courts; as such, they are rarely, if ever, appropriate subjects for judicial review." ** The Court relied on its prior decision in *Greenholtz v. Inmates of Neb. Penal and Correctional Complex*, 442 U.S. 1 (1979), where it rejected the claim "that a constitutional entitlement to release [on parole] exists independently of a right explicitly conferred by the State." ** The individual's interest in release or commutation " 'is indistinguishable from the initial resistance to being confined,' " and that interest has already been extinguished by the conviction and sentence. ** The Court therefore concluded that a petition for commutation, like an appeal for clemency, "is simply a unilateral hope." **

Respondent's claim of a broader due process interest in Ohio's clemency proceedings is barred by *Dumschat*. The process respondent seeks would be inconsistent with the heart of executive clemency, which is to grant clemency as a matter of grace, thus allowing the executive to consider a wide range of factors not comprehended by earlier judicial proceedings and sentencing determinations. The dissent agrees with respondent that because "a living person" has a constitutionally protected life interest, it is incorrect to assert that respondent's life interest has been "extinguished." ** We agree that respondent maintains a residual life interest, *e.g.,* in not being summarily executed by prison guards. However, as *Greenholtz* helps to make clear, respondent cannot use his interest in not being executed in accord with his sentence to challenge the clemency determination by requiring the procedural protections he seeks. ***

The reasoning of *Dumschat* did not depend on the fact that it was not a capital case. The distinctions accorded a life interest to which respondent and the dissent point ** are primarily relevant to trial. And this Court has generally rejected attempts to expand any distinctions further. ***

Respondent also asserts that, as in *Greenholtz*, Ohio has created protected interests by establishing mandatory clemency application and review procedures. In *Greenholtz*, ** the Court held that the expectancy of release on parole created by the mandatory language of the Nebraska statute was entitled to some measure of constitutional protection.

Ohio's clemency procedures do not violate due process. Despite the Authority's mandatory procedures, the ultimate decisionmaker, the Governor, retains broad discretion. Under any analysis, the Governor's executive discretion need not be fettered by the types of procedural protections sought by respondent. ** There is thus no substantive expectation of clemency. Moreover, *** the availability of clemency, or the manner in which the State conducts clemency proceedings, does not impose "atypical and significant hardship on the inmate in relation to the ordinary incidents of prison life." ** A denial of clemency merely means that the inmate must serve the sentence originally imposed.

Respondent also relies on the "second strand" of due process analysis adopted by the Court of Appeals. He claims that under the rationale of *Evitts v. Lucey*, 469 U.S. 387 (1985), clemency is an integral part of Ohio's system of adjudicating the guilt or innocence of the defendant and is therefore entitled to due process protection. Clemency, he says, is an integral part of the judicial system because it has historically been available as a significant remedy, its availability impacts earlier stages of the criminal justice system, and it enhances the reliability of convictions and sentences. Respondent further suggests, as did the Sixth Circuit, that *Evitts* established a due process continuum across all phases of the judicial process.

In *Evitts*, the Court held that there is a constitutional right to effective assistance of counsel on a first appeal as of right. ** This holding, however, was expressly based on the combination of two lines of prior decisions. One line of cases held that the Fourteenth Amendment guarantees a criminal defendant pursuing a first appeal as of right certain minimum safeguards necessary to make that appeal adequate and effective, including the right to counsel. ** The second line of cases held that the Sixth Amendment right to counsel at trial comprehended the right to effective assistance of counsel. ** These two lines of cases justified the Court's conclusion that a criminal defendant has a right to effective assistance of counsel on a first appeal as of right. **

The Court did not thereby purport to create a new "strand" of due process analysis. And it did not rely on the notion of a continuum of due process rights. Instead, the Court evaluated the function and significance of a first appeal as of right, in light of prior cases. Related decisions similarly make clear that there is no continuum requiring varying levels of process at every conceivable phase of the criminal system. **

***

Thus, clemency proceedings are not "'an integral part of the...system for finally adjudicating the guilt or innocence of a defendant,'" *Evitts, supra,* at 393. Procedures mandated under the Due Process Clause should be consistent with the nature of the governmental power being invoked. Here, the executive's clemency authority would cease to be a matter of grace committed to the executive authority if it were constrained by the sort of procedural requirements that respondent urges. Respondent is already under a sentence of death, determined to have been lawfully imposed. If clemency is granted, he obtains a benefit; if it is denied, he is no worse off than he was before. ***

III

Respondent also presses on us the Court of Appeals' conclusion that the provision of a voluntary inmate interview, without the benefit of counsel or a grant of immunity for any statements made by the inmate, implicates the inmate's Fifth and Fourteenth Amendment right not to incriminate himself. Because there is only one guaranteed clemency review, respondent asserts, his decision to participate is not truly voluntary. And in the interview he may be forced to answer questions; or, if he remains silent, his silence may be used against him. Respondent further asserts there is a substantial risk of incrimination since postconviction proceedings are in progress and since he could potentially incriminate himself on other crimes. Respondent therefore concludes that the interview unconstitutionally conditions his assertion of the right to pursue clemency on his waiver of the right to remain silent. While the Court of Appeals accepted respondent's rubric of "unconstitutional conditions," we find it unnecessary to address it in deciding this case. In our opinion, the procedures of the Authority do not under any view violate the Fifth Amendment privilege.

The Fifth Amendment protects against compelled self-incrimination. ** The record itself does not tell us what, if any, use is made by the board of the clemency interview, or of an inmate's refusal to answer questions posed to him at that interview. But the Authority in its brief dispels much of the uncertainty:

> Nothing in the procedure grants clemency applicants immunity for what they might say or makes the interview in any way confidential. Ohio has permissibly chosen not to allow the inmate to say one thing in the interview and another in a habeas petition, and no amount of discovery will alter this feature of the procedure. **

Assuming also that the Authority will draw adverse inferences from respondent's refusal to answer questions—which it may do in a civil proceeding without offending the Fifth Amendment **—we do not think that respondent's testimony at a clemency interview would be "compelled" within the meaning of the Fifth Amendment. It is difficult to see how a voluntary interview could "compel" respondent to speak. He merely faces a choice quite similar to the sorts of choices that a criminal defendant must make in the course of criminal proceedings, none of which has ever been held to violate the Fifth Amendment.

***

IV

We hold that neither the Due Process Clause nor the Fifth Amendment privilege against self-incrimination is violated by Ohio's clemency proceedings. The judgment of the Court of Appeals is therefore

Reversed.

[An opinion by JUSTICE O'CONNOR, concurring in part and concurring in the judgment, with whom JUSTICES SOUTER, GINSBURG, AND BREYER join, is omitted. An opinion by JUSTICE STEVENS, concurring in part and dissenting in part, is also omitted.]

Notes

1. *Subsequent case history*

Eugene Woodard is currently on death row in Ohio. *See* Website of the Ohio Department of Corrections, http://www.drc.state.oh.us.

2. *Politics and procedure*

The rationale of *Evitts v. Lucey*, Chapter 5, *supra*, would seem to compel that since Ohio created an obligatory capital case hearing, some modicum of due process would be required. What political factors may have caused the Court to reach a different conclusion?

3. *O'Connor concurring in part and concurring in the judgment*

A selection from Justice O'Connor's opinion (joined by Justices Souter, Ginsburg, and Breyer) follows:

> A prisoner under a death sentence remains a living person and consequently has an interest in his life. The question this case raises is the issue of what process is constitutionally necessary to protect that interest in the context of Ohio's clemency procedures. It is clear that "once society has validly convicted an individual of a crime and therefore established its right to punish, the demands of due process are reduced accordingly." ** I do not, however, agree with the suggestion in the principal opinion that, because clemency is committed to the discretion of the executive, the Due Process Clause provides no constitutional safeguards. ***
> When a person has been fairly convicted and sentenced, his liberty interest, in being free from such confinement, has been extinguished. But it is incorrect, as JUSTICE STEVENS' dissent notes, to say that a prisoner has been deprived of all interest in his life before his execution. ** Thus, although it is true that "pardon and commutation decisions have not traditionally been the business of courts," ** and that the decision whether to grant clemency is entrusted to the Governor under Ohio law, I believe that the Court of Appeals correctly concluded that some minimal procedural safeguards apply to clemency proceedings. Judicial intervention might, for example, be warranted in the face of a scheme whereby a state official flipped a coin to determine whether to grant clemency, or in a case where the State arbitrarily denied a prisoner any access to its clemency process. ***

What is the significance of Justice O'Connor's decision to write separately in order to include this observation?

4. *Excerpt from Justice Stevens, concurring in part and dissenting in part*

> When a parole board conducts a hearing to determine whether the State shall actually execute one of its death row inmates—in other words, whether the State shall deprive that person of life—does it have an obligation to comply with the Due Process Clause of the Fourteenth Amendment? In my judgment, the text of the Clause provides the answer to that question. It expressly provides that no State has the power to "deprive any person of life, liberty, or property, without due process of law."

Without deciding what "minimal, perhaps even barely perceptible" procedural safeguards are required in clemency proceedings, the Court of Appeals correctly answered the basic question presented and remanded the case to the District Court to determine whether Ohio's procedures meet the "minimal" requirements of due process. *** In Part II of his opinion today, however, the CHIEF JUSTICE takes a different view—essentially concluding that a clemency proceeding could *never* violate the Due Process Clause. Thus, under such reasoning, even procedures infected by bribery, personal or political animosity, or the deliberate fabrication of false evidence would be constitutionally acceptable. Like JUSTICE O'CONNOR, I respectfully disagree with that conclusion.

***

The text of the Due Process Clause properly directs our attention to state action that may "deprive" a person of life, liberty, or property. When we are evaluating claims that the State has unfairly deprived someone of liberty or property, it is appropriate first to ask whether the state action adversely affected any constitutionally protected interest. Thus, we may conclude, for example, that a prisoner has no "liberty interest" in the place where he is confined, ** or that an at-will employee has no "property interest" in his job. ** There is, however, no room for legitimate debate about whether a living person has a constitutionally protected interest in life. He obviously does."

Is Justice Stevens correct?

Faith in Fantasy:
The Supreme Court's Reliance on Commutation
to Ensure Justice in Death Penalty Cases

Victoria J. Palacios
49 Vanderbilt Law Review 311 (March 1996)
Copyright ©1996 by Vanderbilt Law Review

I. INTRODUCTION

Since scarcely a decade after *Furman v. Georgia*, [408 U.S. 238 (1972)] the Supreme Court has struggled to avoid review of death penalty cases by narrowing the grounds defendants can use to challenge their sentences, as well as the procedures they can use to make those challenges. The Court supports its jurisprudence and the deregulation of death with an important but unexamined assumption: whatever shortcomings exist in the administration of the death penalty, ultimately injustice can and will be avoided by the exercise of the commutation power at the state level. *** This Article argues that such an assumption is unwarranted. By substituting the fantasy of commutation for meaningful appellate review, the Court has perpetuated a system in which capital convictions and sentences lack integrity, while capital defendants suffer injustice.

The Supreme Court's commutation jurisprudence has led to increased deregulation of death penalty decision making. It has delegated those decisions to states that are politically unable to deliver justice in death penalty cases. By doing so, the Court has abdicated its role as protector of powerless minorities. It has also made the imposition of a death penalty more likely. In eschewing constitutional limits and relying on the political process, the Court has sanctioned a process in which many people play a small role in death decisions, no one takes sole, personal responsibility for the decision, and the final decision makers are subject to strong political pressure.

Part II of this article argues that, under current law, death penalty convictions and sentences are unreliable. The system produces wrongful convictions and maldistribution because it is administered unfairly at every level. Further, there is serious doubt that the penalty can ever be administered fairly. Reduced access to habeas corpus review makes these problems more difficult to correct. All of these factors make commutation essential to achieving justice in the capital punishment system. It is often the only mechanism available to correct unjust results.

Part III examines the potential benefits of a meaningful commutation process and proceeds to analyze the Supreme Court's commutation cases. The Court clearly looks at commutation as if the potential benefits were real and as if commutation actually corrects injustices.

Part IV corrects the Supreme Court's rosy picture by looking at commutation as it operates in reality. The fact is that the commutation power is virtually dead because of the belief that "super due process" *** has virtually eliminated error and because the political consequences of granting commutations are too great. ***

Part V explores the implications of the Court's death penalty and commutation jurisprudence. The Court's view of commutation advances the deregulation of death by delegating power to non-functioning state commutation systems. Instead of providing meaningful review, the Court fosters a bureaucratic process under which death decisions cannot be attributed to any decision maker. By doing so, the Court has failed to protect the powerless on death row.

This Article's focus is the commutation of death sentences. *** "Commutation" is used to denote a reduction of a sentence to a lesser one. *** In the capital punishment context, it means reducing a death sentence to life imprisonment. "Clemency," on the other hand, denotes "leniency or mercy in the exercise of authority or power." *** Commutation is a more limited form of clemency *** but shares many attributes of its parent power. *** The terms "commutation" and "clemency" are used interchangeably in this Article to mean a reduction of sentence, unless otherwise noted.

II. THE CONTINUING IMPORTANCE OF DEATH PENALTY COMMUTATION

Despite improved crime detection technology and due process protection afforded to criminal defendants, *** evidence of wrongful convictions unfolds with disturbing frequency. Soon after the Supreme Court reinstated the constitutionality of the death penalty, it stated that because of the qualitative difference between imprisonment and death, there is a "corresponding difference in the need for reliability *** in the determination that death is the appropriate punishment in a specific case." *** Notwithstanding efforts to ameliorate arbitrariness and to provide juries with sufficient guidance to impose death sentences evenhandedly, it remains as true today as it was when *Furman v. Georgia* *** was decided that a poor African-American tried for the capital murder of a white victim in the South is far more likely to be sentenced to death than is his middle-class, Northern counterpart whose victim was black, regardless of the aggravating or mitigating factors present in each case. *** In what has been described as a "rush to judgment," members of the Supreme Court, notably Chief Justice Rehnquist and Justice Scalia, have vowed to expedite the imposition of death penalties by, among other things, curtailing habeas corpus review. *** The emergence of the death penalty as a campaign issue and abundant public support for capital punishment create an atmosphere that subordinates reliability and fairness to political posturing and expedience. The combination of these forces makes it increasingly difficult for a condemned inmate to correct problems that survive post-conviction review.

A. Wrongful Convictions

Commutation should remain a vital component of American criminal justice because errors occur at every point in the conviction and sentencing process. *** These errors are simply part of the risk that attends living in a democracy. *** When errors lead to the conviction of innocent defendants, these cases are designated as wrongful convictions or false positives. It is impossible to eliminate the false positives from the criminal justice system. A system that never caught any innocent people would probably catch few guilty ones. *** Wrongful convictions occur, of course, in capital cases as well, *** but imposition of a death sentence removes all opportunity to correct a miscarriage of justice. This fact warrants the often repeated statement, "Death is different." ***

   ***

Wrongful convictions include not only those that are inaccurate, but also those that are inequitable. For example, plea bargaining for a co-defendant's testimony can lead to the conviction of an innocent or less culpable person. ***

Police misconduct accounts for a number of wrongful convictions. While *Brady v. Maryland*, [373 U.S. 83 (1963),] condemns the *prosecution*'s suppression of exculpatory evidence requested by the defendant, the rule in that decision does not protect the defendant from deceptive *police* reports. *** In fact, the discretion of the police to fail to report exculpatory evidence has not been subjected to the same scrutiny as the prosecutor's duty to disclose such evidence. ***

The poor quality of legal representation given to indigents at state trials and sentencing hearings, particularly in the South, accounts for some wrongful convictions and inappropriate death sentences. ***

   ***

The impact of errors inherent in the criminal justice system is amplified and ratified by other factors. Some suspect that public opinion and the fear of crime raise our tolerance for wrongful convictions. *** Furthermore, it is likely that as a case reaches higher levels of review, there is less chance that an error will be discovered and corrected. *** This ratification of error has led one commentator to describe our criminal justice system with the metaphor of a manufacturing line without quality control. ***

[Palacios then examines the fairness of the administration of the death penalty, arguing that it is not fair and can never be fair.]

III. THE SUPREME COURT'S FLAWED BELIEF THAT COMMUTATION REMEDIES INJUSTICE

   ***

A. The Purposes of Commutation

There was a time when the need for commutations was fairly well accepted, though not entirely unquestioned. *** Today, however, discussions of clemency are frequently prefaced with an apologia. *** The controversy is invited perhaps by the very nature of the commutation power—it operates in derogation of the law. *** It is the antithesis of the rule of law because it is called upon when legal rules have failed to do justice. It is inherently paradoxical because it enhances justice in general by overriding the justice system in a specific case. *** Of course, the ultimate critiques are that commutation is discretionary *** and operates largely without standards or review. ***

Because certain historic applications of commutation are no longer necessary, *** because the power's roots are ancient, and because capital defendants under the Warren and Burger Courts came to enjoy "super due process," *** many have come to view commutation as redundant, outdated, and unsuitable in light of the nation's concern over violent crime. ***

Reasons supporting grants of clemency have varied with the executive and with the times. *** A review of the literature on the history of the clemency power *** suggests that the reasons that authorities grant commutations are widely varied, but fall into three categories relevant to this Article: (1) to promote justice where the reliability of the conviction is in question, (2) to promote justice where the reliability of the sentence *** is in question, and (3) to promote justice where neither the reliability of the conviction nor the sentence is implicated. *** Commutations may be granted for justice-neutral reasons as well, such as administrative expedience. *** Grants of clemency may be said to fall into at least one and sometimes more than one of these categories.

1. Justice-Promoting Commutations that Implicate the Reliability of the Conviction

This category consists of commutations granted to promote justice in an individual case where the reliability of the conviction is questionable. *** Examples include wrongful convictions brought to light by new evidence and convictions that are unreliable because of technical errors, doubt as to guilt, or an unfair trial. *** Sometimes a dissenting judge provides particularly strong doubt about guilt. *** Commutations granted in anticipation of rights not yet recognized *** are appropriately included in this group, as are those granted because of the diminished mental capacity of the offender or his status as a juvenile at the time of the crime. ***

2. Justice-Promoting Commutations that Implicate the Reliability of the Sentence

In this category are commutations granted to promote justice in an individual case where the reliability of the sentence is in doubt. This group includes unfair sentences remitted because the punishment outweighs the seriousness of the offense *** or because sentences among co-defendants are disparate in light of their relative culpability. *** When mitigating factors have not been given appropriate weight by the sentencer, *** reductions of such sentences would fall into this classification. This category also includes commutations that promote equalization of sentences within a jurisdiction and those that recognize and reward rehabilitation efforts. *** Finally, commutations may be granted for sentences that result from an unfair trial and for sentences about which the presiding trial judge recommends leniency to the clemency authority.

3. Justice-Promoting Commutations that Do Not Implicate Reliability

Not all justice-promoting clemency relates to the reliability of an offender's conviction or sentence. Justice may be promoted by a grant of commutation that rewards an offender's testimony against his co-defendant *** or because of the post-conviction mental condition of the offender. *** Commutations of sentences to ameliorate the affects of maldistribution *** or to give sway to the recommendations of judges and prosecutors may promote justice by improving the system rather than individual results. ***

Retributivists might argue that in a case in which public and political pressure favor commutation, granting it preserves the value of fairness that underpins the popular conception of justice. *** A grant of clemency made in keeping with the clemency authority's past practices promotes justice to the extent that uniform classifications mete out like punishment for like crimes. ***

The wide range of purposes for commutation strongly suggest that we would be well served to employ it for at least some of these reasons. Commutation provides a unique opportunity to assess the fairness of a given death sentence and the process that produced it. ***

B. The Supreme Court's Commutation Jurisprudence

Numerous holdings, dicta, and separate opinions express views of the Supreme Court and individual justices on clemency and commutation. These views raise three points relevant to this discussion. First, the Court's vision of clemency is sufficiently broad to allow its use for any of the justice-enhancing purposes outlined above. Each time the court has written of clemency it has employed terms like justice and fairness liberally. Second, the Court has deregulated capital punishment *** and left formulation of death penalty policy, including the exercise of clemency, to the states. Finally, the Court clearly sees commutation as a real option for authorities who possess the power. *** The Court uses the availability of commutation to support its denial of remedies and its overall deregulation of death. ***

1. The Breadth of the Commutation Power

The Court's view of the clemency power has undergone change over time. Early on, the justices saw it as something akin to a divine power. *** Perhaps the broadest characterization of clemency appears in *Ex Parte Garland*. *** Upholding the presidential pardon of a confederate legislator, the Court wrote:

> The power thus conferred is unlimited, with the exception stated [impeachment]. It extends to every offence known to the law, and may be exercised at any time after its commission, either before legal proceedings are taken, or during their pendency, or after conviction and judgment. This power of the President is not subject to legislative control. Congress can neither limit the effect of his pardon, nor exclude from its exercise any class of offenders. The benign prerogative of mercy reposed in him cannot be fettered by any legislative restrictions. ***

Six decades later the Court restricted its view of clemency and eschewed the notion that clemency was an act of grace. In *Biddle v. Perovich*, 274 U.S. 480 (1927), the Court wrote, "A pardon in our days is not a private act of grace from an individual happening to possess power. It is part of the Constitutional scheme." *** Thus, the power was not something to be wielded with absolutely unfettered discretion, but rather was somehow tied to the Constitution. Its purpose was broadly construed to better serve the public welfare by "inflicting less than what the judgment fixed." *** The shift in *Biddle* was barely discernible as the power continued to be interpreted rather generously. ***

The Supreme Court has characterized clemency as a nearly absolute power and a "solemn responsibility." *** Indeed, it has designated clemency an indicium of executive power. *** The Court's jurisprudence instructs that, because it is discretionary, *** clemency may be granted conditionally, *** and grants or denials *** are not subject to judicial review. *** Though abuses of the clemency power are possible and happen from time to time, the Supreme Court has said that the check for such abuse is impeachment rather than a constrictive judicial interpretation of the executive's clemency power. ***

The Court interprets the clemency power broadly in other ways. It sees clemency as an indispensable part of the criminal justice system, *** although offenders usually have no right other than to *seek* commutation. *** As a general matter, supreme court jurisprudence establishes that clemency is a means to accomplish justice in criminal matters. In *Ex parte Grossman*, *** the Court stated:

> Executive clemency exists to afford relief from undue harshness or evident mistake in the operation or enforcement of the criminal law. The administration of justice by the courts is not necessarily always wise or certainly considerate of circumstances which may properly mitigate guilt. To afford a remedy, it has always been thought essential in popular government...to vest in some other authority than the courts power to ameliorate or avoid particular criminal judgments. It is a check entrusted to the executive for special cases. ***

Finally, the Court has found that clemency's special justice-enhancing character makes it distinct from legal remedies. ***

The Court's vision is that the clemency power is one with broad discretion, beyond judicial review, and capable of preventing injustice in appropriate cases. The importance of this awesome power in death penalty jurisprudence is compounded by the Court's deregulation of the death penalty. Because the Supreme Court ultimately relies on commutation to insure that justice is done, *** the tale of deregulation is worth retelling at this point.

2. The Deregulation of Death

Early in his tenure on the court, then-Associate Justice Rehnquist advocated a limited role for federal courts in death penalty matters. In *Coleman v. Balkcom*, [451 U.S. 949 (1981) (Rehnquist, J., dissenting)] he departed from the majority in denying a petition for certiorari explaining that the case raised significant issues about the administration of capital punishment and reflected the increasing delay in the enforcement of death penalty statutes. *** He argued that once the Court had granted certiorari to decide questions involving federal rights, cases should then be returned to state decision makers for execution or commutation. "In any event," he wrote, "the decision would then be in the hands of the State which had initially imposed the death penalty, not in the hands of the federal courts." *** Justice Rehnquist got his wish just over a decade later. In a "startling" group of cases decided at the close of the 1982 term, the Court went "out of the business of telling the states how to administer the death penalty." ***

In retrospect, the Court's decision to deregulate death was not surprising. Deregulation may have been foreshadowed even before the Court first undertook regulation of the death penalty in *Furman*. ***

***

The absence of a single, unified position in *Furman*, as well as the five cases decided in 1976 *** and others that followed, lead inescapably to one of two interpretations. Either the Court demonstrated commitment to disciplining state death penalty procedures, or it never intended to do more than eradicate the most prejudicial of the states' procedures, all the time acknowledging that constitutional legal principles cannot make death penalty practice rational. ***

Whatever one's interpretation of *McGautha* and *Furman*, it is clear that in 1983 the Court repudiated the romantic account and announced that federal courts should stop regulating the imposition of the death penalty. *** The decision to deregulate death told capital defendants to look to the states to administer the death penalty fairly and to provide a remedy for injustices that survive post conviction review. ***

3. The Court's Reliance on Commutation

As the Supreme Court limits its review of death penalty cases, it simultaneously recommends the idealized remedy of commutation to death row inmates. This recommendation appears in majority opinions denying legal relief and in dissents where justices do not agree that a legal remedy is constitutionally required. In either context the message is clear: an injustice the Court does not address can be remedied by commutation.

Dissenters in some cases support their position that relief is inappropriate by arguing that offenders can resort to commutation. In *Fay v. Noia*, [372 U.S. 391 (1963),] for example, the Court held that a state prisoner's failure to appeal his felony murder conviction was not intelligent and knowing and did not justify denying his right to seek federal habeas corpus review. Justice Harlan dissented and, joined by Justices Clark and Stewart, wrote, "I recognize that Noia's predicament may well be thought one that strongly calls for correction. But the proper course to that end lies with the New York Governor's powers of executive clemency, not with the federal courts." ***

***

In the landmark case of *Herrera v. Collins*, [506 U.S. 390 (1993),] the Court made it clear that the federal courts are not ultimately responsible for preventing the execution of arguably innocent people. It held that habeas corpus relief is not available for a claim of innocence based on newly discovered evidence. *** The petitioner had argued that the Eighth and Fourteenth Amendments prohibit the execution of an innocent man and that he, in fact, was innocent according to evidence that had not been heard at his trial. Chief Justice Rehnquist, writing for the majority, pointed out that the presumption of innocence disappears after a fair trial and conviction *** and that due process does not mandate that all possible precautions be taken to avoid convicting the innocent. *** Chief Justice Rehnquist noted that the claim of innocence was cognizable in Texas courts but that the time for raising this claim had passed. *** The thirty-day period Texas provided for raising the claim was not constitutionally objectionable, Justice Rehnquist concluded, noting that fourteen other states had periods of thirty days or shorter for petitioning for a new trial based on new evidence. *** Therefore, Texas's refusal to hear the new evidence did not transgress a "principle of fundamental fairness 'rooted in the traditions and conscience of our people.'" *** Chief Justice Rehnquist maintained that, absent an independent constitutional violation, federal habeas corpus relief was not available to Mr. Herrera, all the while insisting that the Court's habeas corpus jurisprudence does not cast "a blind eye towards innocence." ***

***

IV. THE REALITY OF COMMUTATION PRACTICE

This Part describes the operation of state commutation practices generally. It notes a decline in the number of commutations granted and explores reasons that may account for this decline. It culminates with a case study—the commutation petition of William Andrews.

A. *The Operation of State Commutation Practices*

Describing the "typical" state commutation process is challenging. Diversity is a hallmark of statutes that govern clemency throughout the states. Nevertheless, the statutes have these features in common: procedures are largely standardless, decisions are discretionary, and results are unreviewable. ***

In the American system of government, the clemency power is not inherent in any particular branch of government, *** although it is usually associated with the executive branch. *** Today, state laws fall into one of three basic models. In the first model, the governor has primary or exclusive authority to grant commutations in death penalty cases. *** Most states follow this approach. *** In the second model, a parole or pardons board has primary or exclusive jurisdiction over the commutation of capital sentences. *** In the third model, the clemency power is shared by the governor and the parole or pardons board. ***

The use of the commutation power is more or less vulnerable to public pressure depending upon where the power is vested and who appoints the decision makers. *** The *Guide to Executive Clemency Among the American States* indicates that in most of the states that vest the clemency power in a board, its members are appointed by the governor. *** That most states continue to vest primary clemency power in the governor was borne out by a recent study by the Association of Paroling Authorities International. *** The 1994 survey of paroling authorities asked representatives from fifty-two boards *** whether they were empowered to commute sentences. Five responded that they were, twelve replied they were not, and thirty-five said that they could recommend commutation to the governor. ***

Typically, clemency requests require investigation to ensure that sufficient facts are available to the decision maker. *** The investigation is usually conducted by the staff of the decision maker. *** A clemency investigation typically inquires into the circumstances surrounding the crime, the petitioner's biography, reports of psychological and psychiatric examinations, and comments from the trial judge and prosecuting attorney. *** More recently, investigations have included input from victims. *** Some of the information garnered may be confidential. ***

Few state or federal courts have considered whether the Due Process Clause requires fair procedures in the consideration of clemency petitions. Those courts that have considered the issue have provided no constitutional protection. *** Commutation procedures are therefore quite varied. *** Procedures for clemency application range from informal to formal submission of an official petition. The greater the formality, the greater the burden on the applicant and, seemingly, the greater the need for legal representation. At one time, virtually all petitioners were represented by counsel. *** Today, state statutes regarding representation range from prohibiting representatives of applicants from receiving fees *** to providing counsel for an applicant who is indigent. ***

There is great variation in clemency hearings, as well. Usually, the clemency authority is not required to conduct a hearing. *** If a hearing is held, some states allow the petitioner to attend the clemency hearing; *** others do not. Those who do not allow the petitioner to attend the hearing may conduct an interview and include the transcript or report in the file prior to the hearing. *** In the overwhelming number of states, clemency hearings are public *** and informal. Some states have written procedures, *** but many do not. *** The course of the hearing is determined by the presiding official, and the rules of evidence do not apply. *** Officials conducting clemency hearings often have subpoena power, *** although few states make a transcript or other record of the clemency hearing. *** Most states require clemency decisions to be reported to the legislature or filed with the Secretary of State. ***

***

B. The Decline in the Use of Commutation

If at one time the commutation power was a meaningful source of justice, this is no longer the case. The heyday of commutations was the early- and mid-1940s, during which twenty to twenty-five percent of death penalties were commuted. *** Though not written at this time, books by former California Governor Edmund (Pat) Brown *** and former Ohio Governor Michael V. DiSalle *** illustrate that, while commutations were not commonplace during the 1960s, they were sufficiently frequent that, at least in some states, meritorious cases were carefully considered and commuted. Members of the *Furman* Court noted that commutations accounted for a decline in the number of annual executions in the years prior to 1972. *** Commutation was one of several reasons that executions had dwindled to approximately eighteen cases a year prior to *Furman*. *** By Justice Brennan's account, governors had "regularly commuted a substantial number" of death cases. *** Long after commutations ceased to be common, however, writers have continued to promote the belief that they occur with great frequency. ***

In the last quarter century, there has been a dramatic decline in death penalty commutations—so much so that some say the clemency power is now defunct. Michael Radelet, a noted University of Florida sociologist, believes that "clemency is not a component of the modern death-sentencing process." *** Experiences in Florida and Louisiana illustrate how sharp the decline has been. Between 1920 and 1972, Florida governors commuted from twenty to forty percent of death sentences. After the penalty was reinstated in 1976, only six sentences were commuted by Governor Bob Graham, and neither of his successors have commuted any capital sentences. *** Writing in 1974, William J. Bowers observed that about one in four or five death sentences was commuted to life imprisonment. *** By 1988, data collected by Hugo Adam Bedau demonstrated that the frequency had dwindled to one in forty. The decline has prompted some to declare that clemency, like UFOs and Bigfoot, exists only in theory. ***

***

A death row inmate who petitions for commutation to a life sentence has only the remotest hope for relief. ***

C. The Reasons for the Decline

There are many circumstances that have contributed to the atrophy of commutation power. First and foremost, the political consequences of granting commutations are simply too great. This is evident from the experiences of those who have granted commutations and from the efforts of legislatures to abolish or limit clemency. *** The political pressure is, at least in part, a reaction to past abuses of the power. *** Second, many believe that commutation is no longer necessary. They mistakenly believe that the judicial system is flexible enough to render full justice *** and that injustice cannot survive "super due process." *** Third, there is a conservative philosophy among executives that the judgments of courts and juries should not be overridden. *** This Section explores the political ramifications of commutations and argues that, standing alone, they can and have prevented appropriate exercises of commutation.

Some governors have been generous in their exercise of clemency, *** but serious political consequences can follow when a governor grants clemency against the popular will. Pat Brown held office as the governor of California from 1959 to 1966. He believed that his death row decisions played a part in his sound defeat by Ronald Reagan. *** Republican Dave Treen challenged incumbent Louisiana Governor Edwin Edwards in 1979 and used Edwards's clemency record to help defeat him. ***

Commuting a death sentence can pose personal risks as well. When New Mexico's Governor Tony Anaya had made up his mind to commute the sentences of the five offenders on death row, he spoke with no one about his intention because of threats of physical injury and even death he had received, presumably to deter or prevent his exercising the commutation power. *** Just *considering* commutation can be risky as well. When the Utah board conducted its commutation hearing for William Andrews in 1989, the community was in a furor and board members were advised to take security precautions. Officers, some with trained guard dogs, stood watch at the homes of some board members twenty-four hours a day while the matter was pending. ***

President Clinton may be among those who have found opposing the death penalty politically untenable. During his first term as governor of Arkansas, Clinton refused to set execution dates for two dozen death-row inmates and commuted forty-four life-without-parole sentences to make them parole eligible. *** Between the start of his second term and 1992, Clinton moved quickly to set execution dates, declined to stop the executions of three men, and reduced life sentences only seven times. *** During his presidential campaign, Clinton denied the commutation request of Ricky Ray Rector who had "effectively lobotomized himself with a self-inflicted gunshot to the head, after he shot and killed a police officer." *** There is substantial doubt about whether Rector realized he was about to die. On the way to the execution chamber he said he intended to vote for Mr. Clinton. ***

For governors, the choice is a pragmatic one. When a "tough on crime" policy prevails in a state, commutations are reduced. *** In all likelihood, wariness of political fallout accounts for some of the decline in commutations, despite the increase in the number of persons slated for execution. ***

Public opposition to commutation can affect more than just the governor or board. It can have repercussions for the decision maker's office itself. Public outcry has prompted state legislators to introduce bills to abolish or limit the commutation power. After New Mexico's Governor Anaya issued two stays of execution, constitutional amendments and bills limiting the governor's power were introduced in the legislature, although none were passed. *** Similarly, the Utah legislature considered and rejected abolition of commutation after a high-profile, though unsuccessful, commutation hearing. *** Some years later the Utah legislature succeeded in limiting the power. *** This legislative action was a major encroachment on the authority of one of the most powerful parole boards in the country. ***

Though there may be disagreement about why governors seldom grant clemency, there is no refuting that the incidence of clemency grants has slowed to a trickle. Yet, applications for clemency are filed by death row inmates as routinely as are petitions for appellate review. ***
***

V. IMPLICATIONS OF THE COURT'S COMMUTATION JURISPRUDENCE

It is well established that the administration of criminal justice, and particularly the death penalty, is filled with infirmities. There is evidence of a disturbing number of unreliable capital convictions and sentences, *** despite the heightened reliability the Supreme Court has said is necessary for constitutional imposition of the death penalty. *** There is also evidence to believe that many death sentences have resulted from a process that is unfair. *** No one's objectives-neither those who favor the death penalty nor those who oppose it—are served by executing people convicted by an unfair process, some of whom may be innocent. ***

Many of the system's flaws are inherent in the task of adjudicating and punishing wrongdoers. Nevertheless, the inevitability of the errors produced by the system does not obviate the need for a remedy when injustice results in an individual case. The nation's highest court pretends *** that there is an effective safety net that enables state systems to save the unfairly and wrongfully convicted, yet there is little evidence that intervention in fact occurs.

[There are] four consequences of the Court's fantasy. First, the Court's view of commutation advances the deregulation of death. Second, the Court has left the business of commutation to state systems, but those systems are inherently unable to satisfy the need to ameliorate injustice. Third, death penalty decisions are largely decisions without attribution. Because no one feels responsible for imposing the death penalty, injustices are allowed to go uncorrected. Finally, the Court has abdicated its constitutional responsibility to protect discrete and insular minorities, namely those living on death rows throughout the thirty-six jurisdictions that have imposed death sentences. ***

 ***

B. Justice the States Cannot Deliver
***

Surveys show that nearly eighty percent of the American population voices support for capital punishment. *** Not surprisingly, Texans' approval of the death penalty is ninety-two percent, according to one poll. *** American politicians are likely to follow public opinion, rather than try to change it. *** No participant in death sentence decisions is immune from the political pressure that accompanies those decisions. Almost always, the political winds blow in favor of execution. While some public officials have been elected despite anti-death-penalty beliefs, they are the exception rather than the rule. *** The pressure put upon these decision makers begins early in the process with the prosecutor's initial decision to seek capital punishment. Since the death penalty is requested in only a small fraction of all capital murders, this decision is the most critical juncture for homicide defendants. *** Recent highly publicized cases illustrate that prosecutors face close public scrutiny while making these decisions and are often vilified for declining to seek capital punishment. ***

Elected judges face the pressure as well. At the ABA Symposium on politics and the death penalty, Bryan Stevenson, Executive Director of the Alabama Capital Representation Resource Center, observed:

> Approximately one hundred and twenty people are on death row in the State of Alabama. Nearly twenty-five percent of those people received life verdicts from juries. *** When you do a statistical study, a mini-multiple regression analysis of how the death penalty is applied and how override is applied, there is a statistically significant correlation between judicial override and election years in most of the counties where these overrides take place. And it is one of the clearest examples of the precise dynamic of politics in the administration of the death penalty. ***

State supreme court justices have been replaced because of their view on the death penalty. Chief Justice Rose Bird and her two liberal colleagues were voted out of office in 1986, following a period during which the California Supreme Court had reversed sixty-four of the sixty-eight capital sentences it had reviewed. The California Supreme Court now upholds seventy-five percent of the capital sentences it reviews. *** Candidates for state supreme court justice positions are keenly aware of the public's strong approval of capital punishment. In a recent primary campaign, a candidate for the Texas Supreme Court boasted her enthusiastic support for the death penalty, an odd "qualification" in light of the fact that the Texas Court of Criminal Appeals, and not the Texas Supreme Court, has exclusive jurisdiction over criminal cases. ***

Governors appear to be particularly vulnerable to political pressure, although New York's former Governor Mario Cuomo managed to "take the moral high ground" *** before he was ultimately defeated, in part at least, for his anti-death-penalty stance. *** When Florida's former Governor Bob Graham was running for the United States Senate, he signed four death warrants between February and the November election. *** In Governor Bob Martinez's 1989 campaign, Martinez stated, "I now have signed ninety death warrants in the state of Florida." *** During the 1990 election campaigns, gubernatorial candidates indulged in what has been called "ghoulish rivalry" in support of the death penalty. *** California's candidates each vowed to keep the gas chamber busy. When Texas gubernatorial candidate Ann Richards received unsolicited support from a prison newspaper, her rival Jim Mattox adopted the slogan: "Jim Mattox. There are not endorsements for him on death row." *** In their eagerness to jump on the death penalty bandwagon, candidates have made absurd claims. According to Governor Anaya's report, the newly elected New Mexico governor, Garrey Carruthers, stated publicly that he was eager to assume office. The first act he would perform, he announced, would be to sign a death warrant. *** But judges, not governors, sign death warrants in New Mexico. ***

The public's overwhelming approval of capital punishment affects commutation decision makers with full force because states provide little or no insulation to buffer clemency officials from public ire. Although a decision maker in a representative republic should generally be accountable to citizens, he or she should not be so sensitive to public opinion that paralysis results. *** Perhaps the Supreme Court recognized the danger of officials' oversubscribing to public opinion when it suggested that impeachment should be the only check on their reasons for granting clemency. ***

Unfortunately, an appropriate balance has not been struck in capital clemency decision making. A governor who wields the commutation power alone or shares it with others faces re-election periodically. Board members who have the power to grant clemency eventually face reappointment by an elected governor. No matter how much merit these officials see in a case, the fallout of a commutation could be fearsome, or even politically fatal. By ignoring the political pressure against commutations and by pretending commutation authorities are free to grant clemency in meritorious cases, the Supreme Court obscures the reality of commutation practice and promotes the fantasy of the commutation ideal. As long as that is the case, state commutation decision making will continue to be the slave of public opinion and an empty promise to death row inmates seeking justice.

C. Responsibility for Death Penalty Decisions

Who decides who dies? The Court's commutation jurisprudence contributes to a disturbing phenomenon. Modern death penalty practice diffuses responsibility among multiple actors, each of whom legitimizes the decision of the actor preceding it, until responsibility never really settles anywhere, and no one actually appears to do the killing. ***

***

Commutation is the last resort for the condemned prisoner. It is here where the strength of the many previous affirmations of the conviction and sentence weighs most heavily. A nearly irrebuttable presumption of validity exists. Because it is unthinkable that a meritorious claim could have gone unrecognized during the course of many appellate and habeas corpus proceedings, governors and boards are loath to commute a sentence. Commutation decision makers, then, take their place among the many others who had nothing to do with the execution of a person whose conviction and sentence may have been seriously flawed.

***

VI. CONCLUSION

Wrongful convictions, unfair distribution of the death penalty, and a restricted review of death sentences reaffirm the need for a mechanism to provide a remedy for those who are innocent, and those whose proceedings, though constitutional, were seriously flawed. This is particularly true where certain arguments never found a forum. According to the literature on commutations and the Supreme Court's clemency jurisprudence, commutation should be the ideal mechanism for ensuring justice because a power so broad could be used for many justice-enhancing reasons. The Court's decisions demonstrate further that it assumes that commutation currently operates as the idealized process for enhancing justice. In fact, commutation does not so operate because strong pro-death-penalty public opinion stands in the way and states have not provided insulation from public opinion for commutation decision makers.

Unfortunately, the rosy but inaccurate picture painted by the Court has these deleterious effects: (1) by failing to acknowledge that its decisions can leave petitioners without a remedy, the Court quells legitimate criticism of its actions and proceeds apace with the deregulation of death, (2) the Court's obscured reality maintains the tie between commutation decisions and popular opinion via the political process and therefore the states do not provide the hoped for fail-safe mechanism, (3) a non-functioning commutation process does harm because it contributes another bureaucratic layer to insulate those who so strongly support the death penalty from responsibility for all of its consequences, and finally (4) by maintaining the fiction of idealized commutation, the Court adds to the growing evidence that it has abandoned its role as protector of the politically powerless by refusing to prevent an execution. One undertaking of this Article has been to inform the emperors that they have no clothes. *** The Court's stated reliance on commutation is a smoke screen that draws attention from the consequences of its refusal to regulate the death penalty.

The message having been delivered to the emperors, what can be done about miscarriages of justice in light of the Court's position? I add my voice to those of others who have suggested that commutation can be revived. *** It can be reinstituted to some degree by insulating decision makers from the political consequences of granting commutation in an unpopular case. Only then can decision makers render judgments based more on the merits and less on political pressure.

This Article argues that the traditional governor-appointed board is an insufficient buffer against strong public opinion. Better protection against public opinion can be provided if the governor appoints a selection board, *** comprised primarily of unpaid citizens, which would then appoint the commutation authority. The selection board would follow statutory qualifications and other selection factors to ensure balanced representation on the clemency board. For example, candidates for the clemency board should have to meet qualifications relating to education and experience. Additionally, the number of appointments from a single political party should be limited, and representation by a variety of races and genders should be encouraged. Although the governor would still appoint the selection board, the collectiveness of that board's appointment decisions would make each individual less vulnerable to retaliation and political pressure. Further, the commutation decision itself would be made by the clemency board, which would be sufficiently far removed from the governor to attenuate his or her possible influence.

The strengths of a citizen selection board are its independence from state criminal justice agencies, its ability to reflect public sentiment in a tempered fashion, and its potential for attracting useful expertise to the problems of criminal justice policy. Its shortcoming is that its members may lack insight into the ongoing, every-day problems of criminal justice administration. For this reason, a minority of the selection board should include criminal justice professionals such as judges, correctional administrators, and parole board members.

***

When justices of the Supreme Court have uttered phrases such as "heightened reliability" and "death is different," they acknowledge the truly awesome nature of the death penalty. With the decline in the use of the commutation power, we have lost an important means of ensuring that executions occur only when the process and its outcome are fair.

Notes

1. *Clemency through a citizens' selection board*

What is your assessment of the pros and cons of Palacios's recommendation that the governor appoint a selection board, comprised primarily of unpaid citizens, which would then appoint the commutation authority?

2. *Reliance on clemency*

Are there reasons that courts should continue to rely on clemency as a fail safe? What are the dangers in doing so?

Text of Governor George Ryan's
DePaul University College of Law Speech
Pardoning Four on Death Row

Copyright ©2003 by former Governor George Ryan
Delivered on January 10, 2003
Provided by Ryan's Press Office to DePaul University College of Law
This address was not delivered verbatim.

Thank you very much Andrea Lyon for that introduction and thank you Father Minogue for hosting us today.

I want to acknowledge Larry Marshall from Northwestern Law School who is here today. He has long been a tireless advocate for justice for the hardest cases. I want to welcome him. I believe Paul Ciolino may be here. Paul is a private investigator, and a pretty tenacious one at that. He worked on several important cases of death row inmates and he is known for teaching his tricks to law and journalism students. I want to acknowledge him.

I want to thank you all for joining us today.

It means a lot to be here. Although governors work all the time, this is my last full business day in office. At noon on Monday, a new governor will be inaugurated and my time in office will be completed. I'm glad I can spend some time with law students—people who can make a difference in the future.

I know Andrea is dedicated to teaching the next generation of lawyers about the law and about justice. She knows about both and I want to congratulate her for starting an innocence project here, the Center for Justice in Capital Cases.

As you know, I have been learning about the Illinois capital punishment system. It has been an arduous journey.

Four years ago I was taking the oath of office. I had great ambitions for an agenda to build a new Illinois. We succeeded in most of those goals: investing 51 percent of new revenues for education, developing a program to invest in the schools, roads and transit systems of this state—that program became Illinois FIRST.

There were many things we wanted to do. But the death penalty was nowhere on the radar screen. I had no intention of grappling with such a difficult topic. As I have said, the death penalty was just one of those things that was there, in the abstract.

Little did I know what lay ahead.

Three years ago, I was faced with startling information. We had exonerated not one, not two, but 13 men from death row. They were found innocent. Innocent of the charges for which they were sentenced to die.

Can you imagine?

The state nearly killed innocent people, nearly injected them with a cocktail of deadly poisons so that they could die in front of witnesses on a gurney in the state's death chamber.

You have heard some of the stories. I won't dwell on them today because I have so much to report, but the exonerated included Anthony Porter, wrongfully convicted and 48 hours away from being executed.

His lawyer Larry Marshall won a stay of execution so that journalism students led by their professor, David Protess, and Investigator Paul Ciolino could prove his innocence.

Rolando Cruz and Alex Hernandez, wrongly convicted for killing a little girl even as a convicted child killer, Brian Dugan, offered to plead guilty to the horrible crime. Prosecutors, who were zealously committed to sending Cruz and Hernandez to death row, would not accept Dugan's offer of a guilty plea in exchange for life. A courageous Du-Page county judge acquitted Cruz and Hernandez in 1995. Since then, DNA evidence conclusively points to Dugan, who remains uncharged.

There were others—Dennis Williams and Verneal Jimerson. The case against them had hinged on the testimony of a 17-year-old, impoverished, mentally challenged woman who, according to her lawyers, was coerced at gunpoint by investigators into testifying against four of her friends.

When she tried to come clean, the state charged her with perjury (and) sent her off to prison, where she spent eight years in hell. She finally got out when she agreed to go back to her coerced testimony, even though it was false. Twenty years later, the state's attorney was still fighting her effort to clear her name of the perjury charge.

Another co-defendant, Kenny Adams, was sentenced to 75 years in prison. He was offered a get-out-of-jail-free card if he would only testify against one of his co-defendants during one of their retrials. He showed enormous strength of character by refusing that bargain. Adams, Willie Rainge, Williams and Patterson—the Ford Heights Four—were rescued from their nightmare.

Finally, Paul Ciolino and Dave Protess and their students got the evidence to free the Ford Heights Four. They found the witnesses who recanted their claims and, with their lawyers, fought for DNA testing. It's a good thing. The Ford Heights Four were cleared by DNA evidence after an 18-year battle.

Gary Gauger was sentenced to die for killing his parents. But there was no evidence, just an alleged vision statement that was never committed to writing by investigators. Federal Alcohol, Tobacco and Firearms investigators saved him by catching members of the Outlaw motorcycle gang on tape confessing to killing Gauger's parents and laughing about how Gary took the rap.

The category of horrors was hard to believe. If I hadn't reviewed the cases myself, I wouldn't believe it.

I've repeated many times the findings of reporters Steve Mills and Ken Armstrong of the Chicago Tribune who conducted an exhaustive investigation in the flaws of the system in November of 1999. Half of the nearly 300 capital cases in Illinois had been reversed for a new trial or re-sentencing. Nearly half!

Thirty-three of the death row inmates were represented at trial by attorneys who had later been disbarred or at some point suspended from practicing law.

Of the more than 160 death row inmates, 35 were African-American defendants who had been convicted or condemned to die by all-white juries.

More than two-thirds of the inmates on death row are African-American.

Forty-six inmates were convicted on the basis of testimony from jailhouse informants.

I'm not a lawyer, but I don't think you need to be one to be appalled by those statistics.

I have one question. How does that happen?

We had executed 12 people since capital punishment was reinstated here in Illinois in 1977. With the thirteenth exonerated inmate in January of 2000, we had released more innocent men from death row than those hopefully guilty people we had executed.

Three years ago I described it as a shameful scorecard. Truly shameful.

So I did the only thing I could, I called for what is, in effect, a moratorium.

A lot of people called that courageous.

It wasn't. It was just the right thing to do. I have a feeling that's what Father Minogue, Andrea Lyon and the other law professors here at DePaul are teaching you to do.

I wish I had better news to report to you today. But I don't.

In fact I must share with you some startling information. There are more innocent people on death row.

Let me talk to you about Madison Hobley.

In January 1987, 16 years ago, Madison Hobley lived with his wife and infant son in an apartment building on Chicago's south side, where he worked for a medical supply company. Madison had no previous convictions. He had married his childhood sweetheart.

Madison had a steady job, installing medical equipment in people's homes. He was studying to become a medical technician. His only indiscretion was a brief extramarital affair, which he had ended and for which his wife and her parents had forgiven him. By January they were back together, trying to build their lives together as family.

On the sixth, Madison awoke to the sound of a fire alarm. Dressed only in shorts and a t-shirt, he went into the hall to investigate. The couple's apartment was at the top of the stairway on the third floor, and he thought he saw smoke coming from under the door of an apartment across from his. Suddenly, he heard a whoosh and a cracking noise. A stairway door failed. There was a wall of fire and smoke between him and his wife and young son. Shouting to them to head for a window, he crawled down the hall to the back stairs. He hoped he could rescue them. He prayed his wife could drop the baby to him out the window.

But it was not to be. He never saw his family again. Seven people died, including Madison's wife and baby. Yet, in the confusion of the inferno around him, Madison helped to catch a neighbor's baby and save its life.

Because he survived and his family did not, the police immediately focused on Madison Hobley as a suspect, ignoring information about a disgruntled former tenant evicted months before for selling drugs. The now infamous Area 2 detectives, under the command of Lt. [Jon] Burge, grilled Hobley, beat him, "bagged" him and tried to get him to confess.

Bagging involves taking a plastic typewriter cover over a suspect's face and head until the suspect loses consciousness from lack of oxygen. Burge and his men practiced it regularly, we know this now from the Chicago Police Office of Professional Standards.

The police said Madison confessed, but the only writing that survived was his denial. A detective said the purported confession got coffee spilled on it, was "wet and torn" and so he threw it away.

Two men came forward to claim they saw Madison purchase gasoline the night of the fire. One could not be certain of his identification. The other, it turned out, was being "helped" by Chicago police in his own criminal problems, including an arson that had occurred six weeks later and within a few blocks of the apartment building where Hobley lived.

Madison's trial lawyers had no idea that the testimony of this witness was tainted. Nor did they know that a gasoline can introduced into evidence during Madison's trial was not used to start the fatal fire, but rather had been seized earlier at another unrelated fire. That's because his lawyer and investigator, Andrea Lyon and her team and Paul Ciolino, uncovered this new evidence.

The gas can used to convict Madison was in pristine condition, showing no signs that it had "survived" the blaze that killed his family. The defense also did not receive a fingerprint report from the can that could prove Madison's prints were not on the can. A Cook County judge has refused to acknowledge any of this new evidence in hearings ordered by the state supreme court.

So Madison Hobley has sat on death row and waited. Waited for justice.

Madison's troubles even spread to the jury room. The foreman of the jury, a suburban police officer, intimidated some jurors by laying his gun on the jury table and announcing: "We'll reach a verdict." The jury finally came back with a guilty verdict after four days of strained deliberations.

Madison Hobley was convicted on the basis of flawed evidence. He was convicted because the jury did not have the benefit of all existing evidence, which would have served to exonerate him.

The case against Madison evaporated only after years of investigation by Professor Andrea Lyon, from here at DePaul, and Attorney Kurt Feuer, a DePaul law alum, and many of Professor Lyon's students.

Madison Hobley professed his innocence from the first day that Chicago police arrested him.

Evidence uncovered after trial similarly presents a compelling case that Stanley Howard did not commit the crime for which he faces execution.

He was charged with coming up to a man in a car, asking for a match, and then shooting the man in a fit of temper when the man refused the request. However, witnesses subsequently were located who heard the crime unfold and whose testimony establishes that the shooter knew the victim and his companion and that the shooter had been stalking them so that he could, in his words, "catch" them.

There was no physical evidence of any kind against Howard. The state's case consisted entirely of two items of evidence. First, there was an alleged identification by a single eyewitness, the victim's companion. Eyewitness identifications are never very reliable, but here the identification was particularly unreliable. The witness had been drinking heavily at the time of the shooting. She also had a restricted ability and a limited opportunity to see the shooter in the dark at night.

More importantly, she made her identification of Howard six months after the shooting and at the time was only able to make a tentative identification that Howard looked similar to the shooter. Finally, her version of what happened was directly contradicted by ballistics evidence and the testimony of the witnesses who heard what happened that night.

The only other evidence against Howard was his so-called confession, which he has maintained from the beginning was obtained by brutal torture. Like Madison Hobley, Stanley Howard was suffocated with a plastic bag until he confessed. There is strong evidence that corroborates his account. His confession was obtained by Area 2 detectives. In Howard's case, medical evidence uncovered after trial directly establishes that Howard was physically harmed while in the custody of the Area 2 detectives.

He called his father and said these "detectives are killing me." His father immediately called OPS and the FBI.

In addition, witnesses have come forward after trial who corroborate that Howard was in a battered condition during his Area 2 interrogation. Having looked at all of the evidence of torture, even an investigator for the Chicago Police Department's own Office of Professional Standards has concluded that Howard indeed was abused by Area 2 detectives before he gave his so-called confession.

In April of 1986, Aaron Patterson was tortured by Area 2 Violent Crimes detectives, under the direct supervision and with the active participation of Commander Burge.

During the initial interrogation, Patterson repeatedly denied his involvement in the murder of a south side couple who had allegedly been selling illegal weapons.

Detectives subsequently handcuffed Patterson behind his back, turned out the lights, suffocated him with a gray plastic typewriter cover over his head and struck him in the chest.

When Patterson refused to confess, he was suffocated and beaten about his body again. He also was threatened with a gun by Burge himself.

When Patterson was left alone in the interrogation room he scratched into a bench with a paper clip that he was tortured and that his statements to the police were false. Listen to these chilling words: "I lie about murders, police threaten me with violence, slapped and suffocated me with plastic signed false statement to murders."

The record in Mr. Patterson's case shows that he was one of the last of the approximately 60 known victims who have alleged torture by Chicago Police detectives at Area 2 Police Headquarters from 1972 to 1986. Mr. Patterson's father was a Chicago Police Lieutenant, but perhaps he was the wrong color. Despite repeatedly calling for his father, there was no mercy, no benefit of a doubt. The beatings continued.

As a direct result of his torture, the detectives claim to have obtained an oral confession, which was introduced at Patterson's trial and which is the only remaining "evidence" which supports his conviction.

There is no physical or forensic evidence which links Patterson to the crimes. Further, Marva Hall, a young girl who testified at trial that Patterson made an admission to her, has recanted, and has accused the police and a former Assistant Cook County State's Attorney of coercing this false testimony from her.

In addition, there is an affidavit that another man, who was an acquaintance of the victims, actually committed the crimes. That suspect has subsequently committed a very similar crime.

Finally, fingerprints from the scene were previously tested and did not match Patterson's. If tested today these fingerprints could help to identify the real killer, but the state's attorneys office reports that this evidence has been lost.

Unfortunately, much of the evidence of this systematic Area 2 torture and abuse had not emerged at the time of Mr. Patterson's trial in 1989. It was on the basis of this evidence, as well as the incompetence of his trial lawyers, that the Illinois Supreme Court sent Mr. Patterson's case back to the Cook County courts for a new hearing into whether this evidence requires that Mr. Patterson receive a new trial a year ago. There clearly has, however, been no rush to do justice.

Aaron's case is another one in which Dave Protess, Paul Ciolino and the Northwestern students have been investigating.

Leroy Orange was convicted of murder and sentenced to death in 1985 based exclusively on a confession obtained at Area 2 Police Headquarters. Orange consistently maintained that his confession was false and that he gave it only because he was tortured by Jon Burge. At his first court appearance in 1984, Orange told his public defender and the judge that he had been tortured by the police. The lawyer, who he retained after his first court appearance, told the press that the police obtained a confession from Orange by electro-shocking him using a black box.

The only evidence against Orange was his confession. Ordinarily, the admissibility of a confession would be challenged by a defense lawyer, especially when his client claims that his confession was coerced. Coerced confessions are notoriously unreliable. However, Orange's lawyer, who has repeatedly been disciplined, never demanded a hearing to determine the admissibility of Orange's confession. Thus Mr. Orange's confession was introduced into evidence without being challenged by defense counsel.

During the 17 years since his conviction, Orange has sought a hearing to prove that his confession was false. Despite the fact that during this time overwhelming evidence of a pattern and practice of torture at Area 2 has emerged, Illinois courts have repeatedly denied Orange's request for a hearing on his confession. The prosecution has opposed Orange's repeated requests on procedural grounds and even seeks to bar evidence of the torture that led to...Orange's [conviction].

In other words, the prosecution intends to ask a jury to execute Orange based on his confession, but the courts will not allow Orange to inform the jury about the torture that led to the confession.

I'm not a lawyer, I am a pharmacist. But how does this happen? It appears to me, the system has failed Orange by relying on procedural technicalities at the exclusion of the quest for truth.

The system has failed all four men. It has failed the people of this state.

In some way, I can see how rogue cops, 20 years ago, can run wild. I can see how, in a different time, they perhaps were able to manipulate the system.

What I can't understand is why the courts can't find a way to act in the interest of justice. Here we have four more men who were wrongfully convicted and sentenced to die by the state for crimes the courts should have seen they did not commit. We have evidence from four men who did not know each other, all getting beaten and tortured and convicted on the basis of the confessions they allegedly provide.

They are perfect examples of what is so terribly broken about our system. These cases call out for someone to act. They call out for justice, they cry out for reform.

Their cries have fallen on deaf ears, until now.

It reminds me of a story I heard about President Lincoln, in Sen. Robert Dole's recent book.

As President Lincoln shouldered the burden of trying to fight the bloody civil war and saving our young republic, he often had to review individual cases of men who were to face the firing squad.

These were young men who were found guilty of crimes such as desertion while serving the Union in battles in which brother fought brother spilling their blood and dying on grisly battlefields.

President Lincoln reviewed one such case with a senior army officer and noticed that there were no letters or pleas for mercy or pardon from anyone on behalf of the accused soldier. "It's true," the officer said, "He has no friends."

To that President Lincoln replied, "Then I shall be his friend" and signed the pardon request.

Today, I shall be a friend to Madison Hobley, Stanley Howard, Aaron Patterson and Leroy Orange. Today I am pardoning them of the crimes for which they were wrongfully prosecuted and sentenced to die.

I have reviewed these cases and I believe a manifest injustice has occurred. I have reviewed these cases and I believe these men are innocent. I still have some faith in the system that eventually these men would have received justice in our courts. But the old adage is true: justice delayed is justice denied.

There is another tragedy here[, and] because of the brutal police work of [Jon] Burge[,] it almost ensures that the truth will never really be found. The tragedy is compounded and the families of the victims of these long ago murders may never know what happened to their loved ones and why.

Stanley Howard will unfortunately not be released from prison today. He will still need to serve time for a robbery, kidnap, sex assault case. However, the evidence in that case is also very troubling. He has not yet petitioned for relief in that case. I would recommend his lawyers do so, and I urge the next administration pick up where I am leaving off. That case may well be as tainted as his murder conviction. If so, let us right those wrongs and quickly. Let's promote justice.

A few weeks after I announced the moratorium, I appointed the smartest, most dedicated citizens I could find—prosecutors, defense lawyers, former elected officials and business people—to a special commission. It was chaired by former Federal Judge Frank McGarr and co-chaired by former U.S. Attorney Thomas Sullivan and former U.S. Senator Paul Simon.

I asked them to do only one thing: to study the system from top to bottom. I told them until I can be sure with moral certainty that no innocent person will be sent to death row and executed by the state, no one would meet that fate.

They worked for more than two years. They studied every aspect of the system, from the time the police arrive at the scene of a murder, to the last ditch appeals to the supreme court, and all points in between.

Over two years they reviewed each and every case of the exonerated inmates, the inmates on death [row] and...the nearly 150 cases that had been reversed or remanded. Every single case!

After all of that, they developed 85 recommendations. Eighty-five ways to improve our badly broken system. They acknowledged they could never make it perfect, but they said their recommendations could dramatically reduce the chance that we would wrongfully convict and execute an innocent person.

The recommendations included the creation of a statewide panel to review prosecutors' requests for the death penalty; banning death sentences on the mentally retarded; significantly reducing the number of death eligibility factors; videotaping interrogations of homicide suspects; and controlling the use of testimony by jail house informants.

I mention it now so that you will understand the thoroughness of our review. And that was only the beginning.

We took the commission's recommendations and drafted legislation. It was a damn good package [that] would have dramatically improved our state's capital punishment system.

We introduced that bill three times last spring and this fall. Three times. And each time, the legislature punted.

I do not understand that. Thirteen innocent men were nearly executed. Countless flaws are highlighted. The system has proved itself to be wildly inaccurate, unjust, unable to separate the innocent from the guilty and, at times, racist. And yet we couldn't pass a package in Springfield.

What does it take? Now that we can say the number of wrongfully convicted men is 17, will that be enough?

Last spring there was talk of what to do with the inmates currently on death row convicted in our deeply flawed system. I was challenged by a young prosecutor at a conference in Oregon who asked me why, if I was so concerned about the state of our capital punishment system, I didn't just commute the cases of all inmates on death row. I said that was something we would have to look at.

In fact, defense lawyers, like Andrea and Larry, had long planned to petition the prisoner review board to do just that, to fight for clemency for their clients because they could not obtain justice in any other way.

My power to grant these pardons is constitutionally provided. The state Supreme Court has cited the Governor's power in explaining their restraint in acting in some death penalty cases they review.

What has been most troubling is that this is most clearly not limited to our capital cases. They only have received the most attention.

There have been at least 33 inmates, convicted of murder and serving sentences other than the sentence of death, who have been found innocent and released from prison since 1977.

We are adding to that number today, with other cases that we have reviewed, through the normal cases we review from the Prisoner Review Board.

There is the case of Miguel Castillo who spent 11 years behind bars for murder. A Cuban immigrant, Mr. Castillo was arrested for the murder of another Cuban émigré. He was charged, convicted and sentenced to 48 years in prison.

There is only one problem. Mr. Castillo was in jail the night of the murder, serving a 60-day sentence for breaking into a store.

Mr. Castillo said nothing will bring back the 11 years of his life he lost. It seems a travesty to me that it should take so long. But a pardon will at least acknowledge the state made a mistake.

And finally there is the landmark case of Gary Dotson, the first real DNA case in Illinois. My friend, who I served under, Gov. James R. Thompson, released Gary Dotson from prison after the rape victim, Cathy Crowell Webb, recanted her testimony and said she made up the story of being raped by Gary Dotson while she was a teenager in order to cover her relationship with her then-boyfriend. Gary served 12 years in prison. After the recantation, Gov. Thompson held clemency hearings. It was before the advent of reliable DNA evidence, so Gary was never pardoned. He has struggled to rebuild his life ever since. Now we have the DNA evidence that proves Gary is innocent. We will clear Gary's name once and for all.

I have acted today in what I believe is the interest of justice. It is not only the right thing to do. I believe it is on the only thing to do.

If you learn nothing else, follow the example of your teacher, Andrea Lyon, or of Larry Marshall, or Dave Protess. Realize the tremendous opportunity it is to be allowed to practice law. Realize the tremendous power that you have to do good. Remember, whether you are a prosecutor, a defender, that when you step into a courtroom, you should be engaged in a passionate search for the truth, rather than a zealous pursuit of a victory for victory's sake.

Lives hang in the balance.

I have finished my review of the capital cases. It has been a thorough, exhaustive process. We have gone over cases again and again, each and every case.

At stake is whether some, all or none of these inmates on death row will have their sentences commuted from death to life without parole.

One of the things discussed with family members was [that] life without parole was seen as a life filled with perks and benefits.

But I would point out for you a suit in Livingston County where a judge ruled the state corrections department cannot force feed two corrections inmates who are on a hunger strike. The judge ruled that suicide by hunger strike was not an irrational action by the inmates, given what their future holds.

I will tell you there are prisons where there is no air conditioning and the conditions are pretty stark. And in every prison, the inmates are told what to do at all times. They have no freedom. Let's keep things in perspective.

Today I have taken extraordinary action to correct manifest wrongs. As we speak, letters are being prepared and sent for overnight delivery to the survivors of victims and relatives of inmates, to inform them first of my decision in the mass petitions for commutation. Tomorrow, after families have received those letters, I will make my decision public.

Four years ago, I never would have guessed the road would lead me here today. To championing reforms of our capital punishment system, to intervening in the effort to help four death row inmates and four other men find justice where the courts would not grant relief.

You too will see many twists and turns in the road ahead of you. I can't say that I would wish upon you the experience such as the burdens I have faced in this process. But remember that each day you live, your experience will prepare you for a challenge you may not foresee. Grab it with gusto. And fight for justice.

Thank you and God bless you.

Thank you.

Text of Governor George Ryan's Commutation Announcement

Delivered on January 11, 2003, at Northwestern University School of Law
Northwestern Law News
Northwestern University School of Law
Copyright ©2002 by Northwestern University

Four years ago I was sworn in as the 39th Governor of Illinois. That was just four short years ago—that's when I was a firm believer in the American system of justice and the death penalty. I believed that the ultimate penalty for the taking of a life was administrated in a just and fair manner.

Today—three days before I end my term as Governor, I stand before you to explain my frustrations and deep concerns about both the administration and the penalty of death. It is fitting that we are gathered here today at Northwestern University with the students, teachers, lawyers and investigators who first shed light on the sorrowful condition of Illinois' death penalty system. Professors Larry Marshall, Dave Protess and their students along with investigators Paul Ciolino have gone above and beyond the call. They freed the falsely accused, Ford Heights Four. They saved Anthony Porter's life and they fought for Rolondo Cruz and Alex Fernandez.

And before I go on, I'd like to take just a minute to talk about Larry and Dave. Never have I met anyone with more passion but with a fiercer sense of justice than these two men. They have a vision for what the justice system can be and they're an inspiration. And I want to say thanks, again, especially thanks to them for their hard work and dedication and their long hours and their deep seeded belief in what we're doing here today.

I think it's more than proper also that we're together with dedicated people like Andrea Lyon, who I had the opportunity to be with yesterday, who's labored long in the front lines of trying capital cases for many years and who is now devoting her passion to creating an innocence center at DePaul University. Andrea Lyon — there she is. Andrea Lyon saved Madison Hobley's life.

Together, she spared the life and secured the freedom of 17 men who were wrongfully convicted and rotting in the condemned units of our state's prison. Andrea, what you have achieved is of the highest calling. Thank you, thank you very much for all you've done.

Yes, I believe it's right that if I'm here with you, where in a manner of speaking that my journey from a staunch supporter of a capital punishment system to a reformer all began. Since the beginning of our journey, my thoughts and feelings about the death penalty have changed many, many times. And I realize that over the course of my reviews, I had said that I would not do blanket commutations.... But I've always said that it was an option. And it was there. And it was an option that I wanted to keep on the table and have to consider.

During my time in public office, I have always reserved my right to be in the best interest of public policy, to change my mind when I thought it was necessary to do so. And I have done it on a lot of occasions and certainly this is one of those occasions. But I must confess that the debate with myself, I think, has really been the toughest concerning the death penalty. And I suppose the reason that the death penalty has been the toughest is because it's so final. It is. It's absolutely final. And it's the only public policy that determines who lives and dies. And you can talk about whatever you want to talk about, but that's the public policy. It's life and death. It is the only issue that attracts most of the legal minds all across the country. And I can tell you that I have received more advice on this issue than any other policy issue that I've dealt with in my 35 years of public service. I have kept an open mind on both sides of the issue of commutation for life or for death.

I have read, listened to and discussed issues with the families of the victims as well as the families of the condemned. And I know that any decision that I'll make today will not be accepted by one side or the other. I know that my decision will be just that, my decision based on all of the facts that I could gather over the past three years. I may never be comfortable with the decision that I make in the final decision, but I'll know in my heart that I did my very best to do the right thing.

Now, having said that I want to share with you a program or a story that I want to tell you about. As you all know, you have heard me say I grew up in Kankakee, Illinois. And Kankakee is not far from Chicago, but it's still a thousand miles away in terms of a lot of things. It is still a small mid-western town, a place where people tend to know each other. And I had a great neighbor and his name was Steve Small. He and his wife would look after our young children when Laura Lynn and I were out of town. I['ve] got to tell you that wasn't for the faint of heart because we had six kids and five of them were under the age of three. But he was a bright young man who helped run the family business. And he and his wife had three children of their own. And Laura Lynn was especially close because we knew that we were there for each other.

One September midnight, Steve received a call at his home. And he had bought an old Frank Lloyd Wright house in Kankakee and he was in the process of restoring it to its original form. And they said that there had been a break-in at that house. And so, he had to leave his house to go sign a complaint with the police. And when he got to the garage and opened the door, there was a man standing there with a gun and they put the gun on him and threw him in the trunk of the car. And they took him out and buried him in a very shallow grave alive and he died before police could find him.

His killer eventually led police to where Steve's body was buried. The young man's name was Danny Edward. He was also from my hometown of Kankakee. And he now sits on death row. I know his family. I know his brother. I know his mother and father. I share this story with you so that you know that I don't come to this as a neophyte without having expected and experienced the small bit of the bitter pill the survivors of murder must swallow.

But my responsibilities and obligations are more than my neighbors and my family. I represent all of the people of Illinois and the decision that I make about our criminal justice system is felt not only here but as I found out, the world over.

As I said the other day, I received a call from Nelson Mandela. I was at Manny's having a corn beef sandwich, as a matter of fact. And I had a chat with Nelson Mandela for about 20 minutes. But the message that he basically delivered was that the United States sets the example for justice and fairness for the rest of the world. And today, the United States is not in league with most of our allies when it comes to the death penalty. We're not in league with Europe or South Africa or Canada or Mexico, most South and Central American countries. These countries have rejected the death penalty. We're partners ·in death with several third world countries. As you all know, even Russia has now called a moratorium.

The death penalty has been abolished in 12 states and in none of those states has the homicide rate increased. Now, here's a good number for you to remember, in Illinois last year we had about 1,000 murders and only two percent were sentenced to death. I want to know, where is the fairness and the equality in that? The death penalty in Illinois is not imposed fairly or uniformly because of the absence of standards for 102 counties in this state, state attorneys who must decide whether to request a death sentence. Should geography be a factor in determining who gets the death sentence? I don't think it should. But in Illinois it makes a difference. You are five times more likely to get a death sentence for the first-degree murder in the rural areas of the state than you are here in Cook County. Five times more. Where's the fairness in that? Where is the fairness in the justice system? Where is the proportionality?

You know the most—Reverend Desmond Tutu wrote to me this week stating that— he said and I quote—"To take a life when a life has been lost is revenge. It's not justice." He says "justice allows for mercy and clemency and compassion. These virtues are not weaknesses."

"In fact, the most blurring weakness is that no matter how efficient and how fair the death penalty may seem in theory, in actual practice, it's primarily inflicted upon the weak, the poor, the ignorant and against racial minorities." Now that was a quote from former California Governor Pat Brown. He wrote a book and his daughter sent it to me a couple months ago and the book was titled "Public Justice and Private Mercy." And he wrote that—nearly 50 years ago he wrote that. Fifty years ago. Now what's changed in 50 years? Not much. Why not? I don't know. I don't have the answer.

I never intended to be an activist on this issue, needless to say. But soon after taking office, I watched in surprise and amazement as the free death row inmate Anthony Porter was released from jail. As a free man, he ran into Northwestern University professor, David Protess. Where's David? Where are you, David? David's right here.

David, it was a memory I'll never forget, seeing little Anthony Porter run out and jump in your arms as a free man out of prison. He poured his heart and soul; David did, in providing Porter's innocence with his journalism students.

Anthony Porter was 48 hours away from being wheeled into the execution chamber where the state would kill him.

It would be [all so] antiseptic that most of us wouldn't have even paused for a second except that Anthony Porter was innocent. He was innocent for the double murder for which he had been condemned by the State of Illinois to die.

And after Mr. Porter's cause, there was a report by Chicago Tribune reporters, Steve Mills and Ken Armstrong, that documented the systemic failures of our capital punishment system and you've all read it. I can't imagine it. Half, if you will, of the nearly 300 capital cases in Illinois have been reversed for a new trial or for some re-sentencing.

Now, how many of you people here today that are professionals can get by and call your life a success if you're only 50 percent successful? Certainly, I can't as a pharmacist. I don't think doctors can. I don't know how the Justice Department can think they've a system that works when 50 percent of the cases are sent back for fixing.

Thirty-three percent of the death row inmates were represented at trial by an attorney who had later been disbarred or at some point, suspended from the practice of law.

Of the more than 160 death row inmates, 35 were African-American defendants, who had been convicted or condemned to die not by a jury of their peers, but by all white juries.

More than two-thirds of the inmates on death row were African-Americans.

Forty-six inmates were convicted on the basis of testimony from jailhouse informants.

I can recall looking at these cases and the information from the Mills/Armstrong series and I ask myself and my staff, how does that happen? How in God's name does that happen? In America, how does it happen?

I've been asking this question for nearly three years and so far nobody's answered the question. Even as I stand here today nobody's answered the question.

So then over the next few months there were three more exonerated men freed because their...sentences hinged on a jailhouse informant or some new DNA technology that proved beyond a shadow of a doubt that they were innocent.

Thirteen men found innocent and 12 executed. And as I reported yesterday, there's not a doubt in my mind that the number of innocent men freed from our death row stands at 17 now because yesterday we pardoned Aaron Patterson, and Madison Hobley and Stanley Howard and Leroy Orange.

And if you really want to know what's outrageous and unconscionable...it's [that] 17 exonerated death row inmates is nothing short of a catastrophic failure. But to then 13 and now 17 men, it is just the beginning of our sad arithmetic in prosecuting murder cases in this state. During the time that we've had capital punishment in Illinois, there were at least 33 other people wrongfully convicted on murder charges and exonerated, 33. You don't read about those people because they didn't make death row. Since we reinstated the death penalty, there are also 93 people, 93, for our criminal justice to impose the most severe sanction and then rescinded the sentence or even release the prisoners from custody because they were innocent—93.

How many more cases of wrongful conviction have to occur before we can all agree that this system in Illinois is broken?

Throughout this process, I have heard many different points of view expressed and I've had the opportunity to review all of the cases involving the inmates on death row. I have conducted private group hearings, one in Springfield and one in Chicago, with the surviving of the members of the homicide victims. Everyone in that room, who wanted to speak, had the opportunity to do so. Some wanted to express their grief while others wanted to express their anger, but I took it all in.

My commission, myself, my staff had been reviewing each and every case for three years. But I redoubled my effort to review each case personally in order to represent and to respond to the concerns of prosecutors and victims' families. This individual review also naturally resulted in a collective examination of our entire death penalty system.

I also had a meeting with a group of people who are less often heard from and who are not as popular with the media. The family members of death row inmates have a special challenge to face and I spent an afternoon with those family members at a church here in Chicago on the south side. And at that meeting, I heard a different kind of pain expressed. Many of these families live with the twin pain of knowing not only that in some cases their family members were responsible for inflicting a terrible trauma on another family but also the pain of knowing that society has called for another killing. These parents, siblings and children are not to blame for the crime that has been committed. If these innocent have to stand with their loved ones,...they have to stand with their loved ones wondering whether they're going to be killed by the state. And as Mr. Mandela told me, they're also branded and scarred for the rest of their [lives] because of the awful crime that's been committed by their family member.

Others were even more tormented by the fact that their loved one was another victim, but that their loved one was truly innocent of the crime for which they had been sentenced to die.

It was at that meeting that I looked into the face of Claude Lee, another Kankakee citizen, Claude Lee, who's the father of Eric Lee, who was convicted of killing a Kankakee police officer. His name was Anthony Samfay. And a few years ago, it happened. It was a traumatic moment, once again, for my hometown of Kankakee. A brave officer, part of that thin blue line that protects all of us from being struck down by [wanton] violence. And if you will, kill a police officer, you have absolutely no respect for the law nor do you have any respect for man nor his laws nor any respect for God.

I have known the Lee family for many years in Kankakee. There does not appear to be a whole lot of question about the guilt of Eric Lee. He killed that officer. However, I can say now that after our review there is also not much question that Eric is and has been for some time very seriously ill. With the history of treatment for mental illness going back a number of years.

The crime he committed was a terrible crime, killing a police officer. And society demands that the highest penalty be paid.

But I had to ask myself, could I send another man's son to death under the deeply flawed system of capital punishment that we have in Illinois, a troubled young man with the history of mental illness? Could I rely on the system of justice that we have in this state not to make another horrible mistake? Could I rely on a fair sentencing program? Could I rely on a fair sentencing program in the United States?

In the United States, the overwhelming majority of those executed are psychotic, alcoholic, drug addicted or mentally unstable. And they're frequently raised in an impoverished and abusive environment.

Seldom are people with money or prestige convicted of capital offenses, but even more seldom are they executed.

To quote Pat Brown again, he said—and I quote—"Society has both the right and the moral duty to protect itself against its enemies. This natural and prehistoric axiom has never successfully been refuted. If by ordered death, society is really protected and our homes and institutions guarded, then even the most extreme of all penalties can be justified."

"Beyond its honor and incredibility, it has neither protected the innocent nor destroyed the killers. Public sanction[ed] killing has cheapened human life and dignity without the redeeming grace that comes from justice delivered evenly, swiftly and humanely."

At stake throughout the clemency process was whether some, all or none of these inmates on death row could have their sentences commuted from death to life, without the possibility of parole. And one of the things that was discussed with family members was life without parole was seen as a life filled with perks and benefits.

Some inmates on death row don't want a sentence of life without parole. Danny Edwards, from Kankakee, wrote me a letter. Said: "If you can't pardon me, don't condemn me to a life in prison. Leave me on death row. Don't do me any favors," he said, because he didn't want to face the prospect of a life in prison without parole. They'll be confined in a cell about six feet by twelve feet. Usually double-bunked. Our prisons have no air conditioning, except at one of our supermax facilities where inmates are kept in their cell 24 hours a day, and in summer months, the temperature gets as high as 100 degrees. It's a stark and dreary existence, and they can think about their crimes for the rest of their life. Life without parole has even, at times, been described by prosecutors as a fate worse than death.

Yesterday, I mentioned a lawsuit in Livingston County, where a judge ruled the State Corrections Department couldn't force-feed two corrections inmates who were on a hunger strike. The judge ruled that suicide by hunger strike was not an irrational action by the inmates, given what their future holds—life in a six by twelve cell.

Earlier this year, the U.S. Supreme Court held that it's unconstitutional, and cruel and unusual punishment to execute the mentally retarded. It's now the law of this land. How many people have we already executed who were mentally retarded and are now dead and buried? Although we now know that they have been killed by the state unconstitutionally and illegally. Is that fair? Is that right?

This court decision was last spring. The General Assembly of the state of Illinois has failed to pass any measure defining what constitutes mental retardation. We are a rudderless ship, because they failed to act.

This was even after the Illinois Supreme Court also told lawmakers that it was their job, and it must be done.

I started with this issue because I was and still am concerned about innocence, but once I studied, I pondered what had become of our justice system, I came to care above all about fairness. Fairness is fundamental to the American system of justice and to our way of life.

The facts that I've seen in reviewing each and every one of these cases questions not only about the innocence of people on death row, but about the fairness of the death penalty system as a whole.

In a system that's working, if it was working, so many errors in determining whether someone was guilty in the first place, how fairly and accurately was it determining which guilty defendants deserved to live and which deserved to die? And what effect was race having? What effect was poverty having?

And almost every one of the exonerated 17, we'd not only had breakdowns with police and prosecutors and judges, we have terrible cases of shabby defense lawyers. There is no way to sugarcoat what goes on. There are defense attorneys that did not consult with their clients. They didn't investigate the cases that they had, and they were completely unqualified to handle complex death penalty cases. They often don't put much effort into fighting a death sentence, and if your life is on the line, your lawyer certainly ought to be working a little extra hard to make sure that your life is saved. And as I've said before, there's more than enough blame to go around about our failures with this system.

I had more questions in Illinois.

I have learned that we have 102 decision-makers. Each of them are politically elected. Each beholding to the demands of their community, and in some cases, to the media or especially vocal victims' families. And I ask you, in cases that have the attention of the media and the public, are decisions to seek the death penalty more likely to occur? What standards are these prosecutors using?

Some people have assailed my power to commute sentences. A power that literally hundreds of legal scholars from across the country have defended. The prosecutors in Illinois have the ultimate commutation power, a power that is exercised every day. They decide who's going to be the subject to the death penalty, who will get a plea deal, or even who may get a complete pass on prosecution. Every day in this state that happens. They make these—these decisions, and I ask about what standards do they make these decisions on? We don't know. They're not public.... [T]here is no doubt that all murders are cruel and they're wrong, yet less than 2 percent of those murder defendants are going to receive the death penalty. That means that more than 98 percent of victims' families don't get and will not receive whatever satisfaction can be derived from the execution of the murderer. Moreover, if you look at the cases as I have done, both individually and collectively, a killing within the same circumstances might get you 40 years in one county and the death sentence in another county. I have also seen co-defendants who are equally guilty, where one gets sentenced to a term of years, while another ends up on death row.

Supreme Court Justice Potter Stewart has said that the imposition of the death penalty on defendants in this country is as freakish and arbitrary as who gets hit by a bolt of lightning. In my case-by-case review, I found three cases that struck me as particularly unfair, troublesome and deserving of some form of commutation.

In one of them, the murder victims's family had publicly and privately urged me to act more aggressively than I will today. In the cases of Montell Johnson and Mario Flores and William Franklin. I am today commuting their sentence to a term of 40 years to fairly bring their sentences into line with their co-defendants and to reflect the other extraordinary circumstances of each of these cases.

It's an example of what can happen. For years, the criminal justice system defended and upheld the imposition of the death penalty for the 17 exonerated inmates from Illinois. Yet when the real killers are charged, prosecutors have often sought sentences of less than death. In the Ford Heights Four case, Verneal Jimerson and Dennis Williams fought the death sentences imposed upon them for 18 years before they were exonerated, and later Cook County prosecutors sought life in prison for the real killers and sentenced them to 80 years.

What a differen[t] murder for which the Ford Heights Four were sentenced to die. Why is that less worthy of the death penalty 20 years later with a new set of defendants?

I don't understand the arbitrariness of the system. We've come very close to having our state Supreme Court rule the death penalty statute unconstitutional. It was a statute that I helped pass in 1977. Former State Supreme Court Justice Seymour Simon wrote to me just recently that it was only happenstance that our statute was not struck down by the state's high court. When he joined the bench in 1980, three other justices had already said Illinois's death penalty was unconstitutional, but they got cold feet when a case came along to revisit the question. One judge wrote that he wanted to wait and see if the Supreme Court of the United States would rule on the constitutionality of the new Illinois law. Another said that precedent required him to follow the old state Supreme Court ruling with which he had disagreed.

Even a pharmacist knows that that doesn't make a whole lot of sense. We wouldn't have a death penalty today and we wouldn't all be struggling with the issue if these votes had been different. Pretty arbitrary.

Several years ago, we enacted our death penalty statute, a fellow by the name of Girvies Davis was executed. Justice Simon wrote to me that he was executed because this unconstitutional aspect of Illinois law, the wide latitude that each Illinois state's attorney has to determine what cases qualify for the death penalty. One state's attorney decided not to seek the death sentence when Davis' first sentencing was sent back to the trial court for a new sentencing hearing. Instead, he was going to ask for a life sentence, the state's attorney.

But in the interim, a new state's attorney was elected or appointed, somehow became the new state's attorney. And he wanted the death penalty. And he was successful in charging the death penalty, and he was successful in getting the death penalty against Girvies Davis, and Girvies Davis was executed.

I ask you, how fair is that?

After the flaws of our death penalty system were exposed, the Supreme Court of Illinois began to reform its rules and to improve the procedures for trying capital cases. It changed the rule to require that states' attorneys give advance notice to defendants that they plan to seek the death penalty, before trial, instead of after conviction. The Supreme Court also enacted new discovery rules designed to prevent trials by ambush and to allow for better investigation of cases from the very beginning.

Shouldn't that mean that you were tried or sentenced before these important essential reforms were enacted to correct a clearly flawed system that you ought to get a new trial or sentencing that will be more fair or just as accurate? This issue has divided the Supreme Court. Some saying yes, but a majority saying no. These justices have a lifetime of experience with the criminal justice system. And it concerns me that these great minds so strenuously differ on an issue of such importance, especially where life or death hangs in the balance.

What are we to make of the studies that showed that more than 50 percent of Illinois jurors couldn't understand the confusing and obscure sentencing instructions that were being used? What effect did that problem have on the trustworthiness of death sentences? A review of the cases shows that often even the lawyers and the judges are confused about the instruction, let alone the jurors sitting in judgment. Cases still come before the Supreme Court with arguments about whether the jury instructions were proper.

And as I have said, I've spent a good deal of time reviewing these death row cases. My staff, many of whom are lawyers, spent busy days and many sleepless nights answering questions, providing me with information and giving me a lot of great advice.

And it became very clear to me that whatever decision I made I would be criticized for. And it also became very clear to me that it was impossible to make reliable choices about whether our capital punishment system had really done its job.

As I came closer to my decision, I knew that I was going to have to face the question of whether I believed so completely in the choice I wanted to make that I could face the prospect of even commuting the death sentence of Danny Edwards, a man who had killed a close family friend of mine. My wife was even angry and disappointed at my decision, like many of the other families are going to be.

I was struck by the anger of the families of murder victims. To a family, they talked about closure. They pleaded with me to allow the state to kill an inmate in its name to provide the families with closure. But is that the purpose of capital punishment? Is it to soothe the families? And is that truly the families' experience?

I can't imagine losing a family member to murder, nor can I imagine spending every waking day for 20 years with a single-minded focus to execute the killer. The system of death in Illinois is so unsure that it's not unusual for cases to take 20 years before they are resolved. Thank God. Because if it moved any faster, then Anthony Porter, the Ford Heights Four, Ronald Jones, Madison Hobley and all the other innocent men that we've exonerated might already be dead and buried.

But it is cruel and unusual punishment for family members to go through this pain, this legal limbo for 20 years. Perhaps it would be less cruel if we sentenced the killers to life in a six by 12 cell and used our resources to better serve victims.

My heart ached when I heard one grandmother who lost children in an arson fire. She said that she couldn't afford proper grave markers for her grandchildren who died. I question, why can't the state help families provide a proper burial?

Another crime victim came to our family meeting. He believed an inmate sent to death row for another crime also shot and paralyzed him. The inmate, he says, gets free medicine, free health care, while the victim that he shot struggles to pay his substantial medical bills, and as a result, he has forgone getting proper medical care to alleviate the physical pain that he endures.

What kinds of victim services are we providing? Are all of our resources geared toward providing this notion of closure by an eye for an eye? Closure by execution instead of tending to the physical and social needs of family victims? And what kind of values are we instilling in those wounded families and in the young people? You know what Gandhi said about an eye for an eye. He said, that leaves the whole world blind.

President Lincoln often talked of binding up wounds as he sought to preserve the union. He said: "We're not enemies, but friends. We must not be enemies. Though passion may have strained, it must not break our bonds of affection."

I have had to consider not only the horrible nature of the crimes that put men on death row in the first place, the terrible suffering family members of the victims, the despair of the family members of the inmates, but I have had also to watch [in] frustration [as] members of the Illinois General Assembly failed to pass even one substantive death penalty reform in the state! Not one! People like Tom Sullivan and great minds, legal minds and business people in this state put together a great package and our General Assembly thumbed their nose at us, and not even passed one of those! And we gave them three occasions to do it. They couldn't even agree on one—one way to make the system better. And I don't know how much more evidence is needed before that General Assembly will take its responsibility in this area seriously. It's a charge that they've got to look after pretty quick.

The fact is that the failure of the General Assembly to act is merely a symptom of the larger problem. Many people express the desire to have capital punishment. Few, however, seem to prepare to address the tough questions that arise when the system fails. It's easier and more comfortable for politicians to be tough on crime and to support the death penalty. It brings votes. But when it comes to admitting that we have a problem, most run for cover. Prosecutors across our state continue to deny that our death penalty system is broken, or they say if there is a problem, it's merely a small problem, and we can fix it somehow some day. It's difficult to see how the system can be fixed when not one single one of the new reforms proposed by our commission has been adopted....

So when will the system be fixed? When is it going to be made better? We know that it's worse than 50 percent. How much more risk can we afford? And will we actually have to execute an innocent person before the tragedy that is our capital punishment system in Illinois [is] really understood? This summer, the United States district court judge held the federal death penalty was unconstitutional, and noted that with the number of recent exonerations based on DNA and new scientific technology that we, without a doubt, executed innocent people before this technology emerged.

And as I prepare to leave the office of governor, I had to ask myself whether I could really live with the prospect of knowing that I had the opportunity to act but that I failed to do so because I might be criticized. Could I take the chance that our capital punishment system might be reformed, that wrongful convictions might not occur, that enterprising journalism students might free more men from death row? The system that's so fragile that it depends on young journalism students is seriously flawed.

"There is no honorable way to kill, and there is no gentle way to destroy. There is nothing good in war, except its ending."

And that's what Abraham Lincoln said. That's what Abraham Lincoln said about the bloody war between the states. It was a war fought to end the sorriest chapter in American history, the institution of slavery. And while we're not in Civil War now, we're facing what is shaping up to be one of the great civil rights struggles of our time. Stephen Bright of the Southern Center for Human Rights has taken the position that the death penalty is sought with increasing frequency against the poor and minorities.

Our own studies showed that juries were more likely to sentence to death if the victim were white than if the victim were black, three and a half times more likely to be exact, three and a half times more likely. We're not alone. Just this month, the state of Maryland released a study that their death penalty system and racial disparity absolutely exists in their system.

And this week, Mamie Till-Mobley died. She's being buried this morning, I believe. Her son, Emmett, was lynched in Mississippi in the 1950s. She was a strong advocate for civil rights and reconciliation, and in fact just three weeks ago, she was a keynote speaker at the Murder Victims Families for Reconciliation right here in Chicago. This group opposes the death penalty even though their family members have been lost to some senseless killings. Mamie's strength and her grace not only ignited the civil rights movement, including inspiring Rosa Parks to refuse to go to the back of the bus, but inspired murder victims until her dying day.

Is our system fair to all? Is justice blind? These are important human rights issues, ones that need answers.

Another issue that came up at my individual case-by-case review was the issue of international law. The Vienna Convention protects U.S. citizens abroad and foreign nationals in the United States. It provides that if you are arrested, you should be afforded the opportunity to contact your consulate. There are five men on death row who were denied that internationally recognized human right. Today with us we have the consul general from Mexico—where is he? Carlos Sada. Carlos, thank you. Carlos is just back from Mexico, where he was with President Fox, and they called me while he was there to express their deep concern for the Vienna Convention violations. And based on the commission's findings and recommendations, this year I prepared and distributed to police agencies and prosecutors training materials to ensure compliance with the Vienna Convention. If we don't uphold international law here, we can't expect our citizens to be protected outside of the United States. And I think that's especially important in the world today.

My commission recommended the Supreme Court conduct a proportionality review of our system in Illinois. And while our appellate courts perform a case-by-case review of the appellate record, they've not done such a big picture study. Instead, they tinker with a case-by-case review as each appeal lands on their docket.

In 1994, near the end of his very distinguished career as a Supreme Court justice of the United States, Justice Harry Blackmun wrote an influential dissent in the body of law in capital punishment. Twenty years earlier, he was part of the court that issued the landmark *Furman* decision. The court decided that the death penalty statutes in use throughout the country were fraught with severe flaws that rendered them unconstitutional, and quite frankly, they were the same problems that we see right here in Illinois. To many, it looked like the *Furman* decision meant the end of the death penalty in the United States.

This was not the case. Many states responded to *Furman* by developing and enhancing new and improved death penalty statutes. And in 1976, four years after it had decided *Furman*, Justice Blackmun joined the majority of the United States Supreme Court in deciding to give the states a chance with these new and improved death penalty statutes. And there was great optimism in the air.

This was the climate in 1977, when the Illinois legislature was faced with the momentous decision of whether to reinstate the death penalty in Illinois. I was a member of that General Assembly. And at that time, I voted green. I pushed my button green, in favor of reinstating the death penalty. I did so with the belief that whatever problems that plagued the capital punishment system in the past were now being cured. I'm sure that most of my colleagues who voted with me on that day shared the same view.

But 20 years later, after affirming hundreds of death penalty decisions, Justice Blackmun came to the realization in the twilight of his very distinguished career that the death penalty remains fraught with arbitrariness, discrimination, caprice and mistake. He expressed frustration with the 20-year struggle to develop procedural and substantive safeguards. In a now very famous [dissent], he wrote in 1994, "From this day forward, I no longer shall tinker with the machinery of death."

One of the few disappointments of my legislative and executive career is that the General Assembly failed to work with me to reform our system, after we had such a complete and thorough study done by able and competent people.

I don't know how or why legislators could not find the need of the rising voices for reform. I don't know how many more systemic flaws we need to uncover before they need to be spurred to action. Three times I proposed reforming the system with a package that would restrict the use of jailhouse snitches, create a statewide panel to determine death eligible cases, reduce the number of crimes eligible for death. These reforms would not have created a perfect system, but they would have dramatically reduced the chance for error in the administration of the ultimate penalty.

The governor has the constitutional role in our state of acting in the interest of justice and fairness. Our state Constitution provides broad power to the governor to issue reprieves, pardons and commutations. Our Supreme Court has reminded inmates petitioning that while errors and fairness questions may actually exist and cannot be recognized under judicial rules and procedural mandates. The last court, the last resort for relief is the governor. Pretty awesome power.

At times, the executive clemency power has perhaps been a crutch for courts to avoid making the kind of major change that I believe this system needs.

Our systemic case-by-case review has found more cases of innocent men wrongfully sentenced to death row, and because our three-year study has found only more questions about the fairness of the sentencing, and because of the spectacular failure to reform the system, because we have seen justice delayed for countless death row inmates with potentially meritorious claims, and because the Illinois death penalty system is arbitrary and capricious, and therefore, immoral, I no longer shall tinker with the machinery of death.

Thank you. Thank you. I didn't say that as eloquently as Justice Blackmun did, but I've got to tell you:

The legislature couldn't reform it.

Lawmakers won't repeal it.

And I won't stand for it.

I've been asked why I waited for the last 48 hours before I made this decision. There are a lot of reasons, but one was that I wanted to go as far as I could and learn and know as much as I could. But I also thought that I couldn't leave without getting something done. I had to act.

Our capital system is haunted by the demon of error, error in determining guilt, error in determining who among the guilty deserves to die. Because of all of these reasons today, I'm commuting the sentence of all death row inmates, 157 of them.

Thank you. As I said earlier, this was blanket commutation. And I said earlier that I promised the people of Illinois at some point that I wouldn't use it, at some point it was on the front burner, at some point it was on the back burner, but I always said it was an option that I may use and exercise, never really believing as long ago as a week or 10 days that I would blanket commute these sentences. I didn't believe I would do it myself. But I realize that my decision will draw ridicule and scorn and anger from many who oppose this decision. And they'll say that I'm usurping the decision of judges and juries and state legislators. But as I have said, the people of our state have invested in me the power to act in the interests of justice. It's the only place in the Constitution done that way. And even if the exercise of my power becomes my burden, I'll bear it.

Because our Constitution compels it. I sought this office, and even in my final days of holding it, I can't shrink from the obligations to justice and fairness that it demands. There have been many things and many nights where my staff and I have been deprived of sleep in order to conduct the exhaustive review of this system. But I can tell you this—I'm going to sleep well tonight, knowing that I made the right decision.

Thank you. I'm going to quit here in a minute.

As I said when I declared the moratorium, its time for a rational discussion on the death penalty. Here in Illinois and all across America, we must do that. And while our experience in Illinois has indeed sparked a debate, we have fallen short of a rational discussion. Yet if I didn't take this action, I feared that there would be no comprehensive and thorough inquiry into the guilt of the individuals on death row or of the fairness of the sentences applied.

To say it plainly one more time—the Illinois capital punishment system is broken. It has taken innocent men to a hair['s] breath escape from their unjust execution. Legislatures past have refused to fix it. Our new legislature and our new governor must act to rid our state of the shame of threatening the innocent with execution and the guilty with unfairness.

I had an opportunity to—not an opportunity, I had an obligation to oversee the election of the new president of the Senate last week. Last Wednesday. And I had an opportunity to spend a few minutes talking with my good friend Emil Jones. Emil and have been friends for 25, 30 years. He said that one of his top priorities is going to be to do the reform package that will be put together by our commission. He even talked about abolition. Now, I'm not sure what he's going to do about that. That would be very tough.

So I guess that in the days ahead, I'm going [to] pray that we can open our hearts and provide something for victims' families, other than the hope of revenge.

You know, Abraham Lincoln was a hell of a guy. He took this state through some of the toughest—and this country through the toughest times and the toughest part of our history we've ever known. And so I like to quote him a lot. He was always criticized, the press was always on him. That sounds familiar. His party was after him all the time. His cabinet was after him. He couldn't do anything right. But he always came up with the right solutions to tough problems, and he said once, "I have always found that mercy bears richer fruits than strict justice." I can only hope with God's help that will be so. God bless all of you. Work hard for the program. Thank you.

Notes

1. Outgoing Governor Ryan

According to Professor Palacios, clemency "can be reinstituted to some degree by insulating decision makers from the political consequences of granting commutation in an unpopular case. Only then can decision makers render judgments based more on the merits and less on political pressure." Would it have been possible for Governor Ryan to take this action had he not been leaving office?

2. *Subsequent developments*

The Attorney General of Illinois challenged Governor Ryan's actions in two classes of cases in the Illinois Supreme Court. One class of commutees had failed to sign a clemency request as required by statute. The second class were death row inmates whose sentences had been reversed for a new sentencing hearing. In *People ex rel. Madigan v. Snyder*, 804 N.E.2d 546 (Ill. 2004), issued on January 23, 2004, a unanimous Illinois Supreme Court upheld the former Governor's actions. The Court held that the Illinois constitution allowed the legislature to pass requirements for applying for clemency, but did "not purport to give the legislature the power to regulate the Governor's authority to grant clemency. Further, the 1970 Illinois Constitution does not provide that the Governor's power to grant clemency is subject to the legislature's regulation of the application process, as did the 1870 constitution." The Illinois Supreme Court went on to say that the commutations granted to those who had their sentences reversed for new hearings were proper exercises of that constitutional power.

Chapter 15

Politics and Race

Discussions of comity and finality in case law often are present in response not only to legal doctrine but to perceived political consequences. This chapter provides a brief introduction that explores how politics and race interweave with habeas corpus jurisprudence. Because appealing capital sentences is an important function of habeas corpus litigation, the seminal study by James Liebman et al., *A Broken System: Part I and Part II,* included in Part A, highlights some of the political dimensions in both capital cases and habeas corpus jurisprudence. The first statistical study ever undertaken of modern American capital appeals, Liebman's report goes beyond simply documenting that capital appeals take a long time to wind through the system because American capital sentences are replete with error. His report includes the observation that "capital trials produce so many mistakes that it takes three judicial inspections to catch them—leaving grave doubt whether we *do* catch them all." Liebman also notes that some of the "disturbing sources of pressure to overuse the death penalty are political pressures on elected judges, well-founded doubts about the state's ability to convict serious criminals, and the race of the state's residents and homicide victims."

Part B explores the issue of race through both *McCleskey v. Kemp* and *Miller-El v. Cockrell.* Although acknowledging that a study conducted by Professor David Baldus et al., widely referred to as the "Baldus Study," indicates a disparity in the imposition of the death sentence in Georgia based on the race of the victim, *McCleskey* finds that "apparent disparities in sentencing are an inevitable part of our criminal justice system" and that constitutional guarantees were met in McCleskey's case because the state attempted to make his sentencing "as fair as possible." In *Miller-El,* the Court examines when a state prisoner can appeal the denial or dismissal of his petition for writ of habeas corpus within the context of a claim that includes district attorneys using peremptory strikes to exclude 10 of the 11 African-Americans eligible to serve on Miller-El's jury.

A. Politics

A Broken System: Error Rates in Capital Cases, 1973–1995
James S. Liebman, Jeffrey Fagan, and Valerie West
June 12, 2000
Executive Summary
Copyright ©2000 by James S. Liebman, et al.

There is a growing bipartisan consensus that flaws in America's death-penalty system have reached crisis proportions. Many fear that capital trials put people on death

row who don't belong there. Others say capital appeals take too long. This report—
the first statistical study ever undertaken of modern American capital appeals (4,578
of them in state capital cases between 1973 and 1995)—suggests that *both* claims are
correct.

Capital sentences do spend a long time under judicial review. As this study documents, however, **judicial review takes so long precisely *because* American capital sentences are so persistently and systematically fraught with error that seriously undermines their reliability.**

Our 23 years worth of results reveal a death penalty system collapsing under the weight
of its own mistakes. They reveal a system in which lives and public order are at stake, yet
for decades has made more mistakes than we would tolerate in far less important activities. They reveal a system that is wasteful and broken and needs to be addressed.

Our central findings are as follows:

- Nationally, during the 23-year study period, **the overall rate of prejudicial error
  in the American capital punishment system was 68%.** In other words, courts
  found **serious, reversible error in nearly 7 of every 10 of the thousands of capital sentences that were fully reviewed during the period.**

- Capital trials produce **so many mistakes** that it takes three judicial inspections to
  catch them—leaving **grave doubt whether we *do* catch them all.** After state
  courts threw out 47% of death sentences due to serious flaws, a later federal review found "serious error"—error undermining the reliability of the outcome—
  in **40%** of the *remaining* sentences.

- Because state courts come first and see *all* the cases, they do most of the work of
  correcting erroneous death sentences. Of the **2,370 death sentences** thrown out
  due to serious error, **90%** were overturned by **state judges**—many of whom
  were the very judges who imposed the death sentence in the first place; nearly all
  of whom were directly beholden to the electorate; and none of whom, consequently, were disposed to overturn death sentences except for very good reason.
  This does not mean that federal review is unnecessary. Precisely *because* of the
  huge amounts of serious capital error that state appellate judges are called upon
  to catch, it is not surprising that **a substantial number of the capital judgments
  they let through to the federal stage are still seriously flawed.**

- To lead to reversal, error must be serious, indeed. The most common errors—
  prompting a **majority of reversals** at the state post-conviction stage—are (1)
  **egregiously incompetent defense lawyers who didn't even look for—*and
  demonstrably missed*—important evidence that the defendant was innocent or
  did not deserve to die; and (2) police or prosecutors who *did* discover that kind
  of evidence but *suppressed* it, again keeping it from the jury.** [Hundreds of examples of these and other serious errors are collected in Appendix C and D to
  this Report.]

- High error rates put many individuals at risk of wrongful execution: 82% of the
  people whose capital judgments were overturned by state post-conviction courts
  due to serious error were found to deserve a sentence **less than death** when the
  errors were cured on retrial; *7% were found to be innocent of the capital crime.*

- High error rates persist over time. More than **50%** of all cases reviewed were
  found seriously flawed in **20 of the 23 study years,** including 17 of the last 19. In
  half the years, including the **most recent one,** the error rate was **over 60%.**

- High error rates exist across the country. **Over 90%** of American death-sentenc-ing states have overall error rates of **52% or higher**. 85% have error rates of **60% or higher. Three-fifths** have error rates of **70% or higher**.

- Illinois (whose governor recently declared a moratorium on executions after a spate of death-row exonerations) does not produce atypically faulty death sen-tences. **The overall rate of serious error found in Illinois capital sentences (66%) is very close to**—and slightly *lower* than—**the national average (68%)**.

- Catching so much error takes time—a national average of **9 years** from death sentence to the last inspection and execution. By the end of the study period, that average had risen to **10.6 years. In *most* cases, death row inmates wait for years for the lengthy review procedures needed to uncover all this error. Then, their death sentences are *reversed*.**

- This much error, and the time needed to cure it, impose **terrible costs on tax-payers, victims' families, the judicial system, and the wrongly condemned. And it renders unattainable the finality, retribution and deterrence that are the rea-sons usually given for having a death penalty.**

Erroneously trying capital defendants the first time around, operating the multi-tiered inspection process needed to catch the mistakes, warehousing thousands under costly death row conditions in the meantime, and having to try **two out of three cases** *again* is irrational.

This report describes the extent of the problem. A subsequent report will examine its causes and their implications for resolving the death penalty crisis.

A Broken System, Part II: Why There Is So Much Error in Capital Cases, and What Can Be Done About It

James S. Liebman, Jeffrey Fagan, Andrew Gelman,
Valerie West, Garth Davies, and Alexander Kiss
February 11, 2002
Executive Summary

There is growing awareness that serious, reversible error permeates America's death penalty system, putting innocent lives at risk, heightening the suffering of victims, leav-ing killers at large, wasting tax dollars, and failing citizens, the courts and the justice system.

Our June 2000 Report shows how often mistakes occur and how serious it is: 68% of all death verdicts imposed and fully reviewed during the 1973–1995 study period were reversed by courts due to serious errors.

Analyses presented for the first time here reveal that 76% of the reversals at the two appeal stages where data are available for study were because defense lawyers had been egregiously incompetent, police and prosecutors had suppressed exculpatory evidence or committed other professional misconduct, jurors had been misinformed about the law, or judges and jurors had been biased. Half of those reversals tainted the verdict finding the defendant guilty of a capital crime as well as the verdict imposing the death penalty. *82%* of the cases sent back for retrial at the second appeal phase ended in sen-tences less than death, including 9% that ended in *not guilty verdicts*.

Part II of our study addresses two critical questions: Why does our death penalty system make so many mistakes? How can these mistakes be prevented, if at all? Our findings are based on the most comprehensive set of data ever assembled on factors related to capital error—or other trial error.

Our main finding indicates that if we are going to have the death penalty, it should be reserved for the worst of the worst: **Heavy and indiscriminate use of the death penalty creates a high risk that mistakes will occur.** The more often officials use the death penalty, the wider the range of crimes to which it is applied, and the more it is imposed for offenses that are not highly aggravated, the greater the risk that capital convictions and sentences will be seriously flawed.

Most disturbing of all, we find that **the conditions evidently pressuring counties and states to overuse the death penalty and thus increase the risk of unreliability and error include** *race, politics* **and** *poorly performing law enforcement systems.* Error also is linked to overburdened and underfunded state courts.

MAIN FINDING

The higher the rate at which a state imposes death verdicts, the greater the probability that *each* **death verdict will have to be reversed because of serious error.**

- The overproduction of death penalty verdicts has a powerful effect in increasing the risk of error. Our best analysis predicts that:
  - Capital error rates more than *triple* when the death-sentencing rate increases from a quarter of the national average to the national average, holding other factors constant.
  - When death sentencing increases from a quarter of the national average to the highest rate for a state in our study, the predicted increase in reversal rates is *six-fold*—to *about 80%.*

In particular, the more often states impose death sentences in cases that are not highly aggravated, the higher the risk of serious error.

- At the federal habeas stage, the probability of reversal grows substantially as the crimes resulting in capital verdicts are less aggravated. For each additional aggravating factor, the probability of reversal drops by about 15%, when other conditions are held constant at their averages. Imposing the death penalty in cases that are not the worst of the worst is a recipe for unreliability and error.

Comparisons of particular states' capital-sentencing and capital-error rates illustrate the strong relationship between frequent death sentencing and error. ***

- All but one of the 10 states with the highest death-sentencing rates during the 23-year study period had overall capital reversal rates at or above the average rate of 68%.

PRESSURES ASSOCIATED WITH OVERUSE OF THE DEATH PENALTY

Four disturbing conditions are strongly associated with high rates of serious capital error. Their common capacity to pressure officials to use the death penalty aggressively in response to fears about crime and regardless of how weak any particular case for a death verdict is, may explain their relationship to high capital error rates.

- **The closer the homicide risk to whites in a state comes to equaling or surpassing the risk to blacks, the higher the error rate.** Other things equal, reversal rates are *twice as high* where homicides are most heavily concentrated on whites compared to blacks, than where they are the most heavily concentrated on blacks.

- The higher the proportion of African-Americans in a state—and in one analysis, the more welfare recipients in a state—the higher the rate of serious capital error. Because this effect has to do with traits of the population at large, not those of particular trial participants, it appears to be an indicator of crime fears driven by racial and economic conditions.

- The lower the rate at which states apprehend, convict and imprison serious criminals, the higher their capital error rates. Predicted capital error rates for states with only 1 prisoner per 100 FBI Index Crimes are about 75%, holding other factors constant. Error rates drop to 36% for states with 4 prisoners per 100 crimes, and to 13% for those with the highest rate of prisoners to crimes. Evidently, officials who do a poor job fighting crime also conduct poor capital investigations and trials. Well-founded doubts about a state's ability to catch criminals may lead officials to extend the death penalty to a wider array of weaker cases—at huge cost in error and delay.

- The more often and directly state trial judges are subject to popular election, and the more partisan those elections are, the higher the state's rate of serious capital error.

ADDITIONAL FINDINGS

Heavy use of the death penalty causes delay, increases cost, and keeps the system from doing its job. High numbers of death verdicts waiting to be reviewed paralyze appeals. Holding other factors constant, the process of moving capital verdicts from trial to a final result seems to come to a halt in states with more than 20 verdicts under review at one time.

Poor quality trial proceedings increase the risk of serious, reversible error. Poorly funded courts, high capital and non-capital caseloads, and unreliable procedures for finding the facts all increase the chance that serious error will be found. In contrast, high quality, well-funded private lawyers from out of state significantly increase a defendant's chance of showing a federal court that his death verdict is seriously flawed and has to be retried.

Chronic capital error rates have persisted over time. Overall reversal rates were high and fairly steady throughout the second half of the 23-year study period, averaging 60%. When all significant factors are considered, state high courts on direct appeal—where 79% of the 2349 reversals occurred—found significantly more reversible error in *recent* death verdicts than in verdicts imposed earlier in the study period. Other things equal, direct appeal reversal rates were increasing 9% a year during the study period.

State and federal appeals judges cannot be relied upon to catch all serious trial errors in capital cases. Like trial judges, appeals judges are susceptible to political pressure and make mistakes. And the rules appeals judges use to decide whether errors are serious enough to require death verdicts to be reversed are so strict that egregious errors slip through. We study four illustrative cases in which *the courts approved the convictions and death sentences of innocent men* despite *a full set of appeals.** These case studies show

---

* We study the cases of Lloyd Schlup, Earl Washington, Anthony Porter and Frank Lee Smith.

that judges repeatedly recognized that the proceedings were marred by error but affirmed anyway because of stringent rules limiting reversals.

SUMMARY EXPLANATION

The lower the rate at which a state imposes death sentences—and the more it confines those verdicts to the worst of the worst—the less likely it is that serious error will be found. The fewer death verdicts a state imposes, the less overburdened its capital appeal system is, and the more likely it is to carry out the verdicts it imposes. The more often states succumb to pressures to inflict capital sentences in marginal cases, the higher is the risk of error and delay, the lower is the chance verdicts will be carried out, and the greater is the temptation to approve flawed verdicts on appeal. Among the disturbing sources of pressure to overuse the death penalty are political pressures on elected judges, well-founded doubts about the state's ability to convict serious criminals, and the race of the state's residents and homicide victims.

METHODS

We employ an array of statistical methods to identify factors that predict where and when death verdicts are more likely to be found to be seriously flawed, and to assure that the analyses are comprehensive, conservative and reliable: We use several statistical methods with different assumptions about the arrangement of capital reversals and reversal rates to ensure that results are driven by relationships in the data, not statistical methods. We analyze reversals at each separate review stage and at all three stages combined. We use multiple regression to analyze the simultaneous effect on reversal rates of important general factors (state, county, year and time trend) and specific conditions that may explain error rates. We examine factors operating at the state, county and case level. And we check for consistency of results across analyses to determine which factors and sets of significant factors are the most robust and warrant the most confidence.

POLICY OPTIONS

The harms resulting from chronic capital error are costly. Many of its evident causes are not easily addressed head-on (*e.g.*, the complex interaction of a state's racial make-up, its welfare burden and the efficacy of its law enforcement policies). And indirect remedies are unreliable because they demand self-restraint by officials who in the past have succumbed to pressures to extend the death penalty to cases that are not highly aggravated. As a result, some states and counties may conclude that the only answer to chronic capital error is to stop using the death penalty, or to limit it to the very small number of prospective offenses where there is something approaching a social consensus that only the death penalty will do.

In other states and counties, a set of carefully targeted reforms based upon careful study of local conditions might seek to achieve the central goal of limiting the death penalty to "the worst of the worst"—to defendants who can be shown without doubt to have committed an egregiously aggravated murder without extenuating factors. Ten reforms that might help accomplish this goal are:

- Requiring proof beyond *any* doubt that the defendant committed the capital crime.

- Requiring that aggravating factors substantially outweigh mitigating ones before a death sentence may be imposed.

- Barring the death penalty for defendants with inherently extenuating conditions—mentally retarded persons, juveniles, severely mentally ill defendants.

- Making life imprisonment without parole an alternative to the death penalty and clearly informing juries of the option.

- Abolishing judge overrides of jury verdicts imposing life sentences.

- Using comparative review of murder sentences to identify what counts as "the worst of the worst" in the state, and overturning outlying death verdicts.

- Basing charging decisions in potentially capital cases on full and informed deliberations.

- Making all police and prosecution evidence bearing on guilt vs. innocence, and on aggravation vs. mitigation available to the jury at trial.

- Insulating capital-sentencing and appellate judges from political pressure.

- Identifying, appointing and compensating capital defense counsel in ways that attract an adequate number of well-qualified lawyers to do the work.

CONCLUSION

Over decades and across dozens of states, large numbers and proportions of capital verdicts have been reversed because of serious error. The capital system is collapsing under the weight of that error, and the risk of executing the innocent is high. Now that explanations for the problem have been identified and a range of options for responding to it are available, the time is ripe to fix the death penalty, or if it can't be fixed, to end it.

Notes

1. The long road to justice

Liebman's report documents not only the startlingly high error rate in capital convictions but the fact that "[c]atching so much error takes time.... In *most* cases, death row inmates wait for years for the lengthy review procedures needed to uncover all this error. Then, their death sentences are *reversed*." What is your assessment of Liebman's observation that "[t]his much error, and the time needed to cure it, impose terrible costs on taxpayers, victims' families, the judicial system, and the wrongly condemned. And it renders unattainable the finality, retribution and deterrence that are the reasons usually given for having a death penalty"?

Can you envision any way that habeas corpus jurisprudence could be changed in order to address these issues?

2. Judges and the politics of death

In their article *Judges and the Politics of Death: Deciding Between the Bill of Rights and the Next Election in Death Penalty Cases*, 75 B.U. L. Rev. 759 (1995), Stephen B. Bright and Patrick J. Keenan examine the influence of the politics of crime on judicial behavior in capital cases. They observe that in jurisdictions where judges stand for election, judges face the same "hydraulic pressure" of public opinion to which publicly elected prosecutors are subjected. "As a result of the increasing prominence of the death penalty in judicial elections as well as other campaigns for public office," Bright and Keenan maintain, "judges are well aware of the consequences to their careers of unpopular decisions in capital cases."

Assuming that Bright and Keenan are correct, in what ways could the "hydraulic pressure" of public opinion influence the outcome of habeas petitions in capital cases?

B. Race

McCleskey v. Kemp
481 U.S. 279 (1987)

JUSTICE POWELL delivered the opinion of the Court.

This case presents the question whether a complex statistical study that indicates a risk that racial considerations enter into capital sentencing determinations proves that petitioner McCleskey's capital sentence is unconstitutional under the Eighth or Fourteenth Amendment.

I

McCleskey, a black man, was convicted of two counts of armed robbery and one count of murder in the Superior Court of Fulton County, Georgia, on October 12, 1978. McCleskey's convictions arose out of the robbery of a furniture store and the killing of a white police officer during the course of the robbery. The evidence at trial indicated that McCleskey and three accomplices planned and carried out the robbery. All four were armed. McCleskey entered the front of the store while the other three entered the rear. McCleskey secured the front of the store by rounding up the customers and forcing them to lie face down on the floor. The other three rounded up the employees in the rear and tied them up with tape. The manager was forced at gunpoint to turn over the store receipts, his watch, and $6. During the course of the robbery, a police officer, answering a silent alarm, entered the store through the front door. As he was walking down the center aisle of the store, two shots were fired. Both struck the officer. One hit him in the face and killed him.

Several weeks later, McCleskey was arrested in connection with an unrelated offense. He confessed that he had participated in the furniture store robbery, but denied that he had shot the police officer. At trial, the State introduced evidence that at least one of the bullets that struck the officer was fired from a .38 caliber Rossi revolver. This description matched the description of the gun that McCleskey had carried during the robbery. The State also introduced the testimony of two witnesses who had heard McCleskey admit to the shooting.

The jury convicted McCleskey of murder. *** At the penalty hearing, *** the jury heard arguments as to the appropriate sentence. Under Georgia law, the jury could not consider imposing the death penalty unless it found beyond a reasonable doubt that the murder was accompanied by one of the statutory aggravating circumstances. *** The jury in this case found two aggravating circumstances to exist beyond a reasonable doubt: the murder was committed during the course of an armed robbery, ** and the murder was committed upon a peace officer engaged in the performance of his duties. ** In making its decision whether to impose the death sentence, the jury considered the mitigating and aggravating circumstances of McCleskey's conduct. ** McCleskey offered no mitigating evidence. The jury recommended that he be sentenced to death on the murder charge and to consecutive life sentences on the armed robbery charges. The court followed the jury's recommendation and sentenced McCleskey to death. ***

On appeal, the Supreme Court of Georgia affirmed the convictions and the sentences. ** This Court denied a petition for a writ of certiorari. ** The Superior Court of Fulton County denied McCleskey's extraordinary motion for a new trial. McCleskey then filed a petition for a writ of habeas corpus in the Superior Court of Butts County. After holding an evidentiary hearing, the Superior Court denied relief. ** The Supreme

Court of Georgia denied McCleskey's application for a certificate of probable cause to appeal the Superior Court's denial of his petition, ** and this Court again denied certiorari. **

McCleskey next filed a petition for a writ of habeas corpus in the Federal District Court for the Northern District of Georgia. His petition raised 18 claims, one of which was that the Georgia capital sentencing process is administered in a racially discriminatory manner in violation of the Eighth and Fourteenth Amendments to the United States Constitution. In support of his claim, McCleskey proffered a statistical study performed by Professors David C. Baldus, Charles Pulaski, and George Woodworth, (the Baldus study) that purports to show a disparity in the imposition of the death sentence in Georgia based on the race of the murder victim and, to a lesser extent, the race of the defendant. The Baldus study is actually two sophisticated statistical studies that examine over 2,000 murder cases that occurred in Georgia during the 1970's. The raw numbers collected by Professor Baldus indicate that defendants charged with killing white persons received the death penalty in 11% of the cases, but defendants charged with killing blacks received the death penalty in only 1% of the cases. The raw numbers also indicate a reverse racial disparity according to the race of the defendant: 4% of the black defendants received the death penalty, as opposed to 7% of the white defendants.

Baldus also divided the cases according to the combination of the race of the defendant and the race of the victim. He found that the death penalty was assessed in 22% of the cases involving black defendants and white victims; 8% of the cases involving white defendants and white victims; 1% of the cases involving black defendants and black victims; and 3% of the cases involving white defendants and black victims. Similarly, Baldus found that prosecutors sought the death penalty in 70% of the cases involving black defendants and white victims; 32% of the cases involving white defendants and white victims; 15% of the cases involving black defendants and black victims; and 19% of the cases involving white defendants and black victims.

Baldus subjected his data to an extensive analysis, taking account of 230 variables that could have explained the disparities on nonracial grounds. One of his models concludes that, even after taking account of 39 nonracial variables, defendants charged with killing white victims were 4.3 times as likely to receive a death sentence as defendants charged with killing blacks. According to this model, black defendants were 1.1 times as likely to receive a death sentence as other defendants. Thus, the Baldus study indicates that black defendants, such as McCleskey, who kill white victims have the greatest likelihood of receiving the death penalty. ***

The District Court held an extensive evidentiary hearing on McCleskey's petition. Although it believed that McCleskey's Eighth Amendment claim was foreclosed by the Fifth Circuit's decision in *Spinkellink v. Wainwright*, 578 F.2d 582, 612–616 (1978), *cert. denied*, 440 U.S. 976 (1979), it nevertheless considered the Baldus study with care. It concluded that McCleskey's "statistics do not demonstrate a prima facie case in support of the contention that the death penalty was imposed upon him because of his race, because of the race of the victim, or because of any Eighth Amendment concern." ** As to McCleskey's Fourteenth Amendment claim, the court found that the methodology of the Baldus study was flawed in several respects. *** Because of these defects, the court held that the Baldus study "fail[ed] to contribute anything of value" to McCleskey's claim. ** Accordingly, the court denied the petition insofar as it was based upon the Baldus study.

The Court of Appeals for the Eleventh Circuit, sitting en banc, carefully reviewed the District Court's decision on McCleskey's claim. ** It assumed the validity of the study itself and addressed the merits of McCleskey's Eighth and Fourteenth Amendment claims. That is, the court assumed that the study "showed that systematic and substantial disparities existed in the penalties imposed upon homicide defendants in Georgia based on race of the homicide victim, that the disparities existed at a less substantial rate in death sentencing based on race of defendants, and that the factors of race of the victim and defendant were at work in Fulton County." ** Even assuming the study's validity, the Court of Appeals found the statistics "insufficient to demonstrate discriminatory intent or unconstitutional discrimination in the Fourteenth Amendment context, [and] insufficient to show irrationality, arbitrariness and capriciousness under any kind of Eighth Amendment analysis." ** The court noted:

> The very exercise of discretion means that persons exercising discretion may reach different results from exact duplicates. Assuming each result is within the range of discretion, all are correct in the eyes of the law. It would not make sense for the system to require the exercise of discretion in order to be facially constitutional, and at the same time hold a system unconstitutional in application where that discretion achieved different results for what appear to be exact duplicates, absent the state showing the reasons for the difference....

> The Baldus approach...would take the cases with different results on what are contended to be duplicate facts, where the differences could not be otherwise explained, and conclude that the different result was based on race alone.... This approach ignores the realities.... There are, in fact, no exact duplicates in capital crimes and capital defendants. The type of research submitted here tends to show which of the directed factors were effective, but is of restricted use in showing what undirected factors control the exercise of constitutionally required discretion. **

***

The Court of Appeals affirmed the denial by the District Court of McCleskey's petition for a writ of habeas corpus insofar as the petition was based upon the Baldus study, with three judges dissenting as to McCleskey's claims based on the Baldus study. We granted certiorari ** and now affirm.

II

McCleskey's first claim is that the Georgia capital punishment statute violates the Equal Protection Clause of the Fourteenth Amendment. *** He argues that race has infected the administration of Georgia's statute in two ways: persons who murder whites are more likely to be sentenced to death than persons who murder blacks, and black murderers are more likely to be sentenced to death than white murderers. *** As a black defendant who killed a white victim, McCleskey claims that the Baldus study demonstrates that he was discriminated against because of his race and because of the race of his victim. In its broadest form, McCleskey's claim of discrimination extends to every actor in the Georgia capital sentencing process, from the prosecutor who sought the death penalty and the jury that imposed the sentence, to the State itself that enacted the capital punishment statute and allows it to remain in effect despite its allegedly discriminatory application. We agree with the Court of Appeals, and every other court that has considered such a challenge, *** that this claim must fail.

A

Our analysis begins with the basic principle that a defendant who alleges an equal protection violation has the burden of proving "the existence of purposeful discrimination." *Whitus v. Georgia*, 385 U.S. 545, 550 (1967). *** A corollary to this principle is that a criminal defendant must prove that the purposeful discrimination "had a discriminatory effect" on him. *Wayte v. United States*, 470 U.S. 598, 608 (1985). Thus, to prevail under the Equal Protection Clause, McCleskey must prove that the decisionmakers in *his* case acted with discriminatory purpose. He offers no evidence specific to his own case that would support an inference that racial considerations played a part in his sentence. Instead, he relies solely on the Baldus study. *** McCleskey argues that the Baldus study compels an inference that his sentence rests on purposeful discrimination. McCleskey's claim that these statistics are sufficient proof of discrimination, without regard to the facts of a particular case, would extend to all capital cases in Georgia, at least where the victim was white and the defendant is black.

The Court has accepted statistics as proof of intent to discriminate in certain limited contexts. First, this Court has accepted statistical disparities as proof of an equal protection violation in the selection of the jury venire in a particular district. Although statistical proof normally must present a "stark" pattern to be accepted as the sole proof of discriminatory intent under the Constitution, *** *Arlington Heights v. Metropolitan Housing Dev. Corp.*, 429 U.S. 252, 266 (1977), "[b]ecause of the nature of the jury-selection task,…we have permitted a finding of constitutional violation even when the statistical pattern does not approach [such] extremes." *Id.* at 266. *** Second, this Court has accepted statistics in the form of multiple-regression analysis to prove statutory violations under Title VII of the Civil Rights Act of 1964. *Bazemore v. Friday*, 478 U.S. 385, 400–401 (1986) (opinion of BRENNAN, J., concurring in part).

But the nature of the capital sentencing decision, and the relationship of the statistics to that decision, are fundamentally different from the corresponding elements in the venire-selection or Title VII cases. Most importantly, each particular decision to impose the death penalty is made by a petit jury selected from a properly constituted venire. Each jury is unique in its composition, and the Constitution requires that its decision rest on consideration of innumerable factors that vary according to the characteristics of the individual defendant and the facts of the particular capital offense. *See Hitchcock v. Dugger*, [481 U.S. 393,] 398–399 [(1987)]; *Lockett v. Ohio*, 438 U.S. 586, 602–605 (1978) (plurality opinion of Burger, C.J.). Thus, the application of an inference drawn from the general statistics to a specific decision in a trial and sentencing simply is not comparable to the application of an inference drawn from general statistics to a specific venire-selection or Title VII case. In those cases, the statistics relate to fewer entities, *** and fewer variables are relevant to the challenged decisions. ***

Another important difference between the cases in which we have accepted statistics as proof of discriminatory intent and this case is that, in the venire-selection and Title VII contexts, the decisionmaker has an opportunity to explain the statistical disparity. ** Here, the State has no practical opportunity to rebut the Baldus study. "[C]ontrolling considerations of…public policy," *McDonald v. Pless*, 238 U.S. 264, 267 (1915), dictate that jurors "cannot be called…to testify to the motives and influences that led to their verdict." *Chicago, B. & Q. R. Co. v. Babcock*, 204 U.S. 585, 593 (1907). Similarly, the policy considerations behind a prosecutor's traditionally "wide discretion" *** suggest the impropriety of our requiring prosecutors to defend their decisions to seek death penalties, "often years after they were made." *** *See Imbler v. Pachtman*, 424 U.S. 409,

425–426 (1976). *** Moreover, absent far stronger proof, it is unnecessary to seek such a rebuttal, because a legitimate and unchallenged explanation for the decision is apparent from the record: McCleskey committed an act for which the United States Constitution and Georgia laws permit imposition of the death penalty. ***

Finally, McCleskey's statistical proffer must be viewed in the context of his challenge. McCleskey challenges decisions at the heart of the State's criminal justice system. "[O]ne of society's most basic tasks is that of protecting the lives of its citizens and one of the most basic ways in which it achieves the task is through criminal laws against murder." *Gregg v. Georgia*, 428 U.S. 153, 226 (1976) (WHITE, J., concurring). Implementation of these laws necessarily requires discretionary judgments. Because discretion is essential to the criminal justice process, we would demand exceptionally clear proof before we would infer that the discretion has been abused. The unique nature of the decisions at issue in this case also counsels against adopting such an inference from the disparities indicated by the Baldus study. Accordingly, we hold that the Baldus study is clearly insufficient to support an inference that any of the decisionmakers in Mc-Cleskey's case acted with discriminatory purpose.

B

McCleskey also suggests that the Baldus study proves that the State as a whole has acted with a discriminatory purpose. He appears to argue that the State has violated the Equal Protection Clause by adopting the capital punishment statute and allowing it to remain in force despite its allegedly discriminatory application. But "'[d]iscriminatory purpose'… implies more than intent as volition or intent as awareness of consequences. It implies that the decisionmaker, in this case a state legislature, selected or reaffirmed a particular course of action at least in part 'because of,' not merely 'in spite of,' its adverse effects upon an identifiable group." *Personnel Administrator of Massachusetts v. Feeney*, 442 U.S. 256, 279 (1979) (footnote and citation omitted). ** For this claim to prevail, McCleskey would have to prove that the Georgia Legislature enacted or maintained the death penalty statute *because of* an anticipated racially discriminatory effect. In *Gregg v. Georgia, supra,* this Court found that the Georgia capital sentencing system could operate in a fair and neutral manner. There was no evidence then, and there is none now, that the Georgia Legislature enacted the capital punishment statute to further a racially discriminatory purpose. ***

Nor has McCleskey demonstrated that the legislature maintains the capital punishment statute because of the racially disproportionate impact suggested by the Baldus study. As legislatures necessarily have wide discretion in the choice of criminal laws and penalties, and as there were legitimate reasons for the Georgia Legislature to adopt and maintain capital punishment, *see Gregg v. Georgia, supra,* at 183–187 (joint opinion of STEWART, POWELL, and STEVENS, JJ.), we will not infer a discriminatory purpose on the part of the State of Georgia. *** Accordingly, we reject McCleskey's equal protection claims.

III

McCleskey also argues that the Baldus study demonstrates that the Georgia capital sentencing system violates the Eighth Amendment. *** We begin our analysis of this claim by reviewing the restrictions on death sentences established by our prior decisions under that Amendment.

A

The Eighth Amendment prohibits infliction of "cruel and unusual punishments." This Court's early Eighth Amendment cases examined only the "particular methods of execution to determine whether they were too cruel to pass constitutional muster." *Gregg v. Georgia, supra*, at 170. ** Subsequently, the Court recognized that the constitutional prohibition against cruel and unusual punishments "is not fastened to the obsolete but may acquire meaning as public opinion becomes enlightened by a humane justice." *Weems v. United States*, 217 U.S. 349 (1910). In *Weems*, the Court identified a second principle inherent in the Eighth Amendment, "that punishment for crime should be graduated and proportioned to offense." *Id.* at 367.

Chief Justice Warren, writing for the plurality in *Trop v. Dulles*, 356 U.S. 86, 99 (1958), acknowledged the constitutionality of capital punishment. In his view, the "basic concept underlying the Eighth Amendment" in this area is that the penalty must accord with "the dignity of man." *Id.* at 100. ** In applying this mandate, we have been guided by his statement that "[t]he Amendment must draw its meaning from the evolving standards of decency that mark the progress of a maturing society." *Id.* at 101. Thus, our constitutional decisions have been informed by "contemporary values concerning the infliction of a challenged sanction," *Gregg v. Georgia*, 428 U.S. at 173. In assessing contemporary values, we have eschewed subjective judgment, and instead have sought to ascertain "objective indicia that reflect the public attitude toward a given sanction." *Ibid.* First among these indicia are the decisions of state legislatures, "because the... legislative judgment weighs heavily in ascertaining" contemporary standards, *id.* at 175. We also have been guided by the sentencing decisions of juries, because they are "a significant and reliable objective index of contemporary values," *id.* at 181. Most of our recent decisions as to the constitutionality of the death penalty for a particular crime have rested on such an examination of contemporary values. *E.g., Enmund v. Florida*, 458 U.S. 782, 789–796 (1982) (felony murder); *Coker v. Georgia*, 433 U.S. 584, 592–597 (1977) (plurality opinion of WHITE, J.) (rape); *Gregg v. Georgia*, [428 U.S.] at 179–182 (murder).

B

Two principal decisions guide our resolution of McCleskey's Eighth Amendment claim. In *Furman v. Georgia*, 408 U.S. 238 (1972), the Court concluded that the death penalty was so irrationally imposed that any particular death sentence could be presumed excessive. Under the statutes at issue in *Furman*, there was no basis for determining in any particular case whether the penalty was proportionate to the crime: "[T]he death penalty [was] exacted with great infrequency even for the most atrocious crimes and... there [was] no meaningful basis for distinguishing the few cases in which it [was] imposed from the many cases in which it [was] not." *Id.* at 313 (WHITE, J., concurring).

In *Gregg*, the Court specifically addressed the question left open in *Furman*— whether the punishment of death for murder is "under all circumstances, 'cruel and unusual' in violation of the Eighth and Fourteenth Amendments of the Constitution." 428 U.S. at 168. We noted that the imposition of the death penalty for the crime of murder "has a long history of acceptance both in the United States and in England." *Id.* at 176 (joint opinion of STEWART, POWELL, and STEVENS, JJ.). "The most marked indication of society's endorsement of the death penalty for murder [was] the legislative response to *Furman*." *Id.* at 179. During the 4-year period between *Furman* and *Gregg*, at least 35 States had reenacted the death penalty, and Congress had authorized the penalty for aircraft piracy. 428 U.S. at 179–180. *** The "actions of juries" were "fully compatible with the legislative judgments." *Id.* at 182.

We noted that any punishment might be unconstitutionally severe if inflicted without penological justification, but concluded:

Considerations of federalism, as well as respect for the ability of a legislature to evaluate, in terms of its particular State, the moral consensus concerning the death penalty and its social utility as a sanction, require us to conclude, in the absence of more convincing evidence, that the infliction of death as a punishment for murder is not without justification and thus is not unconstitutionally severe. *Id.* at 186–187.

The second question before the Court in *Gregg* was the constitutionality of the particular procedures embodied in the Georgia capital punishment statute. We explained the fundamental principle of *Furman*, that "where discretion is afforded a sentencing body on a matter so grave as the determination of whether a human life should be taken or spared, that discretion must be suitably directed and limited so as to minimize the risk of wholly arbitrary and capricious action." 428 U.S. at 189. Numerous features of the then new Georgia statute met the concerns articulated in *Furman*. *** The Georgia system bifurcates guilt and sentencing proceedings so that the jury can receive all relevant information for sentencing without the risk that evidence irrelevant to the defendant's guilt will influence the jury's consideration of that issue. The statute narrows the class of murders subject to the death penalty to cases in which the jury finds at least one statutory aggravating circumstance beyond a reasonable doubt. Conversely, it allows the defendant to introduce any relevant mitigating evidence that might influence the jury not to impose a death sentence. *See* 428 U.S. at 163–164. The procedures also require a particularized inquiry into "'the circumstances of the offense together with the character and propensities of the offender.'" *Id.* at 189. ** Thus, "while some jury discretion still exists, 'the discretion to be exercised is controlled by clear and objective standards so as to produce non-discriminatory application.'" 428 U.S. at 197–198 (*quoting Coley v. State*, 204 S.E.2d 612, 615 (1974)). Moreover, the Georgia system adds "an important additional safeguard against arbitrariness and caprice" in a provision for automatic appeal of a death sentence to the State Supreme Court. 428 U.S. at 198. The statute requires that court to review each sentence to determine whether it was imposed under the influence of passion or prejudice, whether the evidence supports the jury's finding of a statutory aggravating circumstance, and whether the sentence is disproportionate to sentences imposed in generally similar murder cases. To aid the court's review, the trial judge answers a questionnaire about the trial, including detailed questions as to "the quality of the defendant's representation [and] whether race played a role in the trial." *Id.* at 167.

C

In the cases decided after *Gregg*, the Court has imposed a number of requirements on the capital sentencing process to ensure that capital sentencing decisions rest on the individualized inquiry contemplated in *Gregg*. In *Woodson v. North Carolina*, 428 U.S. 280 (1976), we invalidated a mandatory capital sentencing system, finding that the "respect for humanity underlying the Eighth Amendment requires consideration of the character and record of the individual offender and the circumstances of the particular offense as a constitutionally indispensable part of the process of inflicting the penalty of death." *Id.* at 304 (plurality opinion of STEWART, POWELL, and STEVENS, JJ.) (citation omitted). Similarly, a State must "narrow the class of murderers subject to capital punishment," *Gregg v. Georgia, supra*, 428 U.S. at 196, by providing "specific and detailed guidance" to the sentencer. *** *Proffitt v. Florida*, 428 U.S. 242, 253 (1976) (joint opinion of STEWART, POWELL, and STEVENS, JJ.).

In contrast to the carefully defined standards that must narrow a sentencer's discretion to *impose* the death sentence, the Constitution limits a State's ability to narrow a sentencer's discretion to consider relevant evidence that might cause it to *decline to impose* the death sentence. *** "[T]he sentencer… [cannot] be precluded from considering, *as a mitigating factor*, any aspect of a defendant's character or record and any of the circumstances of the offense that the defendant proffers as a basis for a sentence less than death." *Lockett v. Ohio*, 438 U.S. at 604 (plurality opinion of Burger, C.J.) (emphasis in original; footnote omitted). *See Skipper v. South Carolina*, 476 U.S. 1 (1986). Any exclusion of the "compassionate or mitigating factors stemming from the diverse frailties of humankind" that are relevant to the sentencer's decision would fail to treat all persons as "uniquely individual human beings." *Woodson v. North Carolina, supra*, 428 U.S. at 304.

Although our constitutional inquiry has centered on the procedures by which a death sentence is imposed, we have not stopped at the face of a statute, but have probed the application of statutes to particular cases. For example, in *Godfrey v. Georgia*, 446 U.S. 420 (1980), the Court invalidated a Georgia Supreme Court interpretation of the statutory aggravating circumstance that the murder be "outrageously or wantonly vile, horrible or inhuman in that it involved torture, depravity of mind, or an aggravated battery to the victim." *** Although that court had articulated an adequate limiting definition of this phrase, we concluded that its interpretation in *Godfrey* was so broad that it may have vitiated the role of the aggravating circumstance in guiding the sentencing jury's discretion.

Finally, where the objective indicia of community values have demonstrated a consensus that the death penalty is disproportionate as applied to a certain class of cases, we have established substantive limitations on its application. In *Coker v. Georgia*, 433 U.S. 584 (1977), the Court held that a State may not constitutionally sentence an individual to death for the rape of an adult woman. In *Enmund v. Florida*, 458 U.S. 782 (1982), the Court prohibited imposition of the death penalty on a defendant convicted of felony murder absent a showing that the defendant possessed a sufficiently culpable mental state. Most recently, in *Ford v. Wainwright*, 477 U.S. 399 (1986), we prohibited execution of prisoners who are insane.

D

In sum, our decisions since *Furman* have identified a constitutionally permissible range of discretion in imposing the death penalty. First, there is a required threshold below which the death penalty cannot be imposed. In this context, the State must establish rational criteria that narrow the decisionmaker's judgment as to whether the circumstances of a particular defendant's case meet the threshold. Moreover, a societal consensus that the death penalty is disproportionate to a particular offense prevents a State from imposing the death penalty for that offense. Second, States cannot limit the sentencer's consideration of any relevant circumstance that could cause it to decline to impose the penalty. In this respect, the State cannot channel the sentencer's discretion, but must allow it to consider any relevant information offered by the defendant.

IV
A

In light of our precedents under the Eighth Amendment, McCleskey cannot argue successfully that his sentence is "disproportionate to the crime in the traditional sense." *See Pulley v. Harris*, 465 U.S. 37, 43 (1984). He does not deny that he committed a murder in the course of a planned robbery, a crime for which this Court has determined that the death penalty constitutionally may be imposed. *Gregg v. Georgia*, 428 U.S. at

187. His disproportionality claim "is of a different sort." *Pulley v. Harris*, [465 U.S.] at 43. McCleskey argues that the sentence in his case is disproportionate to the sentences in other murder cases.

On the one hand, he cannot base a constitutional claim on an argument that his case differs from other cases in which defendants *did* receive the death penalty. On automatic appeal, the Georgia Supreme Court found that McCleskey's death sentence was not disproportionate to other death sentences imposed in the State. ** The court supported this conclusion with an appendix containing citations to 13 cases involving generally similar murders. ** Moreover, where the statutory procedures adequately channel the sentencer's discretion, such proportionality review is not constitutionally required. *Pulley v. Harris, supra*, at 50–51.

On the other hand, absent a showing that the Georgia capital punishment system operates in an arbitrary and capricious manner, McCleskey cannot prove a constitutional violation by demonstrating that other defendants who may be similarly situated did *not* receive the death penalty. In *Gregg*, the Court confronted the argument that "the opportunities for discretionary action that are inherent in the processing of any murder case under Georgia law," 428 U.S. at 199, specifically the opportunities for discretionary leniency, rendered the capital sentences imposed arbitrary and capricious. We rejected this contention[.] ***

Because McCleskey's sentence was imposed under Georgia sentencing procedures that focus discretion "on the particularized nature of the crime and the particularized characteristics of the individual defendant," *id.* at 206, we lawfully may presume that McCleskey's death sentence was not "wantonly and freakishly" imposed, *id.* at 207, and thus that the sentence is not disproportionate within any recognized meaning under the Eighth Amendment.

B

Although our decision in *Gregg* as to the facial validity of the Georgia capital punishment statute appears to foreclose McCleskey's disproportionality argument, he further contends that the Georgia capital punishment system is arbitrary and capricious in *application*, and therefore his sentence is excessive, because racial considerations may influence capital sentencing decisions in Georgia. We now address this claim.

To evaluate McCleskey's challenge, we must examine exactly what the Baldus study may show. Even Professor Baldus does not contend that his statistics prove that race enters into any capital sentencing decisions or that race was a factor in McCleskey's particular case. *** Statistics at most may show only a likelihood that a particular factor entered into some decisions. There is, of course, some risk of racial prejudice influencing a jury's decision in a criminal case. There are similar risks that other kinds of prejudice will influence other criminal trials. ** The question "is at what point that risk becomes constitutionally unacceptable," *Turner v. Murray*, 476 U.S. 28, 36 n.8 (1986). McCleskey asks us to accept the likelihood allegedly shown by the Baldus study as the constitutional measure of an unacceptable risk of racial prejudice influencing capital sentencing decisions. This we decline to do.

Because of the risk that the factor of race may enter the criminal justice process, we have engaged in "unceasing efforts" to eradicate racial prejudice from our criminal justice system. *Batson v. Kentucky*, 476 U.S. 79. 85 (1986). *** Our efforts have been guided by our recognition that "the inestimable privilege of trial by jury...is a vital principle, underlying the whole administration of criminal justice," *Ex parte Milligan*, [71 U.S. 2,

123] (1866). *See Duncan v. Louisiana*, 391 U.S. 145, 155 (1968). *** Thus, it is the jury that is a criminal defendant's fundamental "protection of life and liberty against race or color prejudice." *Strauder v. West Virginia*, 100 U.S. 303, 309 (1880). Specifically, a capital sentencing jury representative of a criminal defendant's community assures a " 'diffused impartiality,' " *Taylor v. Louisiana*, 419 U.S. 522, 530 (1975), ** in the jury's task of "express[ing] the conscience of the community on the ultimate question of life or death," *Witherspoon v. Illinois*, 391 U.S. 510, 519 (1968). ***

Individual jurors bring to their deliberations "qualities of human nature and varieties of human experience, the range of which is unknown and perhaps unknowable." *Peters v. Kiff*, 407 U.S. 493, 503 (1972) (opinion of MARSHALL, J.). The capital sentencing decision requires the individual jurors to focus their collective judgment on the unique characteristics of a particular criminal defendant. It is not surprising that such collective judgments often are difficult to explain. But the inherent lack of predictability of jury decisions does not justify their condemnation. On the contrary, it is the jury's function to make the difficult and uniquely human judgments that defy codification and that "buil[d] discretion, equity, and flexibility into a legal system." H. Kalven & H. Zeisel, *The American Jury* 498 (1966).

McCleskey's argument that the Constitution condemns the discretion allowed decisionmakers in the Georgia capital sentencing system is antithetical to the fundamental role of discretion in our criminal justice system. Discretion in the criminal justice system offers substantial benefits to the criminal defendant. Not only can a jury decline to impose the death sentence, it can decline to convict or choose to convict of a lesser offense. Whereas decisions against a defendant's interest may be reversed by the trial judge or on appeal, these discretionary exercises of leniency are final and unreviewable. *** Similarly, the capacity of prosecutorial discretion to provide individualized justice is "firmly entrenched in American law." 2 W. LaFave & J. Israel, *Criminal Procedure* §13.2(a), p. 160 (1984). As we have noted, a prosecutor can decline to charge, offer a plea bargain, *** or decline to seek a death sentence in any particular case. ** Of course, "the power to be lenient [also] is the power to discriminate," K. Davis, *Discretionary Justice* 170 (1973), but a capital punishment system that did not allow for discretionary acts of leniency "would be totally alien to our notions of criminal justice." *Gregg v. Georgia*, 428 U.S. at 200 n.50.

C

At most, the Baldus study indicates a discrepancy that appears to correlate with race. Apparent disparities in sentencing are an inevitable part of our criminal justice system. *** The discrepancy indicated by the Baldus study is "a far cry from the major systemic defects identified in *Furman*," *Pulley v. Harris*, 465 U.S. at 54. *** As this Court has recognized, any mode for determining guilt or punishment "has its weaknesses and the potential for misuse." *Singer v. United States*, 380 U.S. 24, 35 (1965). ** Specifically, "there can be 'no perfect procedure for deciding in which cases governmental authority should be used to impose death.' " *Zant v. Stephens*, 462 U.S. 862, 884 (1983) (*quoting Lockett v. Ohio*, 438 U.S. at 605 (plurality opinion of Burger, C.J.)). Despite these imperfections, our consistent rule has been that constitutional guarantees are met when "the mode [for determining guilt or punishment] itself has been surrounded with safeguards to make it as fair as possible." *Singer v. United States*, 380 U.S. at 35. Where the discretion that is fundamental to our criminal process is involved, we decline to assume that what is unexplained is invidious. In light of the safeguards designed to minimize racial bias in the process, the fundamental value of jury trial in our criminal justice system, and the benefits that discretion provides to criminal defendants, we hold that the Baldus study does not demonstrate a constitutionally significant risk of racial bias affecting the Georgia capital sentencing process. ***

V

Two additional concerns inform our decision in this case. First, McCleskey's claim, taken to its logical conclusion, throws into serious question the principles that underlie our entire criminal justice system. The Eighth Amendment is not limited in application to capital punishment, but applies to all penalties. *Solem v. Helm*, 463 U.S. 277, 289–290 (1983); *see Rummel v. Estelle*, 445 U.S. 263, 293 (1980) (POWELL, J., dissenting). Thus, if we accepted McCleskey's claim that racial bias has impermissibly tainted the capital sentencing decision, we could soon be faced with similar claims as to other types of penalty. *** Moreover, the claim that his sentence rests on the irrelevant factor of race easily could be extended to apply to claims based on unexplained discrepancies that correlate to membership in other minority groups, *** and even to gender. *** Similarly, since McCleskey's claim relates to the race of his victim, other claims could apply with equally logical force to statistical disparities that correlate with the race or sex of other actors in the criminal justice system, such as defense attorneys *** or judges. *** Also, there is no logical reason that such a claim need be limited to racial or sexual bias. If arbitrary and capricious punishment is the touchstone under the Eighth Amendment, such a claim could—at least in theory—be based upon any arbitrary variable, such as the defendant's facial characteristics, *** or the physical attractiveness of the defendant or the victim, *** that some statistical study indicates may be influential in jury decisionmaking. As these examples illustrate, there is no limiting principle to the type of challenge brought by McCleskey. *** The Constitution does not require that a State eliminate any demonstrable disparity that correlates with a potentially irrelevant factor in order to operate a criminal justice system that includes capital punishment. As we have stated specifically in the context of capital punishment, the Constitution does not "plac[e] totally unrealistic conditions on its use." *Gregg v. Georgia*, 428 U.S. at 199 n.50. **

Second, McCleskey's arguments are best presented to the legislative bodies. It is not the responsibility—or indeed even the right—of this Court to determine the appropriate punishment for particular crimes. It is the legislatures, the elected representatives of the people, that are "constituted to respond to the will and consequently the moral values of the people." *Furman v. Georgia*, 408 U.S. at 383 (Burger, C.J., dissenting). Legislatures also are better qualified to weigh and "evaluate the results of statistical studies in terms of their own local conditions and with a flexibility of approach that is not available to the courts," *Gregg v. Georgia*, [428 U.S.] at 186. ** Capital punishment is now the law in more than two-thirds of our States. It is the ultimate duty of courts to determine on a case-by-case basis whether these laws are applied consistently with the Constitution. Despite McCleskey's wide-ranging arguments that basically challenge the validity of capital punishment in our multiracial society, the only question before us is whether in his case ** the law of Georgia was properly applied. We agree with the District Court and the Court of Appeals for the Eleventh Circuit that this was carefully and correctly done in this case.

VI

Accordingly, we affirm the judgment of the Court of Appeals for the Eleventh Circuit.

It is so ordered.

JUSTICE BRENNAN, with whom JUSTICE MARSHALL joins, and with whom JUSTICE BLACKMUN and JUSTICE STEVENS join in all but Part I, dissenting.

I

Adhering to my view that the death penalty is in all circumstances cruel and unusual punishment forbidden by the Eighth and Fourteenth Amendments, I would vacate the decision below insofar as it left undisturbed the death sentence imposed in this case. *Gregg v. Georgia*, 428 U.S. 153, 227 (1976) (BRENNAN, J., dissenting). The Court observes that "[t]he *Gregg*-type statute imposes unprecedented safeguards in the special context of capital punishment," which "ensure a degree of care in the imposition of the death penalty that can be described only as unique." ** Notwithstanding these efforts, murder defendants in Georgia with white victims are more than four times as likely to receive the death sentence as are defendants with black victims. ** Nothing could convey more powerfully the intractable reality of the death penalty: "that the effort to eliminate arbitrariness in the infliction of that ultimate sanction is so plainly doomed to failure that it—and the death penalty—must be abandoned altogether." *Godfrey v. Georgia*, 446 U.S. 420, 442 (1980) (MARSHALL, J., concurring in judgment).

Even if I did not hold this position, however, I would reverse the Court of Appeals, for petitioner McCleskey has clearly demonstrated that his death sentence was imposed in violation of the Eighth and Fourteenth Amendments. While I join Parts I through IV-A of JUSTICE BLACKMUN's dissenting opinion discussing petitioner's Fourteenth Amendment claim, I write separately to emphasize how conclusively McCleskey has also demonstrated precisely the type of risk of irrationality in sentencing that we have consistently condemned in our Eighth Amendment jurisprudence.

II

At some point in this case, Warren McCleskey doubtless asked his lawyer whether a jury was likely to sentence him to die. A candid reply to this question would have been disturbing. First, counsel would have to tell McCleskey that few of the details of the crime or of McCleskey's past criminal conduct were more important than the fact that his victim was white. ** Furthermore, counsel would feel bound to tell McCleskey that defendants charged with killing white victims in Georgia are 4.3 times as likely to be sentenced to death as defendants charged with killing blacks. ** In addition, frankness would compel the disclosure that it was more likely than not that the race of McCleskey's victim would determine whether he received a death sentence: 6 of every 11 defendants convicted of killing a white person would not have received the death penalty if their victims had been black, ** while, among defendants with aggravating and mitigating factors comparable to McCleskey's, 20 of every 34 would not have been sentenced to die if their victims had been black. ** Finally, the assessment would not be complete without the information that cases involving black defendants and white victims are more likely to result in a death sentence than cases featuring any other racial combination of defendant and victim. ** The story could be told in a variety of ways, but McCleskey could not fail to grasp its essential narrative line: there was a significant chance that race would play a prominent role in determining if he lived or died.

The Court today holds that Warren McCleskey's sentence was constitutionally imposed. It finds no fault in a system in which lawyers must tell their clients that race casts a large shadow on the capital sentencing process. The Court arrives at this conclusion by stating that the Baldus study cannot "*prove* that race enters into any capital sentencing decisions or that race was a factor in McCleskey's particular case." ** Since, according to Professor Baldus, we cannot say "to a moral certainty" that race influenced a decision, ** we can identify only "a likelihood that a particular factor entered into some decisions," ** and "a discrepancy that appears to correlate with race." ** This "likelihood" and "discrepancy," holds the Court, is insufficient to establish a constitutional violation. The Court reaches this conclusion by placing four factors on the scales opposite McCleskey's evidence: the desire to encourage sentencing discretion, the existence of "statutory safeguards" in the Georgia scheme, the fear of encouraging widespread challenges to other sentencing decisions, and the limits of the judicial role. The Court's evaluation of the significance of petitioner's evidence is fundamentally at odds with our consistent concern for rationality in capital sentencing, and the considerations that the majority invokes to discount that evidence cannot justify ignoring its force.

***

JUSTICE BLACKMUN, with whom JUSTICE MARSHALL and JUSTICE STEVENS join, and with whom JUSTICE BRENNAN joins in all but Part IV-B, dissenting.

The Court today sanctions the execution of a man despite his presentation of evidence that establishes a constitutionally intolerable level of racially based discrimination leading to the imposition of his death sentence. I am disappointed with the Court's action not only because of its denial of constitutional guarantees to petitioner McCleskey individually, but also because of its departure from what seems to me to be well-developed constitutional jurisprudence.

***

Yet McCleskey's case raises concerns that are central not only to the principles underlying the Eighth Amendment, but also to the principles underlying the Fourteenth Amendment. Analysis of his case in terms of the Fourteenth Amendment is consistent with this Court's recognition that racial discrimination is fundamentally at odds with our constitutional guarantee of equal protection. The protections afforded by the Fourteenth Amendment are not left at the courtroom door. *Hill v. Texas*, 316 U.S. 400, 406 (1942). Nor is equal protection denied to persons convicted of crimes. *Lee v. Washington*, 390 U.S. 333 (1968) (per curiam). The Court in the past has found that racial discrimination within the criminal justice system is particularly abhorrent: "Discrimination on the basis of race, odious in all aspects, is especially pernicious in the administration of justice." *Rose v. Mitchell*, 443 U.S. 545, 555 (1979). ***

I

A

The Court today seems to give a new meaning to our recognition that death is different. Rather than requiring "a correspondingly greater degree of scrutiny of the capital sentencing determination," *California v. Ramos*, 463 U.S. 992, 998–999 (1983), the Court relies on the very fact that this is a case involving capital punishment to apply a *lesser* standard of scrutiny under the Equal Protection Clause. The Court concludes that "legitimate" explanations outweigh McCleskey's claim that his death sentence reflected a constitutionally impermissible risk of racial discrimination. The Court explains that McCleskey's evidence is too weak to require rebuttal "because a legitimate and unchallenged explanation for the decision is apparent from the record: McCleskey committed an act for which the United States Constitution and Georgia laws permit imposition of the death penalty." ** The Court states that it will not infer a discriminatory purpose on the part of the state legislature because "there were legitimate reasons for the Georgia Legislature to adopt and maintain capital punishment." **

The Court's assertion that the fact of McCleskey's conviction undermines his constitutional claim is inconsistent with a long and unbroken line of this Court's case law. ***

***

II

***

B

There can be no dispute that McCleskey has made the requisite showing under the first prong of the standard. The Baldus study demonstrates that black persons are a distinct group that are singled out for different treatment in the Georgia capital sentencing system. The Court acknowledges, as it must, that the raw statistics included in the Baldus study and presented by petitioner indicate that it is much less likely that a death sentence will result from a murder of a black person than from a murder of a white person. ** White-victim cases are nearly 11 times more likely to yield a death sentence than are black-victim cases. ** The raw figures also indicate that even within the group of defendants who are convicted of killing white persons and are thereby more likely to receive a death sentence, black defendants are more likely than white defendants to be sentenced to death. **

With respect to the second prong, McCleskey must prove that there is a substantial likelihood that his death sentence is due to racial factors. *See Hunter v. Underwood*, 471 U.S. 222, 228 (1985). The Court of Appeals assumed the validity of the Baldus study and found that it "showed that systemic and substantial disparities existed in the penalties imposed upon homicide defendants in Georgia based on race of the homicide victim, that the disparities existed at a less substantial rate in death sentencing based on race of defendants, and that the factors of race of the victim and defendant were at work in Fulton County." ** The question remaining therefore is at what point does that disparity become constitutionally unacceptable. *See Turner v. Murray*, 476 U.S. 28, 36 n.8 (1986) (plurality opinion). ***

***

IV
A

One of the final concerns discussed by the Court may be the most disturbing aspect of its opinion. Granting relief to McCleskey in this case, it is said, could lead to further constitutional challenges. ** That, of course, is no reason to deny McCleskey his rights under the Equal Protection Clause. If a grant of relief to him were to lead to a closer examination of the effects of racial considerations throughout the criminal justice system, the system, and hence society, might benefit. Where no such factors come into play, the integrity of the system is enhanced. Where such considerations are shown to be significant, efforts can be made to eradicate their impermissible influence and to ensure an evenhanded application of criminal sanctions.

B

Like JUSTICE STEVENS, I do not believe acceptance of McCleskey's claim would eliminate capital punishment in Georgia. ** JUSTICE STEVENS points out that the evidence presented in this case indicates that in extremely aggravated murders the risk of discriminatory enforcement of the death penalty is minimized. ** I agree that narrowing the class of death-eligible defendants is not too high a price to pay for a death penalty system that does not discriminate on the basis of race. Moreover, the establishment of guidelines for Assistant District Attorneys as to the appropriate basis for exercising their discretion at the various steps in the prosecution of a case would provide at least a measure of consistency. The Court's emphasis on the procedural safeguards in the system ignores the fact that there are none whatsoever during the crucial process leading up to trial. As JUSTICE WHITE stated for the plurality in *Turner v. Murray*, I find "the risk that racial prejudice may have infected petitioner's capital sentencing unacceptable in light of the ease with which that risk could have been minimized." 476 U.S. at 36. I dissent.

JUSTICE STEVENS, with whom JUSTICE BLACKMUN joins, dissenting.

There "is a qualitative difference between death and any other permissible form of punishment," and hence, "'a corresponding difference in the need for reliability in the determination that death is the appropriate punishment in a specific case.'" *Zant v. Stephens*, 462 U.S. 862, 884–885 (1983), *quoting Woodson v. North Carolina*, 428 U.S. 280, 305 (1976) (plurality opinion of STEWART, POWELL, and STEVENS, JJ.). Even when considerations far less repugnant than racial discrimination are involved, we have recognized the "vital importance to the defendant and to the community that any decision to impose the death sentence be, and appear to be, based on reason rather than caprice or emotion." *Gardner v. Florida*, 430 U.S. 349, 358 (1977). "[A]lthough not every imperfection in the deliberative process is sufficient, even in a capital case, to set aside a state-court judgment, the severity of the sentence mandates careful scrutiny in the review of any colorable claim of error." *Zant*, [462 U.S.] at 885.

In this case it is claimed—and the claim is supported by elaborate studies which the Court properly assumes to be valid—that the jury's sentencing process was likely distorted by racial prejudice. The studies demonstrate a strong probability that McCleskey's sentencing jury, which expressed "the community's outrage—its sense that an individual has lost his moral entitlement to live," *Spaziano v. Florida*, 468 U.S. 447, 469 (1984) (STEVENS, J., dissenting)—was influenced by the fact that McCleskey is black and his victim was white, and that this same outrage would not have been generated if he had killed a member of his own race. This sort of disparity is constitutionally intolerable. It flagrantly violates the Court's prior "insistence that capital punishment be imposed fairly, and with reasonable consistency, or not at all." *Eddings v. Oklahoma*, 455 U.S. 104, 112 (1982).

The Court's decision appears to be based on a fear that the acceptance of McCleskey's claim would sound the death knell for capital punishment in Georgia. If society were indeed forced to choose between a racially discriminatory death penalty (one that provides heightened protection against murder "for whites only") and no death penalty at all, the choice mandated by the Constitution would be plain. *Eddings v. Oklahoma*, *supra*. But the Court's fear is unfounded. One of the lessons of the Baldus study is that there exist certain categories of extremely serious crimes for which prosecutors consistently seek, and juries consistently impose, the death penalty without regard to the race of the victim or the race of the offender. If Georgia were to narrow the class of death-eligible defendants to those categories, the danger of arbitrary and discriminatory imposition of the death penalty would be significantly decreased, if not eradicated. As JUSTICE BRENNAN has demonstrated in his dissenting opinion, such a restructuring of the sentencing scheme is surely not too high a price to pay.

Like JUSTICE BRENNAN, I would therefore reverse the judgment of the Court of Appeals. I believe, however, that further proceedings are necessary in order to determine whether McCleskey's death sentence should be set aside. First, the Court of Appeals must decide whether the Baldus study is valid. I am persuaded that it is, but orderly procedure requires that the Court of Appeals address this issue before we actually decide the question. Second, it is necessary for the District Court to determine whether the particular facts of McCleskey's crime and his background place this case within the range of cases that present an unacceptable risk that race played a decisive role in McCleskey's sentencing.

Accordingly, I respectfully dissent.

Notes

1. *Subsequent case history*

Warren McCleskey was executed on September 25, 1991, by electrocution.

2. *A fear of "too much justice"?*

In her introduction to the *Race to Execution Symposium Issue* published by the DePaul Law Review, Professor Susan Bandes writes that "Bryan Stevenson spoke for many of us who work for reform in the death penalty context when he said: 'I have not yet recovered from reading the *McCleskey* decision.' ** He was deeply troubled by the Court's 'fear of too much justice,' ** its claim that it could not acknowledge racial bias in the capital context because it would then have to deal with racial bias in other criminal contexts as well. But, he went on:

> It was the second thing the Court said that broke my heart, that did something to me that I'm still trying to recover from. The second thing the Court said was a certain amount of bias, a certain quantum of discrimination...is in the Court's opinion inevitable.... And so we are gathered in this room talking about race and the death penalty while the United States Supreme Court has already said it's pointless for you to be here."

Susan Bandes, *Introduction: Race to Execution Symposium*, 53 DePaul L. Rev. 4, 1403 (2004), *citing* Bryan Stevenson, *Keynote Address: Race to Execution Symposium*, 53 DePaul L. Rev. 4, 1699 (2004).

Do you agree with the Court that a certain quantum of discrimination is "inevitable"? In what way does habeas corpus jurisprudence reinforce—or refute—the Court's assertion?

Miller-El v. Cockrell
537 U.S. 322 (2003)

JUSTICE KENNEDY delivered the opinion of the Court.

In this case we once again examine when a state prisoner can appeal the denial or dismissal of his petition for writ of habeas corpus. In 1986 two Dallas County assistant district attorneys used peremptory strikes to exclude 10 of the 11 African-Americans eligible to serve on the jury which tried petitioner Thomas Joe Miller-El. During the ensuing 17 years, petitioner has been unsuccessful in establishing, in either state or federal court, that his conviction and death sentence must be vacated because the jury selection procedures violated the Equal Protection Clause and our holding in *Batson v. Kentucky*, 476 U.S. 79 (1986). The claim now arises in a federal petition for writ of habeas corpus. The procedures and standards applicable in the case are controlled by the habeas corpus statute codified at Title 28, chapter 153 of the United States Code, most recently amended in a substantial manner by the Antiterrorism and Effective Death Penalty Act of 1996 (AEDPA). In the interest of finality AEDPA constrains a federal court's power to disturb state-court convictions.

The United States District Court for the Northern District of Texas, after reviewing the evidence before the state trial court, determined that petitioner failed to establish a constitutional violation warranting habeas relief. The Court of Appeals for the Fifth Circuit, concluding there was insufficient merit to the case, denied a certificate of appealability (COA) from the District Court's determination. The COA denial is the subject of our decision.

At issue here are the standards AEDPA imposes before a court of appeals may issue a COA to review a denial of habeas relief in the district court. Congress mandates that a prisoner seeking postconviction relief under 28 U.S.C. §2254 has no automatic right to appeal a district court's denial or dismissal of the petition. Instead, petitioner must first seek and obtain a COA. In resolving this case we decide again that when a habeas applicant seeks permission to initiate appellate review of the dismissal of his petition, the court of appeals should limit its examination to a threshold inquiry into the underlying merit of his claims. *Slack v. McDaniel*, 529 U.S. 473, 481 (2000). Consistent with our prior precedent and the text of the habeas corpus statute, we reiterate that a prisoner seeking a COA need only demonstrate "a substantial showing of the denial of a constitutional right." 28 U.S.C. §2253(c)(2). A petitioner satisfies this standard by demonstrating that jurists of reason could disagree with the district court's resolution of his constitutional claims or that jurists could conclude the issues presented are adequate to deserve encouragement to proceed further. *Slack, supra*, 529 U.S. at 484. Applying these principles to petitioner's application, we conclude a COA should have issued.

I

A

Petitioner, his wife Dorothy Miller-El, and one Kenneth Flowers robbed a Holiday Inn in Dallas, Texas. They emptied the cash drawers and ordered two employees, Doug Walker and Donald Hall, to lie on the floor. Walker and Hall were gagged with strips of fabric, and their hands and feet were bound. Petitioner asked Flowers if he was going to kill Walker and Hall. When Flowers hesitated or refused, petitioner shot Walker twice in the back and shot Hall in the side. Walker died from his wounds.

The State indicted petitioner for capital murder. He pleaded not guilty, and jury selection took place during five weeks in February and March 1986. When *voir dire* had been concluded, petitioner moved to strike the jury on the grounds that the prosecution had violated the Equal Protection Clause of the Fourteenth Amendment by excluding African-Americans through the use of peremptory challenges. Petitioner's trial occurred before our decision in *Batson, supra*, and *Swain v. Alabama*, 380 U.S. 202 (1965), was then the controlling precedent. As *Swain* required, petitioner sought to show that the prosecution's conduct was part of a larger pattern of discrimination aimed at excluding African-Americans from jury service. In a pretrial hearing held on March 12, 1986, petitioner presented extensive evidence in support of his motion. The trial judge, however, found "no evidence...that indicated any systematic exclusion of blacks as a matter of policy by the District Attorney's office; while it may have been done by individual prosecutors in individual cases." ** The state court then denied petitioner's motion to strike the jury. ** Twelve days later, the jury found petitioner guilty; and the trial court sentenced him to death.

Petitioner appealed to the Texas Court of Criminal Appeals. While the appeal was pending, on April 30, 1986, the Court decided *Batson v. Kentucky* and established its three-part process for evaluating claims that a prosecutor used peremptory challenges in violation of the Equal Protection Clause. First, a defendant must make a prima facie showing that a peremptory challenge has been exercised on the basis of race. 476 U.S. at 96–97. Second, if that showing has been made, the prosecution must offer a race-neutral basis for striking the juror in question. [*Batson*], 476 U.S. at 97–98. Third, in light of the parties' submissions, the trial court must determine whether the defendant has shown purposeful discrimination. *Id.* at 98.

After acknowledging petitioner had established an inference of purposeful discrimination, the Texas Court of Criminal Appeals remanded the case for new findings in light of *Batson*. ** A post-trial hearing was held on May 10, 1988 (a little over two years after petitioner's jury had been empaneled). There, the original trial court admitted all the evidence presented at the *Swain* hearing and further evidence and testimony from the attorneys in the original trial. **

On January 13, 1989, the trial court concluded that petitioner's evidence failed to satisfy step one of *Batson* because it "did not even raise an inference of racial motivation in the use of the state's peremptory challenges" to support a prima facie case. ** Notwithstanding this conclusion, the state court determined that the State would have prevailed on steps two and three because the prosecutors had offered credible, race-neutral explanations for each African-American excluded. The court further found "no disparate prosecutorial examination of any of the venireman in question" and "that the primary reasons for the exercise of the challenges against each of the veniremen in question [was] their reluctance to assess or reservations concerning the imposition of the death penalty." ** There was no discussion of petitioner's other evidence.

The Texas Court of Criminal Appeals denied petitioner's appeal, and we denied certiorari. ** Petitioner's state habeas proceedings fared no better, and he was denied relief by the Texas Court of Criminal Appeals.

Petitioner filed a petition for writ of habeas corpus in Federal District Court pursuant to 28 U.S.C. § 2254. Although petitioner raised four issues, we concern ourselves here with only petitioner's jury selection claim premised on *Batson*. The Federal Magistrate Judge who considered the merits was troubled by some of the evidence adduced in the state-court proceedings. He, nevertheless, recommended, in deference to the state courts' acceptance of the prosecutors' race-neutral justifications for striking the potential jurors, that petitioner be denied relief. The United States District Court adopted the recommendation. Pursuant to § 2253, petitioner sought a COA from the District Court, and the application was denied. Petitioner renewed his request to the Court of Appeals for the Fifth Circuit, and it also denied the COA.

The Court of Appeals noted that, under controlling habeas principles, a COA will issue " 'only if the applicant has made a substantial showing of the denial of a constitutional right.' " *Miller-El v. Johnson*, 261 F.3d 445, 449 (2001) (*quoting* 28 U.S.C. § 2253(c)(2)). Citing our decision in *Slack v. McDaniel*, 529 U.S. 473 (2000), the court reasoned that "[a] petitioner makes a 'substantial showing' when he demonstrates that his petition involves issues which are debatable among jurists of reason, that another court could resolve the issues differently, or that the issues are adequate to deserve encouragement to proceed further." ** The Court of Appeals also interjected the requirements of 28 U.S.C. § 2254 into the COA determination: "As an appellate court reviewing a federal habeas petition, we are required by § 2254(d)(2) to presume the state court findings correct unless we determine that the findings result in a decision which is unreasonable in light of the evidence presented. And the unreasonableness, if any, must be established by clear and convincing evidence. *See* 28 U.S.C. § 2254(e)(1)." **

Applying this framework to petitioner's COA application, the Court of Appeals concluded "that the state court's findings are not unreasonable and that Miller-El has failed to present clear and convincing evidence to the contrary." ** As a consequence, the court "determined that the state court's adjudication neither resulted in a decision that was unreasonable in light of the evidence presented nor resulted in a decision contrary to clearly established federal law as determined by the Supreme Court," ** and it denied petitioner's request for a COA. We granted certiorari. **

B

While a COA ruling is not the occasion for a ruling on the merit of petitioner's claim, our determination to reverse the Court of Appeals counsels us to explain in some detail the extensive evidence concerning the jury selection procedures. Petitioner's evidence falls into two broad categories. First, he presented to the state trial court, at a pretrial *Swain* hearing, evidence relating to a pattern and practice of race discrimination in the *voir dire*. Second, two years later, he presented, to the same state court, evidence that directly related to the conduct of the prosecutors in his case. We discuss the latter first.

A comparative analysis of the venire members demonstrates that African-Americans were excluded from petitioner's jury in a ratio significantly higher than Caucasians were. Of the 108 possible jurors reviewed by the prosecution and defense, 20 were African-American. Nine of them were excused for cause or by agreement of the parties. Of the 11 African-American jurors remaining, however, all but 1 were excluded by peremptory strikes exercised by the prosecutors. On this basis 91% of the eligible black jurors were removed by peremptory strikes. In contrast the prosecutors used their peremptory strikes against just 13% (4 out of 31) of the eligible nonblack prospective jurors qualified to serve on petitioner's jury.

These numbers, while relevant, are not petitioner's whole case. During *voir dire*, the prosecution questioned venire members as to their views concerning the death penalty and their willingness to serve on a capital case. Responses that disclosed reluctance or hesitation to impose capital punishment were cited as a justification for striking a potential juror for cause or by peremptory challenge. *Wainwright v. Witt*, 469 U.S. 412 (1985). The evidence suggests, however, that the manner in which members of the venire were questioned varied by race. To the extent a divergence in responses can be attributed to the racially disparate mode of examination, it is relevant to our inquiry.

Most African-Americans (53%, or 8 out of 15) were first given a detailed description of the mechanics of an execution in Texas:

> If those three [sentencing] questions are answered yes, at some point[,] Thomas Joe Miller-El will be taken to Huntsville, Texas. He will be placed on death row and at some time will be taken to the death house where he will be strapped on a gurney, an IV put into his arm and he will be injected with a substance that will cause his death...as the result of the verdict in this case if those three questions are answered yes. **

Only then were these African-American venire members asked whether they could render a decision leading to a sentence of death. Very few prospective white jurors (6%, or 3 out of 49) were given this preface prior to being asked for their views on capital punishment. Rather, all but three were questioned in vague terms: "Would you share with us...your personal feelings, if you could, in your own words how you do feel about the death penalty and capital punishment and secondly, do you feel you could serve on this type of a jury and actually render a decision that would result in the death of the Defendant in this case based on the evidence?" **

There was an even more pronounced difference, on the apparent basis of race, in the manner the prosecutors questioned members of the venire about their willingness to impose the minimum sentence for murder. Under Texas law at the time of petitioner's trial, an unwillingness to do so warranted removal for cause. *Huffman v. State*, 450 S.W.2d 858, 861 (Tex. Crim. App. 1970), *vacated in part*, 408 U.S. 936 (1972). This strategy normally is used by the defense to weed out pro-state members of the venire, but, ironically, the prosecution employed it here. The prosecutors first identified the statutory minimum sentence of five years' imprisonment to 34 out of 36 (94%) white venire members, and only then asked: "If you hear a case, to your way of thinking [that] calls for and warrants and justifies five years, you'll give it?" ** In contrast, only 1 out of 8 (12.5%) African-American prospective jurors were informed of the statutory minimum before being asked what minimum sentence they would impose. The typical questioning of the other seven black jurors was as follows:

> [Prosecutor]: Now, the maximum sentence for [murder]...is life under the law. Can you give me an idea of just your personal feelings what you feel a minimum sentence should be for the offense of murder the way I've set it out for you?
>
> [Juror]: Well, to me that's almost like it's premeditated. But you said they don't have a premeditated statute here in Texas.
>
> .....
>
> [Prosecutor]: Again, we're not talking about self-defense or accident or insanity or killing in the heat of passion or anything like that. We're talking about the knowing—
>
> [Juror]: I know you said the minimum. The minimum amount that I would say would be at least twenty years. **

Furthermore, petitioner points to the prosecution's use of a Texas criminal procedure practice known as jury shuffling. This practice permits parties to rearrange the order in which members of the venire are examined so as to increase the likelihood that visually preferable venire members will be moved forward and empaneled. With no information about the prospective jurors other than their appearance, the party requesting the procedure literally shuffles the juror cards, and the venire members are then reseated in the new order. Tex. Code Crim. Proc. Ann., Art. 35.11 (Vernon Supp. 2003). Shuffling affects jury composition because any prospective jurors not questioned during *voir dire* are dismissed at the end of the week, and a new panel of jurors appears the following week. So jurors who are shuffled to the back of the panel are less likely to be questioned or to serve.

On at least two occasions the prosecution requested shuffles when there were a predominate number of African-Americans in the front of the panel. On yet another occasion the prosecutors complained about the purported inadequacy of the card shuffle by a defense lawyer but lodged a formal objection only after the postshuffle panel composition revealed that African-American prospective jurors had been moved forward.

Next, we turn to the pattern and practice evidence adduced at petitioner's pretrial *Swain* hearing. Petitioner subpoenaed a number of current and former Dallas County assistant district attorneys, judges, and others who had observed firsthand the prosecution's conduct during jury selection over a number of years. Although most of the witnesses denied the existence of a systematic policy to exclude African-Americans, others disagreed. A Dallas County district judge testified that, when he had served in the District Attorney's Office from the late-1950's to early-1960's, his superior warned him that he would be fired if he permitted any African-Americans to serve on a jury. Similarly, another Dallas County district judge and former assistant district attorney from 1976 to 1978 testified that he believed the office had a systematic policy of excluding African-Americans from juries.

Of more importance, the defense presented evidence that the District Attorney's Office had adopted a formal policy to exclude minorities from jury service. A 1963 circular by the District Attorney's Office instructed its prosecutors to exercise peremptory strikes against minorities: " 'Do not take Jews, Negroes, Dagos, Mexicans or a member of any minority race on a jury, no matter how rich or how well educated.' " ** A manual entitled "Jury Selection in a Criminal Case" was distributed to prosecutors. It contained an article authored by a former prosecutor (and later a judge) under the direction of his superiors in the District Attorney's Office, outlining the reasoning for excluding minorities from jury service. Although the manual was written in 1968, it remained in circulation until 1976, if not later, and was available at least to one of the prosecutors in Miller-El's trial. **

Some testimony casts doubt on the State's claim that these practices had been discontinued before petitioner's trial. For example, a judge testified that, in 1985, he had to exclude a prosecutor from trying cases in his courtroom for race-based discrimination in jury selection. Other testimony indicated that the State, by its own admission, once requested a jury shuffle in order to reduce the number of African-Americans in the venire. ** Concerns over the exclusion of African-Americans by the District Attorney's Office were echoed by Dallas County's Chief Public Defender.

This evidence had been presented by petitioner, in support of his *Batson* claim, to the state and federal courts that denied him relief. It is against this background that we examine whether petitioner's case should be heard by the Court of Appeals.

II

A

As mandated by federal statute, a state prisoner seeking a writ of habeas corpus has no absolute entitlement to appeal a district court's denial of his petition. 28 U.S.C. § 2253. Before an appeal may be entertained, a prisoner who was denied habeas relief in the district court must first seek and obtain a COA from a circuit justice or judge. This is a jurisdictional prerequisite because the COA statute mandates that "unless a circuit justice or judge issues a certificate of appealability, an appeal may not be taken to the court of appeals...." § 2253(c)(1). As a result, until a COA has been issued federal courts of appeals lack jurisdiction to rule on the merits of appeals from habeas petitioners.

A COA will issue only if the requirements of § 2253 have been satisfied. "The COA statute establishes procedural rules and requires a threshold inquiry into whether the circuit court may entertain an appeal." *Slack*, 529 U.S. at 482; *Hohn v. United States*, 524 U.S. 236, 248 (1998). As the Court of Appeals observed in this case, § 2253(c) permits the issuance of a COA only where a petitioner has made a "substantial showing of the denial of a constitutional right." In *Slack, supra*, at 483, we recognized that Congress codified our standard, announced in *Barefoot v. Estelle*, 463 U.S. 880 (1983), for determining what constitutes the requisite showing. Under the controlling standard, a petitioner must "show that reasonable jurists could debate whether (or, for that matter,

agree that) the petition should have been resolved in a different manner or that the issues presented were 'adequate to deserve encouragement to proceed further.'" 529 U.S.
at 484 (*quoting Barefoot, supra*, at 893 n.4).

The COA determination under § 2253(c) requires an overview of the claims in the
habeas petition and a general assessment of their merits. We look to the District Court's
application of AEDPA to petitioner's constitutional claims and ask whether that resolution was debatable amongst jurists of reason. This threshold inquiry does not require
full consideration of the factual or legal bases adduced in support of the claims. In fact,
the statute forbids it. When a court of appeals side steps this process by first deciding
the merits of an appeal, and then justifying its denial of a COA based on its adjudication of the actual merits, it is in essence deciding an appeal without jurisdiction.

To that end, our opinion in *Slack* held that a COA does not require a showing that
the appeal will succeed. Accordingly, a court of appeals should not decline the application for a COA merely because it believes the applicant will not demonstrate an entitlement to relief. The holding in *Slack* would mean very little if appellate review were denied because the prisoner did not convince a judge, or, for that matter, three judges,
that he or she would prevail. It is consistent with § 2253 that a COA will issue in some
instances where there is no certainty of ultimate relief. After all, when a COA is sought,
the whole premise is that the prisoner "'has already failed in that endeavor.'" *Barefoot,
supra*, at 893 n.4.

Our holding should not be misconstrued as directing that a COA always must issue.
Statutes such as AEDPA have placed more, rather than fewer, restrictions on the power of
federal courts to grant writs of habeas corpus to state prisoners. *Duncan v. Walker*, 533
U.S. 167, 178 (2001) ("'AEDPA's purpose [is] to further the principles of comity, finality,
and federalism'") (*quoting Williams v. Taylor*, 529 U.S. 420, 436 (2000)). ** The concept
of a threshold, or gateway, test was not the innovation of AEDPA. Congress established a
threshold prerequisite to appealability in 1908, in large part because it was "concerned
with the increasing number of frivolous habeas corpus petitions challenging capital sentences which delayed execution pending completion of the appellate process...." Barefoot,
supra, at 892 n.3. By enacting AEDPA, using the specific standards the Court had elaborated earlier for the threshold test, Congress confirmed the necessity and the requirement
of differential treatment for those appeals deserving of attention from those that plainly
do not. It follows that issuance of a COA must not be *pro forma* or a matter of course.

A prisoner seeking a COA must prove "'something more than the absence of frivolity'"
or the existence of mere "good faith" on his or her part. *Barefoot, supra*, at 893. We do not
require petitioner to prove, before the issuance of a COA, that some jurists would grant the
petition for habeas corpus. Indeed, a claim can be debatable even though every jurist of
reason might agree, after the COA has been granted and the case has received full consideration, that petitioner will not prevail. As we stated in *Slack*, "where a district court has rejected the constitutional claims on the merits, the showing required to satisfy § 2253(c) is
straightforward: The petitioner must demonstrate that reasonable jurists would find the
district court's assessment of the constitutional claims debatable or wrong." 529 U.S. at 484.

B

Since Miller-El's claim rests on a *Batson* violation, resolution of his COA application
requires a preliminary, though not definitive, consideration of the three-step framework
mandated by *Batson* and reaffirmed in our later precedents. *E.g., Purkett v. Elem*, 514
U.S. 765 (1995) (per curiam); *Hernandez v. New York*, 500 U.S. 352 (1991) (plurality

opinion). Contrary to the state trial court's ruling on remand, the State now concedes that petitioner, Miller-El, satisfied step one: "There is no dispute that Miller-El presented a prima facie claim" that prosecutors used their peremptory challenges to exclude venire members on the basis of race. ** Petitioner, for his part, acknowledges that the State proceeded through step two by proffering facially race-neutral explanations for these strikes. Under *Batson*, then, the question remaining is step three: whether Miller-El "has carried his burden of proving purposeful discrimination." *Hernandez, supra*, at 359.

As we confirmed in *Purkett v. Elem*, 514 U.S. at 768, the critical question in determining whether a prisoner has proved purposeful discrimination at step three is the persuasiveness of the prosecutor's justification for his peremptory strike. At this stage, "implausible or fantastic justifications may (and probably will) be found to be pretexts for purposeful discrimination." *Ibid.* In that instance the issue comes down to whether the trial court finds the prosecutor's race-neutral explanations to be credible. Credibility can be measured by, among other factors, the prosecutor's demeanor; by how reasonable, or how improbable, the explanations are; and by whether the proffered rationale has some basis in accepted trial strategy.

In *Hernandez v. New York*, a plurality of the Court concluded that a state court's finding of the absence of discriminatory intent is "a pure issue of fact" accorded significant deference:

> Deference to trial court findings on the issue of discriminatory intent makes particular sense in this context because, as we noted in *Batson*, the finding "largely will turn on evaluation of credibility." 476 U.S. at 98 n.21. In the typical peremptory challenge inquiry, the decisive question will be whether counsel's race-neutral explanation for a peremptory challenge should be believed. There will seldom be much evidence bearing on that issue, and the best evidence often will be the demeanor of the attorney who exercises the challenge. As with the state of mind of a juror, evaluation of the prosecutor's state of mind based on demeanor and credibility lies "peculiarly within a trial judge's province." *Wainwright v. Witt*, 469 U.S. 412, 428 (1985). **

Deference is necessary because a reviewing court, which analyzes only the transcripts from voir dire, is not as well positioned as the trial court is to make credibility determinations. "If an appellate court accepts a trial court's finding that a prosecutor's race-neutral explanation for his peremptory challenges should be believed, we fail to see how the appellate court nevertheless could find discrimination. The credibility of the prosecutor's explanation goes to the heart of the equal protection analysis, and once that has been settled, there seems nothing left to review." **

In the context of direct review, therefore, we have noted that "the trial court's decision on the ultimate question of discriminatory intent represents a finding of fact of the sort accorded great deference on appeal" and will not be overturned unless clearly erroneous. *Id.* at 364. A federal court's collateral review of a state-court decision must be consistent with the respect due state courts in our federal system. Where 28 U.S.C. § 2254 applies, our habeas jurisprudence embodies this deference. Factual determinations by state courts are presumed correct absent clear and convincing evidence to the contrary, § 2254(e)(1), and a decision adjudicated on the merits in a state court and based on a factual determination will not be overturned on factual grounds unless objectively unreasonable in light of the evidence presented in the state-court proceeding, § 2254(d)(2). **

Even in the context of federal habeas, deference does not imply abandonment or abdication of judicial review. Deference does not by definition preclude relief. A federal court can disagree with a state court's credibility determination and, when guided by AEDPA, conclude the decision was unreasonable or that the factual premise was incorrect by clear and convincing evidence. In the context of the threshold examination in this *Batson* claim the issuance of a COA can be supported by any evidence demonstrating that, despite the neutral explanation of the prosecution, the peremptory strikes in the final analysis were race based. It goes without saying that this includes the facts and circumstances that were adduced in support of the prima facie case. ** Only after a COA is granted will a reviewing court determine whether the trial court's determination of the prosecutor's neutrality with respect to race was objectively unreasonable and has been rebutted by clear and convincing evidence to the contrary. At this stage, however, we only ask whether the District Court's application of AEDPA deference, as stated in §§ 2254(d)(2) and (e)(1), to petitioner's *Batson* claim was debatable amongst jurists of reason.

C

Applying these rules to Miller-El's application, we have no difficulty concluding that a COA should have issued. We conclude, on our review of the record at this stage, that the District Court did not give full consideration to the substantial evidence petitioner put forth in support of the prima facie case. Instead, it accepted without question the state court's evaluation of the demeanor of the prosecutors and jurors in petitioner's trial. The Court of Appeals evaluated Miller-El's application for a COA in the same way. In ruling that petitioner's claim lacked sufficient merit to justify appellate proceedings, the Court of Appeals recited the requirements for granting a writ under § 2254, which it interpreted as requiring petitioner to prove that the state court decision was objectively unreasonable by clear and convincing evidence.

This was too demanding a standard on more than one level. It was incorrect for the Court of Appeals, when looking at the merits, to merge the independent requirements of §§ 2254(d)(2) and (e)(1). AEDPA does not require petitioner to prove that a decision is objectively unreasonable by clear and convincing evidence. The clear and convincing evidence standard is found in § 2254(e)(1), but that subsection pertains only to state-court determinations of factual issues, rather than decisions. Subsection (d)(2) contains the unreasonable requirement and applies to the granting of habeas relief rather than to the granting of a COA.

The Court of Appeals, moreover, was incorrect for an even more fundamental reason. Before the issuance of a COA, the Court of Appeals had no jurisdiction to resolve the merits of petitioner's constitutional claims. True, to the extent that the merits of this case will turn on the agreement or disagreement with a state-court factual finding, the clear and convincing evidence and objective unreasonableness standards will apply. At the COA stage, however, a court need not make a definitive inquiry into this matter. As we have said, a COA determination is a separate proceeding, one distinct from the underlying merits. ** The Court of Appeals should have inquired whether a "substantial showing of the denial of a constitutional right" had been proved. Deciding the substance of an appeal in what should only be a threshold inquiry undermines the concept of a COA. The question is the debatability of the underlying constitutional claim, not the resolution of that debate.

In this case, the statistical evidence alone raises some debate as to whether the prosecution acted with a race-based reason when striking prospective jurors. The prosecutors used their peremptory strikes to exclude 91% of the eligible African-American venire members, and only one served on petitioner's jury. In total, 10 of the prosecutors' 14 peremptory strikes were used against African-Americans. Happenstance is unlikely to produce this disparity.

The case for debatability is not weakened when we examine the State's defense of the disparate treatment. The Court of Appeals held that "the presumption of correctness is especially strong, where, as here, the trial court and state habeas court are one and the same." ** As we have noted, the trial court held its *Batson* hearing two years after the *voir dire*. While the prosecutors had proffered contemporaneous race-neutral justifications for many of their peremptory strikes, the state trial court had no occasion to judge the credibility of these explanations at that time because our equal protection jurisprudence then, dictated by *Swain*, did not require it. As a result, the evidence presented to the trial court at the *Batson* hearing was subject to the usual risks of imprecision and distortion from the passage of time.

In this case, three of the State's proffered race-neutral rationales for striking African-American jurors pertained just as well to some white jurors who were not challenged and who did serve on the jury. The prosecutors explained that their peremptory challenges against six African-American potential jurors were based on ambivalence about the death penalty; hesitancy to vote to execute defendants capable of being rehabilitated; and the jurors' own family history of criminality. In rebuttal of the prosecution's explanation, petitioner identified two empaneled white jurors who expressed ambivalence about the death penalty in a manner similar to their African-American counterparts who were the subject of prosecutorial peremptory challenges. One indicated that capital punishment was not appropriate for a first offense, and another stated that it would be "difficult" to impose a death sentence. Similarly, two white jurors expressed hesitation in sentencing to death a defendant who might be rehabilitated; and four white jurors had family members with criminal histories. As a consequence, even though the prosecution's reasons for striking African-American members of the venire appear race neutral, the application of these rationales to the venire might have been selective and based on racial considerations. Whether a comparative juror analysis would demonstrate the prosecutors' rationales to have been pretexts for discrimination is an unnecessary determination at this stage, but the evidence does make debatable the District Court's conclusion that no purposeful discrimination occurred.

We question the Court of Appeals' and state trial court's dismissive and strained interpretation of petitioner's evidence of disparate questioning. ** Petitioner argues that the prosecutors' sole purpose in using disparate questioning was to elicit responses from the African-American venire members that reflected an opposition to the death penalty or an unwillingness to impose a minimum sentence, either of which justified for-cause challenges by the prosecution under the then applicable state law. This is more than a remote possibility. Disparate questioning did occur. Petitioner submits that disparate questioning created the appearance of divergent opinions even though the venire members' views on the relevant subject might have been the same. It follows that, if the use of disparate questioning is determined by race at the outset, it is likely a justification for a strike based on the resulting divergent views would be pretextual. In this context the differences in the questions posed by the prosecutors are some evidence of purposeful discrimination. **

As a preface to questions about views the prospective jurors held on the death penalty, the prosecution in some instances gave an explicit account of the execution process. Of those prospective jurors who were asked their views on capital punishment, the preface was used for 53% of the African-Americans questioned on the issue but for just 6% of white persons. The State explains the disparity by asserting that a disproportionate number of African-American venire members expressed doubts as to the death penalty on their juror questionnaires. This cannot be accepted without further inquiry, however, for the State's own evidence is inconsistent with that explanation. By the State's calculations, 10 African-American and 10 white prospective jurors expressed some hesitation about the death penalty on their questionnaires; however, of that group, 7 out of 10 African-Americans and only 2 out of 10 whites were given the explicit description.

There is an even greater disparity along racial lines when we consider disparate questioning concerning minimum punishments. Ninety-four percent of whites were informed of the statutory minimum sentence, compared to only twelve and a half percent of African-Americans. No explanation is proffered for the statistical disparity. ** Indeed, while petitioner's appeal was pending before the Texas Court of Criminal Appeals, that court found a *Batson* violation where this precise line of disparate questioning on mandatory minimums was employed by one of the same prosecutors who tried the instant case. ** It follows, in our view, that a fair interpretation of the record on this threshold examination in the COA analysis is that the prosecutors designed their questions to elicit responses that would justify the removal of African-Americans from the venire. *Batson, supra*, at 93 ("Circumstantial evidence of invidious intent may include proof of disproportionate impact.... We have observed that under some circumstances proof of discriminatory impact 'may for all practical purposes demonstrate unconstitutionality because in various circumstances the discrimination is very difficult to explain on nonracial grounds' ").

We agree with petitioner that the prosecution's decision to seek a jury shuffle when a predominate number of African-Americans were seated in the front of the panel, along with its decision to delay a formal objection to the defense's shuffle until after the new racial composition was revealed, raise a suspicion that the State sought to exclude African-Americans from the jury. Our concerns are amplified by the fact that the state court also had before it, and apparently ignored, testimony demonstrating that the Dallas County District Attorney's Office had, by its own admission, used this process to manipulate the racial composition of the jury in the past. ** Even though the practice of jury shuffling might not be denominated as a *Batson* claim because it does not involve a peremptory challenge, the use of the practice here tends to erode the credibility of the prosecution's assertion that race was not a motivating factor in the jury selection.

Finally, in our threshold examination, we accord some weight to petitioner's historical evidence of racial discrimination by the District Attorney's Office. Evidence presented at the *Swain* hearing indicates that African-Americans almost categorically were excluded from jury service. *Batson*, 476 U.S. at 94 ("Proof of systematic exclusion from the venire raises an inference of purposeful discrimination because the 'result bespeaks discrimination.'"). ** Only the Federal Magistrate Judge addressed the import of this evidence in the context of a *Batson* claim; and he found it both unexplained and disturbing. Irrespective of whether the evidence could prove sufficient to support a charge of systematic exclusion of African-Americans, it reveals that the culture of the District Attorney's Office in the past was suffused with bias against African-Americans in jury selection. This evidence, of course, is relevant to the extent it casts doubt on the legitimacy of the motives underlying the State's actions in petitioner's case. Even if we presume at this stage that the prosecutors in Miller-El's case were not part of this culture of discrimination, the evidence suggests they were likely not ignorant of it. Both prosecutors joined the District Attorney's Office when assistant district attorneys received formal training in excluding minorities from juries. The supposition that race was a factor could be reinforced by the fact that the prosecutors marked the race of each prospective juror on their juror cards.

In resolving the equal protection claim against petitioner, the state courts made no mention of either the jury shuffle or the historical record of purposeful discrimination. We adhere to the proposition that a state court need not make detailed findings addressing all the evidence before it. This failure, however, does not diminish its significance. Our concerns here are heightened by the fact that, when presented with this evidence, the state trial court somehow reasoned that there was not even the inference of discrimination to support a prima facie case. This was clear error, and the State declines to defend this particular ruling. "If these general assertions were accepted as rebutting a defendant's prima facie case, the Equal Protection Clause 'would be but a vain and illusory requirement.'" *Batson, supra*, at 98. **

To secure habeas relief, petitioner must demonstrate that a state court's finding of the absence of purposeful discrimination was incorrect by clear and convincing evidence, 28 U.S.C. §2254(e)(1), and that the corresponding factual determination was "objectively unreasonable" in light of the record before the court. The State represents to us that petitioner will not be able to satisfy his burden. That may or may not be the case. It is not, however, the question before us. The COA inquiry asks only if the District Court's decision was debatable. Our threshold examination convinces us that it was.

The judgment of the Fifth Circuit is reversed, and the case is remanded for further proceedings consistent with this opinion.

It is so ordered.

JUSTICE SCALIA, concurring.

I join the Court's opinion, but write separately for two reasons: First, to explain why I believe the Court's willingness to consider the Antiterrorism and Effective Death Penalty Act of 1996's (AEDPA) limits on habeas relief in deciding whether to issue a certificate of appealability (COA) is in accord with the text of 28 U.S.C. §2253(c). Second, to discuss some of the evidence on the State's side of the case—which, though inadequate (as the Court holds) to make the absence of a claimed violation of *Batson v. Kentucky*, 476 U.S. 79 (1986), undebatable, still makes this, in my view, a very close case.

I

***

Section 2253(c)(2)...provides that "[a] certificate of appealability *may issue...only if* the applicant has made a substantial showing of the denial of a constitutional right." (Emphasis added). A "substantial showing" *does not entitle* an applicant to a COA; it is a necessary and not a sufficient condition. Nothing in the text of §2253(c)(2) prohibits a circuit justice or judge from imposing additional requirements, and one such additional requirement has been approved by this Court. *See Slack v. McDaniel*, 529 U.S. 473, 484 (2000) (holding that a habeas petitioner seeking to appeal a district court's denial of habeas relief on procedural grounds must not only make a substantial showing of the denial of a constitutional right but *also* must demonstrate that jurists of reason would find it debatable whether the district court was correct in its procedural ruling).

The Court today imposes another additional requirement: a circuit justice or judge must deny a COA, even when the habeas petitioner has made a substantial showing that his constitutional rights were violated, if all reasonable jurists would conclude that a substantive provision of the federal habeas statute bars relief. ** To give an example, suppose a state prisoner presents a constitutional claim that reasonable jurists might find debatable, but is unable to find any "clearly established"

Supreme Court precedent in support of that claim (which was previously rejected on the merits in state-court proceedings). Under the Court's view, a COA must be denied, *even if* the habeas petitioner satisfies the "substantial showing of the denial of a constitutional right" requirement of § 2253(c)(2), because all reasonable jurists would agree that habeas relief is impossible to obtain under § 2254(d). This approach is consonant with *Slack*, in accord with the COA's purpose of preventing meritless habeas appeals, and compatible with the text of § 2253(c), which does not make the "substantial showing of the denial of a constitutional right" a sufficient condition for a COA.

II

In applying the Court's COA standard to petitioner's case, we must ask whether petitioner has made a substantial showing of a *Batson* violation and also whether reasonable jurists could debate petitioner's ability to obtain habeas relief in light of AEDPA. The facts surrounding petitioner's *Batson* claims, when viewed in light of § 2254(e)(1)'s requirement that state-court factual determinations can be overcome only by clear and convincing evidence to the contrary, reveal this to be a close, rather than a clear, case for the granting of a COA.

Petitioner maintains that the following six African-American jurors were victims of racially motivated peremptory strikes: Edwin Rand, Wayman Kennedy, Roderick Bozeman, Billy Jean Fields, Joe Warren, and Carrol Boggess. As to each of them, the State proffered race-neutral explanations for its peremptory challenge. Five were challenged primarily because of their views on imposing the death penalty (Rand, Kennedy, Bozeman, Warren, and Boggess), and one (Fields) was challenged because (among other reasons) his brother had been convicted of drug offenses and served time in prison. By asserting race-neutral reasons for the challenges, the State satisfied step two of *Batson*. *See Purkett v. Elem*, 514 U.S. 765, 767–768 (1995) (per curiam). Unless petitioner can make a substantial showing that (*i.e.*, a showing that reasonable jurists could debate whether) the State fraudulently recited these explanations as pretext for race discrimination, he has not satisfied the requirement of § 2253(c)(2). Moreover, because the state court entered a finding of fact that the prosecution's purported reasons for exercising its peremptory challenges were not pretextual, ** a COA should not issue unless that finding can reasonably be thought to be contradicted by clear and convincing evidence. *See* § 2254(e)(1) ("[A] determination of a factual issue made by a State court shall be presumed to be correct. The applicant shall have the burden of rebutting the presumption of correctness by clear and convincing evidence"). **

The weakness in petitioner's *Batson* claims stems from his difficulty in identifying any unchallenged white venireman similarly situated to the six aforementioned African-American veniremen. Although petitioner claims that two white veniremen, Sandra Hearn and Marie Mazza, expressed views about the death penalty as ambivalent as those expressed by Rand, Kennedy, Bozeman, Warren, and Boggess, the *voir dire* transcripts do not clearly bear that out. Although Hearn initially stated that she thought the death penalty was inappropriate for first-time offenders, she also said, "I do not see any reason why I couldn't sit on a jury when you're imposing a death penalty." ** She further stated that someone who was an extreme child abuser deserved the death penalty, whether or not it was a first-time offense. ** Hearn also made pro-prosecution statements about her distaste for criminal defendants' use of psychiatric testimony to establish incompetency. ** As for Mazza, her stated views on the death penalty were as follows: "It's kind of hard determining somebody's life, whether they live or die, but I feel that is something that is accepted in our courts now and it is something that—a decision that I think I could make one way or the other." **

Compare those statements with the sentiments expressed by the challenged African-American veniremen. Kennedy supported the death penalty only in cases of mass murder. "Normally I wouldn't say on just the average murder case—I would say no, not the death sentence." ** Bozeman supported the death penalty only "if there's no possible way to rehabilitate a person…I would say somebody mentally disturbed or something like that or say a Manson type or something like that." ** When asked by the prosecutors whether repeated criminal violent conduct would indicate that a person was beyond rehabilitation, Bozeman replied, "No, not really." ** Warren refused to give any clear answer regarding his views on the death penalty despite numerous questions from the prosecutors. ** ("Well, there again, it goes back to the situation, you know, sometimes"). ** When asked whether the death penalty accomplishes anything, Warren answered, "Yes and no. Sometimes I think it does and sometimes I think it don't [sic]. Sometimes you have mixed feelings about things like that." *Ibid.* When asked, "What do you think it accomplishes when you feel it does?," Warren replied, "I don't know." *Ibid.* Boggess referred to the death penalty as "murder" ** and said, "whether or not I could actually go through with murder—with killing another person or taking another person's life, I just don't know. I'd have trouble with that." ** Rand is a closer case. His most ambivalent statement was "Can I do this? You know, right now I say I can, but tomorrow I might not." ** Later on Rand did say that he could impose the death penalty as a juror. ** But Hearn and Mazza (the white jurors who were seated) also said that they could sit on a jury that imposed the death penalty. At most, petitioner has shown that one of these African-American veniremen (Rand) may have been no more ambivalent about the death penalty than white jurors Hearn and Mazza. That perhaps would have been enough to permit the state trial court, deciding the issue *de novo* after observing the demeanor of the prosecutors and the disputed jurors, to find a *Batson* violation. But in a federal habeas case, where a state court has previously entered factfindings that the six African-American jurors were not challenged because of their race, petitioner must provide "clear and convincing evidence" that the state court erred, and, when requesting a COA, must demonstrate that jurists of reason could debate whether this standard was satisfied.

Fields, the sixth African-American venireman who petitioner claims was challenged because of his race, supported capital punishment. However, his brother had several drug convictions and had served time in prison. ** Warren and Boggess, two of the African-American veniremen previously discussed, also had relatives with criminal convictions—Warren's brother had been convicted of fraud in relation to food stamps, ** and Boggess had testified as a defense witness at her nephew's trial for theft ** and reported in her questionnaire that some of her cousins had problems with the law. ** Of the four white veniremen who petitioner claims also had relatives with criminal histories and therefore "should have been struck" by the prosecution— three (Noad Vickery, Cheryl Davis, and Chatta Nix) were actually so pro-prosecution that *they were struck by the petitioner.* ** The fourth, Joan Weiner, had a son who had shoplifted at the age of 10. ** That is hardly comparable to Fields's situation, and Weiner was a strong state's juror for other reasons: She had relatives who worked in law enforcement, ** and her support for the death penalty was clear and unequivocal. **

For the above reasons, my conclusion that there is room for debate as to the merits of petitioner's *Batson* claim is far removed from a judgment that the State's explanations for its peremptory strikes were implausible.

With these observations, I join the Court's opinion.

JUSTICE THOMAS, dissenting.

Unpersuaded by petitioner's claims, the state trial court found that "there was no purposeful discrimination by the prosecution in the use of…peremptory strikes." ** This finding established that petitioner had failed to carry his burden at step three of the inquiry set out in *Batson v. Kentucky*, 476 U.S. 79 (1986). Title 28 U.S.C. §2254(e)(1) requires that a federal habeas court "presume" the state court's findings of fact "to be correct" unless petitioner can rebut the presumption "by clear and convincing evidence." The majority decides, without explanation, to ignore §2254(e)(1)'s explicit command. I cannot. Because petitioner has not shown, by clear and convincing evidence, that any peremptory strikes of black veniremen were exercised because of race, he does not merit a certificate of appealability (COA). I respectfully dissent.

***

II
B

As noted, petitioner argues the prosecution struck six blacks—Rand, Kennedy, Bozeman, Fields, Warren, and Boggess—who were similarly situated to unstruck whites. I see no need to repeat JUSTICE SCALIA's dissection of petitioner's tales of white veniremen as ambivalent about the death penalty as Kennedy, Bozeman, Warren, and Boggess. ** However, the majority's cursory remark that "three of the State's proffered race-neutral rationales for striking [black] jurors pertained *just as well to some white jurors who were not challenged and who did serve on the jury*," (emphasis added), is flatly incorrect and deserves some discussion.

***

C

***

2

***

Quite simply, petitioner's arguments rest on circumstantial evidence and speculation that does not hold up to a thorough review of the record. Far from rebutting §2254(e)(1)'s presumption, petitioner has perhaps not even demonstrated that reasonable jurists could debate whether he has provided the requisite evidence of purposeful discrimination—but that is the majority's inquiry, not mine. Because petitioner has not demonstrated by clear and convincing evidence that even one of the peremptory strikes at issue was the result of racial discrimination, I would affirm the denial of a COA.

Notes

1. *Subsequent case history*

Thomas Miller-El has been on death row in Texas since June 26, 1986. *See* Website of Texas Department of Corrections, http://www.tdcj.state.tx.us. On remand, the Fifth Circuit again found that prosecutors had not intentionally excluded African-Americans from Miller-El's capital jury. *Miller-El v. Cockrell*, 537 U.S. 322 (2003). On June 28,

2004, the Supreme Court granted certiorari a second time. *See Miller-El v. Dretke,* __
U.S. __, 124 S. Ct. 2908 (2004).

2. *Statistics and race*

In *Miller-El,* the Court finds that "the statistical evidence alone raises some debate as
to whether the prosecution acted with a race-based reason when striking prospective jurors" and that "[h]appenstance is unlikely to produce this disparity." Why did the statistics in *Miller-El* affect the Court's ultimate decision, whereas the statistics in *McCleskey*
did not?

3. Hernandez *and* Purkett

In reaching its decision in *Miller-El,* the Court references its prior decisions in *Hernandez v. New York,* 500 U.S. 352 (1991), and *Purkett v. Elem,* 514 U.S. 765 (1995) (*per
curiam*).

Hernandez involved a state trial in New York where the prosecutor used four peremptory challenges to exclude Latino jurors. 500 U.S. 352. Although Hernandez eventually
dropped his *Batson* claim for two of the four Latino jurors (because they had been convicted of crimes), he maintained his claim for the other two jurors. The prosecutor explained that he struck the jurors because they looked away from him and hesitated when
he asked them whether they would be willing to accept the translator's rendition of witness
testimony. The trial court and the state courts reviewing his direct appeal found that the
prosecutor had offered a race-neutral basis for his peremptory challenges. The Court affirmed, noting the importance of deference to the trial judge's evaluation of the prosecutor's state of mind based on demeanor and credibility. At the same time, however, the
Court emphasized that "a policy of striking all who speak a given language, without regard
to the particular circumstances of the trial or the individual responses of the jurors, may
be found by the trial judge to be a pretext for racial discrimination." 500 U.S. at 371–372.

In *Purkett v. Elem,* 514 U.S. 765 (1995) (per curiam), Jimmy Elem filed a habeas petition in which he asserted that the prosecutor in his state trial in Missouri had improperly
used a peremptory challenge to strike a potential black male juror. The race-neutral reason
the prosecutor gave for excusing that juror was his "shoulder-length, curly, unkempt
hair...mustache and goatee type beard." 514 U.S. at 766. Although the trial judge, the state
appellate courts, and the federal district court in which Elem filed his federal habeas petition all found that the proffered race-neutral reason was constitutionally acceptable, the
Eighth Circuit Court of Appeals found that the prosecutor's reason for striking the juror
was pretextual and that the state trial court had " 'clearly erred' in finding that striking [the
juror] had not been intentional discrimination." 514 U.S. at 767. The Court reversed, stating that a "legitimate reason" is "not a reason that makes sense, but a reason that does not
deny equal protection." 514 U.S. at 769. The Court went on to note the following:

> In habeas proceedings in federal courts, the factual findings of state courts are
> presumed to be correct, and may be set aside, absent procedural error, only if
> they are "not fairly supported by the record." 28 U.S.C. §2254(d)(8). ** Here the
> Court of Appeals did not conclude or even attempt to conclude that the state
> court's finding of no racial motive was not fairly supported by the record. For its
> whole focus was upon the *reasonableness* of the asserted nonracial motive (which
> it thought required by step two [of Batson]) rather than the *genuineness* of the
> motive. It gave no proper basis for overturning the state court's finding of no
> racial motive, a finding which turned primarily on an assessment of credibility. **

514 U.S. at 769.

Given the backgrounds of both *Hernandez* and *Purkett*, in which the Court deferred to the trial courts' factual findings regarding prosecutor credibility, what was it about Miller-El's case that enabled the Court to "have no difficulty concluding that a COA should have issued"? Similarly, what led the Court to criticize the federal district court for "not giv[ing] full consideration to the substantial evidence petitioner put forth in support of the prima facie case" and "[i]nstead,...[accepting] without question the state court's evaluation of the demeanor of the prosecutors and jurors in petitioner's trial"?

4. *A close case?*

Although concurring in judgment, Justice Scalia states that "some of the evidence on the State's side of the case—which, though inadequate (as the Court holds) to make the absence of a claimed violation of *Batson v. Kentucky*, 476 U.S. 79 (1986), undebatable, still makes this, in my view, a very close case." Based on the additional facts provided by Justice Scalia, what is your assessment of whether this was a "close case"?

Chapter 16

Innocence

This chapter explores the degree to which a habeas petitioner's claim of innocence factors into the petitioner's ability to receive relief through a federal habeas petition.

In *Sawyer v. Whitley*, the Court is faced with a petitioner who has brought a successive federal habeas petition but who claims he is "actually innocent" of the crime for which he was convicted and sentenced to death. The Court holds that to show "actual innocence" one must show by clear and convincing evidence that, but for a constitutional error, no reasonable juror would have found the petitioner eligible for the death penalty. *Herrera v. Collins* also involves a petitioner who bases his federal habeas petition on newly discovered evidence of actual innocence. The Court holds that claims of actual innocence based on newly discovered evidence are not in and of themselves grounds for federal habeas relief: in addition to an innocence claim (whether based on newly discovered evidence or not), a successful petition must also include an independent constitutional violation from the underlying criminal proceeding. In *Schlup v. Delo*, the petitioner joins his innocence claim with a constitutional claim, alleging that his counsel was ineffective and that the prosecution withheld exculpatory evidence. Although Schlup cannot meet the "cause and prejudice" standard for his successive habeas petition, because Schlup uses his innocence claim as a gateway to litigate his constitutional claim, the Court distinguishes *Schlup* from *Herrera* and rejects *Sawyer*'s "clear and convincing" standard, replacing it with a "more likely than not" standard. The chapter ends with an article by the Honorable Henry J. Friendly, entitled *Is Innocence Irrelevant? Collateral Attack on Criminal Judgments*. Although Judge Friendly's article was published more than twenty years before the three cases in this chapter, his observations continue to inform the Court's contemporary reasoning regarding innocence claims and collateral appeals.

Sawyer v. Whitley
505 U.S. 333 (1992)

CHIEF JUSTICE REHNQUIST delivered the opinion of the Court.

The issue before the Court is the standard for determining whether a petitioner bringing a successive, abusive, or defaulted federal habeas claim has shown he is "actually innocent" of the death penalty to which he has been sentenced so that the court may reach the merits of the claim. Robert Wayne Sawyer, the petitioner in this case, filed a second federal habeas petition containing successive and abusive claims. The Court of Appeals for the Fifth Circuit refused to examine the merits of Sawyer's claims. It held that Sawyer had not shown cause for failure to raise these claims in his earlier petition, and that he had not shown that he was "actually innocent" of the crime of which he was convicted or the penalty which was imposed. ** We affirm the Court of Appeals and hold that to show "actual innocence" one must show by clear and convincing evidence that, but for a constitutional error, no reasonable juror would have found the petitioner eligible for the death penalty under the applicable state law.

In 1979—13 years ago—petitioner and his accomplice, Charles Lane, brutally murdered Frances Arwood, who was a guest in the home petitioner shared with his girlfriend, Cynthia Shano, and Shano's two young children. *** [P]etitioner and Lane returned to petitioner's home after a night of drinking and argued with Arwood, accusing her of drugging one of the children. Petitioner and Lane then attacked Arwood, beat her with their fists, kicked her repeatedly, submerged her in the bathtub, and poured scalding water on her before dragging her back into the living room, pouring lighter fluid on her body and igniting it. Arwood lost consciousness sometime during the attack and remained in a coma until she died of her injuries approximately two months later. Shano and her children were in the home during the attack, and Shano testified that petitioner prevented them from leaving. ***

At trial, the jury failed to credit petitioner's "toxic psychosis" defense, and convicted petitioner of first-degree murder. At the sentencing phase, petitioner testified that he was intoxicated at the time of the murder and remembered only bits and pieces of the events. Petitioner's sister, Glenda White, testified about petitioner's deprived childhood, about his affection and care for her children, and that as a teenager petitioner had been confined to a mental hospital for "no reason," where he had undergone shock therapy. ** The jury found three statutory aggravating factors and no statutory mitigating factors and sentenced petitioner to death. ***

Sawyer's conviction and sentence were affirmed on appeal by the Louisiana Supreme Court. *State v. Sawyer*, 422 So. 2d 95 (1982). We granted certiorari, and vacated and remanded with instructions to reconsider in light of *Zant v. Stephens*, 462 U.S. 862 (1983). ** On remand, the Louisiana Supreme Court reaffirmed the sentence. ** Petitioner's first petition for state postconviction relief was denied. *** In 1986, Sawyer filed his first federal habeas petition, raising 18 claims, all of which were denied on the merits. ** We again granted certiorari and affirmed the Court of Appeals' denial of relief. *** Petitioner next filed a second motion for state postconviction relief. The state trial court summarily denied this petition as repetitive and without merit, and the Louisiana Supreme Court denied discretionary review. **

The present petition before this Court arises out of Sawyer's second petition for federal habeas relief. After granting a stay and holding an evidentiary hearing, the District Court denied one of Sawyer's claims on the merits and held that the others were barred as either abusive or successive. ** The Court of Appeals granted a certificate of probable cause on the issue whether petitioner had shown that he is actually "innocent of the death penalty" such that a court should reach the merits of the claims contained in this successive petition. ** The Court of Appeals held that petitioner had failed to show that he was actually innocent of the death penalty because the evidence he argued had been unconstitutionally kept from the jury failed to show that Sawyer was ineligible for the death penalty under Louisiana law. For the third time we granted Sawyer's petition for certiorari, ** and we now affirm.

Unless a habeas petitioner shows cause and prejudice, *see Wainwright v. Sykes*, 433 U.S. 72 (1977), a court may not reach the merits of: (a) successive claims that raise grounds identical to grounds heard and decided on the merits in a previous petition, *Kuhlmann v. Wilson*, 477 U.S. 436 (1986); (b) new claims, not previously raised, which constitute an *abuse of the writ*, *McCleskey v. Zant*, 499 U.S. 467 (1991); or (c) procedurally defaulted claims in which the petitioner failed to follow applicable state procedural rules in raising the claims, *Murray v. Carrier*, 477 U.S. 478 (1986). These cases are premised on our concerns for the finality of state judgments of conviction and the "significant costs of federal habeas review." *McCleskey, supra*, at 490–491. **

We have previously held that even if a state prisoner cannot meet the cause and prejudice standard, a federal court may hear the merits of the successive claims if the failure to hear the claims would constitute a "miscarriage of justice." In a trio of 1986 decisions, we elaborated on the miscarriage of justice, or "actual innocence," exception. As we explained in *Kuhlmann v. Wilson, supra*, the exception developed from the language of the federal habeas statute, which, prior to 1966, allowed successive claims to be denied without a hearing if the judge were "satisfied that the *ends of justice will not be served by such inquiry*." ** 477 U.S. at 448. We held that despite the removal of this statutory language from 28 U.S.C. §2244(b) in 1966, the miscarriage of justice exception would allow successive claims to be heard if the petitioner "establish[es] that under the probative evidence he has a colorable claim of factual innocence." *Kuhlmann, supra*, at 454. *** In the second of these cases we held that the actual innocence exception also applies to procedurally defaulted claims. *Murray v. Carrier*, [477 U.S. at 496]. ***

In *Smith v. Murray*, 477 U.S. 527 (1986), we found no miscarriage of justice in the failure to examine the merits of procedurally defaulted claims in the capital sentencing context. We emphasized that the miscarriage of justice exception is concerned with actual as compared to legal innocence, and acknowledged that actual innocence "does not translate easily into the context of an alleged error at the sentencing phase of a trial on a capital offense." *Id.* at 537. We decided that the habeas petitioner in that case had failed to show actual innocence of the death penalty because the "alleged constitutional error neither precluded the development of true facts nor resulted in the admission of false ones." *Id.* at 538.

In subsequent cases, we have emphasized the narrow scope of the fundamental miscarriage of justice exception. In *Dugger v. Adams*, 489 U.S. 401 (1989), we rejected the petitioner's claim that his procedural default should be excused because he had shown that he was actually innocent. Without endeavoring to define what it meant to be actually innocent of the death penalty, we stated that "[d]emonstrating that an error is by its nature the kind of error that might have affected the accuracy of a death sentence is far from demonstrating that an individual defendant probably is 'actually innocent' of the sentence he or she received." *Id.* at 412 n.6. Just last Term in *McCleskey v. Zant*, 499 U.S. at 502, we held that the "narrow exception" for miscarriage of justice was of no avail to the petitioner because the constitutional violation, if it occurred, "resulted in the admission at trial of truthful inculpatory evidence which did not affect the reliability of the guilt determination."

The present case requires us to further amplify the meaning of "actual innocence" in the setting of capital punishment. A prototypical example of "actual innocence" in a colloquial sense is the case where the State has convicted the wrong person of the crime. Such claims are of course regularly made on motions for new trial after conviction in both state and federal courts, and quite regularly denied because the evidence adduced in support of them fails to meet the rigorous standards for granting such motions. But in rare instances it may turn out later, for example, that another person has credibly confessed to the crime, and it is evident that the law has made a mistake. In the context of a noncapital case, the concept of "actual innocence" is easy to grasp.

It is more difficult to develop an analogous framework when dealing with a defendant who has been sentenced to death. The phrase "innocent of death" is not a natural usage of those words, but we must strive to construct an analog to the simpler situation represented by the case of a noncapital defendant. In defining this analog, we bear in mind that the exception for "actual innocence" is a very narrow exception, and that to make it workable it must be subject to determination by relatively objective standards. In the every day context of capital penalty proceedings, a federal district judge typically will be presented with a successive or abusive habeas petition a few days before, or even on the day of, a scheduled execution, and will have only a limited time to determine whether a petitioner has shown that his case falls within the "actual innocence" exception if such a claim is made. ***

Since our decision in *Furman v. Georgia*, 408 U.S. 238 (1972), our Eighth Amendment jurisprudence has required those States imposing capital punishment to adopt procedural safeguards protecting against arbitrary and capricious impositions of the death sentence. *See, e.g., Gregg v. Georgia*, 428 U.S. 153 (1976). In response, the States have adopted various narrowing factors that limit the class of offenders upon which the sentencer is authorized to impose the death penalty. For example, the Louisiana statute under which petitioner was convicted defines first-degree murder, a capital offense, as something more than intentional killing. *** In addition, after a defendant is found guilty in Louisiana of capital murder, the jury must also find at the sentencing phase beyond a reasonable doubt at least one of a list of statutory aggravating factors before it may recommend that the death penalty be imposed. ***

But once eligibility for the death penalty has been established to the satisfaction of the jury, its deliberations assume a different tenor. In a series of cases beginning with *Lockett v. Ohio*, 438 U.S. 586, 604 (1978), we have held that the defendant must be permitted to introduce a wide variety of mitigating evidence pertaining to his character and background. The emphasis shifts from narrowing the class of eligible defendants by objective factors to individualized consideration of a particular defendant. Consideration of aggravating factors together with mitigating factors, in various combinations and methods dependent upon state law, results in the jury's or judge's ultimate decision as to what penalty shall be imposed.

Considering Louisiana law as an example, then, there are three possible ways in which "actual innocence" might be defined. The strictest definition would be to limit any showing to the elements of the crime which the State has made a capital offense. The showing would have to negate an essential element of that offense. *** We reject this submission as too narrow, because it is contrary to the statement in *Smith* that the concept of "actual innocence" could be applied to mean "innocent" of the death penalty. 477 U.S. at 537. This statement suggested a more expansive meaning to the term of "actual innocence" in a capital case than simply innocence of the capital offense itself.

The most lenient of the three possibilities would be to allow the showing of "actual innocence" to extend not only to the elements of the crime, but also to the existence of aggravating factors, and to mitigating evidence that bore not on the defendant's eligibility to receive the death penalty, but only on the ultimate discretionary decision between the death penalty and life imprisonment. *** The crucial consideration, according to petitioner, is whether due to constitutional error the sentencer was presented with " 'a *factually inaccurate sentencing profile*' " of the petitioner. **

Insofar as petitioner's standard would include not merely the elements of the crime itself, but the existence of aggravating circumstances, it broadens the extent of the inquiry but not the type of inquiry. Both the elements of the crime and statutory aggravating circumstances in Louisiana are used to narrow the class of defendants eligible for the death penalty. And proof or disproof of aggravating circumstances, like proof of the elements of the crime, is confined by the statutory definitions to a relatively obvious class of relevant evidence. Sensible meaning is given to the term "innocent of the death penalty" by allowing a showing in addition to innocence of the capital crime itself a showing that there was no aggravating circumstance or that some other condition of eligibility had not been met. ***

But we reject petitioner's submission that the showing should extend beyond these elements of the capital sentence to the existence of additional mitigating evidence. In the first place, such an extension would mean that "actual innocence" amounts to little more than what is already required to show "prejudice," a necessary showing for habeas relief for many constitutional errors. ** If federal habeas review of capital sentences is to be at all rational, petitioner must show something more in order for a court to reach the merits of his claims on a successive habeas petition than he would have had to show to obtain relief on his first habeas petition. ***

But, more importantly, petitioner's standard would so broaden the inquiry as to make it anything but a "narrow" exception to the principle of finality that we have previously described it to be. A federal district judge confronted with a claim of actual innocence may with relative ease determine whether a submission, for example, that a killing was not intentional, consists of credible, noncumulative, and admissible evidence negating the element of intent. But it is a far more difficult task to assess how jurors would have reacted to additional showings of mitigating factors, particularly considering the breadth of those factors that a jury under our decisions must be allowed to consider. ***

The Court of Appeals in this case took the middle ground among these three possibilities for defining "actual innocence" of the death penalty, and adopted this test:

> [W]e must require the petitioner to show, based on the evidence proffered plus all record evidence, a fair probability that a rational trier of fact would have entertained a reasonable doubt as to the existence of those facts which are prerequisites under state or federal law for the imposition of the death penalty. **

The Court of Appeals standard therefore hones in on the objective factors or conditions that must be shown to exist before a defendant is eligible to have the death penalty imposed. *** We agree *** that the "actual innocence" requirement must focus on those elements that render a defendant eligible for the death penalty, and not on additional mitigating evidence that was prevented from being introduced as a result of a claimed constitutional error.

In the present petition, Sawyer advances two claims, arising from two distinct groups of evidentiary facts that were not considered by the jury that convicted and sentenced Sawyer. The first group of evidence relates to petitioner's role in the offense and consists of affidavits attacking the credibility of Cynthia Shano and an affidavit claiming that one of Shano's sons told a police officer that Sawyer was not responsible for pouring lighter fluid on Arwood and lighting it, and that in fact Sawyer tried to prevent Charles Lane from lighting Arwood on fire. Sawyer claims that the police failed to produce this exculpatory evidence in violation of his due process rights under *Brady v. Maryland*, 373 U.S. 83 (1963). The second group consists of medical records from Sawyer's stays as a teenager in two different mental health institutions. Sawyer alleges ineffective assistance of counsel in trial counsel's failure to introduce these records in the sentencing phase of his trial.

The Court of Appeals held that petitioner's failure to assert his *Brady* claim in his first petition constituted an abuse of the writ, and that he had not shown cause for failing to raise the claim earlier under *McCleskey*. ** The ineffective-assistance claim was held by the Court of Appeals to be a successive claim because it was rejected on the merits in Sawyer's first petition, and petitioner failed to show cause for not bringing all the evidence in support of this claim earlier. ** Petitioner does not contest these findings of the Court of Appeals. ** Therefore, we must determine if petitioner has shown by clear and convincing evidence that but for constitutional error, no reasonable juror would find him eligible for the death penalty under Louisiana law.

Under Louisiana law, petitioner is eligible for the death penalty because he was convicted of first-degree murder—that is, an intentional killing while in the process of committing an aggravated arson—and because at the sentencing phase the jury found two valid aggravating circumstances: that the murder was committed in the course of an aggravated arson, and that the murder was especially cruel, atrocious, and heinous. The psychological evidence petitioner alleges was kept from the jury due to the ineffective assistance of counsel does not relate to petitioner's guilt or innocence of the crime. *** Neither does it relate to either of the aggravating factors found by the jury that made petitioner eligible for the death penalty. Even if this evidence had been before the jury, it cannot be said that a reasonable juror would not have found both of the aggravating factors that make petitioner eligible for the death penalty. *** Therefore, as to this evidence, petitioner has not shown that there would be a fundamental miscarriage of justice for the Court to fail to reexamine the merits of this successive claim.

We are convinced that the evidence allegedly kept from the jury due to an alleged *Brady* violation also fails to show that the petitioner is actually innocent of the death penalty to which he has been sentenced. Much of the evidence goes to the credibility of Shano, suggesting, *e.g.*, that contrary to her testimony at trial she knew Charles Lane prior to the day of the murder; that she was drinking the day before the murder; and that she testified under a grant of immunity from the prosecutor. ** This sort of latter-day evidence brought forward to impeach a prosecution witness will seldom, if ever, make a clear and convincing showing that no reasonable juror would have believed the heart of Shano's account of petitioner's actions.

The final bit of evidence petitioner alleges was unconstitutionally kept from the jury due to a *Brady* violation was a statement made by Shano's then 4-year-old son, Wayne, to a police officer the day after the murder. Petitioner has submitted an affidavit from one Diane Thibodeaux stating that she was present when Wayne told a police detective who asked who had lit Arwood on fire that "Daddy [Sawyer] tried to help the lady" and that the "other man" had pushed Sawyer back into a chair. ** The affidavit also states that Wayne showed the officer where to find a cigarette lighter and a can of lighter fluid in the trash. ** Because this evidence goes to the jury's finding of aggravated arson, it goes both to petitioner's guilt or innocence of the crime of first-degree murder and the aggravating circumstance of a murder committed in the course of an aggravated arson. However, we conclude that this affidavit, in view of all the other evidence in the record, does not show that no rational juror would find that petitioner committed both of the aggravating circumstances found by the jury. The murder was especially cruel, atrocious, and heinous based on the undisputed evidence of torture before the jury quite apart from the arson (*e.g.*, beating, scalding with boiling water). As for the finding of aggravated arson, we agree with the Court of Appeals that, even crediting the information in the hearsay affidavit, *** it cannot be said that no reasonable juror would have found, in light of all the evidence, that petitioner was guilty of the aggravated arson for his participation under the Louisiana law of principals. ***

We therefore hold that petitioner has failed to show by clear and convincing evidence that but for constitutional error at his sentencing hearing, no reasonable juror would have found him eligible for the death penalty under Louisiana law. The judgment of the Court of Appeals is therefore

Affirmed.

JUSTICE BLACKMUN, concurring in the judgment.

I cannot agree with the majority that a federal court is absolutely barred from reviewing a capital defendant's abusive, successive, or procedurally defaulted claim unless the defendant can show "by clear and convincing evidence that but for a constitutional error, no reasonable juror would have found the petitioner eligible for the death penalty under the applicable state law." ** For the reasons stated by JUSTICE STEVENS in his separate opinion, ** which I join, I believe that the Court today adopts an unduly cramped view of "actual innocence." I write separately not to discuss the specifics of the Court's standard, but instead to reemphasize my opposition to an implicit premise underlying the Court's decision: that the only "fundamental miscarriage of justice" in a capital proceeding that warrants redress is one where the petitioner can make out a claim of "actual innocence." I also write separately to express my ever-growing skepticism that, with each new decision from this Court constricting the ability of the federal courts to remedy constitutional errors, the death penalty really can be imposed fairly and in accordance with the requirements of the Eighth Amendment.

I

The Court repeatedly has recognized that principles of fundamental fairness underlie the writ of habeas corpus. *See Engle v. Isaac*, 456 U.S. 107, 126 (1982); *Sanders v. United States*, 373 U.S. 1, 17–18 (1963). Even as the Court has erected unprecedented and unwarranted barriers to the federal judiciary's review of the merits of claims that state prisoners failed properly to present to the state courts, or failed to raise in their first federal habeas petitions, or previously presented to the federal courts for resolution, it consistently has acknowledged that exceptions to these rules of unreviewability must exist to prevent violations of fundamental fairness. *See Engle*, 456 U.S. at 135 (principles of finality and comity "must yield to the imperative of correcting a fundamentally unjust incarceration"). Thus, the Court has held, federal courts may review procedurally defaulted, abusive, or successive claims absent a showing of cause and prejudice if the failure to do so would thwart the "ends of justice," *see Kuhlmann v. Wilson*, 477 U.S. 436, 455 (1986) (plurality opinion), or work a "fundamental miscarriage of justice," *see Murray v. Carrier*, 477 U.S. 478, 495–496 (1986). **

By the traditional understanding of habeas corpus, a "fundamental miscarriage of justice" occurs whenever a conviction or sentence is secured in violation of a federal constitutional right. *See* 28 U.S.C. § 2254(a) (federal courts "shall entertain" habeas petitions from state prisoners who allege that they are "in custody in violation of the Constitution or laws or treaties of the United States"). ** Justice Holmes explained that the concern of a federal court in reviewing the validity of a conviction and death sentence on a writ of habeas corpus is "solely the question whether [the petitioner's] constitutional rights have been preserved." *Moore v. Dempsey*, 261 U.S. 86, 88 (1923).

In a trio of 1986 decisions, however, the Court ignored these traditional teachings and, out of a purported concern for state sovereignty, for the preservation of state resources, and for the finality of state-court judgments, shifted the focus of federal habeas review of procedurally defaulted, successive, or abusive claims away from the preservation of constitutional rights to a fact-based inquiry into the petitioner's innocence or guilt. ***

The Court itself has acknowledged that "the concept of 'actual,' as distinct from 'legal,' innocence does not translate easily into the context of an alleged error at the sentencing phase of a trial on a capital offense." ** Undaunted by its own illogic, however, the Court adopted just such an approach in *Smith*. *** Because Michael Smith could not demonstrate cause for his procedural default, and because, in the Court's view, he had not made a substantial showing that the alleged constitutional violation "undermined the accuracy of the guilt or sentencing determination," ** his Fifth Amendment claim went unaddressed and he was executed on July 31, 1986.

In *Dugger v. Adams*, the Court continued to equate the notion of a "fundamental miscarriage of justice" in a capital trial with the petitioner's ability to show that he or she "probably is 'actually innocent' of the sentence he or she received" ** but appeared to narrow the inquiry even further. Adams' claim, that the trial judge repeatedly had misinformed the jurors, in violation of the Eighth Amendment and *Caldwell v. Mississippi*, 472 U.S. 320 (1985), that their sentencing vote was strictly advisory in nature (when in fact Florida law permitted the judge to overturn the jury's sentencing decision only upon a clear and convincing showing that its choice was erroneous), surely satisfied the standard articulated in *Smith*: whether petitioner can make out a "substantial claim that the alleged error undermined the accuracy of the guilt or sentencing determination." 477 U.S. at 539. In a cryptic discussion relegated to a footnote at the end of its opinion, the Court in *Adams* rejected this obvious application of the *Smith* standard, apparently for no other reason than its belief that Adams' ability to demonstrate a "fundamental miscarriage of justice" in this case somehow would convert an "extraordinary" exception into an "ordinary" one. ** In rejecting the *Smith* standard, the Court did not even bother to substitute another in its place. *See* 489 U.S. at 412 n.6. ** ("We do not undertake here to define what it means to be 'actually innocent' of a death sentence"). The Court refused to address Aubrey Adams' claim of constitutional error, and he was executed on May 4, 1989.

Just last Term, in *McCleskey v. Zant*, the Court again described the "fundamental miscarriage of justice" exception as a "'safeguard against compelling an innocent man to suffer an unconstitutional loss of liberty,'" 499 U.S. at 495 (*quoting Stone v. Powell*, 428 U.S. 465, 491–492 n.31 (1976)). Although the District Court granted relief to McCleskey on his claim that state authorities deliberately had elicited inculpatory admissions from him in violation of his Sixth Amendment right to counsel, *see Massiah v. United States*, 377 U.S. 201 (1964), and excused his failure to present the claim in his first federal habeas petition because the State had withheld documents and information establishing that claim, ** the Court concluded that McCleskey lacked cause for failing to raise the claim earlier. ** More important for our purposes, the Court concluded that the "narrow exception" by which federal courts may "exercise [their] equitable discretion to correct a miscarriage of justice" was of "no avail" to McCleskey: The "*Massiah* violation, if it be one, resulted in the admission at trial of truthful inculpatory evidence which did not affect the reliability of the guilt determination." ** The Court refused to address Warren McCleskey's claim of constitutional error, and he was executed on September 24, 1991.

The Court today takes for granted that the foregoing decisions correctly limited the concept of a "fundamental miscarriage of justice" to "actual innocence," even as it struggles, by ignoring the "natural usage of those words" and resorting to "analog[s]," ** to make sense of "actual innocence" in the capital context. I continue to believe, however, that the Court's "exaltation of accuracy as the only characteristic of 'fundamental fairness' is deeply flawed." *Smith*, 477 U.S. at 545 (STEVENS, J., dissenting).

As an initial matter, the Court's focus on factual innocence is inconsistent with Congress' grant of habeas corpus jurisdiction, pursuant to which federal courts are instructed to entertain petitions from state prisoners who allege that they are held "in custody in violation of the Constitution or laws or treaties of the United States." 28 U.S.C. §2254(a). The jurisdictional grant contains no support for the Court's decision to narrow the reviewing authority and obligation of the federal courts to claims of factual innocence. *See also* 28 U.S.C. §2243 ("The court shall...dispose of the matter as law and justice require"). In addition, the actual innocence standard requires a reviewing federal court, unnaturally, to "function in much the same capacity as the state trier of fact"; that is, to "make a rough decision on the question of guilt or innocence." *Wilson*, 477 U.S. at 471 n.7 (BRENNAN, J., dissenting).

Most important, however, the focus on innocence assumes, erroneously, that the only value worth protecting through federal habeas review is the accuracy and reliability of the guilt determination. But "[o]ur criminal justice system, and our Constitution, protect other values in addition to the reliability of the guilt or innocence determination, and the statutory duty to serve 'law and justice' should similarly reflect those values." *Smith*, 477 U.S. at 545 (STEVENS, J., dissenting). The accusatorial system of justice adopted by the Founders affords a defendant certain process-based protections that do not have accuracy of truth finding as their primary goal. These protections—including the Fifth Amendment right against compelled self-incrimination, the Eighth Amendment right against the imposition of an arbitrary and capricious sentence, the Fourteenth Amendment right to be tried by an impartial judge, and the Fourteenth Amendment right not to be indicted by a grand jury or tried by a petit jury from which members of the defendant's race have been systematically excluded—are debased, and indeed, rendered largely irrelevant, in a system that values the accuracy of the guilt determination above individual rights.

Nowhere is this single-minded focus on actual innocence more misguided than in a case where a defendant alleges a constitutional error in the sentencing phase of a capital trial. The Court's ongoing struggle to give meaning to "innocence of death" simply reflects the inappropriateness of the inquiry. ** "Guilt or innocence is irrelevant in that context; rather, there is only a decision made by representatives of the community whether the prisoner shall live or die." *Wilson*, 477 U.S. at 471–472 n.7 (BRENNAN, J., dissenting). **

Only by returning to the federal courts' central and traditional function on habeas review, evaluating claims of constitutional error, can the Court ensure that the ends of justice are served and that fundamental miscarriages of justice do not go unremedied. The Court would do well to heed Justice Black's admonition: "[I]t is never too late for courts in habeas corpus proceedings to look straight through procedural screens in order to prevent forfeiture of life or liberty in flagrant defiance of the Constitution." *Brown v. Allen*, 344 U.S. 443, 554 (1953) (dissenting opinion). ***

II

A

When I was on the United States Court of Appeals for the Eighth Circuit, I once observed, in the course of reviewing a death sentence on a writ of habeas corpus, that the decisional process in a capital case is "particularly excruciating" for someone "who is not personally convinced of the rightness of capital punishment and who questions it as an effective deterrent." *Maxwell v. Bishop*, 398 F.2d 138, 153–154 (1968), *vacated*, 398 U.S. 262 (1970). At the same time, however, I stated my then belief that "the advisability of capital punishment is a policy matter ordinarily to be resolved by the legislature." *Id.* at 154. Four years later, as a Member of this Court, I echoed those sentiments in my separate dissenting opinion in *Furman v. Georgia*, 408 U.S. 238, 405 (1972). Although I reiterated my personal distaste for the death penalty and my doubt that it performs any meaningful deterrent function, *see id.* at 405–406, I declined to join my Brethren in declaring the state statutes at issue in those cases unconstitutional. *See id.* at 411 ("We should not allow our personal preferences as to the wisdom of legislative and congressional action, or our distaste for such action, to guide our judicial decision").

My ability in *Maxwell*, *Furman*, and the many other capital cases I have reviewed during my tenure on the federal bench to enforce, notwithstanding my own deep moral reservations, a legislature's considered judgment that capital punishment is an appropriate sanction, has always rested on an understanding that certain procedural safeguards, chief among them the Federal Judiciary's power to reach and correct claims of constitutional error on federal habeas review, would ensure that death sentences are fairly imposed. Today, more than 20 years later, I wonder what is left of that premise underlying my acceptance of the death penalty.

B

Only last Term I had occasion to lament the Court's continuing "crusade to erect petty procedural barriers in the path of any state prisoner seeking review of his federal constitutional claims" and its transformation of "the duty to protect federal rights into a self-fashioned abdication." *Coleman v. Thompson*, 501 U.S. 722, 759, 761 (1991) (dissenting opinion). This Term has witnessed the continued narrowing of the avenues of relief available to federal habeas petitioners seeking redress of their constitutional claims. *See, e.g.*, *Keeney v. Tamayo-Reyes*, 504 U.S. 1 (1992) (*overruling in part Townsend v. Sain*, 372 U.S. 293 (1963)). It has witnessed, as well, the execution of two victims of the "new habeas," Warren McCleskey and Roger Keith Coleman.

Warren McCleskey's case seemed the archetypal "fundamental miscarriage of justice" that the federal courts are charged with remedying. As noted above, McCleskey demonstrated that state officials deliberately had elicited inculpatory admissions from him in violation of his Sixth Amendment rights and had withheld information he needed to present his claim for relief. In addition, McCleskey argued convincingly in his final hours that he could not even obtain an impartial clemency hearing because of threats by state officials against the pardons and parole board. That the Court permitted McCleskey to be executed without ever hearing the merits of his claims starkly reveals the Court's skewed value system, in which finality of judgments, conservation of state resources, and expediency of executions seem to receive greater solicitude than justice and human life. **

The execution of Roger Keith Coleman is no less an affront to principles of fundamental fairness. Last Term, the Court refused to review the merits of Coleman's claims by effectively overruling, at Coleman's expense, precedents holding that state-court decisions are presumed to be based on the merits (and therefore, are subject to federal habeas review) unless they explicitly reveal that they were based on state procedural grounds. *See Coleman*, 501 U.S. at 762–764 (dissenting opinion). Moreover, the Court's refusal last month to grant a temporary stay of execution so that the lower courts could conduct a hearing into Coleman's well-supported claim that he was innocent of the underlying offense demonstrates the resounding hollowness of the Court's professed commitment to employ the "fundamental miscarriage of justice exception" as a "safeguard against compelling an innocent man to suffer an unconstitutional loss of liberty." *McCleskey v. Zant*, 499 U.S. at 495. **

As I review the state of this Court's capital jurisprudence, I thus am left to wonder how the ever-shrinking authority of the federal courts to reach and redress constitutional errors affects the legitimacy of the death penalty itself. Since *Gregg v. Georgia*, the Court has upheld the constitutionality of the death penalty where sufficient procedural safeguards exist to ensure that the State's administration of the penalty is neither arbitrary nor capricious. [*See Gregg v. Georgia* and *Lockett v. Ohio*]. At the time those decisions issued, federal courts possessed much broader authority than they do today to address claims of constitutional error on habeas review and, therefore, to examine the adequacy of a State's capital scheme and the fairness and reliability of its decision to impose the death penalty in a particular case. The more the Court constrains the federal courts' power to reach the constitutional claims of those sentenced to death, the more the Court undermines the very legitimacy of capital punishment itself.

JUSTICE STEVENS, with whom JUSTICE BLACKMUN and JUSTICE O'CONNOR join, concurring in the judgment.

Only 10 years ago, the Court reemphasized that "[t]he writ of habeas corpus indisputably holds an honored position in our jurisprudence. Tracing its roots deep into English common law, it claims a place in Art. I of our Constitution. Today, as in prior centuries, the writ is a bulwark against convictions that violate 'fundamental fairness.' **" *Engle v. Isaac*, 456 U.S. 107, 126 (1982). It is this centrality of "fundamental fairness" that has led the Court to hold that habeas review of a defaulted, successive, or abusive claim is available, even absent a showing of cause, if failure to consider the claim would result in a fundamental miscarriage of justice. *See Sanders v. United States*, 373 U.S. 1, 17–18 (1963); *Engle*, 456 U.S. at 135.

In *Murray v. Carrier*, 477 U.S. 478, 495, 496 (1986), the Court ruled that the concept of "fundamental miscarriage of justice" applies to those cases in which the defendant was "probably…actually innocent." The Court held that "in an extraordinary case, where a constitutional violation has probably resulted in the conviction of one who is actually innocent, a federal habeas court may grant the writ even in the absence of a showing of cause for the procedural default." *Id.* at 496. Having equated the "ends of justice" with "actual innocence," the Court is now confronted with the task of giving meaning to "actual innocence" in the context of a capital sentencing proceeding— hence the phrase "innocence of death."

While the conviction of an innocent person may be the archetypal case of a manifest miscarriage of justice, it is not the only case. There is no reason why "actual innocence" must be both an animating *and the limiting* principle of the work of federal courts in furthering the "ends of justice." As Judge Friendly emphasized, there are contexts in which, irrespective of guilt or innocence, constitutional errors violate fundamental fairness. Friendly, *Is Innocence Irrelevant? Collateral Attack on Criminal Judgments*, 38 U.

Chi. L. Rev. 142, 151–154 (1970). Fundamental fairness is more than accuracy at trial; justice is more than guilt or innocence.

Nowhere is this more true than in capital sentencing proceedings. Because the death penalty is qualitatively and morally different from any other penalty, "[i]t is of vital importance to the defendant and to the community that any decision to impose the death sentence be, and appear to be, the consequence of scrupulously fair procedures." *Smith v. Murray*, 477 U.S. 527, 545–546 (1986) (STEVENS, J., dissenting). Accordingly, the ends of justice dictate that "[w]hen a condemned prisoner raises a substantial, colorable Eighth Amendment violation, there is a special obligation...to consider whether the prisoner's claim would render his sentencing proceeding fundamentally unfair." *Id.* at 546.

Thus the Court's first and most basic error today is that it asks the wrong question. Charged with averting manifest miscarriages of justice, the Court instead narrowly recasts its duty as redressing cases of "actual innocence." This error aside, under a proper interpretation of the *Carrier* analysis, the Court's definition of "innocence of death" is plainly wrong because it disregards well-settled law—both the law of habeas corpus and the law of capital punishment.

I

The Court today holds that, absent a showing of cause, a federal court may not review a capital defendant's defaulted, successive, or abusive claims unless the defendant "show[s] by clear and convincing evidence that, but for a constitutional error, no reasonable juror would have found [him] eligible for the death penalty." **

This definition of "innocence of the death sentence" deviates from our established jurisprudence in two ways. First, the "clear and convincing evidence" standard departs from a line of decisions defining the "actual innocence" exception to the cause-and-prejudice requirement. Second, and more fundamentally, the Court's focus on *eligibility* for the death penalty conflicts with the very structure of the constitutional law of capital punishment.

As noted above, in *Murray v. Carrier*, the Court held that in those cases in which "a constitutional violation has *probably* resulted in the conviction of one who is actually innocent, a federal habeas court may grant the writ even in the absence of a showing of cause for the procedural default." 477 U.S. at 496 (emphasis added). The Court has since frequently confirmed this standard. *See, e.g., Coleman v. Thompson*, 501 U.S. 722, 748 (1991); *Dugger v. Adams*, 489 U.S. 401, 412 n.6 (1989); *Teague v. Lane*, 489 U.S. 288, 313 (1989). In subsequent decisions, both those involving "innocence of the offense" and those involving "innocence of the death sentence," the Court has employed the same standard of proof. For example, in *Smith v. Murray*, 477 U.S. 527 (1986), the Court repeated the *Carrier* standard and applied it in a capital sentencing proceeding. The Court ruled that Smith's claim did not present "the risk of a manifest miscarriage of justice" as it was "devoid of any substantial claim that the alleged error undermined the accuracy of the guilt or sentencing determination." 477 U.S. at 538–539. Similarly, in *Dugger v. Adams*, a case involving "innocence of the death sentence," the Court stated the controlling standard as whether an "individual defendant *probably* is 'actually innocent' of the sentence he or she received." 489 U.S. at 412 n.6 (emphasis added). In sum, in construing both "innocence of the offense" and "innocence of the death sentence," we have consistently required a defendant to show that the alleged constitutional error has *more likely than not* created a fundamental miscarriage of justice.

As we noted in another context, "[t]his outcome-determinative standard has several strengths. It defines the relevant inquiry in a way familiar to courts, though the inquiry, as is inevitable, is anything but precise. The standard also reflects the profound importance of finality in criminal proceedings. Moreover, it comports with the widely used standard for assessing motions for new trial based on newly discovered evidence." *Strickland v. Washington*, 466 U.S. 668, 693–694 (1984).

Equally significant, this "probably resulted" standard is well calibrated to the manifest miscarriage of justice exception. Not only does the standard respect the competing demands of finality and fundamental fairness, it also fits squarely within our habeas jurisprudence. In general, a federal court may entertain a defaulted, successive, or abusive claim if a prisoner demonstrates cause and prejudice. *See generally McCleskey v. Zant*, 499 U.S. 467, 493–495 (1991). To show "prejudice," a defendant must demonstrate "a reasonable probability that, but for [the alleged] erro[r], the result of the proceeding would have been different." *Strickland*, 466 U.S. at 694. ** The "miscarriage of justice" exception to this general rule requires a more substantial showing: The defendant must not simply demonstrate a *reasonable probability of* a different result, he must show that the alleged error more *likely than not* created a manifest miscarriage of justice. This regime makes logical sense. If a defendant cannot show cause and can only show a "reasonable probability" of a different outcome, a federal court should not hear his defaulted, successive, or abusive claim. Only in the "exceptional case" in which a defendant can show that the alleged constitutional error "probably resulted" in the conviction (or sentencing) of one innocent of the offense (or the death sentence) should the court hear the defendant's claim.

The Court today repudiates this established standard of proof and replaces it with a requirement that a defendant "show by *clear and convincing evidence* that…no reasonable juror would have found [him] eligible for the death penalty." ** I see no reason to reject the established and well-functioning "probably resulted" standard and impose such a severe burden on the capital defendant. Although we have frequently recognized the State's strong interest in finality, we have never suggested that that interest is sufficient to outweigh the individual's claim to innocence. To the contrary, the "actual innocence" exception itself manifests our recognition that the criminal justice system occasionally errs and that, when it does, finality must yield to justice.

***

First, there is no basis for requiring a federal court to be virtually certain that the defendant is actually ineligible for the death penalty before *merely entertaining* his claim. We have required a showing by clear and convincing evidence in several contexts: For example, the medical facts underlying a civil commitment must be established by this standard, ** as must "actual malice" in a libel suit brought by a public official. ** And we have required a related showing in cases involving deportation ** and denaturalization. ** In each of these contexts, the interests of the nonmoving party were truly substantial: personal liberty, ** freedom of expression, ** residence, ** and citizenship. ** In my opinion, the State's interest in finality in a capital prosecution is not nearly as great as any of these interests. Indeed, it is important to remember that "innocence of the death sentence" is not a standard for staying or vacating a death sentence, but merely a standard for determining whether or not a court should reach the merits of a defaulted claim. The State's interest in "finality" in this context certainly does not warrant a "clear and convincing" evidentiary standard.

Nor is there any justification for allocating the risk of error to fall so severely upon the capital defendant or attaching greater importance to the initial sentence than to the issue of whether that sentence is appropriate. The States themselves have declined to attach such weight to capital sentences: Most States provide plain-error review for defaulted claims in capital cases. ** In this regard, the Court's requirement that "innocence of death" must be demonstrated by "clear and convincing evidence" fails to respect the uniqueness of death penalty decisions: Nowhere is the need for accuracy greater than when the State exercises its ultimate authority and takes the life of one of its citizens.

Indeed, the Court's ruling creates a perverse double standard. While a defendant raising defaulted claims in a noncapital case must show that constitutional error "probably resulted" in a miscarriage of justice, a capital defendant must present "clear and convincing evidence" that no reasonable juror would find him eligible for the death penalty. It is heartlessly perverse to impose a more stringent standard of proof to avoid a miscarriage of justice in a capital case than in a noncapital case.

In sum, I see no reason to depart from settled law, which clearly requires a defendant pressing a defaulted, successive, or abusive claim to show that a failure to hear his claim will "probably result" in a fundamental miscarriage of justice. In my opinion, a corresponding standard governs a defaulted, successive, or abusive challenge to a capital sentence: The defendant must show that he is probably—that is, more likely than not—"innocent of the death sentence."

II

The Court recognizes that the proper definition of "innocence of the death sentence" must involve a reweighing of the evidence and must focus on the sentencer's likely evaluation of that evidence. Thus, the Court directs federal courts to look to whether a "reasonable juror *would* have found the petitioner eligible for the death penalty." ** Nevertheless, the Court inexplicably limits this inquiry in two ways. First, the Court holds that courts should consider *only* evidence concerning aggravating factors. *** [T]his limitation is wholly without foundation and neglects the central role of mitigating evidence in capital sentencing proceedings. Second, the Court requires a petitioner to refute his *eligibility* for the death penalty. This narrow definition of "innocence of the death sentence" fails to recognize that, in rare cases, even though a defendant is eligible for the death penalty, such a sentence may nonetheless constitute a fundamental miscarriage of justice.

   ***

Against this backdrop of well-settled law, the Court's ruling is a startling anomaly. The Court holds that "innocence of the death sentence" concerns only "those elements that render a defendant *eligible* for the death penalty, and *not...additional mitigating evidence* that [constitutional error precluded] from being introduced." ** Stated bluntly, the Court today respects only one of the two bedrock principles of capital-punishment jurisprudence. As such, the Court's impoverished vision of capital sentencing is at odds with both the doctrine and the theory developed in our many decisions concerning capital punishment.

First, the Court implicitly repudiates the requirement that the sentencer be allowed to consider all relevant mitigating evidence, a constitutive element of our Eighth Amendment jurisprudence. We have reiterated and applied this principle in more than a dozen cases over the last 14 years. ***

Moreover, the Court's holding also clashes with the *theory* underlying our capital-punishment jurisprudence. The nonarbitrariness—and therefore the constitutionality—of the death penalty rests on *individualized* sentencing determinations. *** The Court's definition of "innocence of the death sentence" *** focuses solely on whether the defendant is in a class eligible for the death penalty and disregards the equally important question whether "'death is the appropriate punishment in [the defendant's] specific case.'" *Zant v. Stephens*, 462 U.S. at 885. ***

The Court's definition of "innocent of the death sentence" is flawed in a second, related way. The Court's analysis not only neglects errors that preclude a sentencer's consideration of mitigating factors; it also focuses too narrowly on *eligibility*. The Court requires a defendant to call into question *all* of the aggravating factors found by the sentencer and thereby show himself ineligible for the death penalty.

Contrary to the Court's suggestion, however, there may be cases in which, although the defendant remains eligible for the death penalty, imposition of a death sentence would constitute a manifest miscarriage of justice. If, for example, the sentencer, in assigning a sentence of death, relied heavily on a finding that the defendant severely tortured the victim, but later it is discovered that another person was responsible for the torture, the elimination of the aggravating circumstance will, in some cases, indicate that the death sentence was a miscarriage of justice. By imposing an "all-or-nothing" eligibility test, the Court's definition of "innocent of the death sentence" fails to acknowledge this important possibility.

In sum, the Court's "innocent of the death sentence" standard is flawed both in its failure to consider constitutional errors implicating mitigating factors and in its unduly harsh requirement that a defendant's eligibility for the death penalty be disproved.

III

In my opinion, the "innocence of the death sentence" standard must take into account several factors. First, such a standard must reflect *both* of the basic principles of our capital-punishment jurisprudence. The standard must recognize both the need to define narrowly the class of "death-eligible" defendants and the need to define broadly the scope of mitigating evidence permitted the capital sentencer. Second, the "innocence of the death sentence" standard should also recognize the distinctive character of the capital sentencing decision. While the question of innocence or guilt of the offense is essentially a question of fact, the choice between life imprisonment and capital punishment is both a question of underlying fact and a matter of reasoned moral judgment. Thus, there may be some situations in which, although the defendant remains technically "eligible" for the death sentence, nonetheless, in light of all of the evidence, that sentence constitutes a manifest miscarriage of justice. Finally, the "innocence of the death sentence" standard must also respect the "profound importance of finality in criminal proceedings," *Strickland v. Washington*, 466 U.S. at 693–694, and the "heavy burden" that successive habeas petitions place "on scarce federal judicial resources." *McCleskey v. Zant*, 499 U.S. at 491.

These requirements are best met by a standard that provides that a defendant is "innocent of the death sentence" only if his capital sentence is *clearly erroneous*. This standard encompasses several types of error. A death sentence is clearly erroneous if, taking into account all of the available evidence, the sentencer lacked the legal authority to impose such a sentence because, under state law, the defendant was not eligible for the death penalty. Similarly, in the case of a "jury override," a death sentence is clearly erroneous if, taking into account all of the evidence, the evidentiary prerequisites for that override (as established by state law) were not met. ** A death sentence is also clearly erroneous under a "balancing" regime if, in view of all of the evidence, mitigating circumstances so far outweighed aggravating circumstances that no reasonable sentencer would have imposed the death penalty. ** Such a case might arise if constitutional error either precluded the defendant from demonstrating that aggravating circumstances did not obtain or precluded the sentencer's consideration of important mitigating evidence.

Unlike the standard suggested by the Court, this standard acknowledges both the "aggravation" and "mitigation" aspects of capital-punishment law. It recognizes that, in the extraordinary case, constitutional error may have precluded consideration of mitigating circumstances so substantial as to warrant a court's review of a defaulted, successive, or abusive claim. It also recognizes that, again in the extraordinary case, constitutional error may have inaccurately demonstrated aggravating circumstances so substantial as to warrant review of a defendant's claims.

Moreover, the "clearly-erroneous" standard is duly protective of the State's legitimate interests in finality and respectful of the systemic and institutional costs of successive habeas litigation. The standard is stringent: If the sentence "is plausible in light of the record viewed in its entirety" it is not clearly erroneous "even though [the court is] convinced that had it been sitting as the [sentencer], it would have weighed the evidence differently." ** At the same time, "clearly-erroneous" review allows a federal court to entertain a defaulted claim in the rare case in which the "court on the entire evidence is left with the definite and firm conviction that a mistake has been committed." **

Finally, the "clearly-erroneous" standard is workable. As was true of the cause-and-prejudice standard adopted in *McCleskey v. Zant*, the clear-error standard is "[w]ell-defined in the case law [and] familiar to federal courts.... The standard is an objective one, and can be applied in a manner that comports with the threshold nature of the abuse of the writ inquiry." 499 U.S. at 496. Federal courts have long applied the "clearly-erroneous" standard pursuant to Rule 52 of the Federal Rules of Civil Procedure and have done so "in civil contempt actions, condemnation proceedings, copyright appeals, [and] forfeiture actions for illegal activity." *** This workability supports the application of the "clearly-erroneous" standard to the "innocence of the death sentence" inquiry.

In my opinion, then, the "clearly erroneous" standard is the core of the "innocence of the death sentence" exception. Just as a defendant who presses a defaulted, successive, or abusive claim and who cannot show cause must demonstrate that it is more likely than not that he is actually innocent of the offense, so a capital defendant who presses such a claim and cannot show cause must demonstrate that it is more likely than not that his death sentence was clearly erroneous. Absent such a showing, a federal court may not reach the merits of the defendant's defaulted, successive, or abusive claim.

IV

It remains to apply this standard to the case at hand. As the majority indicates, Sawyer alleges two constitutional errors. First, he contends that the State withheld certain exculpatory evidence, in violation of Sawyer's due process rights as recognized in *Brady v. Maryland*, 373 U.S. 83 (1963). Second, Sawyer argues that his trial counsel's failure to uncover and present records from Sawyer's earlier treatments in psychiatric institutions deprived him of effective assistance of counsel as guaranteed by the Sixth Amendment.

As Sawyer failed to assert his *Brady* claim in an earlier habeas petition and as he cannot show cause for that failure, the court may only reach the merits of that "abusive" claim if Sawyer demonstrates that he is probably actually innocent of the offense or that

it is more likely than not that his death sentence was clearly erroneous. As Sawyer's ineffective-assistance claim was considered and rejected in an earlier habeas proceeding, the
court may only review that "successive" claim upon a similar showing. Upon a review of
the record in its entirety, I conclude that Sawyer has failed to make such a showing.

***

Viewed as a whole, the record does not demonstrate that failure to reach the merits
of Sawyer's claims would constitute a fundamental miscarriage of justice. First, in view
of the other evidence in the record, the Thibodeaux affidavit and questions concerning
Shano's testimony do not establish that Sawyer is "probably...actually innocent" of the
crime of first-degree murder. At most, Thibodeaux's hearsay statements cast slight
doubt on the facts underlying the burning of the victim. Similarly, although the challenges to Shano's testimony raise questions, these affidavits do not demonstrate that
Sawyer probably did not commit first-degree murder. Thus, Sawyer has not met the
standard "actual innocence" exception.

Second, the affidavits and the new medical records do not convince me that
Sawyer's death sentence is clearly erroneous. The jury found two statutory aggravating factors—that the murder was committed in the course of an aggravated arson,
and that the murder was especially heinous, atrocious, and cruel. ** As suggested
above, the Thibodeaux affidavit does not show that it is "more likely than not" that
Sawyer did not commit aggravated arson. Moreover, Sawyer offers no evidence to undermine the jury's finding that the murder was especially heinous, atrocious, and
cruel. In addition, assuming that the new medical evidence would support a finding
of a statutory mitigating factor (diminished capacity due to mental disease or defect),
*** I cannot say that it would be clear error for a sentencer faced with the two unre-
futed aggravating circumstances and that single mitigating circumstance to sentence
Sawyer to death.

In sum, in my opinion Sawyer has failed to demonstrate that it is more likely than
not that his death sentence was clearly erroneous. Accordingly, I conclude that the court
below was correct in declining to reach the merits of Sawyer's successive and abusive
claims.

V

The Court rejects an "innocence of death" standard that recognizes constitutional errors affecting *mitigating* evidence because such a standard "would so broaden the inquiry as to make it anything but a 'narrow' exception to the principle of finality." ** As
the foregoing analysis indicates, however, the Court's concerns are unfounded. ***

Similarly, I do not share the Court's concern that a standard broader than the eligibility standard creates "a far more difficult task" for federal courts. ** As noted above,
both the "probably resulted" standard and the "clearly-erroneous" standard have long
been applied by federal courts in a variety of contexts. Moreover, to the extent that the
"clearly-erroneous" standard is more difficult to apply than the Court's "eligibility" test,
I believe that that cost is far outweighed by the importance of making just decisions in
the few cases that fit within this narrow exception. To my mind, any added administrative burden is surely justified by the overriding interest in minimizing the risk of error
in implementing the sovereign's decision to take the life of one of its citizens. As we observed in *Gardner v. Florida*, 430 U.S. 349, 360 (1977), "if the disputed matter is of critical importance, the time invested in ascertaining the truth would surely be well spent if
it makes the difference between life and death."

Notes

1. *Subsequent case history*

Robert Sawyer was executed on March 5, 1993.

2. *Mitigating evidence*

In footnote 2 of Justice Stevens' concurrence, in which he is joined by Justices Blackmun and O'Connor, Justice Stevens observes:

> The Court rejects the argument that federal courts should also consider *mitigating* evidence because consideration of such evidence involves the "far more difficult task [of] assess[ing] how jurors would have reacted to additional showings." ** I see no such difference between consideration of aggravating and mitigating circumstances; both require the federal courts to reconsider and anticipate a sentencer's decision: By the Court's own standard federal courts must determine whether a "reasonable juror would have found" certain facts. Thus, the Court's reason for barring federal courts from considering mitigating circumstances applies equally to the standard that *it* endorses. Its exclusion of mitigating evidence from consideration is therefore wholly arbitrary.

Is the Court's refusal to consider mitigating evidence wholly arbitrary?

Herrera v. Collins
506 U.S. 390 (1993)

CHIEF JUSTICE REHNQUIST delivered the opinion of the Court.

Petitioner Leonel Torres Herrera was convicted of capital murder and sentenced to death in January 1982. He unsuccessfully challenged the conviction on direct appeal and state collateral proceedings in the Texas state courts, and in a federal habeas petition. In February 1992—10 years after his conviction—he urged in a second federal habeas petition that he was "actually innocent" of the murder for which he was sentenced to death, and that the Eighth Amendment's prohibition against cruel and unusual punishment and the Fourteenth Amendment's guarantee of due process of law therefore forbid his execution. He supported this claim with affidavits tending to show that his now-dead brother, rather than he, had been the perpetrator of the crime. Petitioner urges us to hold that this showing of innocence entitles him to relief in this federal habeas proceeding. We hold that it does not.

Shortly before 11 p.m. on an evening in late September 1981, the body of Texas Department of Public Safety Officer David Rucker was found by a passer-by on a stretch of highway about six miles east of Los Fresnos, Texas, a few miles north of Brownsville in the Rio Grande Valley. Rucker's body was lying beside his patrol car. He had been shot in the head.

At about the same time, Los Fresnos Police Officer Enrique Carrisalez observed a speeding vehicle traveling west towards Los Fresnos, away from the place where Rucker's body had been found, along the same road. Carrisalez, who was accompanied in his patrol car by Enrique Hernandez, turned on his flashing red lights and pursued the speeding vehicle. After the car had stopped briefly at a red light, it signaled that it would pull over and did so. The patrol car pulled up behind it. Carrisalez took a flashlight and walked toward the car of the speeder. The driver opened his door and exchanged a few words with Carrisalez before firing at least one shot at Carrisalez' chest. The officer died nine days later.

(handwritten margin note: found guilty + sent to death)

Petitioner Herrera was arrested a few days after the shootings and charged with the capital murder of both Carrisalez and Rucker. He was tried and found guilty of the capital murder of Carrisalez in January 1982, and sentenced to death. In July 1982, petitioner pleaded guilty to the murder of Rucker.

At petitioner's trial for the murder of Carrisalez, Hernandez, who had witnessed Carrisalez' slaying from the officer's patrol car, identified petitioner as the person who had wielded the gun. A declaration by Officer Carrisalez to the same effect, made while he was in the hospital, was also admitted. Through a license plate check, it was shown that the speeding car involved in Carrisalez' murder was registered to petitioner's "live-in" girlfriend. Petitioner was known to drive this car, and he had a set of keys to the car in his pants pocket when he was arrested. Hernandez identified the car as the vehicle from which the murderer had emerged to fire the fatal shot. He also testified that there had been only one person in the car that night.

The evidence showed that Herrera's Social Security card had been found alongside Rucker's patrol car on the night he was killed. Splatters of blood on the car identified as the vehicle involved in the shootings, and on petitioner's blue jeans and wallet were identified as type A blood—the same type which Rucker had. (Herrera has type O blood.) Similar evidence with respect to strands of hair found in the car indicated that the hair was Rucker's and not Herrera's. A handwritten letter was also found on the person of petitioner when he was arrested, which strongly implied that he had killed Rucker. ***

***

Petitioner *** returned to state court and filed a second habeas petition, raising, among other things, a claim of "actual innocence" based on newly discovered evidence. In support of this claim petitioner presented the affidavits of Hector Villarreal, an attorney who had represented petitioner's brother, Raul Herrera, Sr., and of Juan Franco Palacious, one of Raul, Senior's former cellmates. Both individuals claimed that Raul, Senior, who died in 1984, had told them that he—and not petitioner—had killed Officers Rucker and Carrisalez. *** The State District Court denied this application, finding that "no evidence at trial remotely suggest[ed] that anyone other than [petitioner] committed the offense." ** The Texas Court of Criminal Appeals affirmed, ** and we denied certiorari. **

In February 1992, petitioner lodged the instant habeas petition—his second—in federal court, alleging, among other things, that he is innocent of the murders of Rucker and Carrisalez, and that his execution would thus violate the Eighth and Fourteenth Amendments. In addition to proffering the above affidavits, petitioner presented the affidavits of Raul Herrera, Jr., Raul Senior's son, and Jose Ybarra, Jr., a schoolmate of the Herrera brothers. Raul, Junior, averred that he had witnessed his father shoot Officers Rucker and Carrisalez and petitioner was not present. Raul, Junior, was nine years old at the time of the killings. Ybarra alleged that Raul, Senior, told him one summer night in 1983 that he had shot the two police officers. *** Petitioner alleged that law enforcement officials were aware of this evidence, and had withheld it in violation of *Brady v. Maryland*, 373 U.S. 83 (1963).

The District Court dismissed most of petitioner's claims as an abuse of the writ. ** However, "in order to ensure that Petitioner can assert his constitutional claims and out of a sense of fairness and due process," the District Court granted petitioner's request for a stay of execution so that he could present his claim of actual innocence, along with the Raul, Junior, and Ybarra affidavits, in state court. ** Although it initially dismissed petitioner's *Brady* claim on the ground that petitioner had failed to present "any evidence of withholding exculpatory material by the prosecution," ** the District Court also granted an evidentiary hearing on this claim after reconsideration. **

The Court of Appeals vacated the stay of execution. ** It agreed with the District Court's initial conclusion that there was no evidentiary basis for petitioner's *Brady* claim, and found disingenuous petitioner's attempt to couch his claim of actual innocence in *Brady* terms. ** Absent an accompanying constitutional violation, the Court of Appeals held that petitioner's claim of actual innocence was not cognizable because, under *Townsend v. Sain*, 372 U.S. 293 (1963), "the existence merely of newly discovered evidence relevant to the guilt of a state prisoner is not a ground for relief on federal habeas corpus." *** We granted certiorari, ** and the Texas Court of Criminal Appeals stayed petitioner's execution. We now affirm.

Petitioner asserts that the Eighth and Fourteenth Amendments to the United States Constitution prohibit the execution of a person who is innocent of the crime for which he was convicted. This proposition has an elemental appeal, as would the similar proposition that the Constitution prohibits the imprisonment of one who is innocent of the crime for which he was convicted. After all, the central purpose of any system of criminal justice is to convict the guilty and free the innocent. ** But the evidence upon which petitioner's claim of innocence rests was not produced at his trial, but rather eight years later. In any system of criminal justice, "innocence" or "guilt" must be determined in some sort of a judicial proceeding. Petitioner's showing of innocence, and indeed his constitutional claim for relief based upon that showing, must be evaluated in the light of the previous proceedings in this case, which have stretched over a span of 10 years.

A person when first charged with a crime is entitled to a presumption of innocence, and may insist that his guilt be established beyond a reasonable doubt. ** Other constitutional provisions also have the effect of ensuring against the risk of convicting an innocent person. ** In capital cases, we have required additional protections because of the nature of the penalty at stake. ** All of these constitutional safeguards, of course, make it more difficult for the State to rebut and finally overturn the presumption of innocence which attaches to every criminal defendant. But we have also observed that "[d]ue process does not require that every conceivable step be taken, at whatever cost, to eliminate the possibility of convicting an innocent person." ** To conclude otherwise would all but paralyze our system for enforcement of the criminal law.

Once a defendant has been afforded a fair trial and convicted of the offense for which he was charged, the presumption of innocence disappears. ** Here, it is not disputed that the State met its burden of proving at trial that petitioner was guilty of the capital murder of Officer Carrisalez beyond a reasonable doubt. Thus, in the eyes of the law, petitioner does not come before the Court as one who is "innocent," but, on the contrary, as one who has been convicted by due process of law of two brutal murders.

Based on affidavits here filed, petitioner claims that evidence never presented to the trial court proves him innocent notwithstanding the verdict reached at his trial. Such a claim is not cognizable in the state courts of Texas. For to obtain a new trial based on newly discovered evidence, a defendant must file a motion within 30 days after imposition or suspension of sentence. ** The Texas courts have construed this 30-day time limit as jurisdictional. **

Claims of actual innocence based on newly discovered evidence have never been held to state a ground for federal habeas relief absent an independent constitutional violation occurring in the underlying state criminal proceeding. *** This rule is grounded in the principle that federal habeas courts sit to ensure that individuals are not imprisoned in violation of the Constitution—not to correct errors of fact. **

***

Our decision in *Jackson v. Virginia*, 443 U.S. 307 (1979), comes as close to authorizing evidentiary review of a state-court conviction on federal habeas as any of our cases. There, we held that a federal habeas court may review a claim that the evidence adduced at a state trial was not sufficient to convict a criminal defendant beyond a reasonable doubt. But in so holding, we emphasized:

> [T]his inquiry does not require a court to "ask itself whether *it* believes that the evidence at the trial established guilt beyond a reasonable doubt." Instead, the relevant question is whether, after viewing the evidence in the light most favorable to the prosecution, *any* rational trier of fact could have found the essential elements of the crime beyond a reasonable doubt. This familiar standard gives full play to the responsibility of the trier of fact fairly to resolve conflicts in the testimony, to weigh the evidence, and to draw reasonable inferences from basic facts to ultimate facts. **

We specifically noted that "the standard announced...does not permit a court to make its own subjective determination of guilt or innocence." **

The type of federal habeas review sought by petitioner here is different in critical respects than that authorized by *Jackson*. First, the *Jackson* inquiry is aimed at determining whether there has been an independent constitutional violation—*i.e.*, a conviction based on evidence that fails to meet the *Winship* standard. Thus, federal habeas courts act in their historic capacity—to assure that the habeas petitioner is not being held in violation of his or her federal constitutional rights. Second, the sufficiency of the evidence review authorized by *Jackson* is limited to "record evidence." ** *Jackson* does not extend to nonrecord evidence, including newly discovered evidence. Finally, the *Jackson* inquiry does not focus on whether the trier of fact made the *correct* guilt or innocence determination, but rather whether it made a *rational* decision to convict or acquit.

Petitioner is understandably imprecise in describing the sort of federal relief to which a suitable showing of actual innocence would entitle him. In his brief he states that the federal habeas court should have "an important initial opportunity to hear the evidence and resolve the merits of Petitioner's claim." ** Acceptance of this view would presumably require the habeas court to hear testimony from the witnesses who testified at trial as well as those who made the statements in the affidavits which petitioner has presented, and to determine anew whether or not petitioner is guilty of the murder of Officer Carrisalez.

***

This is not to say that our habeas jurisprudence casts a blind eye toward innocence. In a series of cases culminating with *Sawyer v. Whitley*, 505 U.S. 333 (1992), decided last Term, we have held that a petitioner otherwise subject to defenses of abusive or successive use of the writ may have his federal constitutional claim considered on the merits if he makes a proper showing of actual innocence. This rule, or fundamental miscarriage of justice exception, is grounded in the "equitable discretion" of habeas courts to see that federal constitutional errors do not result in the incarceration of innocent persons. ** But this body of our habeas jurisprudence makes clear that a claim of "actual innocence" is not itself a constitutional claim, but instead a gateway through which a habeas petitioner must pass to have his otherwise barred constitutional claim considered on the merits.

Petitioner in this case is simply not entitled to habeas relief based on the reasoning of this line of cases. For he does not seek excusal of a procedural error so that he may bring an independent constitutional claim challenging his conviction or sentence, but rather argues that he is entitled to habeas relief because newly discovered evidence shows that his conviction is factually incorrect. The fundamental miscarriage of justice exception is available "only where the prisoner *supplements* his constitutional claim with a colorable showing of factual innocence." ** We have never held that it extends to free-standing claims of actual innocence. Therefore, the exception is inapplicable here.

Petitioner asserts that this case is different because he has been sentenced to death. But we have "refused to hold that the fact that a death sentence has been imposed requires a different standard of review on federal habeas corpus." ***

**

Petitioner also relies on *Johnson v. Mississippi*, 486 U.S. 578 (1988), where we held that the Eighth Amendment requires reexamination of a death sentence based in part on a prior felony conviction which was set aside in the rendering State after the capital sentence was imposed. There, the State insisted that it was too late in the day to raise this point. But we pointed out that the Mississippi Supreme Court had previously considered similar claims by writ of error *coram nobis*. Thus, there was no need to override state law relating to newly discovered evidence in order to consider Johnson's claim on the merits. Here, there is no doubt that petitioner seeks additional process—an evidentiary hearing on his claim of "actual innocence" based on newly discovered evidence—which is not available under Texas law more than 30 days after imposition or suspension of sentence. ***

Alternatively, petitioner invokes the Fourteenth Amendment's guarantee of due process of law in support of his claim that his showing of actual innocence entitles him to a new trial, or at least to a vacation of his death sentence. *** "[B]ecause the States have considerable expertise in matters of criminal procedure and the criminal process is grounded in centuries of common-law tradition," we have "exercis[ed] substantial deference to legislative judgments in this area." ** Thus, we have found criminal process lacking only where it " 'offends some principle of justice so rooted in the traditions and conscience of our people as to be ranked as fundamental.' " ** "Historical practice is probative of whether a procedural rule can be characterized as fundamental." **

The Constitution itself, of course, makes no mention of new trials. New trials in criminal cases were not granted in England until the end of the 17th century. And even then, they were available only in misdemeanor cases, though the writ of error *coram nobis* was available for some errors of fact in felony cases. ** The First Congress provided for new trials for "reasons for which new trials have usually been granted in courts of law." ** This rule was early held to extend to criminal cases. ** One of the grounds upon which new trials were granted was newly discovered evidence. **

**

The practice in the States today, while of limited relevance to our historical inquiry, is divergent. Texas is one of 17 States that requires a new trial motion based on newly discovered evidence to be made within 60 days of judgment. *** One State adheres to the common-law rule and requires that such a motion be filed during the term in which judgment was rendered. *** Eighteen jurisdictions have time limits ranging between one and three years, with 10 States and the District of Columbia following the 2-year federal time limit. *** Only 15 States allow a new trial motion based on newly discovered evidence to be filed more than three years after conviction. Of these States, four have waivable time limits of less than 120 days, two have waivable time limits of more than 120 days, and nine States have no time limits. ***

In light of the historical availability of new trials, our own amendments to Rule 33, and the contemporary practice in the States, we cannot say that Texas' refusal to entertain petitioner's newly discovered evidence eight years after his conviction transgresses a principle of fundamental fairness "rooted in the traditions and conscience of our people." ** This is not to say, however, that petitioner is left without a forum to raise his actual innocence claim. For under Texas law, petitioner may file a request for executive clemency. ** Clemency *** is deeply rooted in our Anglo-American tradition of law, and is the historic remedy for preventing miscarriages of justice where judicial process has been exhausted. ***

    ***

Executive clemency has provided the "fail safe" in our criminal justice system. ** It is an unalterable fact that our judicial system, like the human beings who administer it, is fallible. But history is replete with examples of wrongfully convicted persons who have been pardoned in the wake of after-discovered evidence establishing their innocence. In his classic work, Professor Edwin Borchard compiled 65 cases in which it was later determined that individuals had been wrongfully convicted of crimes. Clemency provided the relief mechanism in 47 of these cases; the remaining cases ended in judgments of acquittals after new trials. ** Recent authority confirms that over the past century clemency has been exercised frequently in capital cases in which demonstrations of "actual innocence" have been made. ***

In Texas, the Governor has the power, upon the recommendation of a majority of the Board of Pardons and Paroles, to grant clemency. ** The board's consideration is triggered upon request of the individual sentenced to death, his or her representative, or the Governor herself. In capital cases, a request may be made for a full pardon, ** a commutation of death sentence to life imprisonment or appropriate maximum penalty, ** or a reprieve of execution. ** The Governor has the sole authority to grant one reprieve in any capital case not exceeding 30 days. **

The Texas clemency procedures contain specific guidelines for pardons on the ground of innocence. The board will entertain applications for a recommendation of full pardon because of innocence upon receipt of the following: "(1) a written unanimous recommendation of the current trial officials of the court of conviction; and/or (2) a certified order or judgment of a court having jurisdiction accompanied by certified copy of the findings of fact (if any); and (3) affidavits of witnesses upon which the finding of innocence is based." ** In this case, petitioner has apparently sought a 30-day reprieve from the Governor, but has yet to apply for a pardon, or even a commutation, on the ground of innocence or otherwise. **

As the foregoing discussion illustrates, in state criminal proceedings the trial is the paramount event for determining the guilt or innocence of the defendant. Federal habeas review of state convictions has traditionally been limited to claims of constitutional violations occurring in the course of the underlying state criminal proceedings. Our federal habeas cases have treated claims of "actual innocence," not as an independent constitutional claim, but as a basis upon which a habeas petitioner may have an independent constitutional claim considered on the merits, even though his habeas petition would otherwise be regarded as successive or abusive. History shows that the traditional remedy for claims of innocence based on new evidence, discovered too late in the day to file a new trial motion, has been executive clemency.

We may assume, for the sake of argument in deciding this case, that in a capital case a truly persuasive demonstration of "actual innocence" made after trial would render the execution of a defendant unconstitutional, and warrant federal habeas relief if there were no state avenue open to process such a claim. But because of the very disruptive effect that entertaining claims of actual innocence would have on the need for finality in capital cases, and the enormous burden that having to retry cases based on often stale evidence would place on the States, the threshold showing for such an assumed right would necessarily be extraordinarily high. The showing made by petitioner in this case falls far short of any such threshold.

Petitioner's newly discovered evidence consists of affidavits. In the new trial context, motions based solely upon affidavits are disfavored because the affiants' statements are obtained without the benefit of cross-examination and an opportunity to make credibility determinations. ** Petitioner's affidavits are particularly suspect in this regard because, with the exception of Raul Herrera, Jr.'s affidavit, they consist of hearsay. Likewise, in reviewing petitioner's new evidence, we are mindful that defendants often abuse new trial motions "as a method of delaying enforcement of just sentences." ** Although we are not presented with a new trial motion *per se*, we believe the likelihood of abuse is as great—or greater—here.

        ***

This is not to say that petitioner's affidavits are without probative value. Had this sort of testimony been offered at trial, it could have been weighed by the jury, along with the evidence offered by the State and petitioner, in deliberating upon its verdict. Since the statements in the affidavits contradict the evidence received at trial, the jury would have had to decide important issues of credibility. But coming 10 years after petitioner's trial, this showing of innocence falls far short of that which would have to be made in order to trigger the sort of constitutional claim which we have assumed, *arguendo*, to exist.

The judgment of the Court of Appeals is

Affirmed.

JUSTICE O'CONNOR, with whom JUSTICE KENNEDY joins, concurring.

I cannot disagree with the fundamental legal principle that executing the innocent is inconsistent with the Constitution. Regardless of the verbal formula employed—"contrary to contemporary standards of decency," **—the execution of a legally and factually innocent person would be a constitutionally intolerable event. Dispositive to this case, however, is an equally fundamental fact: Petitioner is not innocent, in any sense of the word.

As the Court explains, ** petitioner is not innocent in the eyes of the law because, in our system of justice, "the trial is the paramount event for determining the guilt or innocence of the defendant." ** In petitioner's case, that paramount event occurred 10 years ago. He was tried before a jury of his peers, with the full panoply of protections that our Constitution affords criminal defendants. At the conclusion of that trial, the jury found petitioner guilty beyond a reasonable doubt. Petitioner therefore does not appear before us as an innocent man on the verge of execution. He is instead a legally guilty one who, refusing to accept the jury's verdict, demands a hearing in which to have his culpability determined once again. **

Consequently, the issue before us is not whether a State can execute the innocent. It is, as the Court notes, whether a fairly convicted and therefore legally guilty person is constitutionally entitled to yet another judicial proceeding in which to adjudicate his guilt anew, 10 years after conviction, notwithstanding his failure to demonstrate that constitutional error infected his trial. ** In most circumstances, that question would answer itself in the negative. Our society has a high degree of confidence in its criminal trials, in no small part because the Constitution offers unparalleled protections against convicting the innocent. ** The question similarly would be answered in the negative today, except for the disturbing nature of the claim before us. Petitioner contends not only that the Constitution's protections "sometimes fail" ** but that their failure in his case will result in his execution—even though he is factually innocent and has evidence to prove it.

***

Nonetheless, the proper disposition of this case is neither difficult nor troubling. No matter what the Court might say about claims of actual innocence today, petitioner could not obtain relief. The record overwhelmingly demonstrates that petitioner deliberately shot and killed Officers Rucker and Carrisalez the night of September 29, 1981; petitioner's new evidence is bereft of credibility. Indeed, despite its stinging criticism of the Court's decision, not even the dissent expresses a belief that petitioner might possibly be actually innocent. Nor could it: The record makes it abundantly clear that petitioner is not somehow the future victim of "simple murder" ** but instead himself the established perpetrator of two brutal and tragic ones.

***

Ultimately, two things about this case are clear. First is what the Court does *not* hold. Nowhere does the Court state that the Constitution permits the execution of an actually innocent person. Instead, the Court assumes for the sake of argument that a truly persuasive demonstration of actual innocence would render any such execution unconstitutional and that federal habeas relief would be warranted if no state avenue were open to process the claim. Second is what petitioner has not demonstrated. Petitioner has failed to make a persuasive showing of actual innocence. Not one judge—no state court judge, not the District Court Judge, none of the three judges of the Court of Appeals, and none of the Justices of this Court—has expressed doubt about petitioner's guilt. Accordingly, the Court has no reason to pass on, and appropriately reserves, the question whether federal courts may entertain convincing claims of actual innocence. That difficult question remains open. If the Constitution's guarantees of fair procedure and the safeguards of clemency and pardon fulfill their historical mission, it may never require resolution at all.

JUSTICE SCALIA, with whom JUSTICE THOMAS joins, concurring.

We granted certiorari on the question whether it violates due process or constitutes cruel and unusual punishment for a State to execute a person who, having been convicted of murder after a full and fair trial, later alleges that newly discovered evidence shows him to be "actually innocent." I would have preferred to decide that question, particularly since, as the Court's discussion shows, it is perfectly clear what the answer is: There is no basis in text, tradition, or even in contemporary practice (if that were enough) for finding in the Constitution a right to demand judicial consideration of newly discovered evidence of innocence brought forward after conviction. In saying that such a right exists, the dissenters apply nothing but their personal opinions to invalidate the rules of more than two-thirds of the States, and a Federal Rule of Criminal Procedure for which this Court itself is responsible. If the system that has been in place for 200 years (and remains widely approved) "shock[s]" the dissenters' consciences, ** perhaps they should doubt the calibration of their consciences, or, better still, the usefulness of "conscience shocking" as a legal test.

I nonetheless join the entirety of the Court's opinion, including the final portion, **
because there is no legal error in deciding a case by assuming, *arguendo*, that an asserted
constitutional right exists, and because I can understand, or at least am accustomed to,
the reluctance of the present Court to admit publicly that Our Perfect Constitution ***
lets stand any injustice, much less the execution of an innocent man who has received,
though to no avail, all the process that our society has traditionally deemed adequate.
With any luck, we shall avoid ever having to face this embarrassing question again, since
it is improbable that evidence of innocence as convincing as today's opinion requires
would fail to produce an executive pardon.

***

JUSTICE WHITE, concurring in the judgment.

In voting to affirm, I assume that a persuasive showing of "actual innocence" made
after trial, even though made after the expiration of the time provided by law for the
presentation of newly discovered evidence, would render unconstitutional the execution of petitioner in this case. To be entitled to relief, however, petitioner would at the
very least be required to show that based on proffered newly discovered evidence and
the entire record before the jury that convicted him, "no rational trier of fact could
[find] proof of guilt beyond a reasonable doubt." ** For the reasons stated in the
Court's opinion, petitioner's showing falls far short of satisfying even that standard, and
I therefore concur in the judgment.

JUSTICE BLACKMUN, with whom JUSTICE STEVENS and JUSTICE SOUTER
join with respect to Parts I–IV, dissenting.

Nothing could be more contrary to contemporary standards of decency ** than to
execute a person who is actually innocent.

I therefore must disagree with the long and general discussion that precedes the
Court's disposition of this case. ** That discussion, of course, is dictum because the
Court assumes, "for the sake of argument in deciding this case, that in a capital case a
truly persuasive demonstration of 'actual innocence' made after trial would render the
execution of a defendant unconstitutional." ** Without articulating the standard it is
applying, however, the Court then decides that this petitioner has not made a sufficiently persuasive case. Because I believe that in the first instance the District Court
should decide whether petitioner is entitled to a hearing and whether he is entitled to
relief on the merits of his claim, I would reverse the order of the Court of Appeals and
remand this case for further proceedings in the District Court.

I

The Court's enumeration ** of the constitutional rights of criminal defendants surely
is entirely beside the point. These protections sometimes fail. *** We really are being
asked to decide whether the Constitution forbids the execution of a person who has
been validly convicted and sentenced but who, nonetheless, can prove his innocence
with newly discovered evidence. Despite the State of Texas' astonishing protestation to
the contrary, ** I do not see how the answer can be anything but "yes."

A

The Eighth Amendment prohibits "cruel and unusual punishments." This proscription
is not static but rather reflects evolving standards of decency. ** I think it is crystal clear
that the execution of an innocent person is "at odds with contemporary standards of fairness and decency." ** Indeed, it is at odds with any standard of decency that I can imagine.

This Court has ruled that punishment is excessive and unconstitutional if it is "nothing more than the purposeless and needless imposition of pain and suffering," or if it is "grossly out of proportion to the severity of the crime." ** It has held that death is an excessive punishment for rape, *Coker v. Georgia*, 433 U.S. [584], 592 [(1977)], and for mere participation in a robbery during which a killing takes place. ** If it is violative of the Eighth Amendment to execute someone who is guilty of those crimes, then it plainly is violative of the Eighth Amendment to execute a person who is actually innocent. Executing an innocent person epitomizes "the purposeless and needless imposition of pain and suffering." ***

***

I believe it contrary to any standard of decency to execute someone who is actually innocent. Because the Eighth Amendment applies to questions of guilt or innocence ** and to persons upon whom a valid sentence of death has been imposed, ** I also believe that petitioner may raise an Eighth Amendment challenge to his punishment on the ground that he is actually innocent.

B

Execution of the innocent is equally offensive to the Due Process Clause of the Fourteenth Amendment. The majority's discussion misinterprets petitioner's Fourteenth Amendment claim as raising a procedural, rather than a substantive, due process challenge. ***

***

II

The majority's discussion of petitioner's constitutional claims is even more perverse when viewed in the light of this Court's recent habeas jurisprudence. Beginning with a trio of decisions in 1986, this Court shifted the focus of federal habeas review of successive, abusive, or defaulted claims away from the preservation of constitutional rights to a fact-based inquiry into the habeas petitioner's guilt or innocence. ** The Court sought to strike a balance between the State's interest in the finality of its criminal judgments and the prisoner's interest in access to a forum to test the basic justice of his sentence. ***

***

*** In other words, even a prisoner who appears to have had a *constitutionally perfect* trial "retains a powerful and legitimate interest in obtaining his release from custody if he is innocent of the charge for which he was incarcerated." It is obvious that this reasoning extends beyond the context of successive, abusive, or defaulted claims to substantive claims of actual innocence. ***

***

III

The Eighth and Fourteenth Amendments, of course, are binding on the States, and one would normally expect the States to adopt procedures to consider claims of actual innocence based on newly discovered evidence. ** The majority's disposition of this case, however, leaves the States uncertain of their constitutional obligations.

A

Whatever procedures a State might adopt to hear actual-innocence claims, one thing is certain: The possibility of executive clemency is *not* sufficient to satisfy the requirements of the Eighth and Fourteenth Amendments. The majority point out: "'A pardon is an act of grace.'" ** The vindication of rights guaranteed by the Constitution has never been made to turn on the unreviewable discretion of an executive official or administrative tribunal. ***

    ***

C

    ***

I think the standard for relief on the merits of an actual-innocence claim must be higher than the threshold standard for merely reaching that claim or any other claim that has been procedurally defaulted or is successive or abusive. I would hold that, to obtain relief on a claim of actual innocence, the petitioner must show that he probably is innocent. This standard is supported by several considerations. First, new evidence of innocence may be discovered long after the defendant's conviction. Given the passage of time, it may be difficult for the State to retry a defendant who obtains relief from his conviction or sentence on an actual-innocence claim. The actual-innocence proceeding thus may constitute the final word on whether the defendant may be punished. In light of this fact, an otherwise constitutionally valid conviction or sentence should not be set aside lightly. Second, conviction after a constitutionally adequate trial strips the defendant of the presumption of innocence. The government bears the burden of proving the defendant's guilt beyond a reasonable doubt, ** but once the government has done so, the burden of proving innocence must shift to the convicted defendant. The actual-innocence inquiry is therefore distinguishable from review for sufficiency of the evidence, where the question is not whether the defendant is innocent but whether the government has met its constitutional burden of proving the defendant's guilt beyond a reasonable doubt. When a defendant seeks to challenge the determination of guilt after he has been validly convicted and sentenced, it is fair to place on him the burden of proving his innocence, not just raising doubt about his guilt.

    ***

V

I have voiced disappointment over this Court's obvious eagerness to do away with any restriction on the States' power to execute whomever and however they please. ** I have also expressed doubts about whether, in the absence of such restrictions, capital punishment remains constitutional at all. ** Of one thing, however, I am certain. Just as an execution without adequate safeguards is unacceptable, so too is an execution when the condemned prisoner can prove that he is innocent. The execution of a person who can show that he is innocent comes perilously close to simple murder.

Notes

1. *Subsequent case history*

Leonel Herrera was executed on May 12, 1993.

2. *The role of habeas review*

According to *Herrera*, the rule that "the existence merely of newly discovered evidence relevant to guilt of a state prisoner is not a ground for relief in federal habeas corpus" is "grounded in the principle that federal habeas courts sit to ensure that individuals are not imprisoned in violation of the Constitution—not to correct errors of fact."

506 U.S. at 400. The Court then parenthetically cites *Moore v. Dempsey*, 261 U.S. 86, 87–88 (1923), for the proposition that "what we have to deal with [on habeas review] is not the petitioners' innocence or guilt but solely the question whether their constitutional rights have been preserved." 506 U.S. at 400.

Do you agree that the proper role of habeas review is to ensure that constitutional rights have been preserved, rather than to address questions of innocence? If the general public perception is that courts exist to correct errors of fact, how does one explain the Court's position in *Herrera* to the general public?

3. The clemency "fail safe"

In light of the considerations explored in Chapter 14, is it reasonable for the Court to rely on executive clemency as a "fail safe" to pardon wrongfully convicted persons who claim that newly discovered evidence establishes their innocence?

4. Fundamental miscarriages of justice

In his article *The Risks of Death: Why Erroneous Convictions Are Common in Capital Cases*, 44 Buff. L. Rev. 469 (1996), Professor Samuel R. Gross identifies a number of causes for the conviction of the innocent (*e.g.*, erroneous identification, clearance rates and pressure on the police, perjurious testimony, and false confessions), then he states:

> The basic conclusion is simple. The steady stream of errors that we see in cases in which defendants are sentenced to death is a predictable consequence of our system of investigation and prosecuting capital murder. And behind those cases, there is no doubt a much larger group of erroneous convictions in cases in which defendants are not sentenced to death. But what about what happens after trial? Everybody knows that direct and collateral review are more painstaking for capital cases than for any others. Isn't it likely that all these mistakes are caught and corrected somewhere in that exacting process? The answer, I'm afraid, is No. At best, we could do an imperfect job of catching errors after they occur, and in many cases, we don't really try. As a result, most miscarriages of justice in capital cases never come to light.

Id. at 497. Considering Professor Gross's observation that "most miscarriages of justice in capital cases never come to light," what is your assessment of the equity of the Court's "fundamental miscarriage of justice exception"?

What are the arguments in favor of extending the "fundamental miscarriage of justice exception" to freestanding claims of actual innocence? What are the arguments against it?

Schlup v. Delo
513 U.S. 298 (1995)

JUSTICE STEVENS delivered the opinion of the Court.

Petitioner Lloyd E. Schlup, Jr., a Missouri prisoner currently under a sentence of death, filed a second federal habeas corpus petition alleging that constitutional error deprived the jury of critical evidence that would have established his innocence. The District Court, without conducting an evidentiary hearing, declined to reach the merits of the petition, holding that petitioner could not satisfy the threshold showing of "actual innocence" required by *Sawyer v. Whitley*, 505 U.S. 333 (1992). Under *Sawyer*, the petitioner must show "by clear and convincing evidence that, but for a constitutional error, no reasonable juror would have found the petitioner" guilty. ** The Court of Appeals affirmed. We granted certiorari to consider whether the *Sawyer* standard provides ade-

quate protection against the kind of miscarriage of justice that would result from the
execution of a person who is actually innocent.

I

On February 3, 1984, on Walk 1 of the high security area of the Missouri State Penitentiary, a black inmate named Arthur Dade was stabbed to death. Three white inmates
from Walk 2, including petitioner, were charged in connection with Dade's murder.

At petitioner's trial in December 1985, the State's evidence consisted principally of
the testimony of two corrections officers who had witnessed the killing. On the day of
the murder, Sergeant Roger Flowers was on duty on Walk 1 and Walk 2, the two walks
on the lower floor of the prison's high security area. Flowers testified that he first released the inmates on Walk 2 for their noon meal and relocked their cells. After unlock-
ing the cells to release the inmates on Walk 1, Flowers noticed an inmate named Rodnie
Stewart moving against the flow of traffic carrying a container of steaming liquid. Flowers watched as Stewart threw the liquid in Dade's face. According to Flowers, Schlup
then jumped on Dade's back, and Robert O'Neal joined in the attack. Flowers shouted
for help, entered the walk, and grabbed Stewart as the two other assailants fled.

Officer John Maylee witnessed the attack from Walk 7, which is three levels and some
40–50 feet above Walks 1 and 2. *** Maylee first noticed Schlup, Stewart, and O'Neal as
they were running from Walk 2 to Walk 1 against the flow of traffic. According to
Maylee's testimony, Stewart threw a container of liquid at Dade's face, and then Schlup
jumped on Dade's back. O'Neal then stabbed Dade several times in the chest, ran down
the walk, and threw the weapon out a window. Maylee did not see what happened to
Schlup or Stewart after the stabbing.

The State produced no physical evidence connecting Schlup to the killing, and no witness other than Flowers and Maylee testified to Schlup's involvement in the murder. ***

Schlup's defense was that the State had the wrong man. *** He relied heavily on a
videotape from a camera in the prisoners' dining room. The tape showed that Schlup
was the first inmate to walk into the dining room for the noon meal, and that he went
through the line and got his food. Approximately 65 seconds after Schlup's entrance,
several guards ran out of the dining room in apparent response to a distress call.
Twenty-six seconds later, O'Neal ran into the dining room, dripping blood. *** Shortly
thereafter, Schlup and O'Neal were taken into custody.

Schlup contended that the videotape, when considered in conjunction with testimony that he had walked at a normal pace from his cell to the dining room, *** demonstrated that he could not have participated in the assault. Because the videotape showed
conclusively that Schlup was in the dining room 65 seconds before the guards responded to the distress call, a critical element of Schlup's defense was determining when
the distress call went out. Had the distress call sounded shortly after the murder, Schlup
would not have had time to get from the prison floor to the dining room, and thus he
could not have participated in the murder. Conversely, had there been a delay of several
minutes between the murder and the distress call, Schlup might have had sufficient
time to participate in the murder and still get to the dining room over a minute before
the distress call went out. ***

The prosecutor adduced evidence tending to establish that such a delay had in fact
occurred. First, Flowers testified that none of the officers on the prison floor had radios,
thus implying that neither he nor any of the other officers on the floor was able to radio
for help when the stabbing occurred. Second, Flowers testified that after he shouted for

help, it took him "a couple [of] minutes" to subdue Stewart. *** Flowers then brought Stewart downstairs, encountered Captain James Eberle, and told Eberle that there had been a "disturbance." *** Eberle testified that he went upstairs to the prison floor, and then radioed for assistance. Eberle estimated that the elapsed time from when he first saw Flowers until he radioed for help was "approximately a minute." *** The prosecution also offered testimony from a prison investigator who testified that he was able to run from the scene of the crime to the dining room in 33 seconds and to walk the distance at a normal pace in a minute and 37 seconds.

After deliberating overnight, the jury returned a verdict of guilty. Following the penalty phase, at which the victim of one of Schlup's prior offenses testified extensively about the sordid details of that offense, *** the jury sentenced Schlup to death. The Missouri Supreme Court affirmed Schlup's conviction and death sentence, ** and this Court denied certiorari. **

II

On January 5, 1989, after exhausting his state collateral remedies, *** Schlup filed a *pro se* petition for a federal writ of habeas corpus, asserting the claim, among others, that his trial counsel was ineffective for failing to interview and to call witnesses who could establish Schlup's innocence. *** The District Court concluded that Schlup's ineffectiveness claim was procedurally barred, and it denied relief on that claim without conducting an evidentiary hearing. *** The Court of Appeals affirmed, though it did not rely on the alleged procedural bar. ** Instead, based on its own examination of the record, the Court found that trial counsel's performance had not been constitutionally ineffective, both because counsel had reviewed statements that Schlup's potential witnesses had given to prison investigators, and because the testimony of those witnesses "would be repetitive of the testimony to be presented at trial." *** The Court of Appeals denied a petition for rehearing and suggestion for rehearing en banc, ** and we denied a petition for certiorari. **

On March 11, 1992, represented by new counsel, Schlup filed a second federal habeas corpus petition. That petition raised a number of claims, including that (1) Schlup was actually innocent of Dade's murder, and that his execution would therefore violate the Eighth and Fourteenth Amendments; ** (2) trial counsel was ineffective for failing to interview alibi witnesses; and (3) the State had failed to disclose critical exculpatory evidence. The petition was supported by numerous affidavits from inmates attesting to Schlup's innocence.

The State filed a response arguing that various procedural bars precluded the District Court from reaching the merits of Schlup's claims and that the claims were in any event meritless. Attached to the State's response were transcripts of inmate interviews conducted by prison investigators just five days after the murder. One of the transcripts contained an interview with John Green, an inmate who at the time was the clerk for the housing unit. In his interview, Green stated that he had been in his office at the end of the walks when the murder occurred. Green stated that Flowers had told him to call for help, and that Green had notified base of the disturbance shortly after it began. ***

Schlup immediately filed a traverse arguing that Green's affidavit provided conclusive proof of Schlup's innocence. Schlup contended that Green's statement demonstrated that a call for help had gone out shortly after the incident. Because the videotape showed that Schlup was in the dining room some 65 seconds before the guards received the distress call, Schlup argued that he could not have been involved in Dade's murder. Schlup emphasized that Green's statement was not likely to have been fabricated, because at the time of Green's interview, neither he nor anyone else would have realized the significance of Green's call to base. Schlup tried to buttress his claim of innocence with affidavits from inmates who stated that they had witnessed the event and that Schlup had not been present. *** Two of those affidavits suggested that Randy Jordan—who occupied the cell between O'Neal and Stewart in Walk 2, and who, as noted above, ** is shown on the videotape arriving at lunch with O'Neal—was the third assailant.

On August 23, 1993, without holding a hearing, the District Court dismissed Schlup's second habeas petition and vacated the stay of execution that was then in effect. The District Court concluded that Schlup's various filings did not provide adequate cause for failing to raise his new claims more promptly. Moreover, the court concluded that Schlup had failed to meet the *Sawyer v. Whitley, supra,* standard for showing that a refusal to entertain those claims would result in a fundamental miscarriage of justice. In its discussion of the evidence, the court made no separate comment on the significance of Green's statement. ***

On September 7, 1993, petitioner filed a motion to set aside the order of dismissal, again calling the court's attention to Green's statement. Two days later, Schlup filed a supplemental motion stating that his counsel had located John Green *** and had obtained an affidavit from him. That affidavit confirmed Green's postincident statement that he had called base shortly after the assault. Green's affidavit also identified Jordan rather than Schlup as the third assailant. *** The District Court denied the motion and the supplemental motion without opinion.

***

On November 17, 1993, the Court of Appeals denied a suggestion for rehearing en banc. Dissenting from that denial, three judges joined an opinion describing the question whether the majority should have applied the standard announced in *Sawyer v. Whitley, supra,* rather than the *Kuhlmann* standard as "a question of great importance in habeas corpus jurisprudence." ** We granted certiorari to consider that question. **

III

As a preliminary matter, it is important to explain the difference between Schlup's claim of actual innocence and the claim of actual innocence asserted in *Herrera v. Collins,* 506 U.S. 390 (1993). In *Herrera,* the petitioner advanced his claim of innocence to support a novel substantive constitutional claim, namely, that the execution of an innocent person would violate the Eighth Amendment. *** Under petitioner's theory in *Herrera,* even if the proceedings that had resulted in his conviction and sentence were entirely fair and error free, his innocence would render his execution a "constitutionally intolerable event." **

Schlup's claim of innocence, on the other hand, is procedural, rather than substantive. His constitutional claims are based not on his innocence, but rather on his contention that the ineffectiveness of his counsel, ** and the withholding of evidence by the prosecution, *see Brady v. Maryland,* 373 U.S. 83 (1963), denied him the full panoply of protections afforded to criminal defendants by the Constitution. Schlup, however, faces procedural obstacles that he must overcome before a federal court may address the merits of those constitutional claims. Because Schlup has been unable to establish "cause and prejudice" sufficient to excuse his failure to present his evidence in support of his first federal petition, *** Schlup may obtain review of his constitutional claims only if he falls within the "narrow class of cases…implicating a fundamental miscarriage of justice." ** Schlup's claim of innocence is offered only to bring him within this "narrow class of cases."

Schlup's claim thus differs in at least two important ways from that presented in *Herrera*. First, Schlup's claim of innocence does not by itself provide a basis for relief. Instead, his claim for relief depends critically on the validity of his *Strickland* and *Brady* claims. *** Schlup's claim of innocence is thus "not itself a constitutional claim, but instead a gateway through which a habeas petitioner must pass to have his otherwise barred constitutional claim considered on the merits." ***

***

*** Without any new evidence of innocence, even the existence of a concededly meritorious constitutional violation is not in itself sufficient to establish a miscarriage of justice that would allow a habeas court to reach the merits of a barred claim. However, if a petitioner such as Schlup presents evidence of innocence so strong that a court cannot have confidence in the outcome of the trial unless the court is also satisfied that the trial was free of nonharmless constitutional error, the petitioner should be allowed to pass through the gateway and argue the merits of his underlying claims.

Consequently, Schlup's evidence of innocence need carry less of a burden. In *Herrera* (on the assumption that petitioner's claim was, in principle, legally well founded), the evidence of innocence would have had to be strong enough to make his execution "constitutionally intolerable" *even if* his conviction was the product of a fair trial. For Schlup, the evidence must establish sufficient doubt about his guilt to justify the conclusion that his execution would be a miscarriage of justice *unless* his conviction was the product of a fair trial.

Our rather full statement of the facts illustrates the foregoing distinction between a substantive *Herrera* claim and Schlup's procedural claim. Three items of evidence are particularly relevant: the affidavit of black inmates attesting to the innocence of a white defendant in a racially motivated killing; the affidavit of Green describing his prompt call for assistance; and the affidavit of Lieutenant Faherty describing Schlup's unhurried walk to the dining room. If there were no question about the fairness of the criminal trial, a *Herrera*-type claim would have to fail unless the federal habeas court is itself convinced that those new facts unquestionably establish Schlup's innocence. On the other hand, if the habeas court were merely convinced that those new facts raised sufficient doubt about Schlup's guilt to undermine confidence in the result of the trial without the assurance that that trial was untainted by constitutional error, Schlup's threshold showing of innocence would justify a review of the merits of the constitutional claims.

IV

***

To ensure that the fundamental miscarriage of justice exception would remain "rare" and would only be applied in the "extraordinary case," while at the same time ensuring that the exception would extend relief to those who were truly deserving, this Court explicitly tied the miscarriage of justice exception to the petitioner's innocence. ***

***

V

***

As we have stated, the fundamental miscarriage of justice exception seeks to balance the societal interests in finality, comity, and conservation of scarce judicial resources with the individual interest in justice that arises in the extraordinary case. We conclude that *Carrier*, rather than *Sawyer*, properly strikes that balance when the claimed injustice is that constitutional error has resulted in the conviction of one who is actually innocent of the crime.

Claims of actual innocence pose less of a threat to scarce judicial resources and to principles of finality and comity than do claims that focus solely on the erroneous imposition of the death penalty. Though challenges to the propriety of imposing a sentence of death are routinely asserted in capital cases, experience has taught us that a substantial claim that constitutional error has caused the conviction of an innocent person is extremely rare. ** To be credible, such a claim requires petitioner to support his allegations of constitutional error with new reliable evidence—whether it be exculpatory scientific evidence, trustworthy eyewitness accounts, or critical physical evidence—that was not presented at trial. Because such evidence is obviously unavailable in the vast majority of cases, claims of actual innocence are rarely successful. Even under the pre-*Sawyer* regime, "in virtually every case, the allegation of actual innocence has been summarily rejected." *** The threat to judicial resources, finality, and comity posed by claims of actual innocence is thus significantly less than that posed by claims relating only to sentencing.

Of greater importance, the individual interest in avoiding injustice is most compelling in the context of actual innocence. The quintessential miscarriage of justice is the execution of a person who is entirely innocent. *** Indeed, concern about the injustice that results from the conviction of an innocent person has long been at the core of our criminal justice system. That concern is reflected, for example, in the "fundamental value determination of our society that it is far worse to convict an innocent man than to let a guilty man go free." **

The overriding importance of this greater individual interest merits protection by imposing a somewhat less exacting standard of proof on a habeas petitioner alleging a fundamental miscarriage of justice than on one alleging that his sentence is too severe. ***

  ***

[W]e hold that the *Carrier* "probably resulted" standard rather than the more stringent *Sawyer* standard must govern the miscarriage of justice inquiry when a petitioner who has been sentenced to death raises a claim of actual innocence to avoid a procedural bar to the consideration of the merits of his constitutional claims.

VI

The *Carrier* standard requires the habeas petitioner to show that "a constitutional violation has probably resulted in the conviction of one who is actually innocent." ** To establish the requisite probability, the petitioner must show that it is more likely than not that no reasonable juror would have convicted him in the light of the new evidence. The petitioner thus is required to make a stronger showing than that needed to establish prejudice. *** At the same time, the showing of "more likely than not" imposes a lower burden of proof than the "clear and convincing" standard required under  *Sawyer*. The *Carrier* standard thus ensures that petitioner's case is truly "extraordinary," ** while still providing petitioner a meaningful avenue by which to avoid a manifest injustice.

Carrier requires a petitioner to show that he is "actually innocent." As used in *Carrier*, actual innocence is closely related to the definition set forth by this Court in

Sawyer. To satisfy the *Carrier* gateway standard, a petitioner must show that it is more likely than not that no reasonable juror would have found petitioner guilty beyond a reasonable doubt.

Several observations about this standard are in order. The *Carrier* standard is intended to focus the inquiry on actual innocence. In assessing the adequacy of petitioner's showing, therefore, the district court is not bound by the rules of admissibility that would govern at trial. Instead, the emphasis on "actual innocence" allows the reviewing tribunal also to consider the probative force of relevant evidence that was either excluded or unavailable at trial. Indeed, with respect to this aspect of the *Carrier* standard, we believe that Judge Friendly's description of the inquiry is appropriate: The habeas court must make its determination concerning the petitioner's innocence "in light of all the evidence, including that alleged to have been illegally admitted (but with due regard to any unreliability of it) and evidence tenably claimed to have been wrongly excluded or to have become available only after the trial." ***

***

We note finally that the *Carrier* standard requires a petitioner to show that it is more likely than not that "no reasonable juror" would have convicted him. The word "reasonable" in that formulation is not without meaning. It must be presumed that a reasonable juror would consider fairly all of the evidence presented. It must also be presumed that such a juror would conscientiously obey the instructions of the trial court requiring proof beyond a reasonable doubt. ***

Though the *Carrier* standard requires a substantial showing, it is by no means equivalent to the standard of *Jackson v. Virginia*, 443 U.S. 307 (1979), that governs review of claims of insufficient evidence. The *Jackson* standard, which focuses on whether any rational juror could have convicted, looks to whether there is sufficient evidence which, if credited, could support the conviction. The *Jackson* standard thus differs in at least two important ways from the *Carrier* standard. First, under *Jackson*, the assessment of the credibility of witnesses is generally beyond the scope of review. In contrast, under the gateway standard we describe today, the newly presented evidence may indeed call into question the credibility of the witnesses presented at trial. In such a case, the habeas court may have to make some credibility assessments. Second, and more fundamentally, the focus of the inquiry is different under *Jackson* than under *Carrier*. Under *Jackson*, the use of the word "could" focuses the inquiry on the power of the trier of fact to reach its conclusion. Under *Carrier*, the use of the word "would" focuses the inquiry on the likely behavior of the trier of fact.

Indeed, our adoption of the phrase "more likely than not" reflects this distinction. Under *Jackson*, the question whether the trier of fact has power to make a finding of guilt requires a binary response: Either the trier of fact has power as a matter of law or it does not. Under *Carrier*, in contrast, the habeas court must consider what reasonable triers of fact are likely to do. Under this probabilistic inquiry, it makes sense to have a probabilistic standard such as "more likely than not." *** Thus, though under *Jackson* the mere existence of sufficient evidence to convict would be determinative of petitioner's claim, that is not true under *Carrier*.

***

Because both the Court of Appeals and the District Court evaluated the record under an improper standard, further proceedings are necessary. The fact-intensive nature of the inquiry, together with the District Court's ability to take testimony from the few key witnesses if it deems that course advisable, convinces us that the most expeditious procedure is to order that the decision of the Court of Appeals be vacated and that the case be remanded to the Court of Appeals with instructions to remand to the District Court for further proceedings consistent with this opinion.

It is so ordered.

JUSTICE O'CONNOR, concurring.

I write to explain, in light of the dissenting opinions, what I understand the Court to decide and what it does not.

The Court holds that, in order to have an abusive or successive habeas claim heard on the merits, a petitioner who cannot demonstrate cause and prejudice "must show that it is more likely than not that no reasonable juror would have convicted him" in light of newly discovered evidence of innocence. ** This standard is higher than that required for prejudice, which requires only "a reasonable probability that, absent the errors, the factfinder would have had a reasonable doubt respecting guilt." *** The Court today does not sow confusion in the law. Rather, it properly balances the dictates of justice with the need to ensure that the actual innocence exception remains only a " 'safety valve' for the 'extraordinary case.' " **

***

CHIEF JUSTICE REHNQUIST, with whom JUSTICE KENNEDY and JUSTICE THOMAS join, dissenting.

The Court decides that the threshold standard for a showing of "actual innocence" in a successive or abusive habeas petition is that set forth in *Murray v. Carrier*, 477 U.S. 478 (1986), rather than that set forth in *Sawyer v. Whitley*, 505 U.S. 333 (1992). For reasons which I later set out, I believe the *Sawyer* standard should be applied to claims of guilt or innocence as well as to challenges to a petitioner's sentence. But, more importantly, I believe the Court's exegesis of the *Carrier* standard both waters down the standard suggested in that case, and will inevitably create confusion in the lower courts.

***

The Court fails to acknowledge expressly the similarities between the standard it has adopted and the *Jackson* standard. A habeas court reviewing a claim of actual innocence does not write on a clean slate. ** Therefore, as the Court acknowledges, a petitioner making a claim of actual innocence under *Carrier* falls short of satisfying his burden if the reviewing court determines that *any* juror reasonably would have found petitioner guilty of the crime. **

***

JUSTICE SCALIA, with whom JUSTICE THOMAS joins, dissenting.

A federal statute entitled "Finality of Determination"—to be found at § 2244 of Title 28 of the United States Code—specifically addresses the problem of second and subsequent petitions for the writ of habeas corpus. The reader of today's opinion will be unencumbered with knowledge of this law, since it is not there discussed or quoted, and indeed is only cited *en passant*. ** Rather than asking what the statute says, or even what we have said the statute says, the Court asks only what is the fairest standard to apply, and answers that question by looking to the various semi-consistent standards articulated in our most recent decisions—minutely parsing phrases, and seeking shades of meaning in the interstices of sentences and words, as though a discursive judicial opinion were a statute. I would proceed differently. Within the very broad limits set by the Suspension Clause, U.S. Const., Art. I, §9, cl. 2, the federal writ of habeas corpus is governed by statute. Section 2244 controls this case; the disposition it announces is plain enough, and our decisions contain nothing that would justify departure from that plain meaning.

Section 2244(b) provides:

> When after an evidentiary hearing on the merits of a material factual issue, or after a hearing on the merits of an issue of law, a person in custody pursuant to the judgment of a State court has been denied by a court of the United States or a justice or judge of the United States release from custody or other remedy on an application for a writ of habeas corpus, a subsequent application for a writ of habeas corpus in behalf of such person need not be entertained by a court of the United States or a justice or judge of the United States unless the application alleges and is predicated on a factual or other ground not adjudicated on the hearing of the earlier application for the writ, and unless the court, justice, or judge is satisfied that the applicant has not on the earlier application deliberately withheld the newly asserted ground or otherwise abused the writ.

A long sentence, but not a difficult one. A federal district court that receives a second or subsequent petition for the writ of habeas corpus, when a prior petition has been denied on the merits, "need not…entertain" (*i.e.*, may dismiss) the petition unless it is neither (to use our shorthand terminology) successive nor abusive. ** Today, however, the Court obliquely but unmistakably pronounces that a successive or abusive petition *must* be entertained and may *not* be dismissed so long as the petitioner makes a sufficiently persuasive showing that a "fundamental miscarriage of justice" has occurred. ** ("If a petitioner such as Schlup presents [adequate] evidence of innocence…the petitioner should be allowed to pass through the gateway and argue the merits"). ** That conclusion flatly contradicts the statute, and is not required by our precedent.

***

Notes

1. *Subsequent case history*

Lloyd Schlup's conviction was vacated by a federal district court. After the state refiled, he pleaded guilty and received a life sentence, which he is currently serving. Assuming Mr. Schlup was in fact innocent, what could have been some of the reasons why he chose to plead guilty?

2. *Equitable remedy*

In what ways did the concept of the writ of habeas corpus as an equitable remedy inform the Court's decision?

3. *The "gateway"*

The Court adopts the *Carrier* gateway standard for Schlup's case, maintaining that a petitioner such as Schlup must show that it is more likely than not that no reasonable juror would have found petitioner guilty beyond a reasonable doubt. Why did the

Court reject the *Sawyer* standard for the *Carrier* standard in this case? After *Schlup*, how clear is the Court's standard for passing through the "gate"?

Is Innocence Irrelevant?
Collateral Attack on Criminal Judgments
Henry J. Friendly
38 U. Chi. L. Rev. 142 (1970)
Copyright © by University of Chicago Law Review

Legal history has many instances where a remedy initially serving a felt need has expanded bit by bit, without much thought being given to any single step, until it has assumed an aspect so different from its origin as to demand reappraisal—agonizing or not. That, in my view, is what has happened with respect to collateral attack on criminal convictions. After trial, conviction, sentence, appeal, affirmance, and denial of certiorari by the Supreme Court, in proceedings where the defendant had the assistance of counsel at every step, the criminal process, in Winston Churchill's phrase, has not reached the end, or even the beginning of the end, but only the end of the beginning. Any murmur of dissatisfaction with this situation provokes immediate incantation of the Great Writ, with the inevitable initial capitals, often accompanied by a suggestion that the objector is the sort of person who would cheerfully desecrate the Ark of the Covenant. My thesis is that, with a few important exceptions, convictions should be subject to collateral attack only when the prisoner supplements his constitutional plea with a colorable claim of innocence.

If there be fear that merely listening to such a proposal may contaminate, let me attempt to establish respectability by quoting two statements of Mr. Justice Black:

> [T]he defendant's guilt or innocence is at least one of the vital considerations in determining whether collateral relief should be available to a convicted defendant. ***

And more strongly:

> In collateral attacks...I would always require that the convicted defendant raise the kind of constitutional claim that casts some shadow of a doubt on his guilt. ***

Incredibly, these statements were made in dissent. Even more incredibly, the two other dissenting Justices expressed qualms about them. *** I believe, with qualifications I will elaborate, that this position ought to be the law and that legislation can and should make it so. When I speak of legislation, I am thinking mainly of federal habeas corpus for state prisoners and its equivalent for federal prisoners, since no other course seems realistic in light of Supreme Court opinions. In many states it may still be possible to reach the proper result by judicial decision. Although, if past experience is any guide, I am sure I will be accused of proposing to abolish habeas corpus, my aim is rather to restore the Great Writ to its deservedly high estate and rescue it from the disrepute invited by current excesses.

Seventeen years ago, in his concurring opinion in *Brown v. Allen*, 344 U.S. 443 (1953), Mr. Justice Jackson expressed deep concern over the "floods of stale, frivolous and repetitious petitions [for federal habeas corpus by state prisoners which] inundate the docket of the lower courts and swell our own." The inundation consisted of 541 such petitions. In 1969, state prisoners filed 7,359 petitions for habeas corpus in the federal district courts, a 100 per cent increase over 1964." ** Federal prisoners filed

2,817 petitions challenging convictions or sentences, a 50 percent increase over 1964. **
Prisoner petitions, including those attacking the conduct of prison officials, totaled
12,924. These "comprise the largest single element in the civil caseload of the district
courts" and "accounted for more than one-sixth of the civil filings." ** There has been a
corresponding increase in the load imposed by post-conviction petitions upon the federal courts of appeals. Despite the safeguard intended to be afforded by the requirement
of a certificate of probable cause, ** there were over twice as many *appeals* by state prisoners in 1969 as there were *petitions* in 1952. ** A similar explosion of collateral attack
has occurred in the courts of many of the states. If 541 annual petitions for federal
habeas corpus by state prisoners were an "inundation," what is the right word for
7,500? **

The proverbial man from Mars would surely think we must consider our system of
criminal justice terribly bad if we are willing to tolerate such efforts at undoing judgments of conviction. He would be surprised, I should suppose, to be told both that it
never was really bad and that it has been steadily improving, particularly because of the
Supreme Court's decision that an accused, whatever his financial means, is entitled to
the assistance of counsel at every critical stage. ** His astonishment would grow when
we told him that the one thing almost never suggested on collateral attack is that the
prisoner was innocent of the crime. ** His surprise would mount when he learned that
collateral attack on a criminal conviction by a court of general jurisdiction is almost unknown in the country that gave us the writ of habeas corpus and has been long admired
for its fair treatment of accused persons. ** With all this, and with the American Bar Association having proposed standards relating to post-conviction remedies ** which, despite some kind words about finality, in effect largely repudiate it, the time is ripe for
reflection on the right road for the future.

I wish to emphasize at the outset that my chief concern is about the basic principle of
collateral attack, rather than with the special problem of federal relief for state prisoners
which has absorbed so much attention since *Brown v. Allen*. I must therefore make my
main analysis in the context of a unitary system. My model will be designed for our
only pure example of a unitary structure, the federal system when dealing with federal
convictions. Later I shall advocate adoption of the same model by the states for their
much larger number of prisoners and of corresponding changes with respect to federal
habeas for state prisoners. I shall conclude by showing that these proposals are wholly
consistent with the Constitution.

I

For many reasons, collateral attack on criminal convictions carries a serious burden of
justification.

First, as Professor Bator has written, "it is essential to the educational and deterrent
functions of the criminal law that we be able to say that one violating the law will swiftly
and certainly become subject to punishment, just punishment," ** It is not an answer
that a convicted defendant generally remains in prison while collateral attack is pending.
Unbounded willingness to entertain attacks on convictions must interfere with at least
one aim of punishment—"a realization by the convict that he is justly subject to sanction, that he stands in need of rehabilitation." This process can hardly begin "if society
continuously tells the convict that he may not be justly subject to reeducation and treatment in the first place." ** Neither is it an adequate answer that repentance and rehabilitation may be thought unlikely in many of today's prisons. That is a separate and serious
problem, demanding our best thought ** but irrelevant to the issue here.

A second set of difficulties arises from the fact that under our present system collateral attack may be long delayed—in *habeas corpus* as long as the custody endures, is in federal *coram nobis* forever. ** The longer the delay, the less the reliability of the determination of any factual issue giving rise to the attack. ** It is chimerical to suppose that police officers can remember what warnings they gave a particular suspect ten years ago, although the prisoner will claim to remember very well. Moreover, although successful attack usually entitles the prisoner only to a retrial, a long delay makes this a matter of theory only." ** Inability to try the prisoner is even more likely in the case of collateral attack on convictions after guilty pleas, since there will be no transcript of testimony of witnesses who are no longer available. ** Although the longer the attack has been postponed, the larger the proportion of the sentence that will have been served, we must assume that the entire sentence was warranted. ** The argument against this, that only a handful of prisoners gain release, whether absolute or conditional, by post-conviction remedies, is essentially self-defeating, ** even if it is factually correct. To such extent as accurate figures might indicate the problem of release to have been exaggerated, they would also show what a gigantic waste of effort a collateral attack has come to be. A remedy that produces no result in the overwhelming majority of cases, apparently well over ninety percent, an unjust one to the state in much of the exceedingly small minority, and a truly good one only rarely, would seem to need reconsideration with a view to caring for the unusual case of the innocent man without being burdened by so much dross in the process.

Indeed, the most serious single evil with today's proliferation of collateral attack is its drain upon the resources of the community—judges, prosecutors, and attorneys appointed to aid the accused, and even of that oft overlooked necessity, courtrooms. Today of all times we should be conscious of the falsity of the bland assumption that these are in endless supply. ** Everyone concerned with the criminal process, whether his interest is with the prosecution, with the defense, or with neither, agrees that our greatest single problem is the long delay in bringing accused persons to trial. ** The time of judges, prosecutors, and lawyers now devoted to collateral attacks, most of them frivolous, would be much better spent trying cases. To say we must provide fully for both has a virtuous sound but ignores the finite amount of funds available in the face of competing demands.

A fourth consideration is Justice Jackson's never refuted observation that "[i]t must prejudice the occasional meritorious application to be buried in a flood of worthless ones." ** The thought may be distasteful but no judge can honestly deny it is real.

Finally, there is the point which, as Professor Bator says, is "difficult to formulate because so easily twisted into an expression of mere complacency." ** This is the human desire that things must sometime come to an end. Mr. Justice Harlan has put it as well as anyone:

> Both the individual criminal defendant and society have an interest in insuring that there will at some point be the certainty that comes with an end to litigation, and that attention will ultimately be focused not on whether a conviction was free from error but rather on whether the prisoner can be restored to a useful place in the community. **

Beyond this, it is difficult to urge public respect for judgments of criminal courts in one breath and to countenance free reopening of them in the next. I say "free" because, as I will later show, the limitation of collateral attack to "constitutional" grounds has become almost meaningless.

These five objections are not all answered by the Supreme Court's conclusory pronouncement: "Conventional notions of finality of litigation have no place where life or liberty is at stake and infringement of constitutional rights is alleged." ** Why do they have *no* place? One will readily agree that "where life or liberty is at stake," different rules should govern the determination of guilt than when only property is at issue: The prosecution must establish guilt beyond a reasonable doubt, the jury must be unanimous, the defendant need not testify, and so on. The defendant must also have a full and fair opportunity to show an infringement of constitutional rights by the prosecution even though his guilt is clear. I would agree that even when he has had all this at trial and on appeal, "[t]he policy against incarcerating or executing an innocent man… should far outweigh the desired termination of litigation." ** But this shows only that "conventional notions of finality" should not have *as much* place in criminal as in civil litigation, not that they should have *none*. A statement like that just quoted, entirely sound with respect to a man who is or may be innocent, is readily metamorphosed into broader ones, such as the Supreme Court's pronouncement mentioned above, ** expansive enough to cover a man steeped in guilt who attacks his conviction years later because of some technical error by the police that was or could have been considered at his trial.

Admittedly, reforms such as I am about to propose might not immediately meet some of these points. Aside from the most drastic measures, ** changes that would narrow the grounds available for collateral attack would not necessarily discourage prisoners from trying; they have everything to gain and nothing to lose. Indeed, collateral attack may have become so much a way of prison life as to have created its own self-generating force: it may now be considered merely something done as a matter of course during long incarceration. Today's growing number of prisoner petitions despite the minute percentage granted points that way. But I would hope that over a period of time the trend could be reversed, although the immediate response might be less than dramatic. Furthermore, a requirement that, with certain exceptions, an applicant for habeas corpus must make a colorable showing of innocence would enable courts of first instance to screen out rather rapidly a great multitude of applications not deserving their attention and devote their time to those few where injustice may have been done, and would affect an even greater reduction in the burden on appellate courts. In any event, if we are dissatisfied with the present efflorescence of collateral attack on criminal convictions and yet are as unwilling as I am to outlaw it and rely as in England, solely on executive clemency, ** it is important to consider reform. If mine is not the best mousetrap, perhaps it may lead others to develop a better one.

II

Broadly speaking, the original sphere for collateral attack on a conviction was where the tribunal lacked jurisdiction either in the usual sense ** or because the statute under which the defendant had been prosecuted was unconstitutional ** or because the sentence was one the court could not lawfully impose. ** Thirty years ago, in approving the use of habeas corpus to invalidate a federal conviction where the defendant had lacked the assistance of counsel, Mr. Justice Black was careful to kiss the jurisdictional book. ** He said that although the court may indeed have had "jurisdiction" at the beginning of the trial, this could be lost "due to failure to complete the court" as the sixth amendment was thought to require. **

*** In such cases the criminal process itself has broken down; the defendant has not had the kind of trial the Constitution guarantees. To be sure, there remains a question why, if the issue could have been raised on appeal and either was not or was decided adversely, the defendant should have a further opportunity to air it. ** Still, in these cases where the attack concerns the very basis of the criminal process, few would object to allowing collateral attack regardless of the defendant's probable guilt. These cases would include all those in which the defendant claims he was without counsel to whom he was constitutionally entitled. This need not rest on Justice Black's "jurisdictional" approach. For, as Justice Schaefer of Illinois has so wisely said, "Of all the rights that an accused person has, the right to be represented by counsel is by far the most pervasive, for it affects his ability to assert any other rights he may have." **

Another area in which collateral attack is readily justified irrespective of any question of innocence is where a denial of constitutional rights is claimed on the basis of facts which "are *dehors* the record and their effect on the judgment was not open to consideration and review on appeal." ** The original judgment is claimed to have been perverted, and collateral attack is the only avenue for the defendant to vindicate his rights. Examples are convictions on pleas of guilty obtained by improper means, ** or on evidence known to the prosecution to be perjured, ** or where it later appears that the defendant was incompetent to stand trial. **

A third justifiable area for collateral attack irrespective of innocence is where the state has failed to provide proper procedure for making a defense at trial and on appeal. The paradigm is *Jackson v. Denno*, 378 U.S. 368 (1964), allowing collateral attack by federal habeas corpus on all New York convictions where the voluntariness of a confession had been submitted to the jury without a proper determination by the judge. Whether the case called for retroactive remedy imposed may be debatable; in my view, the former New York procedure, although surely inferior to that prescribed by the Supreme Court, was a long way from being so shocking that it demanded the hundreds of state *corum nobis* and federal habeas corpus proceedings for past convictions which *Jackson* spawned. ** Still, one can hardly quarrel with the proposition that if a state does not afford a proper way of raising a constitutional defense at trial, it must be afforded one thereafter, and this without a colorable showing of innocence by the defendant.

New constitutional developments relating to criminal procedure are another special case. The American Bar Association Report says that these produce a growing pressure for post-conviction remedies. ** But here the Supreme Court itself has given us the lead. In only a few instances has it determined that its decisions shall be fully retroactive—the right to counsel, *Jackson v. Denno*, equal protections claims, ** the sixth amendment right to confrontation, ** and double jeopardy. ** In most cases the Court has ruled that its new constitutional decisions concerning criminal procedure need not be made available for collateral attack on earlier convictions. These include the extension to the states of the exclusionary rule with respect to illegally seized evidence, ** the prohibition of comment on a defendant's failure to take the stand, ** the rules concerning interrogation of persons in custody, ** the right to a jury trial in state criminal cases, ** the requirement of counsel at line-ups, ** and the application of the fourth amendment to nontrespassory wiretapping. ** While neither a state nor the United States is bound to limit collateral attack on the basis of a new constitutional rule of criminal procedure to what the Supreme Court holds to be demanded, I see no occasion to be holier than the pope.

None of these four important but limited lines of decision supports the broad proposition that collateral attack should always be open for the asserted denial of a "constitutional" right, even though this was or could have been litigated in the criminal trial and on appeal. The belief that it should stems mainly from the Supreme Court's construction of the Habeas Corpus Act of 1867 ** and its successors, ** providing that the writ may issue "in all cases where any person may be restrained of his or her liberty in violation of the constitution, or any other treaty or law of the United States." Despite this language no one supposes that a person who is confined after a proper trial, may mount a collateral attack because the court has misinterpreted a law of the United States; ** indeed the Supreme Court has explicitly decided the contrary even where the error was as apparent as could be. ** In such instances we are content that "conventional notions of finality" should keep an innocent man in prison unless, as one would hope, executive clemency releases him.

As a matter of ordinary reading of language, it is hard to see how the result can be different when a constitutional claim has been rejected, allegedly in error, after thoroughly constitutional proceedings, and the history does not suggest that the statute was so intended. ** The reason why the Supreme Court did so construe the Act in *Brown v. Allen* ** was, I believe, its consciousness that, with the growth of the country and the attendant increase in the Court's business, it could no longer perform its historic function of correcting constitutional error in criminal cases by review of judgments of state courts and had to summon the inferior federal judges to its aid. ** Once it was held that state prisoners could maintain proceedings in the federal courts to attack convictions for constitutional error after full and fair proceedings in the state courts, it was hard to read the same statutory words as meaning less for federal prisoners, even though the policy considerations were quite different. ** And once all this was decided, it was easy to slide into the belief that the states should, or even must, similarly expand their own procedures for collateral attack.

With a commentator's ability to consider policy free from imprisonment by statutory language, I perceive no general principle mandating a second round of attacks simply because the alleged error is a "constitutional" one. We have been conclusorily told there is "an institutional need for separate proceeding—one insulated from inquiry into the guilt or innocence of the defendant and designed specifically to protect constitutional rights." ** No empirical data is cited to support this, and so far as concerns proceeding within the same system, it seems fanciful. The supposition that the judge who has overlooked or disparaged constitutional contentions presented on pre-trial motions to suppress evidence or in the course of trial will avidly entertain claims of his own error after completion of the trial and a guilty verdict defies common sense. **

The dimensions of the problem of collateral attack today are a consequence of two developments. ** One has been the Supreme Court's imposition of the rules of the fourth, fifth, sixth, and eighth amendments concerning unreasonable searches and seizures, double jeopardy, speedy trial, compulsory self-incrimination, jury trial in criminal cases, confrontation of adverse witnesses, assistance of counsel, and cruel and unusual punishments, upon state criminal trials. The other has been a tendency to read these provisions with ever increasing breadth. The Bill of Rights, as I warned in 1965, has become a detailed Code of Criminal Procedure, ** to which a new chapter is added every year. The result of these two developments has been a vast expansion of the claims of error in criminal cases for which a resourceful defense lawyer can find a constitutional basis.

Any claimed violation of the hearsay rule is now regularly presented not as a mere trial error but as an infringement of the sixth amendment right to confrontation. ** Denial of adequate opportunity for impeachment would seem as much a violation of the confrontation clause as other restrictions on cross-examination have been held to be. ** Refusal to give the name and address of an informer can be cast as a denial of the sixth amendment's guarantee of "compulsory process for obtaining witnesses." Inflammatory summations or an erroneous charge on the prosecution's burden of proof ** become denials of due process. So are errors in identification procedures. ** Instructing a deadlocked jury of its duty to attempt to reach a verdict ** or undue participation by the judge in the examination of witnesses can be characterized as violations of the sixth amendment to a jury trial. Examples could readily be multiplied. Today it is the rare criminal appeal that does *not* involve a "constitutional" claim.

I am not now concerned with the merits of these decisions which, whether right or wrong, have become part of our way of life. What I do challenge is the assumption that simply because a claim can be characterized as "constitutional," it should necessarily constitute a basis for collateral attack when there has been fair opportunity to litigate it at trial and on appeal. Whatever may have been true when the Bill of Rights was read to protect a state criminal defendant only if the state had acted in a manner "repugnant to the conscience of mankind," ** the rule prevailing when *Brown v. Allen* was decided, the "constitutional" label no longer assists in appraising how far society should go in permitting relitigation of criminal convictions. It carries a connotation of outrage—the mob-dominated jury, the confession extorted by the rack, the defendant deprived of counsel—which is wholly misplaced when, for example, the claim is a pardonable but allegedly mistaken belief that probable cause existed for an arrest or that a statement by a person not available for cross-examination came within an exception to the hearsay rule. A judge's overly broad construction of a penal statute can be much more harmful to a defendant than unwarranted refusal to compel a prosecution witness on some peripheral element of the case to reveal his address. ** If a second round on the former is not permitted, and no one suggests it should be, I see no justification for one on the latter in the absence of a colorable showing of innocence.

It defies good sense to say that after government has afforded a defendant every means to avoid conviction, not only on the merits but by preventing the prosecution from utilizing probative evidence obtained in violation of his constitutional rights, he is entitled to repeat engagements directed to issues of the latter type even though his guilt is patent. A rule recognizing this would go a long way toward halting the "inundation;" it would permit the speedy elimination of most of the petitions that are hopeless on the facts and the law, themselves a great preponderance of the total, and of others, where, because of previous opportunity to litigate the point, release of a guilty man is not required in the interest of justice even though he might have escaped deserved punishment in the first instance with a brighter lawyer or a different judge.

***

IV

Before going further I should clarify what I mean by a colorable showing of innocence. I can begin with a negative. A defendant would not bring himself within this criterion by showing that he might not, or even would not, have been convicted in the absence of evidence claimed to have been unconstitutionally obtained. Many offenders, for example, could not be convicted without the introduction of property seized from their persons, homes, or offices. On the other hand, except for the usual case where there is an issue with respect to the defendant's connection with the property, such evidence is the clearest proof of guilt, and a defendant would not come within the criterion simply because the jury might not, or even probably would not, have convicted without the seized property being in evidence. Perhaps as good a formulation of the criterion as any is that the petitioner for collateral attack must show a fair probability that, in light of all the evidence, including that alleged to have been illegally admitted (but with due regard to any unreliability of it) and evidence tenably claimed to have been wrongly excluded or to have become available only after the trial, the trier of the facts would have entertained a reasonable doubt of his guilt. **

As indicated, my proposal would almost always preclude collateral attack on claims of illegal search and seizure. ***

***

Another type of claim, certain to be a prodigious litigation breeder, concerning which I would forbid collateral attack in the absence of a colorable showing of innocence, consists of cases arising under *Miranda v. Arizona*, 384 U.S. 436 (1966). Consider, for example, one of the knottiest problems in the application of that case, namely, whether questioning by law enforcement officers without *Miranda* warnings took place "after a person has been taken into custody or otherwise deprived of his freedom of action in any significant way." ** Almost all defense lawyers, indeed many defendants themselves, must be aware of the Supreme Court's new requirements about questioning in the station house. But suppose the lawyer does not know that *Miranda* may apply prior to the defendant's arrival there, or that he does not correctly understand what the field of application is, or that a court properly seized of the problem has held *Miranda* to be inapplicable and this is arguably wrong under existing or later decisions. This is generally not "the kind of constitutional claim that casts some shadow of doubt" upon the defendant's guilt. ** The mere failure to administer *Miranda* warnings in on-the-scene questioning creates little risk of unreliability, and the deterrent value of permitting collateral attack goes beyond the point of diminishing returns. *** I would take the same view on collateral attack based on claims of lack of full warnings or voluntary waiver with respect to station-house questioning where there is no indication of the use of methods that might cast doubt on the reliability of the answers.

The confession involuntary in the pre-*Miranda* sense helps to illustrate where I would draw the line. In a case where the prosecution had no other substantial evidence, as, for example, when identification testimony was weak or conflicting and there was nothing else, I would allow collateral attack regardless of what happened in the original proceedings. Such a case fits the formula that considerations of finality should not keep a possibly innocent man in jail. I would take a contrary view where the state had so much other evidence, even though some of this was obtained as a result of the confession, ** as to eliminate any reasonable doubt of guilt.

Neither your patience nor mine would tolerate similar examination of the application of my proposal to all constitutional claims. Such soundings as I have taken convince me that in other contexts as well the proposal would fully protect the innocent, while relieving the courts of most of the collateral challenges with which they are now unnecessarily burdened.

V

Assuming that collateral attack by federal prisoners should be restricted as I have suggested, what should be done with respect to the far more numerous prisoners held by the states, in whose hands the maintenance of public order largely rests? ** The subject has two aspects: The first is whether any changes should be made with respect to federal habeas corpus for state prisoners. The second is whether, in formulating their own procedures, the states should do what they would deem appropriate in the absence of the likelihood of a federal proceeding or should allow collateral attack in every case where the eyes of the federal big brother may penetrate.

At first blush it might seem that to whatever extent collateral attack on criminal judgments should be restricted within a unitary system, it ought to be even more so when one system operates on the judgments of another. The case to the contrary rests primarily on the practical inability of the Supreme Court to correct "constitutional" errors in state criminal proceedings through the appellate process. ** There is, of course, no such impediment when the issue is an important rule of criminal procedure as contrasted to its application in a particular case. The attack on the New York procedure concerning confessions is a good illustration; ** although the decision chanced to be made in federal habeas corpus, it could have been made just as well when the issue had been presented eleven years earlier on direct review, ** and the problem would surely have again arisen in that form if the *Jackson* case had not come along. Almost all the Court's most important decisions on criminal procedure, for example, those relating to equal protection for indigent defendants, ** comment on a defendant's failure to testify, ** the extension to the states of the exclusionary rule with respect to illegally seized evidence, ** confrontation, ** and custodial interrogation, ** have been made on direct review of state judgments. **

The argument for federal habeas corpus with respect to prisoners who have had a full and fair hearing and determination of their constitutional claims in the state courts thus must relate to two other categories of constitutional claims—disputed determinations of fact and the application of legal standards. The contention is that only federal judges, with the protections of life tenure and supposedly greater knowledge of and sympathy for the Supreme Court's interpretations of the Constitution, can be trusted with the "final say" in such matters, although great deference to state factual determinations is required. ** While, if I were to rely solely on my own limited experience, I would think the case for the final federal say has been considerably exaggerated, ** I do not wish to add to the large amount of literature on this point. **

Assuming the final federal say is here to stay, is there any way to accelerate it and thereby avoid the upsetting of a conviction by a federal court when the state can no longer conduct a retrial? One way would be to route appeals from state criminal decisions, whether on direct or on collateral attack, to a federal appellate tribunal—either the appropriate court of appeals or a newly created court **—and preclude federal habeas corpus as to issues for which that remedy is available. Although a number of different models could be visualized, one possibility would be this: After a state rule but upon a state fact-finding or application of a federal constitutional rule, a petition for review would lie not to the Supreme Court but to the federal appellate court. ** The standard for granting such review would be quite different from the Supreme Court's on certiorari. It would be more like what the courts of appeals now apply with respect to certificates of probable cause in state prisoner cases—not whether the issue was important to the law but whether the appeal raised a substantial claim of violation of constitutional rights. The criterion for such *appellate* review would thus be considerably more liberal than I have proposed with respect to *collateral attack* within a unitary system. When a prisoner had failed to seek such review, or the appellate court had declined to grant it or had decided adversely federal habeas corpus with respect to any issue that could have been so presented would be foreclosed, except for those cases where I would preserve collateral attack within a unitary system, and for them only if the state had not provided means for collateral attack in its own courts. Where it did, the prisoner must use it, and final state decisions would be reviewable in the same manner as proposed for state decisions on direct appeal.

Such a scheme would preserve the original understanding that judgments of the highest courts of the states are to be re-examined only by a federal appellate court rather than at nisi prius. ** More important, it would force the prisoner to use his federal remedy while the record is reasonably fresh and a retrial is practical. While the proposal depends on the state court's having made an adequate record and findings, the court of appeals could remand where it had not. Perhaps the most serious objection is that unless review by the Supreme Court were severely restricted, or stays in non-capital cases pending application for such review were forbidden, insertion of an appeal to a lower federal appellate tribunal would further postpone the date when a convicted prisoner begins to serve his sentence. I advance the suggestion only as one warranting discussion, to take place in the larger context of whether the time has not come when the Supreme Court should be relieved of some of its burdens.

Whether there is merit in this proposal or not, I would subject federal habeas for state prisoners to the same limitations that I have proposed for federal prisoners. With the four exceptions noted at the outset, I see no sufficient reason for federal intervention on behalf of a state prisoner who raised or had an opportunity to raise his constitutional claim in the state courts, in the absence of a colorable showing of innocence. It is sufficient if the benefit of fact-finding and the application of constitutional standards by a federal judge is available in cases of that sort.

Assuming that nothing happens on the federal scene, whether through congressional inertia or otherwise, what should the states do with respect to their own systems for collateral attack on convictions? In my view, if a state considers that its system of post-conviction remedies should take the lines I have proposed, it should feel no obligation to go further simply because this will leave some cases where the only postconviction review will be in a federal court.

I realize this may seem to run counter to what has become the received wisdom, even among many state judges and prosecutors. One part of the angry reaction of the Conference of State Chief Justices to *Brown v. Allen* ** was the recommendation that:

> State statutes should provide a postconviction process at least as broad in scope as existing Federal statutes under which claims of violation of constitutional right asserted by State prisoners are determined in Federal courts under Federal habeas corpus statutes. **

The recommendation for broadening state post-conviction remedies was doubtless salutary in 1954 when many states had few or none. ** As my remarks have made evident, I recognize a considerable area for collateral attack; indeed, I think there are circumstances, such as post-trial discovery of the knowing use of material perjured evidence by the prosecutor or claims of coercion to plead guilty, where failure to provide this would deny due process of law. ** My submission here is simply that when a state has done what it considers right and has met due process standards, it should not feel obliged to do more *merely* because federal habeas may be available in some cases where it declines to allow state collateral attack.

The argument against this is that making the state post-conviction remedy fully congruent with federal habeas for state prisoners (1) will economize judicial time, (2) will reduce state-federal conflict, and (3) will provide a record on which the federal judge can act. Except for the few cases where pursuit of the state remedy will result in a release, absolute or conditional, the first argument rests on the premise that many state prisoners will accept the state's adverse judgment. I know of no solid evidence to support this; ** my impression is that prisoners unsuccessful in their post-conviction applications through the state hierarchy almost inevitably have to go at federal habeas, save when their sentences have expired. In the great majority of cases the job simply has to be done twice. Pleasant though it is for federal judges to have the task initially performed by their state brethren, the over-all result is to increase the claims on judicial and prosecutorial time. The conflict that would otherwise exist is avoided only in the rare instances where the state itself grants release and, more important, in cases where it finds the facts more favorably to the prosecution than a federal judge would do independently, but the latter respects the state determination. ** This last is also the real bite in the point about record making. ** It is, of course, somewhat ironic that after federal habeas has been justified in part on the basis of the superiority of fact determinations by the federal judge, the states should be urged to elaborate their post-conviction remedies so as to enable him to avoid the task. Moreover, conflict is even more acrid when a federal judge rejects not simply a state determination after trial and appeal but also its denial of post-conviction relief. ** It should be remembered also that my proposal contemplates state post-conviction record making when there is new evidence that was not available at trial, and that the state trial or pre-trial proceedings will contain a record whenever the point was then raised. The problem areas would thus largely be cases where the point could have been but was not raised at state trial. ** Be all this as it may, such considerations are for the state to weigh against what it may well consider an excessive expenditure of effort in dealing with collateral attack. While the immediate result of a state's failure to provide the full panoply of post-conviction remedies now available in federal habeas would be an increase in the burdens on the federal courts, this might afford the impetus necessary to prod Congress into action.

VI

***

My submission, therefore, is that innocence should not be irrelevant on collateral attack even though it may continue to be largely so on direct appeal. To such extent as we have gone beyond this, and it is an enormous extent, the system needs revision to prevent abuse by prisoners, a waste of the precious and limited resources available for the criminal process, and public disrespect for the judgments of criminal courts.

Notes

1. *Overuse of the writ?*

Judge Friendly is highly critical of what he perceives to be the overuse of the writ of habeas corpus within the judicial system. He says that labeling an error one of constitutional dimension as a road into the federal courts does nothing to limit the availability of federal review. Is the judge right?

2. *Limitations in federal review*

In advocating federal review only for petitioners who assert innocence claims, Judge Friendly states:

> It defies good sense to say that after government has afforded a defendant every means to avoid conviction, not only on the merits but by preventing the prosecution from utilizing probative evidence obtained in violation of his constitutional rights, he is entitled to repeat engagements directed to issues of the latter type even though his guilt is patent. A rule recognizing this would go a long way toward halting the "inundation;" it would permit the speedy elimination of most of the petitions that are hopeless on the facts and the law, themselves a great preponderance of the total, and of others where, because of previous op-

portunity to litigate the point, release of a guilty man is not required in the interest of justice even though he might have escaped deserved punishment in the first instance with a brighter lawyer or a different judge.

Would limiting federal review to cases involving innocence be a good idea? Why or why not?

Part V

The Future of Habeas Corpus Litigation

Chapter 17

Impact of the AEDPA

On April 24, 1996, President Clinton signed the Antiterrorism and Effective Death Penalty Act into law ("AEDPA"). Because the AEDPA contained several amendments affecting federal habeas corpus law, the Supreme Court soon was asked to decide whether those amendments were constitutional.

Felker v. Turpin was decided on June 28, 1996, a mere two months after the law was enacted. The issue in *Felker* is whether the provisions in the AEDPA concerning second or successive habeas petitions unconstitutionally restrict the jurisdiction of the Court. The Court examines an amendment in the AEDPA that creates a "gatekeeping" mechanism for second or successive applications. Under that amendment, a habeas petitioner must ask a three-judge panel in the court of appeals for leave to file a second or successive habeas application in the district court. Because the new amendment also provided that the panel's decision—either granting or denying permission to file a second or successive application—is not appealable and shall not be the subject of a petition for rehearing or for a writ of certiorari, the Court questions whether such a restriction is constitutional. Ultimately, the Court finds that it is.

In *Clay v. United States*, the Court examines how Sections 2255 and 2244(d)(1) were reshaped by the AEDPA. Prior to the AEDPA, no statute of limitations existed to govern requests for federal habeas corpus relief. The AEDPA established a one-year statute of limitations, although the language of the statute did not clearly state when the one-year limitation period begins. The Court determined that a judgment of conviction becomes final when the time expires for filing a petition for certiorari contesting the appellate court's affirmation of the conviction, and that is the date the Court determined the limitation period begins to run.

In *Lockyer v. Andrade*, which was decided one day after *Clay v. United States*, the Court examines the degree to which the AEDPA limits a federal habeas court's review of a state court decision. After observing that the AEDPA does not require a federal habeas court to adopt any one methodology in deciding whether a state court decision is contrary to, or involved an unreasonable application of, clearly established Federal law, the Court explores what constitutes "clearly established Federal law." The Court then decides that one governing legal principle that is "clearly established" under section 2254(d)(1) is the "gross disproportionality" of sentences. Applying this principle to Andrade's sentence of two consecutive terms of 25 years to life, the Court finds that Andrade's sentence is neither contrary to, nor involved an unreasonable application of, the principle of gross disproportionality—even though his crime was stealing a total of nine videotapes from two different Kmart stores: five on November 4, 1995, and four on November 18, 1995.

Felker v. Turpin

518 U.S. 651 (1996)

CHIEF JUSTICE REHNQUIST delivered the opinion of the Court.

Title I of the Antiterrorism and Effective Death Penalty Act of 1996 (Act) works substantial changes to chapter 153 of Title 28 of the United States Code, which authorizes federal courts to grant the writ of habeas corpus. Pub. L. 104-132, 110 Stat. 1217. We hold that the Act does not preclude this Court from entertaining an application for habeas corpus relief, although it does affect the standards governing the granting of such relief. We also conclude that the availability of such relief in this Court obviates any claim by petitioner under the Exceptions Clause of Article III, §2, of the Constitution, and that the operative provisions of the Act do not violate the Suspension Clause of the Constitution, Art. I, §9.

I

On a night in 1976, petitioner approached Jane W. in his car as she got out of hers. Claiming to be lost and looking for a party nearby, he used a series of deceptions to induce Jane to accompany him to his trailer home in town. Petitioner forcibly subdued her, raped her, and sodomized her. Jane pleaded with petitioner to let her go, but he said he could not because she would notify the police. She escaped later, when petitioner fell asleep. Jane notified the police, and petitioner was eventually convicted of aggravated sodomy and sentenced to 12 years' imprisonment.

Petitioner was paroled four years later. On November 23, 1981, he met Joy Ludlam, a cocktail waitress, at the lounge where she worked. She was interested in changing jobs, and petitioner used a series of deceptions involving offering her a job at "The Leather Shoppe," a business he owned, to induce her to visit him the next day. The last time Joy was seen alive was the evening of the next day. Her dead body was discovered two weeks later in a creek. Forensic analysis established that she had been beaten, raped, and sodomized, and that she had been strangled to death before being left in the creek. Investigators discovered hair resembling petitioner's on Joy's body and clothes, hair resembling Joy's in petitioner's bedroom, and clothing fibers like those in Joy's coat in the hatchback of petitioner's car. One of petitioner's neighbors reported seeing Joy's car at petitioner's house the day she disappeared.

A jury convicted petitioner of murder, rape, aggravated sodomy, and false imprisonment. Petitioner was sentenced to death on the murder charge. The Georgia Supreme Court affirmed petitioner's conviction and death sentence, ** and we denied certiorari. ** A state trial court denied collateral relief, the Georgia Supreme Court declined to issue a certificate of probable cause to appeal the denial, and we again denied certiorari. **

Petitioner then filed a petition for a writ of habeas corpus in the United States District Court for the Middle District of Georgia, alleging that (1) the State's evidence was insufficient to convict him; (2) the State withheld exculpatory evidence, in violation of *Brady v. Maryland*, 373 U.S. 83 (1963); (3) petitioner's counsel rendered ineffective assistance at sentencing; (4) the State improperly used hypnosis to refresh a witness' memory; and (5) the State violated double jeopardy and collateral estoppel principles by using petitioner's crime against Jane W. as evidence at petitioner's trial for crimes against Joy Ludlam. The District Court denied the petition. The United States Court of

Appeals for the Eleventh Circuit affirmed, ** extended on denial of petition for rehearing, ** and we denied certiorari. **

The State scheduled petitioner's execution for the period May 2–9, 1996. On April 29, 1996, petitioner filed a second petition for state collateral relief. The state trial court denied this petition on May 1, and the Georgia Supreme Court denied certiorari on May 2.

On April 24, 1996, the President signed the Act into law. Title I of this Act contained a series of amendments to existing federal habeas corpus law. The provisions of the Act pertinent to this case concern second or successive habeas corpus applications by state prisoners. Section 106(b) specifies the conditions under which claims in second or successive applications must be dismissed, amending 28 U.S.C. §2244(b) to read:

> (1) A claim presented in a second or successive habeas corpus application under section 2254 that was presented in a prior application shall be dismissed.

> (2) A claim presented in a second or successive habeas corpus application under section 2254 that was not presented in a prior application shall be dismissed unless—

>> (A) the applicant shows that the claim relies on a new rule of constitutional law, made retroactive to cases on collateral review by the Supreme Court, that was previously unavailable; or

>> (B)(i) the factual predicate for the claim could not have been discovered previously through the exercise of due diligence; and

>>> (ii) the facts underlying the claim, if proven and viewed in light of the evidence as a whole, would be sufficient to establish by clear and convincing evidence that, but for constitutional error, no reasonable fact-finder would have found the applicant guilty of the underlying offense.

Title 28 U.S.C.A. §2244(b)(3) (July 1996 Supp.) creates a "gatekeeping" mechanism for the consideration of second or successive applications in district court. The prospective applicant must file in the court of appeals a motion for leave to file a second or successive habeas application in the district court. §2244(b)(3)(A). A three-judge panel has 30 days to determine whether "the application makes a prima facie showing that the application satisfies the requirements of" §2244(b). §2244(b)(3)(C); see §§2244(b)(3)(B), (D). Section 2244(b)(3)(E) specifies that "the grant or denial of an authorization by a court of appeals to file a second or successive application shall not be appealable and shall not be the subject of a petition for rehearing or for a writ of certiorari."

On May 2, 1996, petitioner filed in the United States Court of Appeals for the Eleventh Circuit a motion for stay of execution and a motion for leave to file a second or successive federal habeas corpus petition under §2254. Petitioner sought to raise two claims in his second petition, the first being that the state trial court violated due process by equating guilt "beyond a reasonable doubt" with "moral certainty" of guilt in voir dire and jury instructions. See Cage v. Louisiana, 498 U.S. 39 (1990) (per curiam). He also alleged that qualified experts, reviewing the forensic evidence after his conviction, had established that Joy must have died during a period when petitioner was under police surveillance for Joy's disappearance and thus had a valid alibi. He claimed that the testimony of the State's forensic expert at trial was suspect because he is not a licensed physician, and that the new expert testimony so discredited the State's testimony at trial that petitioner had a colorable claim of factual innocence.

The Court of Appeals denied both motions the day they were filed, concluding that petitioner's claims had not been presented in his first habeas petition, that they did not meet the standards of § 2244(b)(2), and that they would not have satisfied pre-Act standards for obtaining review on the merits of second or successive claims. ** Petitioner filed in this Court a pleading styled a "Petition for Writ of Habeas Corpus, for Appellate or Certiorari Review of the Decision of the United States Circuit Court for the Eleventh Circuit, and for Stay of Execution." On May 3, we granted petitioner's stay application and petition for certiorari. We ordered briefing on the extent to which the provisions of Title I of the Act apply to a petition for habeas corpus filed in this Court, whether application of the Act suspended the writ of habeas corpus in this case, and whether Title I of the Act, especially the provision to be codified at § 2244(b)(3)(E), constitutes an unconstitutional restriction on the jurisdiction of this Court. **

II

We first consider to what extent the provisions of Title I of the Act apply to petitions for habeas corpus filed as original matters in this Court pursuant to 28 U.S.C. §§ 2241 and 2254. We conclude that although the Act does impose new conditions on our authority to grant relief, it does not deprive this Court of jurisdiction to entertain original habeas petitions.

A

Section 2244(b)(3)(E) prevents this Court from reviewing a court of appeals order denying leave to file a second habeas petition by appeal or by writ of certiorari. More than a century ago, we considered whether a statute barring review by appeal of the judgment of a circuit court in a habeas case also deprived this Court of power to entertain an original habeas petition. *Ex parte Yerger*, 75 U.S. 85 (1869). We consider the same question here with respect to § 2244(b)(3)(E).

Yerger's holding is best understood in the light of the availability of habeas corpus review at that time. Section 14 of the Judiciary Act of 1789 authorized all federal courts, including this Court, to grant the writ of habeas corpus when prisoners were "in custody, under or by colour of the authority of the United States, or [were] committed for trial before some court of the same." Act of Sept. 24, 1789, ch. 20, § 14, 1 Stat. 82. *** Congress greatly expanded the scope of federal habeas corpus in 1867, authorizing federal courts to grant the writ, "in addition to the authority already conferred by law," "in all cases where any person may be restrained of his or her liberty in violation of the constitution, or of any treaty or law of the United States." Act of Feb. 5, 1867, ch. 28, 14 Stat. 385. *** Before the Act of 1867, the only instances in which a federal court could issue the writ to produce a state prisoner were if the prisoner was "necessary to be brought into court to testify," Act of Sept. 24, 1789, ch. 20, § 14, 1 Stat. 82, was "committed...for any act done...in pursuance of a law of the United States," Act of Mar. 2, 1833, ch. 57, § 7, 4 Stat. 634–635, or was a "subject or citizen of a foreign State, and domiciled therein," and held under state law, Act of Aug. 29, 1842, ch. 257, 5 Stat. 539–540.

The Act of 1867 also expanded our statutory appellate jurisdiction to authorize appeals to this Court from the final decision of any circuit court on a habeas petition. 14 Stat. 386. This enactment changed the result of *Barry v. Mercein*, 46 U.S. 103 (1847), in which we had held that the Judiciary Act of 1789 did not authorize this Court to conduct appellate review of circuit court habeas decisions. However, in 1868, Congress revoked the appellate jurisdiction it had given in 1867, repealing "so much of the [Act of

1867] as authorizes an appeal from the judgment of the circuit court to the Supreme Court of the United States." Act of Mar. 27, 1868, ch. 34, § 2, 15 Stat. 44.

In *Yerger*, we considered whether the Act of 1868 deprived us not only of power to hear an appeal from a inferior court's decision on a habeas petition, but also of power to entertain a habeas petition to this Court under § 14 of the Act of 1789. We concluded that the 1868 Act did not affect our power to entertain such habeas petitions. We explained that the 1868 Act's text addressed only jurisdiction over appeals conferred under the Act of 1867, not habeas jurisdiction conferred under the Acts of 1789 and 1867. We rejected the suggestion that the Act of 1867 had repealed our habeas power by implication. ** Repeals by implication are not favored, we said, and the continued exercise of original habeas jurisdiction was not "repugnant" to a prohibition on review by appeal of circuit court habeas judgments. **

Turning to the present case, we conclude that Title I of the Act has not repealed our authority to entertain original habeas petitions, for reasons similar to those stated in *Yerger*. No provision of Title I mentions our authority to entertain original habeas petitions; in contrast, § 103 amends the Federal Rules of Appellate Procedure to bar consideration of original habeas petitions in the courts of appeals. *** Although § 2244(b)(3)(E) precludes us from reviewing, by appeal or petition for certiorari, a judgment on an application for leave to file a second habeas petition in district court, it makes no mention of our authority to hear habeas petitions filed as original matters in this Court. As we declined to find a repeal of §14 of the Judiciary Act of 1789 as applied to this Court by implication then, we decline to find a similar repeal of § 2241 of Title 28 — its descendant — by implication now.

This conclusion obviates one of the constitutional challenges raised. The critical language of Article III, § 2, of the Constitution provides that, apart from several classes of cases specifically enumerated in this Court's original jurisdiction, "in all the other Cases... the supreme Court shall have appellate Jurisdiction, both as to Law and Fact, with such Exceptions, and under such Regulations as the Congress shall make." Previous decisions construing this clause have said that while our appellate powers "are given by the constitution," "they are limited and regulated by the [Judiciary Act of 1789], and by such other acts as have been passed on the subject." *Durousseau v. United States*, 10 U.S. 307 (1810); *see also United States v. More*, 7 U.S. 159 (1805). The Act does remove our authority to entertain an appeal or a petition for a writ of certiorari to review a decision of a court of appeals exercising its "gatekeeping" function over a second petition. But since it does not repeal our authority to entertain a petition for habeas corpus, there can be no plausible argument that the Act has deprived this Court of appellate jurisdiction in violation of Article III, § 2.

B

We consider next how Title I affects the requirements a state prisoner must satisfy to show he is entitled to a writ of habeas corpus from this Court. Title I of the Act has changed the standards governing our consideration of habeas petitions by imposing new requirements for the granting of relief to state prisoners. Our authority to grant habeas relief to state prisoners is limited by § 2254, which specifies the conditions under which such relief may be granted to "a person in custody pursuant to the judgment of a State court." *** § 2254(a). Several sections of the Act impose new requirements for the granting of relief under this section, and they therefore inform our authority to grant such relief as well.

Section 2244(b) addresses second or successive habeas petitions. Section 2244(b)(3)'s "gatekeeping" system for second petitions does not apply to our consideration of habeas petitions because it applies to applications "filed in the district court." § 2244(b)(3)(A). There is no such limitation, however, on the restrictions on repetitive and new claims imposed by §§ 2244(b)(1) and (2). These restrictions apply without qualification to any "second or successive habeas corpus application under section 2254." §§ 2244(b)(1), (2). Whether or not we are bound by these restrictions, they certainly inform our consideration of original habeas petitions.

III

Next, we consider whether the Act suspends the writ of habeas corpus in violation of Article I, § 9, clause 2, of the Constitution. This clause provides that "the Privilege of the Writ of Habeas Corpus shall not be suspended, unless when in Cases of Rebellion or Invasion the public Safety may require it."

The writ of habeas corpus known to the Framers was quite different from that which exists today. As we explained previously, the first Congress made the writ of habeas corpus available only to prisoners confined under the authority of the United States, not under state authority. ** The class of judicial actions reviewable by the writ was more restricted as well. In *Ex parte Watkins*, 3 Pet. 193 (1830), we denied a petition for a writ of habeas corpus from a prisoner "detained in prison by virtue of the judgment of a court, which court possesses general and final jurisdiction in criminal cases." *Id.* at 202. Reviewing the English common law which informed American courts' understanding of the scope of the writ, we held that "the judgment of the circuit court in a criminal case is of itself evidence of its own legality," and that we could not "usurp that power by the instrumentality of the writ of habeas corpus." *Id.* at 207.

It was not until 1867 that Congress made the writ generally available in "all cases where any person may be restrained of his or her liberty in violation of the constitution, or of any treaty or law of the United States." ** And it was not until well into this century that this Court interpreted that provision to allow a final judgment of conviction in a state court to be collaterally attacked on habeas. *See, e.g., Waley v. Johnston*, 316 U.S. 101 (1942) (*per curiam*); *Brown v. Allen*, 344 U.S. 443 (1953). But we assume, for purposes of decision here, that the Suspension Clause of the Constitution refers to the writ as it exists today, rather than as it existed in 1789. *See Swain v. Pressley*, 430 U.S. 372 (1977).

The Act requires a habeas petitioner to obtain leave from the court of appeals before filing a second habeas petition in the district court. But this requirement simply transfers from the district court to the court of appeals a screening function which would previously have been performed by the district court as required by 28 U.S.C. § 2254 Rule 9(b). The Act also codifies some of the pre-existing limits on successive petitions, and further restricts the availability of relief to habeas petitioners. But we have long recognized that "the power to award the writ by any of the courts of the United States, must be given by written law," *Ex parte Bollman*, 8 U.S. 75 (1807), and we have likewise recognized that judgments about the proper scope of the writ are "normally for Congress to make." *Lonchar v. Thomas*, 517 U.S. 314, 323 (1996).

The new restrictions on successive petitions constitute a modified res judicata rule, a restraint on what is called in habeas corpus practice "abuse of the writ." In *McCleskey v. Zant*, 499 U.S. 467 (1991), we said that "the doctrine of abuse of the writ refers to a complex and evolving body of equitable principles informed and controlled by historical usage, statutory developments, and judicial decisions." *Id.* at 489. The added restrictions which the Act places on second habeas petitions are well within the compass of this evolutionary process, and we hold that they do not amount to a "suspension" of the writ contrary to Article I, §9.

IV

We have answered the questions presented by the petition for certiorari in this case, and we now dispose of the petition for an original writ of habeas corpus. Our Rule 20.4(a) delineates the standards under which we grant such writs:

A petition seeking the issuance of a writ of habeas corpus shall comply with the requirements of 28 U.S.C. §§ 2241 and 2242, and in particular with the provision in the last paragraph of § 2242 requiring a statement of the "reasons for not making application to the district court of the district in which the applicant is held." If the relief sought is from the judgment of a state court, the petition shall set forth specifically how and wherein the petitioner has exhausted available remedies in the state courts or otherwise comes within the provisions of 28 U.S.C. § 2254(b). To justify the granting of a writ of habeas corpus, the petitioner must show exceptional circumstances warranting the exercise of the Court's discretionary powers and must show that adequate relief cannot be obtained in any other form or from any other court. These writs are rarely granted.

Reviewing petitioner's claims here, they do not materially differ from numerous other claims made by successive habeas petitioners which we have had occasion to review on stay applications to this Court. Neither of them satisfies the requirements of the relevant provisions of the Act, let alone the requirement that there be "exceptional circumstances" justifying the issuance of the writ.

* * *

The petition for writ of certiorari is dismissed for want of jurisdiction. The petition for an original writ of habeas corpus is denied.

It is so ordered.

JUSTICE STEVENS, with whom JUSTICE SOUTER and JUSTICE BREYER join, concurring.

While I join the Court's opinion, I believe its response to the argument that the Act has deprived this Court of appellate jurisdiction in violation of Article III, §2, is incomplete. I therefore add this brief comment.

As the Court correctly concludes, the Act does not divest this Court of jurisdiction to grant petitioner relief by issuing a writ of habeas corpus. It does, however, except the category of orders entered by the courts of appeals pursuant to 28 U.S.C.A. § 2244(b)(3) from this Court's statutory jurisdiction to review cases in the courts of appeals pursuant to 28 U.S.C. § 1254(1). The Act does not purport to limit our jurisdiction under that section to review interlocutory orders in such cases, to limit our jurisdiction under § 1254(2), or to limit our jurisdiction under the All Writs Act, 28 U.S.C. § 1651.

Accordingly, there are at least three reasons for rejecting petitioner's argument that the limited exception violates Article III, §2. First, if we retain jurisdiction to review the gatekeeping orders pursuant to the All Writs Act—and petitioner has not suggested otherwise—such orders are not immune from direct review. Second, by entering an appropriate interlocutory order, a court of appeals may provide this Court with an opportunity to review its proposed disposition of a motion for leave to file a second or successive habeas application. Third, in the exercise of our habeas corpus jurisdiction, we may consider earlier gatekeeping orders entered by the court of appeals to inform our judgments and provide the parties with the functional equivalent of direct review. In this case the Court correctly denies the writ of habeas corpus because petitioner's claims do not satisfy the requirements of our pre-Act jurisprudence or the requirements of the Act, including the standards governing the court of appeals' gatekeeping function.

JUSTICE SOUTER, with whom JUSTICE STEVENS and JUSTICE BREYER join, concurring.

I join the Court's opinion. The Court holds today that the Antiterrorism and Effective Death Penalty Act of 1996, Pub. L. 104-132, 110 Stat. 1217, precludes our review, by "certiorari" or by "appeal," over the courts of appeals's "gatekeeper" determinations. *See* provision to be codified at 28 U.S.C. § 2244(b)(3)(E). The statute's text does not necessarily foreclose all of our appellate jurisdiction, *see, e.g.,* 28 U.S.C. § 1254(2) (certified questions from courts of appeals); § 1651(a) (authority to issue appropriate writs in aid of another exercise of appellate jurisdiction); this Court's Rule 20.3 (procedure for petitions for extraordinary writs), nor has Congress repealed our authority to entertain original petitions for writs of habeas corpus. *** Because petitioner sought only a writ of certiorari (which Congress has foreclosed) and a writ of habeas corpus (which, even applying the traditional criteria, we would choose to deny, see *ante*), I have no difficulty with the conclusion that the statute is not on its face, or as applied here, unconstitutional. I write only to add that if it should later turn out that statutory avenues other than certiorari for reviewing a gatekeeping determination were closed, the question whether the statute exceeded Congress's Exceptions Clause power would be open. *** The question could arise if the courts of appeals adopted divergent interpretations of the gatekeeper standard.

Notes

1. *Subsequent case history*

Ellis Wayne Felker was executed by electrocution on November 21, 1996.

2. *"New conditions" on the Court's authority to grant relief*

In his analysis, Justice Rehnquist observed that "although the Act does impose new conditions on our authority to grant relief, it does not deprive this Court of jurisdiction to entertain original habeas petitions." What are the "new conditions" to which Justice Rehnquist is referring?

3. *Souter's concurrence*

In his concurrence, Justice Souter observes that "if it should later turn out that statutory avenues other than certiorari for reviewing a gatekeeping determination were closed, the question whether the statute exceeded Congress's Exceptions Clause power would be open. The question could arise if the courts of appeals adopted divergent interpretations of the gatekeeper standard." What kind of divergent interpretations of the "gatekeeper" standard could the courts of appeals adopt?

Clay v. United States
537 U.S. 522 (2003)

JUSTICE GINSBURG delivered the opinion of the Court.

A motion by a federal prisoner for postconviction relief under 28 U.S.C. § 2255 is subject to a one-year time limitation that generally runs from "the date on which the judgment of conviction becomes final." §2255, P6(1). This case concerns the starting date for the one-year limitation. It presents a narrow but recurring question on which courts of appeals have divided: When a defendant in a federal prosecution takes an unsuccessful direct appeal from a judgment of conviction, but does not next petition for a writ of certiorari from this Court, does the judgment become "final" for postconviction relief purposes (1) when the appellate court issues its mandate affirming the conviction, or, instead, (2) on the date, ordinarily 69 days later, when the time for filing a petition for certiorari expires?

In accord with this Court's consistent understanding of finality in the context of collateral review, and the weight of lower court authority, we reject the issuance of the appellate court mandate as the triggering date. For the purpose of starting the clock on §2255's one-year limitation period, we hold, a judgment of conviction becomes final when the time expires for filing a petition for certiorari contesting the appellate court's affirmation of the conviction.

I

In 1997, petitioner Erick Cornell Clay was convicted of arson and distribution of cocaine base in the United States District Court for the Northern District of Indiana. On November 23, 1998, the Court of Appeals for the Seventh Circuit affirmed his convictions. That court's mandate issued on December 15, 1998. See Fed. Rules App. Proc. 40(a)(1) and 41(b) (when no petition for rehearing is filed, a court of appeals' mandate issues 21 days after entry of judgment). Clay did not file a petition for a writ of certiorari. The time in which he could have petitioned for certiorari expired on February 22, 1999, 90 days after entry of the Court of Appeals' judgment, see this Court's Rule 13(1), and 69 days after the issuance of the appellate court's mandate.

On February 22, 2000—one year and 69 days after the Court of Appeals issued its mandate and exactly one year after the time for seeking certiorari expired—Clay filed a motion in the District Court, pursuant to 28 U.S.C. §2255, to vacate, set aside, or correct his sentence. Congress has prescribed "[a] 1-year period of limitation" for such motions "running from the latest of" four specified dates. §2255, P6. Of the four dates, the only one relevant in this case, as in the generality of cases, is the first: "the date on which the judgment of conviction becomes final." §2255, P6(1).

Relying on *Gendron v. United States*, 154 F.3d 672, 674 (7th Cir. 1998) (*per curiam*), the District Court stated that "when a federal prisoner in this circuit does not seek certiorari..., the conviction becomes 'final' on the date the appellate court issues the mandate in the direct appeal." ** Because Clay filed his §2255 motion more than one year after that date, the court denied the motion as time barred.

The Seventh Circuit affirmed. That court declined Clay's "invitation to reconsider our holding in *Gendron*," although it acknowledged that *Gendron*'s "construction of section 2255 represents the minority view." 30 Fed. Appx. 607, 609 (2002). "Bowing to *stare decisis*," the court expressed "reluctance to overrule [its own] recently-reaffirmed precedent without guidance from the Supreme Court." *Ibid.*

The Fourth Circuit has agreed with *Gendron*'s interpretation of §2255. *See United States v. Torres*, 211 F.3d 836, 838–842 (4th Cir. 2000) (when a federal prisoner does not file a petition for certiorari, his judgment of conviction becomes final for §2255 purposes upon issuance of the court of appeals' mandate). Six Courts of Appeals have parted ways with the Seventh and Fourth Circuits. These courts hold that, for federal prisoners like Clay who do not file petitions for certiorari following affirmance of their convictions, §2255's one-year limitation period begins to run when the defendant's time for seeking review by this Court expires. *** To secure uniformity in the application of §2255's time constraint, we granted certiorari, ** and now reverse the Seventh Circuit's judgment. ***

II

Finality is variously defined; like many legal terms, its precise meaning depends on context. Typically, a federal judgment becomes final for appellate review and claim preclusion purposes when the district court disassociates itself from the case, leaving nothing to be done at the court of first instance save execution of the judgment. *See, e.g., Quackenbush v. Allstate Ins. Co.*, 517 U.S. 706, 712 (1996); Restatement (Second) of Judgments §13, Comment b (1980). For other purposes, finality attaches at a different stage. For example, for certain determinations under the Speedy Trial Act of 1974, 18 U.S.C. §3161 *et seq.*, and under a now-repealed version of Federal Rule of Criminal Procedure 33, several lower courts have held that finality attends issuance of the appellate court's mandate. ** For the purpose of seeking review by this Court, in contrast, "the time to file a petition for a writ of certiorari runs from the date of entry of the judgment or order sought to be reviewed, and not from the issuance date of the mandate (or its equivalent under local practice)." This Court's Rule 13(3).

Here, the relevant context is postconviction relief, a context in which finality has a long-recognized, clear meaning: Finality attaches when this Court affirms a conviction on the merits on direct review or denies a petition for a writ of certiorari, or when the time for filing a certiorari petition expires. *See, e.g., Caspari v. Bohlen*, 510 U.S. 383, 390 (1994); *Griffith v. Kentucky*, 479 U.S. 314, 321 n.6 (1987); *Barefoot v. Estelle*, 463 U.S. 880, 887 (1983); *United States v. Johnson*, 457 U.S. 537, 542 n.8 (1982); *Linkletter v. Walker*, 381 U.S. 618, 622 n.5 (1965). Because "we presume that Congress expects its statutes to be read in conformity with this Court's precedents," *United States v. Wells*, 519 U.S. 482, 495 (1997), our unvarying understanding of finality for collateral review purposes would ordinarily determine the meaning of "becomes final" in §2255.

Amicus urges a different determinant, relying on verbal differences between §2255 and a parallel statutory provision, 28 U.S.C. §2244(d)(1), which governs petitions for federal habeas corpus by state prisoners. ** [Section 2244 sets forth the time limit for Section 2254 petitions.] Sections 2255 and 2244(d)(1), as now formulated, were reshaped by the Antiterrorism and Effective Death Penalty Act of 1996. *See* §§101, 105, 110 Stat. 1217, 1220. Prior to that Act, no statute of limitations governed requests for federal habeas corpus or §2255 habeas-like relief. *See Vasquez v. Hillery*, 474 U.S. 254, 265 (1986). ** Like §2255, §2244(d)(1) establishes a one-year limitation period, running from the latest of four specified dates. Three of the four time triggers under §2244(d)(1) closely track corresponding portions of §2255. Compare §§2244(d)(1)(B)–(D), with §2255, PP6(2)–(4). But where §2255, P6(1), refers simply to "the date on which the judgment of conviction becomes final," §2244(d)(1)(A) speaks of "the date on which the judgment became final by the conclusion of direct review or the expiration of the time for seeking such review." ***

When "Congress includes particular language in one section of a statute but omits it in another section of the same Act," we have recognized, "it is generally presumed that Congress acts intentionally and purposely in the disparate inclusion or exclusion." *Russello v. United States*, 464 U.S. 16, 23 (1983) (quoting *United States v. Wong Kim Bo*, 472 F.2d 720, 722 (5th Cir. 1972)). Invoking the maxim recited in *Russello, amicus* asserts that "becomes final" in §2255, P6(1), cannot mean the same thing as "became final" in

§ 2244(d)(1)(A); reading the two as synonymous, *amicus* maintains, would render superfluous the words "by the conclusion of direct review or the expiration of the time for seeking such review"—words found only in the latter provision. ** We can give effect to the discrete wording of the two prescriptions, *amicus* urges, if we adopt the following rule: When a convicted defendant does not seek certiorari on direct review, § 2255's limitation period starts to run on the date the court of appeals issues its mandate. *Id.* at 36. ***

Amicus would have a stronger argument if § 2255, P6(1), explicitly incorporated the first of § 2244(d)(1)(A)'s finality formulations but not the second, so that the § 2255 text read "becomes final *by the conclusion of direct review*." Had § 2255 explicitly provided for the first of the two finality triggers set forth in § 2244(d)(1)(A), one might indeed question the soundness of interpreting § 2255 implicitly to incorporate § 2244(d)(1)(A)'s second trigger as well. As written, however, § 2255 does not qualify "becomes final" at all. Using neither of the disjunctive phrases that follow the words "became final" in § 2244(d)(1)(A), § 2255 simply leaves "becomes final" undefined.

Russello, we think it plain, hardly warrants the decision *amicus* urges, one that would hold the § 2255 petitioner to a tighter time constraint than the petitioner governed by § 2244(d)(1)(A). ***

    ***

Moreover, as Clay and the Government urge, ** one can readily comprehend why Congress might have found it appropriate to spell out the meaning of "final" in § 2244(d)(1)(A) but not in § 2255. Section 2244(d)(1) governs petitions by state prisoners. In that context, a bare reference to "became final" might have suggested that finality assessments should be made by reference to state law rules that may differ from the general federal rule and vary from State to State. *Cf. Artuz v. Bennett*, 531 U.S. 4, 8 (2000) (an application for state postconviction relief is "properly filed" for purposes of 28 U.S.C. § 2244(d)(2) "when its delivery and acceptance are in compliance with the applicable [state] laws and rules governing filings"). The words "by the conclusion of direct review or the expiration of the time for seeking such review" make it clear that finality for the purpose of § 2244(d)(1)(A) is to be determined by reference to a uniform federal rule. Section 2255, however, governs only petitions by federal prisoners; within the federal system there is no comparable risk of varying rules to guard against.

Amicus also submits that 28 U.S.C. § 2263 "reinforces" the Seventh Circuit's understanding of § 2255. ** Chapter 154 of Title 28 governs certain habeas petitions filed by death-sentenced state prisoners. Section 2263(a) prescribes a 180-day limitation period for such petitions running from "final State court affirmance of the conviction and sentence on direct review or the expiration of the time for seeking such review." That period is tolled, however, "from the date that a petition for certiorari is filed in the Supreme Court until the date of final disposition of the petition if a State prisoner files the petition to secure review by the Supreme Court of the affirmance of a capital sentence on direct review by the court of last resort of the State or other final State court decision on direct review." § 2263(b)(1).

We do not find in § 2263 cause to alter our reading of § 2255. First, *amicus'* reliance on § 2263 encounters essentially the same problem as does his reliance on § 2244(d)(1)(A): Section 2255, P6(1), refers to *neither* of the two events that § 2263(a) identifies as possible starting points for the limitation period—"affirmance of the conviction and sentence on direct review" and "the expiration of the time for seeking such review." Thus, reasoning by negative implication from § 2263 does not justify the con-

8

clusion that § 2255, P6(1)'s limitation period begins to run at one of those times rather than the other. ** Second, § 2263(a) ties the applicable limitation period to "affirmance of the conviction and sentence," while § 2255, P6(1), ties the limitation period to the date when "the judgment of conviction becomes final." *See Torres*, 211 F.3d at 845 (Hamilton, J., dissenting). "The *Russello* presumption — that the presence of a phrase in one provision and its absence in another reveals Congress' design — grows weaker with each difference in the formulation of the provisions under inspection." *Columbus v. Ours Garage & Wrecker Service, Inc.*, 536 U.S. 424, 435–436 (2002).

* * *

We hold that, for federal criminal defendants who do not file a petition for certiorari with this Court on direct review, § 2255's one-year limitation period starts to run when the time for seeking such review expires. Under this rule, Clay's § 2255 petition was timely filed. The judgment of the United States Court of Appeals for the Seventh Circuit is therefore reversed, and the case is remanded for further proceedings consistent with this opinion.

It is so ordered.

Notes

1. *Subsequent case history*

After the Supreme Court remanded the case to the Seventh Circuit, the Seventh Circuit ordered the parties to file Statements of Position. *Clay v. United States*, 69 Fed. Appx. 328 (2003). Both parties then suggested that the Seventh Circuit remand the case to the district court because the district court had never reached any aspect of Clay's section 2255 motion, other than its timeliness. The Seventh Circuit agreed and returned the case to the district court. *Id.* Clay's case was still pending before the district court when this book went to press.

2. *Practical consequences*

What are the practical consequences of this decision for the *pro se* petitioner?

Lockyer v. Andrade
538 U.S. 63 (2003)

JUSTICE O'CONNOR delivered the opinion of the Court.

This case raises the issue whether the United States Court of Appeals for the Ninth Circuit erred in ruling that the California Court of Appeal's decision affirming Leandro Andrade's two consecutive terms of 25 years to life in prison for a "third strike" conviction is contrary to, or an unreasonable application of, clearly established federal law as determined by this Court within the meaning of 28 U.S.C. § 2254(d)(1).

I
A

On November 4, 1995, Leandro Andrade stole five videotapes worth $84.70 from a Kmart store in Ontario, California. Security personnel detained Andrade as he was leaving the store. On November 18, 1995, Andrade entered a different Kmart store in Montclair, California, and placed four videotapes worth $68.84 in the rear waist band of his pants. Again, security guards apprehended Andrade as he was exiting the premises. Police subsequently arrested Andrade for these crimes.

These two incidents were not Andrade's first or only encounters with law enforcement. According to the state probation officer's presentence report, Andrade has been in and out of state and federal prison since 1982. In January 1982, he was convicted of a misdemeanor theft offense and was sentenced to 6 days in jail with 12 months' probation. Andrade was arrested again in November 1982 for multiple counts of first-degree residential burglary. He pleaded guilty to at least three of those counts, and in April of the following year he was sentenced to 120 months in prison. In 1988, Andrade was convicted in federal court of "transportation of marijuana," ** and was sentenced to eight years in federal prison. In 1990, he was convicted in state court for a misdemeanor petty theft offense and was ordered to serve 180 days in jail. In September 1990, Andrade was convicted again in federal court for the same felony of "transportation of marijuana," ** and was sentenced to 2,191 days in federal prison. And in 1991, Andrade was arrested for a state parole violation—escape from federal prison. He was paroled from the state penitentiary system in 1993.

A state probation officer interviewed Andrade after his arrest in this case. The presentence report notes:

> The defendant admitted committing the offense. The defendant further stated he went into the K-Mart Store to steal videos. He took four of them to sell so he could buy heroin. He has been a heroin addict since 1977. He says when he gets out of jail or prison he always does something stupid. He admits his addiction controls his life and he steals for his habit. **

Because of his 1990 misdemeanor conviction, the State charged Andrade in this case with two counts of petty theft with a prior conviction, in violation of Cal. Penal Code Ann. § 666 (West Supp. 2002). ** Under California law, petty theft with a prior conviction is a so-called "wobbler" offense because it is punishable either as a misdemeanor or as a felony. ** The decision to prosecute petty theft with a prior conviction as a misdemeanor or as a felony is in the discretion of the prosecutor. ** The trial court also has discretion to reduce the charge to a misdemeanor at the time of sentencing.

Under California's three strikes law, any felony can constitute the third strike, and thus can subject a defendant to a term of 25 years to life in prison. See Cal. Penal Code Ann. § 667(e)(2)(A) (West 1999). ** In this case, the prosecutor decided to charge the two counts of theft as felonies rather than misdemeanors. The trial court denied Andrade's motion to reduce the offenses to misdemeanors, both before the jury verdict and again in state habeas proceedings.

A jury found Andrade guilty of two counts of petty theft with a prior conviction. According to California law, a jury must also find that a defendant has been convicted of at least two serious or violent felonies that serve as qualifying offenses under the three strikes regime. In this case, the jury made a special finding that Andrade was convicted of three counts of first-degree residential burglary. A conviction for first-degree residential burglary qualifies as a serious or violent felony for the purposes of the three strikes law. Cal. Penal Code Ann. §§ 667.5, 1192.7 (West 1999). ** As a consequence, each of Andrade's convictions for theft under Cal. Penal Code Ann. § 666 (West Supp. 2002) triggered a separate application of the three strikes law. Pursuant to California law, the judge sentenced Andrade to two consecutive terms of 25 years to life in prison. See §§ 667(c)(6), 667(e)(2)(B). The State stated at oral argument that under the decision announced by the Supreme Court of California in *People v. Garcia*, 976 P.2d 831 (1999) — a decision that postdates his conviction and sentence — it remains "available" for Andrade to "file another State habeas corpus petition" arguing that he should serve only one term of 25 years to life in prison because "sentencing courts have a right to dismiss strikes on a count-by-count basis." **

B

On direct appeal in 1997, the California Court of Appeal affirmed Andrade's sentence of two consecutive terms of 25 years to life in prison. It rejected Andrade's claim that his sentence violates the constitutional prohibition against cruel and unusual punishment. The court stated that "the proportionality analysis" of *Solem v. Helm*, 463 U.S. 277 (1983), "is questionable in light of" *Harmelin v. Michigan*, 501 U.S. 957 (1991). ** The court then applied our decision in *Rummel v. Estelle*, 445 U.S. 263 (1980), where we rejected the defendant's claim that a life sentence was " 'grossly disproportionate' to the three felonies that formed the predicate for his sentence." *Id.* at 265. The California Court of Appeal then examined Andrade's claim in light of the facts in *Rummel*: "Comparing [Andrade's] crimes and criminal history with that of defendant Rummel, we cannot say the sentence of 50 years to life at issue in this case is disproportionate and constitutes cruel and unusual punishment under the United States Constitution." **

After the Supreme Court of California denied discretionary review, Andrade filed a petition for a writ of habeas corpus in Federal District Court. The District Court denied his petition. The Ninth Circuit granted Andrade a certificate of appealability as to his claim that his sentence violated the Eighth Amendment, and subsequently reversed the judgment of the District Court. **

   ***

We granted certiorari, ** and now reverse.

II

Andrade's argument in this Court is that two consecutive terms of 25 years to life for stealing approximately $150 in videotapes is grossly disproportionate in violation of the Eighth Amendment. Andrade similarly maintains that the state court decision affirming his sentence is "contrary to, or involved an unreasonable application of, clearly established Federal law, as determined by the Supreme Court of the United States." 28 U.S.C. § 2254(d)(1).

The AEDPA circumscribes a federal habeas court's review of a state-court decision. Section 2254 provides:

   (d) An application for a writ of habeas corpus on behalf of a person in custody pursuant to the judgment of a State court shall not be granted with respect to any claim that was adjudicated on the merits in State court proceedings unless the adjudication of the claim —

   (1) resulted in a decision that was contrary to, or involved an unreasonable application of, clearly established Federal law, as determined by the Supreme Court of the United States.

The Ninth Circuit requires federal habeas courts to review the state court decision *de novo* before applying the AEDPA standard of review. ** We disagree with this approach. The AEDPA does not require a federal habeas court to adopt any one methodology in deciding the only question that matters under § 2254(d)(1) — whether a state court decision is contrary to, or involved an unreasonable application of, clearly established Federal law. *See Weeks v. Angelone*, 528 U.S. 225 (2000). In this case, we do not reach the question whether the state court erred and instead focus solely on whether §2254(d) forecloses habeas relief on Andrade's Eighth Amendment claim.

III

A

As a threshold matter here, we first decide what constitutes "clearly established Federal law, as determined by the Supreme Court of the United States." §2254(d)(1). Andrade relies upon a series of precedents from this Court—*Rummel v. Estelle*, 445 U.S. 263 (1980), *Solem v. Helm*, 463 U.S. 277 (1983), and *Harmelin v. Michigan*, 501 U.S. 957 (1991)—that he claims clearly establish a principle that his sentence is so grossly disproportionate that it violates the Eighth Amendment. Section 2254(d)(1)'s "clearly established" phrase "refers to the holdings, as opposed to the dicta, of this Court's decisions as of the time of the relevant state-court decision." *Williams v. Taylor*, 529 U.S. 362, 412 (2000). In other words, "clearly established Federal law" under §2254(d)(1) is the governing legal principle or principles set forth by the Supreme Court at the time the state court renders its decision. *See id.* at 405, 413; *Bell v. Cone*, 535 U.S. 685, 698 (2002). In most situations, the task of determining what we have clearly established will be straightforward. The difficulty with Andrade's position, however, is that our precedents in this area have not been a model of clarity. *See Harmelin v. Michigan*, 501 U.S. at 965 (opinion of SCALIA, J.); *id.* at 996, 998 (KENNEDY, J., concurring in part and concurring in judgment). Indeed, in determining whether a particular sentence for a term of years can violate the Eighth Amendment, we have not established a clear or consistent path for courts to follow. **

B

Through this thicket of Eighth Amendment jurisprudence, one governing legal principle emerges as "clearly established" under §2254(d)(1): A gross disproportionality principle is applicable to sentences for terms of years.

Our cases exhibit a lack of clarity regarding what factors may indicate gross disproportionality. In *Solem* (the case upon which Andrade relies most heavily), we stated: "It is clear that a 25-year sentence generally is more severe than a 15-year sentence, but in most cases it would be difficult to decide that the former violates the Eighth Amendment while the latter does not." 463 U.S. at 294 (footnote omitted). And in *Harmelin*, both JUSTICE KENNEDY and JUSTICE SCALIA repeatedly emphasized this lack of clarity: that "*Solem* was scarcely the expression of clear...constitutional law," 501 U.S. at 965 (opinion of SCALIA, J.), that in "adhering to the narrow proportionality principle...our proportionality decisions have not been clear or consistent in all respects," *id.* at 996 (KENNEDY, J., concurring in part and concurring in judgment), that "we lack clear objective standards to distinguish between sentences for different terms of years," *id.* at 1001 (KENNEDY, J., concurring in part and concurring in judgment), and that the "precise contours" of the proportionality principle "are unclear," *id.* at 998 (KENNEDY, J., concurring in part and concurring in judgment).

Thus, in this case, the only relevant clearly established law amenable to the "contrary to" or "unreasonable application of " framework is the gross disproportionality principle, the precise contours of which are unclear, applicable only in the "exceedingly rare" and "extreme" case. *Id.* at 1001 (KENNEDY, J., concurring in part and concurring in judgment) (internal quotation marks omitted); *see also Solem v. Helm, supra,* at 290; *Rummel v. Estelle, supra,* at 272.

IV

The final question is whether the California Court of Appeal's decision affirming Andrade's sentence is "contrary to, or involved an unreasonable application of," this clearly established gross disproportionality principle.

First, a state court decision is "contrary to our clearly established precedent if the state court applies a rule that contradicts the governing law set forth in our cases" or "if the state court confronts a set of facts that are materially indistinguishable from a decision of this Court and nevertheless arrives at a result different from our precedent." *Williams v. Taylor, supra,* at 405–406; *see also Bell v. Cone, supra,* at 694. In terms of length of sentence and availability of parole, severity of the underlying offense, and the impact of recidivism, Andrade's sentence implicates factors relevant in both *Rummel* and *Solem.* Because *Harmelin* and *Solem* specifically stated that they did not overrule *Rummel,* it was not contrary to our clearly established law for the California Court of Appeal to turn to *Rummel* in deciding whether a sentence is grossly disproportionate. *See Harmelin, supra,* at 998 (KENNEDY, J., concurring in part and concurring in judgment); *Solem, supra,* at 288 n.13, 303–304 n.32. Indeed, *Harmelin* allows a state court to reasonably rely on *Rummel* in determining whether a sentence is grossly disproportionate. The California Court of Appeal's decision was therefore not "contrary to" the governing legal principles set forth in our cases.

Andrade's sentence also was not materially indistinguishable from the facts in *Solem.* The facts here fall in between the facts in *Rummel* and the facts in *Solem. Solem* involved a sentence of life in prison without the possibility of parole. 463 U.S. at 279. The defendant in *Rummel* was sentenced to life in prison with the possibility of parole. 445 U.S. at 267. Here, Andrade retains the possibility of parole. *Solem* acknowledged that *Rummel* would apply in a "similar factual situation." 463 U.S. at 304 n.32. And while this case resembles to some degree both *Rummel* and *Solem,* it is not materially indistinguishable from either. ** Consequently, the state court did not "confront a set of facts that are materially indistinguishable from a decision of this Court and nevertheless arrive at a result different from our precedent." *Williams v. Taylor,* 529 U.S. at 406. ***

Second, "under the 'unreasonable application' clause, a federal habeas court may grant the writ if the state court identifies the correct governing legal principle from this Court's decisions but unreasonably applies that principle to the facts of the prisoner's case." 529 U.S. 362 at 413. The "unreasonable application" clause requires the state court decision to be more than incorrect or erroneous. *Id.* at 410, 412. The state court's application of clearly established law must be objectively unreasonable. *Id.* at 409.

The Ninth Circuit made an initial error in its "unreasonable application" analysis. In *Van Tran v. Lindsey,* 212 F.3d at 1152–1154, the Ninth Circuit defined "objectively unreasonable" to mean "clear error." These two standards, however, are not the same. The gloss of clear error fails to give proper deference to state courts by conflating error (even clear error) with unreasonableness. **

It is not enough that a federal habeas court, in its "independent review of the legal question" is left with a "'firm conviction'" that the state court was "'erroneous'" 270 F.3d at 753 (quoting *Van Tran v. Lindsey, supra,* at 1153–1154). We have held precisely the opposite: "Under §2254(d)(1)'s 'unreasonable application' clause, then, a federal habeas court may not issue the writ simply because that court concludes in its independent judgment that the relevant state-court decision applied clearly established federal law erroneously or incorrectly." *Williams v. Taylor*, 529 U.S. at 411. Rather, that application must be objectively unreasonable. Id. at 409. **

Section 2254(d)(1) permits a federal court to grant habeas relief based on the application of a governing legal principle to a set of facts different from those of the case in which the principle was announced. ** Here, however, the governing legal principle gives legislatures broad discretion to fashion a sentence that fits within the scope of the proportionality principle—the "precise contours" of which "are unclear." *Harmelin v. Michigan*, 501 U.S. at 998 (KENNEDY, J., concurring in part and concurring in judgment). And it was not objectively unreasonable for the California Court of Appeal to conclude that these "contours" permitted an affirmance of Andrade's sentence.

Indeed, since *Harmelin*, several Members of this Court have expressed "uncertainty" regarding the application of the proportionality principle to the California three strikes law. *Riggs v. California*, 525 U.S. 1114, 1115 (1999) (STEVENS, J., joined by SOUTER and GINSBURG, JJ., respecting denial of certiorari) ("There is some uncertainty about how our cases dealing with the punishment of recidivists should apply"). ***

The gross disproportionality principle reserves a constitutional violation for only the extraordinary case. In applying this principle for §2254(d)(1) purposes, it was not an unreasonable application of our clearly established law for the California Court of Appeal to affirm Andrade's sentence of two consecutive terms of 25 years to life in prison.

V

The judgment of the United States Court of Appeals for the Ninth Circuit, accordingly, is reversed.

It is so ordered.

JUSTICE SOUTER, with whom JUSTICE STEVENS, JUSTICE GINSBURG, and JUSTICE BREYER join, dissenting.

The application of the Eighth Amendment prohibition against cruel and unusual punishment to terms of years is articulated in the "clearly established" principle acknowledged by the Court: a sentence grossly disproportionate to the offense for which it is imposed is unconstitutional. *See ante; Harmelin v. Michigan*, 501 U.S. 957 (1991); *Solem v. Helm*, 463 U.S. 277 (1983); *Rummel v. Estelle*, 445 U.S. 263 (1980). For the reasons set forth in JUSTICE BREYER's dissent in *Ewing v. California*, 538 U.S. 11 (2003), which I joined, Andrade's sentence cannot survive Eighth Amendment review. His criminal history is less grave than Ewing's, and yet he received a prison term twice as long for a less serious triggering offense. To be sure, this is a habeas case and a prohibition couched in terms as general as gross disproportion necessarily leaves state courts with much leeway under the statutory criterion that conditions federal relief upon finding that a state court unreasonably applied clear law, *see* 28 U.S.C. §2254(d). This case nonetheless presents two independent reasons for holding that the disproportionality review by the state court was not only erroneous but unreasonable, entitling Andrade to relief. I respectfully dissent accordingly.

The first reason is the holding in *Solem*, which happens to be our most recent effort at proportionality review of recidivist sentencing, the authority of which was not left in doubt by *Harmelin, see* 501 U.S. at 998. Although *Solem* is important for its instructions about applying objective proportionality analysis, *see* 463 U.S. at 290–292, the case is controlling here because it established a benchmark in applying the general principle. We specifically held that a sentence of life imprisonment without parole for uttering a $100 "no account" check was disproportionate to the crime, even though the defendant had committed six prior nonviolent felonies. In explaining our proportionality review, we contrasted the result with *Rummel*'s on the ground that the life sentence there had included parole eligibility after 12 years, *Solem*, 463 U.S. at 297.

The facts here are on all fours with those of *Solem* and point to the same result. *Id.* at 279–281. Andrade, like the defendant in *Solem*, was a repeat offender who committed theft of fairly trifling value, some $150, and their criminal records are comparable, including burglary (though Andrade's were residential), with no violent crimes or crimes against the person. The respective sentences, too, are strikingly alike. Although Andrade's petty thefts occurred on two separate occasions, his sentence can only be understood as punishment for the total amount he stole. The two thefts were separated by only two weeks; they involved the same victim; they apparently constituted parts of a single, continuing effort to finance drug sales; their seriousness is measured by the dollar value of the things taken; and the government charged both thefts in a single indictment. *Cf.* United States Sentencing Commission, Guidelines Manual §3D1.2 (Nov. 2002) (grouping temporally separated counts as one offense for sentencing purposes). The state court accordingly spoke of his punishment collectively as well, carrying a 50-year minimum before parole eligibility, ** and because Andrade was 37 years old when sentenced, the substantial 50-year period amounts to life without parole. *Solem, supra,* at 287 (quoting *Robinson v. California*, 370 U.S. 660, 667 (1962) (when considering whether a punishment is cruel or unusual "'the questions cannot be considered in the abstract'")); *cf. Rummel, supra,* at 280–281 (defendant's eligibility for parole in 12 years informs a proper assessment of his cruel and unusual punishment claim). The results under the Eighth Amendment should therefore be the same in each case. The only ways to reach a different conclusion are to reject the practical equivalence of a life sentence without parole and one with parole eligibility at 87, *see ante,* ("Andrade retains the possibility of parole"), or to discount the continuing authority of *Solem*'s example, as the California court did. ** The former is unrealistic; an 87-year-old man released after 50 years behind bars will have no real life left, if he survives to be released at all. And the latter, disparaging *Solem* as a point of reference on Eighth Amendment analysis, is wrong as a matter of law.

The second reason that relief is required even under the §2254(d) unreasonable application standard rests on the alternative way of looking at Andrade's 50-year sentence as two separate 25-year applications of the three-strikes law, and construing the challenge here as going to the second, consecutive 25-year minimum term triggered by a petty theft. *** To understand why it is revealing to look at the sentence this way, it helps to recall the basic difficulty inherent in proportionality review. We require the comparison of offense and penalty to disclose a truly gross disproportionality before the constitutional limit is passed, in large part because we believe that legislatures are institutionally equipped with better judgment than courts in deciding what penalty is merited by particular behavior. *Solem*, 463 U.S. at 290. In this case, however, a court is substantially aided in its reviewing function by two determinations made by the State itself.

The first is the State's adoption of a particular penalogical theory as its principal reason for shutting a three-strikes defendant away for at least 25-years. Although the State alludes in passing to retribution or deterrence, ** its only serious justification for the

25-year minimum treats the sentence as a way to incapacitate a given defendant from further crime; the underlying theory is the need to protect the public from a danger demonstrated by the prior record of violent and serious crime. *** The State, in other words, has not chosen 25 to life because of the inherent moral or social reprehensibility of the triggering offense in isolation; the triggering offense is treated so seriously, rather, because of its confirmation of the defendant's danger to society and the need to counter his threat with incapacitation. As to the length of incapacitation, the State has made a second helpful determination, that the public risk or danger posed by someone with the specified predicate record is generally addressed by incapacitation for 25 years before parole eligibility. Cal. Penal Code Ann. §667(e)(2)(A)(ii) (West 1999). The three-strikes law, in sum, responds to a condition of the defendant shown by his prior felony record, his danger to society, and it reflects a judgment that 25 years of incapacitation prior to parole eligibility is appropriate when a defendant exhibiting such a condition commits another felony.

Whether or not one accepts the State's choice of penalogical policy as constitutionally sound, that policy cannot reasonably justify the imposition of a consecutive 25-year minimum for a second minor felony committed soon after the first triggering offense. Andrade did not somehow become twice as dangerous to society when he stole the second handful of videotapes; his dangerousness may justify treating one minor felony as serious and warranting long incapacitation, but a second such felony does not disclose greater danger warranting substantially longer incapacitation. Since the defendant's condition has not changed between the two closely related thefts, the incapacitation penalty is not open to the simple arithmetic of multiplying the punishment by two, without resulting in gross disproportion even under the State's chosen benchmark. Far from attempting a novel penal theory to justify doubling the sentence, the California Court of Appeal offered no comment at all as to the particular penal theory supporting such a punishment. ** Perhaps even more tellingly, no one could seriously argue that the second theft of videotapes provided any basis to think that Andrade would be so dangerous after 25 years, the date on which the consecutive sentence would begin to run, as to require at least 25 years more. I know of no jurisdiction that would add 25 years of imprisonment simply to reflect the fact that the two temporally related thefts took place on two separate occasions, and I am not surprised that California has found no such case, not even under its three-strikes law. ** In sum, the argument that repeating a trivial crime justifies doubling a 25-year minimum incapacitation sentence based on a threat to the public does not raise a seriously debatable point on which judgments might reasonably differ. The argument is irrational, and the state court's acceptance of it in response to a facially gross disproportion between triggering offense and penalty was unreasonable within the meaning of §2254(d).

This is the rare sentence of demonstrable gross disproportionality, as the California Legislature may well have recognized when it specifically provided that a prosecutor may move to dismiss or strike a prior felony conviction "in the furtherance of justice." Cal. Penal Code Ann. §667(f)(2) (West 1999). In this case, the statutory safeguard failed, and the state court was left to ensure that the Eighth Amendment prohibition on grossly disproportionate sentences was met. If Andrade's sentence is not grossly disproportionate, the principle has no meaning. The California court's holding was an unreasonable application of clearly established precedent.

Notes

1. *Subsequent case history*

Leandro Andrade currently is serving his sentence of two consecutive terms of 25 years to life.

2. *"Clear error" and "unreasonableness"*

Justice O'Connor observed that the standards of "clear error" and "unreasonableness" are not the same because the "gloss of clear error fails to give proper deference to state courts by conflating error (even clear error) with unreasonableness." She further clarified that under "'§2254(d)(1)'s "unreasonable application" clause...a federal habeas court may not issue the writ simply because that court concludes in its independent judgment that the relevant state-court decision applied clearly established federal law erroneously or incorrectly'.... Rather, that application must be objectively unreasonable." Does the Court's decision in *Lockyer v. Andrade* give clear guidance to federal habeas courts to distinguish what is "objectively" unreasonable?

Chapter 18

The Future of the Writ of Habeas Corpus

The "Great Writ" has changed in scope and reach since the time of the adoption of the United States Constitution. There was a time when only jurisdictional issues could be reached, and then only for a federal prisoner. As the definition of "jurisdictional" broadened and the application of the writ to state prisoners became more available, tensions mounted over the wish to see even-handed application of federal rights, on the one hand, and comity and finality of (primarily state) judgments on the other.

The United States Supreme Court has tried to balance such concerns in various ways, such as by fashioning the doctrine of procedural default and by engaging in more stringent analysis of successive petitions. The passage of the Antiterrorism and Effective Death Penalty Act of 1996 (AEDPA) reflected a political response to the conservative, and some might say right-wing radical, notion that lower courts were applying the writ too liberally—even though most of the relief being granted to petitioners was being granted by Reagan- and Bush-appointed judges.

The question of the place of the writ of habeas corpus in the history of the United States is complex and has no definitive answer. The following cases reflect some of the current competing concerns. In *Duncan v. Walker*, the Court considers whether the tolling provision of the AEDPA for time limitation purposes applies only to state applications for collateral relief or whether it applies to federal applications as well. In *Zadvydas v. Davis*, the Court considers the reach of the writ in the context of 28 U.S.C. § 2241 and examines whether the post-removal-period detention of a deportee must have a "reasonableness" limitation.

Duncan v. Walker

533 U.S. 167 (2001)

JUSTICE O'CONNOR delivered the opinion of the Court.

Title 28 U.S.C. § 2244(d)(2) (1994 ed., Supp. V) provides: "The time during which a properly filed application for State post-conviction or other collateral review with respect to the pertinent judgment or claim is pending shall not be counted toward any period of limitation under this subsection." This case presents the question whether a federal habeas corpus petition is an "application for State post-conviction or other collateral review" within the meaning of this provision.

I

In 1992, several judgments of conviction for robbery were entered against respondent Sherman Walker in the New York state courts. The last of these convictions came in June 1992, when respondent pleaded guilty to robbery in the first degree in the New York Supreme Court, Queens County. Respondent was sentenced to 7 to 14 years in prison on this conviction.

Respondent unsuccessfully pursued a number of state remedies in connection with his convictions. It is unnecessary to describe all of these proceedings herein. Respondent's last conviction was affirmed on June 12, 1995. Respondent was later denied leave to appeal to the New York Court of Appeals. Respondent also sought a writ of error *coram nobis*, which the Appellate Division denied on March 18, 1996. Respondent's last conviction became final in April 1996, prior to the April 24, 1996, effective date of the Antiterrorism and Effective Death Penalty Act of 1996 (AEDPA), 110 Stat. 1214.

In a single document dated April 10, 1996, respondent filed a complaint under Rev. Stat. §1979, 42 U.S.C. §1983, and a petition for habeas corpus under 28 U.S.C. §2254 in the United States District Court for the Eastern District of New York. On July 9, 1996, the District Court dismissed the complaint and petition without prejudice. With respect to the habeas petition, the District Court, citing §2254(d), concluded that respondent had not adequately set forth his claim because it was not apparent that respondent had exhausted available state remedies. The District Court noted that, for example, respondent had failed to specify the claims litigated in the state appellate proceedings relating to his robbery convictions.

On May 20, 1997, more than one year after the AEDPA's effective date, respondent filed another federal habeas petition in the same District Court. It is undisputed that respondent had not returned to state court since the dismissal of his first federal habeas filing. On May 6, 1998, the District Court dismissed the petition as time barred because respondent had not filed the petition within a "reasonable time" from the AEDPA's effective date.

The United States Court of Appeals for the Second Circuit reversed the District Court's judgment, reinstated the habeas petition, and remanded the case for further proceedings. ** The Court of Appeals noted at the outset that, because respondent's conviction had become final prior to the AEDPA's effective date, he had until April 24, 1997, to file his federal habeas petition. The court also observed that the exclusion from the limitation period of the time during which respondent's first federal habeas petition was pending in the District Court would render the instant habeas petition timely.

The Court of Appeals held that respondent's first federal habeas petition had tolled the limitation period because it was an application for "other collateral review" within the meaning of §2244(d)(2). The court characterized the disjunctive "or" between "post-conviction" and "other collateral" as creating a "distinct break" between two kinds of review. ** The court also stated that application of the word "State" to both "post-conviction" and "other collateral" would create a "linguistic oddity" in the form of the construction "State other collateral review." ** The court further reasoned that the phrase "other collateral review" would be meaningless if it did not refer to federal habeas petitions. The court therefore concluded that the word "State" modified only "post-conviction."

The Court of Appeals also found no conflict between its interpretation of the statute and the purpose of the AEDPA. The court found instead that its construction would promote the goal of encouraging petitioners to file their federal habeas applications as soon as possible.

We granted certiorari ** to resolve a conflict between the Second Circuit's decision and the decisions of three other Courts of Appeals. *** We now reverse.

II

Our task is to construe what Congress has enacted. We begin, as always, with the language of the statute. ** Respondent reads § 2244(d)(2) to apply the word "State" only to the term "post-conviction" and not to the phrase "other collateral." Under this view, a properly filed federal habeas petition tolls the limitation period. Petitioner contends that the word "State" applies to the entire phrase "post-conviction or other collateral review." Under this view, a properly filed federal habeas petition does not toll the limitation period.

We believe that petitioner's interpretation of § 2244(d)(2) is correct for several reasons. To begin with, Congress placed the word "State" before "post-conviction or other collateral review" without specifically naming any kind of "Federal" review. The essence of respondent's position is that Congress used the phrase "other collateral review" to incorporate federal habeas petitions into the class of applications for review that toll the limitation period. But a comparison of the text of § 2244(d)(2) with the language of other AEDPA provisions supplies strong evidence that, had Congress intended to include federal habeas petitions within the scope of § 2244(d)(2), Congress would have mentioned "Federal" review expressly. In several other portions of the AEDPA, Congress specifically used both the words "State" and "Federal" to denote state and federal proceedings. For example, 28 U.S.C. § 2254(i) (1994 ed., Supp. V) provides: "The ineffectiveness or incompetence of counsel during Federal or State collateral post-conviction proceedings shall not be a ground for relief in a proceeding arising under section 2254." Likewise, the first sentence of 28 U.S.C. § 2261(e) (1994 ed., Supp. V) provides: "The ineffectiveness or incompetence of counsel during State or Federal post-conviction proceedings in a capital case shall not be a ground for relief in a proceeding arising under section 2254." The second sentence of § 2261(e) states: "This limitation shall not preclude the appointment of different counsel, on the court's own motion or at the request of the prisoner, at any phase of State or Federal post-conviction proceedings on the basis of the ineffectiveness or incompetence of counsel in such proceedings." Finally, 28 U.S.C. § 2264(a)(3) (1994 ed., Supp. V) excuses a state capital prisoner's failure to raise a claim properly in state court where the failure is "based on a factual predicate that could not have been discovered through the exercise of due diligence in time to present the claim for State or Federal post-conviction review."

Section 2244(d)(2), by contrast, employs the word "State," but not the word "Federal," as a modifier for "review." It is well settled that "'[w]here Congress includes particular language in one section of a statute but omits it in another section of the same Act, it is generally presumed that Congress acts intentionally and purposely in the disparate inclusion or exclusion.'" ** We find no likely explanation for Congress' omission of the word "Federal" in § 2244(d)(2) other than that Congress did not intend properly filed applications for federal review to toll the limitation period. It would be anomalous, to say the least, for Congress to usher in federal review under the generic rubric of "other collateral review" in a statutory provision that refers expressly to "State" review, while denominating expressly both "State" and "Federal" proceedings in other parts of the same statute. The anomaly is underscored by the fact that the words "State" and "Federal" are likely to be of no small import when Congress drafts a statute that governs federal collateral review of state court judgments.

Further, were we to adopt respondent's construction of the statute, we would render the word "State" insignificant, if not wholly superfluous. *** We are thus "reluctan[t] to treat statutory terms as surplusage" in any setting. ** We are especially unwilling to do so when the term occupies so pivotal a place in the statutory scheme as does the word "State" in the federal habeas statute. But under respondent's rendition of §2244(d)(2), Congress' inclusion of the word "State" has no operative effect on the scope of the provision. If the phrase "State post-conviction or other collateral review" is construed to encompass both state and federal collateral review, then the word "State" places no constraint on the class of applications for review that toll the limitation period. The clause instead would have precisely the same content were it to read "post-conviction or other collateral review."

The most that could then be made of the word "State" would be to say that Congress singled out applications for "State post-conviction" review as one example from the universe of applications for collateral review. Under this approach, however, the word "State" still does nothing to delimit the entire class of applications for review that toll the limitation period. A construction under which the word "State" does nothing more than further modify "post-conviction" relegates "State" to quite an insignificant role in the statutory provision. We believe that our duty to "give each word some operative effect" where possible ** requires more in this context.

The Court of Appeals characterized petitioner's interpretation as producing the "linguistic oddity" of "State other collateral review," which is "an ungainly construction that [the Court of Appeals did] not believe Congress intended." ** But nothing precludes the application of the word "State" to the entire phrase "post-conviction or other collateral review," regardless of the resulting construction that one posits. The term "other collateral" is easily understood as a unit to which "State" applies just as "State" applies to "post-conviction." Moreover, petitioner's interpretation does not compel the verbal formula hypothesized by the Court of Appeals. Indeed, the ungainliness of "State other collateral review" is a very good reason why Congress might have avoided that precise verbal formulation in the first place. The application of the word "State" to the phrase "other collateral review" more naturally yields the understanding "other State collateral review."

The Court of Appeals also reasoned that petitioner's reading of the statute fails to give operative effect to the phrase "other collateral review." The court claimed that "the phrase 'other collateral review' would be meaningless if it did not refer to federal habeas petitions." ** This argument, however, fails because it depends on the incorrect premise that there can be no form of state "collateral" review "other" than state "post-conviction" review within the meaning of §2244(d)(2). To the contrary, it is possible for "other collateral review" to include review of a state court judgment that is not a criminal conviction.

Section 2244(d)(1)'s 1-year limitation period applies to "an application for a writ of habeas corpus by a person in custody pursuant to the judgment of a State court." Section 2244(d)(2) provides for tolling during the pendency of "a properly filed application for State post-conviction or other collateral review with respect to the pertinent judgment or claim." Nothing in the language of these provisions requires that the state court judgment pursuant to which a person is in custody be a criminal conviction. Nor does 28 U.S.C. §2254 (1994 ed. and Supp. V) by its terms apply only to those in custody pursuant to a state criminal conviction. See, e.g., §2254(a) ("a person in custody pursuant to the judgment of a State court"); §2254(b)(1) ("a person in custody pursuant to the judgment of a State court"); §2254(d) ("a person in custody pursuant to the judgment of a State court"); §2254(e)(1) ("a person in custody pursuant to the judgment of a State court").

Incarceration pursuant to a state criminal conviction may be by far the most common and most familiar basis for satisfaction of the "in custody" requirement in §2254 cases. But there are other types of state court judgments pursuant to which a person may be held in custody within the meaning of the federal habeas statute. For example, federal habeas corpus review may be available to challenge the legality of a state court order of civil commitment or a state court order of civil contempt. *See, e.g., Francois v. Henderson*, 850 F.2d 231 (5th Cir. 1988) (entertaining a challenge brought in a federal habeas petition under §2254 to a state court's commitment of a person to a mental institution upon a verdict of not guilty by reason of insanity); *Leonard v. Hammond*, 804 F.2d 838 (4th Cir. 1986) (holding that constitutional challenges to civil contempt orders for failure to pay child support were cognizable only in a habeas corpus action). These types of state court judgments neither constitute nor require criminal convictions. Any state collateral review that is available with respect to these judgments, strictly speaking, is not post-conviction review. Accordingly, even if "State post-conviction review" means "all collateral review of a conviction provided by a state," ** the phrase "other collateral review" need not include federal habeas petitions in order to have independent meaning.

Congress also may have employed the construction "post-conviction or other collateral" in recognition of the diverse terminology that different States employ to represent the different forms of collateral review that are available after a conviction. In some jurisdictions, the term "post-conviction" may denote a particular procedure for review of a conviction that is distinct from other forms of what conventionally is considered to be postconviction review. For example, Florida employs a procedure that is officially entitled a "Motion to Vacate, Set Aside, or Correct Sentence." The Florida courts have commonly referred to a motion as a "motion for post-conviction relief" and have distinguished this procedure from other vehicles for collateral review of a criminal conviction, such as a state petition for habeas corpus. ** Congress may have refrained from exclusive reliance on the term "post-conviction" so as to leave no doubt that the tolling provision applies to all types of state collateral review available after a conviction and not just to those denominated "post-conviction" in the parlance of a particular jurisdiction.

Examination of another AEDPA provision also demonstrates that "other collateral" need not refer to any form of federal review in order to have meaning. Title 28 U.S.C. §2263 (1994 ed., Supp. V) establishes the limitation period for filing §2254 petitions in state capital cases that arise from jurisdictions meeting the "opt-in" requirements of §2261. Section 2263(b)(2) provides that the limitation period "shall be tolled from the date on which the first petition for post-conviction review or other collateral relief is filed until the final State court disposition of such petition." The reference to "the final State court disposition of such petition" makes it clear that only petitions filed in state court, and not petitions for federal review, toll the limitation period in capital cases. Congress therefore used the phrases "post-conviction review" and "other collateral relief" in a disjunctive clause where the term "other collateral," whatever its precise content, could not possibly include anything federal within its ambit. This illustration vitiates any suggestion that "other collateral" relief or review must include federal relief or review in order for the term to have any significance apart from "post-conviction" review.

Consideration of the competing constructions in light of the AEDPA's purposes reinforces the conclusion that we draw from the text. Petitioner's interpretation of the statute is consistent with the "AEDPA's purpose to further the principles of comity, finality, and federalism." ** Specifically, under petitioner's construction, §2244(d)(2) promotes the exhaustion of state remedies while respecting the interest in the finality of state court judgments. Under respondent's interpretation, however, the provision would do far less to encourage exhaustion prior to seeking federal habeas review and would hold greater potential to hinder finality.

The exhaustion requirement of § 2254(b) ensures that the state courts have the opportunity fully to consider federal-law challenges to a state custodial judgment before the lower federal courts may entertain a collateral attack upon that judgment. ** This requirement "is principally designed to protect the state courts' role in the enforcement of federal law and prevent disruption of state judicial proceedings." ** The exhaustion rule promotes comity in that " 'it would be unseemly in our dual system of government for a federal district court to upset a state court conviction without an opportunity to the state courts to correct a constitutional violation.' " **

The 1-year limitation period of § 2244(d)(1) quite plainly serves the well-recognized interest in the finality of state court judgments. ** This provision reduces the potential for delay on the road to finality by restricting the time that a prospective federal habeas petitioner has in which to seek federal habeas review.

The tolling provision of § 2244(d)(2) balances the interests served by the exhaustion requirement and the limitation period. Section 2244(d)(2) promotes the exhaustion of state remedies by protecting a state prisoner's ability later to apply for federal habeas relief while state remedies are being pursued. At the same time, the provision limits the harm to the interest in finality by according tolling effect only to "properly filed application[s] for State post-conviction or other collateral review."

By tolling the limitation period for the pursuit of state remedies and not during the pendency of applications for federal review, § 2244(d)(2) provides a powerful incentive for litigants to exhaust all available state remedies before proceeding in the lower federal courts. But if the statute were construed so as to give applications for federal review the same tolling effect as applications for state collateral review, then § 2244(d)(2) would furnish little incentive for individuals to seek relief from the state courts before filing federal habeas petitions. The tolling provision instead would be indifferent between state and federal filings. While other statutory provisions, such as § 2254(b) itself, of course, would still provide individuals with good reason to exhaust, § 2244(d)(2) would be out of step with this design. At the same time, respondent's interpretation would further undermine the interest in finality by creating more potential for delay in the adjudication of federal law claims.

A diminution of statutory incentives to proceed first in state court would also increase the risk of the very piecemeal litigation that the exhaustion requirement is designed to reduce. ** We have observed that "strict enforcement of the exhaustion requirement will encourage habeas petitioners to exhaust all of their claims in state court and to present the federal court with a single habeas petition." *** We do not believe that Congress designed the statute in this manner.

    ***

Respondent contends that petitioner's construction of the statute creates the potential for unfairness to litigants who file timely federal habeas petitions that are dismissed without prejudice after the limitation period has expired. But our sole task in this case is one of statutory construction, and upon examining the language and purpose of the statute, we are convinced that § 2244(d)(2) does not toll the limitation period during the pendency of a federal habeas petition.

We also note that, when the District Court dismissed respondent's first federal habeas petition without prejudice, respondent had more than nine months remaining in the limitation period in which to cure the defects that led to the dismissal. It is undisputed, however, that petitioner neither returned to state court nor filed a nondefective federal habeas petition before this time had elapsed. Respondent's May 1997 federal habeas petition also contained claims different from those presented in his April 1996 petition. In light of these facts, we have no occasion to address the alternative scenarios that respondent describes. ***

We hold that an application for federal habeas corpus review is not an "application for State post-conviction or other collateral review" within the meaning of 28 U.S.C. § 2244(d)(2). Section 2244(d)(2) therefore did not toll the limitation period during the pendency of respondent's first federal habeas petition. The judgment of the Court of Appeals is reversed, and the case is remanded for further proceedings consistent with this opinion.

It is so ordered.

[Concurrence by JUSTICE SOUTER is omitted; concurrence by JUSTICE STEVENS, joined by JUSTICE SOUTER, is omitted; and a dissent by JUSTICE BREYER joined by JUSTICE GINSBERG, is omitted.]

Notes

1. *Subsequent case history*

Sherman Walker is currently in prison in New York, where he is serving a 39-year sentence. *See* http://nysdocslookup.docs.state.ny.us/kinqw00.

2. *Concurring opinion of Justice Stevens*

In a separate opinion, concurring in part and concurring in the judgment, Justice Stevens (joined by Justice Souter) agrees that a better reading of the habeas statute section in question is that it is meant to apply only to state collateral processes. He then goes on to "add two observations regarding the equitable powers of the federal courts, which are unaffected by today's decision construing a single provision of the Antiterrorism and Effective Death Penalty Act of 1996 (AEDPA), 110 Stat. 1214." These two observations are the following:

> [While the pre-AEDPA decision of *Rose v. Lundy*, 455 U.S. 509 (1982), required] dismissal of federal habeas corpus petitions containing unexhausted claims, in our post-AEDPA world there is no reason why a district court should not retain jurisdiction over a meritorious claim and stay further proceedings pending the complete exhaustion of state remedies. Indeed, there is every reason to do so when AEDPA gives a district court the alternative of simply denying a petition containing unexhausted but nonmeritorious claims, and when the failure to retain jurisdiction would foreclose federal review of a meritorious claim because of the lapse of AEDPA's 1-year limitations period.

> Second, despite the Court's suggestion that tolling the limitations period for a first federal habeas petition would undermine the "purposes" of AEDPA, ** neither the Court's narrow holding, nor anything in the text or legislative history of AEDPA, precludes a federal court from deeming the limitations period tolled for such a petition as a matter of equity.

Is Justice Stevens correct in either or both of these assertions? Should a federal district court use equitable tolling to reach the merits of a claim, how would the Court likely rule when the case later came before it for review?

3. *Dissenting opinion by Justice Breyer*

In his dissent, Justice Breyer (joined by Justice Ginsburg) concludes that the statute encompasses the tolling-of-time limitation by the filing of a petition for a writ of habeas corpus in federal district court:

> To understand my conclusion, one must understand why the legal issue before us is significant. Why would a state prisoner ever want federal habeas corpus proceedings to toll the federal habeas corpus limitations period? After all, the very point of tolling is to provide a state prisoner adequate time to file a federal habeas petition. If the prisoner has already filed that petition, what need is there for further tolling?
>
> The answer to this question—and the problem that gives rise to the issue before us—is that a federal court may be required to dismiss a state prisoner's federal habeas petition, not on the merits, but because that prisoner has not exhausted his state collateral remedies for every claim presented in the federal petition. ** Such a dismissal means that a prisoner wishing to pursue the claim must return to state court, pursue his state remedies, and then, if he loses, again file a federal habeas petition in federal court. All this takes time. The statute tolls the 1-year limitations period during the time the prisoner proceeds in the state courts. But unless the statute also tolls the limitations period during the time the defective petition was pending in federal court, the state prisoner may find, when he seeks to return to federal court, that he has run out of time.
>
> This possibility is not purely theoretical. A Justice Department study indicates that 63% of all habeas petitions are dismissed, and 57% of those are dismissed for failure to exhaust state remedies. *See* U.S. Dept. of Justice, Office of Justice Programs, Bureau of Justice Statistics, Federal Habeas Corpus Review: Challenging State Court Criminal Convictions 17 (1995) (hereinafter Federal Habeas Corpus Review). And it can take courts a significant amount of time to dispose of even those petitions that are not addressed on the merits; on the average, district courts took 268 days to dismiss petitions on procedural grounds. *Id.* at 23–24; *see also id.* at 19 (of all habeas petitions, nearly half were pending in the district court for six months or longer; 10% were pending more than two years). Thus, if the words "other collateral review" do not include federal collateral review, a large group of federal habeas petitioners, seeking to return to federal court after subsequent state-court rejection of an unexhausted claim, may find their claims time barred. Moreover, because district courts vary substantially in the time they take to rule on habeas petitions, two identically situated prisoners can receive opposite results. If Prisoner *A* and Prisoner *B* file mixed petitions in different district courts six months before the federal limitations period expires, and the court takes three months to dismiss Prisoner *A*'s petition, but seven months to dismiss Prisoner *B*'s petition, Prisoner *A* will be able to return to federal court after exhausting state remedies, but Prisoner *B*—due to no fault of his own—may not.
>
>   ***
>
> *** The problem arises because the vast majority of federal habeas petitions are brought without legal representation. *See* Federal Habeas Corpus Review 14 (finding that 93% of habeas petitioners in study were *pro se*). Prisoners acting *pro se* will often not know whether a change in wording between state and federal petitions will be seen in federal court as a new claim or a better way of stat-

ing an old one; and they often will not understand whether new facts brought forward in the federal petition reflect a new claim or better support for an old one. Insofar as that is so, the Court's approach is likely to lead not to fewer improper federal petitions, but to increased confusion, as prisoners hesitate to change the language of state petitions or add facts, and to greater unfairness. And it will undercut one significant purpose of the provision before us—to grant state prisoners a fair and reasonable time to bring a first federal habeas corpus petition.

Is Justice Breyer correct? What effect, if any, should the Court accord an examination of the realities of *pro se* representation?

4. *Separation of powers*

In his article *An 'Effective Death Penalty'? AEDPA and Error Detection in Capital Cases*, Professor James S. Liebman states:

> As the likes of James Madison, Alexander Hamilton, and James Wilson structured the Constitution, and as the Court's classic separation of powers decisions have understood and maintained that structure ever since, the most fundamental role of Article III courts is to assure that state law, including state decisional law, does not contravene the U.S. Constitution and other federal law. ** As Hamilton wrote in *The Federalist No. 80*, Article III courts' principal role is to exercise "some effectual power...to restrain or correct" state court "infractions" of federal law and thereby to enforce the Supremacy Clause of the Constitution. *** According to the Supremacy Clause: "This Constitution and the Laws of the United States...and all Treaties...shall be the supreme Law of the Land, and the Judges *in every State shall be bound thereby*, any Thing in the Constitution or the Laws of any State to the Contrary notwithstanding." ***
>
> The Court has repeatedly construed these provisions in such landmark cases as *Marbury v. Madison, Martin v. Hunters Lessee*, 14 U.S. (1 Wheat.) 304 (1816), *Cohens v. Virginia*, 19 U.S. (6 Wheat.) 264 (1821), *Abelman v. Booth*, 62 U.S. (21 How.) 506 (1859), *Crowell v. Benson*, 285 U.S. 22 (1932), and *Yakus v. United States*, 321 U.S. 414 (1944). Together, these decisions define the core attribute of the federal-supremacy-inflected "judicial power" that Article III insulates from congressional control or limitation. That core attribute is a federal court's "effectual power," when granted jurisdiction over a matter, to deny force and effect to state decisional and other law of the land as of the time the state law was made. *** And yet, as Justice Breyer seemed to recognize at the *Penry* oral argument, *** it is precisely that "effectual power" that § 2254(d) *** withholds from federal habeas courts. ***

67 BROOK. L. REV. 411, 420, 421 (2001) (relevant citations inserted).

Do you agree with Professor Leibman's assertion that § 2254(d) withholds the "effectual power" from federal habeas courts?

Zadvydas v. Davis; Ashcroft v. Kim Ho Ma

533 U.S. 678 (2001)

JUSTICE BREYER delivered the opinion of the Court.

When an alien has been found to be unlawfully present in the United States and a final order of removal has been entered, the Government ordinarily secures the alien's removal during a subsequent 90-day statutory "removal period," during which time the alien normally is held in custody.

A special statute authorizes further detention if the Government fails to remove the alien during those 90 days. It says:

> An alien ordered removed [1] who is inadmissible . . . [2] [or] removable [as a result of violations of status requirements or entry conditions, violations of criminal law, or reasons of security or foreign policy] or [3] who has been determined by the Attorney General to be a risk to the community or unlikely to comply with the order of removal, may be detained beyond the removal period and, if released, shall be subject to [certain] terms of supervision. . . .

8 U.S.C. § 1231(a)(6) (1994 ed., Supp. V).

In these cases, we must decide whether this post-removal-period statute authorizes the Attorney General to detain a removable alien *indefinitely* beyond the removal period or only for a period *reasonably necessary* to secure the alien's removal. We deal here with aliens who were admitted to the United States but subsequently ordered removed. Aliens who have not yet gained initial admission to this country would present a very different question. ** Based on our conclusion that indefinite detention of aliens in the former category would raise serious constitutional concerns, we construe the statute to contain an implicit "reasonable time" limitation, the application of which is subject to federal-court review.

I

A

The post-removal-period detention statute is one of a related set of statutes and regulations that govern detention during and after removal proceedings. While removal proceedings are in progress, most aliens may be released on bond or paroled. 66 Stat. 204, as added and amended, 110 Stat. 3009–585, 8 U.S.C. §§ 1226(a)(2), (c) (1994 ed., Supp. V). After entry of a final removal order and during the 90-day removal period, however, aliens must be held in custody. § 1231(a)(2). Subsequently, as the post-removal-period statute provides, the Government "may" continue to detain an alien who still remains here or release that alien under supervision. § 1231(a)(6).

Related Immigration and Naturalization Service (INS) regulations add that the INS District Director will initially review the alien's records to decide whether further detention or release under supervision is warranted after the 90-day removal period expires. 8 C.F.R. §§ 241.4(c)(1), (h), (k)(1)(i) (2001). If the decision is to detain, then an INS panel will review the matter further, at the expiration of a 3-month period or soon thereafter. § 241.4(k)(2)(ii). And the panel will decide, on the basis of records and a possible personal interview, between still further detention or release under supervision. § 241.4(i). In making this decision, the panel will consider, for example, the alien's disciplinary record, criminal record, mental health reports, evidence of rehabilitation, history of flight, prior immigration history, and favorable factors such as family ties. § 241.4(f). To authorize release, the panel must find that the alien is not likely to be violent, to pose a threat to the community, to flee if released, or to violate the conditions of release. § 241.4(e). And the alien must demonstrate "to the satisfaction of the Attorney General" that he will pose no danger or risk of flight. § 241.4(d)(1). If the panel decides against release, it must review the matter again within a year, and can review it earlier if conditions change. §§ 241.4(k)(2)(iii), (v).

B

1

We consider two separate instances of detention. The first concerns Kestutis Zadvydas, a resident alien who was born, apparently of Lithuanian parents, in a displaced persons camp in Germany in 1948. When he was eight years old, Zadvydas immigrated to the United States with his parents and other family members, and he has lived here ever since.

Zadvydas has a long criminal record, involving drug crimes, attempted robbery, attempted burglary, and theft. He has a history of flight, from both criminal and deportation proceedings. Most recently, he was convicted of possessing, with intent to distribute, cocaine; sentenced to 16 years' imprisonment; released on parole after two years; taken into INS custody; and, in 1994, ordered deported to Germany. *See* 8 U.S.C. § 1251(a)(2) (1998 ed., Supp. V) (delineating crimes that make alien deportable).

In 1994, Germany told the INS that it would not accept Zadvydas because he was not a German citizen. Shortly thereafter, Lithuania refused to accept Zadvydas because he was neither a Lithuanian citizen nor a permanent resident. In 1996, the INS asked the Dominican Republic (Zadvydas' wife's country) to accept him, but this effort proved unsuccessful. In 1998, Lithuania rejected, as inadequately documented, Zadvydas' effort to obtain Lithuanian citizenship based on his parents' citizenship; Zadvydas' reapplication is apparently still pending.

The INS kept Zadvydas in custody after expiration of the removal period. In September 1995, Zadvydas filed a petition for a writ of habeas corpus under 28 U.S.C. § 2241 challenging his continued detention. In October 1997, a Federal District Court granted that writ and ordered him released under supervision. ** In its view, the Government would never succeed in its efforts to remove Zadvydas from the United States, leading to his permanent confinement, contrary to the Constitution. **

The Fifth Circuit reversed this decision. ** It concluded that Zadvydas' detention did not violate the Constitution because eventual deportation was not "impossible," good-faith efforts to remove him from the United States continued, and his detention was subject to periodic administrative review. ** The Fifth Circuit stayed its mandate pending potential review in this Court.

2

The second case is that of Kim Ho Ma. Ma was born in Cambodia in 1977. When he was two, his family fled, taking him to refugee camps in Thailand and the Philippines and eventually to the United States, where he has lived as a resident alien since the age of seven. In 1995, at age 17, Ma was involved in a gang-related shooting, convicted of manslaughter, and sentenced to 38 months' imprisonment. He served two years, after which he was released into INS custody.

In light of his conviction of an "aggravated felony," Ma was ordered removed. *See* 8 U.S.C. §§ 1101(a)(43)(F) (defining certain violent crimes as aggravated felonies), 1227(a)(2)(A)(iii) (1994 ed., Supp. IV) (aliens convicted of aggravated felonies are deportable). The 90-day removal period expired in early 1999, but the INS continued to keep Ma in custody, because, in light of his former gang membership, the nature of his crime, and his planned participation in a prison hunger strike, it was "unable to conclude that Mr. Ma would remain nonviolent and not violate the conditions of release." **

In 1999, Ma filed a petition for a writ of habeas corpus under 28 U.S.C. § 2241. A panel of five judges in the Federal District Court for the Western District of Washington, considering Ma's and about 100 similar cases together, issued a joint order holding that the Constitution forbids post-removal-period detention unless there is "a realistic chance that [the] alien will be deported" (thereby permitting classification of the detention as "in aid of deportation"). ** The District Court then held an evidentiary hearing, decided that there was no "realistic chance" that Cambodia (which has no repatriation treaty with the United States) would accept Ma, and ordered Ma released. **

The Ninth Circuit affirmed Ma's release. ** It concluded, based in part on constitutional concerns, that the statute did not authorize detention for more than a "reasonable time" beyond the 90-day period authorized for removal. ** And, given the lack of a repatriation agreement with Cambodia, that time had expired upon passage of the 90 days. **

3

Zadvydas asked us to review the decision of the Fifth Circuit authorizing his continued detention. The Government asked us to review the decision of the Ninth Circuit forbidding Ma's continued detention. We granted writs in both cases, agreeing to consider both statutory and related constitutional questions. ** We consolidated the two cases for argument; and we now decide them together.

II

We note at the outset that the primary federal habeas corpus statute, 28 U.S.C. § 2241, confers jurisdiction upon the federal courts to hear these cases. See § 2241(c)(3) (authorizing any person to claim in federal court that he or she is being held "in custody in violation of the Constitution or laws...of the United States"). Before 1952, the federal courts considered challenges to the lawfulness of immigration-related detention, including challenges to the validity of a deportation order, in habeas proceedings. ** Beginning in 1952, an alternative method for review of *deportation orders*, namely, actions brought in federal district court under the Administrative Procedure Act (APA), became available. ** And in 1961 Congress replaced district court APA review with initial *deportation order* review in courts of appeals. See Act of Sept. 26, 1961, § 5, 75 Stat. 651 (formerly codified at 8 U.S.C. § 1105a(a)) (repealed 1996). The 1961 Act specified that federal habeas courts were also available to hear statutory and constitutional challenges to *deportation* (and exclusion) *orders*. See 8 U.S.C. §§ 1105a(a)(10), (b) (repealed 1996). These statutory changes left habeas untouched as the basic method for obtaining review of continued *custody after* a deportation order had become final. **

More recently, Congress has enacted several statutory provisions that limit the circumstances in which judicial review of deportation decisions is available. But none applies here. One provision, 8 U.S.C. § 1231(h) (1994 ed., Supp. V), simply forbids courts to construe that section "to create any...procedural right or benefit that is legally enforceable"; it does not deprive an alien of the right to rely on 28 U.S.C. § 2241 to challenge detention that is without statutory authority.

Another provision, 8 U.S.C. § 1252(a)(2)(B)(ii) (1994 ed., Supp. V), says that "no court shall have jurisdiction to review" decisions "specified...to be in the discretion of the Attorney General." The aliens here, however, do not seek review of the Attorney General's exercise of discretion; rather, they challenge the extent of the Attorney General's authority under the post-removal-period detention statute. And the extent of that authority is not a matter of discretion. See also, e.g., § 1226(e) (applicable to certain detention-related decisions *in period preceding entry* of final removal order); § 1231(a)(4)(D) (applicable to assertion of causes or claims *under §1231(a)(4)*, which is not at issue here); §§1252(a)(1), (a)(2)(c) (applicable to judicial review of "final order[s] of removal"); §1252(g) (applicable to decisions "to commence proceedings, adjudicate cases, or execute removal orders").

We conclude that §2241 habeas corpus proceedings remain available as a forum for statutory and constitutional challenges to post-removal-period detention. And we turn to the merits of the aliens' claims.

III

The post-removal-period detention statute applies to certain categories of aliens who have been ordered removed, namely, inadmissible aliens, criminal aliens, aliens who have violated their nonimmigrant status conditions, and aliens removable for certain national security or foreign relations reasons, as well as any alien "who has been determined by the Attorney General to be a risk to the community or unlikely to comply with the order of removal." 8 U.S.C. §1231(a)(6) (1994 ed., Supp. V); *see also* 8 C.F.R. §241.4(a) (2001). It says that an alien who falls into one of these categories "may be detained beyond the removal period and, if released, shall be subject to [certain] terms of supervision." 8 U.S.C. §1231(a)(6) (1994 ed., Supp. V).

The Government argues that the statute means what it literally says. It sets no "limit on the length of time beyond the removal period that an alien who falls within one of the Section 1231(a)(6) categories may be detained." ** Hence, "whether to continue to detain such an alien and, if so, in what circumstances and for how long" is up to the Attorney General, not up to the courts. **

"[I]t is a cardinal principle" of statutory interpretation, however, that when an Act of Congress raises "a serious doubt" as to its constitutionality, "this Court will first ascertain whether a construction of the statute is fairly possible by which the question may be avoided." ** We have read significant limitations into other immigration statutes in order to avoid their constitutional invalidation. *See United States v. Witkovich*, 353 U.S. 194, 195, 202 (1957) (construing a grant of authority to the Attorney General to ask aliens whatever questions he "deem[s] fit and proper" as limited to questions "reasonably calculated to keep the Attorney General advised regarding the continued availability for departure of aliens whose deportation is overdue"). For similar reasons, we read an implicit limitation into the statute before us. In our view, the statute, read in light of the Constitution's demands, limits an alien's post-removal-period detention to a period reasonably necessary to bring about that alien's removal from the United States. It does not permit indefinite detention.

A

A statute permitting indefinite detention of an alien would raise a serious constitutional problem. The Fifth Amendment's Due Process Clause forbids the Government to "depriv[e]" any "person...of...liberty...without due process of law." Freedom from imprisonment—from government custody, detention, or other forms of physical restraint—lies at the heart of the liberty that Clause protects. ** And this Court has said that government detention violates that Clause unless the detention is ordered in a *criminal* proceeding with adequate procedural protections, *see United States v. Salerno*, 481 U.S. 739 (1987), or, in certain special and "narrow" nonpunitive "circumstances," ** where a special justification, such as harm-threatening mental illness, outweighs the "individual's constitutionally protected interest in avoiding physical restraint." **

The proceedings at issue here are civil, not criminal, and we assume that they are nonpunitive in purpose and effect. There is no sufficiently strong special justification here for indefinite civil detention—at least as administered under this statute. The statute, says the Government, has two regulatory goals: "ensuring the appearance of aliens at future immigration proceedings" and "[p]reventing danger to the community." ** But by definition the first justification—preventing flight—is weak or nonexistent where removal seems a remote possibility at best. As this Court said in *Jackson v. Indiana*, 406 U.S. 715 (1972), where detention's goal is no longer practically attainable, detention no longer "bear[s][a] reasonable relation to the purpose for which the individual [was] committed." **

The second justification—protecting the community—does not necessarily diminish in force over time. But we have upheld preventive detention based on dangerousness only when limited to specially dangerous individuals and subject to strong procedural protections. ** In cases in which preventive detention is of potentially *indefinite* duration, we have also demanded that the dangerousness rationale be accompanied by some other special circumstance, such as mental illness, that helps to create the danger. **

The civil confinement here at issue is not limited, but potentially permanent. ** The provision authorizing detention does not apply narrowly to "a small segment of particularly dangerous individuals," ** say, suspected terrorists, but broadly to aliens ordered removed for many and various reasons, including tourist visa violations. ** And, once the flight risk justification evaporates, the only special circumstance present is the alien's removable status itself, which bears no relation to a detainee's dangerousness. **

Moreover, the sole procedural protections available to the alien are found in administrative proceedings, where the alien bears the burden of proving he is not dangerous, without (in the Government's view) significant later judicial review. ** This Court has suggested, however, that the Constitution may well preclude granting "an administrative body the unreviewable authority to make determinations implicating fundamental rights." *Superintendent, Mass. Correctional Institution at Walpole v. Hill*, 472 U.S. 445, 450 (1985). *** The serious constitutional problem arising out of a statute that, in these circumstances, permits an indefinite, perhaps permanent, deprivation of human liberty without any such protection is obvious.

The Government argues that, from a constitutional perspective, alien status itself can justify indefinite detention, and points to *Shaughnessy v. United States ex rel. Mezei*, 345 U.S. 206 (1953), as support. That case involved a once lawfully admitted alien who left the United States, returned after a trip abroad, was refused admission, and was left on Ellis Island, indefinitely detained there because the Government could not find another country to accept him. The Court held that Mezei's detention did not violate the Constitution. **

Although *Mezei*, like the present cases, involves indefinite detention, it differs from the present cases in a critical respect. As the Court emphasized, the alien's extended departure from the United States required him to seek entry into this country once again. His presence on Ellis Island did not count as entry into the United States. Hence, he was "treated," for constitutional purposes, "as if stopped at the border." ** And that made all the difference.

The distinction between an alien who has effected an entry into the United States and one who has never entered runs throughout immigration law. ** But once an alien enters the country, the legal circumstance changes, for the Due Process Clause applies to all "persons" within the United States, including aliens, whether their presence here is lawful, unlawful, temporary, or permanent. ***

***

The Government also looks for support to cases holding that Congress has "plenary power" to create immigration law, and that the Judicial Branch must defer to Executive and Legislative Branch decisionmaking in that area. ** But that power is subject to important constitutional limitations. *See INS v. Chadla*, 462 U.S. 919, 941–942 (1983) (Congress must choose "a constitutionally permissible means of implementing" that power); *The Chinese Exclusion Case*, 130 U.S. 581, 604 (1889) (congressional authority limited "by the Constitution itself and considerations of public policy and justice which control, more or less, the conduct of all civilized nations"). In these cases, we focus upon those limitations. In doing so, we nowhere deny the right of Congress to remove aliens, to subject them to supervision with conditions when released from detention, or to incarcerate them where appropriate for violations of those conditions. *** Rather, the issue we address is whether aliens that the Government finds itself unable to remove are to be condemned to an indefinite term of imprisonment within the United States.

Nor do the cases before us require us to consider the political branches' authority to control entry into the United States. Hence we leave no "unprotected spot in the Nation's armor." ** Neither do we consider terrorism or other special circumstances where special arguments might be made for forms of preventive detention and for heightened deference to the judgments of the political branches with respect to matters of national security. The sole foreign policy consideration the Government mentions here is the concern lest courts interfere with "sensitive" repatriation negotiations. ** But neither the Government nor the dissents explain how a habeas court's efforts to determine the likelihood of repatriation, if handled with appropriate sensitivity, could make a significant difference in this respect. **

Finally, the Government argues that, whatever liberty interest the aliens possess, it is "greatly diminished" by their lack of a legal right to "liv[e] at large in this country." ** The choice, however, is not between imprisonment and the alien "living at large." ** It is between imprisonment and supervision under release conditions that may not be violated. ** And, for the reasons we have set forth, we believe that an alien's liberty interest is, at the least, strong enough to raise a serious question as to whether, irrespective of the procedures used, ** the Constitution permits detention that is indefinite and potentially permanent.

B

Despite this constitutional problem, if "Congress has made its intent" in the statute "clear, 'we must give effect to that intent.'" ** We cannot find here, however, any clear indication of congressional intent to grant the Attorney General the power to hold indefinitely in confinement an alien ordered removed. And that is so whether protecting the community from dangerous aliens is a primary or (as we believe) secondary statutory purpose. ** After all, the provision is part of a statute that has as its basic purpose effectuating an alien's removal. Why should we assume that Congress saw the alien's dangerousness as unrelated to this purpose?

The Government points to the statute's word "may." But while "may" suggests discretion, it does not necessarily suggest unlimited discretion. In that respect the word "may" is ambiguous. Indeed, if Congress had meant to authorize long-term detention of unremovable aliens, it certainly could have spoken in clearer terms. *Cf.* 8 U.S.C. § 1537(b)(2)(C) (1994 ed., Supp. V) ("If no country is willing to receive" a terrorist alien ordered removed, "the Attorney General may, notwithstanding any other provision of law, retain the alien in custody" and must review the detention determination every six months).

The Government points to similar related statutes that *require* detention of criminal aliens during removal proceedings and the removal period, and argues that these show that mandatory detention is the rule while discretionary release is the narrow exception. ** But the statute before us applies not only to terrorists and criminals, but also to ordinary visa violators ** and, more importantly, post-removal-period detention, unlike detention pending a determination of removability or during the subsequent 90-day removal period, has no obvious termination point.

The Government also points to the statute's history. That history catalogs a series of changes, from an initial period (before 1952) when lower courts had interpreted statutory silence, Immigration Act of 1917, ch. 29, §§ 19, 20, 39 Stat. 889, 890, to mean that deportation-related detention must end within a reasonable time, ** to a period (from the early 1950's through the late 1980's) when the statutes permitted, but did not require, post-deportation-order detention for up to six months, Immigration and Nationality Act of 1952, § 242(c), 66 Stat. 210, 8 U.S.C. §§ 1252(c), (d) (1982 ed.), ** to more recent statutes that have at times mandated and at other times permitted the post-deportation-order detention of aliens falling into certain categories such as aggravated felons, Anti-Drug Abuse Act of 1988, § 7343(a), 102 Stat. 4470, 8 U.S.C. § 1252(a)(2) (mandating detention); Immigration Act of 1990, § 504(a), 104 Stat. 5049–5050, 8 U.S.C. §§ 1252(a)(2)(A), (B) (permitting release under certain circumstances); Miscellaneous and Technical Immigration and Naturalization Amendments of 1991, § 306(a)(4), 105 Stat. 1751, 8 U.S.C. § 1252(a)(2)(B) (same).

In early 1996, Congress explicitly expanded the group of aliens subject to mandatory detention, eliminating provisions that permitted release of criminal aliens who had at one time been lawfully admitted to the United States. Antiterrorism and Effective Death Penalty Act of 1996, § 439(c), 110 Stat. 1277. And later that year Congress enacted the present law, which liberalizes pre-existing law by shortening the removal period from six months to 90 days, mandates detention of certain criminal aliens during the removal proceedings and for the subsequent 90-day removal period, and adds the post-removal-period provision here at issue. **

We have found nothing in the history of these statutes that clearly demonstrates a congressional intent to authorize indefinite, perhaps permanent, detention. Consequently, interpreting the statute to avoid a serious constitutional threat, we conclude that, once removal is no longer reasonably foreseeable, continued detention is no longer authorized by statute. **

IV

The Government seems to argue that, even under our interpretation of the statute, a federal habeas court would have to accept the Government's view about whether the implicit statutory limitation is satisfied in a particular case, conducting little or no independent review of the matter. In our view, that is not so. Whether a set of particular circumstances amounts to detention within, or beyond, a period reasonably necessary to secure removal is determinative of whether the detention is, or is not, pursuant to statutory authority. The basic federal habeas corpus statute grants the federal courts authority to answer that question. *See* 28 U.S.C. § 2241(c)(3) (granting courts authority to determine whether detention is "in violation of the...laws...of the United States"). In doing so the courts carry out what this Court has described as the "historic purpose of the writ," namely, "to relieve detention by executive authorities without judicial trial." *Brown v. Allen*, 344 U.S. 443, 533 (1953) (Jackson, J., concurring in result).

In answering that basic question, the habeas court must ask whether the detention in question exceeds a period reasonably necessary to secure removal. It should measure reasonableness primarily in terms of the statute's basic purpose, namely, assuring the alien's presence at the moment of removal. Thus, if removal is not reasonably foresee-able, the court should hold continued detention unreasonable and no longer authorized by statute. In that case, of course, the alien's release may and should be conditioned on any of the various forms of supervised release that are appropriate in the circumstances, and the alien may no doubt be returned to custody upon a violation of those condi-tions. ** And if removal is reasonably foreseeable, the habeas court should consider the risk of the alien's committing further crimes as a factor potentially justifying confine-ment within that reasonable removal period. **

We recognize, as the Government points out, that review must take appropriate ac-count of the greater immigration-related expertise of the Executive Branch, of the seri-ous administrative needs and concerns inherent in the necessarily extensive INS efforts to enforce this complex statute, and the Nation's need to "speak with one voice" in im-migration matters. ** But we believe that courts can take appropriate account of such matters without abdicating their legal responsibility to review the lawfulness of an alien's continued detention.

   ***

We realize that recognizing this necessary Executive leeway will often call for difficult judgments. In order to limit the occasions when courts will need to make them, we think it practically necessary to recognize some presumptively reasonable period of de-tention. We have adopted similar presumptions in other contexts to guide lower court determinations. **

While an argument can be made for confining any presumption to 90 days, we doubt that when Congress shortened the removal period to 90 days in 1996 it believed that all reasonably foreseeable removals could be accomplished in that time. We do have reason to believe, however, that Congress previously doubted the constitutionality of detention for more than six months. ** Consequently, for the sake of uniform administration in the federal courts, we recognize that period. After this 6-month period, once the alien provides good reason to believe that there is no significant likelihood of removal in the reasonably foreseeable future, the Government must respond with evidence sufficient to rebut that showing. And for detention to remain reasonable, as the period of prior post-removal confinement grows, what counts as the "reasonably foreseeable future" con-versely would have to shrink. This 6-month presumption, of course, does not mean that every alien not removed must be released after six months. To the contrary, an alien may be held in confinement until it has been determined that there is no signifi-cant likelihood of removal in the reasonably foreseeable future.

V

The Fifth Circuit held Zadvydas' continued detention lawful as long as "good faith efforts to effectuate...deportation continue" and Zadvydas failed to show that deporta-tion will prove "impossible." ** But this standard would seem to require an alien seek-ing release to show the absence of any prospect of removal—no matter how unlikely or unforeseeable—which demands more than our reading of the statute can bear. The Ninth Circuit held that the Government was required to release Ma from detention because there was no reasonable likelihood of his removal in the foreseeable future. ** But its conclusion may have rested solely upon the "absence" of an "extant or pending" repatriation agreement without giving due weight to the likelihood of successful future negotiations. ** Consequently, we vacate the judgments below and remand both cases for further proceedings consistent with this opinion.

It is so ordered.

Notes

1. *Subsequent case history*

On November 14, 2001, the Justice Department announced its publication of an interim rule to implement the Supreme Court's decision in this case. This announcement is available at: http://www.usdoj.gov/opa/pr/2001/November/01_ins_595.htm.

2. *Dissenting opinion by Justice Scalia*

In his dissent, Justice Scalia (joined by Justice Thomas) agrees with Justice Kennedy's dissent, "which establishes the Attorney General's clear statutory authority to detain criminal aliens with no specified time limit." According to Justice Scalia, he writes separately because he does not

> believe that...there may be some situations in which the courts can order release. *** A criminal alien under final order of removal who allegedly will not be accepted by any other country in the reasonably foreseeable future claims a constitutional right of supervised release into the United States. This claim can be repackaged as freedom from "physical restraint" or freedom from "indefinite detention," ** but it is at bottom a claimed right of release into this country by an individual who *concededly* has no legal right to be here. There is no such constitutional right.

What are the competing interests at play here? Since this issue is not a tension between states and the federal government, why is it wrong to set a reasonableness standard under 28 U.S.C. § 2241?

3. *Dissenting opinion by Justice Kennedy*

In his dissent, Justice Kennedy (joined by Justice Rehnquist and, as to Part I only, Justices Scalia and Thomas) chides the majority for rewriting the law:

> The Court says its duty is to avoid a constitutional question. It deems the duty performed by interpreting a statute in obvious disregard of congressional intent; curing the resulting gap by writing a statutory amendment of its own; committing its own grave constitutional error by arrogating to the Judicial Branch the power to summon high officers of the Executive to assess their progress in conducting some of the Nation's most sensitive negotiations with foreign powers; and then likely releasing into our general population at least hundreds of removable or inadmissible aliens who have been found by fair procedures to be flight risks, dangers to the community, or both. Far from avoiding a constitutional question, the Court's ruling causes systemic dislocation in the balance of powers, thus raising serious constitutional concerns not just for the cases at hand but for the Court's own view of its proper authority. Any supposed respect the Court seeks in not reaching the constitutional question is outweighed by the intrusive and erroneous exercise of its own powers. In the guise of judicial restraint the Court ought not to intrude upon the other

branches. The constitutional question the statute presents, it must be acknowledged, may be a significant one in some later case; but it ought not to drive us to an incorrect interpretation of the statute. The Court having reached the wrong result for the wrong reason, this respectful dissent is required.

Should the Court have waited for a different case, and if so, what case?

4. *Habeas petitions and Guantanamo Bay*

In an article published in *The New Republic* on January 26, 2004, entitled "Judge Not," Jeffrey Rosen states:

> In...*Gherebi v. Bush*, the U.S. Court of Appeals for the Ninth Circuit held that the enemy aliens being held in Guantanamo Bay can challenge the constitutionality of their detentions by filing habeas corpus petitions in federal courts. The Supreme Court held in 1950 that German enemy aliens tried for espionage by a U.S. military commission in China and imprisoned in Germany had no right to challenge the legality of their detention, because they were held outside "any territory over which the United States is sovereign." The same logic arguably applies at the Guantanamo Bay Naval Base, which the United States leases from Cuba. But the federal appeals court in California held that, since the lease is perpetual unless both parties agree to break it, the United States had the equivalent of sovereign control over the naval base. (Two other appellate courts had previously reached the opposite conclusion about the status of Guantanamo.) The U.S. Supreme Court will resolve the dispute once and for all this spring, but the Ninth Circuit refused to wait for its decision.

> In practice, if the Supreme Court agrees that federal courts have jurisdiction over Guantanamo, the United States could avoid future judicial scrutiny simply by imprisoning all future enemy combatants at the Diego Garcia U.S. Naval Support Facility, located on British territory in the Indian Ocean. This suggests the impracticality of judicial attempts to create broad constitutional rights for enemy aliens based on geographic technicalities. It's certainly troubling that some detainees might fall into a legal black hole, and it's understandable that justices might therefore be tempted to impose some kind of U.S. judicial oversight on Guantanamo. But, for better or for worse, the Supreme Court has long refused to extend the jurisdiction of federal courts over aliens outside the United States, and it would be naive to expect the Court to revisit that decision on a broad scale.

> Although the Ninth Circuit tried to second-guess the president's decision about the designation of enemy aliens, they failed to review a question where they arguably have more competence: namely, the constitutionality of the military tribunals by which the United States has promised to try at least some of the Guantanamo prisoners. "The Ninth Circuit got it precisely backward by allowing the enemy aliens to contest whether the president has the authority in times of crisis to detain them but not allowing them to contest the trials that they may face," says Neal Katyal of Georgetown University Law Center. "The more principled ruling would have said, the president has a broad warfighting power, where the courts should defer to his judgment, and a narrower law enforcement power, where courts can review the constitutionality of any legal procedures he creates." Katyal argues that only Congress has the power to authorize military tribunals and that the congressional statutes authorizing such tribunals during World War II aren't broad enough to cover the terrorism

charges that the Bush administration seeks to prosecute today. My own view is that Bush should ask Congress to authorize the tribunals, but, if he doesn't, the World War II statutes are arguably broad enough to justify the tribunals today. But it's clear that the ultimate supervision of military tribunals — including provisions governing the appointment of counsel — should ideally come from clear statements by Congress rather than the courts.

Do you agree with Rosen's position that President Bush should have asked Congress to authorize the tribunals, rather than arguing his position before the Supreme Court? How do the concerns raised in *Gherebi* compare to the historical use of the doctrine of habeas corpus?

Index of Cases

Index